A HISTORY OF THE
CATHOLIC CHURCH

PIERS PAUL READ

A HISTORY OF THE
CATHOLIC CHURCH

Meid

© Piers Paul Read, 2023

Published by Meid Books

A CIP catalogue record for this book is available from the British Library.

ISBN 978-1-7394793-0-5

Book layout by Clare Brayshaw

Prepared and printed by:

York Publishing Services Ltd
64 Hallfield Road
Layerthorpe
York YO31 7ZQ

Tel: 01904 431213

Website: www.yps-publishing.co.uk

Preface

The idea of writing a history of the Catholic Church came from my observation that my eldest grandchild, in her last year at a prestigious secondary school in London – named after a Christian saint – knew almost all there is to know about Virginia Woolf but next to nothing about Jesus of Nazareth or the Catholic Church. What she did know was not favourable: as the theologian Edward Norman has observed, in today's secular society Christianity, in particular Catholicism, is considered a bad thing. 'It is regarded,' he wrote, 'often with very insubstantial historical backing, as tainted with racism, sexism, social conservatism, as the agent of slavery, of persecution, and of a large catalogue of evils identified by modern Humanism as inhibiting social progress'[1].

This view is found not just among polemical journalists such as the late Christopher Hitchens, but also professional historians. 'In a lifetime of historical research', wrote the American historian Rodney Stark, 'I kept encountering serious distortions rooted in obvious anti-Catholicism...' Stark regards Edward Gibbon (1737-1794) as 'one of the first of celebrated anti-Catholic scholars', and notes that 'in recent years some of the most malignant contributions to anti-Catholic history have been made by alienated Catholics, many of whom are seminary dropouts, former priests, or ex-nuns...' Stark is not a Catholic. 'I did not write this book in defence of the Church. I wrote it in defence of history'. [2]

The Catholic Church into which I was baptised when I was nine months old was founded more than two thousand years ago, and at present has around 1.25 billion adherents in almost every country of the world. It is unique in that it has had from its inception an identifiable patriarch or pope normally living by the tomb of Christ's Apostle Peter in Rome – the bishop of the city but also pastor of the Universal Church. A history of this institution could

---

1   Edward Norman, *Secularism. Sacred Values in a Godless World*, p. 49

2   Rodney Stark, *Bearing False Witness, Debunking Centuries of anti-Catholic History*, p. 7

follow any one of its many facets. Eamon Duffy, Professor of Christianity at the University of Cambridge in his *Saints and Sinners* (1997) chose the popes. So too the nineteenth century German historian, Ludwig, Freiherr von Pastor. His *History of the Popes* begins at the close of the Middle Ages and ends with the death of Pope Pius VI in 1799. It is a work of sixteen volumes.

Inevitably, in this history which covers a larger timespan but is confined to a single volume, there are many lacunae. There is little about the Church outside Europe and, within Europe, much about the Church in France for reasons that I trust will become apparent. As it reaches the present day, and I write about events that I have witnessed rather than learned about from books, there is more about the Catholic Church in England than elsewhere. I have written little about spirituality and have only touched on theological controversies. I have avoided anachronism – judging the past by the standards of the present; and also using words that might mean nothing to secular readers such as 'hermeneutics', 'exegesis', 'eschatology', 'apologetics', even 'evangelist' and 'incarnation'. My thanks go to Lucy Beckett, James Roberts and Anthony McCarthy for reading this book in manuscript and alerting me to factual errors; to Clare Brayshaw for her patience in seeing the book through the different stages of production; and to my wife Emily for her sharp eye in correcting the proofs.

Two friends who read this history in manuscript – one a Catholic, the other an agnostic – agreed that no one after reading it could possibly want to become a Catholic. I took this as evidence that my efforts to be dispassionate had succeeded.

Contents

Preface

PART ONE

1.   The Chosen People

From the beginning of recorded history, men and women have believed in the existence of supernatural beings who intervene in human affairs. In Babylonia, there were Mardull and Ninurta; in Egypt, Amun and Osiris; in Greece Zeus and Aphrodite; in Rome, Jupiter and Venus. Only one tribe stands out for its faith in a single, omnipotent deity who created the heavens and the earth – the Israelites or Jews. Their faith is the source of the Christian religion.

The story of the Jews is told in a compendium of sacred writings, the Torah. In these God communicates to chosen men and women – either in an inner voice, or as angels in the guise of men, or as a voice speaking from a cloud or a burning bush, or through the inspired pronouncements of a series of prophets. It was around 1850 BC that a prosperous nomad living in Mesopotamia, Abram, was told by God to 'leave your country, your family and your father's house, for the land I will show you. I will make you a great nation; I will bless you and make your name so famous that it will be used as a blessing.'[3] Abram was to change his name Abram, which meant 'High Father', to Abraham, 'Father of a Multitude'; and the name of his wife Sarai, meaning 'my princess', was to be changed to Sarah, 'mother of nations'. God made a covenant with Abraham: 'Now this is my Covenant which you are to maintain between myself and you, and your descendants after you: all your males must be circumcised.'[4] This excision of the foreskin that covers the glans penis of a male child soon after his birth has remained a distinctive and defining practice of both Judaism and Islam.

Abraham obeyed God's command to move to this promised land – 'a stately sheik-like figure moving through Palestine from north to south, with

---

3   *Genesis*, 12:1-2. *The Jerusalem Bible*, General Editor Alexander Jones, L.S.S., S.T.L., I.C.B.

4   *Genesis*, 17: 11

his flocks and his herds and his tents and his wife and his concubines.' [5] Genesis, the first book of the Torah, tells further stories of God's intervention in the life of Abraham. His wife Sarah is barren, and when she overhears a visiting messenger tell her husband that she will conceive, she laughs: 'both were old, well on in years, and Sarah had ceased to have her monthly periods. "Now that I am passed the age of child-bearing, and my husband is an old man, is pleasure to come my way again?"' [6]

Sarah does, as promised, give birth to a son, Isaac – a child particularly beloved by his parents as an unexpected gift from God. Does Abraham love his son more than God? God puts him to the test. 'Take your son, your only child Isaac, whom you love…and offer him as a burnt offering on a mountain I shall point out to you.' Abraham obeys; he prepares the wood for this human sacrifice, and takes a knife to kill his son, but God stays his hand. 'Do not harm him. Now I know that you fear God. You have not refused me your son, your only son'.

Abraham dies. Isaac, grown into manhood, marries Rebecca who gives birth to two sons, Esau and Jacob. Jacob, through trickery, disinherits his older brother. After an encounter with God, he is given the name Israel. In due course, he has twelve sons among whom his favourite is the youngest, Joseph. Joseph's brothers, jealous of their sibling, plan to murder him but instead sell him as a slave to Ishmaelite[7] merchants for twenty pieces of silver. The Ishmaelites take Joseph to Egypt where they sell him on to Potiphar, an official of the reigning Pharaoh. Potiphar's wife takes a fancy to the young Joseph 'who was well-built and handsome' but Joseph resists her advances. Enraged, the spurned wife accuses Joseph of assaulting her. He is thrown into prison.

An ability to interpret dreams – first of a fellow-prisoner, Pharaoh's disgraced cup-bearer, and then of Pharaoh himself – earns Joseph a royal pardon. Thanks to his interpretation of Pharaoh's dreams, the Egyptians store food in advance of a famine. Joseph is made the Pharaoh's vizier – 'governor of the whole land of Egypt'. He is given Asenath, the daughter of Potiphera, priest of On, as his wife. He is only thirty years old.

The famine has also hit Palestine where Jacob, believing Joseph dead, sends his surviving sons to Egypt to buy food. Joseph recognises them, forgives

---

5   Cecil Roth, *A Short History of the Jewish People.* p. 4-5

6   *Genesis*, 18: 12-13

7   Descendants of Ishmael, Abraham's son by Sarah's Egyptian maidservant Hagar: see Genesis 16:3

them and sends for his father. The whole tribe of Jacob/Israel with all their livestock move to Egypt. Jacob dies and in due course 'Joseph died, and his brothers, and all that generation', but their descendants remained in Egypt for three or four hundred years. They 'grew in numbers greatly; they increased and grew so immensely powerful that they filled the land'[8]

Seen as a threat by the indigenous Egyptians, the descendants of Jacob were enslaved and oppressed. 'The sons of Israel, groaning in their slavery, cried out for help and from the depths of their slavery their cry came up to God. God heard their groaning, and he called to mind his covenant with Abraham, Isaac and Jacob.'[9] . He appeared from within a burning bush to an Israelite, Moses, identifying himself as 'I am who I am', a name too sacred to be enunciated and so summarised by its initials which, with consonants added, became Yahweh; or, in subsequent Christian translations of the Torah, as 'the Lord'.

God appoints Moses as the leader of the Israelites, and commands him to lead them back to the promised land. When Pharaoh refuses to release them, he is punished by ten plagues. The final punishment is the death of the first born child in every family. Each Israelite family is told to daub the blood of a lamb on the posts of their doors so that the angel of death will pass them by. After this terrible affliction, the Egyptian Pharaoh relents: the Israelites are free to go; but he then changes his mind and his armies pursue them. The Israelites' path is blocked by the Red Sea: God parts the waters and, once the Jews are on the other side, closes the waters and drowns Pharaoh's pursuing army.

Before reaching the promised land, the Jews spend many years wandering around the Sinai desert. They camp at the foot of Mount Sinai. God summons Moses from the mountain and establishes a covenant with the Jewish people. 'You yourselves have seen what I did with the Egyptians, how I carried you on eagle's wings and brought you to myself. From this you know that now, if you obey my voice and hold fast to my covenant, you of all the nations shall be my very own for all the earth is mine. I will count you a kingdom of priests, a consecrated nation'.[10]

Moses returns from the mountain with stone tablets on which are etched Ten Commandments. The first three concerned fidelity to Yahweh. They were to worship only the one true God. They were not to take his name in vain. They

---

8   *Exodus,* 1: 6-7

9   *Exodus,* 2:23-24

10   *Exodus* 19:3.7

were to keep holy the seventh day of the week, the Sabbath day, abstaining from any kind of labour. The remaining seven commandments laid down the norms for a basic social morality. The Jews were to respect their parents, and the life, marriage and property of their 'neighbour'. They were not to 'bear false witness' against their neighbour, nor 'covet' his wife or his goods.

In subsequent revelations, God added to these basic ten commandments a large number of further rules and regulations to govern the way of life and mode of worship of the Jews. There were dietary prohibitions: they were not to eat pig's flesh or shell-fish or rodents; there were complex rites of purification – they were defiled by contact with corpses, non-Jews or women during their monthly periods. The smallest details of their life were subject to regulation. Transgressions were severely punished, either by the community or by God himself. 'While the sons of Israel were in the wilderness, a man was caught gathering wood on the Sabbath day... The Lord said to Moses, "This man must be put to death. The whole community must stone him outside the camp". The whole community took him outside the camp and stoned him till he was dead, as the Lord had commanded Moses.'[11]

In the different books of the Torah – Genesis, Exodus, Deuteronomy, Kings – God appears as a stern sovereign whose favour comes at a high price. He is a jealous God and, although we are told he is 'slow to anger and quick to forgive', he is often ready to punish with annihilation both transgressors and those who thwart his will. All but Noah and his progeny are drowned in the Great Flood and, despite the intercession of Abraham, the cities of Sodom and Gomorrah are destroyed by fire and brimstone. Not just sinful behaviour but apostasy enrages him: he inveighs against those Jews who break the first and most important of the Ten Commandments and worship false gods – the Golden Calf or, more frequently, Baal, the god of fertility.

Yahweh also intervenes against those who thwart or mistreat his chosen people, the Jews. As we have seen, the Egyptians were afflicted with seven plagues to coerce them into liberating the enslaved Israelites. It was also made clear when, after the death of Moses, Joshua finally leads the Jews into the promised land, that the command 'thou shalt not kill' did not apply to the Canaanites, Hittites, Hivites, Perizzites, Girgashites, Amorites and Jebusites[12] or other indigenous inhabitants who resisted the invasion; indeed, clemency towards the enemies of Israel brings down the wrath of God.

---

11   *Numbers,* 15:32-36
12   *Joshua,* 3:10

What was the purpose – the end game – of Yahweh's intervention in human history? Why did he single out for his favour one Semitic tribe, the Jews? Paramount seems to have been his wish to make himself known to a humanity which, at the time and later in history, worshipped a plethora of different gods, or no god at all. 'I am who am.' The Jews upheld the truth that there was one God who created man in his image and likeness, and he could be known through his revelations to the prophets of Israel. With the help of God, Joshua conquered Palestine and David killed Goliath, the champion of the Philistines. David later succeeded Saul as King of Israel and captured Jerusalem. He seduced Bathsheba, the wife of one of his warriors, Uriah the Hittite, and arranged for Uriah to be killed in battle. Solomon, David's son by Bathsheba, built a magnificent Temple on Mount Zion to house the Tablets of the Law, until then carried by the nomadic Jews in the Ark of the Covenant.

But then providence seemed to falter. After Solomon's death, the kingdom was divided into Israel and Judah. Solomon's son Rehoboam ruled Judah from Jerusalem but, half-Ammonite through his mother, he permitted and himself practiced pagan rites. 'He copied all the shameful practices of the nations whom Yahweh had dispossessed for the sons of Israel.'[13] Shishak, the king of Egypt, invaded Palestine, took Jerusalem and sacked both the palace and the Temple. This was only the first of a series of invasions and defeats. In the 7th century BC, the Jews were conquered by Nebuchadnezzar, king of the Persians, and taken as captives to Babylon. The Temple was destroyed by Nebuchadnezzar and only rebuilt when Persian king Cyrus permitted the Jews to return.

Throughout these ordeals, the Jews were both confirmed as God's chosen people and rebuked for their infidelities by a series of prophets – Isaiah, Haggai, Zechariah, Ezekiel, Jeremiah. They were consoled for the present trials at the hands of pagan invaders by the promise of a deliverer anointed by God, a Messiah or 'anointed one', who would not merely confound Israel's enemies but initiate the rule of God throughout the world. The enemies to the south – the Egyptians – and to the east – the Persians – were replaced by a new enemy to the west, the Greeks, who under the Macedonian king Alexander established an empire stretching from Greece to India. The Jews were now ruled by pagan Greeks. A determined attempt was made to 'Hellenise' the Jews. Decrees were issued by Alexander's successors, the

---

13   *1 Kings*, 14:24

Seleucids, abolishing Jewish practices such as circumcision, and establishing the cult of the Olympian Zeus in the Temple. The Jews rebelled under the priest Mattathias. After his death, his third son, Judas Maccabeus, retook Jerusalem. The Temple was cleansed. The pagan altars were destroyed.

A Jewish state was now established ruled by the descendants of Matthathias, the Hasmoneans. Under the thirty-year rule of John Hyrcanus, the Jewish state expanded beyond the borders of the kingdom ruled by David and Solomon. 'Other parts of the country became completely Judaised, their inhabitants being counted henceforth an integral part of the Jewish people.... The area of the Jewish state was increased perhaps tenfold, and its population in proportion. It is from the ethnic group formed in these years that the Jewish people of today is predominantly descended.'[14]

Even as Judas Maccabeus regained independence for the Jews, and as his Hasmonean kingdom flourished under his successors, a power arose on the Italian peninsula, Rome, that was to prove more enduring than the empire of Alexander. In 63 BC, the Roman general, Gnaeus Pompeius Magnus, or Pompey the Great, led his legions south from Syria and captured Jerusalem. John Hyrcanus lost the title of king but remained High Priest. A rump Jewish state, the provinces of Judea and Galilee, became a tributary of Rome. John Hyrcanus himself ceded what power remained to him to his Idumaean vizir, Antipater, who in turn appointed his two sons, Phasael and Herod as governors of Jerusalem and Galilee. Herod, the younger of the two sons, shrewdly backed Mark Anthony in the civil war that followed the assassination in Rome of Julius Caesar, and then switched his allegiance to Octavius Caesar. He was made tributary King of Judea and, to gain an aura of legitimacy with the Jewish people, married as his second wife a princess of the Hasmonean royal family, Mariamne.

Herod was 'supremely able and energetic' but also 'cold, calculating and cruel'[15]. His great achievement was to retain the favour of Octavius Caesar and at the same time keep his volatile subjects under control. To please the Roman emperor he built a city on the Mediterranean coast, Caesarea. To please the Jews he rebuilt the Temple to a pitch of magnificence that made it rival the Seven Wonders of the World. He was paranoid and ruthless, murdering his wife, his brother-in-law, his mother-in-law, his uncle, his

---

14   Roth, *Op. Cit.* p, 79
15   Roth, *Op. Cit.* p, 92

wife's grandfather, and finally his two sons by Mariamne. He also ordered the slaughter of all male children under the age of two in the town of Bethlehem and its surroundings, after being told by visiting eastern savants that it was here, as had been predicted by the prophet Isaiah, that was to be found the new-born 'infant king of the Jews'.[16]

However, despite Herod's ruthlessness and cunning, Israel was in ferment. To be subject to the pagan Romans, who worshipped not just false idols but their emperor, was intolerable to a people whose whole *raison d'être* was their fidelity to the one true God. In Jerusalem, the Chief Priest and the ruling council, the Sanhedrin, retained considerable power: there was a Temple police force to impose their jurisdiction over their people, with only the death penalty remaining the prerogative of the Roman Procurator. It was in the interest of this religious establishment – the Sadducees – to maintain order, and prevent an uprising against the Roman occupation, but a more radical faction, the Pharisees, seethed with resentment and looked to the promised Messiah to liberate them from the Romans as Moses had led them out of Egypt through the parted waters of the Red Sea.

Wild preachers appeared, including one, John, described by the historian Josephus as 'a strange creature, not like a man at all, who lived like a disembodied spirit…he wore animal hair on those parts of his body not covered by his own'. John castigated the sinfulness of the Jewish establishment: 'Brood of vipers, who warned you to fly from the retribution that is coming?'[17] He denounced the Tetrarch Herod Antipas, a son of King Herod, for marrying his brother's former wife, Herodias. Crowds came out of the cities to see this strange prophet who baptised the repentant, symbolically washing away their sins with the waters of the River Jordan. Was he the promised Messiah? No, he insisted, but rather the precursor predicted by Isaiah – the 'voice that cries in the wilderness: Prepare a way for the Lord'.

---

16   Gospel of Saint Matthew, 2: 2
17   Luke, 3: 7-8

2.   Jesus of Nazareth

A careful reading of the prophecies suggests that those who hoped for a Messiah who would be another Mattathias or Judas Maccabeus might be disappointed. Rather than a triumphant leader, he would be, said Isaiah, 'a thing despised and rejected by men, a man of sorrows and familiar with suffering, a man to make people screen their faces...' [18] Isaiah also predicted that he would be born of a virgin in the small town of Bethlehem which is why King Herod's sages and scholars directed the visitors from the east – the Three Kings, or 'wise men' – towards Bethlehem and, when they failed to report back to him on their return journey, Herod ordered the slaughter of all male infants in the region.

The account of this massacre is told in the first of four accounts of the life and death of Jesus of Nazareth, the Christian Gospels or 'good news'. The authors were the tax-collector, Matthew, one of the first disciples chosen by Jesus; Mark, a companion of Peter; Luke, a doctor; and John, 'the disciple whom Jesus loved'. There is controversy as to when the Gospels were written. All were composed in Greek, the common language of the Roman Empire: the style of Matthew's suggests that it was first written in Aramaic, the author's mother tongue, and later translated into Greek. One theory is that Matthew was commissioned by the other disciples to write an account of the life and death of Jesus soon after the Resurrection: it was 'the manifesto of the Mother Church of Jerusalem and is therefore the fundamental document of the Christian faith'.[19] The author of the second gospel, Mark, is thought to have acted as Peter's secretary, and his Gospel, according to this hypothesis, was based on the shorthand notes taken when Peter was in Rome in AD 62/63. Luke was a doctor and his gospel is a more literary work, written in elegant Greek, intended to make the story of Jesus more intelligible to Gentiles. It goes beyond the recollections of the apostles, containing details that could only have come from Mary, the mother of Jesus. John's gospel stands out from the other three: its author was certainly an eye-witness, most probably 'the disciple whom Jesus loved', aware of the other three Gospels but giving his account 'an eternal perspective by commencing with the heavenly pre-existence of the Son of God'.[20]

---

18   Isaiah, 53:3

19   See Dom Bernard Orchard, *The Evolution of the Gospels. One Scholar's View.* CTS 1990

20   Bernard Orchard, *Op. Cit.* p 15

Much has been written about the veracity of the four Gospels. In the eighteenth century it was claimed that they were fraudulent fictions; that Jesus of Nazareth had never existed; in which case, said the atheist philosopher Jean-Jacques Rousseau, 'the authors were more extraordinary than their subject'. The Gospels are unique testaments, and it would take a literary genius to write four different, and sometimes conflicting accounts of the same story, and create in Jesus a character that is so subtle and paradoxical that he has intrigued the most sophisticated minds for two thousand years.

The Gospels are tendentious – works of propaganda written to persuade their readers that the Messiah had indeed come to Israel, but with a far greater purpose than the liberation of the Jews from the Romans. He was the Christ, the 'anointed one', the 'Word made Flesh', the 'Son of God', indeed God himself, come as a sacrifice to atone for the sins of all mankind. There is no description of Jesus's physical appearance, and only scraps of information about his provenance and early life. His mother Mary was a young woman engaged to marry Joseph, a carpenter or builder living in the town of Nazareth. An angel appeared and told her that she would bear a child. She protested that this was impossible 'since I am a virgin'.[21] The angel explained that, should she consent, she would conceive by the power of the Holy Spirit. 'Let it be done unto me,' said Mary, 'according to thy word'.

Joseph, when he realises that his betrothed is pregnant, decides to discreetly break off the engagement; but in a dream he is told that she has not been unfaithful, but has 'conceived what is in her by the Holy Spirit', and he must take her into his home. 'Joseph woke up and did what the angel of the Lord had told him to do; he took his wife to his home and, though he had not had intercourse with her, she gave birth to a son; and he named him Jesus'.[22]

When Mary's pregnancy was well advanced, the Roman Emperor Augustus called for a census throughout his empire. Joseph, being descended from David, was obliged to register in Bethlehem. He travelled there from Nazareth with his pregnant wife and, since all the inns were full, they were put up in a stable where Mary gave birth to the infant Jesus. It was to this stable that shepherds, after a vision, and later the sages from the east, came to pay their respects. When the time came to leave, the sages – the Three Kings – were told in a dream not to return by way of Jerusalem as Herod had requested. Joseph was also warned by an angel to escape Herod's cruel cull of

---

21   Luke, 1:35

22   Matthew, 1:24-25

the new-born in Nazareth by taking Mary and the infant Jesus to Egypt. They returned to Nazareth only after Herod's death.

The Gospels tell us of Jesus's circumcision, and later his presentation in the Temple in Jerusalem where God's promise to a devout old man, Simeon, that he will not die until he has seen the promised Messiah, is fulfilled. Simeon takes the child Jesus in his arms and says: 'Now, master, you can let your servant depart in peace, just as you promised…' The family then withdraw to Nazareth where 'the child grew to maturity, and he was filled with wisdom…' [23] The only recorded incident in his childhood occurs when, on their return in a caravan from a visit to Jerusalem for the feast of Passover, Mary and Joseph realise that Jesus is not with them: he has been left behind. They return to Jerusalem and find him in the Temple, 'sitting among the doctors, listening to them and asking them questions'. When rebuked by his mother for his truancy he answers: 'Why were you looking for me? Did you not know that I must be busy with my Father's affairs?' [24]

Before starting to preach, Jesus went to the River Jordan and asked to be baptised by John. The two were related. 'Know this too,' the angel had told Mary at the time of the Annunciation. 'Your kinswoman Elizabeth has, in her old age, herself conceived a child, and she whom people called barren is now in her sixth month…' [25] The pregnant Mary had gone to visit the pregnant Elisabeth: at Mary's greeting, the baby had 'leapt in her womb' of the older woman. Now on the banks of the River Jordan, the established prophet John with his many disciples recognised Jesus but was reluctant to baptise him: 'It is I who need baptism from you, and yet you come to me.' But Jesus persuaded him that this is what 'righteousness demands'; and after he was baptised 'a voice spoke from Heaven: "this is my Son, the Beloved; my favour rests with him". [26]

Jesus then withdrew into the desert and fasted for forty days and nights. There he was beset by temptations – to assuage his hunger by turning stones into bread; to prove that he was the Son of God by throwing himself off the parapet of the Temple and be saved by angels; to take supreme power over all worldly domains. Jesus resisted the temptations. The devil left him, and 'angels appeared and looked after him.'

---

23   Luke, 2:40
24   Luke, 2:49
25   Luke, !:16
26   Matthew, 3: 17

Jesus now embarked on a mission which was to last around three years. He had no base – 'the Son of Man has nowhere to rest his head' – but moved around Judea and Samaria accompanied by twelve male disciples and a group of women. Like John the Baptist, he called for repentance: 'Repent, for the kingdom of heaven is close at hand '[27]: however the sins he proscribed were not simply breaches of the Law of Moses. Quite to the contrary, it was not the Law that mattered so much as a man or woman's inner disposition. Obeying the commandments and practising the minutiae of Jewish observance was not enough; indeed, some regulations did not even apply. Thus the ban on any activity during the Sabbath might be ignored 'because the Sabbath was made for man, not man for the Sabbath', and the strict dietary obligations laid down by the Law were also of secondary importance: 'it is not what goes into a man that defiles him, but what comes out of him' – words that are blasphemous, abusive or cruel. The thought is as bad as the deed. To curse a man is as bad as killing him. Looking at a woman 'with lust in your eye' is as bad as sleeping with her.

At the heart of Jesus's teaching was the need to love not just God but 'one's neighbour as oneself'. We must even love enemies: no day should end with hatred in a man's heart. As God forgives men and women, so they must forgive those who sin against them. 'How often must I forgive my neighbour?', asks Peter? 'As many as seven times?' 'No,' answers Jesus, 'Seventy-seven times.' Forgiveness must be without limit and 'from the heart'.

Jesus illustrated his teaching with parables – that of the 'Good Samaritan' to explain what he meant by 'neighbour'; that of the 'Prodigal Son' to illustrate God's mercy; of the 'wheat and the chaff' to warn that in due course the virtuous would be saved and the unrepentant sinner would face eternal torment in a place where the 'fire never goes out and the worm never dies'. Since, at the time, the Sadducees did not believe in life after death, Jesus was here taking the part of the Pharisees who did.

The teaching of Jesus disappointed those who had hoped for a Messiah who would lead the Jews against the pagan Romans: the kingdom of heaven, he said, was not of this world. Our aspirations should be the obverse of what had hitherto been supposed. Instead of money, sex and power as objects of our endeavour in life, Jesus enjoined poverty, chastity and obedience. It is the photographic negative, not the print, that depicts what is real: what is shade is light, what is light is shade. To love one's enemies, to give all one has to the

---

27 Matthew, 4:17

poor, to become 'a eunuch for the sake of the Kingdom', all are the opposite of what Darwin's *homo sapiens* is genetically programmed to achieve. Even suffering is not to be eschewed but embraced.

How did Jesus convince his listeners that what he said was true? First, he spoke with a persuasive authority: even now, writes Gabriel Josipovici, as we read the Gospels, 'he comes across as a force, a whirlwind which drives all before it and compels all who cross his path to reconsider their lives from the root up. He has access, not so much to a secret of wisdom as to a source of power.'[28]

And there were the miracles. Today, even Christians may express scepticism over Jesus's powers over nature; but what seems implausible to the modern mind was more readily accepted in antiquity when, as the scholar Robert Knapp tells us, no one doubted the existence of supernatural beings who intervened in their lives – 'for pagans, a number of gods; for the Jews, Yahweh'.[29] Certainly, there were no doubts in the minds of the Evangelists that Jesus turned water into wine, walked on the waters of the Sea of Galilee, fed five thousand people with five loaves and two fishes, drove demons out of the possessed, cured the sick, and brought the dead back to life. The brief mention of Jesus in Josephus's *History* is as a 'wonder worker', not a teacher; and the Babylonian Talmud refers to him as a magician.

Whether it was thanks to the miracles he performed, or simply the authority with which he spoke, Jesus gained a strong following, and this became a matter of concern for the guardians of Jewish orthodoxy. John, in his Gospel, tells of a meeting between the Chief Priests and Pharisees.

> 'Here is a man,' they said, 'working all these signs, and what action are we taking? If we let him go on in this way everybody will believe in him, and the Romans will come and destroy the Holy Place and our nation'. One of them, Caiaphas, the High Priest that year, said, 'You don't seem to have grasped the situation at all; you fail to see that it is better for one man to die for the people, than for the whole nation to be destroyed'.[30]

The French scholar, Ernest Renan, whose *Life of Jesus* was published in 1863, considered that Caiaphas and his father-in-law Ananias were in fact

28   Gabriel Josipovici, *The Book of God. A Response to the Bible*, p. 225

29   Robert Knapp: *The Dawn of Christianity. People and Gods in an Age of Miracles and Magic*

30   John, 11: 47-50

less concerned with the reaction of the Romans to Jesus's preaching than with the challenge it posed to the Jewish religion. Renan, a one-time seminarian who turned violently against the Catholic Church, claimed that his own researches, and those of German biblical scholars, proved that Jesus was not the Son of God and had never made such a claim. 'That Jesus never dreamed of making himself pass for an incarnation of God, is a matter about which there can be no doubt'.[31] Rather, Jesus was the supreme humanist – gentle, compassionate, with an all-embracing love which contradicted the prevailing particularism of his fellow-Jews at the time.[32]

gosh

Because of Jesus's popularity, the Chief Priests had to move cautiously: they could not arrest him when he was surrounded by a crowd. Fortunately for them, one of Jesus's twelve disciples, Judas, possibly disillusioned by Jesus's failure to lead a political uprising, offered to betray him for thirty pieces of silver. He led the Temple police to the Mount of Olives where Jesus was accompanied by only a few disciples: Judas identified him with a kiss. Jesus was arrested and taken before the High Priests, then Herod Antipas, and the Roman Procurator, Pontius Pilate who alone had the authority to order his execution. Following the narrative in the Gospels, Pilate was reluctant to take the case; he said he could see nothing that merited the death penalty, and told the Jews to settle the matter among themselves; but the Chief Priests organised a clamour to intimidate Pilate who finally gave way, sending Jesus with two thieves to be executed by crucifixion on a hill outside the walls of the city.

Who was responsible for the death of Jesus? Some scholars have claimed that the Gospels, particularly that of John, were written at a time when the Christians wanted to ingratiate themselves with the Roman authorities, and therefore exculpate Pilate and put the blame firmly on the Jews: 'His blood be upon us and our children'.[33] The story of the death of Jesus as told in the New Testament, writes Robert S. Wistrich, 'systematically shifts responsibility for his crucifixion from the Romans to his own people, the Jews'.[34] Ernst Renan, on the other hand, exonerates Pontius Pilate. Jesus, this 'paradigm of all that is best in humanity', was the victim of a judicial assassination by the Jewish establishment – the Sanhedrin, and the Chief Priests, Ananias and Caiaphas.

---

31   Ernest Renan, *The Life of Jesus*, p. 181

32   Renan, *Op. Cit.*, p. 167

33   Matthew, 27:26

34   Robert S. Wistrich. *Anti-Semitism. The Longest Hatred.* London, 1991

'It was Ananias (or the party he represented) who killed Jesus. Ananias was the principal actor in the terrible drama, and far more than Caiaphas, far more than Pilate, ought to bear the maledictions of mankind.'

Renan concedes that by their own lights the Jewish authorities made the right choice. 'In a general sense, Jesus, if he had succeeded, would have really effected the ruin of the Jewish nation.' [35] Jesus had come to realise that

> no union was possible between him and the ancient Jewish religion. The abolition of the sacrifices which had caused him so much disgust, the suppression of an impious and haughty priesthood, and, in a general sense, the abrogation of the law, appeared to him absolutely necessary. From this time on he appears no more as a Jewish reformer, but as a destroyer of Judaism.'[36] 'In the light of orthodox Judaism, he was truly a blasphemer, a destroyer of the established worship.' [37]

After the death of Jesus, a prominent Jew, Joseph of Arimathea, was given permission by Pontius Pilate to take the body of Jesus down from the cross and place it in a nearby tomb. There it was hastily wrapped in a cloth – unanointed because sunset saw the start of the Sabbath when no work of any kind was allowed. When the Sabbath ended, at dawn of the following day, the women who had attended to Jesus during his lifetime went to prepare his body for burial and found the tomb empty. 'They have taken my Lord away,' said Mary of Magdala, 'and I do not know where they have put him.'

> As she said this she turned round and saw Jesus standing there, although she did not recognise him. Jesus said, 'Woman, why are you weeping? Who are you looking for?' Supposing him to be the gardener, she said, 'Sir, if you have taken him away, tell me where you have put him, and I will go and remove him'. Jesus said, 'Mary!' She knew him then and said to him in Hebrew, 'Rabbuni!' – which means Master. Jesus said to her, 'Do not cling to me because I have not yet ascended to the Father. But go and find the brothers and tell them that I am ascending to my Father and your father, to my God and your God'. [38]

---

35   Renan, *Op. Cit.,* p. 255

36   Ibid., p. 167

37   Ibid., p. 273

38   John, 20: 13-18

After being told by Mary of Magdala that the tomb was empty, and that she had seen Jesus, the disciples Peter and John ran to the tomb to see for themselves. The younger John reached it first, but waited for Peter before entering. Peter went into the tomb and 'saw the linen cloths on the ground, and also the cloth that had been over his head... rolled up in a place by itself.' John then followed Peter into the tomb: 'he saw and he believed'.[39]

The empty tomb was not the only evidence that Jesus of Nazareth had risen from the dead. He appeared to his disciples on a number of occasions but in an uniquely mysterious form. They gathered behind a locked door ('for fear of the Jews') and suddenly he was there among them. The wounds remained on his body: the disciple Thomas, who had been sceptical, was told by Jesus to put his fingers into the fissure left by the soldier's spear. Jesus joined two disciples walking from Jerusalem to Emmaus who only recognised him when, as they sat down to eat, he blessed the bread. He was not a ghost: he had an appetite. 'Have you anything here to eat?' he asked his disciples on another occasion. 'And they offered him a piece of grilled fish, which he took and ate before their eyes.'[40] 'He opened their minds to understand the scriptures, and he said to them: "So you see how it was written that the Christ would suffer and on the third day rise from the dead, and that in his name, repentance for the forgiveness of sins would be preached to all the nations"' [41] Finally, after forty days, he took his disciples to the outskirts of Bethany where, 'lifting up his hands he blessed them' and 'as he blessed them, he withdrew from them and was carried to heaven'.[42]

3.   Paul of Tarsus

Luke, who ends his gospel with this succinct account of the Ascension to Heaven of Jesus of Nazareth, wrote a sequel for a friend or patron called Theophilus – *The Acts of the Apostles*. 'In my earlier work, Theophilus, I dealt with everything Jesus had done and taught from the beginning until the day he gave his instructions to the apostles he had chosen through the Holy Spirit

---

39   *Ibid.* 20:6-18
40   Luke, 24:35
41   *Ibid.* 24:45-48
42   *Ibid.,* 24: 30-33

and was taken up to heaven.'[43] He describes how Judas, who had betrayed Jesus, had come to regret it, trying to return the money he had been paid, then hanging himself.

Luke then describes how the Holy Spirit that had been promised by Jesus descended on the apostles as tongues of fire. All at once, they lost their fear of arrest and went out into the street to preach the good news, and were heard by the many foreigners in Jerusalem in their native languages. Peter, the leader of the twelve apostles, spoke to the crowd.

> Men of Israel, listen to what I am going to say. Jesus the Nazarene was a man commended to you by God by the miracles and portents and signs that God worked through him when he was among you, as you all know. This man, who was put into your power by the deliberate intention and foreknowledge of God, you took and had crucified by men outside the Law. You killed him, but God raised him to life, freeing him from the pangs of Hades... For this reason the whole House of Israel can be certain that God has made this Jesus whom you crucified both Lord and Christ.'[44]

There followed many conversions, and a community of believers was formed who were 'united heart and soul', and held all their property in common.

Hearing of the claim that Jesus had risen from the dead, and realising that his subversive teaching had not died with him, the Chief Priests and Pharisees moved against his followers. An early gentile convert, Stephen, was tried by the Sanhedrin and, after an eloquent exposition of his faith, condemned and stoned to death. Peter was imprisoned but miraculously released by an angel. Later, the High Priest, Ananias took advantage of the interregnum between the death of the procurator Porcius Festus who had replaced Pontius Pilate and the arrival of his successor, Lucceius Albinus, to usurp the procurator's prerogative when it came to the death penalty and have James, known as 'the brother of the Lord', thrown from the wall of the Temple and stoned to death.

During the stoning of Stephen, a devout Jew, Saul of Tarsus, stood watch over the discarded coats of Stephen's executioners. He was then sent by the Temple authorities to round up the followers of Jesus the Nazarene in Damascus. 'Suddenly, while he was travelling to Damascus and just before he

---

43   Acts,1: 1-2
44   Acts, 2: 22-24; 36

reached the city, there came a light from heaven all around him. He fell to the ground and heard a voicing saying, "Saul, Saul, why do you persecute me?"[45] There followed a volte-face. Saul changed his name to Paul and subsequently became the leading apologist for the claim made for the resurrected Jesus – that he was the Son of God. After describing the descent of the Holy Spirit on the twelve apostles at Pentecost, Luke's *Acts of the Apostles* centres mainly on the missionary work of Paul – describing his journeys throughout the eastern Mediterranean and disputes with Jewish believers. The chief bone of contention was circumcision: must Christian converts first become Jews? Peter, while visiting a Roman centurion in Caesarea, had a vision of a sheet descending from heaven on which was spread out 'every sort of animal and bird', and had then heard a voice telling him 'kill and eat' – a command that Peter first resisted because many of the creatures – shell fish, beasts with cloven hooves – were forbidden by the Law of Moses. But the voice insisted: 'What God has made clean, you have no right to call profane'. Peter took this to mean, not just that he could eat rabbit or lobster, but that gentiles as well as Jews were welcome in the nascent Church. 'The truth I have now come to realise is that God does not have favourites, but that anybody of any nationality who fears God and does what is right is acceptable to him.'[46]

Later, under pressure from observant Jews in Jerusalem, Peter back-tracked, for which he was chastised by Paul. Though Paul had not known Jesus in the flesh, he had known him in his vision and felt he was as much of an apostle as the other twelve, and one with a particular mission to preach to the gentiles. While he travelled around the eastern Mediterranean, he wrote letters to the different Christian communities – in Corinth, in Ephesus, in Rome – castigating those who held that Christians must obey the Law of Moses. What brought life, said Paul, was not adhering to regulations but faith in Christ. The Law was dead. One did not need to be a Jew to be a disciple of Jesus. Certainly, the Jews ' remain very dear to God, for the sake of the patriarchs,' he wrote, 'since God does not take back the gifts he bestowed or the choice he made'; but the new chosen people were those who believed that Jesus of Nazareth was the promised Messiah, the Christ, the Son of God. Paul's letters are the earliest Christian texts, and gave intellectual substance to the Church's understanding that Jesus of Nazareth was the sacrificial lamb who had redeemed the world.

---

45   Acts, 9: 3-4
46   Acts, 10:23

Paul's apostasy had enraged the Jewish authorities. He was arraigned before Gallio, the Proconsul of Achaea, and charged with 'persuading people to worship God in a way that breaks the Law'; but Gallio dismissed the charges. Paul was re-arrested in Jerusalem, and was to be tried by the Sanhedrin but Paul was a Roman citizen and claimed his right to be tried by a Roman court. Thwarted in their attempt to dispose of him by judicial means, the Jewish authorities planned to assassinate him, but the plot became known and he was transferred from Jerusalem to Caesarea escorted by a cohort of Roman soldiers. There, Paul appeared before the Roman legate, Felix, and was charged by Ananias in person of being 'a ringleader of the Nazarene sect' and making trouble 'among Jews the world over'.[47] Felix listened to Paul with interest, but declined to pass judgment, sending Paul to Rome to be tried by Caesar.

The Acts of the Apostles does not record what happened to Paul when he finally reached Rome. Tradition has it that he was executed during the persecution of Christians by the Emperor Nero, and that his body is buried in the basilica of St. Paul 'outside the walls'. Peter, too, it is believed, went to Rome and was executed in the same persecution – his remains buried on the Vatican hill.

4. The Jewish War

While the rise of a heretical sect was clearly seen as an existential threat by the Chief Priests and Sanhedrin, it played no ostensible role in the catastrophe that now overwhelmed the Jewish people. The endemic loathing for foreign rule, the resentment felt at a heavy burden of taxation, and the outrage felt by devout Pharisees at the insensitivity shown by the Romans when it came to their religious practices and beliefs, erupted in a series of revolts. Herod's successors – his sons Archelaeus, Herod Antipas and Philip – did not show the same skill as their father in keeping their volatile subjects under control. In September of 66 AD, a Roman legion sent from Syria by the Roman legate, Cestius Gallus, to restore order in Jerusalem was defeated by the Jewish insurgents. Israel was once again free.

When the Emperor Nero heard of the humiliating rout of Cestius Gallus, he sent an experienced general, Vespasian, to take command of the Roman

---

47   Acts, 24:5-6

legions in Syria. Assisted by his son Titus, Vespasian fought a war of attrition against the rebellious Jews, reducing the cities held by the insurgents one by one. After the death of Nero, Vespasian returned to Rome as Emperor and Titus took command. Between March and September of AD 70 he besieged Jerusalem. The city was fanatically defended but inexorably the Roman legions prevailed. By the end of August, they had reached the Inner Court of the Temple and Herod's magnificent edifice was set on fire. Those taken prisoner were either killed, enslaved or condemned to hard labour. Celebrating his birthday in Caesarea on 24 October, Titus was entertained by the spectacle of Jewish prisoners being killed by wild animals, or by one another, or being burned alive. Returning to Rome, Titus and his father, the Emperor Vespasian, celebrated a triumph, parading their captives and booty which included the menorah, the seven-branched golden candelabrum taken from the Temple.

In Palestine, pockets of resistance survived for a further two years – the last Essenes holding out in Herod's fortress of Masada. In 73, when it became clear that Masada was about to fall, the defenders committed suicide. But the national spirit of the Jews was not yet extinguished. Less than sixty years later, Simeon Ben Koseba, acclaimed by Rabbi Akiba as the promised Messiah, led a second revolt against Roman rule. The Roman Legate in Britain, Julius Severus, was sent by the Emperor Hadrian to suppress this new uprising. In AD 134 Jerusalem again fell to Roman legions. This time, the Romans took measures to ensure the annihilation of Jerusalem as the capital city of the Jews. It was renamed Aelia Capitolina. No Jews were permitted to live there, and what remained of the Temple was made into a sanctuary of Jupiter, the king of the gods, and the divine Emperor, Hadrian. Over Golgotha, where Jesus of Nazareth had been crucified, and the tomb from which he was said to have risen from the dead, was built a temple for the worship of the gods Jupiter, Juno and Venus, the goddess of love.

5.   The Early Church

Flavius Josephus, a Jewish nobleman who fought against the Romans in AD 70, and then treacherously changed sides, retired to Rome on a pension from the Emperor to write an account of these events in his *The Jewish War*. In it, he makes scant and disputed references to Christians. Most of what we know about their lives in the first two centuries following the founding of the Church comes from accounts written by Christians themselves. *The Acts of the Apostles* ends with the arrival of Paul in Rome. Two hundred years later Eusebius (260-340), the Bishop of Caesarea, wrote a *History of the Church*. A diligent researcher in the libraries of antiquity, Eusebius's history drew on writings which are now lost. He listed the successors to Peter as bishops of Rome – Linus, Anacletus, Clement, Everastus; and from him we learn that a pattern was set in the organisation of the Christian communities which was to be followed throughout the ages. There is 'the same division of the clergy into the three orders of bishops, presbyters and deacons, the same practice of episcopal ordination and consecration, the same insistence on the Apostolic Succession and on the establishment by Christ of One holy Catholic and Apostolic Church'.[48]

Initially, the increase in Christian communities was confined to urban centres in the Roman Empire, particularly in the eastern Mediterranean: the common language of the early Church was Greek. 'We know next to nothing about the earliest Christians in Spain, Germany and Britain', we are told by the historian Robin Lane Fox in his *Pagans and Christians*.[49] The Church was established in Ethiopia in these early years, perhaps by the Ethiopian eunuch, the treasurer of the Queen of the Ethiopians, whose baptism by the Apostle Philip is described in *The Acts of the Apostles*; and although tradition has it that the Apostle Thomas established the Church in India, the only historical evidence is of a mission to the sub-continent comes from the Stoic philosopher from Alexandria, Pantaenus, who converted to Christianity.

Around 110 AD Pliny wrote to the Emperor Trajan that Christians were to be found in Pontus among people 'of every rank and sex': it is thought that at this point 'the hard core of these churches' membership lay in the humbler free classes, people who were far removed from higher education...'[50] Later, 'converts began to be won in higher places', creating a social diversity through its teaching on human equality. 'In church meetings educated people had to sit as equals among other men's slaves and petty artisans'.[51] We know that in Rome, to avoid detection by the authorities, Christians gathered in the underground cemeteries, the catacombs, and it was there that they buried

48   G.A. Williamson, Introduction to *The History of the Church by Eusebius*, p. 9

49   Robin Lane Fox, *Pagans and Christians*, p. 273

50   *Ibid.* p. 301

51   Ibid. p. 336

their dead. It was on the walls of the catacombs that we find depictions not of the Cross but of a fish: the Greek word for fish, ICHTHUS, is also an acronym for the phrase 'Jesus Christ, Son of God, Saviour'.

By the second century, the Church had attracted intellectuals such as Justin Martyr who was born in Nablus but taught in Rome: he was executed under the Emperor Marcus Aurelius for refusing to sacrifice to the pagan gods. In the third century there was Origen of Alexandria and Tertullian from Carthage. Tertullian describes the life of the Christian communities in his time: 'One in mind and soul, we do not hesitate to share our earthly goods with one another. All things are common among us but our wives'.

6.   Persecution

From its inception, under a number of different Roman Emperors, attempts were made to suppress the Christian Church. It was considered seditious. Not only did Christians refuse to sacrifice to the pagan gods, they regarded them as demons. This repudiation of the Romans' beliefs and customs was considered a threat to the stability of the state. The only group excused from making sacrifices to the pagan Gods were the Jews: 'the Romans respected the old and venerable in religion, and nothing was older and more venerable than the Jewish cult.'[52]

The Christians' unpopularity made them vulnerable as scapegoats. The pagan historian Tacitus, described how, after the Great Fire of Rome in AD 64,

Nero fastened the guilt of starting the blaze and inflicted the most exquisite tortures on a class hated for their abominations, called Christians [Chrestians] by the populace. Christus, from whom the name had its origin, suffered the extreme penalty during the reign of Tiberius at the hands of one of our procurators, Pontius Pilatus, and a most mischievous superstition, thus checked for the moment, again broke out not only in Judea, the first source of the evil, but even in Rome, where all things hideous and shameful from every part of the world find their centre and become popular.

Accordingly, an arrest was first made of all who pleaded guilty; then, upon their information, an immense multitude was convicted, not

---

52   Ibid., p. 428

so much of the crime of firing the city, as of hatred against mankind. Mockery of every sort was added to their deaths. Covered with the skins of beasts, they were torn by dogs and perished, or were nailed to crosses, or were doomed to the flames and burnt, to serve as a nightly illumination, when daylight had expired.[53]

It is thought that the two Apostles, Peter and Paul, died in this early persecution; and more was to follow. In the early Church, writes Robin Lane Fox,

> martyrdoms were exceptionally public events, because Christians coincided with a particular phase in the history of public entertainment: they were pitched into the cities' arenas for unarmed combat with gladiators or bulls, leopards and the dreaded bears... People liked it... Violence made excellent viewing, and the crowds could be utterly callous...Christian victims were particularly appealing: they included a good proportion of women, not merely slave girls but well-born women...[54]

'The intransigence of the braver Christians made a great impression on their brethren, and also impressed itself on pagans,' he adds. 'The blood of the martyrs,' wrote Tertullian, ' is the seed of the Church'.

7.   Virgins and Martyrs

Among the martyrs were young women who had taken a vow of perpetual virginity: the titles of virgin and martyr are often coupled together in the Church's litany of saints – Agatha, Lucy, Agnes, Cecilia, Catherine, and Anastasia. This commitment to chastity, and refusal to marry, enraged their pagan parents and would-be husbands. The martyrdom of such a young woman is the subject of the third century 'apocryphal romance', *The Acts of Paul and Thekla*: here the Apostle Paul attaches purity of the body to one of Jesus's Beatitudes: 'blessed are the pure of heart'. This esteem by Christians for celibacy was a relative novelty. The Essene Jewish sect valued celibacy; but in the Old Testament, sexual desire is depicted as a natural part of the human condition, for both good and evil. 'Shall I know pleasure at my old age?' asks

---

53   Tacitus, *Annals* 15.44:

54   Robin Lane Fox, *Pagans and Christians*, p. 420

Sarah when told that she will conceive. There is the celebration of erotic love in the Song of Songs. David sees Bathsheba taking a bath on the roof of her house, summons her, seduces her, and arranges for her husband to be killed in battle. His daughter Tamar is raped by her half-brother, Amnon.

However, in the account of man's creation in Genesis, the first book of the Torah, shame in our nakedness is the immediate consequence of Adam and Eve's act of disobedience to God by eating the forbidden fruit. Eve 'took some of the fruit and ate it. She gave some also to her husband who was with her, and he ate it. Then the eyes of both of them were opened and they realised that they were naked. So they sewed fig-leaves together to make themselves loin-cloths'.[55] To this day, once we reach puberty, we conceal our genitals from public view.

Sexual love is remarkable for its absence in the New Testament. No act of intercourse precedes the birth of Jesus: he is born of a virgin. He befriends women but has no wife or lover. He performs his first miracle, turning water into wine, at a wedding reception in Cana, and, in forbidding divorce, confirms the account in Genesis of how husband and wife become 'one flesh'; but then commends those who make themselves, figuratively, eunuchs 'for the sake of the kingdom'. He allows a woman 'with a bad reputation' to anoint his feet with perfumed ointment, and wash away her tears with her hair. He shows compassion towards the woman taken in adultery, saving her from the stoning that was prescribed by the Law of Moses, but tells her to 'sin no more'. He advises those who look lustfully at a woman to pluck out their eye because it is better to go half-blind into Heaven than fully-sighted into Hell.

And then there is the teaching of Paul of Tarsus: marriage is fine but celibacy is better. He counselled unmarried women and widows among the Christians living in Corinth to remain unmarried, 'even as I am', 'but if they cannot control their sexual urges, they should get married, since it is better to be married than to burn.' [56] He points out that married men and women must devote time and energy to one another, leaving less of both to devote to God. But it is not a matter of mere practicality. A Christian's body is a gift of God and the Temple of the Lord: it must not be used profanely. In a number of his epistles, such as those to the Romans and Ephesians, he inveighs against sexual sins – adultery, fornication, sodomy. 'Among you there must not be even a mention of fornication or impurity in any of its forms, or promiscuity:

---

55   *Genesis*, 3:6-8

56   1 Corinthians, 7:8-9 (translation from Authorised Version of the Bible0

this would hardly become the saints! There must be no coarseness, or salacious talk and jokes – all this is wrong for you: raise your voices in thanksgiving instead. For you can be quite certain that nobody who actually indulges in fornication or impurity or promiscuity…can inherit anything of the kingdom of God.'[57] And it would seem that not just sexual misbehaviour is sinful: a woman's sexual allure is offensive to celestial beings. Her 'long hair [is] her glory', a sexual adornment, and so she should cover her head at public worship because of the presence of 'the angels'.[58] For Paul, writes Tom Wright in his biography of the Apostle, 'Sexual holiness is mandatory, not optional, for followers of Jesus'.[59]

8.   Constantine

Sporadic and often local persecution of Christians had taken place under the emperors Nero, Domitian, Trajan, Hadrian, Marcus Aurelius, Maximus, Decius and Valerian. The final 'great persecution' came under Diocletian who in AD 303 published edicts against the practice of the Christian religion, to be enforced throughout the empire. At first sight, this was a formidable threat to the Church. Diocletian was an exceptionally able ruler who had arrested the chaos caused in the 270s when the Empire had been assailed by barbarian raiders, plague, inflation, and a succession of ineffective emperors: Decius had been killed by the barbarian Goths in 251, and Valerian captured by the Persians in 260. To make the defence of the empire more manageable, Diocletian established a tetrarchy, appointing a co-emperor, Maximinian, with the title of Augustus; and two subordinate co-emperors, Constantius and Galerius with the titles of Caesar. The administrative capital of the eastern Empire was established at Nicomedia in Bythnia, and that of the west was moved from Rome to Milan. It was Galerius, administering the eastern part of the empire, who urged Diocletian to suppress the Christians. Constantius, governing Britain and Gaul, did not enforce the edicts with any rigour; and by 311, even Galerius realised that the repression had failed. He issued an edict of toleration and, suffering from a painful terminal disease, he asked Christians to pray for him.

---

57   Ephesians, 4:35-36
58   1 Corinthians 11: 15
59   Tom Wright. *Paul. A Biography.* P. 217. SPCK, 2018

The Emperor Diocletian, also suffering from a debilitating illness, abdicated in Milan in 305. A year later, the auxiliary Augustus, Constantius, administering Gaul and Britain, died in York. His son Constantine, who had campaigned with his father, was proclaimed his successor by the legions under his command. After six years of campaigns, in 312, the last of Constantine's rivals in the west was defeated outside the walls of Rome in the Battle of the Milvian Bridge.

Before this critical battle, Constantine had had a vision in which he was told to have painted on the shields of his soldiers the Christian symbol, the Chi-Ro – the first and second letters of the name *Christos* superimposed on one another: and he heard the words 'in this sign, conquer'. Constantine did as instructed, and subsequently defeated the superior forces of Maxentius. An American scholar, Robert Knapp, in his book *The Dawn of Christianity*, points out that it was common at the time for warriors to call for aid from the gods: what was unusual here was the gods were not Jupiter or Mars but Jesus of Nazareth. Constantine was not a Christian but must have become aware of Christian teaching from his mother, Helena, with whom he spent much of his childhood at Diocletian's court in Nicomedia while his father Constantius was away on campaigns. Was it Helena who persuaded him that Christ might be a more effective ally than any pagan idol? Constantine was only baptised towards the end of his life; but his defeat of Maxentius, and later over the emperor in the east, Licinius, convinced him of the superior power of the Christian God. The Christian religion, Knapp concludes, 'might well have died but for Constantine's cross in the sky. A second miracle resurrected Jesus a second time. This time the faith he inspired, carried on the shoulders of empire, spread throughout the Mediterranean lands for good.'[60]

Why, if the Christian God had brought him victory, did Constantine delay his reception into the Church? At the time, baptism was deemed to wash away one's sins, and 'after baptism Christians had only one last chance of forgiveness.'[61] Constantine was aware that he could not govern an empire without sinning, and in due course was to order the murder of both his son Crispus and his own wife Fausta. Thus, he was not baptised, and did not make Christianity the religion of the state, but in 313, together with the then co-emperor Licinius, Contantine issued an Edict of Toleration in Milan which brought to an end the many years of the persecution of Christians. Christians

---

60   Robert Knapp, *The Dawn of Christianity*, p.

61   Lane Fox, *Op. Cit.* p. 337

remained a minority: Lane Fox estimates that they probably amounted to no more than five percent of the Empire's population: 'Constantine still lived and ruled among an overwhelming pagan majority. His troops were almost all pagans, and so were his ruling class and the aides he inherited'. [62] He did not ban pagan cults, but Christianity became 'the most favoured recipient of the near-limitless resources of imperial favour':[63] The Church became the beneficiary of lavish patronage: a basilica was built beside the Lateran palace dedicated to the evangelist John, and a 'palace-church', the Sessorian basilica, subsequently *Santa Croce in Gerusalemme*, for his mother Helena. Special privileges were extended to the Christian clergy: bishops were permitted to use imperial post-horses, were exempt from taxation, and were excused the heavy burden of holding civil office.

There was no attempt to coerce pagans into conversion, but it was clear to opportunists where their interest lay. Public celebrations became increasingly Christian in character. Christian churches became centres from which the Gospels' injunctions could be put into practice: 'Swollen by the Emperor's gifts, the Church helped the sick and the old, the infirm and the destitute. By the late fourth century, it had led to great hospitals and charitable centres...' [64] Christian values affected Constantine's legislation. In 325 he abolished crucifixion, public branding and gladiatorial games. Divorce was made more difficult, and infanticide was deemed murder. But brutal punishments remained in force: slaves who had sex with Roman women were burned alive.

9.   Helena

The English novelist Evelyn Waugh wrote a fictional account of the life of Constantine's mother, Helena – portraying her as the daughter of a Celtic chieftain living in Colchester in Roman Britain. She loved horses and was more like a member of the Pony Club in 20th century Somerset than a stable-maid from Bithynia in Asia Minor, where modern historians believe she lived as a child. Constantius, serving under the Emperor Aurelian, was possibly stationed in her home town. They were married around 272 and she subsequently gave birth to a son, Constantine. Some fifteen years later,

62   *Ibid.* p. 626

63   Richard Fletcher, *The Conversion of Europe*, p. 19

64   Lane Fox, *Op. Cit.* p. 668

in 290, Constantius divorced Helena to marry Theodora, the daughter of Maximinian. Helena and her son Constantine went to live in the court of the Emperor Diocletian in Nicomedia.

As soon as Constantine had established himself as Emperor, he summoned his mother to Rome where she received the title of *Augusta Imperatrix* and was installed in a palace attached to the Sessorian basilica. Eusebius states that it was only at this point that she was baptised a Christian, but her piety suggests an earlier familiarity with Christianity and, as I have suggested, it was possibly from her that asking for help in battle from the God of the Christians was implanted in the mind of her son. Not only was Constantine fond of her; she was, in the snake-pit of imperial politics, one of the few people he could trust. It is a sign of his love of his mother that Constantine provided her with limitless funds to travel to Palestine in 326 to uncover the sites visited by Jesus of Nazareth, three centuries before.

The Temple in Jerusalem had been demolished by Titus in AD 70, and the city razed to the ground under Hadrian in AD 130 and renamed Aelia Capitolina: a pagan temple had been built over Calvary. The septuagenarian *Augusta Imperatrix* ordered its demolition, and excavations to uncover the site of the Crucifixion, and of the tomb from which Jesus had risen from the dead. Either through the recollections of a Christian remnant living in Aelia Capitolina, or through divine direction – the latter considered plausible at the time – the sacred sites were uncovered and work started to enshrine them in a basilica, the Church of the Holy Sepulchre. Helena also commanded a church to be built on the Mount of Olives; on the site of the birth of Jesus in Bethlehem; and, further afield, a church in Sinai where God had spoken to Moses from within a burning bush.

Most astonishing of all was Helena's discovery, after excavations on a likely site, of uprights and cross-bars of three wooden crosses in a disused cistern or cave. Were these the instruments of execution of Jesus and the two thieves? Which was which? A woman suffering from a terminal illness was summoned and touched with wood from the different crosses; on contact with the third, she was miraculously cured, thus revealing that this was the True Cross. Further items associated with the Crucifixion were uncovered, among them the nails that had attached Jesus to the Cross, a tunic worn by Jesus which was sent to Trier in Germany, and the notice dictated by Pilate and attached to the Cross stating 'Jesus the Nazarene, King of the Jews'. Half of this *titulus crucis* remains in the church of Santa Croce in Gerusalemme in Rome.

Helena returned to Rome via Cyprus where she founded the Stavrovouni Monastery, leaving there a relic of the True Cross. She reached Rome in 327 and died there three years later with her son the Emperor Constantine at her side.

10.   Constantinople

330 AD, the year of Helena's death, also saw the consecration of the new capital of the Roman Empire which had been built by Constantine on the narrow channel linking the Mediterranean to the Black Sea – the Bosporus. Six years before, when the tetrarchy devised by Diocletian had finally come to an end, Constantine as the sole Emperor decided it was impractical to rule from Rome or Milan. Both strategically and commercially, the centre of gravity of the Empire had moved to the east. The existing capital of the eastern Empire was Nicomedia, 100 kilometres from the Bosporus, but Constantine, after considering the site of Troy, decided upon the Greek town of Byzantium on the Bosporus for his Nova Roma.

Constantine himself drew up the plans for the city, and work was started in 324. There was a palace for the emperor, a new Senate House, an immense Hippodrome for chariot races with seats for over 80,000 spectators. A colonnaded 'Middle Street', or Mese, led from a large square at the centre of the city, the Augustaeum, to the Forum of Constantine with a statue of the Emperor as Helios, the god of the Sun. Constantine was aware that the majority of his subjects remained pagans. There were temples to their gods, and the magnificent Christian basilicas he built in Nova Roma were dedicated not to Christ, the Virgin Mary, or Christian saints, but to universal virtues – *Hagia Eirene*, Holy Peace, *Hagia Dynamis*, Holy Power and *Hagia Sophia*, Holy Wisdom.

11.   The Mass

What went on in the basilicas and churches built by Helena and Constantine in Constantinople, Jerusalem and Rome, and throughout the Empire? Since most of the first Christians were Jews, it is thought that the early liturgy followed the pattern of services in Jewish synagogues with prayers to Yahweh, readings from the Torah and the singing of the Psalms. The Christians would add readings from the Gospels, Epistles, and the singing of hymns. At first, and always in the east, the liturgy was in Greek, but soon, in the west, Latin was used for all but the prayer *Kyrie Eleison* (Lord have mercy). When the liturgy was over, the assembly was dismissed with the words *Ite, missa est* (Go, this is the dismissal). From this, in the Latin west, the ceremony came to be called the Mass.

At the heart of the Mass was the Eucharist – a re-enactment of the sacrifice of Jesus on the Cross, 'not merely in a symbolical form', wrote the German theologian Karl Adam, but as 'a great supra-temporal reality' that 'enters into the immediate present. Space and time are abolished. The same Jesus is here present who died on the Cross'.[65] Accounts of the origin of this rite are given in the Gospels of Matthew, Mark and Luke; but the earliest mention is by Paul of Tarsus in his first letter to the Corinthians. 'For this is what I received from the Lord, and in turn passed on to you,' he wrote,

> That on the same night that he was betrayed, the Lord Jesus took some bread, and thanked God for it and broke it, and he said, 'This is my body, which is for you; do this as a memorial of me'. In the same way he took the cup after supper, and said, 'This cup is the new covenant in my blood. Whenever you drink it, do this as a memorial of me.' Until the Lord comes, therefore, every time you eat this bread and drink this cup, you are proclaiming his death, and so anyone who eats or drinks the cup of the Lord unworthily will be behaving unworthily towards the body and blood of Christ.[66]

The Last Supper is described in the gospels of Matthew, Mark and Luke but not in the gospel of John. However, John goes further than the other evangelists in emphasising its significance. 'I am the bread of life,' says Jesus. ' I am the living bread which has come down from heaven. Anyone who eats this bread will live for ever; and the bread that I shall give is my flesh, for the life of the world'. This seemed preposterous to many at the time. 'The Jews started arguing with one another. "How can this man give us his flesh to eat?"' But Jesus went further. '" I tell you most solemnly, if you do not eat the flesh of the Son of Man and drink his blood, you will not have life in you. Anyone

---

65   Karl Adam, *The Spirit of Catholicism,* p.186
66   1 Corinthians, 11: 23-27

who does eat my flesh and drink my blood has eternal life and I shall raise him up on the last day."[67]

Hearing this, 'many of his followers said, "This is intolerable language. How could anyone accept it?"... After this, many of his disciples left him and stopped going with him'. Then Jesus said to the Twelve, 'What about you, do you want to go away too?' Simon Peter answered, 'Lord, who shall we go to? You have the message of eternal life, and we believe: we know that you are the Holy One of God.'[68]

Here, then, was something astonishing in God's relation to man – quite different to anything that had gone before. No longer does a terrifying God speak to man through an inner voice as he did to Abraham, or from a burning bush as he did to Moses, or by way of angels. Now, under the New Covenant, man ingests the body of 'the Word made flesh': as God became human in Jesus, so man through the Eucharist becomes divine. It is the culmination of the Creator's perplexing love for the most evolved mammal in his multifarious creation: 'What is man that you should keep him in mind, mortal man that you care for him?'[69] Peter's faith in a truth that others at the time found impossible to accept persisted in the belief of Christians that, in obedience to Christ's command to re-enact the sacrifice on Calvary, an ordained priest, through the words of consecration, brings about the miraculous change of bread and wine into the body and blood of Christ.

12.   Apocrypha and Heresy

Although the Eucharist was and remains at the heart of all orthodox Christian celebrations, there were variations in the liturgical language and form between the Greek-speaking East and Latin-speaking West; and between the different patriarchies or areas of ecclesiastical administration. It also took many years for the Church to rule on which of a number of Gospels were the work of the evangelists, and which were fanciful accounts of the life of Jesus. As early as AD 170, Bishop Irenaeus of Lyons insisted that only the Gospels of Matthew, Mark, Luke and John were written with the knowledge and authority of the Apostles. Tertullian (155 AD – 220 AD), a scholarly convert to Christianity,

---

67   John, 6:51-54
68   *Ibid*, 6: 59-69
69   Psalm 8:4

weeded out the true from the false, establishing with a few later changes which books should be included in the Old and New Testaments of the Christian Church. Many apocryphal works, including *The Apocalypse of Peter*, the *Protoevangelium of James*, the *Infancy of Thomas* and the *Acts of Peter*, were excluded. In 367, Bishop Athanasius of Alexandria, in an letter to his flock, listed the works which have been accepted as authentic ever since.

Less easily settled than the composition of the canon of Christian scripture was what precisely it was that Christians believed. From the very start there were divergent views, and we find in the gospel of John, and the letters of Paul, anathemas against false teachers. John warns in his first letter that 'several antichrists have already appeared' – rivals of Christ 'who came out of your own number...' Irenaeus of Lyons maintained that John's gospel was written to refute the teaching of the heretical teacher Cerinthus. The term 'heresy' was used to define teaching that disputed or contradicted the agreed or 'orthodox' teaching of the Church. These heresies were mostly named after their originators – Mani, Donatus, Arius; Gnosticism is an exception. Today their teachings may either seem fanciful or based on abstruse points of doctrine: however, at the time they led not just to arguments, but to riots and wars.

When the Emperors Constantine and Licinius proclaimed the toleration of the Christian religion in the Edict of Milan in 313, the Church, following Diocletian's 'Great Persecution', was in a state of disarray. Many Christians had embraced martyrdom with courage and radiance; the Bishops of Rome Telesphorus (125-131), Fabian (236-250) and Sixtus II (257-258) were martyred, while Pontian (230-235) died a convict in the Sardinian salt mines. However, others had either apostatised, denying Christ and sacrificing to the pagan gods, or had hidden in the countryside, or had bribed officials to let them off the hook. The Bishop of Rome, Marcellinus (296-304), reigning at the cusp of the third and fourth centuries, and the first to be called 'pope', had been gravely compromised, handing over copies of the Scriptures to be destroyed, and apparently offering prayers to the pagan gods.

Other bishops and presbyters (priests) had done the same, and those who had refused and suffered persecution held that these *traditors* or 'surrenderers' had ceased to be Christians, that their power to perform the rites and administer the sacraments of the Church was consequently null and void, and so to be readmitted to the Church they must be re-baptised. The contrary, orthodox view was that baptism and holy orders remained valid, whatever the behaviour of a Christian. The differences came to a head when around 310 a *traditor*, Caecilian, was consecrated as Bishop of Carthage and Primate of North Africa. He was rejected by his flock; a rival bishop, Majorinus, was chosen. He died soon after his consecration and was replaced by Donatus from whom the Donatist schism takes its name.

A second and more widespread heresy derived from the teaching of Arius, a priest and ascetic living in Egypt, and like Donatus of Berber descent. He held that Jesus of Nazareth, as the Son begotten by God, was subordinate to God the Father, and had not existed 'in the beginning' as John had claimed in his Gospel. There were a number of passages in the other Gospels which were said to support his contention; and it seemed only common sense that a father should exist prior to his son and therefore 'there was a time when the Son was not'. This teaching won many supporters and became a source of dissension throughout the Empire.

Constantine, though not as yet a baptised Christian, took a close interest in theology, and recognised that, though the Christians remained a minority, their differences could lead to political instability. At his request, a Council was summoned in Arles to consider who should be recognised as the valid bishop of Carthage; and later one at Nicea in Asia Minor to consider the teaching of Arius. All the dioceses of the Empire, save those in Britain, sent representatives to Nicea. Constantine himself presided over some of its sessions and participated in the debates. Twenty-two bishops supported Arius, but the majority upheld the view that Christ was co-eternal and con-substantial with the Father. They were led by Bishop Alexander of Alexandria, who in turn was advised by a young presbyter, Athanasius. The Council concluded with the publication of the Nicene Creed which declared Jesus of Nazareth 'the Son of God, begotten of the Father, Light of Light, very God of very God, begotten, not made, being of one substance with the Father...'; but this did not mean the end of Arianism which flourished under Constantine's successor, Constantine II. Orthodox bishops such as Hilary of Poitiers, and particularly Athanasius, who succeeded Alexander as bishop of Alexandria, were persecuted and exiled from their diocese by the Arian emperor Constantius II (337-361). Arianism was later suppressed in the east by the orthodox emperor Theodosius, but flourished, as we shall see, among the converts to the Christian religion from outside the Empire.

Epiphanius, the intensely orthodox bishop of Salamis in the late fourth century, drew up a list of eighty heresies extending back over history. Donatism, though strictly speaking a schism rather than a heresy, and Arianism, were the most significant, and so merited the attention of Constantine and subsequent emperors. Also worthy of note was the teaching of Marcion that the vindictive God of the Old Testament was distinct from, and inferior to, the loving God of the New Testament; and, of more enduring influence, that of Mani.

Mani was born in western Iran and, after a visionary experience, and studying Hinduism in India, proclaimed himself a prophet – the Paraclete promised by Jesus. At the core of his teaching is the dualism found in both Gnosticism and Zoroastrianism – the belief that there are two Gods, one good, the other evil, with the good God sovereign over the spirit and the evil God sovereign over matter. By condemning matter outright, Manichaeism permitted a measure of licentiousness because only the elect – the priesthood – were expected to obey the laws enjoining celibacy and strict fasting; the mere followers – 'auditors' or 'hearers' – were not, their sinful engagement with matter during their lifetime being forgiven by a last and unique sacrament as they approached death. Mani's followers were organized into a church, and for a while Mani gained the patronage and protection of the Sasanian Emperor, Shapur I; but after Shapur's death, his son, Bahram I, was persuaded by the Kartir, High Priest of the established Zoroastrian religion, to crucify Mani and persecute his followers.

13.   Augustine of Hippo

The fate of Mani – execution at the instigation of the High Priest of an established religion – was inevitably compared by his followers with that of Jesus. Like the early Christians, they were persecuted after Mani's death, but, as with Christianity, persecution did not destroy the Manichean religion. It spread from Persia into the Roman Empire and, one hundred years after Mani's death, we find among its adherents in Carthage a man, Augustine, who was to have as great an influence on Christian teaching as the apostle, Paul of Tarsus.

'Augustine is the person about whom we know most in the ancient world,'[70] wrote Robin Lane Fox, thanks largely to the *Confessions* which he wrote in middle-age – 'the most famous and influential of all ancient autobiographies'.[71]

---

70   Robin Lane Fox, *Augustine. Conversions and Confessions.* P. xi
71   Henry Chadwick, *Augustine, p. 1*

He was born in 354 in the small town of Thagaste, then in the Roman province of Africa Proconsularis, present-day Souk el Ahras in Algeria. There was at the time more land under cultivation than there is today, producing grain and olive oil; and, despite Berber and other blood in its inhabitants, and a mixture of both languages and religions, the culture was the same as that on the Italian peninsula, a short voyage across the Mediterranean Sea. The language of the elite was Latin and, though Augustine's parents Patricius and Monica were probably Berber, they were Roman citizens and Latin was spoken in the home. Augustine was remote from his father, Patricius, a small land-owner with a bad temper, but close to his mother, a devout Christian. Patricius owned slaves and was a pagan throughout Augustine's childhood, becoming a Christian only on his deathbed. Augustine was then aged seventeen.

Augustine had an older brother and a sister, but his intellectual precocity was recognised by his father who found the money to pay for his extensive education. After his father's death, a rich citizen of Thagaste offered to pay for Augustine's further studies in Carthage. His mother Monica held off arranging a marriage for her son: he could do better than a local girl if he waited. 'Even in his mid-forties,' writes Lane Fox, 'he does not fully realize what his life owed to his mother's social climbing'.[72] However, as Augustine admits in his *Confessions*, he had a highly charged libido, and in Carthage went through a period of promiscuity before settling down with a woman from the lower classes who, though she bore him a son, Adeodatus, remained his concubine and was never his wife.

In Carthage, Augustine's intellectual curiosity led him to the works of Cicero, but also to the teaching of Mani and, to his mother's dismay, he joined the Manichean sect. 'As a young Hearer, he listened to the Elect, sang with them and prayed with them'.[73] Mani's 'Church' was to retain him for at least nine years, and even later was to claim significant time and energy'. [74] Had he become a member of the Elect, he would have had to give up sex. A Hearer was under no such obligation, but he should not perpetuate matter by fathering children. Adeodatus was an aberration.

---

72   *Ibid.* p. 49
73   *Ibid.* p. 103
74   *Ibid.* p. 99

After a brief period teaching grammar at Thagaste between 373-374, Augustine ran a school of Rhetoric in Carthage but, after nine years, exasperated by the failure of his students to pay their fees, he moved to Rome and then Milan, where he secured the post of the city's Professor of Rhetoric. An encounter with the Manichean bishop Faustus led Augustine to doubt the truth of Mani's teaching. He turned to Neoplatonism but, soon after his arrival in Milan, he went with his mother to the Christian basilica to listen to the sermons of the bishop, Ambrose – curious to see if his reputation was deserved. Both were welcomed by Ambrose and in due course, under Ambrose's influence, Augustine became convinced of the truth of the Christian religion. However, he held back from baptism partly because of his addiction to sex: 'make me chaste, O Lord, but not yet'.

His mother Monica was still intent on her son's social advancement but this required money. A marriage was arranged with a ten-year-old heiress; Augustine's mistress of fifteen years who is never named was sent back to North Africa, leaving Adeodatus with his father. While waiting for his intended bride to reach maturity, Augustine reverted to a life of promiscuity but then, in September, 386, while sitting beneath a fig tree, feeling wretched because of his inability to escape from his sins, he heard 'the singing voice of a child in a nearby house' saying '"Take it and read, take it and read"'. He took this to be 'a divine command to open my book of Scripture and read the first passage on which my eyes should fall'. He had been reading Paul's Epistles and now opened it at random and read: 'Not in revelling and drunkenness, not in lust and wantonness, not in quarrels and rivalries. Rather, arm yourselves with the Lord Jesus Christ; spend no more thought on nature and nature's appetites'. [75]

The trajectory of Augustine's life now wholly changed: he would abandon his worldly ambitions and lead a celibate life. He resigned his post as Professor of Rhetoric, and plans for his marriage were abandoned. Augustine was baptised by Ambrose at Easter of 387, after which he set off for Africa with his mother whose prayers of a lifetime had been answered by the conversion of her son. Her 'sadness had been turned into rejoicing, into joy far fuller than her dearest wish, far sweeter and more chaste than any she had hoped to find in children begotten of my flesh'.[76] When they reached the port of Ostia on their return journey, Monica fell ill and died.

---

75   Romans, 13: 13,14

76   Augustine, *Confessions,* Book VIII

Three years after his return to Africa, Augustine was ordained a priest by Bishop Valerius of Hippo, and was appointed his coadjutor. On the death of Valerius in 395, Augustine succeeded him as bishop, and remained in this small port city on the coast of the Mediterranean until his death thirty-five years later. Living frugally in community with his clergy, and conscientious in performing his duties as bishop, Augustine found time to compose sermons, and write works which were to mould Christian thinking in future centuries, among them two masterpieces of western literature – his autobiographical *Confessions* and a philosophical magnum opus, *The City of God*. He drew up a rule for a community of women he founded, and which formed the basis of the Rule of Augustinian canons in the Middle Ages: Martin Luther was an Augustinian friar. Much of Augustine's writing was countering heresies and schisms – Donatism (there were many more Donatists than orthodox Christians in Roman North Africa) and Pelagianism, the teaching of the Briton Pelagius that God's grace was not necessary for Salvation.

It was Augustine who is the source of the Church's teaching on Original Sin – viz. that we are born tainted with the sin of Adam and Eve – conveyed, Augustine believed, by the act of sexual intercourse that brings us into existence. Original Sin was washed away by the water of baptism: the unbaptised, even unbaptised babies, were damned. Critics said that Augustine had been carried away by his polemic against Pelagius in coming to this harsh view: it was an innovation in its day and would later be abandoned. Of greater significance was Augustine's teaching on Predestination which was to lead to a fissure in Christian belief more than a thousand years later.

14.   Doctors of the Church

So great was the influence of Augustine, both in his lifetime and in the centuries that followed, that it is easy to overlook the significance of his near contemporaries who, like Augustine, came to be called Doctors of the Church – Ambrose, who baptised Augustine; Gregory Nazianzen, John Chrysostom and Jerome. Ambrose was born in Augusta Treverorum (today's Trier), the largest Roman city north of the Alps. His parents were Christian; his father, Prefect of the Gauls and a member of the Senatorial aristocracy. Ambrose was sent to Rome to be educated, and in 365 followed his father into the imperial administration. Six years later, at the age of thirty-two, he was sent to Milan as governor of the provinces of Amelia and Liguria.

Two years into Ambrose's posting, in November 373, came the death of the Archbishop of Milan, Auxentius. Though he had reigned for almost twenty years, Auxentius had been an Arian, and so was considered a heretic by the adherents of the Nicene Creed. The assembly of Christians, gathered to choose his successor, was tempestuous and threatened to turn into a riot. Ambrose was summoned to restore calm and mediate between the different factions. The crowd of Christians listened to Ambrose and came to an unanimous conclusion: *he* should be their new bishop. He was elected by universal acclaim. Ambrose had been raised as a Christian but he had not yet been baptised. That was not considered an impediment by his enthusiastic supporters. He was baptised on 24th November, and ordained priest and consecrated as a bishop on 1st December. He would remain Archbishop of Milan until his death in 397.

The influence of Ambrose on the Church was considerable. He was a model pastor; he wrote treatises on virginity and faith; he imported the singing of hymns from the eastern to the western church; composed hymns himself; and drew up an Ambrosian rite still used today. More significant was the way in which a member of the Roman upper-classes should move so easily from a position of secular authority to a comparable position in the Church. Ambrose was familiar with the imperial administration in Milan: he was the friend and mentor of three emperors – of Gratian, the boy Valentian and Theodosius the Great. Giving a foretaste of the bitter disputes that were to take place in the Middle Ages between spiritual and secular leaders of Christendom, Ambrose insisted upon the independence of the Church from the state. 'The Emperor is *in* the church,' he told Theodosius, 'not over it.'

In late 388, a Christian mob in the city of Callinicum on the Euphrates, incited by their Christian bishop, plundered and burned down a synagogue. The Emperor Theodosius ordered his legate to punish those responsible and make the Christian bishop pay for the rebuilding of the synagogue. Ambrose protested. It would be iniquitous to expect a Christian bishop to pay for the re-building of an 'idolatrous' edifice. He insisted that all charges against the rioting Christians should be dropped. Theodosius backed down.

Gregory Nanzianzen and John Chrysostom were Greek-speaking prelates in the eastern Empire, both at one time bishops of Constantinople. Jerome's life was spent in both east and west, but his mother-tongue was Latin, and it was his outstanding proficiency in that language, and his knowledge of both Hebrew and Greek, that led to his unique contribution to Christian civilisation – a scholarly and graceful translation of the Bible.

Like Augustine, Jerome had been thoroughly educated in rhetoric by his Christian parents – a training which, because of his irascible temperament, led to a nastiness in the tone of his polemic. Jerome was an ascetic: at one time he lived as a hermit in the desert in Syria, but like Augustine he was subject to temptation. 'In my mind,' he wrote, 'I often found myself among groups of dancing girls' despite the privations of living among 'scorpions and wild beasts'. To distract himself from 'the fires of lust', he decided to learn Hebrew. He left the desert and studied the Scriptures under Gregory Nazianzen in Constantinople. In 382 he went to Rome to serve as secretary to Pope Damas. He antagonised the Romans by attacking the vanity of their wives and daughters. 'What are rouge and paint doing on the face of a Christian?' Not all the Roman matrons took offence: when, after the death of Pope Damas, Jerome decided to return to the east, he was accompanied by a rich widow, Paula, and her daughter Eustochium. They went to live near the Basilica of the Nativity in Bethlehem, and it was here, over the next thirty-five years, that Jerome worked on his translation of the Bible. When completed, it was adopted by the Catholic Church and called the Vulgate, from *versio vulgata* – the "version commonly used".

15.   Christians and the Jews

It was the Emperor Theodosius (379-395) who established Nicene Christianity as the established religion of the Roman Empire and, under the influence of Ambrose, passed laws against pagan worship. Inexorably, since the reign of Constantine I, Christians had grown in numbers and influence, and as early as 'the 340s we find the first surviving Christian text which asks for…the total intolerance of pagan worship'.[77] There was a momentary setback during the brief reign of the Emperor Julian 'the Apostate', a collateral descendant of the Emperor Constantine, who ruled from 361-363. Julian had been raised as a Christian but rejected the Christian religion in favour of a form of neo-Platonism. He believed that Christianity had sapped the vitality of the Empire which would flourish only if it returned to its pagan roots. Pagan temples were restored, and work started on the rebuilding of the Jewish Temple in Jerusalem. After initial military triumphs in the west, Julian invaded the Persian empire with disastrous results. On his retreat from the Euphrates,

---

77   Lane Fox, *Pagans and Christians*, p. 672

Julian was wounded, and later died. He was succeeded by Jovian, a Christian, who in his short reign re-established Christianity as the established Church.

Julian's intention to rebuild the Temple in Jerusalem was thought to be as much to antagonise the Christians as please the Jews. The enmity felt by Jews for 'the Nazarene sect' had not diminished over the centuries. In Justin Martyr's second century Dialogue with Trypho, a Jew 'confronts Trypho with the simple declaration, "You hate us and, whenever you have the power, kill us"'. Tertullian, another second century Christian scholar and apologist, said that the Jews were 'the seed-plot of all calumnies against us'.[78] Eusebius, a century later, described in his history of the early Church how at the burning of the bishop of Smyrna, Polycarp, during one of the periodic persecutions of Christians by the Roman emperors, 'the crowds rushed to collect logs and faggots...the Jews as usual joining in with more enthusiasm than anyone'.[79]

It was Eusebius who put forward the theory that the destruction of the Temple in Jerusalem was part of God's plan – a physical demonstration, like the tearing of the veil in the Temple at the time of death of Christ, that his Covenant with the Jews had been replaced by a Covenant with the Christians, the new People of God. The idea formed part of 'the polemic between Judaism and Christianity during the first centuries of the Common era,' which, as Israel Jacob Yuval has pointed out, 'in all their varieties and nuances, played a substantial role in the mutual formation of the two religions'.[80] To the Jewish mind, despite their expulsion from the promised land, the destruction of the Temple and the ascendancy of Christianity, Judaism remained alive in their fidelity to their Law, and the study of their sacred books – the Torah and the Talmud. 'The fall of Jerusalem swept away aristocracy and priesthood... The national idea was henceforth not the priest, the warrior, or the landowner, but the student; and aristocracy was reckoned in terms of the learning, rather than the wealth, of a man's family'.[81] 'Having lost the Kingdom of Israel, the Jews turned the Torah into a fortress of the mind and spirit, in which they could dwell in safety and even contentment'.[82]

The Torah is familiar to Christians as the Old Testament: the Talmud was (and to a large extent remains) a 'closed book' to gentiles. Yet it has been described as 'the most important book in Jewish culture, the backbone of

---

78   Flannery, *Op. Cit.*, p. 35

79   Eusebius, *The History of the Church from Christ to Constantine*, p. 171

80   Israel Jacob Yuval, *Two Nations in Your Womb*, p. xvii

81   Roth, *Op. Cit.* p. 125

82   Johnson, *Op. Cit.*, 149

creativity and of national life. No other work has had a comparable influence on the theory and practice of Jewish life, shaping spiritual content and serving as a guide to conduct.'[83]

What is the Talmud? Essentially, it is 'the summary of oral law that evolved after centuries of scholarly effort by sages who lived in Palestine and Babylonia until the beginning of the Middle Ages'. [84]

> The importance in Jewish life of the Talmud ...is not by any means purely academic. It comprises the accumulated wisdom of the Jewish people over many generations. No aspect of Hebrew thought, and no subject of human interest, is unrepresented in it... The way of life which the Talmud so minutely illustrated and prescribed made the whole people of Israel one, wheresoever they might be found and into however many political factions they might be divided. It gave them the characteristic imprint which distinguished them from others, as well as their remarkable powers of resistance and cohesion. Its dialectic sharpened their wits, and conferred upon them a preternatural mental acuteness.[85]

This 'characteristic imprint which distinguished them from others' had made Jews unpopular among the pagan Romans – an unpopularity that took on a theological dimension after the accession of Constantine. Imperial edicts, which had previously referred to Judaism as 'a distinguished religion, certainly permissible', now referred to it as 'a sacrilegious gathering' or 'nefarious sect'. 'Judaism steadily lost ground in competition for the pagan soul. Under the new Christian empire, its privileges were withdrawn.'[86] Discriminatory legislation restricted the civic status of the Jews: they were barred from public functions – the army, the civil service, and, intermittently, the practice of law. Jewish marriage to Christians and any form of proselytism were forbidden under pain of death.

The edict forbidding proselytism and conversion had grave implications for the social and economic status of Jews – hitherto 'a large, well-organised, comparatively wealthy minority...'[87]

---

83   Adin Steinsaltz, *The Essential Talmud*, p. 3

84   Steinsaltz, *Op. Cit.* p. 3

85   Roth, *Op. Cit.* p 132

86   Flannery, *Op. Cit.* p. 45

87   Johnson, *Op. Cit.* p. 164

Jews were prominent in slave trading and also engaged in agriculture and industry, which required the use of slaves. Motivated by proselytic zeal and a wish to avoid legal impurity incurred by household contact with the uncircumcised, they were in the habit of circumcising their slaves. The Church was naturally alarmed at the loss to the fold. The Empire, sharing the worry of the Church, determined to put an end to the practice. The grave consequences for Jewry can be understood. Many were forced from agriculture and industry into small trades and crafts, but not without strong and prolonged resistance to the slavery statutes.[88]

Understandably, the Jews 'greeted with relief' the accession of the Emperor Julian, and welcomed the commissioning of Alypius of Antioch in 363 to rebuild the Temple in Jerusalem. However, the project was thwarted when, as Alypius's masons started work, 'fearful balls of fire, breaking out near their foundations' so scorched the workmen that they had to give up the attempt. Some historians ascribe this setback to the earthquake in Galilee of 363; others suggest sabotage or an accidental fire. Christians saw it as an act of God. 'Christianity saw the destruction of the Temple as a manifestation of God's vengeance for the crucifixion of his son.'[89]

John Chrysostom ('the honey tongued') Patriarch of Constantinople, made much of Julian's failure to rebuild the Temple in his sermons. He saw it as a direct intervention of God to perpetuate Judaism's punishment as prophesied by Jesus in the New Testament. Christians and Jews continued to argue over 'what brought about the destruction of Jerusalem… Just as the Church accused the Jew of the "original sin" of the Crucifixion, so did the Jews charge Rome, and by extension the Church, with the "original sin" of the destruction of Jerusalem and the Temple.'[90]

Was Chrysostom an anti-Semite? Modern scholars now believe that the collection of his sermons given the Greek title of Kata Ioudaiōn (Κατά Ιουδαίων), translated as *Adversus Judaeos* in Latin and *Against the Jews* in English, were in fact directed not against the Jews but members of his own congregation who observed Jewish feasts and fasts; the collection should be properly translated as 'Against Judaizing Christians'. He is said to have 'made

---

88   Flannery, *Op. Cit.* p. 57-58
89   Yuval, *Op. Cit.*, p. 32
90   Yuval, *Op. Cit.*, p. 32

the deicidal theme central to his theology of Judaism' [91], and that the idea of a collective responsibility for the crucifixion of Christ – the sins of the fathers handed down from generation to generation – is to be found among some Christians until the 20th century.

The charge of 'deicide' is gleaned from the Christian Gospels, now newly translated by Jerome. The fourth century Nicene Creed, the agreed summary of belief of all Christian churches after the reign of Theodosius, talks of Jesus 'suffering under Pontius Pilate', not suffering at the hands of the Jews; but there are some passages in the canonical Gospels that gave rise to the view that the Jews as a people were to blame for the death of Christ. In the Gospel of John, writes Paul Johnson in his *History of the Jews*,[92] ' "the Jews" appears to mean many different things – the Sadducees, the Pharisees, or both together, the Temple police, the Jewish establishment, the Sanhedrin, the Jewish ruling class – but also the people.... The most offensive and damaging passage in the Gospels is, in fact, in the Gospel of Matthew who has the Roman procurator, Pontius Pilate, saying "'I have no part in the death of this innocent man; it concerns you only". And the whole people answered, "'His blood be upon us, and upon our children"'.[93]

Robert S. Wistrich, as we have seen, and a number of other authors, find this account 'highly improbable', a shifting blame from Pontius Pilate 'partly for political reasons in order not to antagonise the Romans' [94] at the time the Gospels were written; but in the Babylonian Talmud the Jews not only accept the responsibility but take credit for the crucifixion of Christ: their position was, as Peter Schäfer puts it in his *Jesus in the Talmud*: 'yes, the Roman governor wanted to set him free, but we did not give in. He was a blasphemer and idolater, and although the Romans probably could not care less, we insisted that he get what he deserved. We even convinced the Roman governor (or more precisely forced him to accept) that this heretic and impostor needed to be executed – and we are proud of it'.[95]

The Babylonian Talmud 'was the main source of instruction for Jews everywhere (Palestine alone excepted)' from the time of its compilation in the fifth century and throughout the Middle Ages.[96] From it a clear picture

---

91   Flannery, *Op. Cit.* p. 64

92   Johnson, *Op. Cit.* p. 146

93   Matthew, 27:25-26

94   Robert S. Wistrich, *Antisemitism. The Longest Hatred*, p. 14

95   Peter Schäfer, *Jesus in the Talmud*, p. 74

96   Johnson, *Op. Cit.* p, 163

emerges that is 'a daring and powerful counter Gospel to the New Testament and John in particular'. The Jewish counter-narrative maintains that Joseph and Mary were married, that Mary had a secret lover and that Joseph's initial suspicion was correct. Mary had indeed been unfaithful to him. Mary's lover, Jesus's natural father, was a Roman soldier, Pandera. As punishment for the sin of adultery, she should have been stoned to death as laid down by the Law of Moses; and Jesus, her bastard son, by the same law, become a social outcast: '"No bastard (*mamzer*) shall be admitted into the Congregation of the Lord; even to the tenth generation shall he not be admitted into the Congregation of the Lord. (Deuteronomy, 23:3)'.[97]

According to the Babylonian Talmud – an account also put about by the pagan philosopher, Celsus – Jesus, under the name of Simeon, went to Egypt where he learned the magic with which he worked his 'miracles' when he returned to Israel, and persuaded some to believe that he was the Son of God. 'The worst idolater is someone who … declares himself God or the son of God. This falls under the category of blasphemy, which according to the Bible, deserves the death penalty of stoning.' [98] 'The reason for his execution was because he was convicted of sorcery and of enticing Israel into idolatry.'[99] Nor was Christ's crucifixion the end of the punishment inflicted on this, 'one of the worst heretics that the people of Israel have ever produced'. He is 'punished in Gehinnom … sitting forever in boiling excrement.' [100]

Thus the charge of an undying hatred for Christianity made by Christians in the fourth century AD such as Basil the Great, Gregory Nazianzen and John Chrysostom was not fanciful; and 'even the expulsions and other clearly characteristic violence inflicted on Jews by representatives of Christianity lose something of their horror when we discover the Jews, when conditions lent themselves, did not hesitate to have recourse to these measures themselves.'[101] However, from the accession of Constantine conditions increasingly favoured the Christians who by the end of the fourth century showed the same fanaticism in defence of their religion as had the Jews.

---

97   Schäfer, *Op. Cit.*, p. 97

98   Schäfer, *Op. Cit.*, p. 106

99   Schäfer, *Op. Cit.*, p. 12

100   Schäfer, *Op. Cit.*, p. 13

101   Blumenkrantz, quoted in Flanery, *Op. Cit.p. 79*

16.   The Fall of the Roman Empire

When Augustine lay dying in Hippo in 430, the city was being besieged by the Vandals, a barbarian tribe who the year before had breached the frontiers of the western Empire, and swept through Gaul and the Iberian peninsula into North Africa. The borders of the western Empire had for many centuries been the rivers Rhine and Danube, with a fortified 350-mile *limes Germanicus* running between the two. Roman armies had made incursions beyond this frontier, fighting battles with the barbarian tribes as far east as the Elbe; but by the fourth century all that could be hoped for was containment of the different tribes who, often from sheer want, wished to settle within the Roman Empire. For some time there had been an erosion of the distinction between Roman and barbarian: in 212 AD Roman citizenship had been extended to all inhabitants of the Empire, and barbarians were recruited into the Roman army, but often turned against those they were meant to protect.

This seepage became a flood in the late fourth century when the Visigoths, some of whom had already been allowed to settle in the empire, and who had accepted baptism by Arian Christians, were pressed from the east by another savage tribe, the Huns, and so a further 200,000 were allowed into the Empire. Left to starve, they turned on their hosts and at the Battle of Adrianople in 378 AD defeated the Romans, later starting their pillaging migration west through Spain and North Africa to Corsica, Sardinia and Sicily.

In the winter of 405-406, the river Rhine froze over, permitting many thousands of barbarians to cross into the Empire. Notionally, these tribes considered themselves Roman 'federates' but in reality they took control of the areas where they settled – the Vandals, Visigoths, Ostrogoths, Huns, Burgundians and, in the lowlands at the mouth of the Rhine, the Franks. Britain was abandoned – the last Roman legions withdrawn by the Emperor Honorius in AD 410: 'one of the most telling signs of the times,' writes the historian Richard Fletcher, 'was the building of town walls throughout the western provinces of Gaul, Spain and Britain, furnishing defenses for settlements which had never needed them before'.[102]

The last Roman emperor in the west, Romulus Augustulus, was deposed by the Ostrogoth chieftain, Odacer, in 475 after reigning for only ten months. Odacer then ruled Italy from Ravenna, preserving the Roman administration and enlisting the support of many of the Senatorial families. Assassinated in

---

102   Fletcher, *Op. Cit.* p. 18

Ravenna, he was succeeded by Theodoric who called himself the 'King of the Goths and Romans', and was recognized by the eastern Emperor Anastasias as the ruler of Italy. He, like Odacer, retained the Empire's administrative structure, employing members of the Roman elite, among them the philosopher Boethius. Although an Arian, he took no measures against the Catholic Church. He imposed the rule of law – Roman law for the Romans, Gothic law for the Goths.

Thus, what came to be called 'the Fall of the Roman Empire' was not a single, cataclysmic event like the fall of the Byzantine empire a thousand years later with the capture of Constantinople by the Ottoman Turks. Rome, with almost a million inhabitants, was first besieged and then sacked by the Visigoths under Alaric in 409 and 410, the first time it had fallen to an enemy army in its 800-year history, but those who had fled later returned. In 452 Attila the Hun approached Rome, but was met by the Pope, Leo, and his clergy outside the city walls, and bought off with the promise of tribute. Three years later, a Vandal army under Geneseric besieged the city. Again, it was Leo who treated with Geneseric, persuading him to spare the inhabitants and the buildings if permitted to enter the city unopposed.

A hundred years later, in 547, the Goths under their king Totila captured and plundered the city. The population of Rome declined. Many left the city for fear of further barbarian incursions, but also because the Vandals' conquest of north Africa had stopped the supply of grain. Nevertheless, with around 350,000 inhabitants at the turn of the fifth to the sixth century, it remained the largest city in both the eastern and western empires. Some of the monuments and temples were in ruins, either destroyed by the invaders or cannibalised by the city's inhabitants to build homes and churches; but its schools and academies remained open.

17.   Benedict of Nursia

Around 494, a minor nobleman living in Nursia in the Sabine Hills sent his fourteen-year-old son Benedict to complete his education in Rome, accompanied by his former nurse-maid, Cyrilla. They remained in Rome for two or three years, but Benedict, a devout Christian, was appalled by the decadence of the Romans and with Cyrilla left the city. He decided that he would abandon any worldly ambitions and devote his life to God as a hermit or anchorite. Under the guidance of a monk, Romanus, he exchanged his patrician clothes for a garment made of sheep-skin, and went to live alone in a cave in Subiaco. Cyrilla, it may be assumed, returned to Nursia.

Withdrawing from the world in this way was not new. As early as 320 Paul, a young Christian living in Upper Egypt, had left the home of his prosperous parents for the nearby desert where he found a cave next to a spring in which he lived alone for the next ninety years. Right at the end of his life, he received a visit from Antony, also from Upper Egypt, who too had sold all his property and lived in the desert on a diet of bread and water. Others who wished to emulate Antony's ascetic life gathered around him: a community was formed. His reputation for sanctity reached the Emperor Constantine, who asked for his prayers. Athanasius, Bishop of Alexandria, came to visit him, and enlisted him in his struggle against the Arians. Pachomius (c. 295-346), another Egyptian, inspired by a vision to set up a monastery on the Upper Nile, is credited with the first rule for communal living. It proved so popular that by his death in 346 he is said to have presided over nine monasteries and two communities of religious women.

How do we account for this call to the ascetic life so many years after the death of Christ? 'The first Christian hermits,' we are told by Robin Lane Fox, 'retreated to the desert in order to escape from their fellow Christians.'[103] During the Great Persecution under Diocletian, ardent believers had been horrified to see fellow-Christians lapse or lie or pay bribes rather than suffer for their faith. And when the persecution ended, and Christianity became the Emperor Constantine's favoured religion, there were Christians who profited from his lavish endowments to lead a worldly life. The aim of the first 'holy men' who fled to the desert was to be perfect, to live a life in the 'rank of angels', as the Gospel seemed to define it. 'The monastic life became the main avenue to perfection; at the same time, a far from perfect Christian majority had as great a need as ever for intercessors and agents of blessing and forgiveness.'[104]

In Egypt, the desert was close and familiar; so too in Syria where, rather than retreat into caves, some Christian ascetics lived on the top of pillars, a few remaining there for years. Most celebrated was Simeon Stylites, born around 390, who outdid all others in the mortification of his flesh. He moved from a cell to live on the top of a 67-foot pillar on a platform six feet square. He was imitated by other 'Stylites' in the eastern church over many centuries. More

---

103   Lane Fox, *Pagans and Christians*, p. 602
104   Ibid., p. 604

conventional monasteries were founded in the east by Basil (329-379) with a rule more balanced and humane than that of Pachomius. In the west, the first monastery was founded by Martin, Bishop of Tours, in Ligugé near Poitiers in 360. Augustine of Hippo, as we have seen, drew up a rule for communities of both men and women at the end of the fourth century. By the fifth century, the heads and necks of monks were shaved, leaving a rim of hair encircling a bald patch on the top of the skull. This was called the tonsure; its origin is uncertain; but it became the mark of admission into Holy Orders – first for monks, and later for secular clergy. Women religious had all their hair shaved off. 'A woman…thinks long hair her glory', Paul of Tarsus had said – a glory unfitting for those who had renounced the world.

The significance of Benedict of Nursia, then, was not that he founded the first monastery in western Europe, but rather that he drew up a Rule that was followed by almost all future monastic foundations. His reputation for holiness drew others to join him at Subiaco but, because of dissension with another monk, Benedict and some chosen companions left Subiaco and travelled south to the town of Cassinium. Towering above the city, was a mountain, Montecassino, crowned with a pagan temple of Apollo. Benedict and his followers climbed the mountain, smashed the statue of Apollo, destroyed the temple, and in its ruins built a church and monastery. He remained there until his death in 547, and it was there that he wrote his Rule.

What accounts for the Rule's success?

It is a remarkable document, Roman in its strength and balance, and in its sound practical detail; exquisitely charitable, fervent in faith. St. Benedict laid his emphasis upon community life. He divided the monks' day between prayer, study and manual labour. He mitigated the austerities of the Egyptian desert, urging the abbot, whose rule was to be paternal and monarchic, 'so to temper all things that the strong may still have something to long after, and the weak may not draw back in alarm'. If no detail was too trivial to interest him – from the clothes and shoes of the brethren to their portions of food and drink – he could point the way to great spiritual heights, as in his *Prologue* and in his famous 72nd chapter, *On Good Zeal*. The virtues he specially enjoined were those of obedience and humility.[105]

---

105   *The Saints*. A Concise Biographical Dictionary. Edited by John Coulson. London, 1957

'The care of the sick shall come before and above all else, so that in the very deed they be served as Christ…' , Benedict wrote in Chapter 36 of his Rule – thereby establishing monasteries and religious orders as the principal purveyors of social welfare until the end of the nineteenth century. The Rule's insistence upon manual labour would have a significant effect on the development of agriculture, and hence the economic development of western Europe, but much of this was yet to come. Even as Benedict wrote his Rule, western Europe was passing 'from the twilight of the ancient world into the darkness that preceded the dawn of mediaeval civilization.' 'In the chaos and turmoil of the age that followed, the monasteries of western Europe, from being places of withdrawal from a world that was seething with political and social activity, gradually became centres of light and life in a simple, static, semi-barbarian world, preserving and later diffusing what remained of ancient culture and spirituality.' The Rule was established as a template for Roman order and Christian love. 'While kingdoms changed hands and great estates were broken up, the monastery, self-supporting and self-sufficient, could often remain. It became a nucleus that could escape destruction…and prosper in times of peace.'[106]

18.   Gregory the Great

Within fifty years of the death of Benedict of Nursia in 547, a Benedictine monk was chosen as pope – Gregory I, the second of only three popes to be called 'the great'[107]. Gregory was the son of a rich Roman patrician, the senator Gordianus: the family had provided two popes earlier in the century. After studying law, Gregory had been made Prefect of the city but in his early 30s he withdrew from public life to become a Benedictine monk. He was no ordinary monk because by then his father had died and he was the heir to large estates throughout Italy and Sicily, and a mansion on the Coelian hill. The resources were sufficient to found six monasteries in Sicily: his family home became a monastery dedicated to St. Andrew. There he hoped to lead a life of hermetic seclusion but was summoned to serve the pope, Benedict I, who ordained him as a deacon; and soon after he was sent by Benedict's successor, Pelagius II, as his ambassador to the Eastern emperor in Constantinople. He

---

106   David Knowles, *Christian Monasticism*, p. 37

107   The other two were Leo (440-461)and Nicholas (858-867).

remained there seven years, returning to Rome in 585. When Pope Pelagius died five years later, he was unanimously chosen as the new pope.

'Gregory,' wrote the historian Richard Fletcher, 'was a Roman through and through'[108] and he administered the patrimony of the Church as if it was an empire. 'The Church was by now the largest single landowner in the west, its property built up by the imperial bounty in the Constantinian era, and then from donations and legacies of great families like Gregory's own.'[109] With exceptional energy and administrative skill, Gregory reorganized and deployed these resources to feed the hungry and care for the poor. During the last years of the sixth century, 'he became virtually civil ruler of Italy, negotiating treaties, paying troops and appointing generals'.[110] He upheld the primacy of the popes as the successors of the apostle Peter, insisted upon clerical celibacy and, when Jews were mistreated in Palermo, Gregory rebuked the bishop, reminding him that 'Jews had the legal right to observe the solemnities handed down to them by their ancestors'.[111] Jews were not to be allowed to proselytize, but there were to be no forced conversions to Christianity or seizure of their property, and they could practice their religion. '[112] The words *sicut Judaeis* ('and thus to the Jews'), first used by Gregory in this letter, brought Augustine of Hippo's teachings on the Jews into Roman Law. Gregory published a bull which became the foundation of Catholic teaching in relation to the Jews and specified that, although the Jews had not accepted salvation through Christ, and were therefore condemned by God until such time as they accepted salvation, Christians were nevertheless duty-bound to protect them as, following Augustine, living evidence of the Church's origins: 'like fossils for the naturalist, the Jews' continued presence on the earth is proof of an earlier stage, now superseded, in salvation's evolution'.[113]

In 596, intent on the conversion of pagans, Gregory dispatched the prior of his monastery on the Coelian Hill, Augustine, with a company of forty monks, on a mission to the pagan Anglo-Saxons in England. Briton had been Christian when part of the Roman empire, but the invasion of the Angles, Saxons and Jutes in the fourth and fifth centuries had driven the Christians to retreat to remote parts of the British Isles. They were cut off from Rome.

---

108   Fletcher, *Op. Cit.*, p. 114

109   Eamon Duffy, *Saints and Sinners*, p. 64

110   *Dictionary of the Saints*, p. 66

111   J.M. Wallace-Hadrill, *The Frankish Church*, p. 392

112   Epistolæ, vii. 25, Sicut Judæis

113   David Nirenberg, *Anti-Judaism. The History of a Way of Thinking*, p. 129

When Augustine and his forty monks landed on the Isle of Thanet in Kent, they were welcomed by the local king, Aethelbert, whose wife Bertha, the daughter of the Frankish Count of Paris, was a Christian. After a tricky start, Aethelbert and his entourage were baptised; dioceses were established in Canterbury and Rochester, and later London and York. Contact was made with the Christians on the Celtic fringes who treated the Italian missionaries with great suspicion and only over time came to align their practices to those of Rome.

In the course of his reign, Gregory established some changes to the liturgy, and initiated the pious devotion of the Stations of the Cross. He left a considerable correspondence – around 850 letters – and many sermons and homilies. His *Pastoral Care* outlining the duties of bishops was translated into Anglo-Saxon by King Alfred, and became the set text on the subject for centuries to come. His theology followed closely that of Augustine of Hippo, but his greatest devotion was to Benedict of Nursia who had died only half a century before. Gregory's *Dialogues* is 'a set of miracle-encrusted lives of the early Italian monks, in particular St. Benedict' – revealing a piety 'colourful, receptive to miracles and marvels, readily moved to awe' [114] – this judgement made by the historian, Eamon Duffy, in the 20th century and addressed to a generation less receptive to miracles and marvels or moved to awe. Less receptive, too, to Benedict's remedy for the temptation of the flesh as described by Gregory: once, when lascivious thoughts about a woman entered his imagination, he stripped naked and threw his body in a thorn bush. Such thoughts never returned.

19.   The Franks

Of the barbarian tribes that overran the western Roman empire in the course of the fifth and sixth centuries, some like the Huns did not settle, others like the Gepids, Thuringians, and Alamans were defeated and absorbed by the larger tribes, and a few like the Sueves, Burgundians and Bavarians became these larger tribes' allies. By the fifth century, the Vandals remained in north Africa; the Visigoths ruled most of the Iberian peninsula; and the Ostrogoths had established a kingdom in Italy and Sicily. In the mid-sixth century, the armies of the Eastern Emperor Justinian under his general Belisarius

---

114   Duffy, *Op. Cit.* p. 6

reconquered Italy, north Africa and parts of the south coast of the Iberian peninsula; but his hold on these territories did not last. In 624 the Visigoths finally evicted the Byzantines from Spain, and a new tribe, the Lombards, successfully invaded Italy, leaving Justinian in control only of Ravenna, and the land around it.

We have now moved into what historians once called 'the Dark Ages' – five or six centuries with few extant monuments to mark their passing, and few records of what took place. And yet it is wrong to assume a complete breakdown in governance, learning or civilization of any kind. Benedict of Nursia, as we have seen, studied in Rome where, in the sporadic absence of a secular ruler, the popes like Gregory took control of the city. However, the fate of Italy, the future of the Catholic Church, and indeed of western Europe, was determined by what took place north of the Alps.

A barbarian tribe, the Salian Franks, had under their king Clovis emerged from their homeland in the Rhine delta to conquer the whole of Gaul. The dynasty was called Merovingian after its semi-mythical founder, Merovech. Clovis was married to a Catholic Burgundian princess, Chrotechildis, who had their two sons baptized. The first died just after his baptism which Clovis saw as the punishment by his pagan gods. However in 496, at Tolbiac, when Clovis faced a superior force of Alamans, Queen Chrotechildis persuaded him to call for help from Christ. The predicted defeat became a victory: Tolbiac was Clovis's Milvian Bridge. He was baptized together with his retinue of warriors by Bishop Remigius at Rheims.

As we can see from the role of Bishop Remigius, the Church had not been dispossessed by the pagan Franks; indeed, 'the churches and monasteries of Roman Gaul emerged from the barbarian invasions and settlements as landed proprietors on a large scale. Roman law defined and protected their properties and moveable wealth.'[115] Normally the Gallo-Roman bishops and sometimes abbots were men of rank and personal wealth. They lived in cities where most Christians were to be found – the population of the countryside often remained pagan[116] – living in compounds which included the cathedral, their residence and the *hôtel dieu* which could 'refer to a number of different functions, including what we today would call a hospital, a hospice, a hostelry, an orphanage or a place for the care of abandoned children.'

---

115   J.M. Wallace-Hadrill, *Op. Cit.*, p. 123

116   The French word for peasant – *paysan* – comes from *païen*, pagan.

In the Roman empire, the local administration or, to be more precise, the prefect, was responsible for offering assistance to the unfortunate. However, as city government collapsed, the Church, and thus the bishop, inherited such charitable functions, for which it was well suited through the mission entrusted to it by Christ. From the fourth century, it assumed full responsibility for such tasks, redefining and extending them as society evolved in new directions. There was no mistaking the recommendations that popes made in regard to these matters, for they had strongly emphasised the obligation to bring succour to God's disinherited. Thus, under Pope Simplicius (468-83), Gelasius stipulated that bishops should reserve a quarter of their church's income in *hospitalitas*, a term here interpreted in a very wide sense. Such rulings were reiterated at regular intervals, for example at the Councils of Orleans (511), Tours (567) and Mâcon (585). In 583, at the Council of Lyons, the care of lepers was added to the list. These exhortations were not only repeated but, in addition, they became prescriptions or even threats. At the Council of Orleans (511), those prelates who failed to fulfil their duties risked being demoted.[117]

Not all bishops in Gaul were local notables. Hilary of Poitiers, himself from an eminent pagan family, was succeeded as bishop by Martin, a native of Pannonia (present day Hungary). Martin had been a soldier in the imperial army who, when stationed in Amiens, had taken pity on a shivering beggar and given him half his cloak. The next day, he had a dream or vision in which he saw the same half of his cloak covering the shoulders of Jesus. Still only a Christian catechumen at the time, Martin was baptized and asked to leave the army. He was accused of cowardice. To prove his courage, he stood unarmed before his cohort during a military encounter.

Released from the army, Martin went to Poitiers where he was ordained priest by Hilary. He founded a monastery at Ligué near Poitiers, the first in mainland France. On the death of Hilary, he was chosen as his successor. His life as recounted by his biographer, Sulpicius Severus, describes a sequence of confrontations – with the pagans in the countryside whose sacred trees, shrines and temples he demolished; with 'well heeled, well connected, well read and groomed'[118] fellow bishops, appalled at his beggar's attire; and with imperial officials over his demands for clemency for prisoners. His visions, and the miracles he performed, together with his ascetic lifestyle and patent

---

117   Alain Erland-Brandenburg, *The Cathedral. The Social and Architectural Dynamics of Construction*, CUP, 1994

118   Fletcher, *Op. Cit.* p. 39

holiness, meant that he was held in awe by Christians in all stations of life. Helen, the devout wife of the usurping Emperor Maximus, visited Martin at Tours, and waited on him at table.

Martin died on 8th November, 397, and was at once acclaimed as a saint: his tomb became the most venerated in France. He was not a martyr; he had not died for his faith; but in the fourth and fifth centuries, 'asceticism assumed the function of martyrdom as the road to sanctity'.[119] Pagan superstition had been supplanted by Christian belief in the intercession of the saints. Relics were prized for their magical powers. At the instigation of Genevieve, a holy woman living in Paris, an abbey was built north of Paris to house the relics of Dionysius or Denis on the site of his execution during the persecution of the Emperor Decius in the mid-third century[120]. It would become the mausoleum of the French kings.

A holy and influential figure in Paris, Genevieve exemplifies the esteem in which women were held by the Franks.

> Aside from her natural gifts and abilities, the Germanic woman was a prophetess. So, too, were Celtic women. Married, the Frankish woman…was no mere chattel. She could hold and administer land, defend herself in court, act as a compurgator, make donations and free her slaves if she wished.[121]

Pope Gregory had made use of Christian queens such as the Bavarian Theudelinda, married to two successive Lombard kings; and Bertha, the wife of the Kentish ruler, Aethelbert. Devout women, not just saintly men, were the agents of the Christianisation of Europe.

After Clovis's victory over the Visigoths at Vouille in 507, the Emperor Anastasius in Constantinople conferred on him the office of honorary consul of the Roman Empire. The barbarian was now a Roman: the pagan now a Catholic – and by no means a nominal Catholic, but one who promoted and protected missions to his as yet unconquered pagan neighbours. This was in contrast to the absence of missionary zeal in the early centuries when the identities of Roman and Christian were conflated, and 'there could be no

---

119   J.M. Wallace-Hadrill, *Op. Cit.* p. 37

120   Legend had it that Denis was decapitated in Montmartre, and walked holding his head to the site of his interment prompting the observation by Mme du Deffand in the eighteenth century: 'ce n'est que le premier pas qui coute'. It is only the first step that matters.

121   J.M. Wallace-Hadrill, *Op. Cit.* p. 404

question of taking the faith to the heathen barbarian'. There was not a single example, we are told by Richard Fletcher, 'of a man who was appointed bishop with the specific task of going beyond the frontier of a wholly pagan region in order to convert the barbarians living there.'[122]

It was a Briton, Patrick, 'who crossed the threshold'. Kidnapped from his home near the Severn estuary in then Roman Britain by pirates, he was enslaved in Ireland, but later escaped, and returned as priest and bishop to convert his former captors, dying with his task accomplished in 492. One of his spiritual progeny, Columba (521-597), left Ireland to convert the Scots and northern English, founding a monastery on Iona. Another Irishman, Columbanus, went further afield to the continent of Europe. Welcomed by the Franks, he founded a monastery at Luxeuil in the bleak uplands of northern Burgundy close to the source of the Saône. The monastery flourished but, after antagonizing the King of Burgundy by rebuking him for fathering four children out of wedlock, Columbanus was obliged to leave Luxeuil. He sailed up the Rhine, preaching the Christian faith, reaching Bregenz on Lake Constance. Here it was antagonistic pagans who drove him out. He crossed the Alps and was welcomed by the Arian Lombard king. He and his companions were given a ruined oratory in the Apennines which became the great monastery of Bobbio. Asked to mediate between the Arians and the pope in Rome, he declined, proclaiming his total fidelity to the see of Peter. 'We, Irish, living disciples of Saint Peter and Saint Paul... are bound to the chair of Saint Peter; for however great and glorious Rome may be, it is this chair which makes her great and glorious in our eyes.'

Another monk who looked to Rome was Wilfrid, the son of a Northumbrian nobleman, who in his youth studied at the monastery of Lindisfarne and Canterbury, but also in France and at Rome. Latin was the language of the Church, and so an Englishman could converse with any bishop or priest. In 664 a synod was summoned by King Oswiu or Northumberland to meet at the Abbey of Whitby where his relative Hilda was the abbess. At issue was the date of Easter, calculated in different ways by the Roman and the Celtic Churches. The synod was described by the Benedictine monk, known as the Venerable Bede, in his *Historia ecclesiastica gentis Anglorum* (*Ecclesiastical History of the English People*) written in the monastery of St. Peter in Jarrow on the Wear. Wilfrid was successful at the synod: the English Church adopted the same formula for calculating Easter as the pope in Rome.

---

122   Fletcher, *Op. Cit.*, p. 25

Willibrord, another Northumbrian nobleman (657-739), was educated at Wilfrid's monastery at Ripon, and he had the same 'strong sense of allegiance to Rome'. In 678 he moved to Ireland and twelve years later, at the age of thirty-two, travelled to the Continent where he gained the support of the Franks for a mission to the pagan Frisians. Before embarking on this mission, he travelled to Rome to obtain the pope's approval. There he was consecrated under the name Clement as the archbishop of the Frisians with his see at Utrecht where he remained until his death in 739 at the age of eighty-one.

Although Willibrord did not himself make many converts among the pagans, he inspired others to come from England to preach the Gospel to their Continental cousins. Among them was Wynfrid (675-674), a West Saxon born in Crediton in Devon. A monk from an early age, he was elected abbot of the community at Nursling but declined the post to join Willibrord on the mission to the Frisians. He too went to Rome to ensure papal approval, where he was consecrated bishop and given the name Boniface. Rather than join Willibrord in Utrecht, Boniface went to Hesse in Thuringia where, in a spectacular gesture, he chopped down an oak tree sacred to the Norse god Donar. It enraged the pagan Germans but Boniface was protected by the Franks. He went on to preach, baptize and recruit a native clergy, mingling neophytes with the experienced in the monasteries he founded – most notably Fulda. He was bishop of two new sees, Cologne and Mainz, but also undertook the reform of the Frankish church, reinforcing its links to Rome. Richard Fletcher ascribes the initially peaceable conversion of the pagans in Germany to Boniface: it was therefore an irony that in 754, by then an old man, while administering the sacrament of confirmation to his most recent converts, he was attacked and killed by a party of pagan marauders.

20.   Relics

The body of Boniface was buried at the abbey at Fulda and, immediately after his interment, pilgrims came to venerate his earthly remains. From the earliest days of the Church, dead bodies of holy men and women, particularly martyrs, were preserved and venerated and deemed to have miraculous powers. After the martyrdom of Polycarp in 156 AD his bones and ashes were recovered and revered. When Cyprian of Carthage was beheaded in 258 AD 'the Christians laid out cloths to receive his blood as a relic'. [123] Miracles were ascribed to the remains of saints, and pilgrims from all over Christendom came to their tombs, starting with that of Peter beneath the altar of the basilica on the Vatican hill, and Paul in the basilica *fuori le Mura* – outside the walls of Rome.

The greatest of all relics was the Cross upon which Christ had been crucified, discovered as we have seen by Helena, the mother of the Emperor Constantine, together with the nails that had been driven through his hands and feet, and the *titulus* – the placard ordered by Pontius Pilate to be nailed to the cross on which was written 'Jesus the Nazarene, King of the Jews'. [124] The nails sent by Helena to her son Constantine were embedded in the imperial crown. The True Cross, like the *titulus,* was divided. One half was carried into battle by the Byzantines, captured by the Persians but recovered by the Emperor Heraclius. It was once again in the van of the Crusaders army that faced Saladin on the heights of Hattin but failed to prevent its defeat.

Fragments of the True Cross were to be found in reliquaries throughout Europe, and later Protestant and Enlightenment sceptics would claim that if reassembled they would suffice to build Noah's Ark. Unquestionably, truth and legend, a distinction that meant less in the past than it does to us today, were always hard to disentangle, but it is interesting that the inscription on half of the titulus kept as a relic in the Church of the Holy Cross in Rome, itself built over Helena's palace, written in both Hebrew and Latin, contains certain Hebrew characters unique to the 1st Century AD, and the Latin, like the Hebrew, is written from right to left. The German historian, Michael Hesemann, after consulting Jewish and secular experts in 1997, concluded that 'the Titulus Crucis is indeed the authentic relic'. [125]

Many of the tombs such as those of Boniface, Benedict of Nursia or Martin of Tours contained their remains, less fragments of bones or cloth that had been subtracted and sent elsewhere: one of Boniface's spinal vertebra enclosed in a silver mounted glass dome is found today in the Benedictine Abbey of Downside in England. Some bones had been re-interred such as those of the martyr Denis by the Frankish king Dagobert in the seventh century: over his tomb in the twelfth century the Abbot Suger built the first Gothic church, the Abbey of St. Denis. The tomb of Thomas Becket, murdered in Canterbury in

---

123   John Coulson, *A Dictionary of the Saints,* p. 141

124   John, 19:19

125   See Michael Hesemann, *Die Jesus-Tafel,* 1999

1170, drew large numbers of pilgrims whose donations led to its adornment with gold, silver and precious stones. Among the finest artefacts of this period are the gold and silver reliquaries – sometimes bejewelled or enamelled – which contained the often fragmentary remains of a saint.

The veneration of relics was to be an acute point of difference between Catholics and Protestants at the time of the Reformation, and was mocked by the *philosophes* of the French Enlightenment. That many were fake is beyond dispute and, although Augustine of Hippo and his mentor Ambrose of Milan had both witnessed miraculous cures after contact with relics, and despite the account in the Old Testament of how a corpse was brought back to life by falling on the bones of Elisha when thrown into his tomb, miracles were dismissed by Luther and Calvin as yet another means for the unscrupulous clergy to exploit the credulous laity.

The Catholic Church did not deny that there were fakes; attempts were made to discover and destroy them, often with unfortunate results such as those which followed the Synod of Pistoia in 1786. There is a poignant scene in Guiseppe di Lampedusa's novel, *The Leopard,* set in Sicily in the nineteenth century, when the hero's devout aunts are forced to relinquish relics considered inauthentic.

However, the veneration of authentic relics, and their miraculous powers, was consistently upheld by the Church. Thomas Aquinas rejected the idea of a relic as some kind of magical talisman but wrote that 'God fittingly does honour to such relics by performing miracles in their presence'. A belief in the Resurrection of the Dead enhanced the value of a saint's body which on occasions when exhumed were found to be incorrupt. Incorruptibility was held to establish the sanctity of the deceased. When the Council of Trent in its 25th session issued a decree on relics, it showed some of Aquinas's caution, insisting that all claims of miraculous cures must be investigated by the bishops of the diocese in which it took place, but it approved the veneration of relics and condemned those who dismissed it as superstition. Indeed, it was established that relics should be placed in a small cavity carved out of every altar stone upon which Mass was said.

Pilgrims, like today's tourists, spent money, and there was competition for their custom. It was said that the house of the Virgin Mary had been carried by angels, first to Croatia, then to Loreto in Italy: a fine basilica was built over its four walls. It was while on pilgrimage to the cave on Mount Gargano in Italy where the Archangel Michael had appeared to the local bishop in the fifth century that Norman knights saw that the surrounding territory was ripe for the taking. It was said that after the beheading of the Apostle James the Greater in Jerusalem around AD 42, a group of Christ's companions, among them Mary Magdalen, sailed from Palestine to Provence to escape the persecution. There Mary Magdalen retired to a cave, and after her death was interred in a church named after the Roman martyr, Maximin. From here her remains were stolen by a monk and reburied in the Abbey of Vézelay in Burgundy.

This narrative was among a plethora of different accounts of the later life of Mary Magdalen.[126] However, the claims of Vézelay were accepted by the popes, and so drew pilgrims from throughout Latin Christendom. Vezelay also became one of the starting points for one of the greatest and most enduring of all pilgrimages – that to the tomb of the Apostle James the Greater in Galicia in the north-eastern corner of the Iberian peninsula. Given the year of his death in Jerusalem, recorded by both the Jewish historian Josephus and *The Acts of the Apostles*, it is implausible to suggest that he crossed the Mediterranean to evangelise the westernmost province of the Roman empire as some claimed; but if unlikely it is not impossible that his body was taken to Spain and buried in a tomb which was miraculously revealed by the appearance of a star in a field in the eighth century – leading to the construction of a church, later a great basilica, dedicated to *Santiago de Compostela* – St. James of the field of a star. The authenticity of this discovery was accepted by Pope Leo III and the emperor Charlemagne. Because of the Apostle's reputed appearance to aid the Christians in a battle against the Muslims , he became known in Spain as *Santiago Matomoros* – St. James killer of the Moors.

Pilgrimage was encouraged by the Church. In the 11th century the monks of Cluny saw it as a form of penitence that would enhance devotion to Christ, and pilgrimages to the Holy Land presaged the First Crusade. Pilgrims also sustained the economies of towns and villages along the pilgrim routes. The religious orders provided food and shelter *gratis*, and on *el Camino de Santiago* pilgrims were protected by outposts manned by the Templar Knights. Relics attracted pilgrims and so had a considerable value. They were prized booty when the Latin crusaders sacked Constantinople in 1453, and Baldwin II, the Latin emperor of Byzantium, chronically short of funds, sent Christ's Crown of Thorns to Venice as security for a loan of 13,134 gold pieces. It was redeemed with Baldwin's consent by his cousin, the devout Louis IX of France who, to house the relic, built in Paris the exquisite Sainte Chapelle.

---

126   See Susan Haskins, *Mary Magdalen,* p. 106 *et seq.*

PART TWO

21. Islam

While the northern frontiers of Christendom were being extended beyond those of the former Roman empire under the devout Merovingian king Dagobert, the eastern emperors ruling from Constantinople were engaged in endemic conflict with the Sassasian rulers of the Persian empire. The Persians were Zoroastrians, a monotheistic religion older than Christianity, and when in 614 with Jewish allies they captured Jerusalem, Christian shrines were desecrated or demolished; 35,000 of its Christian inhabitants, among them the Patriarch, were deported to Persia; and around 60,000 slain. The Persians reached the Bosphorus and besieged Constantinople; but the Byzantines, under the Emperor Heraclius, mounted a counter-attack and the Persians were finally defeated at the Battle of Nineveh in 627. Precious relics taken from Jerusalem were recovered and taken back in triumph to Constantinople.

However, the years of war had left the Byzantine armies enfeebled, and endemic plague, which killed around a third of the empire's population, diminished the source of new recruits. The body politic too was sapped by religious disputes: the Monophysite heresy, which held that Jesus of Nazareth had one nature, not two as defined by the Council of Chalcedon, was rife throughout the Empire, particularly in the southern provinces of Egypt, Syria and Palestine. South of Palestine was Arabia, whose indigenous population was pagan, worshipping stars, idols and sacred stones, in particular a black stone of great antiquity, the fragment of a meteorite, housed in a temple, the Ka'bah, in the city of Mecca, and sacred to a deity known simply as Allah – 'the god'. The Arabs' loyalty was to their tribe and the chief source of their income was the plunder gained on *razzias* or raids on other tribes. The Quraysh, the tribe which controlled Mecca, had established that, because it housed the sacred Ka'bah and attracted pilgrims, Mecca should be exempt from attack.

'Far from Islam having been born in the full light of history,' wrote the historian Tom Holland, 'its [Islam's] birth was shrouded in what has appeared to an increasing number of scholars, an almost impenetrable darkness.'[127] There

---

127   Tom Holland, *In the Shadow of the Sword*, p. 41

is, however, a traditional account, which states that a certain Muhammad was born in Mecca around AD 570 into a minor clan of the Quraysh tribe. His father died before he was born, and his mother when he was still a child. An orphan, he was raised first by his grandfather, then an uncle, Abu Talib, who took him on trading trips to Syria where he came across communities of Christians (Nazarenes) and Jews. At the age of twenty-five, Muhammad married a widow, Khadijah, fifteen years older than he was. She provided Muhammad with the resources to trade on his own behalf but he showed less interest in business than religion, withdrawing every now and then to a cave in the desert outside Mecca to meditate and pray to the one true god, Allah. On one occasion, he fell into a trance and saw an ethereal being whom he later identified as the Angel Gabriel. Gabriel told Muhammad that he was to be 'the messenger of God' and there began a series of revelations that were to last until Muhammad's death. At some point – precisely when is the subject of controversy – these were assembled in written form as the Qur'an or Koran. To the followers of Muhammad, they were the word of God.

Antagonizing the pagan merchants of Mecca with his denunciation of riches, injustice and the worship of idols, Muhammad and the growing number of those who believed in the authenticity of his visions were driven out of Mecca and moved first to Ta'if and then Medina. In time, Muhammad took control of Medina, formed alliances by taking wives from Medina's indigenous tribes, and led *razzias* on the caravans of the merchants of Mecca. In 624, an army of 800 sent from Mecca against the Muhammadans was defeated at the Battle of Badr. This victory enhanced Muhammad's prestige and persuaded many to accept his claim to be the messenger of Allah: the name given to this new religion was 'submission' or Islam. Muhammad dealt harshly with his defeated enemies. All the men of the Jewish clan of Qurayzah who had conspired against Muhammad were executed, and their wives and children sold as slaves. Two poets, custodians of the oral history of their tribe, who had criticized Muhammad were executed following the Battle of Badr.

In 630, Mecca finally capitulated and Muhammad with ten thousand followers entered the Ka'bah in triumph. All the pagan idols were destroyed except the fragment of a meteorite: 'veneration of the black stone was the only concession that Muhammad made to the Arabs' ancient pagan beliefs'.[128] Not all Meccans embraced Islam, but there was every incentive to do so.

---

128   Gusatav E. von Grunebaum, *Medieval Islam. A Study in Cultural Orientation.* Chicago, 1947, p. 68

Muhammad now led his expanded army on *razzias* against those tribes that still opposed him and, following their defeat, shared the booty among his followers. After these victories, all the Arabian tribes united under Islam. Booty would now have to come from beyond Arabia: 'for its continuing welfare the Islamic state must find an outlet northwards for the energy of the Arabs.'[129] In 630, Mohammad led an army of 30,000 north to Tabuk, about three hundred miles northwest of Medina, and took the rich city of Adhruh on the borders of the Byzantine Empire. This was Muhammad's largest expedition but also his last; he died after returning to Arabia in 632 having clearly indicated the path that Islam was to follow.

How do we account for the appeal of Muhammad? Unlike Jesus, he performed no miracles. His vision in the year 620, in which he rode on a heavenly steed, el-Buruq, with the Angel Gabriel, to the Temple Mount in Jerusalem to meet Abraham, Moses and Jesus, and from there ascended past the seven heavens to the throne of God, 'seems to have been a personal experience for Muhammad himself because it contained no revelation for inclusion in the Koran.'[130] There were no witnesses as there were to Jesus's Transfiguration.

Rather, Muhammad's success came not from the exercise of supernatural power over nature but from his adroit appeal to both the spiritual and material self-interest of the Arabs of his time. Muhammad promised paradise for those who died in battle, and plunder for those who did not. When his forces reached a critical mass, it became advantageous for other tribes to join them; and his straightforward monotheism – there is only one God, and Muhammad is his Prophet – was far easier to comprehend than the Trinitarian beliefs of bickering Christians. The authority of the Prophet not only ended the incessant feuding of the tribes: it also gave a sense of identity to the Arabs like that already possessed by the Abyssinians, Persians, Byzantine Christians and Jews. Islam was an Arab religion, not, like the other faiths on offer, an import from abroad.

The choice for pagans conquered by the armies of Islam was also simple: conversion or death, with slavery and concubinage for their wives and daughters. Jews and Christians, 'the Peoples of the Book' – the Bible – could secure the Prophet's protection by the payment of a tax. Mohammad saw himself as the last in the line of Israel's prophets. His revelations drew heavily

---

129   W. Montgomery Watt, *Muhammad. Prophet and Statesman.* Oxford, 1961
130   Karen Armstrong, *Muhammad: A Biography of the Prophet*, London, p. 139

on the Torah, and initially Muhammad told his followers to pray facing Jerusalem. But the Jews were scornful of Muhammad's use of their scripture and found the improvisation of the Angel Gabriel self-evidently absurd. When they rejected his claims to be the messenger of God, Mohammad accused them of falsifying scripture to conceal the fact that the Ka'bah had in fact been built by Abraham, and instructed Muslims to pray facing Mecca. To Muhammad, 'Islam was the resurrected uncontaminated religion of Abraham, which the Jews had deserted'.[131]

Christians, too, found it impossible to give credence to revelations that so arbitrarily drew on the Torah, the New Testament and the Apocryphal Gospels. Most offensive of all was Muhammad's insistence that Jesus was not the son of God; indeed, he considered it blasphemous to suggest that God would deign to appear in human form. It was not that he dismissed Jesus as a fraud: quite to the contrary, he was a prophet in the line of Abraham and Moses; his mother Mary was a virgin; but because God so loved the son of Mary the crucifixion of Jesus had been an illusion. God would not permit such a painful and ignoble fate for one he loved.

Beyond the question of the divinity of Jesus, there were a number of other differences between the two religions, in particular Mohammad's teaching on the use of violence. Jesus enjoined love of one's enemies[132] and, when encountering violence, 'turning the other cheek'. For the first three-and-a-half centuries of the Church's existence, his followers had adhered to this teaching, and meekly accepted persecution. The Byzantine Emperor Manuel II Palaiologus (1392-1420) later said that the only novelty in Islam, 'a cruel and inhuman religion', was conversion at the point of a sword.

Another significant difference was the two religions' teaching on sexual morality. Jesus had been celibate and recommended celibacy 'for the sake of the kingdom'. Muhammad condemned it. Jesus insisted upon lifelong monogamy for those who married, rescinding the Law of Moses that allowed divorce. Muhammad allowed a man to have up to four wives, any number of concubines, and could end a marriage with a simple declaration. He himself had a Christian concubine and nine wives. No doubt many of his marriages were of convenience, made to form bonds with hitherto hostile clans. Nonetheless, it shocked his contemporaries that one of Muhammad's wives had been married to his adopted son, and another, A'ishah, he married

---

131   Von Grunebaum, *Op. Cit.*, p. 78

132   See Luke 6:27-38

when he was aged fifty-three and she only nine years old. He had a separate room or small suites built for each of his wives around the courtyard of his house in Medina, and was reputedly proud of his ability to satisfy all his wives on a single night. When one of them became jealous at his dalliance with an Egyptian captive, the Angel Gabriel commanded Muhammad to rebuke her. 'God's interest in detail, and particularly in detail concerning the Prophet's personal life, occasionally bewildered the faithful but Allah supported the Prophet and silenced his critics'.[133]

Christian propagandists were to make much of these aspects of Muhammad's life, as well as certain instances of treachery which suggest that, in the cause of Islam, he believed the end justified the means: but it is clear that he was not considered immoral by his contemporaries, and in fact raised the ethical standards of the society into which he was born. He enjoined honesty, frugality and humility: he swept out his own tent. He forbade infanticide and insisted on the care of vulnerable members of the community, in particular widows and orphans. He created a family structure and a form of social security that were a major advance on what went before, and made of the nomadic tribes of Arabia a nation that conquered a vast empire and founded a great civilization.

The choice of a successor to Muhammad (caliph, from the Arabic *Khalifahi)* was disputed between different members of his family, and was to lead to the division of Islam into the Sunnis, the followers of Abu Bakr, the father of Muhammad's young wife A'ishah; and the Shia, the followers of Ali, the husband of Muhammad's daughter Fatimah. At first, Ali and his supporters accepted the election of Abu Bakr and on his death, two years after that of Muhammad, the election of another of the Prophet's fathers-in-law, Umar. It was Umar who led the Muslims on a triumphant campaign of conquest, establishing 'the last, the climactic, and the most enduring empire of antiquity'.[134] Byzantine Syria capitulated in 636 and Mesopotamia the same year. In 641 Egypt fell to Umar's army, and in the following year he was master of Persia.

How was it that the two ancient empires of Persia and Byzantium were unable to resist the onslaught of Islam? Both were enfeebled after the long wars between the two and, in the case of Byzantium, against encircling tribes of barbarians to the north. The Emperor Heraclius, triumphant against the

133   *Ibid*, p. 79-80
134   Tom Holland, *Op. Cit.* p. 55

Persians, suffered one defeat after another, and in 637, only eight years after it had been liberated from the Persians, Jerusalem surrendered to the besieging armies of the Caliph Umar. However, its fate was very different from before. The lives and property of the Christians were preserved, their churches and shrines protected. If the Peoples of the Book paid the requisite tax, which was often lower than that levied by the Byzantines, they were left to follow their own religious practices and be governed by their own laws. The Muslim Arabs remained the ruling caste, and were sustained by their subjects' taxes, but they mostly remained in fortresses on the borders of their empire.

The regime of moderate taxation and religious liberty appealed to those like the Egyptians who had adopted the Monophysite beliefs, and had their own patriarch in Alexandria. The city surrendered to the Muslims armies in 646 which, having secured the prosperous and populous province of Egypt, were free to move west along the southern coast of the Mediterranean. In the next decades, while in the east the ancient Persian empire succumbed to Islam with Muslim armies reaching Central Asia and Northern India, in the west the Berber population of north Africa accepted Islam and, in 711, under their leader, Tariq ibn Ziyad, crossed the Strait of Gibraltar and defeated the Christian Visigoths led by their king Roderick. By 716, most of the Iberian peninsula was under Muslim control. A remnant of Visigoths held out in Asturias in the north, and the Basques in the foothills of the Pyrenees.

22.   Charlemagne

The advance of the armies of Islam into western Europe was halted by their defeat at a battle outside Poitiers in France by a Christian Frankish army led by Charles Martel. The king of the Franks was Theuderic IV; however, although they retained the mystique of their descent from the semi-mythical Merovech, the Merovingian kings had become ineffective as leaders of their tribe – beset by a supine decadence and branded with the epithet *les rois fainéant* – the do-nothing or idle kings. Power and authority were exercised by the 'Mayors of the Palace', or major domos – a position that had itself become hereditary, devolving from Pepin of Herstal (635-714) to his son Charles Martel.[135]

---

135   We have seen this with the Hasmonean kings who ceded power to Antapiter and his son Herod

Pepin himself had been a successful warlord who, after defeating rivals in 683, took the title Duke of the Franks. Charles Martel, who succeeded his father as Mayor of the Palace in 715, was distinguished from the other great men of the late Merovingian period by his 'heroic vigour. He had some of the qualities of a Beowulf, and stood nearer to that heroic figure than to the administrator-kings of the Middle Ages'.[136] Some historians consider that the seeds of the feudal system stem from his need to sustain his armies which, without sufficient funds, he did largely through the distribution of land . Alongside his secular commitments there was his role as protector of the Catholic Church so that, although some lands were taken from the Church to reward his warriors, others were given to monasteries and shrines. Charles had certainly no wish to alienate the mediators between an earth and a heaven to whose intervention he ascribed his triumphs. It was as the champion of the Church that he not only defeated the Muslims outside Poitiers, but at the request of Pope Gregory III went outside the Frankish domains to end a siege of Rome by hostile Lombards.

The Lombards were a new tribe of barbarians who had migrated from southern Scandinavia through Austria and Slovakia to defeat the Ostrogoths and Byzantines and establish a kingdom ruled from Pavia in the valley of the Po. Converted to Catholicism in 653, they nonetheless came into conflict with the popes in Rome who, after the Lombards had defeated the forces of the Byzantine emperor, claimed Ravenna as part of their emerging domain. The Lombards under their king Liutprand twice besieged and took Rome in 729 and 739. On the first occasion, filled with remorse, Liutprand left his armour as a votive offering on the altar of St. Peter's basilica; on the second, when relations with the papacy had further soured, he allowed his soldiers to loot the basilica, making off with 'its ornaments, even its lights'.[137]

With the eastern emperor powerless to protect them, the popes called first on Charles Martel and, after his death in 741, on Charles's son Pepin who succeeded his father as Mayor of the Palace. Educated by the monks of St. Denis, Pepin was a devout Catholic but also a shrewd ruler. Finding his notional subjection as Mayor of the Palace to the idle Merovingian king Childeric III irksome, he wrote to Pope Zachary asking if a king could any longer be considered a king if he exercised no royal power? The pope replied in the negative. Childeric was deposed and Pepin elected king of the Franks

---

136   J.M. Wallace-Hadrill, *The Barbarian West.*, p. 86
137   Duffy, *Op. Cit.*, p. 86

by an assembly of Frankish nobles. He was anointed first by the English missionary Boniface; and a year later, in 754, Pope Zachary's successor, Stephen II, travelled to Paris for a second consecration in the basilica of St. Denis. That same year, and again two years later, Pepin led armies into Italy and defeated the Lombards. 'The exarchate of Ravenna was handed over to the Pope. A papal state had been created: it would endure in the form Pepin gave it for more than a thousand years'.[138]

This bond between the popes and the Franks continued under Pepin's two sons Carloman and Charles – the latter becoming sole ruler after 774 when Carloman withdrew to a monastery. Charles, known to history as Charlemagne, or Charles the Great, was as devout as his brother: 'Charlemagne's sense of Christian mission was a central feature of his reign…'[139] His ideal was a Christian society living at peace under a monarch, but he was aware of the 'huge gap between the concept of peace and the fact of bloodshed'. Throughout his long reign, he was constantly at war, conquering Aquitaine and territory on the far side of the Pyrenees in the west; and Frisia, Burgundy, and Bavaria in the east. Of particular significance to the Catholic Church was his final confrontation with the Lombards in Italy: they were emphatically defeated. Charlemagne took the title of King of the Lombards, and Lombardy became part of the Frankish empire.

'The annexation of Lombardy brought Charlemagne in contact with a court more sophisticated than his own'[140] This encouraged him to invite scholars and artists to his own court in Aachen (Aix-la-Chapelle), leading to what historians call 'the Carolingian renaissance'. Alcuin, a priest, poet and theologian was summoned to Aachen from the great missionary school in York. He became Charlemagne's friend and principal advisor. 'There are no surprises about Alcuin. He was a straightforward exponent of what he found in Saint Augustine, Saint Benedict, Cassiodorus and Gregory the Great…'[141] The only known difference between Alcuin and Charlemagne was on the question of forced conversions to Christianity – not of the Jews, whom Charlemagne favoured, but of the pagan Saxons in the north against whom he fought a series of protracted and sanguinary campaigns after which the defeated were compelled to accept baptism.

---

138   *Ibid.* p. 88
139   J.M. Wallace-Hadrill, *The Barbarian West*, p. 99
140   J.M. Wallace-Hadrill, *The Frankish Church,* p. 191
141   J. M. Wallace-Hadrill, *The Barbarian West*, p. 101

'It is a striking feature of the spread of Christianity,' wrote Richard Fletcher, 'that it was, before Saxony, so tranquil a process. That is why Boniface mattered so much'. Now, 'for the first time in Christian history, a state-sponsored mission used the faith quite unashamedly as an instrument for the subjugation of a conquered people.'[142] The Saxons 'fought hard to preserve their pagan religion and its bloodthirsty rites with a tenacity the Franks called obduracy'.[143] In his first campaign in 782, Charlemagne destroyed the Irminsul, the tree-trunk that supported the Saxon heaven, just as Boniface had chopped down the sacred Donar Oak at Geismar. The faith of the Saxons did not fall with their sacred tree; they stubbornly held on to their pagan beliefs and continued to resist Charlemagne. Ten years later, after defeating a Saxon force near Verdun on the Allier, Charlemagne ordered the massacre of 4,500 obdurate prisoners. The Saxon chieftain Widukind escaped and took refuge in Denmark, but returned three years later to face the Franks for a third time. Again he was defeated and this time he and his people accepted baptism.

Although in theory opposed to forced conversions, and despite the 'unmatched brutality'[144] shown by Charlemagne, the Church participated in Charlemagne's imposition of the Catholic religion. Attending Mass on Sundays and feast days became obligatory for the Saxons. Refusing baptism now became a capital offence: so too cremation, attacks on churches, the killing of clergy and eating meat during Lent. It is difficult to know how this regime compared to what had preceded it, but 'Saxons appear to have settled down to make the best of a bad job. Saxon nobles were stout supporters of the East Frankish Carolingian kings throughout most of the ninth century.'[145]

On hearing the news of Widukind's conversion, the Pope Hadrian I ordered three days of thanksgiving. He died soon after, and was succeeded by Leo III, a Roman of modest origins who had served in the Curia from childhood and pursued the policies of his predecessor. Like Hadrian, he understood the importance of the papacy's bond with the Franks: when announcing his election he reminded Charlemagne of his role as defender of the Church. Although he had been unanimously elected, Hadrian soon alienated the aristocratic courtiers of the previous pope. In 799 he was kidnapped and imprisoned in a monastery. He escaped, and took refuge with Charlemagne in

---

142   Richard Fletcher, *Op. Cit.* p. 195

143   J.M. Wallace-Hadrill, *The Barbarian West*, p.97

144   Fletcher, *Op. Cit.* p. 195

145   J.M. Wallace-Hadrill, *The Frankish Church*, p. 184

Paderborn. Agents of his enemies followed, charging him before Charlemagne with perjury and adultery. Alcuin advised Charlemagne that no one could pass judgement on the successor of St. Peter. Leo was escorted back to Rome and in the year 800 Charlemagne followed. At Mass on Christmas Day, as Charlemagne rose from praying at the tomb of St. Peter, Hadrian stepped forward and placed a crown upon his head, proclaiming him Emperor.

Charlemagne later claimed that this coronation came as a surprise. Historians consider this unlikely. There was clearly a vacancy. Not only had the Byzantine emperor been ousted from Ravenna, but the eastern empire was now ruled by a woman, the Empress-regent Irene. To Leo it was clear that the western empire required a powerful emperor, both to counter the threat from the Muslim Arabs, now called Saracens, but also to guarantee the popes' right to the papal states – rights which, he claimed, had been bestowed by the Emperor Constantine on the successors of St. Peter in perpetuity. The coronation of Charlemagne, as a successor to Constantine, seemed wise at the time, but was to cause trouble in the future.

23. Iconoclasm

Around twenty years before, and again twenty years after the coronation of Charlemagne, the popes in Rome became involved in a theological debate that raged in the Byzantine empire, leading to persecution, torture, blinding and executions. The issue was whether or not Christians should venerate man-made images of Christ, the Virgin Mary or the Saints. Increasingly, such icons had become the object not just of veneration but a belief that they themselves possessed miraculous powers. Mohammad had condemned this as idolatry, and Islam forbade any depiction of Mohammad or the prophets, including Christ. It may have been that some Byzantine Christians came to feel the same misgivings, and wonder whether or not the defeat of their armies by the Muslims was punishment by God for their worship of icons. Or perhaps God had expressed his anger at this idolatry with an earthquake in the Aegean in 726 after which many thousands were drowned in the subsequent tsunami.

Whatever the origins of iconoclasm, it gained many partisans, among them the Emperor Leo III, the Isaurian (717-741), who ordered the removal of the image of Christ placed over the ceremonial gate into his palace in

Constantinople. Germanos, the Patriarch of Constantinople, opposed Leo's action and was deposed. The main opponents of Leo's iconoclast policies were monks. Iconophile monasteries were suppressed, monks tortured and executed, the bodies of saints exhumed and burned, and relics thrown into the sea. Many monks fled abroad. The great Christian theologian, John Damascene, out of reach of the Emperor's wrath in the monastery of St. Saba in the Muslim Caliphate, denounced the Emperor's destruction and persecution.

The Patriarch Germanos had appealed to the pope, Gregory II (713-31) against his deposition, while the Byzantine emperor Leo had written to pope Gregory, commanding him to summon an ecumenical council to condemn the worship of images, and in the meantime destroy all those in Rome. Gregory replied in 727, defending the veneration of religious images, and chastising the emperor for his persecution of the iconophiles. After the death of Gregory II, his successor Gregory III continued the defence of icons. Leo, whose rule at the time covered southern Italy and Sicily, retaliated by confiscating lands owned by the Holy See. In 731 the pope summoned a synod in Rome which excommunicated all those who destroyed images of Christ and his mother Mary.

A papal legate was sent to Constantinople to convey this edict to the emperor, but he was arrested and imprisoned by the Byzantine governor in Sicily. Leo sent a fleet to attack Rome and oust the pope, but it was dispersed in a storm. Other misfortunes – plague, earthquakes, famine, and further Saracen successes – did not suggest that God was on the side of the eastern emperor; but when Leo died of dropsy in 741, another misfortune, his iconoclast policies were pursued with even greater vigour by his son Constantine V. Synods were held in both Rome and Constantinople which passed resolutions supporting the different parties. It was only on the death of Constantine V in 775, that the persecution of iconophiles was moderated by his son Leo IV whose wife Irene venerated holy images that she concealed in her quarters. When Leo died, Irene became regent for her son Constantine VI. She summoned a church Council, the Second Council of Nicaea, which restored the veneration of icons.

A second phase of iconoclasm was instigated in 815 by the Emperor Leo V, known as the Armenian, again as a result of military defeats which he ascribed to the veneration of images. Leo V's successors continued his iconoclast policies until 843 when another woman, Theodora, acting as regent for the infant Michael III, reversed the policies and icons were once more revered in the Orthodox Church.

Iconoclasm would return, this time in the west, not the east, many hundreds of years later. The lasting consequence of the Iconoclast conflict in the ninth century was the severance of ties between the papacy and the Byzantine emperor. Hitherto, since the reign of Justinian I, the choice of a pope in Rome had to be endorsed by the Emperor in Constantinople, and a number of popes had Greek as their mother tongue. Now the patronage of the papacy passed to the new western emperors.

Another consequence of the defeat of Iconoclasm, of momentous cultural significance, lay in the evolution of western art. Depictions of Christ, the Mother of God, and the saints in Christendom in western Christendom led to icons and magnificent mosaics in Ravenna, Rome and Monreale in Sicily; and to the art of Giotto, Masaccio, Raphael, Leonardo da Vinci, Memling and many others; and to the statuary of Brunelleschi, Michelangelo and the anonymous sculptors who adorned Christian churches and Cathedrals. Under Islam, no depictions of Muhammad or other human beings were permitted in mosques and palaces, only geometric patterns and decorative lettering.

24.   After Charlemagne

Charlemagne died in 814, leaving his crown and empire to his eldest son Louis the Pious who then, three years later, divided the empire into three – one kingdom to the west, another to the east, and in the centre a middle kingdom stretching from the mouth of the Rhine right across the continent to the papal states. This central *tranche*, the core of the empire, was ruled by his son Lothar who shared the imperial authority inherited by his father. However, on the death of Louis the Pious, his sons fell out and only resolved their differences first with the Treaty of Verdun in 843 and later the Treaty of Mersen in 870. The west and east portions developed into France and Germany, while the Middle Kingdom, Lotharingia, on the death of Lothar without an heir, was shared by his two brothers, and was fought over until the middle of the 20th century.

Distracted by their quarrels with one another, the Frankish kings were unable to live up to Charlemagne's commitment to protect the pope in

Rome. The Byzantine emperors were equally powerless, losing their territory adjacent to the papal states in southern Italy, and Sicily, to the Saracens. The Saracens had also established a base, Fraxinentum or Fraxinet (today's La Garde-Freinet) on the south coast of France, from which they raided travellers crossing the Alps. In 846, a force of 500 Saracen horsemen landed at the mouth of the Tiber and attacked Rome. The pope took refuge in the Castel Sant' Angelo, and watched impotently as a group of Saxon pilgrims were massacred, and the tombs of the Apostles Peter and Paul were vandalised and plundered.

Pope Leo IV (847-55), determined to prevent a repetition of this humiliation, summoned labourers from the cities and monasteries of the papal states to build a massive wall around the Vatican. The 'Leonine' wall, forty feet high and twelve feet thick, was 'in some ways the most remarkable monument of papal Rome in the early Middle Ages.'[146] It remains standing today.

King Lothair of Lorraine helped pay for the wall, but this bought no favours from Leo's successor, Nicholas I (858-67), the third and last pope after Leo and Gregory to be given the title 'Great'. Lothair divorced his wife, Theutberga, the daughter of the King of Burgundy, who had proved unable to provide an heir, and married his mistress Waltrada by whom he already had three children. Theutberga appealed to Pope Nicholas: he ruled in her favour, and excommunicated the archbishops of Cologne and Trier who had approved Lothair's divorce and remarriage. Nicholas's intransigence paid off: Lothair dismissed his concubine and took back his wife. The sanctity of Christian marriage was confirmed – at least for a time.

Nicholas's firm stance was less effective in dealing with the Byzantine Emperor Michael III who had deposed the Patriarch of Constantinople, Ignatius, and appointed in his place a layman – a young high-flyer in the Imperial civil service called Photius. Ignatius appealed to Rome, and Pope Nicholas ruled in his favour. Photius was excommunicated but, with the backing of the emperor, remained in place. It was a misfortune for the western Church that Photius turned out to be a learned, able and holy man and is regarded as a saint by the Orthodox Church. The other differences between the Catholic and Orthodox Church over clerical celibacy, fasting laws, the use of unleavened bread in the Mass, and the inclusion of the 'Filioque' clause in the Creed of the Western church, were not enough to cause a breach: but in 867 Photius presided over

---

146   Duffy, *Op. Cit.* p. 99

a synod at Constantinople which excommunicated and deposed the pope. Nicholas had died before the news reached Rome but it meant that 'Rome and Constantinople were now formally separated.'[147]

The death of Pope Nicholas the Great, writes the British historian, Eamon Duffy, 'marks a watershed in the history of the papacy'. His successor, Hadrian II (867-72), was weak and there was now no secular authority able to buttress that of the pope. The titular Roman emperors north of the Alps were caught up in 'a wild dance of uprising, alliances, usurpations, restorations, family feuds, solemn vows and blatant oath-breaking in which the great empire broke up into the national outlines of modern Europe.'[148] Freed from Frankish domination, Italy disintegrated into small states ruled by self-appointed dukes or kings. The popes were left 'defenceless in the snake pit of Italian politics… and the papacy became the possession of the Great Roman families, a ticket to local dominance for which men were prepared to rape, murder and steal'.

A third of the popes elected between 872 and 1012 died in suspicious circumstances, John VIII (872-82) bludgeoned to death by his own entourage, Stephen VI (896-7) strangled, Leo V (903) murdered by his successor, Sergius III (904-11), John X (914-28) suffocated, Stephen VIII (939-42) horribly mutilated, a fate shared by the Greek antipope John XVI who, unfortunately for him, did not die from the removal of his eyes, nose, lips and hands. [149]

In March, 896, Pope Stephen VII disinterred the corpse of an earlier pope and rival, Formosus which, clothed in priestly vestments, was propped up on the throne in the Council Chamber to stand trial before a synod of bishops for the supposed crimes of his reign. The corpse was condemned. The three fingers that had blessed the faithful when alive were cut off, and the rotting corpse thrown by the supporters of Pope Stephen into the Tiber from which it was retrieved by fishermen and reburied.

From the turn of the tenth century, one family, the Theophylacts, came to dominate both the city of Rome and the papacy. Originally from Tusculum, the head of Theophylact family, 'a wan and shadowy figure', is named as senator and *dux* in the scant records of the time, but it was not the father but his wife Theodora and daughter Marozia who came to rule Rome. Much of what is known about these two women comes from a hostile source, the

---

147   Duffy, *Op. Cit.* p. 103

148   James Hawes, *The Shortest History of Germany*, p. 36.

149   Duffy, *Op.Cit.*, p. 103

chronicle of Liutprand of Cremona; but 'the "monarchy of Theodora" is an undoubted fact: from the year 900 onwards it is her name, not her husband's, that predominates in the sparse annals of the city'.[150] 'A certain shameless strumpet called Theodora, at one time was sole monarch of Rome and – shame though it is to write it – exercised power like a man.'[151] She had two daughters, Marozia and Theodora. Marozia, shortly after puberty, caught the eye of Pope Sergius, became his mistress and had a male child. The influence exercised by Theodora through her daughter's liaison with the pontiff continued after his death. It was her candidates Anastasius III and Lando who succeeded Sergius III on the throne of St. Peter, but each died within a year. Theodora now summoned her protégé and lover, John, Bishop of Ravenna, and in 914 he was installed as pope, John X.

Having provided her lover with the papal throne, Theodora now found a husband for her daughter Marozia, a mother but still in her teens. He was a soldier of fortune, Alberic, self-styled Marquis of Camerino, whose soldiers provided a useful prop to the power of the Theophylacts. Marozia had another child, also a boy, who took the name of his father, Alberic. John X and Marozia's father, still a senator and judge, ruled as a triumvirate and, in a rare moment of co-operation and good sense, led a coalition against the Saracens in southern Italy and 'destroyed them utterly, thus removing the menace that had hovered over Italy for two generations.' [152]

The older generation of the Theophylacts, and the warlord Alberic, now disappear from the chronicles and it is Marozia who takes centre stage. With Alberic gone – dead or banished – she took as a second husband Guy of Tuscany. This soldier enabled Marozia to take the Castel Sant' Angelo and as *senatrix* become the *de facto* ruler of Rome. She loathed Pope John X, her mother's lover, and had him imprisoned in the dungeons of the Castel Sant' Angelo where he died, either from starvation or suffocation. Two nondescript popes were now appointed by Marozia – stop-gaps prior to her most shameless and audacious move – the elevation to the papacy of her son by Pope Sergius III, now in his early twenties, as Pope John XI.

On the death of Guy of Tuscany, Marozia married his half-brother, Hugh of Provence: her son, the pope, officiated at his mother's wedding. Hugh was

150   Hawes, *Op. Cit.* p. 27

151   Liutprand, *Antopodosis*, Chapter xlviii

152   Hawes, *Op. Cit.* p. 30

a powerful and ambitious potentate, and had persuaded his step-son, Pope John, to proclaim him King of Italy. But the deep passions of sibling rivalry were at work. By favouring her son John, Marozia had neglected his brother Alberic who now exploited the Romans' dislike of the foreign influence of Hugh of Provence to foment a riot. The mob stormed the Castel Sant' Angelo and seized the newlywed couple. Hugh escaped but not Marozia or the pope. Alberic, proclaiming himself Prince of Rome, Senator of all the Romans, Count and Patrician, had his mother and half-brother, Pope John XI, imprisoned. Marozia now disappears from the chronicles. John was released but confined to the Lateran palace and limited to ecclesiastical functions. Alberic turned out to be an effective ruler and, of the five popes he appointed, two were sincere reformers; but the reality was that the popes had become 'harassed Italian prince-bishops, desperately struggling to preserve the territory of St. Peter, sometimes responding to but never initiating reforms which were beginning to stir within Christendom'. [153]

25.   Cluny

The Papacy was not the Catholic Church, and among the contemporaries of the degenerate Theophylacts were many devout Christians, some of whom died in defence of their faith. In the north, marauding Vikings from Scandinavia raided the coasts of Britain, destroying monasteries and butchering or enslaving the Christians. Danish invaders settled in the north of England, forming the pagan kingdom of Northumbria, constantly at war with the Christian kingdoms of Mercia and Wessex. In the south, Saracens continued to rule Sicily, and made raids from their bases on the south coast of France. It was only in 972 that their base in Fraxinet on the coast of Provence was finally taken by Christian forces and demolished.

But setbacks for the Church in one part of Europe were balanced by gains in another. On 14 April, the Holy Saturday of 966, the first king of a united Polish state, Mieszko I, was baptised along with many of his followers, while the Magyars, one of the most recent and ferocious of the marauding barbarian tribes, had settled to form the kingdom of Hungary and were successfully evangelised by Catholic missionaries between 970 and 1040.

---

153   Duffy, *Op. Cit.* p. 108

There were saintly bishops[154], holy women, and two martyred kings – the East Anglian king, Edmund, killed defending his Christian kingdom against pagan Vikings in 869, and Wenceslaus, Duke of Bohemia and king of the Czechs, assassinated in 935.

In the monasteries of northern Europe there were some holy monks such as Bertin, from a monastery in St. Omer (died 903), Notker the Stammerer from the Abbey of St. Gall (died 912), and Gérard of Brogne (died 959). If there were not more saints from the monasteries, it was because many had fallen into decline. 'The sunlight of the Carolingian age,' wrote David Knowles, 'was followed by the century which for Gaul-Frankland was the darkest of all (850-950) when the empire fell into feudalism and monasteries decayed or were secularised.'[155] The descendants of those Frankish barons who had had endowed monasteries, resented the transfer by their forefathers of land from the family's estates. Some clawed back the land; others, preferring to avoid confrontation with the Church, put pressure on the monastic communities to elect as abbot their landless younger sons who on occasions moved into the abbot's lodgings with their families and hunting dogs. With no commitment to sanctity in their abbot, the monks modified the rigours of the Benedictine rule, exchanging their rough habits for softer, warmer clothes, abandoning the strict regime of fasting and abstinence, and rescheduling the office of matins so that they could get a good night's sleep.

In 910, William, Duke of Aquitaine, known as William the Pious, decided to found a monastery that would keep to the rule of Benedict of Nursia to atone for the sins of his youth. By inheritance, he was the Count of Auvergne but in 893 he had conquered Poitou and Aquitaine and was proclaimed Duke of Aquitaine. He therefore ruled a large swathe of France extending in the east to the Mâconnais, and it was at Cluny, on the site of a hunting lodge in a wooded valley fifteen miles west of the river Saône at Mâcon, that he chose a site for his new foundation. As abbot, he recruited Berno of Baume, a Burgundian nobleman who had built an abbey on his own estates at Gigny, and had established his credentials as a reforming abbot of Baume in the

---

154   Betto of Auxerre (died 918), Radbod, Bishop of Utrecht (died 918), Forannan, Bishop of Domhnach (died 932), Frithestan, Bishop of Winchester (died 934), Huno, Archbishop of Bremen-Hamburg (died 936), Alphege, Bishop of of Winchester (died 951), Bruno the Great of Cologne (died 965), Ulrich of Augsburg (died 973, Conrad (died 975) and Gebhard (died 995), both bishops of Constance, Wolfgang Bishop of Regensburg (died 994).

155   Knowles, *Op. Cit.* p. 47

Jura. Both William and Berno knew that while William was committed to the Benedictine rule that a community of monks should elect its own abbot, William's successors might take a different view and impose an abbot of their choice. They therefore went to Rome to ask for a charter making the new community answerable only to the pope in Rome. The pope to whom they made this request was John XI, the son of Marozia by Pope Sergius. Though still in his twenties, and preoccupied with the poisonous politics of the city state, he was conscious of his duties as the successor of Peter, and duly agreed to the request of Berno and William of Aquitaine.

The community at Cluny, under a succession of outstanding abbots, was to become the engine of reform, not just of western monasticism but of the whole Catholic Church. Berno was followed by Odo, a fellow Benedictine from Baume, who 'set the characteristic "tone" of the Cluniacs – aristocratic but genuinely humble, politic but utterly devout, with a pervasive, sophisticated simplicity. He had an extraordinary spiritual gaiety – he sometimes made his monks laugh till they cried and could as easily move them to tears of compassion.'[156] He was followed by Aymard, Mayeul, Odilo, and Hugh. It was Mayeul who was kidnapped by Saracens as he crossed the Alps, leading – after he had been ransomed – to the destruction of the Saracen base at Fraxinentum. That Mayeul should be making such a journey shows how the abbots of Cluny were constantly called upon to advise popes and oversee the reform of other monasteries. Cluny itself became the mother house of around a thousand foundations, among them fifty in England. The influence of Cluny inspired other reformers such as Dunstan, Ethelwold and Oswald in England.

Under Hugh, who succeeded Odilo in 1049, the number of monks in the Cluny community increased from sixty to three hundred, and with continuous construction it became the largest and most impressive monastic establishment in the west.

> Its church, as rebuilt by Hugh, was the culmination in splendour and magnitude of the Romanesque basilica, and it remained the largest church in Christendom until the sixteenth century, when St. Peter's was given of set purpose a length surpassing it by a few feet.[157]

---

156   *The Saints. A Concise Biographical Dictionary.* Edited by John Coulson. P.131
157   David Knowles, *Op. Cit.* p. 50

To be a monk at Cluny, we are told by the Benedictine historian, Dom David Knowles, 'was a distinction such as is, in an army devoted to its drill, membership of the Brigade of Guards'. Their mission was to sanctify society through a life of adoration, intercession and prayer.

> Life at Cluny around the year 1050 had reached a degree of liturgical splendour unequalled before or since. It has been calculated that more than eight hours, excluding any private prayer, were spent in church and chapters on normal weekdays, and if at least eight hours were allowed for sleep and toilet, and another hour for meals, it will be seen that the time available for reading and such skills as copying and illuminating manuscripts must have been small. Manual labour was practically non-existent …Contemporaries within and without the community bear witness to the exacting, almost breathless, round of offices…[158]

There was a demand for the services of members of this elite from elsewhere in the Church. Pope Gregory VII wrote to Abbot Hugh asking 'for some wise men from among his monks to appoint as bishops'. Among the reforms that spread from Cluny to the whole Church under Pope Gregory VII was the strict imposition of clerical celibacy: the Church now had no place for priests with wives. Pope Gregory VII was briefly a monk at Cluny, and Urban II was prior of Cluny before Gregory summoned him to Rome, making him cardinal bishop of Ostia, and sending him as papal legate to Germany. Both men were of the greatest significance in the developing history of the Church.

26.   The Investiture Crisis

Charlemagne had been crowned Roman Emperor in 800; however his empire was never the single administrative entity of antiquity, but a nexus of tribal loyalties, and after his death, as we have seen, it was divided into what were to become the nation states of Germany and France. Yet it remained universally believed that western Christendom required an emperor to defend it with the sword. Thus, when the last of Charlemagne's descendants, Louis, died childless in 911, the German chieftains reverted to the ancient custom of electing a monarch. They chose Conrad, Duke of Franconia, only distantly related to the Carolingian dynasty through his mother.

---

158   *Ibid.* p.50

A monarch that depends on the nobility for his crown is inevitably weak: he rules by the will of an oligarchy, not by the right of inheritance. After Conrad's death, the regional potentates chose Henry the Fowler, the Duke of Saxony, whose successful campaigns in the east against the Magyars gave him sufficient authority to impose his son Otto as his successor. Otto was crowned King in Aachen in 936, but Emperor only in 962. When the last of the Ottonians, Henry II, died childless, the imperial crown went to the successful warlord, Conrad II, founder of the Salian dynasty. The nobility accepted that his son, Henry III, should succeed him but Henry died when his son, also called Henry, was still a child. At first his mother, Agnes of Poitou, acted as regent, but in a *coup d'état*, a group of German nobles, led by Anno, Archbishop of Cologne, and Adalbert, Archbishop of Bremen, kidnapped the young king and sent his mother to a convent.

This blatant interference in politics by these bishops shows just how involved they had become in the affairs of the world. Bishops, particularly in Germany, had become not just spiritual leaders but 'prince' bishops, absolute rulers of their own principalities and peers of the realm. Who appointed these powerful bishops? The canons of the cathedral? The German king? Or the pope? When Hildebrand became pope as Gregory VII in 1073, he determined to push through the Cluniac reforms, among them the exclusive right of the pope to appoint bishops. He went further. In his *Dictatus Papae*, issued two years after his accession to the throne of the apostle Peter, he asserted not just the pope's right to appoint bishops, but to depose all princes, temporal as well as spiritual. All Christians were subject to the pope, who had supreme legislative and judicial power.

Using papal legates and provincial synods, Gregory set out to impose his reforms, among them a ban on clerical marriage. The German King, Henry IV, feeling empowered by his defeat of a Saxon revolt, defied Pope Gregory, appointing bishops to sees in Italy as well as Germany and, when chastised by the pope, summoning a synod of German bishops to depose him. Gregory retaliated by excommunicating Henry, and releasing his subjects from their oaths of allegiance. Henry's enemies in Germany now felt able to move against him. Henry realised that he could only hold on to his crown if he came to terms with the pope. In a dramatic gesture of repentance, he crossed the Alps in mid-winter of 1077, and stood, barefoot and wearing a hair shirt, at the gates of the castle of Canossa in northern Italy where Pope Gregory was a guest of the powerful Queen Matilda of Tuscany.

After three days, the gates of the castle were opened and Henry, with his wife Bertha and son Conrad, were let into the castle. There Henry went on his knees to ask for the pope's forgiveness. It was granted. The excommunication was lifted: Henry, Gregory and Matilda received communion together at Mass in the castle chapel. However, the reconciliation between pope and emperor did not last, and the conflict spread to England and above all Italy where rivalry between the supporters of the pope, known as the Guelphs, and the supporters of the Emperor, the Ghibellines, persisted into the fifteenth century. Although the papacy always retained the right to admit a bishop into communion with the Holy See by the conferring of the *pallium* – a woollen shawl – the choice of bishops was frequently made by powerful Catholic monarchs such as the King of France or the Emperor of Austria well into the nineteenth century. Indeed it persists in the present day: in 2019, Pope Francis agreed that the Communist government in Beijing should have the power to veto the appointment of bishops in China.

27.   The Normans

In England in 1107 King Henry I came to a compromise settlement with Pope Gregory VII on the question of investiture at the Concordat of London. Henry was the fourth son of William of Normandy, known as William the Conqueror, who in 1066 had defeated the Saxon King Harold at Hastings and established Norman rule. The Normans – Norsemen or 'men from the north' – were not Franks but Vikings who, after frequent raids on the coast of France in the ninth century – at one point besieging Paris – had been bought off by the French king Charles the Simple by the allocation of territory at the mouth of the river Seine with its capital at Rouen. The founder of this duchy was Rollo, who upon being baptised a Christian took the name Robert. He married Popa, the daughter of Count Berenger of Bayeux, and thereafter there was some intermarriage between his descendants and barons with the Franks; but this did not dilute the formidable strength of the Norman knights. They were brutal, fearless but also devout. The father of William the Conqueror, Robert, fearing for his salvation after pillaging Church property in his early years, made a pilgrimage to Jerusalem and died on the return journey.

Palestine was under Muslim rule but Christianity was one of the Religions of the Book and so Christian pilgrims were permitted to visit the holy sites.

The overland journey was long and hazardous but a regular trade by sea had been established by merchants of the Duchy of Amalfi in southern Italy. In 999, a group of Norman knights, after disembarking in Amalfi on their return from Jerusalem, were invited to stay by Prince Guaimar III of nearby Salerno. While they were there, Saracens from North Africa arrived to claim the annual tribute from Guaimar. Guaimar was persuaded by his Norman guests to refuse the tribute and attack the Saracens camped outside the city. The Saracens were duly routed, and lessons were learned as to what Norman pugnacity could achieve.

It was the same in 1016 when a group of Norman knights came on pilgrimage to Mount Gargano on the other side of the Italian peninsula – an ancient shrine in a grotto where the Archangel Michael was said to have appeared. Here too the knights were struck by the weakness of the notional rule of the Byzantine emperor. Restless at home – with little opportunity for the customary pillage that was in their blood – the pilgrims went back to Normandy, gathered together a larger party of knights, and, disguised as pilgrims, returned to southern Italy to make their fortunes. Other groups came to southern Italy not as pilgrims but mercenaries, and in due course some took over the principalities of their employers. Robert Guiscard (1015-1085), the sixth son of a poor Norman baron, Tancred d'Hauteville, became Duke of Apulia. He drove the Byzantines out of Calabria, capturing Bari and Brindisi. In 1077 he took the principality of Salerno, and in 1081 crossed the Adriatic Sea to defeat an army led by the Byzantine Emperor, Alexius Comnenus. Meanwhile his younger brother Roger captured Sicily. By 1130 there had come into being a state governed by the Normans encompassing the whole of Sicily and Italy south of the Papal States.

The right of the Normans to their conquests was obtained from the popes in Rome who granted them the duchies of Apulia and Calabria, and the lordship of Sicily, as feudal fiefs of the patrimony of St. Peter. It return, the Normans swore loyalty to the popes and promised assistance should it be required. 'This was a daring move,' writes Eamon Duffy, 'because the popes had never been sovereigns of southern Italy or of Sicily, and in strict law had no right to give what did not belong to them.'[159] It was justified by a document held by the popes known as the Donation of Constantine by which the first Christian emperor had given all Italy to the popes. Its authenticity was yet to be questioned, and its value at the time was immediately apparent.

---

159   Duffy, *Op. Cit.* p. 119

Ecclesiastical obedience which, under Byzantine rule had been to the Patriarch of Constantinople, was now transferred to the pope in Rome, and a military force was available as a counterweight to that of the German emperors. Pope Alexander II (1061-73) was able to call on Norman troops to put down a revolt in the city instigated by the German regent, the Empress Agnes; and he further forged his alliance with the Normans by supporting Duke William's claim to the English throne, sending him a papal banner to be raised aloft at the Battle of Hastings.

28. The Great Schism and the First Crusade

The year 1054 saw the final separation of the eastern Orthodox and the western Latin Churches when Orthodox Christians in Sicily refused to adopt the beliefs and practices of the Latin Church, and the Orthodox patriarch in retaliation ordered the closure of all Latin churches in Constantinople. The differences between the two, apparent as far back as 867 (see page 72), had not been resolved over the years which followed. Some were theological (the filioque clause in the Creed); some liturgical (the use of unleavened bread for the Eucharist); and some canonical – in particular the rejection by the Orthodox Churches of the claims to supreme authority by the pope.

Initially, the division barely affected religious life in either wast or west; nor was it a source of particular animosity. In 1095 the Byzantine emperor Alexus Comnenus sent a delegation to a Council of the Latin Church presided over by the then Pope, Urban II, being held in the city of Piacenza, to ask for help against a new horde of Islamic invaders that was threatening Constantinople.

This represented an extraordinary reversal of fortune for the empire in the east. For many years, after the first wave of Muslim conquests, a relatively stable frontier had been established between the Byzantine empire and the Abbasid caliphate of Baghdad in the Taurus Mountains above Antioch. In the early tenth century, the Byzantines had embarked on a campaign of reconquest, capturing Cyprus and the city of Aleppo. By 1025, the Byzantine empire had stretched from the straits of Messina in the west to the Danube and Crimea in the north, and to beyond the Euphrates in the east. However, the Byzantine' hold on this empire was precarious; their armies depended largely upon mercenaries; and in 1071, though superior in numbers and strength, they had been routed by a new force of marauders at Manzikert near Lake Van in Armenia.

These marauders were the Seljuk Turks who, emerging from the steppes of Asia, had conquered territory of the Baghdad caliphate, but then converted to Islam and now attacked the Christian Byzantine Empire with the same mix of religious zeal and love of plunder as the early leaders of their adopted religion. Manzikert was a catastrophe for the Byzantines: their emperor, Romanus IV Diogenes, was taken prisoner by the Seljuk chieftain, Alp Arslan. Nothing could stop the Seljuks' advance. By 1081, they had captured Nicea, less than a hundred miles from Constantinople.

The strength of the Byzantines had been sapped by having to fight a war on two fronts. The Norman adventurer, Robert Guiscard, after taking Bari had crossed the Adriatic and was advancing towards Thessaloniki. Only the death of both Robert Guiscard and Arp Arslan provided a breathing space during which the Byzantines raised their ablest general, Alexius Comnenus, to the throne of what was now a small Greek state facing annihilation. Robert, Count of Flanders, returning from a pilgrimage to the Holy Land, came to the emperor's aid with a contingent of knights, but it was not enough to alter the balance of power now so favourable to the Seljuk Turks. More useful was Count Robert's advice: if the Emperor wanted help from the west, he should turn not to the German emperor whose affairs were in chaos but to the pope, Urban II.

Pope Urban II, born Odo of Lagery in Châtillon-sur-Marne in eastern France, came from a noble family and was prepared for high office in the Church by his uncle, the Archbishop of Rheims. He studied at Rheims under Bruno, founder of the austere Carthusian order; was made a canon, then archdeacon before taking the tonsure – the shaving of the hair from the top of his head – as a Benedictine monk at Cluny. There he became prior but after a dozen years or so was summoned to Rome by the zealous reformer, Gregory VII, who made him Cardinal Bishop of Ostia in 1080. In 1088, though the anti-pope Clement III held Rome, Urban was chosen at Terracina by acclamation as Victor III's legitimate successor. In 1093, Urban returned to Rome and took possession of the Lateran Palace and the Castel Sant' Angelo. By the time of the Synod of Piacenza in 1095, his rule was secure.

A handsome, courteous and conciliatory man, Urban shared the same high estimate of his office as his mentor, Gregory VII, but was more tactful in the exercise of his authority. He had already improved relations with the Byzantine Empire, and was minded to come to Alexius Comnenus's aid. But how? There had been endemic war between Christians and Muslims since the seventh century, with frequent changes of the frontiers between the territory adhering to the two religions. In the west, the Saracens had been ousted from Italy and Sicily, and in Spain a *Reconquista* – a Christian reconquest of Iberia – had made significant progress. The Christian kingdoms in the north of Leon-Castile and the County of Barcelona had made inroads into the territory of the Caliphate of Cordoba, which on the death of the Caliph Abd al'Rahman, fragmented into independent states or *ta'ifas*. The popes had sent banners to the Christian armies; and had contributed their own forces to fight the Saracens in Italy, but never before had they marshalled a Christian army.

Urban came from a warrior caste. His kinsmen were knights, and, had he not been a monk and a priest, he too would have been a knight. He was therefore familiar with the mentality of the Frankish barons, and indeed had been trying to tame their belligerence – the incessant vendettas, quarrels and disputes which, even if brought to court, were often settled in a primitive fashion by a duel, or trial by ordeal. Attempts by the Church to curb this fratricidal violence with interdicts, excommunications and the designation of certain holy days, or penitential seasons such as Lent and Advent, when knights were obliged to keep a Truce of God under pain of sin, met with little success. There was much to be learned from the example of the Norman Hautevilles who channelled their aggression by fighting the enemies of Christendom.

After the closing of the Synod of Piacenza, Pope Urban set out on a tour of France, going first to Valence on the Rhône, then turning up into the inhospitable hills of the Auvergne to visit the Bishop of Le Puy, Adhemar of Monteil. Adhemar came from the same caste as Urban and some years before had been on pilgrimage to Jerusalem. From Le Puy, Pope Urban issued a summons to all the bishops of the Catholic Church to assemble at Clermont in November of the same year.

Urban had decided upon a crusade, but how could he persuade Frankish warriors to risk their lives for the eastern Emperor? The Byzantines were much disliked by the Franks – seen as devious, decadent and corrupt. Liutprant of Cremona had described Constantinople as 'a city full of lies, tricks, perjury and greed, a city rapacious, avaricious and vainglorious'. The emperors had been corrupted by oriental decadence, employing eunuchs as their ministers, and putting out the eyes of their enemies. No western knight would be willing to die for Constantinople.

However, Jerusalem was a different matter. It was the prize destination for every Christian pilgrim – the hazards and hardships of the journey a penance embraced as atonement for sins. 'The most important expression of the renewed spirituality in the eleventh century – which originated in Cluny – was the penitential pilgrimage'[160] The monks at Cluny had encouraged pilgrimage as 'a form of martyrdom'.[161] 'In fact the attitude of the eleventh-century Christian towards Jerusalem and the Holy Land had become obsessive.'[162] On the whole, during the four centuries of Islamic rule over Palestine, Christians had made pilgrimages to Jerusalem unimpeded. The only outright persecution of Christians had taken place around a hundred years before during the reign of the fanatical Egyptian Caliph, al-Hakim; although more recently seven thousand pilgrims from northern Europe led by the Bishops of Utrecht, Bamberg and Ratisbon had been ambushed by Muslims near Rabieh and had fought back in self-defence.

On Tuesday 25 November, 1099, the three hundred or so bishops who had responded to Pope Urban's summons assembled at Clermont. A week was spent dealing with Church business, passing the usual edicts against simony, lay investiture and the marriage of priests; a vote was passed in favour of the Truce of God; and a decree excommunicating King Philip of France for his adulterous liaison with Bertrade de Montfort. Then, on 27 November, the bishops and their entourage were told to assemble in a field outside the city's eastern gate. Here, from a throne raised on a platform, in a session of the Council open to all, Urban addressed a huge gathering of clergy and laity. He told the crowd of the reverses suffered by their co-religionists in the East, and the suffering they had endured at the hands of the Seljuk Turks. He went on to describe the harassment of Christian pilgrims to the holy city of Jerusalem. Should they be left undefended? With the eloquence of an experienced preacher, he called upon them to emulate their ancestors who had fought with Charlemagne, turning away from fratricidal strife to fight the enemies of the Christian faith in the east. He in his turn, as the successor of St. Peter, with his God-given powers to bind and loose on this earth, promised that those who committed themselves to this campaign in a spirit of penitence would be let off all punishment due to them for their past sins.

---

160   Joshua Prawer, *The Latin Kingdom of Jerusalem*, p.7
161   Richard Fletcher, *Op. Cit.*, p. 262
162   Jonathan Riley-Smith, *The First Crusade and the Idea of Crusading*, p. 21

Urban's appeal met with an enthusiastic, even rapturous reception. A cry of *Deus le volt!* (God wills it) arose from the crowd. Adhemar of Le Puy, Urban's host at Clermont, fell on his knees and begged the pope to be allowed to join this Holy War. Cloth was torn into strips and crosses sewn on to the doublets of those who there and then vowed to join the crusade. As word spread from Clermont to the outermost limits of Europe, Christians vowed to take the Cross. Urban's promise of an indulgence was a considerable incentive for 'hard boiled and violent men in a world much preoccupied with sin and its consequences.'[163] However, as Eamon Duffy points out in his history of the Popes, the indulgence was taken to promise more than Urban had originally intended. He had said that a crusader would be excused the punishment due for his transgression, in this world and in purgatory in the next: it presupposed repentance, confession and absolution. However it was understood as a promise that the sins themselves would be forgiven, and thus was born the concept of the papal *indulgence* which would be so misused in later years.

Pope Urban's call for a crusade was momentous, 'a shock to the communal system' and 'something different from anything that had been attempted before'.[164] It was taken up by preachers throughout Europe, with an immediate impact not only on the knights and nobleman who Urban hoped to inspire, but also on the uneducated poor who, led by a charismatic preacher from Picardy known as Peter the Hermit, formed an ill-armed and undisciplined horde that set off forthwith to liberate Jerusalem. Bishops and abbots did what they could to restrain them but the movement was out of their control. The lure of adventure and promise of spiritual rewards proved irresistible. The clergy forbade married men to leave their wives and children, but they were ignored.

Peter the Hermit was joined at the head of this ramshackle army by a knight called Walter Sans-Avoir. As it passed through Germany, it was joined by a contingent led by a monk called Gottschalk, and a minor baron, Count Emicho of Leiningen. The army now contained 'crusaders from all parts of western Europe, led by experienced captains'[165] but they had not the authority, and perhaps not the will, to prevent their followers attacking the Jewish

---

163   Eamon Duffy, *Op. Cit.*. p. 137

164   Bull, *The Oxford Illustrated History of the Crusades*, p. 17

165   Jonathan Riley-Smith, *The First Crusade and the Idea of Crusading*, p. 52

communities in the cities of Cologne and Trier. Urban might have anticipated the danger; a predecessor, Pope Alexander, had written to the bishops in Spain ordering them to protect the Jews in their diocese 'lest they be killed by those who are setting out to fight against the Saracens...' [166] Now, on the Rhine, the prince bishops and local nobility took in Jews for their protection, but the threat of excommunication did not prevent the pogroms. The peasant crusaders were unable to distinguish between a Jew and a Muslim. Moreover, as was customary, looting was the means by which they were to pay for their endeavour: 'it can be assumed that for many crusaders the loot taken from the Jews provided their only means of financing such a journey' and that frequently 'religious zeal of the murderous mob was merely a feeble attempt to conceal the real motive: greed'. [167] But they did not stop at pillage. Men, women and children were slaughtered and, as at Masada in AD 73, and in York a century or so later, Jews themselves 'massacred their own' rather than 'succumb to the blows of the uncircumcised'.[168]

The murderous attacks on Jews spread from the Rhineland to other German cities such as Speyer and Worms; then to the Norman capital, Rouen; and to Prague, the capital of Bohemia. Although the Jews were not the only victims of the peasants' crusade – in Hungary the crusaders attacked the local gentile inhabitants – it was a traumatic experience for European Jews. And worse was to come.

By the time the army led by Peter the Hermit and Walter Sans-Avoir reached Constantinople, the Emperor Alexius had been alerted to the danger posed by these supposed saviours, and so appointed his Pecheneg cavalry to act as military police. When the crusaders started to loot the suburbs of Constantinople, the Pechenegs escorted them to a military camp on the eastern side of the Bosphorus. From there the crusaders launched an attack on the Seljuk Turks. On 21 October 1096, at Xerigordon close to Nicea. the army of the People's Crusade was annihilated.

Two months later, the kind of force that Pope Urban had had in mind began to assemble at Constantinople. First came a cousin of the King of France, Hugh of Vermandois, with a small group of knights and men-at-arms; then a larger force led by Godfrey of Bouillon, Duke of Lower Lorraine; his brother

---

166   Fletcher, *Op. Cit.* p. 232

167   Mayer, *The Crusades*, p.44

168   Albert of Aix, quoted in Daniel Cohn-Sherbok, *The Crucified Jew: Twenty Centuries of Christian anti-Semitism*, London 1992, p. 40

Eustace: Baldwin of Boulogne, and his cousin Baldwin of Bourg. They were all descended on both sides of the family from Charlemagne – classic exemplars of Frankish warrior-champions of the Church. Charlemagne's empire might now be divided into Germany and France, but none would describe themselves as German or French. All were Christians, and among their retinue were both French-speaking and German-speaking knights.

Next came a contingent of Normans from southern Italy led by the eldest son of Robert Guiscard, the forty-year-old Bohemond of Taranto, accompanied by his dashing young nephew, Tancred. Given that Robert Guiscard had recently invaded the Byzantine empire, their presence aroused misgivings in the Emperor Alexius; but Bohemond seemed sincere in his commitment to the crusade. Following them on the same route from Italy across the Adriatic to Dyrrachium on the Dalmatian coast, and then to Thessalonica, came a body of powerful noblemen led by Robert II, Count of Flanders, whose father had fought with the Emperor Alexius; Robert, Duke of Normandy, brother of the English King, William Rufus; and Stephen, Count of Blois, the son-in-law of William the Conqueror. The largest contingent was led by Raymond, Count of Toulouse. With him came Adhemar, Bishop of Le Puy, who had been the first to take the Cross, and had been appointed by Pope Urban as his legate and spiritual leader of the Crusade.

In April, 1097, the crusading army crossed the Bosphorus and, like the People's Crusade before them, came up against the army of the Turkish sultan, Kilij Arslan, outside Nicea. If Kirij Arslan imagined that a second victory over the Crusaders would be as easy as the first, he was unpleasantly surprised. As Anna Comnena, the daughter of the Emperor Alexius, would write in her memoir of her father, 'the irresistible first shock of a charge by Frankish knights would make a hole through the walls of Babylon'. [169] The Turks were routed and abandoned Nicaea. True to their promise to the Emperor Alexius, the crusaders allowed Byzantine troops to invest the city. There was no pillaging, no booty but rich gifts from the Emperor. The Crusaders marched on across Anatolia, harassed by the Turks, and reached the great city of Antioch – its battlements with four hundred towers three miles long and one mile deep, and a citadel a thousand feet above the town. It had a largely Christian population but was garrisoned by the Seljuk Turks. Bohemond of Taranto had recruited a spy within the city who under cover of dark admitted the crusaders. Antioch was taken without a fight.

---

169   Quoted in R.C. Smail, *Crusading Warfare, 1097-1193*, p. 115.n

It was mid-summer and to avoid the great heat the crusaders decided to remain in Antioch until All Saints Day, November 1st. Then the plague hit the city, and the Papal Legate, Adhemar of Le Puy, was among its victims. All Saints Day came and went. The leaders quarrelled, and many left the city to avoid the plague. Finally, under pressure from the rank-and-file, Raymond of Toulouse took command and on 13 January, 1099, the crusading army set off from Antioch for Jerusalem, marching between the mountains and the Mediterranean sea. They were unopposed. The emirs of Damascus, Aleppo and Mosul watched and waited: it was not in their interest to help the Fatimid caliph in Cairo retain Jerusalem.

Only one third of those who had set out from western Europe to liberate Jerusalem two years before remained alive, leaving around twelve thousand foot soldiers and twelve or thirteen hundred knights for the assault on Jeruslem. They had brought no siege materials with them but as luck would have it, a ship from England and two galleys from Genoa had docked in Jaffa, providing nuts, bolts and nails for the construction of wooden towers. The Crusaders stormed the city. The Fatimid governor and his entourage, given a safe-conduct, were the only Muslims to escape with their lives. Intoxicated by their victory, and still charged with the passions of battle, the crusaders set about the slaughter of the city's inhabitants with the same indifference to age or gender as had been shown by Titus's legions a thousand years before. Tancred had captured the al-Aqsa mosque, and raised his banner to signify that those Muslims who had taken refuge there were under his protection: it was ignored. All were slaughtered. So too the Jews who had fled to their synagogue. It was set on fire. All were burned alive.

The chaplain of Raymond of Toulouse, Raymond of Aguilers, would later describe how he had walked up to his ankles in blood: 'in all the streets and squares of the city, mounds of heads, hands and feet were to be seen. People were walking quite openly over dead men and horses.' To him, the slaughter was no more than the Muslims had deserved. 'What an apt punishment! The very place that endured for so long blasphemies against God was now masked in the blood of the blasphemers.' The crusaders were jubilant. After three years of suffering and hardship, a journey of two thousand miles in savage climates and through inhospitable terrain, Pope Urban's mission had been accomplished. On 17 July, the princes, barons, bishops, priests, preachers, visionaries and camp-followers, processed through the streets of the deserted city to the Church of the Holy Sepulchre to attend Mass at the holiest shrine of their religion, and give thanks for their astonishing victory.

29.   The Military Orders

Pope Urban II died two weeks after the crusaders' triumph but before the news had reached Rome. His successor, Paschal II, an Italian from a modest background, welcomed the news but he was too preoccupied with his dispute with the German emperors, Henry IV and his son Henry V, and the anti-popes they set up against him, to play a significant role in what came to be called '*outremer*' – overseas. There the Latin barons established their own principalities in Edessa, Antioch, Tripoli and the kingdom of Jerusalem – the last ruled first by Godfrey of Bouillon and then Baldwin of Boulogne. The security of these Latin possessions was enhanced by the presence in the eastern Mediterranean of Venetian and Pisan fleets. A combined assault by land and sea quickly reduced the ports and cities on the coast of Palestine.

However, most of the crusaders, their vows fulfilled, now returned to Europe and the King of Jerusalem was left with an army of only around three hundred knights and a thousand foot-soldiers. There might have been no immediate prospect of external aggression, but internal security was another matter. A growing number of pilgrims arrived from Europe on boats from Pisa and Venice equipped only with a pouch and staff. In Jerusalem they were safe enough, but on the route from Jaffa to Jerusalem, or once on the road to the many sites of events in the life of Jesus of Nazareth, they were vulnerable to attack from disaffected Muslims or Bedouin brigands living in caves in the Judean hills. The question of security for pilgrims became acute.

In 1104, Hugh Count of Champagne came to the Holy Land with a retinue of knights. Among them was Hugh of Payns who, when Count Hugh returned to Europe in 1108, remained in Jerusalem with a fellow-knight, Godfrey of St.-Omer. Possibly they meant to become monks but, seeing the need to defend the pilgrims from Europe, proposed the formation of a community of knights that would follow the rule of a religious order. The King and Patriarch approved the idea, and on Christmas Day, 1119 Hugh, Godfrey and eight other knights took vows of poverty, chastity and obedience before the Patriarch in the Church of the Holy Sepulchre. To provide them with an income, they were endowed with a number of benefices, and were housed in what had been the al-Aqsa mosque on the southern edge of the Temple Mount. The name given to this body of warrior monks was 'The Poor Fellow-Soldiers of Jesus Christ and the temple of Solomon', later 'The Knights of the Temple of Solomon', and 'The Knights of the Temple', or simply 'The Templars'.

The idea of knights subject to monastic discipline, with no family or possessions, combined both the spiritual and the practical needs of those magnates such as Hugh of Champagne and Fulk of Anjou. Fulk enrolled as an associate of the order, and Hugh, having repudiated his unfaithful wife and having made over his county to his nephew Theobald, disinheriting the son he believed was by his wife's lover, returned to the Holy Land and took vows of poverty, chastity and obedience as a Poor Fellow-Soldier of Jesus Christ.

In Jerusalem itself, prior to the First Crusades, Amalfi merchants and pilgrim knights had established a hospice to care for pilgrims dedicated to St. John. After the taking of Jerusalem by the crusaders, this was reconstituted as a military order known as the Knights of the Hospital of St. John or the Hospitallers. Later, in 1190 in the coastal city of Acre, a third military order was formed by German knights, the Brothers of the German House of St. Mary in Jerusalem, or the Teutonic Knights.

In 1127, Hugh of Payns went to Europe to raise funds for his new order, the Knights of the Temple. Equipping a knight involved considerable expense – he required not just a horse, arms and armour but also a sergeant and squire. The magnates of western Europe understood this and a number of those who would like to have taken the Cross, but feared for what might happen in their realms in their absence, were happy to pay for proxies. Hugh of Payns thus raised substantial sums of money – Henry I of England was particularly generous, giving him 'great treasures of gold and silver'. There were also endowments of land, and a structure was established to administer the Templars' estates – with 'Commanderies' throughout western Europe, often with a circular chapel modelled on the Church of the Holy Sepulchre in Jerusalem.

Most important of all, Hugh secured the endorsement of his order at the Council of Troyes in 1129. It was by no means a foregone conclusion. A number of churchmen, among them the founder of the Carthusian order, Bruno, had doubts about the morality of war: had not Jesus rebuked Peter for drawing a sword in his defence? However, the most influential Catholic leader at the time, Bernard, Abbot of Clairvaux – coming from the same knightly milieu as Hugh of Payns, and a friend of Hugh of Champagne – was persuaded, and persuaded others, of the righteousness of a military order. What was required *outremer*, he wrote to an abbot thinking of founding a monastery in the Holy

Land, 'are fighting knights not singing and wailing monks'[170] – an army of chaste warriors who would be subject to their Grand Master, and he only to the pope. Hugh persuaded Bernard to write a Rule for the Templars, *De Laude*. In the introduction, Bernard warns the Templar knights to reject any doubts cast on their motives as the work of the Devil. Certainly, their vocation was a novelty in the life of the Church, 'clean different from the ordinary way of knighthood',[171] but the purity of their motives transferred 'homicide, which was evil, into malecide – the killing of evil – which was good.' There was no doubt in Bernard's mind but that the Saracens were the agents of the Devil.

30.   Bernard of Clairvaux

Bernard of Clairvaux was the most illustrious member of a new monastic order, the Cistercians. The constant quest for Christian perfection that had started in the deserts of Egypt – the founding, flourishing and then decline of such communities – had seen its most long-lasting model in Monte Cassino: but time and again compromise and corruption eroded the original idea, driving those such as Berno of Cluny to return to Benedict's austere rule. But even Cluny, by the twelfth century, although ruled by a saintly abbot, Peter the Venerable, had been compromised by the huge sums pouring into its coffers from rents, tithes and feudal rights, and the contributions of pilgrims who set off from Cluny and passed the Cluniac staging posts on their way to the shrine of Santiago de Compostella. The abbots of Cluny were often absent from their communities, called away to serve the wider Church. The monks had abandoned the manual labour enjoined by the Benedictine rule, leaving serfs to till their land while they served either as officials or 'choir monks', singing a superb liturgy elaborated with a plethora of new devotions in their large and richly decorated abbey church.

The early years of the eleventh century saw yet again a yearning among some monks to escape the business of the modern monastery, and return to the simplicity, solitude and asceticism of the original anchorites. One such monk was Bruno, born in Cologne, who first studied and then taught at Rheims – Pope Urban II was one of his pupils. He was made a canon of the

---

170   Quoted in Malcolm Barber, *The New Knighthood. A History of the Order of the Temple*, p. 13

171   Maurice Keen, *Chivalry*, p.8

cathedral, and chancellor of the diocese, but repelled by the worldliness of a new archbishop, he left Rheims in 1084 and found the solitude he had longed for high in the Chartreuse mountains in Savoy. Here, with six companions, he built a chapel and six wooden huts. As the monastery grew, the huts became three-roomed dwellings opening onto a common cloister. The monks remained hermits, meeting only to sing the office, take a walk together once a week, and eat together on feast days. The monastery, La Grande Chartreuse, became the mother house of the Carthusian order.

For a time, between leaving Rheims and founding La Grande Chartreuse, Bruno is thought to have lived as a hermit close to the Abbey of Molesme. This had been founded by an austere and devout Burgundian, Robert, from a group of hermits living in the forest of Colan in eastern France. Disputes within this community at one point drove Robert to leave Molesme and, with a French monk, Alberic, and a Saxon from Dorset, Stephen Harding, form a community at Cîteaux, around fifteen miles south of Dijon. However, at the instigation of the Archbishop of Lyon, Pope Urban II ordered Robert to return to Molesme which in his absence had gone into decline. Robert obeyed, leaving first Alberic, then Stephen, as abbots of Cîteaux. The community, known now as Cistercians, adopted a habit of white, un-dyed wool and established a precarious self-sufficiency through cultivation of the land.

These early Cistercians struggled to survive. Their aloofness alienated the local nobility and the rigours of their regime deterred potential recruits. There came a point, under Stephen Harding, when it was thought that the project might fail . Then suddenly, in 1113, a young local nobleman, Bernard de Fontaines from nearby Fontaines-lès-Dijon, appeared with thirty relatives and friends as postulants at the gates of Cîteaux. They were admitted and from that moment the order flourished.

Bernard was born in 1091, the third son of Tescelin le Roux and Aleth of Montbard. Handsome, learned, neurotic and charismatic, he was twenty-two-years old when he became a Cistercian monk. His example set a fashion. Other young noblemen joined the Cistercians, and after only three years Stephen Harding despatched Bernard with twelve other monks to establish a new Cistercian community in a remote valley near Bar-sur-Aube. Bernard named it Clairvaux – the Valley of Light.

The early years at Clairvaux were hard – both physically and on the level of human relations. Bernard himself would write later in life that he had chosen the harsher regime of the Cistercians to that of, say, the Benedictines at Cluny because only such a regime could curb his passionate nature. Bernard's vast correspondence with churchmen throughout Christendom reveals a man who spoke his mind, had a sharp wit, and was impatient with his spiritual and intellectual inferiors. Though he claimed that he chose the ascetic rule for personal reasons, he betrayed a measure of contempt for the easier-going life of monks in less austere orders. In the course of a dispute with the Abbot of Cluny, Peter the Venerable, over a young novice, he said that the very beauty of Cluny – its fine liturgy and rich décor – were a form of decadence. '*Vous faites le luxe pour Dieu*' – you live in luxury for God. The austerity of the Cistercian rule remains apparent in the severe beauty of the ruins we see today of the Cistercian foundations which sprang up throughout Europe.

Such was Bernard's magnetism, that young and old flocked to join his community. His uncle, one of the original party of thirty who had accompanied Bernard to Citeaux, was now followed by all his brothers and his ageing father, Tescelin le Roux. One might feel a certain sympathy for the young women of the region who saw their potential husbands disappear though the gates of Clairvaux, but Bernard had a solution. He established a community of nuns at Jully close to Molesme, installing his younger sister Humbeline as superior. Humbeline was married, but took her vows with her husband's consent. Bernard's older brother Guy was also married and had two daughters, yet was persuaded by Bernard to renounce them and join the community at Clairvaux.

Although Bernard was to write a commentary on the erotic poem in the Bible, the Song of Songs, he seemed at times to share the view of his contemporary, Peter Damian, that 'marriage was a doubtful cover for sin'. Perhaps Bernard had suffered from temptations of the flesh in his youth: certainly, he thought any contact with women perilous, and forbade his monks from embracing even their mothers and sisters. Indeed, it seemed clear to Bernard that salvation was only possible if a man or woman was shut away from any worldly temptation behind the high walls of a monastery.

Bernard's fame spread throughout Europe – his intellect, piety and asceticism qualifying him to act as the conscience of Christendom. He was inexorable in his denunciation of heretical ideas, such as those of Peter Abelard and Henry of Lausanne. To some modern historians, he comes across as a self-righteous zealot: 'he saw the world,' wrote John Julius Norwich, 'with the eye of a fanatic'. To David Knowles, however, Bernard was' one of the small class of supremely great men whose gifts and opportunities have been exactly matched… For forty years, Cîteaux-Clairvaux was the spiritual centre of Europe, and at one time Bernard had among his ex-monks the pope, the archbishop of York and cardinals and bishops in plenty.' By the time of his death in 1163, three hundred and thirty-nine Cistercian monasteries had been established throughout Europe, sixty-eight of them from Clairvaux.

31.   The Second Crusade

In 1144 the Latin principality of Edessa fell to the Muslim Emir of Mosul. This prompted the Pope, Eugenius III, to ask Louis VII, the King of France to lead a new crusade. Louis, only twenty-five years old, and married to the lively heiress of a domain larger than his own, Eleanor of Aquitaine, found little enthusiasm for the idea among his barons, and was advised against it by his sage counsellor, Abbot Suger of St. Denis who feared that the barons would make trouble in Louis's absence. Undeterred, Louis turned to Bernard of Clairvaux: Louis' brother Henry had joined the community at Clairvaux; Pope Eugenius had been one of his monks. On 31 March, 1146, the French nobility, summoned by their king, gathered in Vézelay in Burgundy: the church, containing the relics of Mary Magdalen, was a place of pilgrimage, and a staging post on the route to Compostella. There, speaking from a raised platform outside the town, they heard Bernard preach a new crusade.

His eloquence had the desired effect: not just the nobility but also commoners took the Cross. 'Villages and towns are now deserted,' Bernard wrote to Pope Eugenius. 'You will scarcely find one man for every seven women. Everywhere you will see widows whose husbands are still alive.' [172] The crusade started badly, as had the First Crusade, with attacks on the Jewish communities in the Rhineland. Bernard condemned the pogroms, and went to Germany, summoned by the Archbishop of Mainz, to discipline a Cistercian monk Rudolf who had been inciting the attacks on the Jews. While there, he persuaded the Hohenstaufen King of Germany, Conrad III, to join his fellow monarch Louis on the crusade.

In May, 1147, Conrad led an army of around twenty thousand crusaders out of the city of Regensberg to follow the overland route taken by the First Crusade to Constantinople. The French followed from Metz a few weeks

---

172   Quoted in Steven Runciman, *A History of the Crusades, Vol. 2.* p. 254

later, led by King Louis who was accompanied by his wife Eleanor. Conrad was impatient, and crossed the Bosphorus into Anatolia. At Dorylaeum his army was attacked by the Seljuk Turks and defeated. The survivors, including Conrad, retreated to Nicea where they were joined by the French. Louis, still accompanied by Eleanor, proceeded east, escorted by a strong force of Templar Knights, now wearing their uniforms of a red cross on a white tunic. It was wet and cold. They were harassed by the Turks' light cavalry. Conrad fell ill and returned to Constantinople. When the crusaders reached the Byzantine port of Attalia, Louis and Eleanor with their entourage sailed to Antioch.

Antioch, a Latin principality since the time of the First Crusade, was now ruled by Eleanor's uncle, Raymond of Poitiers. He and his barons were particularly pleased to have the company of Eleanor and her ladies-in-waiting, and they to enjoy the ease and distractions of Raymond's court after the discomfort and privations of their journey across Asia Minor.

Worse than the discomfort and privations had been the effect on Eleanor's feelings for her petulant and indecisive husband, Louis. Eleanor was twenty-five years old – intelligent, vivacious, high-spirited and clearly drawn to her courageous uncle Raymond who, in turn, appreciated the flirtatious gaiety of his niece. Gossip began to circulate in the court at Antioch that their affection for one another had transgressed the bounds of propriety. The feelings of Raymond's wife Constance are not known: she was much younger than her husband, and perhaps unaware of what was going on. Not so King Louis, whose jealousy was exacerbated by Eleanor's support for Raymond's views as to how the crusade should proceed. Raymond wanted to attack Aleppo; Louis ordered his army to March south towards Jerusalem and, when Eleanor refused to accompany him, took her with him by force.

In June, 1148, the French and German crusading armies gathered at Acre together with contingents from Provence, Savoy, Flanders and England. This dazzling array of European monarchs and princes was joined by the young King of Jerusalem, Baldwin III, and the principal barons of his kingdom. However, its commanders could not agree as to what to do with this host. If its objective was the retaking of Edessa, then it should move against Aleppo as Raymond had suggested; if it was to pre-empt a threat to Jerusalem from the Fatimid caliphs in Cairo, then it should take their fortress at Ascalon. There was a third possibility – Damascus. This appealed to the Europeans because of its biblical connotations, and to the barons of *outremer* because it controlled large swathes of fertile land.

The siege of Damascus was a catastrophe. The Damascenes remained behind their ramparts, avoiding an outright confrontation which would have favoured the Franks, but harassed the crusaders with sorties by their light cavalry. Too weak to storm the city's ramparts, and hearing that a Muslim force from Aleppo was on its way to relieve the city, the great Christian army returned to Galilee with nothing accomplished.

King Conrad now left the Holy Land in disgust. King Louis lingered, convinced that the Byzantines were somehow to blame for the fiasco. His only achievement was the ending of his marriage to Eleanor of Aquitaine. Passing through Rome on their way back to France, Louis and Eleanor received counselling from the ageing pope Eugenius: he insisted that they sleep in the same bed. To no avail. Their marriage was annulled in 1152 on the grounds of consanguinity, and Eleanor went on to marry the Duke of Normandy who in due course became King Henry II of England.

32.   The Third Crusade

Edessa was never recovered by the Latin Christians, and the Kingdom of Jerusalem itself came under threat with the rise to power of the Fatimid's vizier, Saladin – an inspired general of mixed Kurdish and Turkish descent who in 1171 abolished the Fatimid dynasty in Cairo and proclaimed himself Caliph. His conquests included Yemen but, more ominously for the Latins, Syria: until then the quarrelling rulers of the region had never combined against them. In 1187, Saladin marched into Palestine and attacked the Latin army assembled by the weak and indecisive King Guy of Jerusalem on the Heights of Hattin near Lake Tiberias. The Muslims triumphed. Saladin led his victorious army into Jerusalem. In deliberate contrast to the behaviour of the crusaders when they first took the city, Saladin was magnanimous towards the conquered Latins. The inhabitants were spared. The cross was removed from the Dome of the Rock but the Church of the Holy Sepulchre remained in the hands of orthodox Christians. His magnanimity had its limits: after their defeat at Hattin, the 230 knights of the Temple and St. John were given the choice of submission to Islam or death. None denied Christ. All were then decapitated to the wild cries of ecstatic Sufis.

At first it seemed as if the fall of Jerusalem would mean the end of any Latin presence in the Holy Land; but a number of coastal cities such as

Antioch, Tripoli and Tyre remained in the hands of the Latins, as well as some fortresses held by the military orders. Acre had fallen to Saladin's army but in June of 1187, after taking a vow that he would leave Palestine, King Guy was released by Saladin. The vow, made to a Muslim and under duress, was judged invalid; and, showing an unusual resolve, Guy gathered a force to re-take Acre. He established a fortified encirclement of the city which withstood the assaults of what remained of Saladin's army.

The besieging Latin army was not strong enough to take Acre, but it held out until reinforcements arrived from western Europe. News of the fall of Jerusalem had traumatised Christendom, and at once the pope called for a new crusade. The response was overwhelming. Among the first to take the Cross was Richard, the third son of Henry II of England and Eleanor of Aquitaine. Richard, now Duke of Aquitaine and King of England, was famous throughout Europe as a skilled strategist and ferocious warrior. The alacrity with which he responded to the pope's call came less from devotion to the Catholic religion than a sense of *noblesse oblige*. The prestige of his dynasty demanded that he go on crusade: he took the Cross in the cathedral in Tours on the same spot from which his great-grandfather, Fulk of Anjou, had set out for Jerusalem.

King Philip Augustus of France joined Richard, together with a large number of French and German barons – many of them descendants of earlier crusaders. In 1189, the German Emperor, Frederick I of Hohenstaufen, known as Barbarossa or Red Beard, set off for the Holy Land from Regensburg with 'the largest single force ever to leave on a crusade.' [173]. As a young man, he had accompanied his uncle Conrad on the disastrous Second Crusade. Now aged sixty-six, he led his army through Hungary and the Balkans to Constantinople. Relations between the Latins and Byzantines were unsatisfactory. Five years earlier, there had been a pogrom of Latins living in Constantinople by its Greek inhabitants: many were slaughtered, their houses and churches burned. When Saladin captured Jerusalem, the Byzantine emperor Isaac Angelus had written to congratulate him.

However, the Byzantines did not want to tangle with an army as strong as that of Frederick Barbarossa which therefore crossed the Bosporos unmolested and marched into Anatolia. Saladin's son-in-law, Malik Shah, was sent to oppose it, but was decisively defeated. The victorious Barbarossa led his crusaders down from the Taurus mountains onto the plain of Seleucia

---

173   Steven Runciman, *A History of the Crusades. Vol. 3. The Kingdom of Acre* p. 11

but, while crossing the River Calycadnus, fell from his horse and, weighed down by his armour, drowned.

With the death of their king, many of the German crusaders lost heart and, when they reached the ports of Cilicia and Syria on the Mediterranean, took ship and returned home. Barbarossa's son, Frederick of Swabia, continued first to Antioch where he buried his father's body, and then on to join his fellow crusaders besieging Acre. There he caught the fever, thought to be malaria, rampant in the camp and on 20 February, 1191, he died. Two months later, King Philip II August of France reached Acre and, seven weeks after that King Richard of England – Richard having seized Cyprus from its Byzantine ruler *en route*. Acre was taken. The triumphant monarchs raised their banners on the ramparts, among them Leopold, the Archduke of Austria. Richard thought Leopold did not merit a share in the glory, and so the spoils, and had Leopold's banner torn down and thrown into the moat.

After this humiliation, Leopold of Austria returned home. So too did the sardonic, hypochondriacal French king, Philip August. Richard was left in command of the crusading army. There was a delay in the payment of an indemnity and exchange of prisoners agreed with Saladin: Richard saw it as a ruse to tie up part of his army, and had 2,700 Muslim captives – men, women and children – slaughtered by his English soldiers. Unencumbered, he then marched south along the coast, supplied by a Christian fleet. At Arsuf, south of Caesarea, Saladin attacked but was beaten back – his first defeat since Hattin. But his army was not destroyed and Richard, though he came within sight of Jerusalem, lacked the strength to move inland and take the Holy City. Even if it could be taken, it could not be held once Richard and his army had returned to England. News of troubles in England put pressure on Richard to do so. Both he and Saladin, who felt a mutual esteem, realised that they had reached a stalemate. A treaty was signed whereby the Christians retained possession of the coastal cities they had taken, and Christian pilgrims would have free access to Jerusalem.

Richard returned to Acre, settled his affairs in the city, dispatched his wife and sister on a boat to France. He himself set sail on 9 October: he had been in the Holy Land for sixteen months and, if he had not retaken Jerusalem, he had done what he could: his vow was fulfilled. His route to England was problematic: the Byzantine Emperor, the German Emperor, the Count of Toulouse who controlled the ports on the south coast of France – all were his enemies. It was too late in the year to sail through the straits of Gibraltar and across the Bay of Biscay. Adverse winds blew his boat to the island of Corfu, a province of the Byzantine Emperor. There Richard and his escort of four Templar knights took ship with pirates heading for Venice. The ship went aground at Aquileia at the northern end of the Adriatic Sea. From here, disguised as returning pilgrims, they went north over the Alps. Richard, who had failed to remove his royal ring, was recognised in Vienna, apprehended, and handed over to Leopold whom he had humiliated in Acre. Leopold imprisoned him in the castle of Dürrenstein, then passed him on to his overlord, the Emperor Henry VI, who set his ransom at 150,000 marks. King Philip August of France, and Richard's brother John, lobbied the Emperor to keep him under lock and key; but Richard charmed the nobles in the Emperor's entourage, made all the assurances demanded of him and, when most of the ransom was paid, was released. King Philip wrote to John: 'Beware, the devil is out'.

While Richard was imprisoned, Saladin died. Richard, five years after his release, was fatally wounded by a bolt from a cross-bow while besieging the castle of a recalcitrant vassal. He died on 6 April, 1199, forty-two years old.

33.   The Fourth Crusade

The year before Richard's death, a Roman nobleman, Lothar of Segni, was elected pope, taking the name Innocent III. Highly intelligent, and a man of absolute personal integrity, his reign would mark the 'pinnacle of papal power and influence'.[174] He was 'a man born to rule, uniting exceptional gifts of intellect and character with determination, flexibility, rare skill in handling men, and also humaneness'. He had 'an exalted conception of his position as Vicar of Christ', set 'midway between God and man' with 'not just the Church but the whole world to govern'.[175]

Innocent's objectives were the pursuit of the Cluniac reforms of the Church, and to assert the primacy of the papacy, but there was also what had now become an obsession of every pope – the return of Jerusalem to Christian rule. To that end he proclaimed a new crusade. The maritime republic of Venice was contracted to provide a fleet to transport a large army to Egypt whose defeat, the crusaders believed, was the key to the conquest of

---

174   Eamon Duffy, *Op. Cit.* p. 145

175   J.N.D. Kelly (ed.), *Op. Cit.* p.186

Palestine. However, the army that assembled in Venice in 1202 was smaller than had been expected; many crusaders had taken ship in other ports; and those in Venice found they had insufficient funds to pay the sum agreed with the Venetians.

To pay off the debt, the Venetians proposed that the crusaders, *en route* to Egypt, should help them retake the city of Zara on the Dalmatian coast that had defected to the Hungarians. The inhabitants were Catholics, but despite a clear ruling by Innocent III that those who fought fellow-Christians would be excommunicated, the crusaders complied. Zara was taken. The fleet moved on to Constantinople, and there the Crusaders became enmeshed in further Levantine intrigue. A deposed emperor promised military assistance and rich rewards if the crusaders would restore him to the throne. Short of funds, the crusaders agreed but the plan went awry: the pretender was killed. Manipulated by the Venetian Doge, who had been blinded by the Byzantines during the pogrom of Latins living in Constantinople thirty years before, the crusading army besieged, captured and sacked the city – the first time it had fallen to an enemy since it was built by the Emperor Constantine. The Greek historian, Speros Vryonis, describes how

> For three days they murdered, raped, looted and destroyed on a scale which even the ancient Vandals and Goths would have found unbelievable. Constantinople had become a veritable museum of ancient and Byzantine art, an emporium of such incredible wealth that the Latins were astounded at the riches they found. Though the Venetians had an appreciation for the art which they discovered (they were themselves semi-Byzantines) and saved much of it, the French and others destroyed indiscriminately, halting to refresh themselves with wine, violation of nuns, and murder of Orthodox clerics. The Crusaders vented their hatred for the Greeks most spectacularly in the desecration of the greatest Church in Christendom. They smashed the silver iconostasis, the icons and the holy books of <u>Hagia Sophia</u>, and seated upon the patriarchal throne a whore who sang coarse songs as they drank wine from the Church's holy vessels.[176]

---

176   Vryonis, Speros (1967). *Byzantium and Europe*. New York: Harcourt, Brace & World. p. 152.

The English historian of the Crusades, Sir Stephen Runciman, judged it 'an act of gigantic political folly',[177] thwarting any move to help the Christians in Palestine, fragmenting the forces available to counter the Muslim powers, and leading to an enduring hatred of Orthodox Greeks for Latin Catholics. 'There was never a greater crime against humanity', he wrote, 'than the Fourth Crusade' – a questionable judgement given that it was made in the wake of the atrocities of Hitler's Third Reich.

Innocent III was appalled by the crusade's perversion into an attack on a Christian power, but he decided some good could be gained from the catastrophe. The Ayyubid sultans might remain safe in Cairo, and the Muslims retain possession of Jerusalem, but Latin rule of the Byzantine empire, which followed the sack of Constantinople, might end the schism between the eastern and western branches of Christendom.

34. The Albigensian Crusade

'The decades which followed the fourth crusade', wrote the historian Maurice Keen, 'saw Latin dominion extended to the furthest limits it ever achieved in the Middle Ages'. Europe appeared 'united as a single religious and political society, to a degree which was never surpassed.'[178] Pope Gregory VII's ambition for the Church's governance over both religious and secular affairs seemed to have been realised in Innocent III: 'He is the successor', wrote a visitor to Rome from Byzantium, 'not of Peter but of Constantine'.

But even at this moment of papal triumph, there were signs that in some areas western Christendom was rotting from within. There was growing criticism of the lavish display, lax morals and greed of the clergy. The criticism led to disaffection, and adherence to new or long-dormant heretical sects. In 1144 highly organized heterodox churches came to light in Liège and Cologne, and were suppressed with considerable violence. In 1173, a rich merchant in Lyon, Peter Waldo, suddenly renounced his riches to lead a life of apostolic poverty. He had a translation made of the Bible and urged his followers to follow its precepts rather than the teaching of the Church. Communities of Waldensians flourished in the cities of northern Italy. They

---

177   Steven Runciman, *Op. Cit.* Vol 3, p. 131

178   Maurice Keen, *Penguin History of Medieval Europe*, p. 135

were condemned as heretics in a Bull issued in Verona by Pope Lucius III in 1184, but Waldensian communities survived, forerunners of the Reformers of the sixteenth century.

If the Waldensians were precursors of the Protestants, the second heresy that flourished in the twelfth century had roots far in the past. Manichaeism, the religion founded by Mani in the third century AD which had engaged Augustine of Hippo before his conversion to Christianity, had not been extinguished by persecution, but had survived in various forms, spreading from the east to west. The core belief was that there were two co-equal deities – a good God who was pure spirit, an evil God whose province was matter. Communities of these dualists had flourished in Armenia where they were known as Paulicians, and later among the Slav peasants in Bulgaria where a certain Bogomil founded a dualist church. Bogomil missionaries spread throughout the Balkans and established a church in Constantinople.

The bacillus, as orthodox Christians saw it, was then carried west either by merchants or returning crusaders. At first sight a religion which taught that all matter was evil might seem unattractive to human beings encased by nature in flesh: but it was only a small number of *perfecti* who eschewed matter in so far as possible, leading austere lives as celibate vegans. They ministered to, and were sustained by, the ordinary believers – the *credentes* – who at some point in their lives would join the *perfecti* in a ceremony called the *consolamentum* – the only sacrament of the Manichaean church – which enabled them to enter into the realm of pure spirit. Since the reception of the *consolamentum* was usually postponed until one's dying days, there was an implicit opening for licentiousness: one had might as well be hung for a sheep as for a lamb. The moral constraints of marriage enjoined by the Catholic Church were neither here nor there because to procreate was to perpetuate matter and so was evil. 'Marriage they saw as the ultimate compromise with the body, and the pregnant woman was their *pariah*.' Better to avoid conception: 'buggery', the English word for anal intercourse, stems from the French word for the Manichaeans, 'bougre'.

The name given to the dualist religion when it reached Languedoc, the region in the south of France between the River Rhône and the Pyrenees, was Cathar which means 'pure' or 'purified'; and there can be no doubt but that the ascetic lives of the *perfecti* impressed many at a time when the secular priesthood was ignorant and indulgent. The general decadence and lassitude of the clergy was shared by that of the nobility headed by the indulgent

Counts of Toulouse. The era of chivalry and romance that had enchanted the troubadours was coming to an end. By the mid-12th century 'Languedoc was a society in an advanced stage of disintegration which still clung to the husk of a civilization that had all but disappeared'[179].

By 1167, the Cathars in Languedoc were sufficiently numerous and organized to hold a conference in St. Felix-de-Caraman near Castelnaudary presided over by the dualist 'pope' Niquinta from Constantinople. Two Cathar 'bishops' from northern France attended, and further bishops were appointed for the region. This establishment of a rival church did not go unnoticed: in a letter to the General Chapter of the Cistercian order, Raymond V of Toulouse blamed the debility and decay of the Church in his domains for a situation 'where few still believe in the Resurrection; the sacraments are despised and the religion of the two principles has everywhere established its hold.'[180] Raymond's solution was a crusade led by the French king: 'I will show him where the heretics are to be found'.

Force or persuasion? As early as 1145, Bernard of Clairvaux, who had preached against heresy in the Rhine Valley, spent two months touring Languedoc, urging the heretical Cathars to return to the Catholic faith: 'errors are refuted by argument, not by force.' He had been received with enthusiasm in the large cities, but in the small hill towns congregations walked out of the church when he started his sermons, and when he preached in the streets the inhabitants hammered on their doors to smother his words. Bernard changed his mind about coercion: 'if the heretics would prefer to die than to believe, then let them die'. It now seemed clear from their obduracy that Raymond V had been right. The heresy would have to be suppressed by force.

The difficulty here was that the Church depended on the civil authorities to punish those it had exposed as heretics, and in Languedoc the civil authorities – the local nobility – were unwilling to take on the task, either because they were *credentes* themselves, or because there were Cathars among their families and neighbours. 'How can we expel the *perfecti*,' a southern knight told Bishop Foulques of Toulouse. 'We were brought up with them and we count our relatives among them – and we see that they live honourably'. This unwillingness to expel or punish the Cathars in their midst was apparent to Raymond VI, Count of Toulouse, who had succeeded his father in 1194.

---

179   Jonathan Sumption, *The Albigensian Crusade,* p. 31
180   Quoted in Sumption, *Op. Cit.,* p. 34

Raymond VI, whose mother Constance was the daughter of King Louis VI of France, was attractive, easy-going and self-indulgent. He liked luxury and women, seducing his father's mistresses, committing incest with his sister, and repudiating two of his five wives. His religious convictions are unknown, but he clearly had no objection to Cathars. His second wife, Beatrice of Béziers, was a Cathar and there were Cathars in his court; yet he was also a generous benefactor of Cistercian abbeys and the military orders.

As sovereign of the county of Toulouse, it was Raymond's duty to deal with heretics when they were pointed out to him by the Church. It was therefore to him that Pope Innocent III first issued a command to extirpate the Cathars from his domain. Jonathan Sumption in his history of the Albigensian Crusade, talks of Innocent's 'fanatical, even hysterical hatred of heresy'[181] which suggests it was unreasonable; but it should be remembered that there was no doubt in his mind, or that of any orthodox Catholic at the time, that a heretic who died unrepentant would spend eternity in Hell. As pope, Innocent was responsible for protecting his flock from this fate: hence his sense of urgency when it came to dealing with the Cathars.

As Sumption recognises, Innocent was more cautious in his actions than in his words: he had trained in Bologna as a canon lawyer, and at times pedantically kept to the letter of that law. Also a canon lawyer as well as a theologian was the Cistercian monk, Peter of Castelnau, whom Innocent sent in 1203 as his Legate together with another Cistercian, the primate of his order, Arnaud-Amaury, Abbot of Cîteaux. The Legates had full powers, and in the first months of their visitation a number of bishops who were deemed to be corrupt, or had otherwise fallen short of expectations of the austere Cistercians, were removed from their posts. Little time was left for preaching, and what there was proved as ineffective as had that of Bernard of Clairvaux fifty years earlier.

Raymond VI made promises when it came to suppressing the Cathars but they were not fulfilled and in 1207, their patience at an end, he was excommunicated by the Legates. Pope Innocent III had also lost patience, and was putting out feelers for a crusade. This alarmed Raymond more than the excommunication, and he sent word to Peter of Castelnau that he was ready to give in to all the Church's demands. Peter went to St. Gilles near the River Rhône where Raymond, also Marquis of Provence, was holding court to receive his submission; but Raymond procrastinated as before, and by the

---

181   Sumption, *Op. Cit.* p. 67

end of the day Peter and his entourage departed with little achieved along the banks of a tributary of the River Rhône. A member of Raymond's entourage galloped after them and, as they awaited the ferry to cross the river, thrust his lance into Peter of Castelnau.

Raymond VI denied that he had ordered the assassination of the papal legate, but his failure to identify the assassin led Pope Innocent III to conclude that this was another of his lies. His excommunication was confirmed, and on 10 March, 1208, Innocent proclaimed a crusade. 'Forward soldiers of Christ! Go forth with the Church's cry of anguish ringing in their ears...' Their reward would be the lands of convicted heretics and, as with crusaders in the Holy Land, the forgiveness of their past sins.

The Albigensian Crusade lasted twenty years: it was, wrote Jonathan Sumption, 'one of the most savage of all mediaeval wars'.[182] Pope Innocent had hoped it would be led by the King of France, but was disappointed: Philip Augustus was preoccupied with his conflict with King John of England, who was also a menacing vassal as Duke of Aquitaine. Prominent and powerful princes who had joined the crusade to liberate Jerusalem, such as Odo III duke of Burgundy, were offered the post but all declined. A French baron and veteran crusader, Simon de Montfort, was chosen, to act in tandem with the second papal legate, the Cistercian Abbot Arnaud-Amaury. Simon had claims through his mother to be the Earl of Leicester, and had taken part in the Fourth Crusade – honourably refusing to take part in the attacks on Zara and Constantinople, and sailing straight to Palestine.

Simon was personally courageous, always ready to leap into the melee of battle. He was unquestionably devout but his desire to extirpate heresy was mixed with an ambition to establish a principality for his family from the expropriated lands of the heretics and their protectors. Dynastic interests bedevilled the crusade: vassals of Raymond such as Raymond-Roger, Count of Foix, and magnates whose lands straddled the Pyrenees such as King Pedro of Aragon, sent armies into the fray. To the usual slaughter that went with battles and sieges was added the burning of unrepentant Cathars when their cities were taken.

Death by immolation was now the accepted punishment for heretics, a form of capital punishment inherited from the Roman empire: it was the fate of the Christian martyr, Polycarp (see Chapter 15). In the Middle Ages it

---

182   Sumption, *Op. Cit.* p. 16

seemed an appropriate punishment for heretics: 'How ludicrous would it have been to threaten and punish with death mere counterfeiters, arsonists, thieves, or murderers, but not resolute subverters of God's truth?'[183] The Cistercian monk, Arnaud-Amaury, was relentless in the pursuit of the heretics. When the city of Beziers, home to both Cathars and Catholics, fell to the crusaders, it was Arnaud-Amaury who was said to have told his soldiers: 'kill them all, the Lord will know his own'.

The crusade only came to an end when the young king of France, Louis VIII, who had succeeded his father in 1226 led an army into Languedoc which then became a fief of the French Crown. The last Cathars held out in the apparently impregnable mountain fortress of Montségur; but in early January of 1244 a force of Basque volunteers, familiar with the Pyrenees, climbed the rocks, killed the sentries and occupied the eastern barbican of the castle. When by March it was clear that they could not be dislodged, the commander of the garrison, Pierre-Roger of Mirepoix, surrendered. Two hundred Cathars who refused to recant were burned on pyres outside the castle. Some *perfecti* had fled abroad, and some dogged dualists were to be found well into the fourteenth century, but in Languedoc the Cathar religion ceased to exist – thanks not just to the military triumphs of the crusade but to the work in the aftermath of its victories of a new ecclesiastical institution founded by Pope Innocent in 1228 to root out heresy – the Inquisition.

35.   Dominic Guzman

In 1206, early in their mission to the Cathars, the Papal Legates Peter of Castelnau and Arnaud-Amaury, conferring with local clergy outside the church of Notre-Dame des Tables in Montpellier, were joined by a party of Spanish clerics returning from a diplomatic mission on behalf of their king, Alfonso VIII of Castile. The leader of the delegation, Diego, bishop of Osma, was accompanied by a canon of his cathedral, Dominic de Guzman. Their mission had been a failure; so too the work of the papal legates whose morale was at a low ebb. Diego and Dominic had been shocked by the evidence of the spread of heresy as they passed through Languedoc, and now learned from the legates of the failure of the secular powers to do anything about it. They returned to Castile, but after a second mission on behalf of the king, were

---

183   Brad S. Gregory, *The Unintended Reformation*, p.159

relieved of their diplomatic duties. In 1204, both men went to Rome – Diego to ask to be relieved of his bishopric so that he might work on the missions. Pope Innocent III agreed to his request but sent both men not to the pagan fringes of Christendom but back to Languedoc to assist his Legates.

It was Dominic Guzman who decided that a wholly new approach was required to deal with the heretical Cathars. He came from a devout family of the Castilian nobility. He had spent ten years studying at the University of Palencia, and was considered serious-minded by his fellow students, betraying his great faith with the occasional extravagant gesture – selling his books to raise money to feed the poor, and offering to sell himself as a slave to ransom captives held by the Moors. The waste of such a talent was not allowed: instead, after his ordination, he was made a canon of the cathedral of Osma.

Dominic was already in his early thirties when he arrived in Languedoc to preach to the heretics. His analysis of why the mission had as yet made no headway was harsh. First, the native clergy were ignorant, unable to defeat the Cathar *parfaits* in argument, and living comfortably on their stipends, a poor contrast to their ascetic way of life. The Cistercian monks who had come from monasteries in northern France were better educated, but they were well fed and travelled in style. Their order with its monasteries throughout Europe had done great things; the insistence upon manual labour for the monks, which came from Benedict of Nursia's original rule, had meant the clearance of forests for arable land which provided food for Europe's growing population: but it had made the monasteries rich and the austerity enjoined by the early Cistericians, such as Bernard of Clairvaux, might, for all we know, have inspired the personal devotions of an abbot like the Papal Legate Arnaud-Amaury, but did not inhibit him from co-commanding an army and travelling with the entourage of a prince.

Dominic therefore enjoined on himself and his followers a vow of poverty, and admitted only those followers trained in theology or canon law. He soon perceived that the bacillus of heresy was frequently passed from women to their children who were educated in Cathar convents. Therefore, in 1206, with the help of Bishop Foulques of Toulouse, he established a convent at Prouille deep in Cathar territory. Prouille was endowed by the bishop and local landowners, and housed not just a community of nuns, who followed an Augustinian rule amended by Dominic; but was also became the headquarters of the growing number of itinerant preachers. After the assassination of the

Papal Legate, Pierre de Castenau, Dominic joined the crusaders, befriending Simon de Montfort, and working to restore the Catholic faith and religious practice in the wake of de Montfort's conquests. He was present at the Battle of Muret, and de Monfort ascribed the crusaders' unlikely victory to Dominic's prayers.

After the victory at Muret, Dominic's long-held ambition to found a religious order devoted to the extirpation of heresy and teaching of true doctrine was put into effect under the aegis of Bishop Foulques in Toulouse. This Order of Preachers was at first a diocesan fraternity, but Dominic's ambitions extended beyond Languedoc. Attending the Lateran Council in 1215, his petition for the establishment of a new order was at first refused; but a year later he appealed in person to Pope Innocent III who was sufficiently impressed to issue a Papal Bull establishing the new order on 22 December 1216.

Innocent III's successor as pope, Honorious III, was so impressed by Dominic's preaching in Rome that he gave his order the church of St. Sixtus, and asked Dominic to undertake the reform of convents and monasteries in the Holy City. But Dominic's ambitions extended beyond the reform of existing institutions: he wished his followers to establish the beauty of truth through learning. In 1217, he established a Dominican house at the University of Paris, and later another at Europe's oldest university at Bologna. It was at Bologna that the first General Chapter was held in 1219, and Dominic was chosen as Master General of the Order. Dominic died in the city two years later.

36.　Francis of Assisi

Until now, those who wished to devote themselves to the religious life became either secular priests, confined to a diocese and obedient to their bishops; or tonsured monks, obedient to their abbots and, except under unusual circumstances, required to reside in their monasteries for life. The members of Dominic's Order of Preachers, the Dominicans, were of necessity peripatetic, subject to the head of their order who in turn was subject only to the Pope. They begged for their sustenance, and so were thus known as 'mendicant' friars (brothers), but they were not the first such confraternity. Six years before the Bull that established the Order of Preachers, Pope Innocent had approved the foundation of another order of mendicant friars, the Franciscans – so named after their founder, Francesco Bernadone.

Francesco – Francis – was born in Assisi in 1181, the son of a prosperous silk merchant, Pietro Bernardone. He was christened Giovanni but in his infancy his father changed his name to Francesco because of his admiration for France. Francis received a rudimentary education but unlike Dominic showed little aptitude for learning. Nor did he take to trade. In adolescence, he was something of a playboy, indulged by his parents – handsome, cheerful, gallant, a favourite among the *jeunesse dorée* of Assisi. His aspirations were those of a knight, not a draper, and at the age of twenty he joined a force sent out to fight the army of nearby Perugia. It was defeated; Francis was taken prisoner and spent a year imprisoned as a hostage. Upon his release, he planned to pursue martial glory in the entourage of Count Walter of Brienne, but ill-health held him back. Two prophetic dreams, and a growing disenchantment with his indulgent way of life, led to a series of extravagant gestures while on pilgrimage to Rome – embracing a leper, emptying his pockets for beggars, and finally exchanging his elegant clothes for their rags.

Returning to Assisi, he stopped to pray at a ruined chapel on the approach to the city dedicated to St. Damian. As he prayed, he heard a voice: 'Go, Francis, and repair my house which as you see is falling into ruin'. When he reached Assisi, he went to his father's warehouse, seized bales of valuable fabrics, and sold them at the market at Foligno to raise money for the repairs to the chapel. His father was incensed, and in due course arraigned Francis before the city magistrates. 'Hitherto I have called you my father on earth,' Francis said to Pietro Bernadone. 'Now I answer only to Our Father who art in Heaven'. Before the magistrates, he disowned his inheritance and all his possessions, including the clothes he was wearing, removing them in their presence. From then on, he lived and dressed as a beggar, appealing for money to rebuild St. Damian's chapel and care of the destitute and sick.

'Go away from me, with your curse upon you, to the eternal fire prepared for the devil and his angels. For I was hungry and you never gave me food; I was thirsty and you never gave me anything to drink; I was a stranger and you never made me welcome, naked and you never clothed me, sick and in prison and you never visited me… I tell you most solemnly, in so far as you neglected to do this to one of the least of these, you neglected to do it to me'.[184] These

---

184   Matthew, 25: 42-45

sombre words from Jesus of Nazareth's teaching on the Last Judgement in the Gospel of Matthew were the inspiration of Francis of Assisi, and his audacity in taking Jesus at his word electrified those around him. Others joined him in sufficient numbers for Francis to draw up a rule. He went to Rome to seek the endorsement of Pope Innocent III for his new venture. Innocent was cautious – heresy was still rife in Lombardy – but Francis's originality was in his behaviour, not his beliefs. He also had a champion in the pope's nephew, Cardinal Ugolino, who vouched for his orthodoxy. There are some amusing accounts of Francis's encounter with Innocent which may or may not be true; but the outcome was papal approval. Before leaving Rome, Francis and his companions received the ecclesiastic tonsure, and Francis was ordained a deacon: he never felt worthy to become a priest.

In 1211, the Benedictines of Monte Subasio gave Francis a chapel at Porziuncola near Assisi around which arose the first Franciscan convent – small huts of wattle, straw and mud enclosed by a hedge. The following year, an eighteen-year-old heiress from Assisi, moved by Francis' preaching, secretly left her father's house by night and with two friends went to Francis at Porziuncola, asking him to establish a community of women committed to the same ideals. There and then, by the light of torches held by the friars, Francis cut off Clare's fine hair, clothed her in the rough habit of a nun, and sent her to live temporarily in a nearby monastery. This was the foundation of the Second Franciscan Order of Poor Ladies or, as they came to be known, the Poor Clares.

Francis was a man who embodied a number of disparate qualities. He clearly retained the great charm that had made him so popular in his youth, to which was now added an otherworldliness that came with his contact through dreams and visions of God. Yet he could also lead, organise and command; and there was a confidence when dealing with cardinals and even the pope that came from a certainty that he was the instrument of divine providence. He was not immune to temptation. On one night in mid-winter, the pleasant thought of having a wife and a family led him to leave his hut and model the form of a woman and three children in the snow – this to remind himself of how a family would be an encumbrance that would impede his total dedication to the service of God.[185]

---

185 Benedict of Nursia, when he had felt tempted by the thought of a woman, had thrown himself naked into a thorn-bush.

With Francis's simplicity went a certain naivete. He preached to birds and animals, extending to them the love he felt due to any creature of God's creation. Towards the end of his life, he apologised to a mule, whom he called a 'brother ass', for having treated it so harshly. He wished to convert the Saracens, and in 1219, with eleven companions, joined the crusading army then besieging Damietta on the Nile delta. Francis's reputation had extended beyond Christendom: the Ayyubid sultan let him pass through the lines, and listened as Francis sought to persuade him of the truth of the Christian faith. His preaching failed. Francis returned to the Latin army with only an assurance of better treatment for the sultan's Christian prisoners. There is no evidence that Francis disapproved of the crusade against the Saracens, any more than Dominic disapproved of the crusade against the Cathars. It is thought that Francis went on to Acre in Palestine where he secured rights for his friars to act as guardians of the sites of Jesus's life and Passion – the Holy Places.

In contrast to Dominic Guzman, Francis saw little value in learning, fearing that it stifled the spirit of prayer: his friars should preach by example rather than argument. Yet he himself was a poet: his *Canticle of the Sun* is among the earliest works of vernacular Italian literature. Above all he was a mystic, coming so close to Christ through prayer and mortification, and immersing himself so profoundly in the Passion that Jesus's wounds appeared on his body – the stigmata. 'The saint's right side is described as bearing an open wound which looked as if made by a lance, while through his hands and feet were black nails of flesh, the points of which were bent backward.'

Francis's constant worry in his later years was that the purity and simplicity of his rule, above all the commitment to complete poverty, should not be compromised by practical considerations. The order had flourished: five thousand friars attended an assembly held at Porziuncola in 1220. The order founded universities with teachers as learned as any Dominican: Bonaventure, Duns Scotus, William of Ockham and Roger Bacon were Franciscans. Francis himself was a poet, not a theologian. Nor was he an administrator. After the assembly at Porziuncola, recognising his inability to manage such a large organisation, Francis passed on his position as general of the order to others. His health was deteriorating; he was going blind. He paid a last visit to Clare at St. Damian's and it was while visiting her that he wrote the *Canticle of the Sun*. In July, 1226, Francis was taken to Assisi, but then, at his request, to Portziuncola where his mission had begun. There, on 3 October, at the age of forty-five, Francis died – summoned from this world to the next by 'Sister Death'.

37. The Making of Saints

Francis was declared a saint two years after his death by his friend and champion, Cardinal Ugolino, by then Pope Gregory IX. The process of canonisation whereby it became an article of faith that a man or a woman was in Heaven, had only recently been reserved for the Holy See. In the early Church, a martyr was always a saint – thus Peter, Paul, Stephen and the many who died for their faith in the Roman persecutions, whose names were cited in the Catholic Mass. Later, men and women of conspicuous virtue were proclaimed saints by popular acclaim, often as a result of miracles performed in their name – Hilary of Poitiers, for example, or Martin of Tours. Their claims were validated by the metropolitan or diocesan bishop; but a decree of Pope Alexander III in 1170 reserved the power for the pope, a ruling confirmed by Gregory IX's uncle, Innocent III, when canonising Cunigunde of Luxembourg, the wife of the German Emperor Henry II. Miracles were, and still are, required as evidence that the saint is indeed in heaven: in the case of Francis, there were many. So too those worked in the name of Dominic Guzman who, six years after the canonisation of Francis, was also declared a saint.

The entries in today's dictionaries of Catholic saints are overwhelmingly those of Europeans. It was during the centuries which followed the mission of Francis Xavier that indigenous priests and converts were killed – often with refined cruelty – for their Catholic faith. In Japan, there was Paul Miki and his companions; in China Augustine Zhao Rong; in Korea Andrew, Kim Tae-gŏn and Paul Chŏng Ha-Sang; in Vietnam Andrew Dũng-Lac; and in Africa 44 young men were executed on the command of the Kabaka, Mwanga II.

Virginity as well as martyrdom was esteemed by the Church: in Peru there was the mystic Rose of Lima, canonised in the seventeenth century; and in Sudan, Josephine Bakhita, once a slave, in the year 2000. These canonisations demonstrate that the Church did not only value male Europeans, and was not indifferent to the plight of the sick and the poor. Cunigunde was celebrated for her charitable works; so too Elisabeth, Queen of Hungary and contemporary of Francis of Assisi, who was canonised by Pope Gregory four years after her death in 1231. Elisabeth of Portugal was named after her great-aunt Elisabeth of Hungary, and followed her example in charitable work later in the fourteeth century, and was also declared a saint. Another queen, Margaret of Scotland, who had lived in the second half of the eleventh century, was canonised many years after her death in 1250. The Swedish noblewoman, Birgitta, was declared a saint in 1391, her daughter Catherine in 1484.

The charitable works of these Christian queens and members of the nobility were combined with other virtues – asceticism, prayer and in many cases a tempering influence on their less pious husbands. It is also true that as queens they had resources at their disposal. So too did devout kings such as the English Edward the Confessor or the French Louis IX. They endowed monasteries and convents, and often the queens when widowed ended their days in religious communities they had founded. Thus it was never the case that Jesus's command to care for the poor and the sick was abandoned; some in the Church may have wallowed in its wealth, but it was to provide rudimentary welfare from the Church's inception during the Roman Empire until the nineteenth and twentieth centuries when in what was once Latin Christendom welfare became the responsibility of the state.

38.   The Emperor Frederick II

Much of the Church's resources in the Middle Ages were consumed by two running obsessions – first, the never-ending struggle between the popes and the German emperors, and second the crusades. The shameful perversion of the Fourth Crusade, which had led to the sack of Constantinople, and the placing of a Latin emperor on the throne of the Byzantine Empire, did not deter Pope Innocent III from calling for a Fifth Crusade to oust the Muslims from Jerusalem. Plans were laid at the Lateran Council of 1215, and in 1217 a contingent of crusaders led by King Andrew of Hungary reached Acre, the city on the Palestinian coast still in Christian hands.

It was now generally accepted that the route to Jerusalem lay through Cairo – in other words, that the Holy City could only be liberated if the major Muslim power in the region was defeated. The crusading army, its command disputed between the Latin King of Jerusalem, John of Brienne and the Papal Legate, Cardinal Pelagius, marched on Damietta, the city that controlled the entry to the delta of the river Nile. Damietta fell on 5 November, 1219: it was at this point Francis of Assisi joined the crusaders and was allowed through the lines to preach before the sultan, Al-Malik al Kamil. Cardinal Pelagius now led the army towards Cairo. It camped in wetlands. The Egyptians opened the sluice gates. The army sank into the mud and was forced to surrender.

A Sixth Crusade, which followed closely upon the Fifth, was bedevilled by the antagonism between the papacy and the Hohenstaufen Emperor Frederick II, the son of the Emperor Henry VI and grandson of Barbarossa, Frederick II. His mother Constance had been the heir to the Norman King Roger of Sicily, and Frederick was born in Italy and raised haphazardly in Palermo. Sicily at the time was among the most prosperous areas of Europe, and its population reflected its particular history – having been ruled by Byzantine Greeks, Saracens, Normans and Germans. The Saracen influence remained strong: the Norman kings had created a court in Palermo more like those of the emirs of Cordoba and Granada in Muslim Spain than anything in Italy or north of the Alps. Frederick was taught to ride and fight, but he also developed an intellectual curiosity which was unusual for a prince at the time. He was an omnivorous reader, fluent in several languages, and fascinated by science.

Both Frederick's parents died when he was still a child. As an orphan, he was a ward of Pope Innocent III and even after coming of age on his fourteenth birthday, 26 December, 1208, took his guardian's advice and married a widow in her '20s, Constance of Aragon: it is thought that Constance rubbed off his rough edges, and brought out his 'charm and personal fascination'.[186] Constance gave birth to a son, Henry, and soon after came the first of Frederick's eleven illegitimate children, Enzio. A sensualist as well as a scholar, Frederick astonished his contemporaries by his cleanliness, taking a bath every day. He was no idler. From childhood, he had had a strong sense of his rights and duties as heir to the crown of Sicily, and at once set about asserting his authority, reclaiming stolen estates, and establishing an efficient, centralised system of government and taxation.

Frederick was also conscious of his rights and duties as the heir to the imperial crown of his father and grandfather. Soon after his birth, his baby son Henry was crowned King of Sicily, and Constance appointed regent while Frederick travelled north to Rome. There he swore fealty to the pope, Innocent III, promising the pope at the pope's request that he would keep

---

186   Georgina Masson, *Frederick II of Hohenstaufen, A Life*. p. 39.

his realms distinct by leaving his son as sovereign in Sicily while he went north to claim his rights north of the Alps. As the eighteen-year-old ward of one of the most powerful and sagacious popes the Church had known, Frederick had little choice but to acquiesce in his guardian's plans; but he was only feigning submission and biding his time. Dodging his enemies – the Pisans and Milanese – who blocked his path, Frederick crossed the Alps to his duchy of Swabia. Over the course of the following eight years, he saw off his rivals for the Imperial crown. He was crowned emperor by the pope in Rome in return for a promise to go on crusade.

Frederick procrastinated when it came to a crusade, or was thought to have procrastinated. He failed to send reinforcements to the Sixth Crusade, and it was not until 1227 that he gathered an army at Brindisi to lead to the Holy Land. However, on embarking himself at Brindisi Frederick fell ill, or said he fell ill, and returned home. This was seen as a ruse to avoid a solemn commitment, and he was excommunicated by the new pope, Gregory IX, who as Cardinal Ugolino had been the champion of Francis of Assisi.

A year later, Frederick tried again to set off for Palestine which only further enraged the pope – an excommunicate could not lead a Christian crusade – and Frederick was excommunicated again. He ignored the anathemas hurled at him from Rome, and also the refusal of the barons of *outremer* and the military orders to cooperate. It hardly mattered, because Frederick achieved through diplomacy what previous crusades had failed to achieve through force of arms. In 1229 he signed a treaty with the Ayyubid sultan, Al Kamil, which returned Jerusalem, Nazareth, Bethlehem, and a narrow strip connecting Jerusalem to the coast, to Latin control. Muslim shrines in Jerusalem remained in their hands – a clause in the treaty which enraged the Templars because one of these was their headquarters on the Temple Mount, the Al Aqsa mosque.

It was a paradox that 'once again pilgrims were able to travel to the Holy Land and visit the scene of Christ's Passion and Resurrection, thanks to the efforts of the man whom the head of the church had condemned.'[187] However, the very ease with which Frederick had reached an agreement with the Muslim sultan increased misgivings about Frederick's Christian faith. He spoke Arabic; he had debated questions of science and philosophy with Muslim scholars; he had a Saracen bodyguard, recruited from the Saracen

---

187   *Ibid*, p. 147

community from western Sicily which, after it had rebelled and been defeated by Frederick, had been transported to Lucera in southern Italy.

Frederick was not an imposing figure like his grandfather, Barbarossa. He was short and clean-shaven with reddish hair, already inclining to baldness, and 'would have appeared ugly in the extreme to the Oriental taste'. But he lived in the style of an oriental despot, keeping his four consecutive wives in a harem guarded by eunuchs, and including in his peripatetic court a troupe of Saracen dancing girls, as well as a menagerie including lions, tigers, panthers, an elephant, and 'a host of other strange animals and birds that in mediaeval eyes contributed in no small part to the glamour of the imperial court'. He proceeded in a dazzling cavalcade, and wherever the court settled there was feasting, jousting, dancing, and hunting which was his passion. He was known as *stupor mundi* – the wonder of the world!

Frederick's admirers, such as his 20th century biographer, Georgina Masson, see him as a forerunner of the Italian Renaissance: 'he was the first, not only of his generation but for another century and a half, to recognise and appreciate the glories of classical sculpture...'[188] But there was a touch of a Mengele as well as a Leonardo. Curious to know what might be the default mother tongue of the human race, he ordered a group of children to be raised from birth in complete silence: they died before the experiment was completed. To learn about life in the depths of the ocean, he ordered a diver to plunge deeper and deeper into the straights of Messina until he failed to return. In order to learn about the process of digestion, he had two condemned prisoners given the same meal, then one told to exercise, the other to remain still, before being cut open to see the effects on the contents of their stomachs.

It was a cruel age, but it seems clear that Frederick was untroubled by a Christian conscience. 'In public, Frederick always conformed of necessity to the role of a Catholic prince – the eldest son of the Church – but there is little doubt that in private his views were very different. Towards the end of his life, when his conflict with the popes was at its most rancorous, he was said to have dismissed Moses, Muhammad and Jesus of Nazareth as 'the three imposters'. Certainly, Frederick seemed unconcerned about the consequences of the popes' excommunications for his prospects for salvation: they were inconveniences only because the Church was so powerful. Even so, he might have shrugged off the popes' anathemas, and in time conquered Rome – to

---

188   *Ibid*, p. 188

his mind, the proper seat of government for a Roman emperor – had not the popes been joined by his other implacable enemies, the Lombard cities, in particular Milan. Throughout Italy, there was a recurring conflict between the Guelphs (the supporters of the popes) and the Ghibellines (supporters of the emperor), and neither was able to triumph over the other.

Frederick's epic struggle with the papacy in Italy meant that he neglected his duties in Germany. It had been many centuries since barbarians had swept into Europe from the east, but suddenly between 1241 and 1242 a new and ferocious tribe of nomads, the Mongols, who had conquered Muscovy under their leader, Genghis Khan, invaded Poland and then Hungary. The King of Hungary called for help from Frederick but none was forthcoming. Frederick expressed admiration for the Mongols' courage and discipline, and told his vassals in Germany to fortify their castles, judging that they would be defeated in open battle. This inadequate response to a grave crisis for Christendom diminished his prestige and so his authority in Germany. It was left to Austrian knights, after several engagements, to bring the Mongol invasion of western Europe to an end.

In Italy, by 1247, the advantage seemed to be to Frederick. He besieged the city of Parma, building a small town, Vittoria, to house the encircling army: but on 18 February, 1248, when he was out hunting, the Parma garrison made a sortie, took and plundered Vittoria, and returned to Parma with the imperial treasure and regalia. Frederick was not defeated, but he was disheartened. One of his sons had been killed; another captured by the Bolognese; his most loyal and long-serving minister, Pietro della Vigna, appeared to have betrayed him. He died two years later, dressed in the habit of a Cistercian monk, and after receiving the Last Sacrament of the Church from his childhood friend, Archbishop Berardus de Castacca of Palermo.

At great cost, the successors of the Apostle Peter had thwarted the attempt of the Roman Emperor to form an efficient, well-governed state that incorporated Italy and Germany. Georgina Masson judged that 'there is no doubt that the popes were right in thinking that in an age when brute force reigned supreme, the papacy would have been reduced politically to the position of a mere cipher if it had been shorn of its territorial possessions and its great wealth – a pensioner of the all-powerful Emperor.'[189] However, Masson also points out that Frederick's determination to incorporate the whole of Italy into his

---

189   *Ibid.* p. 355

empire led to the weakening of his position in Germany, with his relinquishing many imperial rights and prerogatives to appease the German princes so that, unlike France, Spain or England, Germany remained a fragmented nation. It would be over seven hundred years before either Germany or Italy were established as unitary states.

39.   King Louis IX of France

Born in 1214, twenty years after Frederick, but with a partially contiguous reign, was Louis IX of France. Like Frederick, Louis inherited the throne when still a child, and like Frederick he grew up to be an able ruler; but in all other respects the contrast between the two men could not have been greater. Louis was a devout Catholic, and his faith inspired all he did. Like so many other leading figures in the history of the Church, Louis had a formidable mother, Blanche of Castile, who acted as regent during his minority, and later during the six years he was away on crusade. It was she who raised Louis to love and fear God. 'I love you, my dear son, as much as a mother can love her child; but I would rather see you dead at my feet than that you should ever commit a mortal sin'. Her only apparent weakness was jealousy of her daughter-in-law, Margaret of Provence, whom Louis married in 1234. In the early years of their married life, they would creep out of their separate quarters at night to meet on the staircase, posting servants to warn of the approach of the queen mother. Margaret shared Louis' piety and, unlike Frederick, Louis proved a loving and attentive husband, spending as much time as he could with his wife and their eleven children.

In the early years of his reign, Louis and his mother successfully put down revolts by powerful vassals, among them Louis' future brother-in-law, Henry III of England, whom in 1242 he defeated at the Battle of Taillebourg. He took seriously Christ's blessing of those who 'hunger and thirst after righteousness', establishing an impartial administration of justice under the king, with severe punishments for judges who showed favour towards the rich, the powerful or their friends. He abolished trial by ordeal, and introduced laws against blasphemy, usury and prostitution – founding a refuge for 'fallen' women. Among other religious foundations were the abbeys of Royaumont, Lys and Maubuisson; a hospital at Vernon; an asylum for the blind in Paris; and on the Île-de-la-Cité in Paris he built the beautiful Sainte-Chapelle to house the relics he bought for a high price from the Latin emperor of Constantinople – a fragment of the True Cross and the Crown of Thorns.

Louis was punctilious in his care for the poor, feeding up to a hundred each day from his own table, and himself eating the scraps that they left over. His strong faith did not make him subservient to the Catholic clergy: quite to the contrary, he was frequently critical of their failure to live according to the precepts of the Gospels. Far from being a bigot, Louis was kind and forgiving: the treaty that followed the Battle of Taillebourg was generous towards the defeated. On the other hand he was implacable when it came to the remaining Cathars in the lands in Provence whose absorption into the kingdom of France was completed during his reign; and inter-religious exchanges with Jewish rabbis went badly. A Jewish convert to Catholicism, Nicholas Donin, made a translation of the Talmud which led to a disputation in Paris, after which the King ordered all copies of the Talmud to be burned – perhaps because of the passages in which Christ is consigned to a vat of boiling excrement for all eternity.

After another conference with Jewish scholars, organised by the abbot of Cluny, an old knight belaboured a rabbi with his crutch after he denied the perpetual virginity of Mary, and that she was the Mother of God. When rebuked by the abbot for his belligerence, the knight blamed him for calling the conference in the first place 'because there were many good Christians there who, before the discussion ended, would have gone away with doubts about their own religion through not fully understanding the Jews' – a view with which King Louis concurred: 'No one, unless he is an expert theologian, should venture to argue with these people. But a layman, whenever he hears the Christian religion abused, should not attempt to defend its tenets, except with his sword, and that he should thrust into the scoundrel's belly, and as far as it will enter.'[190]

This account comes from *The Life of St. Louis* by Jean, Lord of Joinville, Louis' Seneschal[191] in Champagne. The son and grandson of crusaders, Joinville's response was immediate when in 1248, after an apparently miraculous recovery from an illness, King Louis took the Cross. Joinville mortgaged his estates to pay for nine knights to accompany him on crusade, sending their war horses and armour in barges down the rivers Saône and

---

190   Joinville, *The Life of St. Louis*, from *Chronicles of the Crusades*, translated by M.R.B. Shaw, p. 175

191   A post much like that of a Lord-Lieutenant in modern Britain

Rhône to Marseille. A thousand boats sailed to Cyprus where the crusaders were joined by the barons from Outremer. It was still accepted that the defeat of the Ayyubid sultan in Cairo was prerequisite to the liberation of Jerusalem, and so the crusaders sailed to Egypt, landing at the eastern end of the Nile delta. They took the city of Damietta, abandoned by the Muslims, and then marched towards Cairo in the sweltering heat beside the rising waters of the Nile. At Al Mansurah they encountered the Muslim army. 'King Louis came up at the head of his battalions,' wrote Joinville, 'with a great sound of shouting, trumpets and kettledrums. He halted with his troops on a raised causeway. Never have I seen a finer or more handsome knight! He seemed to tower head and shoulders above all his people; on his head was a gilded helmet, and a sword of German steel was in his hand.'[192]

However, rivalry between the Templars and Louis' brother, the Comte d'Artois, led to the latter's death. Ferocious fighting, vividly described by Joinville, led Louis to command a retreat to Damietta; but the Muslims had hauled galleys from one branch of the Nile to another and the crusaders were cut off. Louis had no alternative but to surrender: both he and Joinville were taken prisoner. Joinville's life was saved because, questioned by his captors as to whether he was related to the Emperor Frederick, he said he thought his wife was his cousin: Frederick's reputation as a friend of the Saracens persisted. A ransom for the French king was agreed: 400,000 *livres tournois* and the surrender of Damietta.

Once the ransom was paid and he was set free, Louis sailed to Acre where he remained with his wife and children for four years, supervising the reinforcement of the coastal cities of Jaffa, Caesarea and Acre itself. His surviving brothers, including the Comte d'Anjou who would be invested by the pope with the crown of Sicily, returned to France. Joinville remained with his king. By 1254, Louis decided that he had done all that he could for the Latin kingdoms in the Holy Land and with Joinville returned to France. Fifteen years or so later, now in his mid-forties, Louis again took the Cross, and in 1270 attacked Carthage on the coast of North Africa. This, the Eighth Crusade, was no more successful than the Seventh: disease spread in the besieging army and on 25 August, 1270, took the life of its leader, King Louis IX.

Jean de Joinville admired and revered the subject of his *Life*, and was plainly regarded by the king as his friend. However, the many stories and anecdotes

---

192   Ibid., p. 222

in his narrative which show the king's piety, humour and scrupulous commitment to justice do not amount to a hagiography. Joinville's graphic descriptions of what he had witnessed are interspersed with stories he had heard from other sources, but he always makes clear which is which. He is sometimes critical of Louis, and describes, for example, how he lost his temper with his brother who on the voyage to the east preferred to play card games than join in worthy conversation. Moreover, Joinville's admiration of Louis was shared throughout Europe. The devout king might not have proved an inspired strategist on crusade, but there is no doubting his personal courage, or his concern for the men under his command. He could assemble the largest army in Europe, and established stability through diplomacy and his commitment to peace.

The prestige and respect felt in Europe for King Louis IX were due more to the attraction that his personality created than to military domination. For his contemporaries he was the quintessential example of the Christian prince and embodied the whole of Christendom in his person.[193]

40.   Thomas Aquinas

Accompanying King Louis on the crusade in Egypt was his chaplain and confessor, Robert de Sorbon, a devout priest from a poor rural family in the Ardennes. On his return to France, with the support of the king, he founded a college in Paris, the Maison de Sorbonne, which in due course gave its name to the university of Paris.

Corporations of scholars had been formed in the previous century. The earliest to receive a charter as a university was Bologna in 1088. Oxford traces its origins to 1096, but was accredited in 1167; Cambridge in 1209, Padua in 1222. In Paris, prior to the Maison de Sorbonne, there had been a body of scholars attached to the cathedral of Notre Dame which received a royal charter from King Philip II in 1200, and papal endorsement by Pope Innocent III in 1215. In 1224, the Emperor Frederick II had founded a university in Naples.

The Dominicans – the Order of Preachers – whose vocation was to study and propagate the Catholic Faith, established houses in the university cities, and sent their ablest members as teachers. Most celebrated, in the thirteenth

---

193   Georges Goyau, *St. Louis IX*

century, was the German Albert of Lauingen who in 1245 was appointed professor of Theology in Paris, and in 1254, provincial of the Dominicans. In 1260 he served briefly as Bishop of Regensburg, and he was employed by the popes on diplomatic missions; but it was as a scholar that he gained renown – with treatises not just on philosophy and theology, but also astrology, botany, music, mineralogy, alchemy, zoology, physiology, phrenology , justice, friendship and love. He engaged in academic disputes, particularly while in Paris: his study of pagan philosophers such as Aristotle was considered scandalous by many conservative theologians, but his great erudition gained him the sobriquet of *Doctor Universalis* and, towards the end of his life, *Albertus Magnus* – Albert the Great.

However, Albert's reputation, and his standing in the Catholic Church, was soon overtaken by one of his pupils, Thomas Aquinas. Thomas, the youngest son of the Count of Aquino, a vassal of the Emperor Frederick II, was born in his father's castle in Roccasecca in southern Italy. At the age of five, he was sent to be raised by the monks of the nearby monastery of Monte Cassino, with the intention that in due course he would become one of their number: 'He was a large and heavy and quiet boy, and phenomenally silent; scarcely opening his mouth except to suddenly say to his schoolmaster in an explosive manner: "What is God?"'[194]

At one point, during the wars between the pope and Thomas's second cousin, the Emperor Frederick II, the abbey was closed and Thomas was sent to continue his studies at the university of Naples. Unlike the other universities founded at the time, this was not an ecclesiastical foundation but a secular institution, intended by the irreligious Frederick II for the training of his civil servants. Here, there was none of the mistrust of pagan philosophers felt by many devout scholars at the time: Naples was then the only university to teach the works of Aristotle, and Islamic and Jewish philosophers such as Averroes and Maimonides, brought to Sicily with Frederick's encouragement by Islamic scholars from Spain.

Here Thomas came across the Dominicans, founded only twenty years before, but already a dynamic force in the Church. He determined to join them but was opposed by his parents who were appalled that a member of their family should become a mendicant friar when in due course, as a Benedictine, he might well rise like his uncle Sinibald to become Abbot of

194   G.K. Chesterton, *Saint Thomas Aquinas,* London, 1933

Monte Cassino. The Dominicans in Naples were eager to accept a recruit who already showed an unusual intellectual precocity, and prepared to send Thomas to Rome; but soon after he left Naples, he was kidnapped by his brothers at their mother Theodora's request, and imprisoned in the castles of Monte San Giovanni and Roccasecca. Here he continued his studies, tutored his sisters and drove away with a red-hot fire-iron a girl of easy virtue sent by his brothers into his bedroom.

In 1244, after a year of incarceration, Theodora realised that that her son would not change his mind and, unwilling to lose face by releasing him, arranged his escape. Thomas reached Rome, accepted the Dominican habit from the Master General of the Order, Johannes von Wildeshausen, and was sent to further his studies under Albert the Great in Paris. He was twenty years old and so large and silent that his fellow-students called him the 'Dumb Ox'. 'You call him a Dumb Ox,' said Albert. 'I tell you this Dumb Ox shall bellow so loud that his bellowings will fill the world.'[195] After three years, Thomas accompanied Albert to Cologne. Four years after that he returned to Paris where, after three more years of study, he received his master's degree, and was appointed Regent Master in Theology. 'So began one of the most packed and prolific philosophical and theological careers in history'.[196]

Thomas taught not just in Paris, where he befriended his near contemporary, the Franciscan friar Bonaventure, but spent six years attached to the papal court, then in Orvieto; two in Rome, founding a new college, then two years back at the papal court which had moved to Viterbo. In 1269 he was back in Paris, and in 1279 returned to his *alma mater*, the University of Naples. He wrote many treatises and commentaries which were disseminated throughout Europe: his output was prodigious, amounting to several million words. An early work was an examination of the theology of Peter Lombard; later came *Summa Contra Gentiles,* a defence of Christianity directed at Muslims, Jews and unbelievers; and later still a majestic exposition of the Catholic faith intended for students, his *Summa Theologiae* – 'a cathedral in words'[197].

In his writing Thomas avoids rhetoric and exposes little of his personality in the relentless logic and thoroughness with which his great works unfold. Unlike Augustine he does not offer insights into his own character – there is none of Augustine's dramatic and tortuous struggle to be chaste. To Thomas, sexual morality is no more than common sense.

---

195   *Ibid.* p. 79
196   Timothy McDermott, *Summa Theologiae. A Concise Translation.* p. x.
197   *Ibid.* p. xvii

Use of food properly ordered for the body's welfare is no sin; and in the same way, use of sex properly ordered for its purpose of human reproduction is no sin…. Not even our distraction from spiritual matters at the moment of enjoying such pleasure makes it unvirtuous; for it is not unvirtuous to suspend reason for a time for a good reason, otherwise sleeping would be a vice. [198]

The greatest and most enduring achievement of Thomas Aquinas, wrote Charles Freeman in *The Closing of the Western Mind*, was to 'incorporate Aristotle into Christian and above all Catholic, tradition with such intellectual power and coherence that in some areas of thought Aristotelianism and Catholicism became virtually indistinguishable.'[199] It was with Aquinas that the western mind was re-opened to reason after a thousand years of Christian obscurantism. Did Aquinas 'baptise Aristotle', as the Church later claimed? Or might it rather be said 'that Aquinas was converted to Aristotelianism'?[200] 'It is arguable,' writes Freeman, 'that Thomas Aquinas revived the Aristotelian approach to knowing things so successfully that he unwittingly laid the foundations of the scientific revolution that was to transform western thought.'[201]

But this judgement overlooks the sanctity of Thomas Aquinas. There may have been no *stigmata*, but throughout his adult life, while immersed in prayer, he had fallen into trances, or ecstasies. He had a particular reverence for the Eucharist, and took time off from writing his theological treatises to compose hymns in its praise. The term 'transubstantiation' had been first used in the Lateran Council of 1215, but it was Thomas who proposed to Pope Urban IV a feast to celebrate this transformation, which led to promulgation of the feast of Corpus Christi in 1264. 'If in this world there be any knowledge of this sacrament stronger than faith,' he said, 'I wish now to use it in affirming that I firmly believe as certain that Jesus Christ, True God and True Man, Son of God, and son of the Virgin Mary, is in this Sacrament…' To Gabriel Josipovici, 'the mediaeval Church can be said to have reached its high-water mark …by instituting the feast of Corpus Christi'. [202]

---

198   *Ibid.* p. 432
199   Charles Freeman, *Op. Cit.* p. 333
200   *Ibid.* p. 333
201   *Ibid.* p. 333
202   Gabriel Jospipovici, *The World and the Book*, p. 59

The longest and last of Thomas's ecstasies occurred while he was saying Mass in Naples in December, 1273. Such was the power of this vision that, although his *Summa Theologiae* was not yet complete, he told his friend Father Reginald, that he could write no more. 'Such secrets have been revealed to me that all I have written now appears to be so much straw'. Three months later, in May, 1274, Thomas was summoned by Pope Gregory X to attend a Church Council in Lyons. He set out on foot, but fell ill near Terracina. He was taken to the nearby Castle of Maienza, the home of his niece, the Countess Francesca Ceccano. The monks of the nearby Abbey of Fossa Nuova thought it more appropriate that he should stay in a monastery, and Thomas agreed. 'If the Lord wishes to take me away, it is better that I be found in a religious house than in the dwelling of a lay person'. There he received the Sacred *Viaticum*, the Last Sacrament, and it was as he received the consecrated host that he made his profession of faith in the True Presence, and an act of submission to the Holy Roman Church, 'in whose obedience I now pass from this life'. He died on 7 March, 1274.

41.   Cathedrals

If Thomas Aquinas was the master architect whose *Summa Theologiae* became the verbal cathedral of the Catholic faith, there were in both preceding and subsequent centuries real if unknown architects who expressed their faith not in words but in brick and stone. We have seen how the Emperor Constantine and his mother Helena built large basilicas throughout the empire. So too the Emperor Charlemagne and his successors: 'The Carolingian period 'was one of frenetic architectural activity'.[203] Again, we have seen how reforming fervour emanating from the monastery at Cluny found architectural expression in the building there of the largest church in Christendom, and the many satellite abbeys and parish churches – these with the rounded arches, carved tympanums, and richly decorated interiors of the Romanesque style which 'was not the heir of Roman architecture; it sought rather, to rival it.'[204]

However, by the beginning of the thirteenth century – the time of Francis of Assisi, Dominic Guzman, Thomas Aquinas and King Louis IX of France – the Romanesque style had given way to what has been described as "the most

---

203   Alain Erland-Brandenburg, *Op. Cit.* p. 85
204   *Ibid.* p. 99

consummate art of building which the world has achieved"[205] – the 'Gothic' cathedral. Its progenitor was Suger, the abbot of St. Denis, the monastery north of Paris. Suger had entered the community at the age of ten, was elected abbot at the age of thirty-one and, because of his great learning, sagacity and experience, became the friend, counsellor and confidant of two French kings, Louis VI and VII. He had helped arrange the marriage of Louis VII to Eleanor of Aquitaine, acted as regent when the couple went on crusade, and unsuccessfully opposed the annulment of their marriage upon their return.

Suger brought about reforms in his community of St. Denis, but was also faced with the deteriorating fabric of the abbey church which contained the tombs of the French kings and queens going back to the Merovingian Dagobert. Rather than simply repair the existing structure, Suger decided in 1137 to re-build it using innovative new techniques – the pointed arch, the ribbed vault, the ambulatory with radiating chapels, and the flying buttress which made possible the insertion of large clerestory windows, suffusing the huge edifice with light. The name of the architect of St. Denis is unknown, but there can be no doubt but that Suger was the inspiration: he would later write an account of what had been achieved.[206] The rebuilding of the basilica was completed in seven years, and dedicated in 1144 in the presence of the king.

The abbey of St. Denis became the prototype for the cathedrals which were built over the next three or four hundred years – buildings expressing the transcendental yearning of a people imbued with the Christian faith – the towers and spires reaching to heaven, the light of truth entering through the great windows, the sculptures and stained glass illustrating the story of God made man . 'The motives which inspired these great buildings of this period, the principles which underlay their forms, the general character of the forms themselves were in their essential nature the same throughout Western Europe from Italy to England'.[207] All over Europe there arose unique and magnificent buildings – in France in Amiens, Bourges, Beauvais, Chartres and Rheims where the kings were crowned, and in Paris itself, on the Ile-de-la-cité, the cathedral of Notre Dame. In Germany, Aachen, Strasburg and Cologne; in England Canterbury, York, Lincoln, Salisbury; in Italy Milan; in Spain Burgos – there was hardly a major city that did not construct a superb cathedral in

---

205   Edward S. Prior, *History of Gothic Art in England*, I, 7

206   *Libellus de consecratione ecclesiae S. Dionysii*

207   Charles Eliot Norton, *Historical Studies of Church Building in the Middle Ages*, I, 10

the Gothic style. Here was an unique artistic product of Christian civilization which 'advanced with constant increase of power of expression, of pliability and variety of adaptation, of beauty in design and skill in construction until at last, in the consummate splendour of such a cathedral as that of Our Lady of Chartres or of Amiens, it reached a height of achievement that has never been surpassed'.[208]

The term 'Gothic' was coined at the time of the Renaissance by Vasari, when the classical designs of antiquity were considered civilised and the cathedrals of the Middle Ages primitive, even barbaric. Now they are appreciated as 'the greatest cycle of buildings in a definite and highly developed style that has ever been produced by man, and… the most salient exposition in history of human capacity for evolving a material perfection with absolute beauty and spiritual significance, all under the control and by the impulse of a dominant and undivided religious faith.'

42.   Pope Boniface VIII

Most of the popes during the thirteenth century were Italian – frequently prelates who had pursued a career in the Church. There were exceptions: Clement IV was a Frenchman; John XXI the son of a Portuguese doctor. Secular politics affected the choice of a new pope: there were cardinals who favoured the German Emperor, the King of Sicily or one or other of the powerful Roman clans – the Orsini and the Colonnas. No one now doubted that the election of a pope was a matter for the cardinals alone, but the rule that a successful candidate must receive two thirds of their number meant that there was often deadlock and frequently long delays – so long that there were occasions when the cardinals were locked into the church or palace where they held their deliberations, with ever diminishing supplies of food giving them an incentive to reach a decision. On one occasion, to concentrate their minds, the roof of the church where the conclave was being held was removed, leaving them unprotected from the weather until they came to a decision.

After the death of Honorius IV in 1287, it took the cardinals eleven months to choose the Franciscan Giralomo Masci, who took the name Nicholas IV; and on his death in 1292, the conclave remained deadlocked for twenty-seven

---

208   *Ibid.*, 1, 13

months – half the cardinals being partisans of the Orsinis and half of the Colonnas. The faithful were scandalised. Charles of Anjou, King of Naples and Sicily, and brother of the king of France, made the journey to Perugia to urge them to reach a decision; and a message from a devout hermit, Pietro del Morrone, was conveyed by Cardinal Latino Malabranca that God would punish the cardinals if they did not make up their mind.

Pietro del Morrone was well known for his holiness: why not abandon candidates favoured by the Orsinos and Colonnas, the cardinals asked themselves, and choose him as pope? Certainly, he was eighty-five years old, his parents had been peasants, he struggled to understand Latin, and he had lived much of his life in caves and grottos; but the choice of this ascetic would appeal to those Catholics, such as the 'spiritual' Franciscans, who yearned for the Church to return to the simplicity and asceticism of its roots. Morrone was sought out in his cave and, protesting his inadequacy, escorted by Charles of Anjou to L'Aquila where he was crowned pope. L'Aquila was not in the papal states; it belonged to Charles; and, the new pope, who took the name Celestine V, established his court not in Rome but in Naples.

Here,' the situation quickly descended from comedy, through farce, to tragedy'.[209] Living in a formidable fortress, the Castel Nuovo, Celestine slept in a hut he had had built in one of the castle's great chambers. He was unable to understand what was going on around him. Used to the company of his fellow anchorites, he was easy prey for sophisticated, worldly churchmen clamouring for benefices and lucrative appointments, presenting for his signature documents he did not understand. Eager to please, he made decisions which he later retracted. He was caught between the expectations of his 'spiritual' followers, and the intrigues of the cynical, manipulative officials of the curia; and then there were the interests of his host, Charles of Anjou: of the new cardinals created by Celestine, seven were French.

It quickly became clear, especially to Celestine, that raising him to the throne of St. Peter had been a mistake. Could he abdicate? To advise him on the matter, Celestine turned to the curia's greatest expert on Canon Law, Cardinal Benedict Gaetani. Gaetani was also unusual – even unique – in that, during the protracted conclave that had led to the choice of Celestine, he had sided with neither the Orsinis nor the Colonnas but had remained neutral. Born in Anagni into the minor nobility of the Campagna, he had studied law at Bologna, then joined the papal diplomatic service, accompanying legates

---

209   E.R.Chamberlin, *The Bad Popes*, London, 1970, p. 83

to England and France. His career profited from his family's connections: his mother was the niece of a pope, and he was distantly related to other pontiffs; but he was also an able diplomat, successfully mediating on the pope's behalf in conflicts between European nations.

Benedict Gaetani may or may not have encouraged Celestine to abdicate, but it was he who dealt with the legal complexities involved in this almost unprecedented step; and he was certainly the only one among the cardinals who knew why Celestine summoned them to a consistory on December 13, 1296.

> Pale, trembling, but for once resolute, the old man read a prepared deed of renunciation that he and Gaetani had drawn up. In the astonished silence that followed, he slowly descended the steps from the throne, and with his own hands stripped himself of the gorgeous robes that symbolised for him not power, but imprisonment. He left the chamber, then returned a few moments later, clad in his own familiar close garments.[210]

Ten days later, the cardinals met in conclave and elected Benedict Gaetani as Celestine's successor. He took the name Boniface VIII.

Boniface had been the favoured candidate of Charles of Anjou, and the speed with which he was chosen was due partly to the influence of those French cardinals who had been appointed by Celestine at Charles's prompting. And after the fiasco of Celestine's reign, it made sense to choose a man who had shown himself to be an experienced and competent curial civil servant. However, the 'spirituals' who had hoped for so much from Celestine were incensed by his abdication which they believed had been engineered by Boniface with an eye to the succession. Their outrage spread to the people of Naples; despite the protection of the king, Boniface was not safe in Naples and so left the city so precipitously that his baggage was left behind. Celestine went with him but on the way to Rome he and a band of followers escaped from the papal cavalcade and made for the hills and Celestine's cave on Mount Morrone.

Boniface was welcomed by the Romans who were treated to a coronation as elaborate and grand as that of any emperor in antiquity. Hitherto, as Cardinal Gaetani, he had been known for his accumulation of benefices, exploiting any

---

210   *Ibid.* p. 86

and every source of revenue to buy up land for the Gaetani family: now he was to be more than a worldly cardinal but, in the words pronounced as the papal tiara was placed on his head, 'the father of kings and princes, the ruler of the world'. After the coronation there was a banquet in the Lateran palace as sumptuous as any that had gone before.

There was only one cause for concern: Celestine. The Romans might have welcomed Boniface, but what of the Church at large? There was a substantial party who believed that Celestine's abdication had been made under duress; that he remained the true pope and Boniface was a usurper. King Charles also saw the danger, and sent a force to apprehend the octogenarian hermit in his cave; but Celestine had fled, taking a ship for Greece from a port on the Adriatic coast. A storm drove it back to port where Celestine was recognised by royal officers, arrested and handed over to Boniface who incarcerated him in the fortress of Fumone, close to the base of the Gaetani in Anagni. Celestine was delighted with his prison cell, but recognised the malice of his successor. 'You have entered like a fox,' he told Boniface. 'You will reign like a lion – and you will die like a dog'. [211] He himself lived for only another ten months: it was said that he had been murdered.

Boniface VIII's first act as pope was to annul all the appointments to benefices made by Celestine. He mediated with some success between the kings of France and England, which gained him some prestige abroad, but his core ambition was at home – to aggrandize his family, the Gaetanis – milking the revenues of the Church to buy up land in the Campagna and beyond. By fair means or foul, long-established families were dispossessed, and joined the band of Boniface's enemies led by the ancient and powerful family of Colonna. On Thursday, May 3, 1297, a young firebrand from the Colonnas ambushed a caravan carrying gold intended for the pope. On hearing of this outrage, Boniface summoned the two Colonna cardinals to the Lateran palace, and told them not just to return the gold but accept papal garrisons in their strongholds. The Colonnas rejected the ultimatum. It was a declaration of war. Boniface deposed the two Colonna and excommunicated the entire Colonna family. It was a grotesque misuse of a spiritual sanction, but worse was to follow: Boniface declared a crusade against the Catholic Colonnas which allowed him to access funds raised throughout Europe for a war to liberate Jerusalem from Muslim rule.

---

211   *Analecta Bollandiana*, IX, *Vita et miracula Sancti Petri Caelestini*, pp 147-200

After a cruel campaign, not just the armed men loyal to the Colonnas but 'the peasants on their lands, the women and chi ldren in all the villages which happened to be within the boundaries of their lands' were either killed or sold into slavery, 'their pathetic goods becoming the property of the "crusaders"'.[212] Crops were burned, olive trees cut down, and one by one the fortresses of the Colonnas taken until finally their capital, the ancient city of Palestrina, was besieged. After an offer of amnesty, the Colonnas surrendered. Boniface reneged on his offer: the Colonnas were thrown into dungeons and the ancient city of Palestrina razed to the ground.

Boniface VIII has been described as 'the last of the papal monarchs on an heroic scale'.[213] He was physically imposing – tall, commanding, with eyes expressing his arrogance, and his features set in a sensual sneer. He wore with ease the heavy robes of his office, and the bee-hive shaped triple tiara better suited to an oriental despot than the successor of a Galilean fisherman. He inherited his concept of a papal imperium from his predecessors – Nicholas I, Gregory VII, Innocent III; but in many ways he was more like the Hohenstaufen emperor, Frederick II – a second *stupor mundi*. He shared Frederick's ambition, his self-belief and, like Frederick, seems to have taken the teaching of the Church he headed with a pinch of salt. A man had as much chance of life after death, he told his guests at dinner, 'as the roast fowl on the dining table here' – a remark that particularly shocked the cleric who recorded it because it was a day of fasting and abstinence. Chastity? 'Why, there is no more to going to bed with women and boys than in rubbing the skin of one hand against the other.' Were these just the *risqué* quips of a man who liked witty, pithy speech? 'It is difficult to assess his true beliefs,' writes E.R. Chamberlin, but his table talk seems to reveal 'a learned man who was indifferent to, or even sceptical of, the inner mysteries of the religion he professed'.[214]

On 22 February, 1300, Boniface issued a Papal Bull proclaiming this first year of a new century a Jubilee Year, and granting indulgences to those who made the pilgrimage to Rome. Whatever the reputation of the pope among the cardinals, the kings and the higher clergy, the summons met with an enthusiastic response among the humbler Christians who flocked to 'the

---

212   E.R.Chamberlin, *Op. Cit.* p. 102
213   *Ibid.* p. 106
214   *Ibid.* p. 111

mother city of Europe'. With the Colonna defeated, there was peace and a good harvest which meant that the pilgrims could buy food at a reasonable price. Boniface was an able administrator, and though the numbers far exceeded anything he had anticipated, he ensured that the Holy City's administration rose to the occasion. In the first chaotic weeks, people were crushed to death by the milling crowds, particularly in the stretch of road which ran over the bridge of Sant' Angelo towards St. Peter's and so a breach was made in the Leonine walls to enable a one-way system – the pilgrims entering over one bridge and leaving by another. The Florentine banker, Giovanni Villani, later described the astonishing mix of dress and language from 'the rough furs of Tartars to the silks and brocades of the Venetians'.

Passing through the gates, each was caught up in the slow, inexorable current that took the crowds through the narrow streets, over the bridge, up the great flight of steps that led to the doors of the basilica and through them at length to the tomb of Peter. There, crushed in a solid human mass, they prayed as best they might and, before leaving, cast their offering before the altar. Day and night two clerics stood in front of the altar of St. Peter, holding a rake in their hand with which they gathered in an infinite quantity of money'.[215]

Boniface's enemies believed that the Jubilee was simply a means of making money for the avaricious pope but, as E.R. Chamberlin points out, 'the money gathered was the copper of the poor rather than the gold of the rich, and probably barely covered expenses'.[216] Ominously, no monarch came to pray at the tomb of Peter, or pay homage to the man who believed himself to be not just the successor of Peter but of Constantine.

43.   King Philip the Fair

The challenge to Boniface's pretensions came not from Germany but from France and its king, Philip IV. Modelling himself on his grandfather, Louis IX, he was a devout Catholic, wearing a hair-shirt to mortify his flesh. He was known as *Philippe le Bel* because, wrote Bernard Saisset, Bishop of Pamiers, he was 'more handsome than any man in the world'. But Saisset thought the king's distant manner was the cover for an empty head. A modern historian

---

215   *Ibid.* p. 11
216   *Ibid.* p. 114

describes Philip as 'a captious, sternly moralistic, literalistically scrupulous, humourless, stubborn, aggressive, and vindictive individual, who feared the eternal consequences of his temporal deeds'.[217] At the age of sixteen, a year before he ascended the throne, Philip was married to Joan of Navarre who brought as her dowry Navarre, and the rich province of Champagne. The marriage was happy and, when Joan died in 1305, Philip did not re-marry.

Philip was the heir not just to the piety of his grandfather, but also the policy of the Capetian kings of expanding their realm east into Champagne and south to Toulouse – the second a reward for defeating the Cathars in the Albigensian crusade; and extending his powers within France at the expense of the nobility, the cities and the Church. Effective resistance to this policy came from his most powerful vassal, Edward Duke of Gascony, who was also King Edward I of England. A war between the two kings came to an end in 1298, but conflict continued with Edward's ally, Flanders, which saw the defeat of the French at Courtrai.

Wars as always involved great expense, and every expedient was used to raise money. Philip, like the Emperor Frederick II, employed in his administration not churchmen who had divided loyalties, or members of the nobility who had their own interests and so could not be trusted, but a rising class of lawyers – the *légistes* – who derived their power solely from the favour of the king. Pierre Flotte, who was Chancellor and Keeper of the Seals in the early years of Philip's reign, was killed at the battle of Courtrai. He was succeeded by William of Nogaret from St.-Felix-de-Caraman in the county of Toulouse.

Little is known about the origins of William of Nogaret. Some historians believe that there were skeletons in his cupboard in the form of parents and relatives who had been burned as Cathars. Clearly, given King Philip's piety, it would have been fatal for Nogaret to express any sympathy for heresy. Quite to the contrary, Nogaret lauded his monarch as 'a most Catholic king' descended from 'fervent champions of the faith and strong defenders of the Holy Mother Church'.[218] This no doubt buttressed Philip's belief that his expansionist policy was in accord with the will of God; but he realised that he could not rely on God to provide the means like manna from heaven. He had inherited from his father a large debt, incurred by the war with Aragon; the debt grew with his own conflict with England and Flanders. Every expedient available

---

217   E.A.R.Brown, *Medieval Studies*, 49, p. 282-334
218   Quoted in Malcolm Barber, *The Trial of the Templars*, Cambridge, 1978, p. 29

to him was exploited to the full – taxes on the cities, feudal dues; but the sums raised were not enough. He and his ministers now looked to rich immigrant communities. Lombard merchants living in Paris, who in the early years of Philip's reign had acted as his bankers, raising loans on the security of future taxation, were now made subject to fines and seizures, ending with outright expropriation and expulsion from France.

Next it was the turn of the Jews. In July, 1306, their property was seized and they too were expelled from France. Philip then resorted to the expedient of debasing the currency of *livres, sous* and *deniers*. Money circulating in France lost two-thirds of its value, leading to riots in Paris from which the king took refuge in the *donjon* of the Knights Templar. There now remained only one source of untapped revenue: that of the Church. In principle, no king could tax the clergy without the permission of the pope but both Philip and Edward in England had ignored this principle which prompted Boniface VIII to issue a bull, *Clerico laicos,* confirming the ban. Philip's response was to prohibit all transfer of funds from France to Rome. Since Boniface depended upon revenues from the Church in France, he was obliged to back down; and the canonisation of Philip's grandfather, Louis IX, in 1297, set the seal on the accord between pope and king.

A new *casus belli* arose, however, when in 1301 Bishop Saisset, Bishop of Pamiers, was arrested, charged with blasphemy, heresy, simony and treason, and thrown into goal: his chief crime seems to have been calling the king empty-headed, and comparing him to an owl. The arrest of a bishop was a gross trespass on the rights of the Church. Boniface issued another bull, *Ausculta fili*, summoning the French bishops to a synod in Rome; and on 18 November, 1302, before the thirty-nine bishops who had had the courage to attend, issued the bull *Unam Sanctam* that confirmed all the claims to papal supremacy that popes had made since the reign of Gregory VII: 'It is altogether necessary for salvation that every human creature be subject to the Roman Pontiff'.

The claim was not new; the bull quoted freely from the writings of previous popes, and from Thomas Aquinas and Bernard of Clairvaux; but it was clear that this claim to universal jurisdiction in secular as well as spiritual matters by the pope would be rejected by King Philip IV. Boniface therefore prepared a bull of excommunication, but its publication was thwarted by a coup of stupendous audacity. Early in the morning of 6 September, 1303, while Boniface was residing in his palace in his home town of Anagni, a force of French soldiers led by William of Nogaret, and accompanied by Sciarra, a Colonna who had survived the war of 1298, broke into the city. The papal guard fled. The pope's nephews put up a token resistance, then surrendered, but this had given time for Boniface to put on his robes of office, and have placed on his head the papal crown. They found him, awaiting his fate, seated on the papal throne. Sciarra Colonna wanted to kill him but Nogaret stayed his hand.

However, if Nogaret balked at the assassination of the Supreme Pontiff, he had not expected such an easy and complete success, and so had no clear plan as to what to do next. The favoured option was to take Boniface in chains to Lyon, there to stand trial before a Church council on charges of heresy, sodomy and abuse of power. But during the three days of dithering, the inhabitants of Anagni, all of whom were either relatives or dependants of the Gaetanis, finally organised a force to aid their pope. Outnumbered, the French fled. Boniface was liberated and taken back to Rome. He was now free but the trauma had upset the balance of his mind. He shut himself away in the Lateran palace, convinced that all visitors were covert assassins – his paranoia mixed with plans for revenge. A month after his return to Rome, he died – 'the last of the true Roman emperors'.[219]

The outrage of Anagni horrified Europe. Even Dante, who loathed Boniface because he had been exiled from Florence as a result of Boniface's interference in the city's affairs, denounced this assault on the vicar of Christ. The inhabitants of Anagni were condemned by Boniface's successor, Pope Benedict XI, for their pusillanimous failure to protect their pontiff. The only one to celebrate the scandal was the man who had instigated it, King Philip IV of France. His only regret was that Boniface had not been put on trial by a Church council and, even as his enemy lay in his grave, he demanded that the corpse be exhumed, tried for heresy, and condemned.

44.   The Fall of the Templars

Nine years before the Jubilee year of 1300, in May, 1291, Acre had fallen to the army of the Mameluk sultan, al-Ashraf. Tyre had already been surrendered, and Sidon was abandoned soon after. Haifa fell on 30 July; Beirut a day later. Tortosa was evacuated on 3 August, and eleven days after that the Knights

---

219   E.R.Chamberlin, *Op. Cit.* p. 122

of the Temple abandoned their impregnable fortress on the coast, Castle Pilgrim. All that remained of the Latin presence in the Holy Land was a Templar garrison on the island of Ruad, two miles off the coast by Tortosa.

News of the fall of Acre, and the end of a Latin presence in Palestine, was met with dismay in Rome. Already plans had been laid by Pope Nicholas IV for a new crusade, and somewhat optimistically it was hoped that the Mongols, the tribe from Central Asia that had conquered the east-Slavic state of Kievan Rus and sacked Baghdad in 1158, would convert to Christianity and join a crusade. When it became clear that this was wishful thinking, and a Latin re-conquest was unlikely, there were recriminations with blame falling on the Italian maritime republics and the military orders. The Templars had put up an heroic resistance at the siege of Acre: their Master, William of Beaujeu, had been killed: the Master of the Hospitallers had been wounded: many thought that he too should have died at his post.

When Pope Nicholas IV died in 1293, his plans for a new crusade died with him. His successors, as we have seen, had other priorities such as Boniface VIII's 'crusade' against the Colonnas. The Military Orders remained – the Templars, the Hospitallers or Knights of St. John and the Teutonic Knights on the Baltic who, after converting the pagan Prussians and Lithuanians to Christianity at the point of a sword, made them their serfs. The Grand Master of Teutonic Knights, Hermann von Salza, had acted as the chief minister of the Emperor Frederick II who in turn gave privileges to the order which then became a significant power in north-eastern Europe.

After the fall of Acre, the Teutonic Order moved its headquarters first to Venice and then in 1309 to Marienburg, its formidable brick fortress in Prussia. The Hospitallers first withdrew to Limassol in Cyprus but, having built up a substantial fleet of galleys, its Grand Master, Foulques de Villaret, decided that the order's future lay as a naval power with a base beyond the reach of the King of Cyprus or any other European power. His eye fell on the Island of Rhodes, off the coast of Asia Minor. It was notionally part of the Byzantine Empire; but following the Fourth Crusade, southern Greece was ruled by Latin princes, Crete and some of the Ionian islands by Venice, and Rhodes by freebooting Genoese. In June, 1306, a force of Hospitallers landed on the island, and by the end of the year it had taken the capital, Filermo. In 1307, Pope Clement V endorsed their right to the island. The Knights of St. John were in possession of a well-fortified and self-sufficient principality free from any extraneous control.

James de Molay, the Grand Master of the Templars, who could neither read nor write, lacked the prescience and shrewdness of the Hospitallers Grand Master, Foulques de Villaret. He thought only of a new crusade launched from the Templar base on the island of Ruad. To that end, he reinforced its garrison to make up for those lost in the siege of Acre, and toured the European capitals to drum up support. He was in Rome when Celestine V abdicated, and he persuaded Boniface VIII to oblige King Amaury of Cyprus to grant the order the same privileges and exemptions they had enjoyed in the Holy Land. In Cyprus, as elsewhere, the Templars were resented for these privileges and exceptions, and the unimaginative, inflexible and arrogant de Molay did nothing to smooth ruffled feathers.

King Philip the Fair of France was not against the idea of a new crusade; quite to the contrary, he envisaged a French empire in the eastern Mediterranean with his brother Charles de Valois on the throne in Constantinople. A prerequisite to this plan, in the mind of the French king, was to combine the knights of the Temple and the Hospital into a force which he would command. The idea of a merger had widespread support, but it was rejected by James de Molay.

There was now a new pope, Clement V – a Frenchman, Bernard de Got, hitherto Archbishop of Bordeaux and the subject not of the King of France but of the Duke of Aquitaine, King Edward I of England. 'Intelligent, but indecisive and weak'[220], Clement's initial intention to take up residence in Rome was never fulfilled. He remained in cities on the fringes of King Philip's domain: he was crowned in Lyon, resided for a time in Poitiers, and finally settled in Avignon, the city adjacent to the papal enclave, the *Comtat Venaissan*, and notionally, as a dependence of Arles, within the borders of the Holy Roman Empire. There was, however, no imperial force to protect him: he was therefore vulnerable to the French king who, having seized one pope in Anagni, would not hesitate to apprehend another in Avignon.

On 12 October, 1307, the Grand Master of the Templars, James de Molay, was in Paris where he acted as a pall-bearer at the funeral of King Philip's sister-in-law, Catherine de Courtenay, the wife of Charles of Valois. The next day, Friday 13 October, the king's *baillis* and seneschals throughout France put into effect the secret orders they had received three weeks before, to arrest all members of the Templar order, holding them to face charges 'horrible to contemplate,

---

220   *The Oxford History of the Popes,* p. 212

terrible to hear of…an abominable work, a detestable disgrace, a thing almost inhuman, indeed set apart from all humanity'. With remarkable efficiency, 15,000 knights together with sergeants, chaplains, *confrères,* servants and labourers were rounded up in a single day. The Grand Master, James de Molay, was arrested in the Temple fortress outside Paris by William of Nogaret.

Earlier, charges of gross impropriety had been made by expelled members of the Order which had been relayed to King Philip and by him to Pope Clement – the improprieties being sodomy, blasphemy, and worship of the Devil. Whether or not Philip believed them to be true, they served as a pretext for his assault on the order. His principal motive was his continuing need for money: the Temple, which had essentially lost its *raison d'être* since the fall of Acre, remained a rich and powerful corporation. No doubt Philip also wished to get rid of the stubborn James de Molay, but his principal motive was revealed by his command to sequester the property of the Temple as he had that of the Lombards and the Jews.

Of course, the Templar knights were not foreigners like the Lombards or infidels like the Jews, nor by law did they come under the jurisdiction of the King but were subject only to the pope. Philip claimed that his actions had been taken in consultation 'with our most holy father in Christ, the pope', but this claim was rebutted by Clement. 'You, our dear son,…have violated every rule and laid hands on the persons and properties of the Templars… Your hasty act is seen by all, and rightly so, as an act of contempt towards ourselves and the Roman Church'.[221] It is not clear whether or not Clement gave any credence to the charges made against the Templars: his chief objection was to the king's trespass on his prerogatives. As the investigation into the supposed crimes of the Templars was undertaken by the Inquisition, and under torture some knights, among them James de Molay, confessed to blasphemy, Devil worship, collaboration with the Saracens – but not sodomy! – Clement either became convinced, or deemed it prudent to appear to be convinced, of their guilt. Edward, the King of England, was persuaded by Philip and Clement to arrest the Templars within his domain but could find no evidence against them. Pope Clement recommended torture. Edward replied that torture was not permitted by English law. So too the King of Aragon who had received the same advice.

The use of torture proved effective in France where James de Molay, though he denied sodomy, admitted to denying Christ and spitting on his image at

---

221   Quoted in Menache, *Clement V*, p. 207

the time of his reception into the order in Baune. Other confessions followed, but were retracted when Pope Clement V, then residing in Poitiers, sent three cardinals to Paris to investigate the charges. It seemed that Clement was prepared to accept that the Templars were innocent, but he had to move cautiously: 'Poitiers was nearer to Paris than Anagni and the *de jure* powers of the Pope were paltry compared to the *de facto* powers of the king.'[222] Clement was in no position to take on King Philip, as his predecessors had taken on the German emperors: he therefore resorted to the only tools at his disposal – patience and procrastination. He agreed to the king's demand of a posthumous trial of Boniface VIII, and the canonisation of Boniface's predecessor, Celestine V, but not as Saint Celestine, martyr, as Philip had wanted, but as Saint Pietro da Morrone, Confessor.

On Saturday, 16 October, 1311, an ecumenical council of the Catholic Church summoned by Pope Clement assembled at the city of Vienne, twenty kilometres south of Lyon on the river Rhône. The turnout was disappointing; over a third of those invited failed to turn up. The agenda was much the same as that of many other councils – reform of the Church, a new crusade – the idea of reform hard to sustain when the pope had appointed three relatives to the College of Cardinals. The only unusual item was the third – the dissolution of the Order of the Temple. Prelates from outside France, who had found no credible evidence against the Templars in their diocese, nonetheless acquiesced when, on 3 April, 1312, Pope Clement read out the Bull *Vox in Excelso* which abolished the order. The bull was apologetic in tone, and the great wealth of the Order was not surrendered to the French king but transferred to the Knights of St. John, the Hospitallers. The pope's policy of patience and procrastination might not have saved the Templars, but it had largely thwarted King Philip's attempts to seize their property as he had that of the Lombards and the Jews

During the protracted proceedings of the Council of Vienne, James de Molay remained incarcerated in Philip the Fair's dungeons in Paris. De Molay continued to insist that, as Master of the Order of the Temple, he was answerable to the pope alone, and would give an account of his actions to the pope face-to-face. Such a meeting was never to take place. Towards the end of December, 1313, Pope Clement sent a commission of three cardinals to Paris who ruled that, since the recalcitrant knights had publicly and openly

---

222   Piers Paul Read, *The Templars*, p. 269

confessed their crimes, 'they were adjudged to be thrust into harsh and perpetual imprisonment.'[223]

The severity of the sentence was too much for James de Molay. Now an old man, well into his seventies, what profit was there in submission if the reward was a lingering death? The Pope had betrayed him; all he could hope for now was the justice of God. He retracted his confession, and with the Preceptor of Normandy, Geoffrey de Charney, who had done the same, was taken to an island on the river Seine, the Île-du-Javeau, now the Île-de-la-Cité, where they were burned at the stake. It was later said that James de Molay, before he died, summoned King Philip and Pope Clement to appear before the tribunal of God before the year was out. Pope Clement died a few months later, on 20 April, 1314. King Philip followed on 29 November of the same year after an accident out hunting.

45.   Catherine of Siena

Following the conversion of the Emperor Constantine, the history of the Catholic Church tends to follow the lives of popes, emperors, kings, bishops and those few men such as Augustine of Hippo, Benedict of Nursia, Dominic Guzman and Francis of Assisi who founded religious orders. The influence of devout women such as Constantine's mother Helena or Augustine's mother Monica is clear; and there is the founding by Benedict's sister Scholastica, or Francis's disciple Clare, of religious orders for women: there are also those founded by queens such as Brigid of Sweden. Catholic women, though excluded from the ministerial priesthood because of their gender, could exert great influence as queens or abbesses of rich and powerful religious foundations – an example is Hilda of Whitby in the seventh century – or simply by the power of a personality combined with the example of a patently holy way of life.

Catherine di Benincasa was the youngest child of a Sienese dyer, Giacomo di Benincasa, and Mona Lapa, the daughter of a poet. Temperamentally cheerful, Catherine was drawn to the devout life from childhood, refusing to follow the life mapped out by her parents leading to marriage and a family of her own, but making a pledge of perpetual virginity and withdrawing into a small room in her parents' large house where she practised the austere life

---

223   *The Chronicle of William of Nangis,* quoted in Barber, *Op. Cit.* p. 241

of a recluse. Her mother was dismayed; she regarded Catherine as a difficult adolescent; but at the age of sixteen she was allowed to join the Third Order of the Dominicans – a means by which members of the laity could participate in the life of the friars, wearing the same black and white habit but living at home. There she practised great austerities, leaving only to nurse the sick, help the poor and urge sinners to repent.

By the time she reached her early twenties, Catherine suffered not just from the pain and weakness brought on by her mortifications, but from the envy of others in the Dominican order. This did not suppress her cheerful personality, and her growing reputation for practical wisdom and spiritual insight. All her contemporaries bear witness to her extraordinary personal charm…and she began to gather disciples round her, both men and women, who formed an informal association known as the *bella brigata* or the Club of Fortebranda – Fortebranda being the neighbourhood in which she lived. Among the members of the club were members of prominent families, soldiers, artists, lawyers, politicians as well as priests, and members of religious orders, among them an English Augustinian friar, William Flete.

During the summer of 1370, when Catherine was still only twenty-three years old, she had a series of visions in which she saw Hell, Purgatory and Heaven, and heard a Divine Command to address the problems of the world around her. These were considerable. The city states of northern Italy were constantly at war with one another and the Holy See, employing bands of mercenaries or *condottieri*, many from the other side of the Alps – such as the Bretons employed by Pope Clement VII, Germans under Werner von Urslingen and the White company commanded by an English soldier of fortune, Sir John Hawkwood. To avert wars, and potential civil wars, Catherine, who could not read or write, dictated letters to kings and princes, even to Hawkwood, but above all to the pope, Gregory XI, a Frenchman, Pierre Roger de Beaufort. Addressing him in her letters as *dulcissimo babbo* – 'my sweet Daddy'- she showed no deference to the Prince of the Apostles.

> Even if you have not been very faithful in the past, begin now to follow Christ, whose vicar you are, in real earnest. And do not be afraid. Attend to things spiritual, appointing good shepherds and good rulers in the cities under your jurisdiction…. Above all, delay no longer in returning to Rome and proclaiming the Crusade.[224]

---

224 Kenelm Foster and Maryu John Ronaye (eds.), *Selected Writings of Catherine of Siena*, p. 94. Quoted in Eamon Duffy, *Op. Cit.* p. 168

In 1375, war broke out between Florence and the papal states. At the request of the Florentines, Catherine travelled to Avignon to mediate between the pope and the coalition of city states that opposed him. She was accompanied by twenty-three members of her *bella brigata*, among them four priests, but she was mocked for her simplicity by the sophisticated women in the papal court, and treated with suspicion as a mystic by the Inquisition. Official delegates from Florence undermined her authority as a representative of their city, but diplomatic matters were of secondary importance to Catherine. Her chief objective was to persuade Pope Gregory to return to Rome. The king of France, the College of Cardinals and the pope's own family were all against it, but the increasingly frail pontiff was persuaded by this holy and zealous young woman. On September 13th, 1376, he left Avignon for Rome, thus ending what the poet Petrarch called the papacy's 'Babylonian captivity'.

46.   The Avignon Popes

It was said by the French churchmen in Pope Gregory's entourage that, though he lived for only eighteen months after his return to Rome, it was long enough to regret it. Catherine had said that Italy yearned for his return like a child for its father, but in reality he found his subjects in a state of simmering insurrection – resenting the brutal rule of the legates who had governed them in his absence. Mercenaries employed on the pope's behalf by Robert, the Cardinal Archbishop of Geneva, had massacred four thousand of the inhabitants of the city of Cesena who had objected to the presence of the Breton *condottieri*.

Gregory XI died on 27 March, 1378. The rules for the conclave electing a new pope were precise: it had to take place where the previous pope had died. Five cardinals had been left in Avignon, but sixteen – most of them Frenchmen – were in Rome. The sixteen assembled in the Vatican, the first conclave to be held in Rome since 1303. Agitated crowds filled the streets, and the city's magistrates warned the cardinals that their hold on the populace was precarious. The Romans were determined that the cardinals should not elect another French pope: 'A Roman or an Italian,' was the cry from the mob. 'Give us a Roman pope or we will make your heads redder than your hats.'[225]

---

225   Jean Froissart, quoted in E.R.Chamberlin, *Op. Cit.* p. 137

While the cardinals gathered on the first floor of the Vatican palace, the mob burst into the ground floor. The bell of the Capitol sounded a call to arms; the bells of St. Peter's responded. There was pandemonium. Terrified, the cardinals settled on the Italian Archbishop of Bari, Bartolomeo Prignano, as the new pope. He was a Neapolitan lawyer who had served at the heart of the curial administration in Avignon- ' a short, plump man, heavy-featured, his naturally sallow complexion muddied by years of indifferent food and confinement in airless, cluttered offices.' Born in a slum, he had no royal or princely patron and held his post purely as a result of his administrative skills. 'Buried deep within him, almost strangled by the legal web in which he moved, was a very genuine piety that was offended by the gross luxury of the Avignonese court.' He knew better than any the workings of the fiscal machinery of the Church – 'perhaps the most efficient system ever devised for a continent-wide extraction of gold'[226], and was disgusted by the way it was spent.

Thus the cardinals in conclave had come up with a pope who was both Italian and intent on reform, but Prignano was brought down by his personality – impatient, irascible, taciturn towards his superiors, bullying towards his inferiors. Now that he was pope, all were his inferiors. Nine days after his election, Prignano was crowned as Urban VI, and all at once, as his secretary Dietrich von Niem observed, the short-tempered bureaucrat was transformed into a raging tyrant. At the first consistory, all the pent-up contempt for the corrupt curia that had built up during the years in Avignon burst as a torrent of abuse delivered in the coarse language of the Neapolitan slums. The insults might have been deserved, but they were ill-advised when the cardinals retained so much wealth and power.

As the weeks went by, Urban's behaviour grew worse – he physically attacked a cardinal during another consistory – and one by one the cardinals left Rome, gathering in the palace at Anagni which had witnessed the humiliation of Boniface VIII. There they considered whether or not the election of Urban had in fact been valid, or had been made under duress, concluding that they had chosen Prignano, an Italian, only from fear for their lives. The election was therefore invalid. A new conclave was held in which, while the few Italian cardinals abstained, the French majority elected a new pope, the butcher of Cesena, Robert, Cardinal Archbishop of Geneva, who took the name Clement VII.

---

226   E.R.Chamberlin, *Op. Cit.* p. 129

When the news reached Siena, Catherine denounced the rebel cardinals as demons, and appealed to the *condottiero*, Alberico da Barbiano, to come to the aid of Pope Urban. His was the first force of purely Italian mercenaries and, after defeating a foreign force backing Clement VII, was welcomed by Urban in Rome with a banner inscribed 'Italy delivered from the Barbarians'. The French garrison in the Castel Sant' Angelo surrendered. Clement fled first to Naples and then to Avignon: much of the Curia went with him. Urban responded by creating twenty-nine new cardinals from different parts of Europe. There had been anti-popes before, but not two pontiffs elected by the same college of cardinals, each with his own administrations. The different nations had to choose whom to obey. France and its allies such as Scotland recognised Clement, while France's enemies, such as England, remained loyal to Urban. The schism was to last for thirty-nine years.

'Thou art Peter and upon this rock I shall build my church.' Since the earliest years of its existence, the Bishops of Rome had been at the apex of the Church's administration – a position, it was believed, not contrived by men but designed by Christ himself in appointing Peter the first among the twelve apostles, and conferring on him the powers to bind and loose. The Church in the East might deny this pre-eminence, but it was the unifying concept in Latin Christendom. Emperors had never accepted that they reigned at the pope's pleasure, but of a nation's three estates, the clergy was the first, the nobility only second, and the commons third. The pope's ultimate authority over the vast and pervasive ecclesiastical structures was unquestioned.

But who now was the pope? Each excommunicated the other, so which was bound for Heaven and which for Hell? Which of the two possessed the powers conferred by Christ to appoint bishops, to grant indulgences, to pass final judgement in disputes over doctrine? It could not be both. Perhaps it was neither. Perhaps the powers claimed by the popes belonged in fact to the Church as a whole? In England, a priest and scholar, John Wycliffe, gained considerable support when he questioned the powers of the pope and the wealth of the clergy. As the schism persisted, and new popes were elected to replace Urban and Clement, opinion turned towards the idea of a Council that would depose the popes in both Avignon and Rome and choose a third. One was held in Pisa in 1409. It deposed both the Roman pope Gregory XII, and the Avignon pope Benedict XIII, and elected a third, Alexander V: but neither of the established popes were willing to relinquish their thrones. The successor to the third pope, John XXIII, was persuaded by Sigismund, the

King of Hungary, to summon a Council in Constance, an ancient diocese on the great lake bearing its name.

Sigismund, the son of the Holy Roman Emperor Charles IV, and himself Emperor designate with the title King of Rome, had acquired the crown of Hungary through his marriage to Mary, Queen of Hungary. He was related through his mother to the kings of Poland and Grand Dukes of Lithuania; he became in due course King of Croatia, Bohemia and Germany and Holy Roman Emperor. In 1396 he had led a crusade against the Ottoman Turks that was defeated at Nicopolis, leaving Constantinople surrounded by Muslim forces.

Involved throughout his life in interminable campaigns, Sigismund hoped that once the schism was ended and Christendom reunited, it would join him on a new crusade against the Turks. Twenty-nine cardinals, one hundred doctors of theology, one hundred and thirty-four abbots and one hundred and eighty-three archbishops and bishops assembled at Constance. The Council deposed the Avignon pope Benedict XIII and John XXIII, the successor to the Pisan pope, Benedict XIII; while the Roman pope, Gregory XII agreed to abdicate. An electoral commission appointed by the Council then chose Cardinal Oddo Colonna as the sole legitimate pontiff. He took the name Martin V. The Great Schism was at an end.

There were other matters on the Council's agenda – notably the question of heresy. The preaching of John Wycliffe in England against the avarice and corruption of the clergy; his insistence on the right of the laity to receive communion in both kinds, and to read the Bible in a vernacular translation (he himself had translated large parts into English), had developed in the 1380s into a denial of transubstantiation – the teaching that after the words of consecration by a priest, the bread becomes the flesh of Jesus and the wine his blood. This was a step too far for most of his supporters. The doctors of divinity in the University of Oxford who had initially commended his teaching, now condemned it. Bulls were issued by the Roman pontiffs pronouncing him a heretic and his followers, known as Lollards, were obliged to retract their support. Wycliffe was banned from preaching but he continued to publish tracts from his rich living at Lutterworth in Leicestershire until his death in 1384. However, Wycliffe was pursued beyond the grave. On 4 May, 1415, the Council of Constance declared him a heretic. It ordered that his writings be burned, and his corpse removed from consecrated ground.[227]

---

227   The order was carried out in 1428. Wycliffe's remains were exhumed, burned, and his ashes thrown into the River Swift that ran through Lutterworth.

Although Wycliffe's teaching was successfully curtailed in England, it had spread to Bohemia where Jan Hus, a priest and scholar who had served at one time as the regent of Prague University, had translated a number of Wycliffe's works into Czech and preached the same demands for reform. In 1411 Hus condemned the sale of indulgences promoted by the anti-Pope John XXIII and questioned the authority of the pope and bishops, saying that all teaching should be based on the Bible alone. Like Wycliffe, he too demanded Communion in both kinds. His teaching spread rapidly throughout Bohemia and Moravia, and seeped into Austria and Hungary.

Aware of an impending collapse of the authority of the Church, the emperor-elect Sigismund placed the question of Hus's orthodoxy on the agenda of the Council of Constance. Since much of Hus's writing was based on the teaching of Wycliffe – his *De Ecclesia* published two years before the Council followed closely Wycliffe's heretical *De potentate papae* – the judgement of the Council was predictable; but Hus nonetheless accepted King Sigismund's offer of a safe conduct and travelled to Constance. Here he continued to preach and say Mass. When it was thought that he might flee, he was imprisoned in the castle of the Bishop of Constance. Sigismund was persuaded that no promise made to a heretic could be considered valid. In June, 1415, Hus was put on trial for heresy and, after refusing to recant, he was stripped of his priestly vestments at a plenary session of the Council and, with a paper hat inscribed with the word *Haeresiarcha* – a leader of heretics – he was burned at the stake, and his ashes thrown into the River Rhine.

The twentieth-century historian Eamon Duffy judged that the views of Wycliffe and Hus 'on predestination and membership of the Church…were heretical by the standards of the late medieval Church', but that many of his proposed reforms such as giving the laity Communion in both kinds 'were in no way heretical, and had widespread support among reform-minded intellectuals'.[228] Even the heretical teachings, such as those on Predestination and the symbolic nature of the Eucharist, were not comparable to the bizarre dualistic beliefs of the Cathars that had swept in from Persia.

If the fathers of the Council of Constance had thought the burning of Jan Hus would be the timely stitch that would save nine, they were to be disappointed. Outraged by his cruel death, and the Emperor's reneging on his promise of a safe conduct, Hus's followers in Bohemia took up arms against

---

228   Eamon Duffy, *Op. Cit.* p. 172

the government and, under able commanders, defeated the forces raised by the king. Pope Martin V proclaimed a Hussite crusade but five sallies into Bohemia, one led by Cardinal Henry Beaufort, the illegitimate son of John of Gaunt, were defeated. The Hussite wars came to an end in 1436 when, at the Council of Basel, it was agreed that Catholics in Bohemia and Moravia could receive Communion in both kinds – a privilege confined to that part of Europe where 'academic anti-clericalism and popular piety really made common cause'.[229]

Sixteen years after the burning of Jan Hus, in 1431, a young French woman suffered the same fate in the market place of Rouen. This was Joan of Arc, who a few years before had left her home in Domrémy in eastern France, directed she claimed by the 'voices' of saints and the Archangel Michael, to revive the morale of the French army engaged in the Hundred Years War against the English and Burgundians. The hardened veterans, roused by her rhetoric, followed her to relieve the English siege of Orléans. At her urging, the long-postponed coronation of the Dauphin took place in Rheims Cathedral in 1429: France now had a king, Charles VII.

Returning to the field of battle, Joan was captured by the Burgundians, who handed her over to their allies, the English, and after a long imprisonment and a trial by the episcopal court of the Bishop of Beauvais, Peter Cauchon, she was condemned as a witch and a heretic, and burned at the stake. She was less than twenty years old. Charles VII made no attempt to save her. Joan's condemnation was soon recognised as a travesty; she was exonerated by Pope Callistus III in 1456, and four hundred and fifty years later she was declared a saint. Charles VII went on to be an able monarch: the English were finally thrown out of France.

We speak now of the English rather than the Plantagenets because what had started as competition for territory and the French crown between two rival but related dynasties had ended as a war between nations. The European who at the time of the First Crusade thought of himself only as a Christian, and rallied to the call to liberate Jerusalem, now identified as a member of a nation – England, say, or France – and fought for the interests of his king. He or she might retain a nagging anxiety about his or her fate in a world to come, and sustain a market in indulgences, but interdicts and excommunications had lost their sting: the immediate needs of the body were now more pressing

---

229 Maurice Keen, *Op. Cit.* p. 292

than those of the soul. Both the size of the population of Western Europe and its prosperity were now in decline – eroded by the rampaging *condottieri* in Italy, the Hundred Years War between England and France, and by recurrent outbreaks of the bubonic plague, starting with the Black Death (1347-49). Urban populations were decimated and rural communities wiped out. A shortage of labour led to a rise in wages, and laws to limit these led to peasant uprisings in France (the *Jacquerie*) and England (the Peasants' Revolt). 'This growing gulf between the men who tilled the soil and their masters was perhaps the most marked development of agrarian history in the later Middle Ages...'[230]

There might now be only be one pope in Rome, but his authority had been irreparably diminished. Those who had hoped that, after the ending of the Great Schism, a reformed conciliar Church might attract the principal loyalties of Catholics had failed: 'the universal Church of the west, as it emerged from the period of the schism and the councils, was really a confederation of national churches in all but name', [231] much of its wealth and power appropriated by individual monarchs. The conciliarism manifest in the Council of Constance, and linked reforms, persisted in the subsequent Councils held in Basel in 1431 but most of those who attended were theologians, not bishops. It reconvened in Basel, then Ferrara, Florence and finally to the Lateran Palace in Rome. Some significant decrees were passed by these councils: the number of sacraments was fixed at seven at the Council of Florence, and decrees were passed concerning religious education and the selection of bishops, but the popes of the period, Julius II and Leo X, had no particular interest in enacting these reforms, and had anyway lost their moral authority over the universal Church. When, after the devastating defeat by the Turks of a crusading army at Nicopolis in 1396, a call had gone out for a new crusade, it fell on deaf ears. The rulers of western nations had other priorities. In 1453 Constantinople – for a thousand years the capital of the eastern empire, and of orthodox Christendom – fell to the Ottoman Turks.

---

230   Maurice Keen, *Op. Cit.* p. 235
231   Maurice Keen, *Op. Cit.* p. 298

47.   A Catholic Culture

'In the Middle Ages,' wrote the historian Tom Holland, 'no civilisation in Eurasia was as congruent with a single set of beliefs as was the Latin West with its own distinctive form of Christianity.' In Europe, 'in the lands that acknowledged the primacy of the pope, there was only the occasional community of Jews to disrupt the otherwise total monopoly of the Roman Church.'[232]

The contribution of the Jews, often physically confined to ghettos and intellectually by the Talmud, was small: greater by far, once their works had been freed from the taint of paganism by Albert the Great and Thomas Aquinas, was the influence of the authors of ancient Greece and Rome, leading to a focus on man as the acme of God's creation. This rediscovery of the art and architecture of antiquity led to what came to be called the Renaissance. It was not that Christendom had hitherto been without art: there had been the vivid if naïve statuary and dazzling stained glass of the Gothic cathedrals; the astonishing Byzantine mosaics in Ravenna or Palermo; murals by unnamed artists in churches and cathedrals; and the icons of the Orthodox Church. Had the iconoclasts triumphed in the eighth century, these would have been erased and, as in the Islamic world where the depiction of Christ and his saints was forbidden, the development of art and architecture confined to calligraphy and geometric designs.

It was in the prosperous Tuscan cities of Siena and Florence that the first flourishing of the Renaissance took place, and we have the names of these early masters – Giotto, Fra Angelico, Piero della Francesca, Signorelli, Simone Martini … The subjects they chose were almost all taken from Scripture or the lives of the saints; it was often the Church that commissioned their work, and many of the artists were themselves devout: but artists, like authors and architects, came increasingly to look back to pagan antiquity for their inspiration. The cathedral church in Florence, Santa Maria del Fiore, began in the Gothic style but the plans envisaged a dome like that extant in the Pantheon in Rome – once a temple, now a church. Around a hundred years after the start of the cathedral's construction, a dome was finally built to the design of a young goldsmith in his twenties, Filipo Brunelleschi: it was the first since the fall of the Roman empire. Flying buttresses were now out of fashion: some said it was a painter of the later Renaissance, Raphael, not Vasari, who

---

232   Tom Holland, *Dominion. The Making of the Western Mind*, p. xxii

had come up with the disparaging term 'Gothic' for the cathedrals of the thirteenth and fourteenth centuries.

Parallel to the rebirth of art and architecture was that of music and literature. Mediaeval music encompassed the romance of the lute-playing troubadours, but it was the liturgy of the Church – the daily singing of the office by monks, and of the *Kyrie, Credo, Sanctus* and *Agnus Dei* during the Mass, that was the source of musical evolution in western Europe. The ubiquitous use of plainchant developed in the eighth and ninth centuries, with musical annotation devised by a monk Guido d'Arezzo in the 11th century.

While Latin remained the language of the Church, and French the language of the court, the development of literature in the course of the fourteenth century saw the increasing use of vernacular tongues. There had been Viking sagas, and French romances – *Le Roman de la Rose* (1230), *La Chanson de Roland* (c. 1240); but, as with painting and sculpture, the first and finest author of the Renaissance was found in Tuscany, Dante Alighieri. Dante was a citizen of Florence, deeply involved in the city's politics – a Guelph (a supporter of the Pope) who was exiled from his native city after the triumph of the Ghibellines (supporters of the Emperor). Already an established poet, he wrote his *Divine Comedy* while in exile, completing it in 1320, a year before he died. It is a work infused with Catholic teaching on the afterlife, and the philosophy of Thomas Aquinas, but it is Virgil, a poet from ancient Rome, who leads Dante, the narrator, through Hell, Purgatory and Heaven.

The Divine Comedy was written in the vernacular, and was instrumental in the establishing of the Tuscan dialect as classic Italian. So too was the work of his younger contemporary Petrarch, and that of Dante's friend Boccaccio, author of *The Decameron*. The printing press had yet to be invented: their works were copied and recopied, gaining a widespread circulation. The same was true of the work of the Englishman, Geoffrey Chaucer, the son of a London wine merchant with a training in law, and a reputation as an astronomer as well as a poet. He had links to the court, and was sent on diplomatic missions by the king, among them one to the English *condottiero* Sir John Hawkwood who also corresponded, as we have seen, with Catherine of Siena. In 1368 Geoffrey Chaucer represented King Edward III at the wedding of the king's son Lionel of Antwerp to Violante Visconti in Milan: also present were Petrarch and Boccaccio whose influence is apparent when Chaucer himself came to write *Troilus and Criseyde*, virtually a translation of Boccaccio's work of the same name; and his *magnum opus*, *The Canterbury Tales* – a series of stories told by pilgrims as they travel from London to the shrine of Thomas Becket in Canterbury.

Chaucer wrote in the Middle English vernacular and, like Dante and Boccaccio, was instrumental in the formation of the language of his native land. However, Chaucer did not think of himself as an Englishman, or even an European. For Chaucer, the defining element of larger human community was not geographical proximity but religious faith. The Latin culture of the western Roman empire had never disappeared. However, we find in *The Canterbury Tales* passages such as those in 'The Miller's Tale' which, described as 'bawdy', verge on the pornographic: so too, of course, in Boccaccio's *Decameron*. It is not just sex that it is given its due as a powerful force in nature, but like the swearing and 'explosive farting' they are regarded as *peccadillos*. The graphic depictions of sexual encounters may seem crude, but they were not heretical, which is no doubt why the Church raised no objection. It might have sensed that the narrator's Christian faith was somewhat *pro forma*, but it was real.

For historians, *The Canterbury Tales* are invaluable as a 'snapshot' of life in the fourteenth century, and while the teaching of the Church was unquestioned, there is, in the characters of the Friar, the Summoner and the Pardoner, a scathing denunciation of corrupt clerics. There was perhaps a flaw in the concept of mendicant orders: begging for a living invariably antagonises those who work for theirs. Dante placed both Dominic Guzman and Francis of Assisi in paradise in his *Divine Comedy*: it is nevertheless painful to see through the eyes of Chaucer how degraded their ideals had become by the beginning of the fourteenth century.

It cannot be said that Chaucer was merely expressing the gripes of the merchant class from which he came: the same censure of clerical corruption is found in *Piers Plowman*, a long allegorical poem by William Langland, an obscure and impoverished cleric who was Chaucer's contemporary. Here we have a pilgrimage not from London to Canterbury but through life in pursuit of truth. Piers encounters allegorical characters such as Conscience, Reason, Guile, Sloth and Fraud. There is satire but not Chaucer's cynicism or bawdy: in its forcefulness, its pathos, its grim humour, its realism and occasional dramatic moments and above all its sincerity, *Piers Plowman* is clearly the work of a man deeply imbued with the Catholic faith.

48.   The Reconquista

Constantinople fell to the Ottoman Turks in 1453, and with it the remnants of the Byzantine Empire. Justinian's great basilica, the Hagia Sophia, became a mosque. Defence of the frontiers of Christendom from Islamic expansion now devolved upon Catholic powers – the kingdom of Hungary in central Europe and the Republic of Venice in the Mediterranean.

The Venetians, putting their commercial interests before a defence of the faith, signed a peace treaty with the Ottomans in 1479, and so the following year failed to stop a Turkish fleet of 120 ships reaching the coast of southern Italy, and landing a force of 20,000 Muslim soldiers commanded by Gedik Ahmed Pasha. This besieged and captured the city of Otranto, massacring 12,000 of its male inhabitants and enslaving 5,000 women and children. Further attacks by the Ottomans were made on Lecce, Taranto and Brindisi. A fear that Rome might suffer the same fate as Constantinople led Pope Sixtus IV to preach a crusade. Neapolitan forces were joined by French and Hungarian contingents sent by their king, Matthias Corvinus. In September, 1481, Otranto was retaken, and eleven years later Granada, the last Muslim principality on the Iberian peninsula fell to the armies of King Ferdinand of Aragon and his wife, Queen Isabella of Castile.

The fall of Granada was the culmination of the *Reconquista* (re-conquest) that had started soon after the Muslim Tariq ibn Ziyad in 711 had conquered virtually the whole peninsula with its population of Christian Visigoths, Goths and Romano-Iberians. The Muslim incursion reached its limit when, as we have seen, an army led by Abd al 'Rahman was defeated near Poitiers in Aquitaine by Charles Martel in 732 and the Muslims were driven back over the Pyrenees. On the Iberian peninsula itself, a remnant of Visigoths had held out in the far north, a base from which the *Reconquista* began; and formed the kernel of the Kingdom of Asturias which, by the mid-ninth century, had established its southern frontier on the River Douro.

In the east, the Franks under Charlemagne captured Barcelona, Tortosa and Pamplona, extending the frontier between Christendom and the Muslim Emirate of al-Andalus to the River Ebro. Over the next seven centuries, different Christian kingdoms were established in the north of the peninsula, expanding into the territory of the Emirate of Cordoba. In the tenth century the Kingdom of Asturias had become that of Leon, while the small independent Christian kingdoms of Navarre and Aragon were formed astride the Pyrenees. In the eleventh century, there arose, between Leon and Navarre, the small kingdom of Castile, while a state of Catalonia was formed from Barcelona and its hinterland.

Originally Cordoba had been an emirate, recognizing the suzerainty of the caliph in Baghdad, but in the tenth century it was proclaimed an independent caliphate by the emir Abd ar-Rahman. There followed a period of prosperity and stability. The caliphate, stretching into north Africa, became a centre of Islamic culture and learning, preserving many of the writings of ancient Greece and Rome that had been lost in the Christian west. It established a reputation for relative tolerance: the Peoples of the Book – the Christians and Jews – were permitted to practise their religion upon the payment of a tax as prescribed by the Prophet Muhammad. However, this tolerance had its limits. In 786, the caliph Abd-er Rahman I drew up plans for an imposing mosque in Cordoba, and conscripted Christians to help in its construction. Some Christians objected and between 850 and 859 forty-eight were executed for proclaiming their Christian beliefs. Most were monks, priests or deacons, but two women, Flora and Maria, the daughters of mixed marriages who had chosen their mothers' religion, were executed for apostasy.

The *Reconquista* was in part a war of conquest, in part a crusade, but there were long periods of *conviviencia* when Muslims, Christians and Jews lived together in relative amity. Christian and Muslim states made temporary alliances. At one time in his career, the eleventh century Castilian warlord, Rodrigo Diaz de Vivar, better known as El Cid, fought for Muslim Zaragoza against Christian Aragon. When he captured Valencia in 1094, he established an independent principality with the support of both Christians and Muslims. His son Diego died fighting for King Alfonso of Castile against the Muslim Amoravids.

The *Reconquista* as a crusade was encouraged by a number of popes even before Pope Urban II preached the First Crusade at the Council of Clermont in 1095: Pope Alexander II had promised an indulgence to Christians fighting against the Muslims of al-Andalus. After the Council of Clermont, Pope Urban II had to reassure the knights fighting Islam on the Iberian peninsula that they would receive the same indulgences to prevent them joining the army making for Jerusalem. The Knights Templar established bases in Spain, and similar indigenous military orders followed – the Orders of Santiago, of Montesa, of Calatrava, of Saint James. After the overwhelming defeat of the Muslim army at the battle of Las Navas de Tolosa in 1212, large swathes of territory were awarded to the military orders in the Spanish kingdoms; and in Portugal which had been recognised by the pope as an independent kingdom in 1179. When the Templars were suppressed in 1312, rather than appropriate the assets of the order, King Denis of Portugal settled them on a new order, the Knights of Christ. So too in Castile and Aragon, which added the Templars' property to the other orders' already considerable holdings. In Aragon, the Knights of Saint John were the largest single landowner; while in Castile the Order of Alcántara owned half the province of Extremadura.[233]

The Christian powers were also distracted from the *Reconquista* by their ambitions beyond the Iberian peninsula. The kingdom of Aragon, which by the thirteenth century incorporated Valencia and Catalonia, conquered the island kingdom of Majorca. After the revolt against the French in Palermo (the 'Sicilian Vespers') the Aragonese took the island, and in 1435 the kingdom of Naples passed to King Alfonso of Aragon. Fifty years later, a body of Catalan mercenaries led by Roger de Flor became the rulers of the Duchy of Athens.

By the fifteenth century, four Christian kingdoms were established on the Iberian peninsula – Portugal, Castile, Aragon, Navarre – and one remaining Muslim state, the emirate of Granada. There were skirmishes between the Christian states and Granada, but no attempt at conquest: Granada was well-defended by mountain ranges, and fortresses along its borders, among them the supposedly impregnable Ronda. Granada was also a useful conduit for trade with north Africa and beyond, and so for more than a century no attempt was made by the Christian powers to take it .

Change came with the marriage in 1469 in Valladolid of Isabella of Castile and Ferdinand of Aragon. Isabella, half-sister of King Henry IV of Castile, and heir-apparent, was a devout but formidable young woman who, at the age of seventeen, rejected the suitors proposed by her half-brother Henry, and secretly arranged with the King of Aragon a marriage to his son Ferdinand. On a flimsy excuse, she fled from Henry's court to Valladolid where the marriage took place. Ferdinand had had to cross Castile to Valladolid disguised as a servant.

The marriage of Ferdinand and Isabella 'was thought a marvel at the time', wrote the historian Hugh Thomas: he thought it 'difficult to think of two married sovereigns acting so successfully together'.[234] *Tanto monta, monta tanto, Isabel como Fernando.* (It comes to the same thing. Isabella is the same as

233   Piers Paul Read, *Op. Cit.*, p. 320s

234   *Ibid.*, p. 14

Ferdinand). Both proved to be competent rulers of their own domains. When Isabella's half-brother Henry IV died in 1474, the King of Portugal invaded Castile in support of the claim of his grand-daughter, Isabella's half-sister, Juana 'La Beltraneja' – so named after her mother's lover who was assumed to be her natural father. The intruders were defeated and returned to Portugal. Isabella then turned her attention to putting down more localized revolts, taming the nobility, reforming the finances of the kingdom, and curbing the ubiquitous lawlessness with the formation of a police force answerable not to the municipalities but to the crown. Ferdinand too proved an able ruler of Aragon, and also a successful military commander. He too was a committed Catholic, if not as devout as Isabella. His numerous infidelities did not appear to affect his marriage: he and Isabella had five children.

In 1469, the year of her marriage, Isabella chose as her confessor the Dominican friar, Tomás de Torquemada – the devout and orthodox prior of the monastery of the Holy Cross in Segovia. He and the queen were like-minded, and he certainly supported her – and may have influenced her – in dealing with the intractable problems posed by the influential Jewish community, and the *conversos* – those Jews who had been converted to the Catholic religion. Some were descendants of those brought into the Church a century earlier by the 'strenuous and successful, if not wholly creditable'[235] mission of the half-English Dominican friar Vincent Ferrer: a rabbi converted by Ferrer later became Bishop of Burgos.

Ferrer had been canonized in 1455, but converts from Judaism, though many worked as farmers or artisans, and had intermarried within the Catholic community, were nonetheless identified as *conversos*, and were suspected of secretly reverting to their Jewish religion. Popular antipathy was fueled by envy: many *conversos* had become rich and powerful under the patronage of the crown, being appointed as tax farmers and ministers of the government. In the 1440s there were anti-*converso* riots in Toledo; in 1449 in Cuidad Real and again in 1464, 1467 and 1474. The problem was complex because many *conversos* 'were indeed secret Jews'.[236] Blasphemous rituals were ascribed to them such as stealing and desecrating the consecrated host: 'Again, we see fear of the Jew, especially in his concealed form as a *converso*, fomenting disorder, dissent and doubt in society'.[237]

---

235   John Coulson (ed.), *The Saints. A Concise Biographical Dictionary,* p 443

236   Paul Johnson, *A History of the Jews*, p. 225

237   *Ibid.*, p. 226

The two monarchs, Ferdinand and Isabella, 'were never personally anti-Semitic...' Ferdinand's personal physician was a Jew, and both he and Isabella 'continued to have Jewish doctors and financiers as their closest collaborators....' The agitation against the Jews and *conversos* came from the municipalities, and here 'the interventions of the crown in local politics presents an impressive picture of the monarch[y?] protecting its Jews.' [238] However, they had first to deal with the social tensions caused by the enmity that existed between Christians and Jews, Christians and *conversos,* and Jews and *conversos* whom they considered apostates. There was also the fear of 'Judaizing' Jews luring Catholics away from their religion. Therefore in 1478 Ferdinand and Isabella asked Pope Sixtus IV for a bull establishing an inquisition in Spain. Sixtus reluctantly complied, proposing caveats which Ferdinand ignored. In 1483 a Council was established to administer this Inquisition, with the queen's confessor, Tomás de Torquemada, as its president.

Already, attempts had been made to ensure that Jews and Christians were segregated in the municipalities; and Jews were now expelled from selected cities in Andalusia – among them Seville, Cordoba and Cadiz. 'It is possible that the expulsions were in part motivated by fear of Jewish collaboration with the Muslim kingdom of Granada, then under attack by Ferdinand's forces...' [239] An army of 80,000 led by the grandees of church and state – among them Cardinal Mendoza, the Archbishop of Toledo, 'a coat of mail over his surplice'[240] – had assembled at Santa Fé for the final act of the *Reconquista* – the taking of Granada. Cut off from all supplies, with no prospect of relief from North Africa, the outcome was not in doubt. In January, 1492, the long siege finally came to an end: the emir Muhammad XII of Granada, known as King Boabdil, capitulated and handed over the keys to his magnificent palace, the *Alhambra.*

Prior to the surrender, Ferdinand and Isabella had agreed that the Muslim inhabitants of Granada would be free to leave the city unmolested. King Boabdil was to be granted a small principality in the as yet unconquered Alpujarras mountains, and there were to be no forced conversions. However, elated by what seemed a signal of divine favour, and upon the insistent advice of Torquemada, Ferdinand and Isabella changed their minds. On 31 March, they issued an edict giving all Jews under their jurisdiction the choice of

---

238   Henry Kamen, *The Spanish Inquisition. An Historical Revision.* p. 16
239   *Ibid.* p. 19
240   Hugh Thomas, *Op. Cit.* p. 21

converting to Catholicism or leaving their realms. They were to make their choice by the 31 July.

The expulsion of Jews from Christian countries was not a novelty. Usury – the lending of money for interest – was condemned in the Bible as a form of exploitation of the poor. It was therefore considered sinful for Christians to charge interest to Christians, and by Jews to Jews, but not for Christians to borrow money at interest from Jews. Excluded from most other ways of earning their living by both Christian laws and their own regulations on defilement, the Jews took to money-lending and prospered. Their wealth attracted the cupidity of the perpetually insolvent monarchs. As direct subjects of the Christian monarchs, Jews could be taxed without the sanction of parliaments or estates general. Charging high rates of interest, the money-lenders were resented by their creditors: there were riots and pogroms, notably the massacre in England of March, 1190 – in fact not a massacre but the self-immolation of Jews taking refuge in the keep of the king's fortress in York, Clifford's Tower – an echo of the mass suicide at Masada at the end of the Jewish War in 74 AD.[241]

By and large, Jews were protected by the Christian monarchs as a source of revenue, but in due course throughout Europe expulsion accompanied by expropriation of their property proved both popular and lucrative. Jews had been expelled from England and Gascony by Edward III in 1294; from France by King Philip Augustus in 1182, and again by Louis IX in 1254, by Philip IV in 1306, by Charles V in 1322, and Charles VI in 1394; from the Kingdom of Naples in 1293, Hungary in 1360; and in the fifteenth century from the Italian duchies of Parma and Milan; the duchies of Austria, Upper Bavaria, Passau, and Ravenna.

Thus the expulsion of Jews from Christian states was not without precedent: however, the Jewish communities in these cities and principalities, as in the kingdoms of England and France, had been small, whereas in Spain there were around 200,000 Jews who for centuries had been integrated into the economy if not the society of the different kingdoms. Estimates of those who chose to leave range from 60,000 to 80,000, although the Spanish historian Henry Kamen believes that 'the Jews of Spain on the eve of the expulsion in 1492 numbered just over eight thousand souls, a far cry from the totals

---

241   See R.B. Dobson, *The Jews of Medieval York and the Massacre of March 1190*.

offered by their own leaders or by most subsequent scholars'.[242] It would seem that Ferdinand and Isabella expected most Jews to convert: their edict 'did not seek to expel a people but to eliminate a religion'.

Certainly, Ferdinand and Isabella and their advisers did not anticipate that the expulsion 'would be a traumatic experience that left its impact for centuries in the western mind.'[243] Forced conversions had been consistently forbidden by the popes in Rome, but with their property and skills their only livelihood, around half the Jews in Spain were effectively coerced into the Catholic religion, while around a third of the 9,000 Jews in Aragon chose to emigrate. In 1496, Portugal enacted the same policy towards the Jews as Castile and Aragon. Those Jews who left endured great suffering, and a number eventually decided to return and convert. The majority, to be known as Sephardic Jews as opposed to the Ashkenazi Jews of Central and Eastern Europe, either remained in north Africa, moved to the Ottoman Empire, or settled in tolerant Christian states: paradoxically, they were given refuge by the popes in Rome, the papal states and that papal enclave attached to Avignon, the *Comtat Venaissin*.

Far larger than the number of Jews in the kingdom of Castile after the fall of Granada was that of Muslims who had been assured that they could continue to practise their religion unmolested. King Boabdil, as we have seen, was given his own small principality in the mountains of Las Alpujarras, but after the comfort and grandeur of the Alhambra, he found it insufferable and in October, 1493, he moved to Morocco where he lived for another forty years.

The primate of Spain, Cardinal Archbishop Pedro Gonzalez de Mendoza, who had fought in the siege of Granada – a Spanish grandee who as a bishop had fathered two sons by one mistress and a third by another – died on 11 January, 1495. He was succeeded by Cardinal Francisco Jiménez de Cisneros, a prelate of quite a different kind – an ascetic who had tried to escape worldly entanglements by becoming a Franciscan friar, living virtually as a hermit, sleeping on the floor, wearing a hair-shirt under his habit and subjecting himself to rigorous fasts.

The new archbishop's rigour had appealed to Queen Isabella who had made him her confessor; and on the death of Cardinal Mendoza, put him

---

242   Kamen, *Op. Cit.*, p. 23
243   Kamen, *Op. Cit.*, p. 22

forward for the see of Toledo. Cisneros was horrified; he fled from the court but was brought back by Isabella's retainers, and accepted only after being commanded to do so by the pope. He immediately embarked upon the reform of his order, the Franciscans: his insistence upon celibacy led a number of friars to flee to north Africa with their concubines and convert to Islam. He was to found the Complutense University in Madrid, and commission the first printed polyglot edition of the Bible, but more immediately he directed his religious zeal on the many followers of Muhammad remaining in Castile.

Ignoring the assurances made by Ferdinand and Isabella prior to the surrender of Granada, Cisneros ordered mass conversions and the burning of Islamic manuscripts. The Muslims rebelled and were violently suppressed. Again, in breach of the Alhambra Decree, they were now offered the same choice as the Jews: conversion, execution or exile. Most were too poor to abandon the source of their livelihood as peasants or artisans, and accepted baptism. This new and large group of converts were known as *Moriscos*.

Three months or so after the fall of Granada, on 17 April, 1492, with their peripatetic court still at Santa Fé, Ferdinand and Isabella signed an agreement with a middle-aged Genoese mariner, Christopher Columbus, known as the *Capitulaciones*. Under its terms, the monarchs would approve and largely finance an expedition to the west across the unexplored ocean in search of a new route to the Indies. For *los reyes Católicos* it was essentially a commercial venture . They could not have foreseen that it would vastly enlarge the size of Christendom, and bring many million souls into the Catholic Church.

49.   The Renaissance Popes

When Ferdinand's father, King Alfonso of Aragon, had entered into secret negotiations with Isabella of Castile for her marriage to his son Ferdinand in 1469, he had come up against the problem of consanguinity: Isabella and Ferdinand were second cousins and the marriage of a couple so closely related was forbidden by the Church's canon law. The pope could grant a dispensation, and an application was made to Pope Pius II, but it was slow in coming. The Cardinal Archbishop of Valencia, Rodrigo Borgia, as a favour to King Alfonso, declared that the dispensation had been granted and so the wedding could go ahead.

Rodrigo Borgia was the nephew of Pope Callistus III, and had been made a cardinal by his uncle at the age of twenty-five. He was a man of great ability and considerable charm, with an undisguised weakness for women. One of his uncle's successors, Pope Sixtus, wrote to rebuke the young cardinal for attending an orgy in Siena to which 'the husbands, fathers, brothers and kinsmen of the young women were not admitted'. 'We have heard that the most licentious dances were indulged in, none of the allurements of love were lacking and you conducted yourself in a wholly worldly manner. Shame forbids mention of all that took place. [244]

Having been made vice-Chancellor of the Church by his uncle, Rodrigo Borgia had by the time of the conclave in 1492 amassed a vast fortune which he used to bribe a majority of the cardinals to choose him as pope: this sin of simony – paying for a benefice – was nothing new, but never before had the papacy been so openly auctioned for such large sums of money. Having achieved his objective – the papacy – and taking the name Alexander, he proceeded to endear himself to the Romans with lavish entertainments and celebrations.

At the time of his accession Alexander VI had eight children by a number of different women, but it was the fortunes of the four born to his self-effacing mistress of twenty-five years standing, Vannozza de' Cattanei, who came to obsess him – Cesare, Giovanni, Lucrezia and Joffré. Vannozza de' Catenei had been dropped in 1486, and a year or two later replaced by the sixteen-year-old Guilia Farnese – brought to Rome as the bride for the son of Madonna Adriana, Rodrigo's cousin and life-long friend. The marriage went ahead but Guilia became Borgia's *maitresse en titre* who 'sparkled in the foreground of his life'.[245]

Alexander started his reign with good intentions – reform of the Church and a crusade against the Turks – but was soon distracted by his pursuit of carnal pleasures and dynastic ambitions. Like Boniface VIII before him, he planned to establish principalities for his children, not seized from existing families such as the Colonnas but from the papal states. Advantageous marriages were arranged for his children: 'Within a year of his election, Alexander had linked his family to the three dominant houses of Italy and Spain.'[246] He settled the duchy of Benevento as well as that of Gandia on his

---

244   Quoted in E.R.Chamberlin, *Op. Cit.*, p. 161

245   *Op. Cit.*, p. 176

246   *Op. Cit.* p. 179

son Giovanni, but in 1497 Giovanni went absent late at night with only a groom: his body was later dragged from the River Tiber with its throat cut and a number of lacerations – a victim possibly of a jealous husband, or his ambitious brother.

Cesare now became the heir to his father's ambitions. He was dispensed of his vows as a cleric and transformed from a cardinal archbishop to a secular prince. Both he and his father envisaged the expropriation by the Borgias of the entire papal state that straddled central Italy, and to further this ambition they made alliances with both France and Spain, thereby bringing French armies into the Italian peninsula.

Despite his preoccupation with establishing a dynasty, Alexander was drawn into the wider affairs of the Church and the world. In 1494, in the Treaty of Tordesillas, he drew up a line a hundred leagues[247] west of the Cape Verde Islands dividing the New World between the Spanish and the Portuguese – the latter having penetrated far down the coast of Africa decades before the discoveries of Columbus, and taken possession of the Madeira islands and the Azores. He also excommunicated Savonarola, a troublesome friar whose preaching had aroused a penitential hysteria in Florence, leading to the surrender and public burning of adornments by both men and women – a 'bonfire of the vanities' . Penitence was one thing: heresy another. After calling for a Council to depose the debauched pontiff, Savonarola was arrested, tortured and hanged.

The Florentine author, Niccolo Machiavelli, is said to have modelled his exemplary ruler in his *The Prince* on Cesare Borgia – ruthless, cynical, amoral. At first Machiavelli's esteem seemed merited as Cesare took the cities which resisted his rule – his campaigns paid for by the sale of cardinal's hats by his father, and the pious contributions of the pilgrims who flocked to Rome for the jubilee year of 1500. Sustaining the ambitions of her father and brother was the enigmatic figure of Lucrezia Borgia. Rumours spread after the pope's death of an incestuous relationship between father and daughter are now considered spurious; but she was at her father's side when he judged a copulating competition between prostitutes and palace servants; and she watched from a balcony in the Vatican palace while Cesare shot unarmed criminals in the courtyard below.

---

247   Five hundred and fifty kilometers or 345 miles

Alexander VI, Cesare Borgia and a Cardinal Corneto all fell ill after dining together in the summer of 1503 – possibly after accidentally ingesting arsenic intended for the Cardinal alone. Cesare recovered; his father did not, and his ambitions for his family died with him.

After a reign of only a few months, Alexander's successor, Pius III, was succeeded by Alexander's implacable enemy, Giuliano della Rovere, who took the name Julius II. Ruthless, violent, sensual – Julius became known known as *il papa terribile* – the awesome pope. Though as a cardinal he had fathered three daughters, his ambitions were not to form fiefs for his family, but to recover from the Borgias the cities and territories alienated from the papal states. In this he succeeded. Cesare Borgia fled to Spain and three years after the death of his father was killed fighting as a mercenary. The French, brought into Italy by the Borgias, were driven out by Pope Julius. He himself led his army into battle wearing full armour, and was later esteemed as the liberator of Italy from foreign domination. More a soldier than a priest, he nonetheless fulfilled his role as supreme pontiff, banning simony in the election of popes, establishing the first bishoprics in South America, and granting a dispensation to prince Henry of England to marry Catherine of Aragon, the wife of his deceased older brother Arthur.

Julius II, the warrior pope, was also a great patron of the arts – encouraging and patronising artists, in particular Raphael, Michelangelo and Bramante. The Renaissance, started in Florence around 1400, had spread to Rome by the middle of the century – promoted in particular by the scholarly, patient and politically adroit pope, Nicholas V (1447-1455), who had enjoyed the company of humanists and scholars, and was a passionate bibliophile, spending large sums on classical manuscripts which formed the basis of the Vatican Library. To adorn the churches he built or restored, he employed artists such as Fra Angelico and Benozzo Gozzoli.

Subsequent popes followed Nicholas's example, appropriating this revival of a pagan culture for the greater glory of the Church. However, the rediscovery of the authors of antiquity had its dangers: the 'western mind', restricted for so long to the study of Scripture and the early Church Fathers, now came to revere the work of philosophers who had known nothing of Jesus Christ. 'The new culture became a fashion….The worship of ancient Rome permeated the higher strata of society. Scholarly snobs laced their letters and conversation and even their prayers with classical allusions: God again became Jupiter, Christ was transformed into Apollo, saints into gods, nuns into vestal virgins.'[248] Some scholars, among them the pre-eminent intellectual of the period, Erasmus of Rotterdam, did not succumb to this craze for the pre-Christian past but rather satirised it and, though well aware of the depth of corruption among popes and prelates, remained loyal to the Church.

The city of Rome itself, so frequently destroyed, had buildings from every period of its history. A domed pagan temple, the Pantheon, built during the reign of the emperor Hadrian, was consecrated as a church in the seventh century and remained standing. So too the great barn-like basilicas built by the Emperor Constantine – among them the city's cathedral, St. John Lateran; St. Mary Major, and the basilica built over the tomb of St. Peter on the Vatican Hill. The focus of pilgrims from all over Europe, St. Peter's too had been commissioned by Constantine, and had a similar structure to St. John Lateran.

During the Great Schism, St. Peter's had fallen into disrepair, and it was Nicholas V who first proposed not just restoring the basilica but replacing it altogether. He did not live long enough to proceed with his plans, but they were taken up by *il papa terribile*, Julius II. A competition held to decide upon an architect was won by Donato Bramante, and the foundation stone was laid in 1506. After Bramante's death, he was replaced by Raphael; after him came Antonio da Sangallo; and after him, during the reign of Pope Paul III, Michelangelo. Michelangelo's design for the dome was influenced by that of the Pantheon and also by Brunelleschi's dome in Florence: it was not completed until 1590, and remains the tallest in the world. Around the inside of the dome, written in letters 1.4 metres high, were the words addressed by Jesus of Nazareth to the Apostle Peter. *Tu es Petrus et Super Hanc Petram Aedificabo Ecclesiam Meam. Tibi dabo claves regni Caelorum.* You are Peter and on this rock I will build my church. I will give you the keys to the kingdom of heaven.

The construction of the new basilica over the tomb of the Apostle Peter, the crowning glory of the visible Church, was to lead to a fissure in the faith itself. The project incurred immense costs and Pope Julius, practical and frugal though he was, also had to pay for the mercenaries who fought his many wars, and for the splendours appropriate for a pope. His sensual and extravagant successor, Giovanni de Medici, Leo X, decided to raise money for the re-building through the sale of indulgences – viz. scrips that assured the

---

248   *Op. Cit.* p. 164

purchaser that, through the exercise of the power given by Jesus to Peter, the pope spared a sinner the punishment in purgatory for his or her sins. The sale of indulgences had appealed to would-be crusaders who dared not absent themselves for any length of time from their domains: they were assured of the same spiritual benefits if they paid for others to go in their place.

Subsequently the concept of an indulgence had been extended by popes to raise funds for other projects – in particular, their own wars against Christian princes. By the sixteenth century, 'Raising donations for Church projects by dispensing spiritual blessings was a long-established practice, and few people questioned it.'[249] In the Archdiocese of Magdeburg, the Archbishop Albert von Brandenburg, the twenty-three-year-old son of the Elector of Brandenburg, reached an agreement with Pope Leo X that he should keep half the proceeds of the sale of indulgences in his diocese to pay back to the Fugger Bank in Augsburg money he had borrowed to buy his appointment to another archdiocese, that of Mainz. An archbishop of Mainz was one of the seven Electors of the Holy Roman Emperor, and therefore eligible for substantial bribes when it came to an election. The young archbishop had appointed a Dominican friar, Johann Tetzel, to market the new indulgence.

Tetzel was an experienced salesman of indulgences – he had sold the Jubilee indulgences for Pope Leo X – and like salesmen throughout history, larded his product with exaggerated claims. An indulgence could be bought, not just to save the purchaser from punishment due for his sins, but a deceased member of his family: 'he even set the promise to a German rhyme which roughly translates as 'Place your penny on the drum/ The pearly gates open, and in strolls mum.'[250]

Devout Catholics were appalled that the faithful could be misled in this way, among them an Augustinian friar, professor of Theology at the University of Wittenberg in Saxony, Martin Luther. Luther denounced the sale of indulgences in his lectures and sermons; and on 31 October, 1517, published ninety-five questions he wanted to be considered in an academic disputation. It was later claimed that he nailed these to the door of Wittenberg Cathedral, but 'much is uncertain in the anecdotes of these tumultuous years, and not even the doors themselves can bear witness, having been destroyed in a fire in 1760.' [251]

249   Eamon Duffy, *Op. Cit.* p. 200

250   *Ibid.* p. 200

251   Diarmaid MacCulloch, *Reformation. Europe's House Divided, 1490-1700*, p. 123

50.   The Netherlands on the eve of the Reformation

Living alongside the corrupt and avaricious churchmen in the fifteenth
century, there were, particularly in Poland and Hungary, men engaged in the
heroic defence of Christendom against the advancing Muslim Ottomans, and
also throughout Christendom men and women who devoted their lives to
prayer, to preaching, and to care of the poor and the sick. In the prosperous and
peaceable Netherlands[252] were to be found centres of spiritual regeneration,
though not in the quondam centres of devotion and spirituality, the great
Benedictine and Cistercian monasteries. Monasticism in Western Europe
had become 'spiritually weak, shackled both by its roots in landed wealth
and by its close dependence upon monarchs and nobles through the system
of commendam'[253] whereby a layman was appointed to a monastic office as a
protector and caretaker during an abbatial inter-regnum, enjoying its income
-originally a temporary measure but in due course becoming permanent. It
was used by popes and later by kings to reward their retainers. By a concordat
of 1517, the rights to all abbatial appointments in France were given by Pope
Leo X to King Francis I.

There remained sufficient well-endowed posts for the clergy, and a career
in the Church was the obvious choice for Geert Groote, the precocious
son of a civil servant in the city of Deventer in the episcopal principality
of Utrecht in the Netherlands. Groote studied first at Aachen and then at
Paris, graduating in 1358 at the age of fifteen. He taught in Deventer, then
Cologne, accumulating stipends that enabled him to lead a comfortable,
even luxurious life. But in 1374, he had a change of heart. He abandoned all
comforts and luxuries, turned his family home in Deventer into a refuge for
destitute women and, after three years living as a Carthusian monk, set out
on a mission to denounce avarice and concubinage among the clergy, and
preach repentance to the people of Utrecht. Influenced by the mystic prior of
a community of Augustinian canons, John Ruysbroeck, he and his followers
founded a new religious community following the Augustinian rule – the
Brethren of the Common Life.

---

252   The Netherlands, or Low Countries, consisted of a number of small states – the
county of Flanders, the episcopal bishoprics of Utrecht and Liege, as well as Holland,
Hainault, Brabant, Friesland, Zealand, Picardy, Guelders and Zutphen. In the course of
the fifteenth century they came under the rule of the Dukes of Burgundy.

253   David Knowles, *Op. Cit.*, p. 142

In 1384, the plague came to Deventer. Groote nursed the victims and caught the disease, dying that year aged 44. His principal disciple, Florens Radewyns, continued his work: in the course of the fifteenth century, more than a hundred communities were established throughout the Netherlands, Lower Saxony and Westphalia; and the movement, known as the *Devotio Moderna*, led to the reform of existing monastic foundations. Two brothers, the sons of a blacksmith and school-teacher from Kempen, after coming across followers of the *Devotio Moderna* in Deventer, entered the Brethren of the Common Life in the monastery of Mount Saint Agnes in Zwolle. The older, Johann, would become prior, the younger, Thomas, world-famous as the author of 'perhaps the finest expression of a renovated piety, based upon communal living and prayer',[254] *The Imitation of Christ*.

Thomas à Kempis (Thomas from Kempen) was a monk and Catholic priest but, while *The Imitation of Christ* became the handbook for the attainment of holiness of his co-religionists such as Thomas More, Ignatius Loyola and Francis Xavier, it was to be esteemed equally by non-Catholic Christians such as Samuel Johnson, John Wesley and General Gordon, going into many editions, and published in many translations from the Latin, selling more copies than any other work of Christian literature apart from the Bible itself.

The Imitation of Christ was addressed to Thomas's fellow religious and, while many of its precepts applied equally to the laity, some – for example the advice to eschew all particular affection for one's fellow human beings – were not appropriate for a married couple. However, for both the clergy and laity, *The Imitation of Christ* made clear, life's purpose is to know God through the contemplation of Christ. This knowledge came from the Grace of God, and the Grace of God from self-denial. At times Thomas seems to suggest a two-way valve which, when open to one's appetites, ambitions and desires is closed to God, and when prized open by asceticism and self-denial enables the Grace of God to pour into the soul.

The power of Thomas's writing comes from its simplicity: the path to sanctity may be hard but it is straight-forward. He mistrusted theology: 'Of what use is it to discourse learnedly on the Trinity, if you lack humility and therefore displease the Trinity? Lofty words do not make a man just or holy, but a good life makes him dear to God... If you knew the whole bible by heart, and all the teachings of the philosophers, how would this help you

---

254   Peter Ackroyd, *The Life of Thomas More*, p. 98

without the grace and love of God?'[255] Yet Thomas, who in his early years in the monastery of St. Agnes worked as a copyist, knew the Bible inside out, and he was familiar with the works of the philosophers of antiquity; but while 'true learning is good in itself and ordained by God, a good conscience and a holy life is always to be preferred'. [256]

The fourth and last part of *The Imitation of Christ* is an encomium on the Eucharist – 'A devout exhortation to Holy Communion' – 'which does far more than encourage the faithful to regular and devout Communion.. but shows this sacred rite to be the central sun around which all the worship and sacraments of the Church revolve.' 'I acknowledge my need for two things – food and light. You have therefore given me in my weakness Your sacred Body as the refreshment of my soul and body, and have set Your Word as a light for my feet. Without these two I cannot rightly live.' The nature of the Eucharist would become one of the most significant differences between the Catholic Church and the Reformers: *The Imitation of Christ* warns against 'curious and unprofitable inquiries' into the nature of Christ's presence in the Sacrament. 'God can do more than man can comprehend.' [257]

In the next generation, an author from the same region, Erasmus Gerritszoon, born in Rotterdam and so known to history as Erasmus of Rotterdam, achieved an even greater renown than Thomas á Kempis. The son of a priest and a doctor's daughter, Erasmus, like Thomas, was educated in the Dutch town of Deventer – possibly in the school run by the Brethren of the Common Life, or more probably in one directed by the celebrated humanist, Hegius. His parents died when he was still an adolescent, and he was persuaded by his guardians to become a monk. He had no vocation, and loathed the monastic life, but was able to pursue his studies of the classics of antiquity. His fluency in Latin led the Bishop of Cambrai to employ him as his secretary, and later to send him to Paris to complete his studies. He was ordained a priest, but here again he had no true vocation, refusing ecclesiastical appointments which might have brought him an income, and instead leading a life of an independent, peripatetic scholar: 'Erasmus was the first, and for long the only, author who could live by his pen'.[258]

---

255   Thomas á Kempis, *The Imitation of Christ*, Translated by Leo Sherley-Price, p. 27

256   *Ibid.*, p. 31

257   *Ibid.*, p. 18

258   G.R. Elton: *Europe from Renaissance to Reformation*, p.249

Between 1498-1499 Erasmus visited England, complaining about the food and the cold weather, but, conversing in Latin, forming lifelong friendships with English humanists – John Fisher, a priest and scholar; John Colet, a cleric and educationist; Thomas Linacre, the king's physician; and Thomas More, a scholar and lawyer. He then pursued his study of Greek in Paris but already he was a celebrity, courted by kings, princes and advocates of the 'new learning' throughout Europe. On a visit to Italy, he was lionised by humanist scholars and made a Doctor of Divinity in Turin: 'It must never be forgotten that the use of Latin and the awareness of a common Christian purpose did more to unite these scholars and reformers than their mother tongues or places of origin could ever achieve in dividing them.'[259]

Now proficient in Greek as well as Latin, Erasmus embarked upon a revised translation of the New Testament, mixing and matching the Greek in which the Gospels and Epistles had been written with Jerome's Latin translation, the Vulgate. It was published in Basel in 1516, with a second edition in 1519: 3,300 copies were sold. It is thought that this version of the Bible was used by both Luther and Tyndale for their translations into German and English.

In 1511 Erasmus returned to England, where he was made the Lady Margaret Beaufort Professor of Divinity at Cambridge – Lady Margaret being the king Henry VIII's grandmother, a devout reader of *The Imitation of Christ,* and patron of the priest and scholar, John Fisher: Fisher was the first holder of the post she created. Staying with Thomas More on his way to Cambridge, he wrote, in the space of three days, his *Moriae Encomium (In Praise of Folly)* which satirized the absurdities of society, in particular the clergy. In the view of a Catholic commentator, Joseph Sauer, it was 'a cold-blooded attempt to discredit the Church'[260] ; yet there was no evidence that it was seen as such at the time – certainly not by the devout More. It became a best-seller throughout Europe, and was said to have amused the pope himself, Leo X, and the ferociously orthodox Cardinal Cisneros.

Erasmus's patron, the Bishop of Cambrai, was the brother of one of the two godfathers of the young Archduke Charles of Habsburg, who was raised, together with his sisters, by his aunt, Margaret of Austria, in the court at Mechelen (Malines) outside Brussels. Erasmus was appointed a councillor to the young prince with a stipend of 200 guilders, and lived close to the court

259   *Ibid.* p. 183
260   Joseph Sauer, *Catholic Encyclopaedia*

at Leuven, where he was appointed as Professor of Theology at the university in 1517.[261]

Erasmus was vain, and he enjoyed the praise of prelates and princes, but though eager for patronage he was in no one's pay. With a call for a return to the simplicity of a religion based on Scripture, and a disregard, even contempt, for peripheral accoutrements of Catholic practice – fasts, pilgrimages, relics, the veneration of saints, celibacy – Erasmus was expected by many to support Luther and the Reformers but, after at first showing some sympathy for Luther's rebellion, he later dithered and finally fell out with Luther, affirming his own orthodoxy and loyalty to the Church and the Pope.

51.   Charles V

Queen Isabella of Castile, the grandmother of Erasmus's pupil, Charles of Habsburg, died in 1504. Her husband Ferdinand remained alive for another twelve years and, to cement relations with France, married Germaine de Foix, the niece of the French King, Louis XII. She was thirty-eight years younger than he was. To Ferdinand's disappointment, the only child born of their union died in infancy. Of his five children by Isabella, the eldest two had died as teenagers. The youngest child, Catherine, had married Arthur, the eldest son of the English King Henry VII. The middle daughter, Joanna, had married Philip of Habsburg, known as 'Philip the handsome', the son of the Holy Roman Emperor, Archduke Maximilian I of Austria: Erasmus's pupil Charles was the eldest of their several children. Due to the death of her siblings, Joanna inherited the throne of Castile, and later Aragon, but suffering, it is now thought, from depression and possibly schizophrenia, she was declared insane and confined by her father, and later her son, in the Royal Palace of Tordesillas.

Philip the handsome, Joanna's husband, died in 1506 at the age of twenty-eight. Charles thus became the heir of his maternal grandparents, Ferdinand and Isabella, but also of his paternal grandparents, the Holy Roman Emperor, Archduke Maximilian, and Maximilian's deceased wife, Mary of Burgundy. Ferdinand died in 1516, and Maximilian in 1519: thus at the age of nineteen, Charles was the ruler of the largest European domain since the disintegration of the Roman empire – Austria, the Netherlands, the Burgundian territory

---

261   Wim Blockmans, *The Emperor Charles V*, p. 17

of the Franche-Comté (though not Burgundy itself which had be taken by France); Milan, Naples and Sicily; and Spain with its possessions in the Americas.

The heir to this prodigious inheritance was not himself a prodigy. He lacked his father's good looks – his physiognomy was marred by the protruding 'Habsburg jaw'. His *beau ideal* as a boy was his Burgundian grandfather, Charles the Bold, and the court at Mechelen outside Brussels was still wholly Burgundian in style. Charles himself was well trained in the martial skills of a Mediaeval knight. 'He took part in the great processions of knights, in their hunts, tournaments and feasts and spoke the same language as this cultivated elite.'[262] The greatest honour he could bestow was admission to the chivalric Order of the Knights of the Golden Fleece. He was intelligent but 'there is no trace of…cultural leanings in Charles as a young man.'[263] He was fortunate that his guardian, the regent of the Netherlands, Margaret of Austria, 'was the wisest of women and possessed one of the most astute political minds of her epoch.'[264] This led Charles to trust women, appointing his sister, Mary of Hungary, to succeed his aunt as regent of the Netherlands, and his wife, Isabella of Portugal, to govern Spain during his long absences in Germany.

With an inadequate understanding of the dangers of in-breeding, Charles became obsessed with retaining the integrity of the Habsburg dynasty by arranging marriages between first and second cousins in successive generations of his family, ignoring the Church's ban on unions within the fourth degree of kinship. In this respect, 'Charles was authoritarian, cool and manipulative with female members of the dynasty: their own feelings must always yield to the Habsburg interests as Charles saw them.'[265] Although an unquestioning and increasingly devout Catholic, he fathered a number of illegitimate children. At the age of seventeen, when he left the Netherlands to establish his rights in Spain, he made a 'Joyous Entry' to the kingdom in Valladolid and there began a liaison with his step-grandmother, the twenty-nine-year-old widow of Ferdinand, Germaine de Foix. A covered wooden bridge was built between her residence and the Royal Palace to enable the lovers to exchange visits unobserved. A daughter, Isabella, was the result who was brought up in the court: she was both Charles's daughter and aunt.

---

262   Otto von Hapsburg, *Charles V*, p. 14

263   Wim Bockmans, *Op. Cit.*.p. 170

264   Otto von Bismarck, *Op. Cit.* p. 21

265   Blockmans, *Op. Cit.* p. 122

At the siege of Tournai, in 1521, an affair with Joanna van der Gheynst, the daughter of a tapestry maker, led to the birth of another daughter, Margaret, who was raised in the court of her namesake, the regent Margaret of Austria, and was later married off by Charles at the age of fourteen to Pope Clement VII's debauched nephew, Alexander de Medici; and, when he was assassinated a year later, to the grandson of Pope Paul III, Ottavio Farnese, Duke of Parma. He was thirteen years old.

Three other daughters were born as a result of Charles' amorous liaisons with three different women and, when Charles was forty-seven, the daughter of a Dutch girdle-maker, Barbara Blomberg, bore him a son John. He was raised in the court at Valencia with Charles' legitimate son Philip, and was to gain renown as Don John of Austria, the victor of the naval battle of Lepanto. Charles' wife Isabella, bore him three children but suffered during the long periods when her husband was absent, grew depressed and died in childbirth in 1539.

When Charles' grandfather, the Archduke Maximilian of Austria and Holy Roman Emperor, died in 1519, Charles, so conscious of his honour and that of his dynasty, thought it only proper that he should succeed him as emperor, but the imperial crown was not hereditary: it remained, as it had always been, in the gift of the German princes. Since the Golden Bull of 1265 the choice had been made by seven hereditary Electors designated by the pope – three ecclesiastics, the Archbishops of Mainz, Trier and Cologne; and four secular Electors, the King of Bohemia, the Count Palatine of the Rhine, the Duke of Saxony and the Margrave of Brandenburg. Charles faced competition from both Henry VIII of England and particularly Francis 1 of France, and was obliged to borrow large sums from the Augsburg banker, Jakob Fugger, to fund inducements to the Electors to make him their choice – '850,000 Rhine guilders, 2.1 tonnes of pure silver, four times the amount of silver exported from the Americas at that time, or 62 per cent of his total annual income from the Low Countries in 1531'.[266]

On 28 June, 1519, in Frankfurt-am-Main, the seven Electors unanimously chose Charles as Emperor. Charles was in Spain when he heard the news, and he immediately returned to the Netherlands. He was crowned King of the Romans in Charlemagne's capital, Aachen, the following year, making him titular overlord of a realm stretching from the border of Denmark in the

---

266   *Ibid.,* p. 51

north to Italy in the south; and from the border with France in the west to that of Bohemia and Hungary in the east. It seemed that Latin Christendom was now finally within an inch of an united imperium under one emperor and one pope.

However, while the imperial crown brought honour, prestige, moral authority and certain judicial rights, there was no standing imperial army, no capital city, no central administration, no reliable source of income, and no means of enforcing edicts except through the rulers of the many principalities. The Swiss Confederation, at the geographical heart of the empire withdrew with impunity, ceasing to attend sessions of the imperial parliament, the Diet. The emperor's greatest judicial authority was in the 60 or so free imperial cities, but these tenaciously held on to their established rights. The emperor's means of coercion depended upon his *Hausmacht* – the resources of territories under his direct rule; but even though those were considerable, containing within them most productive silver mines, the greatest trading centres of Europe, and the increasing flow of gold from the Americas, there were unique impediments not found in other emerging nations. Communicating from one part of the empire to another was difficult: France and England lay astride both the land and northern sea routes from Spain to the Netherlands, and the Moors from north Africa harassed ships in the Mediterranean sailing from Spain to Italy. Neither France nor England might have resources equal to those of the Habsburgs but they were compact with centralised administrations and standing armies.

France was the largest and most populous individual nation in Europe. Francis I, the king of France and Charles' contemporary, did not see the combination of so many nations under one ruler as the coming to fruition of a Christian ideal, but rather as the encirclement of his realm by a rival. He decided that the weak link in the chain was Italy, and it was here that Francis sought to thwart the ambitions of the emperor. In the six wars between France and the Empire in the course of the first half of the sixteenth century, France was invariably the aggressor. The conflict over Naples and Milan led in 1525 to a battle outside Pavia in which the French were defeated and King Francis taken prisoner and taken to Spain. Peace was made in Madrid, and Francis was released, leaving his son as hostage; but once free, Francis reneged on his promises on the grounds that they had been made under duress. Charles was enraged. War was renewed.

The popes in Rome also feared encirclement of the papal states if the Habsburgs ruled in both Naples and Milan, and so mostly sided with the

French: it was only during the brief reign of Hadrian VI, Charles' one-time tutor, the Flemish Adriaan Florensz Boeyens – incidentally the last non-Italian pontiff until the 20th century – that the papacy was allied to Charles. Hadrian's successor, Clement VII, the grandson of the Medici Lorenzo the Magnificent, who had been Charles' favoured candidate in the conclave, switched to and fro between Charles and the French, fatefully joining France, Milan, Florence and Venice in the League of Cognac against the Emperor. This led to a fresh invasion by an imperial army of mercenaries – 14,000 German *Landsknechte* and 16,000 Spaniards under the Constable of Bourbon. In 1527, this army, though victorious, went unpaid. Cold and hungry, the soldiers mutinied and forced the Constable to lead them on a march on Rome. Clement VII had no money to pay their wages, and withdrew into the Castel Sant' Angelo, watching from its ramparts the sack of the Holy City – slaughter, rape and plunder equal to anything inflicted by the barbarian Visigoths in the fifth century. The destruction and debauch of the Holy City caused consternation throughout Europe, and brought to an end the period of Rome's cultural glory that had come with the Renaissance. Charles expressed regret though some scholars question whether this regret was sincere.[267]

Did Charles see the sack of Rome as God's punishment of a pope who thwarted a reform of the Church by refusing to summon a council and failing to preach a crusade, putting the interests of his own principality, the papal states, before those of Christendom itself? It was frustrating for Charles that the wars against Catholics he felt obliged to wage in Italy thwarted his ambition to lead a crusade against the Ottoman Turks. The threat was real. In 1521 the Turks took Belgrade; in 1522 they ousted the Knights Hospitaller from the island of Rhodes who then retreated with their galleys to Malta, given to them by Charles. In 1526 a Muslim army under Suleiman the Magnificent defeated the Hungarians at the battle of Mohacs: Charles' brother-in-law, King Louis of Hungary, was killed and half that Catholic country came under Ottoman control. In 1529, the Turks besieged Vienna, the capital of the Habsburg homelands but failed to take it. 'This development was a cause of constant anxiety to Charles. As Emperor, he above all had the task of defending the Christian faith, especially the Catholic Church'.[268]

The war between Christendom and Islam had been endemic since the seventh century: wholly unanticipated, and slow to be recognised as a serious

---

267   See Geoffrey Parker, *Emperor. A New Life of Charles V.*

268   *Blockmans, Op Cit.*, p. 40

threat to the Church, was Martin Luther's defiance of the Pope. Luther himself did not at first see his ninety-five theses as the opening salvos of a barrage that would divide the Catholic Church, but rather questions for academic debate. However, his penchant for pungent phrases took what he wrote beyond the tepid language of academe. 'If the pope knew the exactions of the preachers of indulgences, he would rather have the basilica of St. Peter reduced to ashes than built with the skin, flesh and bones of his sheep.'[269]

As we have seen, Charles was a Catholic but hardly a fanatic. In response to Luther's complaints, he had summoned him to appear under a safe-conduct guarantee before the imperial Diet, which met in 1521 in the German city of Worms on the upper Rhine. Luther had made his case, had been condemned and placed under the ban of the Empire. Charles honoured the safe-conduct, and Luther left Worms for Saxony where the Duke gave him refuge in the Wartburg castle at Eisenach in Thuringia. Here was a case when the character, personality and convictions of one man – Charles of Habsburg – altered the history of Europe, for there were those who thought that Luther, like Hus at the Council of Constance, should have been seized and burned or at least imprisoned. 'If Luther and Calvin had been locked up when they began to dogmatize,' said the French Cardinal Richelieu many years later, 'the State would have been spared a great deal of trouble.'[270]

But Charles, with his *beau ideal* of Burgundian knighthood, was a man of his word and honoured Luther's safe-conduct. He may also have believed that he had dealt with Luther by placing him under the ban of the Empire; but it was ignored by the Elector of Saxony. Lying low in the Wartburg castle, Luther spent his time translating Erasmus's Bible into inspired German prose.

Charles had also failed to understand the significance of that new technological invention, the printing press. It is estimated that during the five years following 1517, ten million pamphlets were printed and circulated in the German empire. And Charles got no help from the popes in Rome who remained unaware of 'the needs of the masses for a fervent religious revival.'[271] Luther was declared a heretic, but dealing with heretics was the responsibility of the secular rulers. He was Charles' problem, but Charles was off in Spain and had more pressing political problems on his plate. 'Right until the end, Charles and his advisors underestimated the seriousness of the

---

269 Quoted in Diarmaid MacCulloch, *Reformation. Europe's House Divided. 1490-1700*
270 Sainte-Beuve, *Port Royal*, quoted in R.A.Knox's *Enthusiasm*, p. 185
271 *Op. Cit.*, p. 42

religious differences and the determination of the reformers.' When he finally realised how far Luther's heresy had spread, he could only come up with brutal coercion as a means to suppress it. 'If we do not take a strong line,' he wrote to his sister Mary, 'the risk to the faith is enormous. The consequences could be so harmful that there could be no turning back, namely the estrangement of the rest of Germany from our Holy Faith.'

PART THREE

52. The Reformation

The Church founded by the followers of Jesus of Nazareth had faced divisions in the course of its rise to be the dominant religion of the western world. The Arian heresy had flourished in the fourth century and, after several centuries of increasing estrangement, the Eastern Orthodox and Western Catholic Church had finally separated with the Great Schism in 1054. However, Arianism had been successfully eradicated, and the differences in belief and practice between the eastern and western Churches were small.

What came to be called the Reformation was of a different order for Luther rejected not only the authority of the Pope but also that of Church Councils, insisting that God's word could only be found in scripture – *sola scriptura*; and that a man or woman was 'justified', in other words saved from damnation, not by good deeds but, as he claimed Saint Paul had made clear, by 'faith alone'. There was no purgatory where a soul was punished and purified, and all those prayers and Masses said for the salvation of souls were a confidence trick whereby the clergy extracted money from a gullible laity. Revering the images of Christ, his mother Mary, or the saints verged on idolatry condemned in the Old Testament. Pointless too as a means of earning salvation were pilgrimages, the veneration of relics, fasting and asceticism, or the care of the sick and the poor. God does not keep a ledger in which he enters sins in one column and good deeds in another. By his grace alone, he saves those who believe in him, and damns those who do not.

The Mass was also called into question. Luther had found no evidence in the Gospels that it was a re-enactment of Christ's sacrifice on the Cross, and rejected the Church's teaching that consecration by a priest turned bread into the flesh of Christ, and wine into his blood – what Thomas Aquinas had termed *transubstantiation* – believing instead in *consubstantiation* – a kind of infusion of the divine body and blood into the bread and wine rather than a material change: in this he differed from subsequent reformers who believed that the bread and wine remained just that.

Thanks to the printing press, pamphlets expressing Luther's revolutionary views spread rapidly throughout Europe. In the great free cities of the Holy Roman Empire, other preachers took up his ideas and added some of their own. Inspired sermons in the huge cathedrals by learned reformers convinced burgers and peasants of the truth of the new teaching. Catholic bishops were ousted and theocratic states established – in Zurich by Huldrych Zwingli; in Strasbourg by Martin Bucer; and in Geneva by John Calvin.

In 1520 Martin Luther had written a tract in vernacular German entitled 'To the Christian Nobility of the German Nation' in which he condemned the concept of a ministerial priesthood, asserting instead the 'priesthood of the people'. As the legitimate rulers of the people, the German princes were now to exercise authority over the Church. The first ruler to adopt Lutheranism as his state's religion was not in fact a king or a prince but the Grand Master of the Teutonic Order, Albert of Brandenburg, a nephew of the King of Poland, and cousin of the sovereign of the adjacent 'Royal' Prussia, the Elector of Brandenburg. Albert declared himself Duke of Prussia and his principality a secular Lutheran state. The knights took wives and were allotted estates.

The bond between Luther and the German nobility was put to the test when, partly incited by Luther's teaching, the German peasantry rebelled against their rulers. Luther himself, after an initial hesitation, supported the nobility in their brutal suppression of the revolt, publishing a tract 'Against the Murderous, Thieving Hordes of Peasants' (*Wider die Mordischen und Reubischen Rotten der Bauern*). Reassured, some major German princes converted to Lutheranism. In the Imperial Diet held in Speyer in 1529, presided over not by the Emperor Charles but by his brother the Archduke Ferdinand of Austria, it was decided that a period of relative tolerance towards Lutherans was to be abandoned. The assembled rulers were enjoined to suppress heresy in their domains. A number, among them the Elector of Saxony, the Elector of Brandenburg, the Landgrave of Hesse and the Prince of Anhalt, together with representatives of fourteen free Imperial cities, protested – giving the name Protestant to those throughout Europe who repudiated the pope and the Catholic church.

At the request of the Emperor, Charles V, a compendium of Lutheran beliefs was drawn up, largely by a colleague of Luther at Wittenberg, Philip Melanchthon. It was published in both Latin and German, and endorsed by a number of free cities and the leading Protestant princes, and presented to the Emperor at the Diet held at Augsburg in 1530. With its twenty-eight articles, it was to become the foundational document of the Lutheran religion. The twenty-third article permitted the marriage of priests: in 1525 Luther had married a Cistercian nun, Katerina von Bora, whom he had helped escape with some of her sisters from their convent at Marienthron.

During the Diet at Augsburg, the two most powerful Protestant princes – Philip of Hesse and John Frederick I of Saxony – formed an alliance named after the small town of Schmalkalden in Thuringia, which committed them to mutual support should the Habsburgs attempt to suppress Lutheranism with military force. In 1535, the states of Anhalt, Württemberg and Pomerania; and the cities of Augsburg, Frankfurt-am-Main and the Kempten joined the Schmalkaldic League. The Emperor Charles and his brother Ferdinand were unable to move against this heretical and treasonous alliance because of a more immediate threat from the Turks under Suleiman the Magnificent. Only in 1547 did Charles face and defeat the armies of the league at Mühlberg. It was an outstanding victory, but it was now too late to suppress Lutheranism by military force.

Charles recognised that he had failed. Disillusioned, between 1554 and 1558, he abdicated as monarch of his many domains – those in Italy and the Netherlands, together with Spain and its American possessions, went to his son Philip; and the Habsburg possessions in eastern Europe and the imperial crown to his brother Ferdinand. In 1557 Charles withdrew to the monastery of Yuste in Spain. Suffering acutely from gout, and sensing that his death was imminent, he slept with an empty coffin next to his bed. In 1558, he fell ill and on 21 September he died, holding the cross that his wife Queen Isabella had in her hands on her death. He had hoped to bring peace to Europe but his life had seen a succession of conflicts; and those with the Protestant princes were to lead 'to an unintended disaster that has fundamentally shaped the subsequent course of Western history in ways they could not have foreseen and which nearly all of them would have deplored'. [272]

---

272   Brad Gregory, *The Unintended Reformation*, p. 160

53. The Spread of the Reformation

The Reformation was established in different states by different means. Most peaceably, it came about when established rulers such as the Grand Master of the Teutonic Knights, Philip of Hesse and John Frederick of Saxony together with most of their nobility accepted Luther's teaching and disestablished the Catholic Church. The appropriation of the Church property was an incentive. 'Inevitably there was much cynical and greedy robbing of the Church's wealth, and not everyone can have arrived at the Reformation through idealism, but we should respect the possibility that many did.' No doubt German cities, once it was decided that 'the mass was blasphemous and chantries for the dead were a waste of money, could redeploy a good deal of Church wealth for worthy purposes: schools, hospitals, rebuilding the city walls and gates'.[273] There was also fledgling nationalism: 'German speakers in northern Europe had long despised the supposedly debauched culture and decadent habits of people south of the Alps, and resented the large sums of money which their rulers' previous deals with Rome allowed to travel south from the Empire to the papacy'.[274]

It should be remembered that many of the sovereign states within the Holy Roman Empire were in fact ruled by their Catholic Bishops who were invariably members of the German nobility. Herman von Wied, Prince Bishop of Cologne, one of the seven Electors who had chosen Charles as Emperor, and who had crowned him as King of Rome in Aachen, had at first condemned Luther's teaching but then became more sympathetic, inviting Martin Bucer and Philip Melanchthon to preach in his city. Charles respected the archbishop's piety, but thought him ignorant and a political menace. Archbishop von Wied hoped to achieve a compromise between Catholics and Protestants but, when that became unlikely, opted for a break with Rome. However, his Lutheran beliefs were not popular in Cologne. He was excommunicated by Pope Paul III and deposed, retiring in 1547 to his family estates, dying 'a declared evangelical' in 1552. This left the English Archbishop of Canterbury, Thomas Cranmer, 'the only leading archbishop in Europe to declare for the Reformation'.[275]

---

273   Diarmaid MacCulloch, *Reformation. Europe's House Divided, p. 172*

274   *Ibid.*, p. 129

275   *Ibid.* p. 271

In the episcopal principality of Münster, one hundred and fifty kilometres north of Cologne, the Prince Bishop, Franz von Waldeck, was expelled from the city by radical Protestants in 1532. The leaders were followers of a Strasbourg preacher, Melchior Hoffman, and, believing in the re-baptism of adults, were known as Anabaptists. Their beliefs went far beyond Luther's, encompassing polygamy and an abolition of social distinctions. Moderate Lutherans were banished and Anabaptists from elsewhere welcomed to this new Jerusalem, forming a police force to protect the leaders. A second baptism became compulsory, and laws were passed to punish blasphemy, swearing and adultery with death. All books other than the Bible were burned. Polygamy became compulsory: unmarried women had to accept the first man who proposed to them. One of the Millennial leaders, John Beukel, had a number of young wives and held banquets at which he distributed communion and then personally carried out executions: forty-nine women were dispatched for breaking the laws on polygamy.[276]

The rule of the Anabaptists in Münster was short-lived. The Archbishop, Franz von Waldeck, assembled an army and besieged the city. It fell on 24 June, 1535. A number of the leaders were captured, imprisoned and later tortured and executed in the market place. Their bodies were left to rot in iron cages hanging from the steeple of the church of Saint Lambert. The corpses were later removed but the cages remain to this day.

Women were abused by the Anabaptists, but elsewhere they played a significant role in the spread of the new religion. Two hundred kilometres or so from Münster was the small principality of East Friesland with its capital the port of Emden facing the Netherlands across the estuary of the Emse. On the death of its ruler in 1540, his widow, Countess Anna von Oldenberg, ruled as regent, and, like Archbishop von Wied of Cologne, set out to establish a compromise between Catholicism and Lutheranism in her small state. To this end she invited a distinguished Polish churchman, Jan Łaski, to direct her. He had been an archdeacon of the cathedral in Warsaw, but had been drawn to the evangelicals' teaching, having to leave Poland when he took a wife. Łaski came from the Polish nobility – his uncle had been primate of Poland – and also – something which enhanced his prestige in the eyes of Countess Anna – had been the patron, friend and favourite of Desiderius Erasmus when he had studied in Basel. In 1550, after two years in Emden, Łaski sailed to England

---

276   See Paul Johnson, *A History of Christianity*, p. 263

where, since the death of King Henry VIII and the accession of his son by his third wife, Jane Seymour, the boy king, Edward VI, Protestants were now welcome. He was put in charge of a large 'Strangers' Church' to cater for the Protestant refugees from the Continent. His preaching and the liturgy of this parish 'had a great influence throughout Reformed Protestantism'.[277]

The ascendancy of the Reformers in England was a paradox because Henry VIII in the early years of his reign had been an orthodox Catholic – so orthodox, indeed, that when Luther had stated that there were only two sacraments, Henry – humanistic scholar and amateur theologian – had written a refutation, *Assertio Septem Sacramentorum adversus Martin Lutherum*. It was presented to Pope Leo X with the assurance that 'there is no nation which more impugns this monster, and the heresies broached by him.'[278] Leo rewarded 'this great prince' with the title of *Fidei Defensor* – Defender of the Faith – a tribute retained by Henry's successors, and to be found imprinted on British coinage to this day.

However, this warm bond with the popes in Rome did not survive their failure to annul Henry's first marriage to Catherine of Aragon, the daughter of King Ferdinand and Isabella and therefore the aunt of the Emperor Charles V. Catherine had first married Henry's older brother Arthur when both were aged fifteen. Despite a 'bedding ceremony' after the wedding, Catherine was to insist that the marriage was never consummated. As Prince of Wales, Arthur had taken his bride to live in Ludlow Castle. Six months later, both fell ill. Catherine recovered. Arthur did not. Reluctant to undo the alliance with Spain, Arthur's father, King Henry VII, obtained an annulment from the pope to enable Catherine to marry his younger son Henry. This marriage was consummated. A daughter, Mary, was born but thereafter only stillborn babies.

Henry VIII therefore had no male heir. This troubled him for a number of reasons. The bloodshed and chaos of the Wars of the Roses remained vivid memories. The right to the throne, established by Henry Tudor after his victory at the Battle of Bosworth, could be questioned: a line of strong kings was essential to establish the dynasty. Added to this were the scruples of Henry VIII about the validity of the annulment that enabled him to marry his brother's widow. Was it not possible that the birth of a girl instead of a boy,

---

277   Diarmaid MacCulloch, *Op. Cit.* p. 258

278   Quoted in Peter Ackroyd, *The Life of Thomas More*, p. 222

and the subsequent still births, were God's punishment for flouting his law? Henry called upon theologians to advise him, and sent to Rome to have the annulment annulled. A certain urgency was added to the matter when Henry fell in love with a young woman at court, Anne Boleyn. Unlike her sister, who had been the king's mistress, Anne would only sleep with him as his wife.

On a number of previous occasions – one has only to think of Pope Eugene III's annulment of the marriage of the French king Louis VII and Eleanor of Aquitaine – popes had been prepared to annul marriages at the request of monarchs, or in this case, annul annulments. However, the Queen of England, Catherine of Aragon, was the niece of the Emperor Charles V. To rule that she was not the Queen of England; that her marriage had been invalid and her daughter Mary illegitimate, would be an insult to the Emperor. The popes prevaricated. Henry's able Chancellor, Cardinal Wolsey, used every means available to settle 'the king's great matter' but he failed. He died on his way south to be deposed and possibly executed by his exasperated master. He was replaced as Lord Chancellor by the king's friend, the lawyer and humanist scholar, Thomas More.

More, as we have seen, had been, like Jan Łaski, a close friend of Erasmus, but unlike Łaski he abhorred Lutheranism. As Lord Chancellor he vigorously pursued heretics and where he could saw to it that they were punished according to the law. His conviction that the papacy was of divine origin and the cornerstone of Christendom was shared by his friend John Fisher, the exemplary Bishop of Rochester, who was writing 'a great theological tract against Luther'. More too, on the instructions of the king, joined in the polemic, using the same crude language as Luther, 'trading text for text, and insult for insult'.[279] More thought as a lawyer: heresy was not just sinful but seditious. 'It was a form of disorder on every level. His duty to his religion and to his country came together, lending him a double strength and authority'.[280]

However that strength and authority was being progressively undermined at court. Anne Boleyn, who had been partly educated in the Netherlands, was sympathetic to Lutheranism and had the ear of the king. It was clear that, if the pope would not sanction Henry's marriage to Anne, then the Church in England must dispense with the pope. Under the guidance of a new royal minister, Thomas Cromwell, a compliant parliament proclaimed that the King was now head of the church and his marriage to Catherine of

279   Ackroyd, *Op. Cit.* p. 223
280   Ackroyd, *Op. Cit.* p. 291

Aragon invalid. When William Warham, the Archbishop of Canterbury, who had been as assiduous as More in the pursuit of heretics, died in 1532, he was replaced by the covert Protestant Thomas Cranmer. More saw the writing on the wall and resigned as Lord Chancellor. Cranmer, who had smuggled a wife into England from the Netherlands, officiated at the marriage of Henry to Anne Boleyn. More sent his best wishes to the king but would not attend the wedding. He declined to swear the oath accepting an Act of Succession which repudiated the authority of the pope and declared Anne the legitimate queen of England. So too did a group of Carthusian monks, and John Fisher, recently made a cardinal by the pope. This was deemed treason. Both More and Fisher were executed on Tower Hill. Three Carthusians were hanged, drawn and quartered at Tyburn. Fifteen more Carthusian monks were starved to death in Newgate prison.

Cranmer and Cromwell, with the queen's connivance and under Henry's nose, promoted the evangelical cause in England and the destruction of the Catholic Church. Although Henry still thought of himself as a Catholic, there were advantages to permitting the Reform – in particular the dissolution of the monasteries which raised huge sums for the exchequer. 'There were in 1535 some 800 religious houses of all kinds and sizes in England and Wales. A few were enormously wealthy in both land and treasures; a few were below subsistence level; while the rest were comfortably off. Altogether their net income considerably exceeded the annual income of the Crown, that is, the king and his government.' [281] The largest single landowner after the Crown were the Knights of Saint John.[282]

All was over by March 1540. Little is known of the fate of the evicted monks and nuns. Diarmaid MacCulloch suggested that 'in countless monasteries and convents, the notion of Christian liberty fused with long evenings spent reading the refined sarcasm of Erasmus about monastic life to send monks and nuns joyfully out into the world to start a new Christian life, which for many meant exploring Christian liberty inside Christian marriage.'[283] This had been the case of Luther's wife, Katerina von Bora. David Knowles wrote that 'very few monks actually defected to the Reform'.[284]

---

281   David Knowles, *Op. Cit.* p. 143

282   See Michael Hodges, *The Knights Hospitaller in Great Britain in 1540.. A Survey of the Houses and Churches etc. of St. John of Jerusalem including those earlier belonging to the Knights Templar.* The Grand Priory of England.

283   MacCulloch, *Op. Cit.*, p. 154

284   David Knowles, *Op. Cit.* p. 143

An important contribution to the spread of the Reformation was the dissemination throughout the country of an English translation of the Bible by William Tyndale. Tyndale, a scholar fluent in many languages who had studied and taught at both Oxford and Cambridge, had come across Erasmus's edition of the Greek New Testament, and determined that its study and interpretation should not be reserved to the clergy, but be available to all in their own tongue – in his case, English. "'I defy the Pope, and all his laws; and if God spares my life, ere many years, I will cause the boy that driveth the plow to know more of the Scriptures than thou dost!" Finding no patron, he went to the Continent – first to Wittenberg, then Worms and finally Antwerp. He worked not only on a translation of the Bible but Protestant polemic, disputing with Thomas More in a series of pamphlets: More's *The Confutation of Tyndale's Answer* having 'the distinction of being the longest religious polemic in the English language'.[285]

Tyndale was admired by Thomas Cromwell, and might well have found a prominent place among the 'new men' in England had not 'this courteous and unworldly man…diffident on his own account' but 'fervent for the truth' written a pamphlet denouncing the annulment of Henry VIII's marriage to Catherine of Aragon. This enraged Henry who asked the Emperor Charles V to extradite Tyndale from Antwerp. At first Charles demurred, but he had no love of heretics and in 1535 Tyndale was arrested in the Netherlands, and a year later tried and condemned to be strangled at the stake – his body then burned.

There was a posthumous triumph: by the time of his death, it is thought that as many as 16,000 copies of Tyndale's Bible had been smuggled into England and, despite the king's antipathy for Tyndale, Cromwell was able to persuade him that a copy should be placed every parish in the realm. Cromwell also recruited and paid preachers to read the Bible to the largely illiterate population: 'the resulting popular enthusiasm was sufficiently noticeable for the King to take fright', persuading Parliament to pass an Act restricting the reading of the Bible to 'upper status groups in society, deemed to be less excitable'.[286]

Was the Reformation welcomed by the English people or not? The victorious Protestants would later insist that the break with Rome and all that followed

---

285   Ackroyd, *Op. Cit.* p. 299
286   MacCulloch, *Op. Cit.* p. 203

had delighted a populace that had long since resented the power and riches of the Church, and the authority exercised by the popes in Rome. The lands of the dissolved monasteries were either given or sold at knock-down prices to the king's or Cromwell's friends and clients, whose descendants thus had an interest in promoting this view of the Reformation. In the twentieth century, some historians disputed – even overturned – this 'Whig' view of sixteenth century history – notably Jack Scarisbrick in his *Henry VIII* and Eamon Duffy in *The Stripping of the Altars*. Besides the meticulous research of these revisionist historians, there is the evidence of the Pilgrimage of Grace in 1536, a popular rising in the north of England which nearly toppled Henry from his throne.

This 'rising of the commons with a leavening of gentlemen'[287] started in Louth in the Lincolnshire Wolds, but gained substance in Yorkshire and parts of Lancashire. It was provoked by the dissolution of the monasteries by agents of Thomas Cromwell – the monks evicted, their land and treasures confiscated, bells melted down, the lead torn from the roofs and stained-glass windows. The north was poorer than the south of England, and it was the monasteries that 'provided help to those in need of charitable assistance'.[288] There were general grievances such as the raising of taxes, but it was the brutal destruction of the buildings that had been part of the landscape for centuries, the callous termination of a culture and way of life, that principally inspired the revolt. The abolition of feast days, part of Cromwell's de-mystification of religious practice, was greatly resented, and so too cases where Cromwell's agents had 'stripped the precious metals from a much venerated shrine and thrown away the bones of the incumbent saint.' Henry's attack 'on the Roman Church's traditions, its wealth, its liturgies and beliefs, its monastic and other social structures, was the one thing common to all the uprising.'[289] There was no violence. The 'oath of honourable men' taken by the rebels at the instigation of one of the leaders, Robert Aske, stated that 'You shall not enter into this our Pilgrimage of Grace for the Commonwealth, but only for the love that ye do bear until Almighty God, his faith, and to the Holy Church militant.' The emblems on the pilgrims' banner were the Seven Wounds of Christ, together with the consecrated host and the chalice from the mass.

---

287   Geoffrey Moorhouse, *The Pilgrimage of Grace*, p. 86

288   *Ibid.,* p 37

289   *Ibid., Op. Cit.* p. 101

The city of York fell to the rebels, and the formidable fortress at Pontefract was surrendered without a siege. An army of between 40,000 and 50,000 marched on towards London, halting at the bridge over the River Don at Doncaster to parley with the commander of the king's greatly inferior forces, the Duke of Norfolk. Promises were made, and pardons assured. Naively, the leaders of the Pilgrimage accepted Henry's word and, while their army disbanded, 'the three leading figures of the Pilgrimage of Grace…went to London of their own volition after being summoned by the king.'[290]

It was a trap: Henry saw no reason to keep his word to traitors. The leaders were arrested and later executed – Robert Aske at Clifford's Tower in York. Arrests and cruel executions were pursued throughout the north. Eventually the only physical evidence of a once rich monastic culture were the *bare ruined choirs, where late the sweet birds sang*.[291]

54.   Jean Calvin

Along with Martin Luther, the most influential Reformer was a Frenchman from Picardy, Jean Calvin. He was born in 1509, twenty-seven years after Luther, and so belonged to a second generation of Protestant divines; and while Luther's origins were in the Saxon peasantry, Calvin's were middle-class – his father a lawyer. He was originally intended for the priesthood, but his studies were redirected to the law when his father decided that a legal practice would earn him a better living. Thanks to the patronage of a rich family, the de Montmors, he was able to study Latin and philosophy, first in Paris, later in Orleans where he learned Greek, and later Hebrew – essential for a study of Scripture. In 1529 he underwent a spiritual crisis, promising God that to avert eternal damnation he would 'betake myself to your way, condemning my past life, not without groans and tears…'

Calvin gained his degree in Law in 1532, taught for a time at Orleans, and published his first book – an academic treatise on Seneca. It was a time of turmoil in French universities with many academics opting for evangelical reforms while the king, Francis I, growing increasingly alarmed at the spread of heresy, took harsh measures to suppress it. In 1533, Calvin moved to the Collège Royale in Paris but, associated with its reforming rector, Nicholas

---

290   *Ibid.c, Ibid.* p. 196

291   William Shakespeare, *Sonnet LXXIII*

Cop, fled to Basel, Strasbourg and finally Geneva. In 1536, he published his *Institutes of the Christian Religion*, a first edition in Latin, later editions translated into French. Just as the *Augsburg Confession* defined Luther's Evangelical Protestantism that became the religion of swathes of northern Germany and Scandinavia, so the *Institutes* expressed the beliefs of the more austere Reformed religion adopted by French Protestants, and also the followers of John Knox in Scotland.

When Calvin settled in Geneva, its 15,000 inhabitants were divided on matters of faith. Neither Catholics nor Protestants envisaged a mutual tolerance: in a letter addressed to Francis I, the king of France, Calvin had argued not for toleration but the extinction of the Catholic religion. Geneva had been ruled by its bishop with its feudal overlord the Counts of Savoy. The bishop had fled the city in 1519; it had proclaimed its independence from Savoy in 1530, and the Catholic party was finally defeated in 1534. Catholic altars were desecrated, sacred statues and images destroyed, priests imprisoned, and citizens fined if they did not attend the sermons of the Reformers.

There were ructions: at one time, Calvin had to leave Geneva and take refuge in Strasbourg. He returned in 1541, and thereafter his ascendancy was assured. Religious enthusiasts flocked to Geneva 'in a manner strikingly reminiscent of Münster in its Anabaptist days. Soon all the ministers in the city were immigrants, mostly French: between the 1540 and 1594, the Genevan ministry did not include a single native Genevan'.[292] The city's Council declared that Calvin's *Institutes* were a 'holy doctrine which no man might speak against'. A dissident, Jean Gouet, was imprisoned, tortured and executed in 1547. 'Within five years fifty-eight sentences of death and seventy-six of exile, besides numerous committals of the most eminent citizens to prison, took place in Geneva.'

Calvin's ascendancy stemmed from his learning, his determination and 'his extraordinary abilities as a preacher'.[293] In appearance he is described as 'of medium height with bent shoulders, piercing eyes, auburn hair and a large forehead'. His sermons were as persuasive as Luther's but in a wholly different style – the German earthy, even coarse; the Frenchman classical, logical, lucid. While in Geneva, he preached over two thousand sermons, each

---

292   MacCulloch, *Op. Cit.* p. 239
293   *Ibid.* p. 246

without notes and lasting at least an hour. Of his extensive correspondence, 4271 letters survive. He was briefly married to a widow, Idelette Stordeur de Bure. She bore a son who died soon after his birth, followed by his mother Idelette in 1549. Calvin did not marry again, and imposed an austere regimen on the inhabitants of Geneva. Voltaire would later claim that 'for more than two hundred years there was not a single musical instrument allowed in the city of Geneva'. Certainly dancing was banned. There was opposition but dissidents were either exiled, imprisoned or, in the case of Jacques Gruet, arrested for sedition, tortured and condemned to death.

Calvin had not instigated but he had approved the execution of Gruet. In the more notorious case of Michael Servetus, which scandalized Voltaire and later Edward Gibbon, Calvin was the prime mover. Servetus was a Spanish scientist, physician and theologian who like the Anabaptists questioned infant baptism but more radically denied that God was Father, Son and Holy Spirit: God was one. His publication of a pamphlet denying the Trinity had led to his expulsion from both Basel and Strasbourg. He had corresponded with Calvin, and unwisely had sent him a copy of the *Institutes* with marginal notes pointing out his errors. Calvin was therefore ill-disposed towards Servetus when, fleeing from the Inquisition in Lyon where he had been living under an assumed name, he decided to visit Calvin in Geneva on his way to Italy. Calvin was displeased. 'If he comes here,' he said, 'and I have any authority, I will never let him leave the place alive.' On his arrival in Geneva, Servetus was arrested at the instigation of Calvin's secretary, charged with heresy and burned at the stake. Calvin's fellow divines, Bullinger and Melanchton, approved.

Calvin's teaching was spread throughout Europe by missionaries emanating from Geneva. 'Between 1565 and 1600, nearly half of all Calvin's publications were English, German or Dutch translations from the original Latin and French.[294] Calvin's many correspondents included the young Protestant king of England, Edward VI, and he contributed to the revision of Cranmer's *Book of Common Prayer*. The Scottish divine, John Knox, after ministering to his compatriots in Geneva, brought Calvinism to Scotland. The English Puritans, the Scots-Irish Ulstermen, and the pilgrims on the *Mayflower* were all the progeny of Jean Calvin, and the imprint of the tastes and temperament of this Frenchman from Poitou – his dislike of theatres, dancing, and celebrations such as Christmas – have left their imprint on societies to this day.

---

294   MacCulloch, *Op. Cit.*, p. 318

55.   The French Wars of Religion

Calvin's influence was greatest in his native France. His sermons and treatises were dispatched from the printing presses of Geneva to every corner of France and to the French-speaking cantons of Switzerland. There were seventy-seven editions of forty-six titles of his works before 1551: he was one of the most widely read contemporary authors in French. His *Institutes* – 'rational, modern in method but traditional in its grounding in scripture...a towering intellectual achievement, placing him among the supreme doctors of the church'[295] – was accepted as the formulation of the beliefs of all French Protestants who for reasons that are obscure became known as Huguenots.[296]

As elsewhere in Europe, there were a number of reasons for dissatisfaction with the Catholic religion. The Church served the state. At the Concordat of Bologna in 1516, as we have seen, Leo X had conceded to Francis I the right to appoint to all ecclesiastical benefices: as a result, 93 of the 129 bishops were either princes of the blood or from the *noblesse de d'épée*. Of the eighty bishops appointed by Francis's successor, Henry II, only three had degrees in theology, and only 15 had studied canon law. Few resided in their diocese: most used their revenues for grandiose living, contrasting poorly with the austere evangelical missionaries from Geneva. 'There is at the heart of the matter: the failure of the institutional church to match the spirit of the hour.'[297]

Again, as elsewhere in Europe, respect for the Church's teaching had been undermined by the spread of humanism among scholars and theologians. Lefèvre d'Étaples, an esteemed teacher, turned to biblical exegesis in his old age: the preface to his Latin commentary on the Gospels with its denigration of the Mass, insistence on *sola scriptura*, and assertion of justification through faith alone came to be regarded as the founding manifesto of the Reformation in France. It appalled the orthodox theologians of the Sorbonne who wanted him to be tried as a heretic, but he was admired by Francis and protected by the king's sister Margaret, queen of the small principality in the Pyrenees, Navarre.

It was when Francis, after his defeat at the Battle of Pavia, was taken as a prisoner of war to Madrid, that his wife Claude, acting as regent, took stronger measures against the spread of heresy – leading Lefèvre and other dissidents

---

295   Geoffrey Treasure, *The Huguenots*, p. 82

296   The name probably derives from the word '*eyguenots*', 'confederates' in the *patois* of Geneva. The confederates those who favoured of an alliance with other Protestant cities in Switzerland rather than their notional overlord, the King of Savoy.

297   *Ibid.*, p. 52

to flee from France – Lefèvre to Strasbourg, William Farel to Zurich and eventually Geneva, and others to the safe haven of Navarre. When Francis was released and returned to France, the persecution eased but then came 'the affair of the placards' when on 18 October 1534 Lutherans put up posters in Paris and some provincial cities ridiculing the Mass and other Catholic practices. One was pasted on a wall outside the apartment where the king was staying in the Chateau of Amboise.

Catholics were outraged, but so too was the king. He led a solemn procession of expiation during which six heretics were burned, and unleashed the ultra-Catholic *parlement* who burned eighteen more. An edict was issued ordering the extermination of heretics, and those who protected them. 'Francis was now lost to the cause of reform'[298] , but despite the repression the Protestants were not crushed. The modest group of disorganised Lutherans had grown into a substantial minority of committed Reformers, now directed by Jean Calvin in Geneva. The first national synod of the French Reformed Church was held in Paris in 1559. Most delegates came from the urban middle-classes – lawyers, academics, merchants, financiers, artisans and some apostate priests and monks. Outside the cities, illiteracy impeded the spread of Protestant ideas: moreover, 'peasant culture was inherently hostile to novelty.'[299]

From the start, there was no desire by either Catholics or Protestants to live together in mutual tolerance. To Catholics, Protestantism 'appeared less as a movement than a widespread disorder: essentially foreign though fomented by resolute Frenchmen, some trained abroad'. Heresy was not just blasphemous and sacrilegious but *seditious*: the Huguenots were repudiating the France of Clovis, Charlemagne, Saint Louis and Joan of Arc. To the Huguenots the Catholics were corrupt, superstitious and idolatrous: they made their views plain not just with posters but by passive resistance – refusing, as was customary, to hang rich drapery from their windows on the feast of Corpus Christi; and then more aggressively by desecrating shrines, throwing garbage at religious processions, putting faeces in holy water stoops, smashing statues, stained glass windows, rood screens, reliquaries; hacking the heads off the angels and saints on the great Gothic cathedrals; and, when they could, whitewashing the walls of churches to cover up the idolatrous murals and frescos.

---

298   *Ibid.*, p. 71

299   *Ibid.*, p. 6

If the measures taken by Francis I and, after his death, his son Henry II, to suppress the Huguenots did not succeed, it was first because they were too many, and second because of they came to be protected by powerful and semi-autonomous members of the nobility. Among the converts to Calvinism, there was Francis I's sister, Marguerite, queen of Navarre, and her formidable daughter, Jeanne d'Albret, who publicly proclaimed her conversion to Calvinism in 1560. Jeanne's husband, Antoine de Bourbon, dithered but Antoine's younger brother Louis, Prince of Condé, hearing a sermon in Geneva on his way back to France after campaigning in Italy, became a Protestant and a leader of the Huguenots. Condé was an experienced soldier; so too Gaspard de Coligny, a Burgundian whose family had a long history of military service for the French kings. He too had fought in Italy, and courageously if unsuccessfully in the defence of Saint-Quentin in north-eastern France. King Francis I made him Admiral of France.

The leaders of the Catholic faction were the Guise, grandees from Lorraine, that middle kingdom created after the death of Charlemagne from whom they claimed descent. They were accepted in the French court as *princes étranger*, and Claude of Lorraine was made Duke of Guise by Francis I. In March, 1563, on his way from Lorraine to join the French court in Paris, he came across a group of around 700 Huguenots holding an illegal service outside the town of Vassy in Champagne. There was an exchange of insults, then blows and finally a conflict which left twenty-three Huguenots dead and a hundred wounded. This was the start of open conflict with the Huguenots and the first of eight religious wars. They took large number of cities – among them Orleans, Angers, Tours, Blois, Sens, Rouen, Le Havre, Lyons, Valence, Grenoble, Vienne, Nimes, Montpellier. Where the Huguenots triumphed, priests and monks were slaughtered, churches pillaged, relics burned, statues smashed, and chalices and monstrances[300] either sold or used in the performance of profane lampoons. While laying siege to Orleans, held by the Huguenots, the duke of Guise was stabbed by an assassin, Poitrot de Méré, and died six days later. De Méré admitted that his scheme had been approved by the Huguenot leaders, Coligny and Condé. Coligny rejoiced in the assassination as 'a manifest miracle of God'.

Intransigence in both parties meant that treaties made did not last, with periods of peace being followed by new conflicts. Both sides called in help

---

300   The gold or gilt receptacle in which a consecrated host is placed when venerated on
       the altar

from abroad – the Huguenots from England, now ruled by the Protestant Queen Elisabeth; and the Catholics from Spain, in particular the Duke of Alva who was campaigning against Protestants in the Netherlands. The third of these religious wars ended when in 1569 the Prince of Condé was killed at the Battle of Jarnac in 1569. At a treaty signed in Saint-Germain-en-Laye on 5 August, 1570, King Charles IX for the Catholics and Admiral Coligny for the Huguenots agreed on a compromise whereby the Huguenots would be able to hold public office, and they would retain control of four fortified cities – La Rochelle, Cognac, Montauban and La Charité on the Loire.

Throughout the wars of religion, King Charles's mother, Catherine de Medici had worked for a compromise between the warring factions and, to set a seal on the pact made at Saint-Germain-in-Laye it was agreed that her daughter, the king's sister, Marguerite de Valois, would marry Jeanne d'Albret's son, now a Huguenot leader, Henry de Bourbon. The Pope, King Philip II of Spain and many French Catholics were appalled that the Catholic Marguerite should marry a heretic; nonetheless, the plans for the marriage went ahead. Reluctantly, because of the Pope's disapproval, the Cardinal of Bourbon – Henry of Navarre's paternal uncle – agreed to conduct the ceremony. The Huguenot grandees and their armed entourages came to Paris to attend the wedding.

The ceremony passed off peaceably on 18 August: however, a number of Huguenots remained in Paris to negotiate the details of the treaty of Saint-Germain-en-Laye. On 22 August, Admiral Coligny, on his way back to his lodgings from the Louvre, was shot from an upstairs window of a house belonging to the Guises. It was a slight wound; King Charles, who was fond of Coligny, visited him on his sick-bed; but both he and his mother feared that, with an army of 3,000 camped outside the city, the Huguenots would take revenge for this attempt on the life of their leader. Therefore on 23 August, the eve of the Feast of Saint Bartholomew, they decided upon a pre-emptive strike. An order was issued to close the gates of the city, and the king's mercenary Swiss Guard were given a list of Huguenot leaders who were to be killed.

It is possible that the king and his mother meant to limit the executions to the names on the list; but the eviction of the leaders from the Louvre to be slaughtered in the street ignited a pogrom of Protestants by Catholics. Henry of Guise led a group to the house where Admiral Coligny lay recovering from his wounds, dragged him from his bed, killed him with their swords and threw his corpse though the window into the street. Where Guise led, the Catholic populace of Paris followed. For three days and nights, Protestants –

men, women and children – were hunted down and slaughtered. Their bodies were thrown onto carts and then dropped into the River Seine. There were similar pogroms in many provincial cities. 'At the very least, two thousand Huguenots were killed in Paris; three to four thousand in the provinces. French Protestantism was decapitated...'[301] Among the Huguenot leaders, only Henry of Navarre, now the king's brother-in-law, and his cousin, the Prince of Condé, were spared and smuggled out of the city.

King Charles did not deny that he had ordered the killing of Huguenots, insisting that it was to pre-empt a Protestant coup. This claim was accepted by Pope Gregory XIII who ordered a *Te Deum* to celebrate this victory over the enemies of the Church: he issued a medal and commissioned three frescoes depicting the event from the artist Georgio Vasari. However, moderate Catholics were dismayed by what had occurred: King Charles' father-in-law, the Emperor Maximilian II, talked of 'a shameful bloodbath'. To Protestants throughout Europe, the Massacre of Saint Bartholomew was an act of infamy: Sir Francis Walsingham, the English ambassador in Paris, narrowly escaped with his life, and the massacre stiffened the resolve of his monarch, Queen Elisabeth, to suppress the Catholic Church in England.

Charles IX died in 1574 at the age of twenty-four. He was succeeded by his brother Henry III, the last of the childless Valois monarchs, *les rois maudits* – the accursed kings. There would be five more wars between French Catholics and Protestants. Outside forces were again drawn into the conflicts from England, Germany and Spain, and Huguenots became embroiled in the Protestant revolt against the King of Spain in the Netherlands. When the Guise thought that too many concessions were being made to the Huguenots, they formed a Catholic League. 1584 saw the death of the king's younger brother, the Duke of Anjou, making the heir to the throne the Huguenot leader, Henry de Bourbon. This was unacceptable to the Catholic League, as it was to the people of Paris, and pressure was put on the king to exclude him from the succession.

Henry and his mother now considered the Guise over-mighty subjects and, when the court was in the Chateau of Blois, Henry of Guise and his brother, the Cardinal de Guise, were summoned to the royal apartments and there killed by the king's guards. War was resumed in which Henry III, the last Valois, combined with the Huguenot Henry of Navarre against the Catholic

---

301   *Ibid.*, p. 179

League. Theologians at the Sorbonne declared that by allying himself with a heretic, the king had forfeited his right to the throne. A Dominican friar, Jacques Clément, granted an audience with the king, stabbed him in the spleen, killing him, and was then himself killed by the royal guards.

Henry of Bourbon under Salic law was now the legitimate king of France but much of his realm was controlled by the Catholic League which refused to accept him. The League was now led by a younger son of the Duke of Guise, the Duke of Mayenne, and was aided by Spanish troops under the Duke of Parma. Henry was largely successful in the field against the forces of the League, but it was clear that he would never take Paris which remained implacably Catholic. He therefore decided to convert. With his many mistresses, he was never a model Calvinist but the decision 'was both anxious and painful'.[302] It was made from expediency: *Paris vaut bien une messe*, he said: Paris is worth a mass. Absolved of his sins by Pope Clement VIII in 1593, there was no longer any reason for Catholics to reject him. He was crowned king of France at Chartres and entered Paris in March, 1594.

Henry of Bourbon remains hard to read. He reached an understanding with the pope who annulled his marriage to Marguerite de Valois, thereby enabling him to marry – not, as he had promised, his mistress Gabrielle d'Estrées, but another daughter of the rulers of Florence, Marie de Medici. His entourage was largely Protestant, but he had a Jesuit confessor, Père Coton.

The war with Spain and die-hard members of the League continued for another three years, concluding with the Peace of Vervins in 1598. In the same year, Henry had issued an Edict while in the city of Nantes which finally brought to an end the French wars of religion. The Huguenots were to be recognised as subjects with the same rights as Catholics. They were confirmed in their possession of certain fortified cities such as La Rochelle as *places de sûreté*, and one hundred and fifty lesser strongholds as *places de refuge*. Catholicism remained the state religion – Huguenots were free to worship only in certain areas – but the law now decreed that in France Catholics and Protestants were to live together in the same nation.

---

302   *Ibid.*, p. 16

56.   Poland

France was not, with the Edict of Nantes, the first European nation to confer equal rights with Catholics to members of the Reformed religion. More than two decades earlier, in 1573, the Polish parliament, the *Sjem*, had passed a law enjoining religious tolerance, the Warsaw Convention.

Poland, at the time of the Reformation, was a large and powerful nation – a realm then united with Lithuania stretching from the Baltic to the Black Sea. Lithuania had been the last pagan nation in Europe, constantly at war with the Teutonic Knights who, after the fall of Acre, had established their headquarters at the fortress of Marienburg in Prussia. Knights from throughout Europe, among them Henry Bolingbroke, later King Henry IV of England, would spend a a season fighting the pagans. The subdued Lithuanians, once the had become Christians, became the serfs of their German conquerors..

In 1386 the Lithuanian Grand Duke Jogaila, when elected King of Poland, had been baptised a Catholic and thereafter was known by his baptismal name, Wladyslaw; the dynasty he founded were known as the Jagiellonians. Under Wladyslaw and his successors, the Polish-Lithuanian commonwealth developed into a powerful, prosperous and cultured state. There were no natural frontiers, and wars were fought to prevent the encroachment of Muscovy to the East, the Tartars of Crimea to the South, and to the north the Teutonic Knights who, with the conversion of the Lithuanians to Christianity, had lost their *raison d'être* and had 'degenerated into a drunken and licentious Order'.[303] In the Battle of Grunwald (Tannenberg) the Knights were defeated by a combined force of Poles and Lithuanians, with a contingent from Kievian Rus, but a siege of the fortress of at Marienburg failed. In the sixteenth century, as we have seen, the Knights adopted the Reformed religion, abjured their vows, married and converted the estates they had managed for the Order into hereditary possessions. The last Grand Master, Albert of Brandenburg, declared himself Duke of Prussia with his capital in Königsberg.

Poland had fine institutes of higher education – the great Polish astronomer Copernicus attended the University of Krakow between 1491 and 1495 – but by and large the schools in Poland were poor and so Polish noblemen sent their sons to be educated in East Prussia. 'The best and most enterprising young men of the nobility, therefore, were being educated in the Reformed

---

303   George Slocombe, *A History of Poland*, p. 97

faith'[304] and upon their return not only spread their views throughout Poland, but on occasions evicted Catholic priests from their livings and appointed Protestant preachers. At the same time, Protestantism was promoted by the Bohemian Brothers 'whose preachers invaded the kingdom of Poland in great numbers'.[305] There were individual conversions: the most powerful nobleman in Lithuania, Prince Michael Radziwill, became a prominent Calvinist, paying for the first translation of the Bible into Polish. The Catholic Church remained influential – 'the only factor of union and stability' – but there was a widespread resentment of its power and wealth: even Catholic members of the *schlacta* – the all-powerful nobility – joined with the 'dissidents' – the name given to members of the Reformed religion – in coveting the wealth of the Church, and resenting the powers of Church courts which in due course were abolished.

The chief reason for the failure to prevent the spread of Lutheranism and Calvinism in Poland and Lithuania was the weakness of the crown. Polish kings were elected by members of the nobility and, to gain their electors' support, the candidates agreed to constitutional concessions by which the powers of the crown were successively diminished. The principle of *cuius regio, eius religio* (the religion of the ruler should be the religion of the state) that prevailed in Germany was never applied in Poland where royal edicts were subject to the veto of parliament, the *sjem*, which at one time had a majority of Protestant members.

A second reason was that the Catholic Church had since the union of Poland and Lithuania in 1386 been obliged to co-exist with members of other religions – the schismatic Orthodox Church in Lithuania and the Jewish communities which in the fourteenth century had been invited by an earlier king, Casimir, to settle in Poland. Thus a measure of religious toleration already existed in the Polish-Lithuanian commonwealth prior to the Reformation.

Initially, attempts were made to stem the spread of heresy. There were frequent hangings of 'dissidents' in the reign of Sigismund I, but upon his accession, Sigismund II, although a devout Catholic, decided that his father's measures to stem the growth of the Reformed religion had failed. He also faced a dilemma: he wanted to marry the beautiful and cultivated Lithuanian, Barbara Radziwill, and one of the concessions won by the *schlachta* was that

---

304   *Ibid.*, p.122

305   *Ibid.*, p. 120

the king could only marry with the consent of the Polish parliament, the *sjem*. Sigismund was half-Italian through his mother, Bona Sforza, and had good relations with the popes in Rome. Upon the advice of a prudent Papal Legate, Sigismund settled on a policy to deal with the Protestants: he did nothing. 'The policy of the king, and the wisdom of the representatives of the Holy See...saved Poland from the bloodshed caused elsewhere by religious intolerance.'[306]

57.   The Dutch Revolt

Contiguous, both geographically and historically, with the religious conflicts in France were the risings in the Netherlands against the rule of the Habsburg King Philip of Spain. This group of city states, secular principalities, and episcopal domains, had been conquered by the Dukes of Burgundy and, as we have seen, were part of the vast inheritance of Charles V. Charles had been born and raised in Flanders, spoke Dutch as well as French, Spanish and some German, and that part of his empire was dearest to his heart. However, when he divided his empire in 1556, the seventeen provinces were given to his son Philip who had been raised in Spain, spoke neither Dutch nor French, and regarded the Netherlands as mere provinces of the Spanish Empire. They were among the most prosperous and, like his father Charles, he taxed them to cover expenses in other parts of the empire – notably wars against the Ottomans, the Protestant princes in Germany, and the neighbouring French. Frequently the interests of Charles, as Holy Roman Emperor, and Philip, as King of Spain, did not coincide with those of the mercantile Dutch. Thus the taxes were resented not just for their weight, but for the purposes to which they were put.

A second factor was religion. The Protestantism of both Luther and Calvin which spread to the Low Countries was regarded by both Charles and Philip as a heresy that should be suppressed. There were periodic burnings and executions but as in France the Protestants became too many to be crushed by force. Just across the Ems estuary was the safe-haven of Emden, and the Calvinist missionaries from Geneva were indistinguishable from the many merchants plying their wares throughout Europe except, perhaps, by the greater sobriety of their attire. Philip's regent in the Netherlands, his half-

---

306   *Ibid.*, p. 124

sister Margaret of Parma, ruled through a council of notables, many of whom opposed the harsh measures taken against the Reformers. But the Reformers themselves did not help the cause of toleration: in August, 1566, a mob led by a Calvinist preacher Sebastian Matte sacked the monastery and church of Steenvoorde, destroying all the 'graven images' – the statues, stained glass, and relics. Further iconoclastic tumults followed, with churches and cathedrals vandalised throughout the Netherlands. Little was done to restrain them. Philip, realising that he could no longer rely on the local nobility to maintain order, despatched an army of 10,00 men from Spain led by the third Duke of Alba.

Alba took the stern measures he thought necessary, among them the establishment of a special court, known as the Council of Troubles. Superseded by Alba, Margaret of Parma resigned as regent and so was unable to prevent the execution for treason of two prominent Dutch noblemen, the Counts of Egmont and Horne – the treason being their tolerance of Protestantism. A thousand further executions followed: the Council of Troubles became known as the Council of Blood. This only served to increase the spirit of revolt, and in 1568, the former *Stadtholder* of the provinces of Holland, Zeeland and Utrecht, the taciturn Lutheran William of Orange, known as William the Silent, returned from Saxony, where he had sought refuge with his father-in-law, the Elector, to lead the rebellion – not, as yet, against King Philip but against Alba.

Aid came from an army of French Huguenots who invaded the Netherlands from the south, and contingents from Germany led by William's brothers. So began a conflict that was to last for eighty years. One battle was lost, another won, but William was obliged to withdraw because of lack of resources. Four years later, in 1572, he returned to the Netherlands and set up a base of operations in Delft. An attempt by Alba to raise a new tax had soured his relations with the Dutch and improved the prospects for a second rebellion. Moreover, William had allies abroad: he had sought help from the Ottoman Turks who were attracted by the iconoclasm of the Calvinists and welcomed any support in their incessant conflict with the Habsburgs. 'Better Turkish than Papist' was inscribed on a silver medallion by Calvinists who increasingly became the animating spirit of the rebellion. In 1573 William converted from Lutheranism to Calvinism.

The war between the now Calvinist northern provinces, and armies sent from Spain, continued well into the next century. Foreign nations became involved:

England's Queen Elizabeth, after an initial reluctance, backed her Protestant co-religionist in the north. When Antwerp was retaken by the Spanish, many of its merchants and entrepreneurs moved to Amsterdam. To protect their trade, the Dutch Protestants had built a formidable navy, able to take on the Spanish but also the English in later disputes over trade and their colonial empires. It was not until 1648, with the Treaty of Münster – an adjunct to the pan-European Treaty of Westphalia that brought the Thirty Years War to an end – that the Protestant Dutch Republic was recognised as an independent state.

58.   Michel de Montaigne

'See how the Christians love one another!', exclaimed the Roman author Tertullian in the third century AD. A detached spectator of the civil wars that followed the Reformation would rather have observed: 'See how the Christians hate one another!' The slaughter of Catholics by Protestants, and Protestants by Catholics, both parties convinced that they were acting according to the will God, was not as yet seen as an indictment of Christianity as such. Neither side doubted that Jesus of Nazareth was the Son of God, or that every human being born into the world was ultimately destined for Heaven or Hell. There had always been reasons for men to hate and kill each other, and others quite as sanguinary would emerge in the future with nationalism, colonialism and the atheist ideologies of the nineteenth and twentieth centuries. And while Protestantism and Islam were the most immediate threats to the Catholic Church in the sixteenth century, there was also a less obvious but equally insidious danger of an *indifference* to religion as such – an indifference that 'has become so common among the educated in our own world as to be now quite unremarkable'[307] but was rare prior to the sixteenth century.

If the seed of this skepticism was sown by Erasmus, the plant flourished during the French wars of religion in the mind of a Gascon lawyer and author, Michel de Montaigne – described by the critic Erich Auerbach as 'the first modern man'. Montaigne was born in the Château de Montaigne close to Bordeaux in south-western France which had been bought by his grand-father, rich from trading in herrings. His father, Pierre Eyquem de Montaigne, was a soldier who had fought in Italy against the armies of Charles V, and was

---

307   Lucy Beckett, *In the Light of Christ. Writings in the Western Tradition*, p.312

later elected mayor of Bordeaux. He was said to have had forefathers from the Marrano community – Spanish and Portuguese *conversos* who continued to practice the Jewish religion in secret; so too his mother, Antoinette Lopez de Villanueva, whose father was a rich Marrano merchant from Zaragoza. In the nineteenth century, the polemical anti-Semite, Édouard Drumont, ascribed Montaigne's skepticism to his Jewish antecedents, describing him as 'a destroyer…who highlighted the vices and absurdities of humanity without proposing any better attainable ideals'.[308] However, there is no evidence that Michel's parents' Catholicism was insincere. Michel's father, of whom he was fond, was determined that his son should be fluent in Latin and hired a German tutor who could not speak French. Michel was sent first to the University of Bordeaux, then to that of Toulouse. Upon graduating, he obtained a legal post in Périgeux, moving to Bordeaux when his father was elected mayor. There he formed a close friendship with the lawyer and philosopher, Étienne de la Boétie whose premature death was to inspire reflections on friendship and death in Montaigne's writings.

In 1570 he married the daughter of a prosperous merchant, Françoise de la Cassaigne, and in 1570, upon his father's death, he resigned his posts in Bordeaux and retired to live as a recluse in the Château de Montaigne. He assembled his extensive library in a round tower and began his *essais* – discursive attempts to define the limits of what can and cannot be known: his motto was *Que Sais Je?* – what do I know?.

'Montaigne was no scholar. He seldom read books through'[309] but he dipped into a vast number of works by the thinkers of antiquity – Seneca, Horace, Ovid, Plutarch – mixing their experience with his own, and adopting from Socrates and the Stoics his own philosophy of moderation and self-restraint. He emerges from his essays as 'modest, truthful, humorous, and objective; he is clear-sighted, unprejudiced, and a great conversationalist.'[310] His work was read and admired throughout France, and the influence of both the content, and the form he invented – the essay – is seen in the work of authors such Bacon, Hazlitt, Emerson, Nietzsche, and Zweig. Some critics have detected his influence in the later plays of Shakespeare.

What is notably scarce or even absent from Montaigne's essays are references to the Scriptures or the Church fathers: it was as if the Renaissance

---

308   Édouard Drumont, *La France Juive*, p. 222
309   J.M.Cohen, Introduction to Montaigne's *Essays*, p. 14
310   *Ibid.*, p. 9

had followed Antiquity with nothing in between. What did he know? Only what he had learned through experience, or could accept from the trustworthy evidence presented by others. 'The religions of worship and mystical revelation, whether Greek or Christian, were incomprehensible to him. He found no virtue in asceticism, but saw every reason to grant the mind and the body their ordinary comforts'.[311]

Montaigne never fell out with the Catholic Church. Although he had friends and relatives who were Huguenots, his religion remained 'a conforming Catholicism'. After ten years reading and writing in his tower at the Chateau of Montaigne, the pain caused by kidney stones forced him to travel to Germany, Switzerland and Italy in search of a cure. In Italy he visited the Holy House of Loreto and left a silver relief depicting him praying with his family to the Madonna. In Rome, his *Essays* were read by the Dominican theologian, Sisto Fabri, and returned with only two critical comments. It was not until 1676 that the they were placed on the Vatican's *Librorum Prohibitorum*, the List of Prohibited Books (the Index), after theologians came to appreciate just how corrosive were Montaigne's beliefs to the Catholic faith. 'Montaigne's faults are great', wrote Blaise Pascal:

> He inspires indifference regarding salvation without fear or repentance...one may excuse his somewhat free and licentious views on certain situations in life...but his completely pagan views on death are inexcusable; for all hope of piety must be abandoned if we are not at least willing to die as Christians. Now, through his book, he thinks of dying a death of cowardly ease.[312]

In answer to his question, 'What do I know?', Montaigne's answer was 'very little' – certainly very little about the nature of God. Those who rely on reason, Montaigne observed, never agree, so reason is demonstrably an unsound guide. Truth is undiscoverable and 'religion can be bracketed off from civilized life as a mere cause of contention among the educated'. 'Prayer was clearly not his way'.[313] However, despite this 'relaxed, pessimistic skepticism', Montaigne regarded the Catholic Religion as a source of stability: 'without the path pointed out by the Church', he told Étienne Pasquier, 'reason is lost, embarrassed, shackled. ' When recalled from Italy to be mayor of Bordeaux,

---

311   *Ibid.*, p. 17
312   Blaise Pascal, *Pensées*, Translated by A.J.Krailsheimer, p. 215
313   J.M.Cohen, *Op. Cit.* p 17

as his father had been before him, he held it for the Catholics against the Huguenots, but later for Henry of Navarre against the Catholic League: both Francis I and Henry IV regarded him as a friend. At the age of 59, he fell ill with a throat infection (quinsy) and, realizing that he was dying, did not send for a priest but called for a mass to be said and died during its celebration.

59.   The Counter-Reformation

It is a paradox that the Protestant Reformation did not spread to Italy where the corrupt practices within the Church outdid those elsewhere in Christendom, in particular those perpetrated by the popes in Rome. Fortunately for Europe's cultural heritage, the ideas of the Reformers, though they appealed to some theologians, did not thrive among the mercantile and artisan circles south of the Alps: one need not be a partisan Catholic but simply a lover of art to shudder at the thought of Lutheran or Calvinist iconoclasts let loose among the religious artworks of the Renaissance. In Italy 'militant mass support and a charismatic leadership prepared to make a break with the old structures were both lacking'. Indeed, many of the guilds of late Medieval Italy had developed into oratories with 'an intense, activist and Eucharistically centered piety'.[314]

Another reason is that the popes of the period, although slow to realise the scale of disaffection north of the Alps, were aware of the need for reform. The Council of Florence of 1438 had 'made provision for the worship and rites of the Church, focusing on the Sacraments' which were 'fixed at seven'. It had 'highlighted the sacramental ministry of bishops'[315] and condemned those who acted not as pastors but as politicians. Some, like John Fisher in England, lived up to these expectations, conscientiously caring for the people of his impoverished diocese of Rochester, and refusing all offers of advancement.

The paradox is embodied in Alessandro Farnese, elected pope as Paul III in 1534. A man of great charm and intelligence, 'he was emphatically the product of the old corruption'. [316] He was the brother of Giulia Farnese, the last mistress of Pope Alexander VI, and as a cardinal had fathered four children. He built for himself one of the finest mansions in Rome – the Palazzo Farnese. Like the worst of the Renaissance popes, he endowed his

---

314   Diarmaid MacCulloch, *Op Cit.*, p. 216

315   Michael A. Mullet, *The Catholic Reformation*, p. 3

316   Eamon Duffy, *Op. Cit.* p. 209

children with properties from the papal states, and early in his reign made cardinals of his two teenage grandsons. He reinstated the Carnival in 1538 – 'firework displays, masked balls, risqué plays'[317] – and invited women to the banquets he gave for his sons and their wives.

But Paul III was intelligent and, after a briefing from the papal nuncio in Vienna, decided that the only way to stem the spread of heretical Protestantism was to summon a Council. This had already been mooted as a way to prevent a schism, but the idea had been opposed not only by the cardinals who feared that any reform would threaten their privileges but also by King Francis I of France who encouraged the religious conflict in Germany that weakened his adversary, the Emperor Charles V. Some hoped that the Council would establish a religious compromise, but the Lutherans and Calvinists refused to attend a Council presided over by the pope or one of his legates. Finally, in December 1545, it was agreed that a Council would be convened in Trent – a city notionally within the Holy Roman Empire but on the south side of the Alps.

To prepare for the Council, Paul III appointed to the College of Cardinals a group of reform-minded humanists – a pious layman from Venice, Gasparo Contarini; a learned Englishman, Reginald Pole – a cousin of King Henry VIII; another scholar working within the Curial administration, Matteo Giberti; Jacopo Sadoleto who had established his reformist credentials as a model bishop in Carpentras; and Giampietro Caraffa, a Neapolitan nobleman, formerly the Archbishop of Brindisi and papal legate in England, Spain and the Netherlands, who had founded a religious order devoted to reform, the Theatines. This group, from which members of the Curia were excluded, became a Reform Commission whose report, delivered in March, 1537, placed the responsibility for the travails of the Church squarely on the cardinals and popes. The curial cardinals tried but failed to prevent the report's publication. In 1538 Luther published a German translation,' with a lip-smacking introduction and notes…'[318]

Within the Reform Commission, however, there were differences. Cardinal Caraffa was determined to eradicate heresy through traditional means: he persuaded Paul III to found a Roman Inquisition with himself as one of the six Inquisitors. Cardinals Contarini and Pole, on the other hand, were inclined to sift the good from the bad in Luther's teaching. 'Heretics are

---

317   *Ibid.* p. 209

318   *Ibid.* p. 211

not heretics in everything', said Pole. He thought Luther was probably right on the question of Justification through Faith alone.

Only thirty-one bishops assembled in Trent in December 1545 for the opening of the Council, only one of whom was from Germany. The Lutherans and Calvinists regarded it as a farce and did not attend, but many of the decrees of the Council were in response to their teaching. It abolished many of the abuses condemned and ridiculed by the humanists and the reformers – calling for an improvement in both the spiritual and intellectual calibre of the clergy through the establishment of seminaries. When it came to the dogmatic differences with the Protestants such as purgatory, justification, transubstantiation and the number of the sacraments, 'it was uncompromising, but clear and cogent' [319] in re-iterating traditional teaching. For Cardinal Pole, it was too clear and cogent on the question of Justification upon which he had pinned his hopes for a reconciliation with the Lutherans. He had been one of the three papal legates presiding over the opening of the Council, but his hopes for a compromise were dashed by the decree published in 1547 which insisted that 'God's grace is available through the good works which humans can perform, including participation in the Church's sacraments of baptism and penance...' Anticipating this ruling, Cardinal Pole suffered a 'virtual nervous breakdown' and pleading illness left the Council, never to return. [320]

'The Church after Trent,' wrote the historian Eamon Duffy, 'would be better organised, better staffed, more clerical, more vigilant, more repressive, altogether a more formidable institution. As its reforms took effect, the advance of Protestantism would be halted, and then, partly reversed.' [321] It was not a clear-cut process. The strands of rigour and compromise remained intertwined. The moderate Cardinal Pole was one vote short of being chosen as the new pope at the conclave following the death of Paul III in 1549. Three years later, on the death of the Protestant King Edward VI of England, and the accession of his Catholic half-sister, Mary, Pole was despatched to England as Papal Legate to help the Queen bring her realm back to the Catholic Faith. No attempt was made to restore the property of the Church expropriated on Henry VIII's behalf by Cromwell and given or sold to the 'new men', but Cranmer was deposed as Archbishop of Canterbury and replaced by Pole:

319   *Ibid.* P. 214

320   Diarmid MacCulloch, *Op. Cit.* p. 235-236

321   Eamon Duffy, *Op. Cit.* p. 215

it was only now that Pole was ordained a priest. In effect, he became Mary's chief minister, seeing her married to King Philip of Spain – a match that brought Philip to England but resulted only in a phantom pregnancy.

Pole, if he did not encourage, acquiesced in the burning or execution of 220 men and 60 women for the crime of heresy. Among them was Cranmer, who was burned despite his recantation – the victim some said of Mary's revenge for the treatment of her mother, Catherine of Aragon. These cruel if traditional measures earned her the name 'Bloody Mary' and were used by English Protestants to discredit the Catholic Church. Pole's appointment of excellent bishops might, given time, have re-established Catholicism in England, but Mary's reign was short: she died on 17 November, 1558, and Pole from influenza twelve hours later.

The conclave following the death of Pope Paul III in 1549, at which Reginald Pole narrowly missed election, chose instead a Roman jurist, Giovanni del Monte, who took the name Julius III. The choice of the name of one of the worst of the Renaissance popes indicated a return to type: Julius was 'a typical Renaissance pontiff, generous to relatives, devoted to banquets, the theatre, hunting'[322]. He was besotted with a youth he had picked up off the streets of Parma and made him both the keeper of his monkeys and a cardinal. His reign of five years was followed by one of only 21 days of the 'first real reform pope', Marcellus II; and then Giampietro Caraffa, the fiercely orthodox cardinal from Naples who had persuaded Paul III to establish a Roman Inquisition. Now he established an Index of Prohibited Books on which were placed the works of Erasmus and, later, Montaigne.

60.   New Religious Orders

When the Council of Trent came to an end in 1563, many of its reforms were under way but far from completed. It had become clear that there was to be no compromise with either the Lutherans or Calvinists: the western Church was now irrevocably split. It had also become clear that the secular leaders of Christendom, who hitherto had been charged with the suppression of heresy, were now either unwilling or unable to continue to do so. 'It fell to the popes to organise and promote the missionary drive to recover the lost

---

322   J.N.D.Kelly, *Op. Cit.* p.263

populations of Europe. Rome became, what it had never before been, the working headquarters of the most vital movements for reform and renewal in the Church.'[323]

However, the revival of Catholic faith and practice in what came to be called the Counter-Reformation, was not wholly or even largely the work or popes and bishops 'nor was it only a response to the Reformation: even before Luther posted his theses in Wittenberg, individual Catholics, many of them women, had on their own initiative worked for reform. Angela Merici, an orphan born on Lake Garda in northern Italy in 1474, had by the end of the fifteenth century established a religious association of women to perform spiritual and religious works of mercy, in particular the education of girls in their homes. Already a member of the Third Order of Saint Francis, and influenced by eremitical women, the Beguines,in the Netherlands, Angela and her companions committed themselves to meet, to take 'Holy Communion once a month, to lead frugal lives and to carry out social works of charity, including service in hospitals, orphanages and hostels for prostitutes and, especially, the teaching of religion to girls.'[324] The women placed themselves under the patronage of Saint Ursula, a dedicated virgin from the fourth century who was said to have been martyred with eleven thousand companions (probably only eleven) by barbarian Huns on their way from England to Rome.

Angela was ahead of her time in despatching her Ursuline nuns to minister in people's homes: until then, women who had taken religious vows were obliged to remain enclosed in their convents, and the Fathers of the Council of Trent ruled that they should continue to do so. Thus in time the Ursulines came to live in convents, and lay clothes were replaced by a habit. However, their work continued: by 1584, 600 sisters ran eighteen schools in the archdiocese of Milan alone and 'the Ursulines clung on to some of their distinctive features, not least a social recruitment from middling and lower-middle-class families...contrasting this organisation with long-standing patterns of treating convents as refined dumping grounds for the unmarried daughters of European élites.'[325]

With a more aristocratic membership, but equally dedicated to care of the poor, were the Theatines, founded by Gaetano Cajetan (1480-1547) and

---

323   Eamon Duffy, *Op. Cit.* p. 221

324   Michael A. Mullet, *Op. Cit.* p.106

325   *Ibid.*, p. 107

Giampietro Caraffa; and the Clerks Regular of Somascha, the Somaschans, founded by a former Venetian soldier Jerome Emiliani in 1529 and devoted to the care of orphans. The 1530s saw the foundation in Milan by Anthony Mary Zaccaria and his companions of a congregation dedicated to the reinvigoration of the Catholic faith called the Regular Clerics of Saint Paul or, after establishing themselves in the monastery of Saint Barnabas in Milan, the Barnabites. Matteo di Bascio (1495-1552), a member of the stricter branch of the Franciscans, the Conventuals, came to Rome after working among the victims of plague, and established with the consent of Pope Clement VII a community of hermits, even more austere than the Conventuals. They preached among the poor barefoot and wore the rough hooded tunic of Francis of Assisi, and so became known as 'the hooded men', *i scapuccini* or *cappuccino*, finally the Capuchin friars. Like the Ursulines, they were to encounter many trials (in 1547 their fourth General converted to Protestantism) but again like the Ursulines they survived these crises, grew in numbers and established houses throughout Italy and abroad.

Italy had need of the new orders because of its dire condition after the wars between France and the Empire. Rome in particular took many years to recover from its sack in 1525. In 1553, a young Florentine, Philip Neri, came to Rome after training as a businessman with an uncle near Naples. He worked as a tutor for a Florentine family living in the city – living a frugal life of study and prayer. While praying, at Pentecost, 1544, he felt that a ball of fire had come into his heart. This led to an apostolate of an unique kind: he would walk through the streets of Rome looking in on cafés, inns and brothels, appealing to those he met to reform their lives. He was no priest preaching from a pulpit but a man of great charm who invited those he befriended to visit his lodgings to talk and pray. He and his companions worked to restore Rome as a holy city, reviving the ancient pilgrimages to the catacombs and seven basilicas. As their numbers grew, they moved to a larger room which they called their 'oratory', or place of prayer.

There were priests among Philip's admirers and in due course Pope Gregory XIII provided them with a newly restored church, the *Chiesa Nova*. Philip would not found an order – he thought there were enough already; but he laid down a few rules for his Congregation of the Oratory, the Oratorians. In 1551, he was ordained as a priest, and became a discerning confessor. He was beloved throughout the city, and became known as 'the apostle of Rome'.

He died on 26th May, 1595, after living and ministering in his adopted city for sixty years.

A case of how the good (genuine sanctity) and the bad (nepotistic patronage) mingled during this period of transition in the Church was Charles Borromeo, the son of the Count of Arona, and a member of one of the noblest and richest families in Lombardy. Devout, even as a child, he was made a cardinal at the age of twenty-one by his maternal uncle, Giovanni Angelo Medici, Pope Pius IV. He was given important posts within the curia, and directed the final session of the Council of Trent. He was made first administrator and later Archbishop of Milan, then the largest diocese in Italy but in a state of decay after decades of absentee bishops. Charles embarked on a vigorous programme of reform which encompassed both the secular clergy and religious orders. He organised aid for the Milanese when the city was hit first by famine, and then the plague. He sheltered English victims of persecution, and kept on his person a portrait of John Fisher. He sought to improve the standard of education of his diocesan clergy so that they too could pass on to their parishioners the truths of the Catholic Faith. He founded a congregation of devout laymen named after his great predecessor, Saint Ambrose; and established seminaries, colleges and Sunday schools for children where they could be taught the Catechism drawn up by the Dutch Jesuit, Peter Canisius. Borromeo was described as austere, dedicated and uncompromising; members of a religious order he antagonised attempted to assassinate him. However, he earned the respect of both popes and monarchs and was the model for reforming bishops envisaged by the Fathers of the Council of Trent.

Another reforming churchman from a noble family was Francis of Sales, the eldest son of a soldier and statesman in the then independent Alpine Duchy of Savoy. As the eldest son, Francis was prepared for a career as a lawyer and statesman: his initial schooling was in Annecy, but at the age of twenty-six he was sent with a servant and a tutor, the Abbé Déage, to study in Paris. He learned the worldly pastimes of riding, fencing and dancing but went to lectures in theology as well as law and, after only a year, suffered a spiritual crisis, fearing that perhaps the Huguenots were right about predestination, and that he was one of the damned. In the small church of Saint-Etienne-des-Grès, he prayed to the Virgin Mary, and all at once the terror left him: he accepted that the essence of God was not punishment but love.

To persuade others of God's overwhelming love became Francis's life-long vocation. He committed himself to a celibate life, and determined to become a priest – hesitating only because he knew that it would disappoint his father. The old soldier was only persuaded to consent to his son's ordination when the Prince Bishop of Geneva, Claude de Granier, exiled to Annecy by the Calvinists, proposed that Francis should be made first Provost and then his Coadjutor. When Granier died in 1602, Francois of Sales succeeded him and, despite many offers of preferment from popes and kings, remained the bishop of this remote and truncated diocese for the rest of his life.

Calvinist Geneva was inaccessible to its Catholic bishop, and the Reformed religion had spread beyond the city. The Château de Sales, where Francis had been born and raised, was close to the Chablais, the region south of the Lake of Geneva that had become Calvinist, but which Francis after his ordination determined to bring back to the Catholic fold. As a young priest, he set out on this mission, enduring hardships and often in great danger. He was, to some extent, protected by his rank, and the support of Charles-Emmanuel I, the Duke of Savoy. At night, he could withdraw into the fortress of Allinges, but he never called upon soldiers to coerce conversions. 'All through love and nothing through force,' he told Pierre Camus, the Bishop of Belley. It was solely through his preaching and writing and kindness that he eventually re-established the Catholic religion in the towns and villages of the Chablais as far as the shores of Lake Leman.

Francis's nobility, together with his attractive personality, also eased his path with the King of France, Henri IV, who was the ruler of the northern part of his diocese, the Gex. The two men were hardly like-minded. Francis regarded chastity as the Lily of the virtues[326]; the king had three children by his favourite mistress, Gabrielle d'Estrées, whose sister Angélique, Abbess of Maubuisson, reputedly had six children by six different men. 'I have an utter contempt for the court,' wrote Francis, 'since more and more do I abhor the ruling pleasures of the world, the world itself, its spirit, its maxims, its silliness'. Nonetheless, the two men became friends. 'A rare bird indeed,' said the king of Francis. 'Devout, learned and a gentleman into the bargain.'

Many saints before Francis had felt this abhorrence of the world, but thought the only escape was into a monastery or convent. What was revolutionary in Francis was his belief that one could remain in the world

---

326   'The symbolism of the lily…is instantly recognisable as an attribute of Mary's purity and chastity.' Sarah Drummond, *Divine Conception. The Art of the Annunciation*, p. 88

and yet be holy, and that and that this was true for women as well as men. It was the advice he gave to Jeanne-Françoise Frémont de Chantal, a young widow he met on a visit to Dijon. He became her spiritual director and in due course founded and wrote the rule for a new order for religious women, the Sisters of the Visitation, with Jeanne-Françoise as its first superior. The nuns were not to be enclosed, but were free to leave their convent to help the sick and the poor.

The long and profound friendship of Francis de Sales and Jeanne-François de Chantal shows how a chaste love is possible between a man and a woman. Earlier Doctors of the Church such as Jerome, Augustine of Hippo and Bernard of Clairvaux appeared to regard women largely as occasions of sin – to be discarded when one's passions were mastered (Augustine); or shut out behind a twelve-foot wall (Bernard). Francis believed that women could serve God living among both women and men. He advised his mother to permit his sister Joanna, then aged twelve, to return home from a convent. 'It is unreasonable that a girl should be allowed to stay so long in a convent, if she does not intend to spend her whole life there.'[327]

However, neither Jeanne-Françoise de Chantal nor Joanna de Sales was the Philothea to whom Francis addressed his classic of spiritual advice, *Introduction to the Devout Life*. Louise de Charmoisy, the young wife of a cousin of Francis's, had put herself under his spiritual direction in Annecy. When obliged to move to Chambéry, she showed her many letters from Francis to Père Fourier who had been Francis's own spiritual director. It was Father Fourier who persuaded Francis to make the letters the basis for a work of spiritual counsel.

First published in 1609, the *Introduction to the Devout Life* became a best-seller and made the Bishop of Annecy famous throughout Europe. Francis's teaching that lay people could and should aspire to spiritual perfection was novel and controversial. Some of his teachings, which seem harsh in the 21st century, were thought dangerously easy-going at the time. He tells Philothea that, while dancing was innocent in itself, she should recall at a ball 'that many souls are suffering for sins committed at a dance...' There is no talk of predestination, but he displays a vivid belief in the Devil and the possibility of damnation: 'Consider that you are most truly standing between Hell and Paradise, and that both the one and the other are open to receive you, according to the choice you make in this life'.

---

327   See Piers Paul Read, Preface to *Introduction to the Devout Life*, SPCK, p. xi

Francis was canonised by Pope Alexander VII in 1665, declared a Doctor of the Church by Pope Pius IX in 1877, and proclaimed the patron saint of writers by Pope Pius XI in 1923. The refinement of his language and the brilliant play on words may be lost in translation, but there remains the psychological insight of a great novelist, and in any language there emerges from his prose the optimism, kindness and charm – his love of his fellow human beings, and, above all, his love of God.

The Sisters of the Visitation founded by Francis of Sales and Jeanne-François de Chantal would face the same difficulties as Angela Merici's Ursuline nuns – the Church's insistence, confirmed by the Council of Trent, that nuns must live enclosed in a convent. So too did Mary Ward, a woman born in the village of Mulwith in North Yorkshire in Protestant Elizabethan England. At the age of fifteen, she felt drawn to the religious life and entered a convent in the Spanish Netherlands. Deciding that she was called to an active rather than a contemplative life, she left the convent and established a community in Saint-Omer which ran a school for girls. The project was successful: further Institutes of the Blessed Virgin Mary were established in Flanders, Bavaria, Austria, Bohemia and Italy. In 1637 she returned to England with an introduction to Queen Henrietta Maria from Pope Urban VIII, founding schools, visiting prisoners and nursing the sick. In 1642 she returned to her native Yorkshire, dying in York three years later.

And finally, among the formidable women who worked for the reform of the Church, was Teresa of Avila who in the mid-sixteenth century led a reform of the Carmelite order. Coming from a partly Jewish family living in Avila in Spain, Teresa became a Carmelite in 1536 at the age of twenty, and in the course of contemplative prayer experienced ecstasies and mystic visions, among them the penetration of her heart by a spear of divine love. In early middle age, encouraged by a devout Franciscan Peter of Alcántara, she founded in 1562 a convent which would emulate the ascetic practices of the early Carmelites, among them going bare-foot – hence becoming known as the 'discalced' or slipperless Carmelites. Unlike the Ursulines or the Sisters of the Visitation, the discalced Carmelites were strictly enclosed with emphasis laid on prayer and contemplation. In the following twenty years, seventeen further communities were established by Teresa in Spain, and there were foundations in France and the Spanish Netherlands.

'By her Carmelite reform Teresa inaugurated a reform of the organized religious life of women and in the framework of spirituality in general that has had immense influence throughout the Church.'[328] She was not just a reformer but also a mystic whose book the *Interior Castle* describes the development of mystical prayer, and whose autobiographical *Life* became a classic of Spanish Renaissance literature: from it emerges a personality of honesty, common-sense, determination, wit and charm. Her reforms were opposed by the easy-going 'calced' Carmelite nuns; so too the unreformed orders of male Carmelites, who imprisoned and mistreated John de Yepes, known as John of the Cross, a friar who worked to emulate Teresa's reforms. John of the Cross was also a poet and mystic whose *The Dark Night of the Soul* is considered a classic of Spanish Renaissance literature. In due course both Teresa of Avila and John of the Cross would be proclaimed Doctors of the Church.

61.   Ignatius of Loyola

A third Spaniard whose influence was to be greater than that of any of the other Catholic reformers was Ignatius of Loyola. Born Don Iñigo Lopez de Recalde in 1491 in the castle of Loyola, he was the youngest of the thirteen children of Beltrán de Loyola and Marina Sanchez de Lincona: both his parents were from ancient noble families in the province of Guipuzcoa in north-eastern Spain. His mother died soon after his birth and he was farmed out to a wet nurse, the blacksmith's wife. Despite spending the first years of his life with the blacksmith's children, 'young Iñigo was instilled with the pride of the Loyolas, which called them to be leaders, heroes, extraordinary men'. This heritage included a profound, almost instinctive religious faith. Despite fathering three illegitimate children, Iñigo's father Beltran 'was a man of deep faith.'[329]

As was the custom among the nobility at the time, Iñigo was sent around the age of fourteen to serve as a page in the household of the Majordomo of Queen Isabella, and Treasurer of the Kingdom of Castile, Velázquez de Cuéllar at Arévalo. Here, in an atmosphere of splendour and royal magnificence, he learned the arts of war and courtly manners, but also to dance and to flirt – his imagination fired by the chivalric romance, *Amadis de Gaula*. Maria, the

---

328   John Coulson, (Ed.), *Op. Cit.* p. 425

329   W.W.Meissner, SJ. *Ignatius Loyola. The Psychology of a Saint.* P. 16

wife of Velázquez de Cuéllar – a kinswoman of the Loyolas – was a confidante of Germaine de Foix who, it will be recalled, had a child by her step-grandson, the emperor Charles V, and introduced 'many of the dissolute manners of the ladies of Valencia…to the court of Castile'.[330] In the court at Arévalo, 'Staunch Catholic faith and sexual license stood side by side'. [331]

Iñigo thus became 'a product of his culture and his time' – 'a man of arms, courageous and loyal', caught up in the romance of chivalry, but also 'a gallant, a libertine whose morals were questionable but whose *machismo* as never in doubt'. [332] He 'was particularly reckless in gambling, in his dealings with women, in quarrelling and with the sword'[333] but in the household of Velázquez he gained the confidence to move at ease among the higher nobility.

Iñigo would later confess to 'a great and vain desire of winning glory' and the opportunity came when Spain went to war with France. He passed from the service of Velázquez de Cuéllar to that of Antonio Manrique de Lara, Duke of Nájera who, as Charles V's viceroy in Navarre, was charged with suppressing the revolt of the *Communeros* – Spaniards resentful of the Flemish officials placed over them by Charles. Francis I, the King of France, seeing an opportunity to weaken Charles, supported the *Communeros*, and also the ruling dynasty of Navarre which had been ousted when the Pyrenean kingdom had been annexed by Spain. A French army of over twelve thousand men, equipped with heavy artillery, invaded Navarre and besieged its capital, Pamplona. The city surrendered but the citadel, whose garrison included a contingent led by Iñigo, held out at Iñigo's insistence. The French canon blew a breach in the walls. Iñigo stood, sword in hand, ready to repel the invaders when '"a cannon ball struck him in the leg, crushing its bones and because it passed between his legs it also seriously wounded the other"'.[334]

The citadel of Pamplona fell to the French. Iñigo, now a prisoner, was treated well by his captors: his bones were set and in due course he was carried on a litter to convalesce in the Castle of Loyola. There the doctors decided that the bones in his leg must be re-set: the operation, carried out without anaesthetic, left an unsightly protuberance which Iñigo, ever the vain *hidalgo*, insisted must be removed with a saw. But it was the last demand of

330   Philip Caraman, SJ: *Ignatius of Loyola*, p. 13

331   W.W.Meissner, SJ. *Op. Cit.* p. 22

332   *Ibid.* p.23

333   Philip Caraman, *Op. Cit.*, p.13

334   Ignatius of Loyola, *Vita*, I: quoted in W.W.Meissner, *Op. Cit.* p. 35

the narcissistic gallant, for 'the impact of the cannon ball at Pamplona set in motion a series of events that were to have far-reaching consequences'. [335]

Bed-ridden for many months, Iñigo's only distractions were works of Christian authors in the Castle's library – the four volume *Life of Jesus* by the Carthusian Rudolph of Saxony, and a book describing the lives of the saints, *Flos Sanctorum*, by Jacobus Voragine, translated by another Cistercian, Fray Gauberto Vagad. 'By the frequent reading of these books,' Iñigo would write in his autobiography – referring to himself in the third person as 'the pilgrim', 'he conceived some affection for what he found there narrated. Pausing in his reading, he gave himself up to thinking over what he had read… Suppose that I should do what Saint Francis did, what Saint Dominic did?' Iñigo was still tempted by dreams of worldly glory, but found that these fantasies left him feeling 'dry and dissatisfied', while the idea of imitating the ascetic practices of the saints left him consoled. 'Thus, step by step, he came to recognize the difference between the two spirits that moved him, the one being from the evil spirit, the other from God.'[336]

During the long period of Iñigo's convalescence, his older brother Martin, now the Lord of Loyola, was away fighting the French. His care was therefore in the hands of Martin's wife Magdalena. 'It is possible,' suggests one of Iñigo's biographers, 'that in his weakened and tormented condition Iñigo might have been erotically stimulated by the tender and intimate ministrations of the beautiful Magdalena.'[337] He appears to have fallen in love with his sister-in-law, and in his seething imagination to have confused her image with that of the Virgin Mary. Many years later, he told a novice that he had to cover the picture of the mother of Jesus in his prayer book 'so that his intense affection and passion for her might not be aroused.'

The sublimation and purification of Iñigo's incestuous, adulterous passion led to a revulsion at the memories of his past sins of the flesh. He determined to atone for them by making a pilgrimage to Jerusalem. As soon as he was well, he left Loyola on a mule, heading for Barcelona on the Mediterranean on the first leg of his journey to Palestine. Before reaching Barcelona, he stopped at a Benedictine monastery in Montserrat where he placed his sword on the altar, and exchanged his fine clothes for a tunic of sack-cloth. From Monserrat, he walked to the town of Manresa where did menial work in a hospital in exchange for food and lodging, and begged for his livelihood in the street.

---

335   W.W.Meissner, *Op. Cit.* p. 54

336   Ignatius of Loyola, *Op. Cit.* V. quoted in W.W. Meissner, *Op. Cit.* p. 47

337   W.W. Meissner, *Op. Cit.* p. 57

Much of his time at Manresa was spent in a nearby cave where he undertook savage penances and prayed for many hours at a time. He followed a programme of fasts, sleepless nights, vigils, flagellation and other assaults on his body to subdue the source of physical desire. He kept a record of his spiritual progress which became, in due course, his *Spiritual Exercises* – 'a book not *on* spirituality but rather a book *of* spirituality', 'a guide for spiritual renewal in the Roman church during the entire Counter-Reformation…' and 'one of the most influential works in Western civilisation'.[338]

It was now that Iñigo came across the equally influential *Imitation of Christ* by Thomas à Kempis, accepting, like the Flemish mystic, that 'without victory over self, there can be no rationality, no belief, no salvation'. The *Spiritual Exercises* dwell on the reality of the Devil; of the real danger of damnation for those who fail to realise that 'man is created to praise, reverence, and serve God our Lord, and by this means save his soul.'[339]

The months Iñigo spent at Manresa 'proved to be the decisive period of his remarkable conversion'. Now a penniless pilgrim, he made his way to Venice and from there took passage to Palestine. Christian pilgrims were tolerated by the Ottoman authorities, but the Franciscans who retained their role as guardians of the Holy places gave short shrift to Iñigo's idea of a mission to convert the Muslims and, with an authority delegated by the pope, sent him back to Europe. Here Iñigo decided that the education he had received as a young *hidalgo* was inadequate. He went back to school in Barcelona, and then studied at a number of schools and universities – Barcelona, Alcalá, Salamanca and finally at the Collège de Montaigu at the University of Paris. It was at Paris that there formed around him a group of men who shared his values and ambitions. On the Feast of the Assumption of the Virgin Mary, 15 August 1534, in the small chapel of Saint Denis in Montmartre, they took vows of poverty, chastity and obedience, and made a commitment to band together to work for the salvation of lost souls.

Throughout his years of study, Iñigo – who took the name, Ignatius – was sustained by the charity of his admirers, many of them formidable women: 'there seems little doubt that throughout his career Ignatius had a special effect on women and exercised an unusual attraction on them.'[340]

---

338   *Ibid.* p. 87
339   *Ibid.* p. 91
340   *Ibid.* p. 245

Ignatius's 'skills as a preacher were limited, but in intimate conversation or discussion in small groups, the force of his personality found ample play.' As with Francis of Sales, his background eased his path with kings, cardinals and popes. He was small but good-looking: 'his character was Basque to the core – headstrong, obstinate, passionate, stern, taciturn, but even so at times charming and playful'; and 'always the noble knight, the man of breeding and courtly manners, bearing himself with dignity and respect for his fellows. Despite his detachment, men were drawn to him irresistibly.'[341]

The ambition to work for the conversion of Muslims in the Holy Land died hard; Ignatius and his followers had assembled in Venice, intending to sail to Palestine, but found their path blocked by the war that had broken out between Venice and the Ottomans. They therefore decided to turn to the pope to direct their vocation, and added to the three vows they had taken of poverty, chastity and obedience to their religious superior a fourth of absolute obedience to the successor of Peter: 'every one of the company was to be under obedience to Paul III and his successors, without hesitation, irresolution or excuse, in whatever pertained to the progress of souls and the propagation of the faith.'[342] Five years after taking their vows at the chapel in Montmartre, Ignatius and his companions formed the Society of Jesus with Ignatius as its first Superior General. Sponsored by Ignatius's friend, Cardinal Contarini, it was approved by Pope Paul III in 1540 in the Bull *Regimini militantis Ecclesiae*.

Given a house and church in Rome by the pope, Ignatius now devoted himself to drawing up the *Constitutions* for the Society – 'legal documents, regulations…without emotion, personal reflection, nuance or suggestion about the man who poured his life's blood and even dying breath into them.'[343] They reflect his military training, and the authoritarian trait in his character: 'to a certain extent freedom was threatening in the mind of Ignatius'. Other religious orders, of course, took vows of obedience but this was obedience to a religious superior within a closed community. Obedience for a Jesuit was to a superior many miles away for, while Ignatius remained in Rome, his companions dispersed throughout the world, to counter the Reformation in Germany and, in the case of Ignatius's fellow Basque, Francis Xavier, to

341 *Ibid.* p. 188
342 Philip Caraman, *Op. Cit.* p. 124
343 W.W. Meissner, *Op. Cit.*, p. 220

convert the pagans in India, China, Borneo and Japan The criteria for entry into the Society of Jesus were strict, and the training of a Jesuit long and arduous, but the order attracted the men of the highest calibre from the social elite – among them the 4th Duke of Gandia, Francis of Borgia, the great-grandson of Rodrigo de Borgia, Pope Alexander VI.

Ignatius founded two colleges in Rome – one Roman, one German – and these 'were perhaps Ignatius's principal contribution to the Counter-Reformation...' Although the Jesuits would become the zealous adversaries of the Protestants, 'their founder was not animated by any anti-Lutheran ardour.'[344] Education was to become the prime means by which the Society would re-invigorate the Catholic Church. At the time of Ignatius's death, there were already twenty-two Jesuit houses in Italy, nineteen in Spain and Portugal, five in Japan. At its inception, the Society was to be limited to sixty members but this was repeatedly amended as demand grew for Jesuits as teachers, missionaries and confessors of kings. In due course the Society would become the largest and most powerful of all Catholic orders – to its enemies arrogant, scheming, manipulative – justifying any action however immoral if it was *ad majorem gloriam Dei* – for the greater glory of God; yet like their founder indifferent to privations and embracing martyrdom as they travelled throughout the world seeking the salvation of souls.

62.   The Spanish Inquisition

Just as the Reformed religions never took root in Italy, so the ideas of Luther and Calvin had little impact in Spain. The Jesuits, founded by the Spaniard Ignatius of Loyola, may have formed the vanguard of the Counter-Reformation, but Ignatius remained for most of his life preoccupied with the salvation of the souls not of Protestants but of Muslims in Palestine. One reason was that there were no precursors of heretical dissent in Spain as there had been elsewhere in Europe with Wycliffe in England and Hus in Bohemia: on the Iberian peninsula, the ideological struggles since the *Reconquista* had been with the minority religions of Judaism and Islam. Another reason was that the Catholic Church itself, in the person of Francisco Jiménez Cisneros, Archbishop of Toledo from 1495, had embraced the new learning.

---

344   Philip Caraman, *Op. Cit.* p. 170

The third and perhaps most conclusive reason was the existence in Spain of a national institution dedicated to the elimination of heresy, the Spanish Inquisition. Modelled in almost all details on the Inquisition first established by Dominic Guzman in the thirteenth century to stamp out the Cathar heresy in Languedoc, it had been established by Queen Isabella of Castile in 1480 to uncover backsliding or, worse, proselytising by Jews who purported to have converted to the Catholic religion. At the request of Ferdinand and Isabella, Pope Sixtus IV published a bull authorising the establishment of the Holy Office of the Inquisition with a Council, Inquisitors and an Inquisitor General – the first, as we have seen, was the Dominican friar Tomas de Torquemada – all appointed by the Crown. The Inquisitors in turn established their own lay auxiliaries known as 'familiars' – in effect an autonomous police force exempt, or claiming to be exempt, from the *fueros* – the established laws of the land. Their tribunals punished transgressors in a number of different ways for a variety of crimes – the most severe being burned at the stake for heresy, with the sentences being carried out not just in public – as elsewhere in Europe – but as the high point of an elaborate ceremony lasting many hours, with a vigil, prayers, processions and a mass, attended by local officials and often the king. Known as an *auto da fé* – an act of faith – it was a spectacle that attracted enthusiastic spectators from the countryside surrounding the cities in which these executions were held. 'There is no doubt that the autos were popular... The auto in its heyday was an event without parallel in any other country'. [345]

The Jewish community on the Iberian peninsula, established during the Roman empire, was the largest in Europe. It had survived and on occasions collaborated with the Muslim invasion of Visigothic Spain in the 7th century, and under the caliphate, and later during the long *Reconquista,* had lived side by side with both Muslims and Christians in what was called the *convivienza.* As in other parts of Europe, the prosperity they established in trade and the professions thanks to their literacy and numeracy made them unpopular. Far from being the fossilized and degraded exemplars of the old but now superseded covenant of Pope Gregory the Great's *sicut Judaeis*, the Jews now lorded it over Christians in a Christian country.

By 1492, as we have seen, it had seemed clear to the Catholic monarchs, Ferdinand and Isabella, that a return to *convivienza* had failed, and that the Jewish presence in their kingdoms posed a threat to the faith of their

---

345   Henry Kamen, *The Spanish Inquisition. An Historical Revision.* p. 205

subjects. They therefore decided on the most drastic measures of all – the total expulsion of the Jews. The move was not against a race but against a religion and the decision was made by the monarchs; but the edict 'came from the Inquisition' – that issued in Aragon 'a ferocious document that…reeks of a virulent anti-Semitism not present in the Castilian text'.[346]

At first the expulsion of the Jews from Spain – 'a traumatic experience that left its impact for centuries on the western mind'[347] – seemed to meet with some success: the Rabbi of Córdoba was received into the Church with the Papal Legate as one of his sponsors; but, while observant Jews may have left the kingdom, the *conversos* community had grown in size. The *conversos* remained not just prominent in commerce and the professions, but also were entwined with the nobility and embedded in the Church itself: at least four bishops were of *converso* origin, and so too a cardinal, Juan de Torquemada, the uncle of the first Inquisitor General. *Conversos* were neither ashamed of nor embarrassed by their Jewish origins; they still provoked the envy and antagonism of their Old Christian compatriots, and there were still cases of them reverting secretly to the customs and practices of their ancestral religion.

Added to the continuing danger of back-sliding among the *conversos* was the growth of Illuminism – the Gnostic belief that the soul can attain a perfect union with God making the Church's sacraments superfluous and sin impossible. Its precepts were declared heretical, and the *alumbrados* were pursued by the Inquisition: Ignatius of Loyola came under suspicion when he was studying at the University of Alcalá. Though there were few Lutherans or Calvinists in Spain, the success of the Reformers during the reign of Charles V in other parts of his domain led him to alert his daughter Joanna, acting as regent in Spain, and advise a ruthless repression of Protestants. 'This historic letter of 25 May 1558…marks the turning point in Spain. From now on…heterodoxy was treated as a threat to the state and the religious establishment'.[348] The Inquisition now drew into their net any Spaniard who had spoken in favour of Luther's ideas. In 1559, the year following Charles V's letter to Joanna, eighty-eight Protestants or crypto-Protestants were condemned by the Inquisition, two of them English sailors. Eighteen of them

---

346   *Ibid.,* p. 20
347   *Ibid.,* p. 22
348   *Ibid.* p. 94

were burnt. It was no doubt the inclusion of the English sailors among those condemned that fostered the infamous reputation of the Spanish Inquisition: in fact, writes Henry Kamen,

> the Protestant crisis in Spain, often presented as a singularly bloody period of repression, seems almost humane when compared with the ferocity of religious persecution in other counties. In Spain probably just short of a hundred persons were condemned to death by the Inquisition between 1559 and 1566. The English authorities under Queen Mary had executed nearly three times as many heretics as died in Spain in the years just after 1559, the French under Henry II at least twice as many. In the Netherlands ten times as many had died.[349]

Kamen's 'historical revision' of the Spanish Inquisition in the 1990s did much to refute the black propaganda of Protestant polemicists over the centuries, but it does not make it seem an attractive institution – it was a precursor in many ways of agencies established by totalitarian regimes in the twentieth century. However, 'the scenes of sadism conjured up by popular writers on the Inquisition have little basis in reality.' [350] It barely impinged on the rural population: most of its victims were urban *conversos*, and since confiscation of their property was part of the punishment for their crimes, 'many ordinary Spaniards came to the conclusion that the Inquisition was devised simply to rob people'.[351]

While the Inquisition's main preoccupation was with heresy, its purpose was also to preserve social stability: for example, it investigated and punished sexual misdemeanours. It may have been staffed largely by clerics but it was established and administered by the crown. While it led a relatively tranquil existence among the people of Spain, its political life was always stormy. Since the distinction between sin and crime was imprecise, the Inquisition was beset throughout its long career with quarrels over jurisdiction.' it had serious disputes with the papacy, the bishops, and virtually every other authority of state.'[352] It became legalistic, recording even the most trifling details of its proceedings and employing lawyers as well as clerics: indeed in 1608 King Philip III 'stipulated that all inquisitors must be *letrados* or jurists.

---

349   *Ibid.* p. 98
350   *Ibid.* p. 189
351   *Ibid.* p. 149
352   *Ibid.* p. 157

This training in the law meant that the popular hysteria which saw tens of thousands of women burned or drowned as witches in other parts of Europe found no traction in Spain. A gathering of lawyers in Granada in 1526 stated that 'the majority of jurists in this realm agree that witches do not exist'. While in Bordeaux in 1609 eighty witches were executed by the judge Pierre de Lancre, judges in Spain dismissed charges of witchcraft for lack of evidence, regarding it as a delusion.

Back-sliding Muslims as well as Jews were subject to scrutiny by the Inquisition. Treated magnanimously after the fall of Granada in 1492, there remained a large population of *Mudéjares* (unconverted Muslims) in the province which resisted assimilation and attempts to convert them to Christianity. Their diet and clothing was distinct from that of their Christian neighbours, and they persisted with their prayers, fasts and ablutions as directed by their clergy, the *alfaquis*. They were protected from the Inquisition by Ferdinand but, after his death, they were forcibly baptized by the *Comunidades*, those who rebelled against the imposition of Flemish officials by Charles V, which freed them from vassalage to the landed nobility who backed the king. Following the defeat of the *Comunidades*, the Inquisition refused to allow these coerced Christians to return to Islam; and 'it now seemed incongruous to tolerate Muslims elsewhere in the kingdom of Aragon. Charles V ordered the baptism of all *Mudéjares*: 'from 1526 the Muslim religion no longer existed in Spain officially: all *Mudéjares* were now *Moriscos*'.[353]

In the decades which followed, measures were taken to forcibly assimilate the *Moriscos* when it came to their diet, their clothing and their use of Arabic. 'How can people be deprived of their natural tongue in which they were born and raised?' complained a Morisco in Granada. 'The Egyptians, Syrians, Maltese and other Christian people speak, read and write in Arabic, and are still as Christian as we are.' In 1568, the oppression of the *Moriscos* led to a revolt in Granada and the neighbouring countryside. It was a brutal conflict with atrocities committed by both parties – priests massacred by the *Moriscos* and *Moriscos* slaughtered or sold as slaves. The *Moriscos* had shown not just that they rejected assimilation, but that they were a potential fifth column should any Muslim army invade across the straights of Gibraltar. That threat was reduced after the defeat of the Turkish fleet at Lepanto in 1571, but it was never wholly absent. *Morisco* bandits remained in the mountains,

---

353   *Ibid.* p. 217

and Aragonese *Moriscos* made contact with the rulers of Morocco and the Huguenots in France.

It was therefore decided in 1609 that the *Moriscos*, like the Jews, should be expelled from Spain. The deportations began in Valencia with half the population of Spanish *Moriscos*, and subsequently continued from the rest of Spain. 'In all about three hundred thousand *Moriscos* were expelled from a peninsula population of some three hundred and twenty thousand.' [354] Now the second of the three cultures of Iberia had been extinguished. Cardinal Richelieu, who had seen many enormities, described the expulsion of the Moors from Spain as 'the most barbarous act in human annals'.

63.   Purity of Blood

Purity of blood – *Limpieza de Sangre* – was a concept that arose out of the enmity between the Old and New Christians in Spain. It was novel in that racial prejudice was unknown in the Roman Empire: the Romans were quite 'insensible as to whether someone had black skin or white, or vice versa.'[355] Citizens were favoured over non-citizens but that had nothing to do with race: Paul of Tarsus was a Jew, Augustine of Hippo a Berber. There was some prejudice against Jews because of their particularism and monotheistic beliefs but, as we have seen, allowances were made by the Roman emperors out of respect for the longevity of their customs and traditions. Similar concessions were made by the popes, and later by Mohammed who regarded Jews, like Christians, as one of the 'peoples of the Book'.

The Jews, however, were not simply members of a religion like Christians or Muslims but a people – a group defined by their Semitic descent as well as their beliefs; and, though they might adopt another religion, qualities inherited from their past were not washed away with the waters of baptism, nor the natural affinity of human beings of like for like. The result was the growth in Spain – particularly after the mass conversions that followed the pogroms of 1391 – of that large, prosperous and influential community of *conversos* that was of such concern to the Inquisition.

The purpose of the Inquisition's tribunals was to sift the wheat from the chaff among the *conversos*, but to many Old Christians there was a simpler

---

354   *Ibid.* p. 227

355   Hugh Thomas, *The Slave Trade. The history of the Atlantic Slave Trade: 1440-1870.*

solution – the exclusion of *conversos* from public office. Statutes passed to this effect were condemned by the leaders of the Church in Spain and by Pope Nicholas V in Rome, but a mistrust of *conversos* entered the bloodstream of Spanish Catholics, and the founding of the Inquisition 'gave a major impetus to the spread of this discrimination'.[356] In 1483 a papal bull reserved the posts of episcopal inquisitors to Old Christians, and at the same time the ancient military orders passed statutes excluding the descendants of both Muslims and Jews. So too the Jeronymites (or Hieronymites), an order following the Augustinian rule and inspired by the irascible translator of the Bible, Jerome. The Inquisitor General Torquemada, when founding the monastery of Saint Thomas Aquinas in Avila in 1496, applied to the pope for a decree excluding the descendants of Jews.

In 1555 and 1556, the Cardinal Archbishop of Toledo, Juan Martinez Siliceo, published purity-of-blood statutes stating that the *converso* 'inherits the bad moral inclinations of his Jewish ancestors' and is therefore unfit to hold any public office.[357] Siliceo was in fact an adopted name to disguise the humble rural origins of Juan Martinez Guijarro who viewed himself as the harbinger of the second Spanish *Reconquista* and made every possible effort, cunning and conspiracy included, to have his anti-*conversos* laws approved by both royal and papal authorities.'[358]

There was strong and effective opposition to anti-*conversos* legislation not just from the *conversos* themselves – embedded in both the Church hierarchy and the royal administration – but also by devout Old Christians who thought it iniquitous to discriminate against blood relatives of Jesus of Nazareth and his disciples. The Italian Dominican, Cardinal Thomas Cajetan, considered it irrational because 'our salvation comes from the Jews, from whom Christ, the Apostles and many fathers of the faith were born according to the flesh. This refusal would generate in Jews an excuse not to convert to Christianity, knowing that their children would be rejected forever'.[359]

Ignatius of Loyola rejected the idea of *limpieza de sangre*. He said he would regard it as an honour to belong to the same race as Jesus. Among Ignatius's six companions who took vows in the church in Montmartre was the

---

356   Robert Aleksander Maryks: *The Jesuit Order as a Synagogue of Jews. Jesuits of Jewish Ancestry and Purity-of-Blood Laws in the Early Society of JesusI*, p. 233

357   *Ibid.*, p. 30

358   *Ibid.*, p. 30

359   Quoted in *Ibid.* p. 196

converso, Diego Lainez, who later became a close collaborator of Ignatius and, on his death, was chosen as his successor. 'Neither for the electors nor for the Judeo-phobic Pope Paul IV, who approved the election with a moving speech, was Lainez's *converso* lineage – which he made public on the occasion – any impediment to the highest administrative post in the Society of Jesus.'[360] Lainez's successor, Francis of Borja, was equally open to the admission of *conversos* leading the king, Philip II, to refer to the Society as 'a synagogue of Hebrews'.[361] Borgia appointed the Portuguese *converso* Ignacio de Azevedo provincial of Portugal and rector of the first Jesuit college in Lisbon. Later, in 1570, sailing as visitor to the new Jesuit province of Brazil, Azevedo's ship was captured by Huguenot pirates led by Jacques Sourie. Azevedo and his thirty-nine young companions, among them a nephew of Teresa of Avila, were stripped naked, cut into pieces and thrown into the sea.

The martyrdom of Azevedo, and the achievements of other *converso* Jesuits holding high office in the Society, should have established beyond doubt the devotion to the Catholic Church of the *converso* Jesuits; but their very prominence provoked envy, particularly among Italian and Portuguese members of the society who did not want the next General to be a Spaniard, and so, on the death of Francis de Borgia in 1572, with the encouragement of Pope Gregory XII, managed to prevent the election of Juan Alfonso de Polanco, Ignatius's secretary and close collaborator, choosing instead a Fleming, Everard Mercurian. Mercurian immediately embarked upon a programme to 'cleanse the house', removing from office *converso* Jesuits in Rome, and also Lombardy where the presence of Spanish *conversos* had caused resentment. Some of the *conversos* sent back to Spain formed a group opposed to Mercurian's policy called the *memorialistas,* calling for an autonomous Jesuit province in Spain. When the Flemish Mercurian died in 1581, an Italian Claudio Acquaviva replaced him, and continued Mercurian's policy of excluding the Spanish *conversos* from positions of power. Coming from the Neapolitan nobility – he was the son of the Duke of Altri – Acquaviva, aged only thirty-seven on his election, proved exceptionally successful during his tenure of office. By the time of his death, the Society had tripled in size with 13,000 members in 550 houses and 15 provinces; and missions either augmented or established in India, China, Japan, Paraguay, Canada and the Protestant nations in Europe – in particular England where Catholics were severely persecuted under Queen Elizabeth I.

360   *Ibid.* p. 94
361   *Ibid.* p. 133

The Spanish *conversos* fought back against their marginalisation, with two of their number, José de Acosta and Francisco de Toleda, calling for a General Congregation in 1594 to recall Acquaviva and his three deputies – among them the anti-*converso* Rhinelander, Paul Hoffaeus. The move backfired. As a punishment for the rebelliousness and disobedience of the Spanish *conversos*, the Congregation passed a law, 'violating Loyola's will as expressed in the Jesuit *Constitutions*, and contradicting the practice of the first three Generals, ruling that any Jewish or Muslim ancestry was an insurmountable impediment for admission to the Society'. Henceforth, even the most sincere converts were to be excluded 'on the basis of ethnic discrimination'. The law provoked outrage and led to a twelve-year campaign to have it repealed. At the Sixth Congregation, held in 1608, it was not repealed but modified: purity-of-blood need now be established only for the previous five generations. This statute remained in force until the 29th Congregation in 1946 when it was finally annulled – 'almost certainly under the sway of the Shoah'.[362]

64.   Slavery

The enslavement of men, women and children is found from pre-history until the end of the nineteenth century, and in some guises persists today. The condition of slaves has varied from that of viziers and potentates to that of beasts of burden. The lives of prisoners taken in war were considered forfeit and slavery better than death. In ancient Egypt slaves built the pyramids and in Athens the Parthenon. In ancient Rome with many captives from its many wars, slave labour sustained the economy, yet slaves were also domestic servants, sometimes on intimate terms with their owners, and could be cultivated and literate: Cicero's indispensable secretary, Tiro, was born a slave.

In Palestine, slavery was as ubiquitous as it was in the rest of the Roman Empire. Jesus of Nazareth, who 'took on the condition of a slave'[363], said nothing about slavery as such. The sick servant about whom the Centurion was so anxious that he sought out Jesus to cure him was almost certainly a slave[364]. Paul of Tarsus told those who could gain their freedom to do so[365] but

---

362   *Ibid.* p. 213
363   Philippians, 2:7
364   Matthew, 8:8
365   1 Corinthians, 7: 21

regarded it as a matter of indifference as to whether a Christian convert was a slave or free: 'there are no more distinctions between Jew and Greek, slave and free, male and female, but all of you are one in Christ Jesus.'[366] Indeed, Paul returned a runaway slave, Onesimus, who 'was like a son to him,'[367] to his owner, Philemon, albeit as a brother, no longer a slave.

The first Christians did not want their movement to appear seditious and so, because 'slavery was entrenched in the social order… Christian leaders did nothing to disturb it'.[368] Yet Christianity appealed to slaves because, though it did not challenge their civic status, it acknowledged their equal worth. To free a slave – manumission – was considered a good work by the Church: under the Emperor Hadrian, a man named Hermes is said to have freed 1,200 slaves one Easter. In 321 a Church decree, *Manumissio in ecclesia,* proposed a simple form of emancipation and was approved by the Emperor Constantine. In the early fifth century, a rich Christian, Melania, liberated 8,000 slaves when she decided to withdraw from the world.[369] In 649, the king of the Franks, Clovis II, married his British slave Bathilda who upon his death acted as regent for her son, and 'used her position to mount a campaign to halt the slave trade and to redeem those in slavery'.

As well as encouraging manumission, the Church dignified manual labour: Christ's foster-father, Joseph, was a carpenter and Paul of Tarsus a tentmaker. The Rule of Benedict of Nursia made labour part of a monk's daily routine: *laborare est orare* – to work is to pray; and though some religious communities relaxed the rule and employed serfs, the land cleared by Cistercian monks and lay-brothers for crops and pasturage led to the birth to the wool trade between England and Flanders, and fed the growing European population. At the same time, the development of windmills and watermills made human labour redundant in the grinding of corn; and, where that labour was still required, it was found that 'serfs not only produced more than slaves did, but they required no permanent guards'.[370] Thomas Aquinas taught that enslavement was an offence against natural law, and the only English pope, Adrian IV, ruled that slaves should receive the sacraments including the sacrament of marriage, and that marriage between slaves '"ought not to

---

366   Galatians, 3: 28

367   Tom Wright, *Paul. A Biography*, p. 281

368   Robin Lane Fox, *Pagans and Christians*, p. 296.

369   Hugh Thomas, *The Slave Trade. The History of the Atlantic Slave Trade: 1440-1870.* p.26

370   Hugh Thomas, *Op. Cit.* p. 26

be in any way prevented": Christendom gasped...' [371] By the eleventh century, slavery had been abandoned in central Italy and Catalonia. In England, the Domesday Book records only 25,000 *servi* and by 1200 slavery had disappeared in England. [372]

Under Islam, slavery was ubiquitous with slaves coming from a number of different sources. It existed in Arabia prior to the advent of the Prophet Mohammad, and was permitted by the Koran if those enslaved were not Muslims. It has been shown that 'the number of concubines taken by Muslims jumped dramatically with the early Islamic conquests' with 'a similar leap in the number of slaves taken more generally. One of the first public buildings erected in the new Muslim garrison city of Fustat (later Cairo) was a slave market'.[373] Africans were brought from the interior of east Africa by Arab slave merchants based on the island of Zanzibar; and from west Africa in caravans across the Sahara desert: 'anything between 5,000 and 20,000 slaves may have been carried north annually from the region of the Niger to the harems, the barracks, the kitchens or the farms of the Muslim Mediterranean and near East during the late Middle Ages'.[374] Raids were made among the Slavs in what is now Ukraine on the north coast of the Black Sea: the English words 'slave', French *esclave*, German *sklave*, are derived from 'Slav'. The Arab term 'Mamluk' was used for slave soldiers, abducted from among Circassians, Abkhazians, Georgians, Albanians and Greeks by Egyptian sultans: they became an elite military force and in 1250, after defeating the crusaders under King Louis IX in the Nile delta, seized power in Cairo, killed the last of Saladin's descendants and, taking Acre in 1291 finally drove the Latin Christians out of Palestine.

A hundred years or so later, the Ottoman Turks formed their own elite force of slave-soldiers, the Janissaries: adolescent boys were taken from their villages in the Balkans, converted to Islam, and trained as members of the Sultan's bodyguard. They were not allowed to marry but were paid a salary and in due course became not just an elite military force but a powerful lobby protecting their own interests in Istanbul. A contingent of 12,000 Janissaries fought at the Ottoman siege of Vienna in 1683 which was raised by the combined forces of the Holy Roman Empire and the Polish-Lithuanian

---

371   Christopher Brooke, *The Medieval Idea of Marriage*, p. 52

372   Hugh Thomas, *Op.Cit.*, p. 36

373   *Slavery and Islam*, location 2605

374   Hugh Thomas, *Op. Cit.* p 44

Commonwealth under Jan Sobieski. This defeat of the Ottomans marked the high point of Islamic expansion into Europe by land; just as in 1571 the defeat of the Turkish fleet at the Battle of Lepanto by a fleet commanded by Charles V's illegitimate son, Don John of Austria, had halted the Ottoman's advance into the western Mediterranean.

The naval victory at Lepanto, and the raising of the siege of Vienna, did not mean that the thousand-year war between Christianity and Islam was at an end: it would be two centuries before the Christian nations within the Ottoman empire would be freed, and Constantinople would never be re-taken. Moreover Muslim regimes remained entrenched in North Africa from Egypt to Morocco, replenishing their supply of slaves by raids on Christian coastal communities in Spain, France, Italy and as far away as Ireland. 'Modern historians…produce reliable estimates that Islamic raiders enslaved around a million western Christian Europeans between 1530 and 1640: this dwarfs the contemporary slave traffic in the other direction, and is about equivalent to the number of west Africans taken by Christian Europeans across the Atlantic at the same time.' [375] Religious orders were founded to ransom abducted slaves; the manacles of some of those so reprieved remain hanging from the walls of the cathedral in Majorca. However, despite the existence of flourishing slave markets in Tunis and Algiers, a combination of Islam's toleration of sexual intercourse between a male owner and his female slave, the similar colour of the skin of those living on both sides of the Mediterranean, and a *hadith* that directed 'Muslims to treat their captives like members of their own family', [376]seems to have blurred over time the distinction between masters and slaves.

Where slavery survived in Europe, it was at the interface between Islam and Christendom on the Iberian peninsula. There had been a mass enslavement of Christians following the Muslim conquest of Visigothic Spain – thirty thousand were said to have been sent to Damascus; and many centuries later, in 1482, during the last war between Christians and Muslims in Spain, the Sultan of Granada enslaved several thousand Christians during a successful raid on the Sierra de Ronda, leading King Ferdinand in retaliation to enslave the entire population of the Muslim city of Benemaquez. He did the same when he conquered Málaga in 1487; a third of the captives were sent to Africa

---

375   Diarmaid MacCulloch, *Op. Cit.* p. 57

376   Karen Armstrong, *Muhammad. A Biography of the Prophet*, p. 180

in exchange for Christian prisoners held there; a third (over 4,000) were sold by the Spanish Crown to help pay for the cost of the war; and a third were distributed through Christendom as gifts – 1000 went to Pope Innocent VIII, fifty girls were sent to Isabella, the Queen of Naples, and thirty to Leonora, the Queen of Portugal. [377] In 1492, the year when Granada fell to Ferdinand and Isabella, and Christopher Columbus sailed to America, the historian Hugh Thomas estimates that 'there must have been about 100,000 slaves in Spain, Seville having the largest such population.'[378] Slavery in Castile was far from defunct.

A new pressing demand for labour followed Columbus's discoveries in the West Indies. The lure was gold, but who was to mine it? Initially the Spanish enslaved the local population: in 1496 Columbus returned from his second voyage with a dozen Indians hoping to sell them on the Spanish market to help repay his investors. The system of *ecominendas* (trusteeship), established in Spain in the wake of the *Reconquista*, whereby the King awarded groups of subject peoples as well as land to his followers, had been transferred to the Spanish conquests in the Americas. However, the *ecominenderos* ran into two difficulties The first was the frailty of the Indians, who suffered from diseases caught from the Europeans (there was an epidemic of smallpox in 1518), but even when healthy were constitutionally unsuited to hard labour: Diego Colon, the son of Christopher, told King Ferdinand that the Indians struggled 'to break the rocks in which gold was found.'[379] The working population of Hispaniola went into precipitous decline, and raids for slaves on neighbouring islands were not enough to replenish the stock. As a result, on 22 January, 1510, King Ferdinand authorised the export of fifty slaves from Spain. 'This was the beginning of slave traffic to the Americas. Gold in Hispaniola was the lure.'[380]

The second obstacle were objections raised by the Church. In 1510, a group of Dominican friars arrived in Santo Domingo from Spain. Horrified by the mistreatment of the Indians that they witnessed, the superior, Pedro de Córdoba, commissioned Friar Antonio de Montesinos to preach a sermon denouncing those who had enslaved Indians.

---

377   Hugh Thomas, *Op. Cit.* p. 83

378   Hugh Thomas, *Rivers of Gold*, p. 29

379   Hugh Thomas, *The Slave Trade*, p. 92

380   *Ibid.*, p. 93

Tell me by what right of justice do you hold these Indians in such a cruel and horrible servitude? On what authority have you waged such detestable wars against these people who dwelt quietly and peacefully on their own lands? Wars in which you have destroyed such an infinite number of them by homicides and slaughters never heard of before. Why do you keep them so oppressed and exhausted, without giving them enough to eat or curing them of the sicknesses they incur from the excessive labour you give them, and they die, or rather you kill them, in order to extract and acquire gold every day?[381]

To perpetrate such injustice, said Montesinos, was a mortal sin, and no Dominican would give absolution to slave-owners who did not repent and make restitution.

Montesinos' sermon outraged the Spanish colonists in the congregation, among them the governor, Diego Colon. He complained to King Ferdinand; the Dominicans were recalled to Spain; but once there persuaded Ferdinand to appoint a commission to investigate the treatment of the Indians. The enquiry led in due course to the Laws of Burgos that regulated the treatment of the indigenous inhabitants of Spain's colonies in the Americas.

Also in the congregation that heard the sermon of Antonio de Montesinos was a young *hacienda* and slave owner, Bartolomé de las Casas, who at the age of eighteen had emigrated with his father from Spain to Hispaniola. He had been allocated land and slaves, and fought against the indigenous Tainos. In 1519 he entered the Dominican order and was ordained a priest – the first to be ordained in the Americas. He noted down the content of the sermon of his fellow friar, Montesinos, but did not agree that the system of *ecominendas* was in itself the cause of injustice. However, in 1513 he took part as a chaplain in the conquest of Cuba and saw for himself the massacres and atrocities perpetrated by the Spaniards. 'I saw here cruelty on a scale no living being has ever seen or expects to see.' Nonetheless he accepted, in partnership with a friend, an *encomienda* on the south coast of Cuba and for a short while lived as both priest and land-owner.

A year later, las Casas had a change of heart. He surrendered his *encomienda* and urged others to do the same. His call fell on deaf ears and, realising that only a change in the law would protect the native population,

---

381   Bartolome de Las Casas. *Witness: Writing of Bartolome de Las Casas*, edited and
        translated by George Sanderlin, (Maryknoll: Orbis books, 1993) p. 66-67

Las Casas returned to Spain to agitate for reform. Many in government, including those in charge of royal policy towards the Indies, were themselves absentee *encomienderos* and were unsympathetic. Las Casas placed his hopes in an appeal to the conscience of the king but Ferdinand died in 25 January, 1516. The crown now passed to Ferdinand's grandson, the underage Charles of Habsburg, who was residing in Malines. Las Casas set out for Flanders, and while passing through Madrid presented a written appeal to the regents acting for Charles still in his minority, Cardinals Ximenes Cisneros and Adrian of Utrecht.

Entitled *Memorial de Remedious para Las Indias,* Las Casas' pamphlet produced a dramatic result. Cardinal Cisneros appointed three Jeronimite monks to govern the Indies, and Las Casas was appointed Protector of the Indians with an annual salary of 100 pesos. However, in his *Memorial* he made one fateful suggestion which he later greatly regretted: if the Indian slaves were to be freed, and were anyway unfit for hard labour, the solution might be to import hardier black slaves from Africa. 'Like all enlightened men of his time, he believed that an African enslaved by Christians was more fortunate than an African in domestic circumstances'.[382]

Las Casas returned to Santa Domingo, arriving two weeks after the Jeronymite monks. Although he had played a role in their selection, and in drawing up the new protocols they were to follow, he found that they had already compromised in the face of the implacable opposition of the Spanish colonists. Las Casas denounced the Jeronymites' inadequate reforms, and accused them of complicity in the kidnapping of Indians. He became so loathed by the settlers that his life was in danger, and he had to withdraw into the Dominican friary. The Jeronymites did adopt that fateful suggestion of Las Casas, writing to the young king Charles that 'all the citizens of Hispaniola demand that Your Majesty give them a licence to be able to import blacks, because the Indians are insufficient to sustain them in the island.'[383] 'These requests were strongly supported by Fra Bartolomé de Las Casas… His desire to protect the Indians from ill-treatment blinded him for many years for the need to guard against similar mistreatment of Africans'.[384]

Charles of Habsburg, now aged eighteen, had taken over from his regents as ruler of his empire. Holding court in Saragossa, he took the advice of his

---

382   Hugh Thomas, *Op. Cit.* p. 98

383   *Ibid.* p. 97

384   *Ibid.* p 98

minister, Rodriguez de Fonseca, and on 18 August, 1518, issued a licence to transport black slaves from Africa directly across the Atlantic to the Indies. The beneficiary of this licence was the governor of Bresse in the Franche-Comté (Burgundy), Laurent de Govenot, making the birth of the transatlantic slave-trade 'in every sense a European enterprise: the grant of the Flemish-born Emperor to a Savoyard, who sold his rights, through a Castilian, to Genoese merchants – who in turn would of course have to arrange for the Portuguese to deliver the slaves'.[385]

The Spanish dependence upon the Portuguese for the supply of slaves was in conformity with the Treaty of Tordesillas of 1494 by which both nations accepted a line of demarcation drawn at the request of Ferdinand and Isabella by Pope Alexander VI between their emerging overseas empires. This allocated the coast of Africa and what became Brazil to Portugal, with the rest of South America and the West Indies to Spain. The Portuguese dominance of trade with west Africa had started with the exploratory voyages of Prince Henry the Navigator in the previous century. The third surviving son of King John I of Portugal, and nephew through his mother Philippa of King Henry IV of England, Henry took part with his father in the capture of Ceuta opposite Gibraltar on the north coast of Africa – hitherto a base for slave raids on the coast of Portugal. As Grand Master of the Military Order of Christ, which had acquired the assets of the Templars after the order's dissolution, Henry developed a new and more manoeuvrable ship, the caravel, to sail down the coast of Africa in search of gold, and make contact with a rumoured Christian king, Prester John.

Madeira and the Azores were colonized by the Portuguese; the Canary Islands by the Spanish. By 1444, Portuguese explorers had sailed past the southern limits of the Sahara desert and the band of Islamic rule, and so established maritime trade-routes to rival the land routes across the Sahara. Portugal, and particularly the port of Lagos, became an *entrepôt* for imported gold but also slaves. A slave trade already existed in Africa, but 'the Portuguese market transformed it and caused an upheaval in the interior of Africa'.[386] The innovation in the issue of a licence to Laurent de Governot by Charles V was not the crown's sanction of the slave-trade as such, but the transport of slaves directly from Africa to the Americas – the start of a trade 'of every-increasing dimensions', a source of profit to the merchant as well as the Crown, that was to last for the next 350 years.

---

385   *Ibid.* p.99
386   *Ibid.* p.110

It should be noted that, throughout those years, though initially some Africans were obtained by raids, the majority were bought from local rulers and were already enslaved. Slavery was not an European invention: not just in Africa but in the Americas 'the indigenous people of the New World did not find the concept of slavery an innovation: slaves, with something close to the European definition of the term, were well known in Mexico, Peru, and most of the other societies... Slaves in Old Mexico, for example, may have constituted a tenth of the population, almost all obtained by capture in war. These captives were primarily required for human sacrifice.'[387] That custom was brought to an end by the Christian *conquistadors*, but not the institution of slavery.

Further protests against slavery were made by churchmen. Charles V's confessor, the Dominican theologian Domingo de Soto, wrote that it was wrong to enslave a free man but his words 'struck few chords at the time'. Another Dominican, Alonso de Montufar, Archbishop of Mexico, wrote to Charles's son Philip that 'We do not know any just cause why negroes should be captives any more than the Indians.' He received no reply. Slavery was condemned in Rome; the acceptance of a thousand slaves by Pope Innocent VIII in 1482, some of which he passed on to his cardinals, proved to be an aberration. The Renaissance pope Leo X wrote that 'not only the Christian religion but nature itself cried out against a state of slavery', and Pope Paul III ascribed slavery to 'Satan, the enemy of the human race, who always opposes all good men so that the race may perish...' In April, 1639, Pope Urban VIII issued a bull *Commissum nobis* reaffirming the edict of 'our predecessor Paul III 'that those who reduced others to slavery were subject to excommunication'. 'Throughout the seventeenth century, letters of protest on the matter of the slave trade continued to arrive at the sacred Congregation for the Doctrine of the Faith in Rome from Capuchins, Jesuits and bishops': 'these isolated denunciations,' wrote Hugh Thomas, 'enables the Catholic Church to present herself as a prefigurement of the abolitionist movement more plausibly than is often allowed.' Indeed, Thomas goes on, 'it is hard not to feel that there were, by 1600 or so, enough hostile voices to have brought the trade to an end within the next generation or so had it not been for the entry into the business of the Northern European Protestants'.[388]

---

387   *Ibid.* p. 104
388   *Ibid.* p. p.147-148

65. The Jesuit Reductions

Before leaving the Americas, two instances of specifically Catholic interventions in the slave-trade should be noted. The first was the work of a Catalonian Jesuit, Peter Claver, who after graduating from the Jesuit college in Catalonia, sailed to Cartagena on the coast of what is now Colombia, then the principal slave market in the New World. Together with another Jesuit in the city, Alonso de Sandoval, Claver began a ministry to the African slaves. He met each slave ship as it docked, overcoming the stench of urine, faeces and putrefying flesh to tend to the slaves. He baptised the sick and dying, 'easing their tortured bodies , his lips meeting their filthy sores with a kiss'. His mission was to restore their dignity as human beings, and save their souls. He trained Africans to act as interpreters and, over his forty years in Cartagena, baptised three hundred thousand slaves.

Unlike Alonso de Sandoval, Claver did not call for the abolition of slavery; 'he accepted it as an inevitable though regrettable element in the social system';[389] but he devoted every waking moment to the most wretched and repulsive segment of humanity. His mission extended from the slave-ships to the prisons and plantations: his compassion from slaves to captive English sailors, and Portuguese prisoners of the Inquisition, though his priority was always the African slave. He loved music, and found it something he could share with those who spoke no European language. He could be 'pig-headed and difficult', and antagonised the colonial establishment, but he was also admired and revered for his uncompromising adherence to the teaching of Christ.

The second intervention was the creation of refuges for the Indians deep in the interior of South America by priests of the Society of Jesus which gave rise to an unique experiment in the ordering of human affairs. As we have seen, following Columbus's discoveries, the pursuit of riches, above all gold, had been accompanied by a drive by missionaries for the salvation of the souls of the indigenous populations of the New World. Though some of the more brutal and less scrupulous Spanish and Portuguese colonists questioned whether Indians, and in particular native Africans, did indeed have souls, it was never doubted by the Church and missionaries were sent to the Americas by different religious orders – the Jeronymites, the Dominicans, the

---

389   John Coulson (Ed.), *Op. Cit.* p. 372

Franciscans. Despite the 1537 Bull of Pope Paul III excommunicating those who enslaved South American Indians, there were clergy who did not think this applied to Africans. As late as 1693, a French priest, Father Labat, on his arrival at the prosperous Caribbean colony of Martinique, described how his monastery, with its nine brothers, owned a sugar mill tended by thirty-five slaves, of whom eight or ten were old or sick, and about fifteen badly nourished children.[390]

The Jesuits, founded in 1540, and growing in strength and numbers only during the second half of the sixteenth century, were late-comers to the missions. They too were known to have African slaves. 'A Jesuit, Frei Miguel Garcia, who arriving in Brazil about 1580, and being among the earliest members of the order to reach that dominion, was horrified to find that his Society owned Africans who, as he thought, had been illegally enslaved. He decided to refuse to hear confession from anyone who owned African slaves. He and a colleague returned to Europe in protest. But nothing more was heard of them'. [391]

The Jesuits were more diligent when they came to evangelise the Guarani Indians in the interior of the South American continent to the south of Brazil. Approached via the tributaries of the Rio de la Plata, and governed notionally by a Spanish governor residing in the precarious settlement of Buenos Aires, the aims of Church and state were the same: to gather the nomadic Indians into settlements called 'reductions' where they could be civilised, evangelised and protected from enslavement by the Spanish colonists and *encomienderos*. As a prelude, Diego de Torres, the Provincial appointed by Acquaviva, the Jesuit General in Rome, ordered the liberation of all Indians held as slaves in the Jesuit *encomiendas*, a move which made him unpopular not just with the colonists but also the Franciscans who had tolerated slavery. In 1612 he secured a legal ruling that 'every Indian, regardless of his former status, was in law a free man who gave his labour in return for a fair wage and humane treatment'. 'If Torres had done nothing else in his life', wrote the Spanish historian, Antonio Astraín, 'he would have a just title to be regarded throughout the world as one of mankind's principal benefactors'.[392]

Three years before, in 1609, three Jesuits and a local Guarani *cadique* (tribal chieftain) had established the first reductions, San Ignacio Guazu. Further

390   *Ibid.* p. 455
391   Hugh Thomas, *Op. Cit.* p. 147
392   Quoted in George O'Neil, *Golden Years on the Paraguay,* p. 20

missions followed. There was resistance, particularly from the shamans, loathe to abandon the powers they enjoyed as priests of their ancestral religion: seven Jesuits were killed by hostile Indians in these early years. However, the semi-nomadic life led by the Guarani in the jungle left them vulnerable to slave-raids, and so many were attracted by the protection offered by the reductions. By nature amenable, the Guaranis were monotheists, 'believing in a Father God', and so had 'a natural aptitude for the Christian experiment'.[393] By the beginning of the eighteenth century, there were around 150,000 Indians living in around forty different reductions in territory that now forms part of Argentina, Brazil and Paraguay.

Each of the reductions followed the same design, with straight streets converging on a central square. In the middle of the square was a cross, and a statue of the mission's patron saint, with the four sides made up of the church, the Jesuits' residence, a hospital, and a home for widows and orphans. The churches were magnificent, and the priests' dwelling palatial on the exterior, but inside furnished with the simplicity of a peasant's cottage in Spain.

Overall direction of the reductions was in the hands of the Jesuit priests – with a minimum of two to each reduction – acting through the Guarani caiques. All property was held in common, but married couples were allocated a house and some land which they could cultivate on those days of the week when they did not work in the communal fields. 'Since the Indian was naturally indolent, the economy could be maintained only by a system of well-regulated labour' [394] 'If a man could work, he was made to work, if not he was supported by public funds.' The morning started with prayers and hymns followed by breakfast, after which one of the priests would lead the Indians to their work in the fields, singing hymns, stopping to pray at shrines – the file growing shorter as the Indians broke away to go to work, until 'finally the priest and acolyte with the musicians returned alone'.

Economically, the reductions were self-sufficient 'while socially they were more advanced than any Indian community since the passing of the Inca Empire. In their hey-day, there were twenty looms at least in each town. Visitors could see at work highly skilful carpenters, goldsmiths, masons, sculptors, stone-cutters, bell-founders, calligraphers, instrument makers, engravers, copyists, even armourers';[395] and of course butchers in the abattoirs

393   Philip Caraman. *The Lost Paradise. An Account of the Jesuits in Paraguay, 1607-1768*, p. 40
394   *Ibid.* p. 158
395   *Ibid.* p. 127

who ensured a supply of beef from the large herds of cattle. The principle export of the reductions was *yerba*, the source of the infusion *maté*, which had grown wild, but which the Jesuits successfully established in plantations close to the reductions.

For the welfare of their citizens, they developed 'a system that European countries took another two centuries to attain.' Many eighteenth-century writers saw the reductions as an attempt to put the ideas expressed by Thomas More in his *Utopia* into practice, and 'certainly the ideas of Thomas More were very much in the air…but in the final analysis, the reductions owed their character more to the practical needs of the missionary situation than to any preconceived utopia'.[396] Visitors were impressed by the absence of beggars, and the good health of the Indians, and also by their cleanliness: their washing and toilet facilities were far in advance of anything in the Spanish towns'. The Indians were prone to infestation by worms because 'their eating habits remained half-savage'. As Christians, they had abandoned cannibalism but 'for the most part they lived on beef which they ate without salt and half-raw'. Nor were they immune to smallpox: a series of epidemics decimated the population of the reductions.

Besides epidemics, the chief threat to the reductions came from slave raids by the Mamelucos – ' the rabble population of São Paulo in Brazil'. Also known as the Paulistas they had made their base into an impregnable fortress so that the Portuguese governor in Rio de Janeiro had 'abandoned not only the desire but all hope of subduing their stronghold'.[397] In the course of a hundred and fifty years, they are thought to have made two million slaves. Their first raid on the reductions was in 1629, and the Indians in the missions were found to be easy prey. As a result, the mission fathers decided to move 12,000 Guarani from reductions vulnerable to the Mamelucos – an heroic trek through the jungle from which only 4,000 survived.

The Jesuits then asked the Spanish crown for permission to form militias armed with European firearms. Despite opposition from the colonists, permission was given: the Spanish kings had consistently backed the Jesuit missions, both to protect the Indians from enslavement but also, to protect their territory from Portuguese incursions. The militias were formed and the reductions cavalry in particular became the crack force at the service of the Spanish crown.

---

396   *Ibid.,* p. 110
397   *Ibid.* p. 56

'For success in the field, the Guarani depended on their Spanish officers. Left to themselves, they were unable even to draw themselves up in battle order; but with Spanish officers they were singularly effective, fending off the Mamelucos and defending the frontier with Brazil. Altogether, between 1637 and 1745, the reduction Indians entered the field at least fifty times on behalf of the king, at considerable sacrifice of lives, working time and money'. On seven occasions, Guarani troops came down the Parana to defend Buenos Aires. 'The system explains how Spain took possession of the new world with a handful of men, while most of her military strength was engaged in Europe'.[398] The Portuguese worked through the Mamelucos, the Spanish used their missionaries.

An irony here was that many of the Jesuit missionaries were not Spanish. An increasing number came from the German-speaking dominions of the Habsburgs and elsewhere in central Europe. Some were 'men who in their home countries would have occupied a university chair or attained eminence in scientific research'. Antonio Sepp came from the Austrian Tyrol. Florian Paucke, an artist and writer, was Swiss. Anton Hals was a German. Peter Pole was an English sea captain who, after landing at Buenos Aires, had become a Catholic and then a Jesuit priest. Philippe Lemaire was a Fleming who had worked as a joiner in naval docks and used his skills in the construction of the reductions' magnificent churches. These were designed by architects among the missionaries – a Czech, Juan Kraus, and Italians José Brasanelli, Andres Blanqui and Juan Primoli who had been professor of architecture in Milan. The fact that these educated Europeans should choose to live in a land infested with ants, snakes, man-eating jaguars, and large toads whose venomous urine, if it touched the eyes, led to blindness, demonstrates the enduring belief of the followers of Ignatius Loyola that any sacrifice is a price worth paying if it brings one soul to faith in Christ and eternal life.

The reductions had internal as well as external enemies. The Spanish colonists resented their exemption from taxes, and that their economies flourished without the use of slaves. There was also envy and resentment to be found among members of the secular clergy. A bishop, Don Bernadino Cárdenas, accused the Jesuits of concealing silver mines worked by Indian labour; of withholding tax due to the Crown; of breaking the seal of the confessional; and of having deceived the King to secure land that should have gone to the

---

398   *Ibid.* p. 106

Spanish settlers. There has been rumours of the Jesuits' secret riches before the charges made by Cardenas: 'to many settlers it had seemed incredible that the Jesuits should bury themselves in the jungle merely to preach to savages.'[399] Official investigations established that the charges were false, but suspicions remained in the public imagination and 'the government at Madrid, from the middle of the seventeenth century, became increasingly suspicious of the Jesuits in Paraguay', with the result that the reductions 'were exposed to the almost perennial threat that their privileges on which they depended for survival would be taken from them.'[400] Cardenas's calumnies would be revived many years later when the Society of Jesus itself came under attack in Europe.

The first of two fatal blows that brought down the reductions was the Border Treaty between Spain and Portugal signed in Madrid in January, 1750. The peaceable King of Spain Ferdinand VI, under the influence of his Portuguese wife, Maria Barbara, agreed to a frontier along the Uruguay river which left a number of the reductions under Portuguese rule. The Jesuits fathers were ordered to comply with the treaty by their General in Rome, but were permitted to move those living in the threatened reductions across the Uruguay into Spanish territory. However, the Guarani themselves refused to leave their homes and rebelled. In 1754, the Guarini forces, led by Sepé Tiaraju, initially defeated a Spanish force sent to evict them; but two years later they were defeated by an army of 3,000 Spanish and Portuguese troops in Rio Grande del Sul. 1,500 Indians were killed, as against two Spaniards and one Portuguese.

The second blow came in 1761 with the expulsion of the Jesuits from all the territories of the King of Spain, and the return to Europe under obedience of the Jesuit missionaries. This came as a result of the campaign against the Society of Jesus by European statesmen, in particular the chief minister of Portugal, the Marquis of Pombal. Anti-clerical pamphleteering revived all the calumnies put about by Bernadino Cárdenas, and were used to justify the recall of the Jesuit missionaries. After their departure, some attempts were made by the Franciscans to preserve the reductions, but in due course they fell into decay, their inhabitants either enslaved or merging with the wider population.

---

399   *Ibid.* p. 89
400   *Ibid.* p. 97

66.   Other Jesuit Missions

At the other end of the Americas was the Jesuit mission in Quebec, the French settlement on the Saint Lawrence River in Canada. Occupied by the English in the early seventeenth century, it was not until Quebec reverted to French rule in 1632 that the Jesuits embarked upon a mission to the Hurons who, with the Iroquois, were the dominant tribe of Indians in the region. The Jesuit superior, Paul Le Jeune, wished to emulate 'the Jesuit utopia, that was being developed in Paraguay' but found the Huron less amenable than the Guarani. 'Do you hunt in heaven?' he was asked 'or make war, or go to feasts?' 'What opposed them was a complete way of life with its trial marriages, tortures and cannibal feasts.'[401]

An outbreak of smallpox that coincided with the arrival of new missionaries from France led the Indians to see the Jesuits in their black soutanes as harbingers of death. Priests were captured by Iroquois, traditional enemies of both the Huron and the French, and died after protracted and refined torture. Eight Jesuits were martyred – one, Charles Garnier, the son of rich Parisians, was known to have walked forty miles in the heat of the summer to baptise a dying Indian and so save him from Hell.

At the same time as the Jesuits in Quebec embarked on their unsuccessful mission to the Huron, the Church in Japan, established by the first of all the Jesuit missionaries, Francis Xavier, in the previous century, suffered a ferocious persecution after a Spanish captain had said that the missions were a cover for the conquest of Japan by Spain. Two hundred and fifty Christians were killed, among them twenty-six priests, and among the priests three Jesuits – Paul Miki, John Goto and James Kisai. Jesuit priests were murdered by the indigenous inhabitants on a mission to Guam and the Marianas Islands. A Jesuit mission to Ajacán on what is now the coast of Virginia was betrayed by their guide, an Indian who, captured in his youth, had been educated by the Jesuits. In Ajacán he returned to his native village and, with a band of native warriors, killed the missionaries.

In quite different parts of the world, the Catholic missionaries not only suffered death but varied forms of torture following the custom of their captors. Cannibalism held a particular horror for Europeans, but at least by the time their flesh was eaten their suffering was over. The twenty-six

401   Coulson, John (Ed.), *Op. Cit.* p. 321

martyrs of Japan were crucified and then stabbed with spears. The Iriquois who captured the party of missionaries in 1642 tore out their fingernails and gnawed at their fingers. 'The refinements or '"caresses" as the Indians called them, of their torture involved hot coals, knives, mutilations; death, the climax of what was more a diabolic rite than a mere display of cruelty, was usually by burning – the body afterwards being divided and eaten.' Jean de Brébeuf had a necklace of red-hot tomahawks placed around his neck and, as he lay dying, the Iroquois drank his blood to ingest his valour. His heart was reserved for their chief.[402]

Compare this to the death of another zealous Catholic, Balthasar Gérard, whose right hand was burned off with a red-hot iron, his flesh torn from his bones with pincers in six different places; his body disembowelled while he remained conscious; his heart torn from his chest and thrown in his face, his body then quartered and his head cut off. Gérard was not a martyr, but the assassin of William the Silent, and his protracted execution was not the work of savages but the God-fearing citizens of the Netherlands. So too another Catholic fanatic, François Ravaillac who, after assassinating Henry IV of France, had his four limbs tied to four different horses which then galloped off in different directions – the prescribed punishment for killing a king.

A death comparable to that of Balthasar Gérard was that of Catholic priests in England following the succession of Elisabeth Tudor to the throne in 1558. Elisabeth's Religious Settlement, though it retained some traces of the old religion, was essentially Protestant. Her own beliefs were opaque: she said she did not want to look through a window into men's souls, and let no one peer into her own. However, her Act of Supremacy confirmed the breach with Rome, and Protestants such as Sir William Cecil were appointed to high office. Under the Act of Supremacy she was proclaimed not Supreme Head but Supreme Governor of the Church in England; and a subsequent Act of Uniformity restored the use of Cranmer's 1552 prayer book, and made it obligatory to attend church on a Sunday. It passed the House of Lords by three votes.

To the disgust of Presbyterian Protestants, the Settlement retained an episcopacy but most of Elisabeth's appointments to vacant bishoprics were Protestants who had left England during the reign of Mary. All the lay commissioners appointed to enforce the Acts were Protestants, leading to a

---

402   *Ibid.* p. 322

wave of iconoclasm – the removal from parish churches of images, statues, rood screens, the replacement of altars with communion tables, and the banning of all vestments other than a surplice. Many parishes were slow to comply: their priests remained Catholic; so too their parishioners who hoped that in due course there would be a return to the old religion. It was not to be. 'By the end of the 1570s, whatever the instincts and nostalgia of their seniors, a generation was growing up which had known nothing else, which believed the Pope to be Antichrist, the Mass a mummery, which did not look back to the Catholic past as their own, but another country, another world.'[403]

Catholics who rejected the settlement, known as 'recusants', formed a significant minority, particularly among the landed gentry who resented the 'new men' brought to power and enriched by the Reformation. They formed an underground Church with links to those who had fled abroad – among them deans, archdeacons, cathedral canons and academics from Oxford and Cambridge who had been dismissed for refusing to swear allegiance to the new laws. Ten years after the accession of Queen Elisabeth, in 1568, an English college was established in Douai in the Spanish Netherlands to provide a Catholic education for the sons of recusant Catholics. As the Protestant nature of the Elizabethan Settlement became apparent, the fathers of the Council of Trent ruled that to attend the services of the Church of England was a grievous sin: 'it is far better to suffer most bitter cruelties than to give the least sign of consent to such wicked and abominable rites'. In 1569, a rebellion led by the Earls of Westmoreland and Northumberland would, if successful, have replaced Elisabeth with Mary Stuart, at one time Queen of France, and by then Queen of Scotland: the rising was defeated. A further conspiracy uncovered by the government's efficient network of informants, involved a Florentine banker, Roberto Ridolfi, and the Duke of Norfolk who planned to bring Spanish troops to England under the Duke of Alva and, like the northern earls, place Mary Stuart on the throne.

These attempts to replace Elisabeth with her Catholic cousin were supported by Pope Pius V who in 1570 issued a bull, *Regnans in Excelsis*, which declared Elisabeth's claim to the throne of England invalid, and released her subjects from any loyalty they felt was due. Raised in poverty, working as a shepherd before becoming a Dominican, Pius was devout, austere, severe. He was one of the last popes to defend the claims of predecessors such as Gregory VII or

---

403   Eamon Duffy, *The Stripping of the Altars*, p. 592

Boniface VIII that his office gave him the right to depose monarchs. The case of Elisabeth Tudor seemed straight-forward: her mother, Anne Boleyn, had not been legitimately married to her father, Henry VIII, and as a bastard she could not be queen. His bull did not please the Catholic kings of France and Spain who had long-since rejected papal claims to a universal sovereignty; and it made life more difficult for those Catholics in England who had not joined the rebellion of the northern earls, and hoped for a measure of tolerance of the practice of their faith in return for loyalty and discretion.

This was never likely: religious uniformity was considered essential, and Presbyterian Protestants also suffered persecution; but they never posed a threat as did the Catholics whose Spanish co-religionists had a large standing army close at hand on the other side of the North Sea. The mass was banned; attending mass, or putting up a priest, was treasonous and Catholic priests by definition subversive agents of foreign powers. In 1571 the executions began. A married layman, John Storey, who had fled to Flanders and taken service with the Duke of Alba, was kidnapped by a ship's captain, taken to England and there condemned to be hanged, drawn and quartered at Tyburn outside London.[404] In 1573, Thomas Woodhouse, a parish priest in Lincolnshire under Queen Mary, was arrested and charged with saying mass. Everard Hanse, raised as a Protestant in Northamptonshire, converted to Catholicism and, after training as a priest in Douai, returned to England where, while ministering to Catholics in the Marshalsea Prison, he came under suspicion because someone recognised the foreign manufacture of his boots. He was hanged, drawn and quartered at Tyburn. Executions took place elsewhere in England. In 1577 Cuthbert Mayne, was hanged, drawn and quartered at Launceston in Cornwall. In 1586, Margaret Clitherow, a butcher's wife in York, was charged with sheltering priests. Hoping to save her family from the confiscation of property that followed conviction for treason, she refused to plead and so was placed naked beneath a board on a bridge over the river Ouse upon which rocks were laid until she was crushed to death.

In 1580, the Society of Jesus decided upon a mission to England. Its first provincial, Robert Persons, a former fellow of Balliol College, Oxford was accompanied by another Oxford scholar, Edmund Campion. Persons was the son of a Somerset farmer; Campion of a bookseller in Paternoster Row close to Saint Paul's Cathedral in London. Campion, made a fellow of Saint

---

404   Now Marble Arch

John's College, Oxford, in 1557 had had no qualms about taking the Oath of Supremacy. In 1566, he was chosen to welcome Queen Elizabeth on a visit to the university, and took part in a public debate in her presence. He impressed not only the queen but her chief minister, William Cecil. Rapid preferment in the Church of England seemed in prospect and in 1564 Campion was ordained as a deacon but, already convinced by Catholic teaching, he did this 'with remorse of conscience and detestation of mind'.

With rising doubts about the Church of England, Campion left Oxford for Ireland and from there escaped to Douai where he was received into the Catholic Church. He joined the English College, founded by William Allen, a former fellow of Oriel College Oxford. Later, he went to Rome on foot and there was accepted into the Society of Jesus. He was assigned to the Austrian province, studied in Brno in Moravia and was ordained priest by the Archbishop of Prague in 1578. He taught at Prague University until 1580 when he joined Robert Persons on the mission to England. Intercepted correspondence alerted the government to their arrival which, coinciding as it with a rising in Ireland backed by the pope, stigmatised them as agents of a foreign power with a political agenda. Campion denied this in a pamphlet entitled *Challenge to the Privy Council*, later known as *Campion's Bragg*; and in another, *Decem Rationes* (*Ten Reasons)* dismissing the claims of the Anglican church which was printed in the home of recusants at Stonor Park near Henley-on-Thames. Pursued by government agents, he moved around the country – saying mass, hearing confessions and preaching to recusant Catholics.

Campion was betrayed when staying at Lyford Grange in Berkshire, arrested and taken to the Tower of London. He was offered glittering posts in the Church of England if he would abjure his Catholic Faith but he refused. During four months imprisonment in the Tower, he was tortured by the rack – a machine which pulled the body apart – to force him to disclose the names of those who had concealed him in their houses. Despite being enfeebled after the torture, he was able to defend the arguments of his pamphlets in a public disputation. He was put on trial for treason in November, 1581, and found guilty. 'In condemning us,' he said, 'you condemn all your own ancestors, all our ancient bishops and kings, all that was once the glory of England – the island of saints, and the most devoted child of the See of Peter'. Together with two other priests, Ralph Sherwin and Alexander Briant, Campion was tied to a hurdle, dragged to Tyburn where the sentence of the Lord Chief Justice, Sir

Christopher Wray, was carried out: you shall 'be hanged and let down alive, and your privy parts cut off, and your entrails taken out and burned in your sight; then your heads to be cut off and your bodies divided into four parts, to be disposed of at Her Majesty's pleasure. And may God have mercy on your souls'.

Queen Elisabeth's anxieties were not unreasonable: the threats to her rule were real. However, providence seemed to favour her. In Edinburgh, Mary Stuart – the Catholics' candidate to replace her – was forced to abdicate in favour of her one-year-old son James. After a failed attempt to recover her throne, she fled to England to seek the protection of her half-cousin Elisabeth Tudor. Confined for the next nineteen years in various strongholds in the north and midlands – a safe distance from both Edinburgh and London – she never met Elisabeth. Willingly or unwillingly, Mary was the constant object of treasonous intrigue. She was finally put on trial in 1587, found guilty of treason, and clumsily beheaded. She believed herself to be a martyr for the Catholic faith.

Mary Stuart's death did not bring the schemes to depose Elisabeth to an end. The year after her execution, a Spanish fleet of 130 ships sailed from Corunna to the Spanish Netherlands to ferry Spanish troops commanded by the Duke of Parma across the North Sea to England. The enterprise failed – the galleons set on fire and scattered by the more nimble English warships. This triumph for the smaller English navy brought an end to a threat of invasion, but did not stop the persecution of Catholics. Elisabeth died in March, 1603. Her successor, James I of Scotland, was the son of Mary Stuart and his accession raised hopes among Catholics of a measure of tolerance. When these hopes were disappointed, a group of fanatical Catholics decided to kill the king and members of parliament with explosives – the Gunpowder Plot whose discovery and subsequent frustration is still celebrated in Britain annually on 5 November with bonfires and fireworks.

Persecution continued under Charles I, an Anglican with a Catholic wife, but harassed by the growing body of Puritanical Protestants in the House of Commons. After his defeat in the English Civil War, Charles was executed and England became a Presbyterian Commonwealth. Measures against Catholics grew more severe under the Commonwealth's Lord Protector, Oliver Cromwell: the Jesuit Peter Wright, and the secular priest John Southworth, were both executed at Tyburn. Nor did the persecution cease when the easy-going Charles II was restored to the throne in 1660. A flare-up of anti-

Papist hysteria came when a renegade Catholic priest, Titus Oates, claimed to have uncovered a Jesuit plot to assassinate Charles II. This resulted in the execution of around fifteen innocent men, among them the last priest to die at Tyburn – the white-haired fifty-five year old Catholic Bishop of Armagh, Oliver Plunkett – hanged, drawn and quartered on 1 July, 1681.

The triumph of Protestantism in England meant that more was made of the burnings under 'Bloody Mary' than the executions under her half-sister Elisabeth. In fact, the body count was roughly equal. 'Elizabeth I burned no Catholics,' wrote Eamon Duffy, 'but she strangled, disembowelled and dismembered more than 200'.[405] Diarmaid MacCulloch estimates that between 1581 and 1681 more than two hundred priests and at least sixty lay men and women were executed as traitors. 'In fact England judicially murdered more Catholics than any other country in Europe, which puts English pride in national tolerance in an interesting perspective.'[406]

67. The Thirty Years War

The suspicion of Queen Elisabeth and her government that the Jesuit priests sent to England were acting as agents for Philip of Spain was largely mistaken but not far-fetched. The first three Generals of the Society of Jesus had been Spanish, and many of the first Jesuits came from provinces governed by the Habsburgs – Spain itself but also Naples, Milan, the Spanish Netherlands, Austria and the Tyrol. The Habsburg rulers both in Madrid and Vienna shared the Jesuits' zeal for countering heresy through preaching, education, example and, where all else failed, the sword. To them little distinction was to be made between the interests of their dynasty and that of the Church – a view contested by other Catholic monarchs, in particular the kings of France and the popes.

On his abdication in 1556, the Emperor Charles V had divided his territories, as we have seen, between his son Philip and his brother Ferdinand – the former being assigned the Habsburg possessions in Italy, the Netherlands and Spain with its overseas empire; the latter receiving the Habsburg states in Germany, Austria, Bohemia and the Crown of the Holy

---

405   Eamon Duffy, *Fires of Faith. England under Mary Tudor*, p. 82
406   Diarmaid MacCulloch, *Op. Cit.* p. 392

Roman Emperor – now customarily going to a Habsburg but still a matter of election and so its possession by no means assured. The religious settlement at Augsburg the year before Charles's abdication had established the principle of *cujus regio, ejus religio* – the religion of the sovereign is the religion of the state – a tricky formula to apply in Germany with its two thousand separate jurisdictions. By and large, Protestantism became established in the north (Saxony, Brandenburg) and Catholicism in the South (Austria, Bavaria). The main point of friction was the Netherlands – a rich province now ruled by Philip and effectively divided between a rebellious Protestant north and a loyal Catholic south. The division was *de facto*, not *de jure*; a twelve-year truce had been agreed by King Philip III of Spain in 1609; but it was only a truce, and by 1620 the Spaniards were preparing to reconquer the north and extirpate heresy when the truce ended.

Armies in this period were no longer the feudal levies of the Middle Ages, nor the national conscripts of later centuries. They were largely mercenary and so expensive to raise and maintain. As in Italy in the previous century, there were able generals north of the Alps, themselves for hire, who would raise *ad hoc* armies of mercenaries and adventurers from throughout Europe: 'no one thought it strange that a French soldier should command an army against the French, and loyalty to a cause, to a religion, even to a master, was more highly esteemed than loyalty to a country.'[407] Critical to any campaign was the availability of funds to pay the solders and here Spain, with bullion coming from Peru, was in a strong position. Its weakness were its lines of communication with the Netherlands. Since the defeat of the Armada by the English, and the growth of the naval power of the Protestant Northern Provinces, the sea route from Spain was hazardous while the land route from Italy over the Alps up the Rhine valley was long and vulnerable to hostile powers – in particular the Val Telline, a valley on the route north through the Alps from Milan, that could be blocked by Venice, Savoy or the Protestant Swiss Grisons (Graubünden).

A second threat came at Heidelberg on the Rhine, the capital of the Palatinate, whose ruler, one of the seven Electors of the Holy Roman Emperor, was a Calvinist. The principality was divided into the Lower Palatinate on the Rhine and Upper Palatinate in the east of Germany bordering Bohemia. The Elector in the last years of the sixteenth century, Frederick IV, had married

---

407   C.V.Wedgwood, *The Thirty Years War*, p. 14

the daughter of William I of Orange. His son, Frederick V, who succeeded his father in 1610, married, at a grand wedding in London, Elizabeth Stuart, the daughter of James 1st of England – reputedly as lively as her grandmother, Mary Queen of Scots but, unlike her, an ardent Calvinist. When they married, both Elisabeth and Frederick were sixteen years old.

On their return to Heidelberg, Elizabeth drew up plans for the renovation and expansion of the royal palace while Frederick, mentored by his minister, Christian of Anhalt, put himself forward as the leader of the Empire's Protestant princes. At issue were the rights of princes *vis-à-vis* the Emperor – who despite the acceptance of the *cuius regio, cuius religio* of the Treaty of Augsburg was thought to be preparing a Habsburg despotism that would re-impose Catholicism by force. The conflict came to a head in Bohemia, the kingdom bordering the Upper Palatinate to the east.

Like the king of Poland, the king of Bohemia was elected by the nobility – the Estates. For over a century, the choice had been a Habsburg – the crown of Bohemia and the Holy Roman Empire worn by the same man; however over that century the religious complexion of the nation had changed: the majority were now Lutherans and Calvinists. This was of little consequence to the Emperor Rudolph who was more interested in art and astrology than religion, and in 1609, under pressure from the Protestants, he issued a *Letter of Majesty* guaranteeing religious liberty in Bohemia. Further pressure led to his abdication – the crowns of Bohemia, Hungary and Austria passing to his younger brother, the Archduke Matthias. On Rudolph's death a year later, Matthias became Holy Roman Emperor and moved the court from Prague to Vienna

Although he was Rupert's younger brother, Matthias was already old and ailing, and so the question now arose as to who should succeed him as Emperor and King of Bohemia. Prosperous and cultivated, Bohemia and Moravia were valuable provinces – Bohemia of particular interest to the Habsburgs because its king was one of the seven Electors of the Holy Roman Emperor. With three votes already in the hands of Protestants – Brandenburg, Saxony and the Palatinate – it was vital that the next king of Bohemia should again be Catholic and a Habsburg. The only plausible candidate was Matthias's young cousin Ferdinand, now the ruler of the Alpine province of Styria with its capital Graz. Educated by the Jesuits, Ferdinand was a zealous Catholic and so likely to be rejected by the Protestant Bohemians; but they put forward no candidate and, with a promise from Ferdinand that he would respect the

Letter of Majesty, he was chosen by the Estates on 17 June, 1617, as Matthias's designated successor.

Things went wrong from the start. The officials left in Bohemia to govern the country when Matthias returned to Vienna and Ferdinand to Graz were Catholics, and at once aroused the wrath of the Protestant nobility by halting the construction of a Lutheran church. Those who objected were arrested and imprisoned. Outraged Protestants demanded their release and on 21st May, 1618, assembled in Prague to press their demands. On the morning of the 22nd, leading Protestants marched towards the royal castle, the Hradschin, followed by an angry crowed. The mob swept through the gates, up the stairs to the audience chamber and into the smaller room where the king's representatives, Jaroslav Martinez and William Slavata, cowered behind the Council Table with their backs against the wall. They were seized and Martinez was thrown out of the window into the courtyard below. 'Jesu Maria,' he cried. 'Let's see if she will protect you,' jeered the crowed; and then, after Martinez's secretary and then Slavata had also be thrown out of the window, 'By God, she has' : their fall, which would otherwise have been fatal, had been broken by a pile of dung.

After this, 'the Defenestration of Prague', the Protestants took control of the government, appointing thirteen Directors and authorising the raising of an army of sixteen thousand men. The only measure taken against the Bohemian Catholics was the expulsion of the Jesuits on June 9th. The response of the Emperor Matthias to this revolt was conciliatory but Ferdinand, the deposed King of Bohemia, called for a crusade to regain his throne.

The Emperor Matthias died the following year, on 20th March, 1619. This led to two elections. The Bohemian Estates met to choose a new king; and, two days later, the seven Electors gathered in Frankfurt to elect a new Emperor. There were few plausible candidates for either post. For the crown of Bohemia, the moderate Lutheran Elector of Saxony was suggested but declined to stand. This left the Elector Palatine Frederick IV who at the earlier election had been considered too young and inexperienced to stand against Ferdinand. Now, promoted by his minister, Christian of Anhalt, he was supported by the Bohemian Calvinists. 'The extremists were in the saddle. Frederick was chosen king by a hundred and forty-six votes to seven.'[408]

---

408   *Ibid.* p. 95

In Frankfurt Ferdinand of Habsburg had the votes of the three Catholic Electors – the Archbishops of Mainz, Cologne and Trier. The vote of Bohemia went to Ferdinand, its deposed king; so too that of the representative of the Lutheran Elector of Saxony who had received no clear instructions from his monarch. The representative of the Elector of Brandenburg followed suit while that of Frederick, the Count Palatine, instructed not to vote for Ferdinand, cast his vote for Maximilian of Bavaria, only to discover that Maximilian had said that votes cast for him should go to Ferdinand. Thus Ferdinand was the unanimous choice for the imperial crown.

In Heidelberg, the young Prince Palatine took counsel as to whether he should accept the crown of Bohemia or not. Most advised against it – among them his father-in-law, King James of England. William of Orange in the Protestant Netherlands urged him to accept; so too his minister, Christian of Anhalt, and Frederick's wife Elisabeth who, while remaining neutral in public, had said that she would rather eat sauerkraut with a king than roast meat with a mere elector. In the end, it was not in the conjugal boudoir, nor even the Council chamber, that the decision was made, but in the youthful conscience of Frederick himself. His co-religionists in Bohemia had put their trust in him: he could not disappoint them. 'It is a divine calling which I must not disobey,' he wrote to his uncle, the Duke of Boullion. 'My only end is to serve God and His Church'.[409] In October, 1620, Frederick left Heidelberg for Prague.

The voice of conscience can err. Was it wise, with the imminent resumption of the war between the Catholic Spanish and the Dutch Protestants, for the leader of Germany's Protestant princes, with his stranglehold on the river Rhine, to become embroiled in an uprising in eastern Europe? To Frederick it was a duty; to Elisabeth, despite being pregnant, an adventure; to Christian of Anhalt an opportunity to make his prince into a king; yet, as the historian C.V. Wedgwood put it, 'were it ever possible in history to single out one action as decisive for the developments which followed it, the acceptance of the Crown of Bohemia by the Elector Frederick was such an act'.[410]

Initially, all went well. Frederick and Elisabeth received a rapturous welcome in Prague. Frederick was recognised as King of Bohemia by the Republic of Venice, and Protestant Denmark, Sweden and the United Provinces of the Netherlands. But he had made one miscalculation: there were

---

409   Quoted in *Ibid.*, p. 98

410   *Ibid.* p. 103

Catholics with consciences too, among them Maximilian von Wittelsbach, the Duke of Bavaria. Maximilian, was a kinsman of the Habsburgs and, like his cousin Ferdinand, a devout Catholic. He was one of the founders of the Catholic League of German princes – a response to the Protestant Union, and modelled on the Guises's Catholic League in France. Maximilian had been educated by the Jesuits; so too Johann, Count of Tilly, a devout Catholic from Brabant in the Spanish Netherlands who had considered becoming a Jesuit but had chosen instead a military career, rising in the service of the Spanish and then the Emperor to the rank of Field Marshal: he was known as 'the monk in armour'. On 23rd of July, 1620, Maximilian and Tilly led an army of twenty-five thousand men from Austria into Bohemia. 'The troops, mercenaries of many tongues, marched to the encouragement of Jesuit preachers; the twelve largest cannon were each called after an apostle, and their general's especial patroness was the Virgin Mary'.[411]

Having crossed the frontier, the Bavarians marched on Prague and, on the night of November 8th, defeated Frederick's army under Christian of Ahalt on a hill outside the city known as the White Mountain. Unaware that a battle was imminent, Frederick and Elisabeth were dining with two English ambassadors in their royal apartments in Prague. The first they knew of the encounter was the arrival of fugitives, and then a hysterical Christian of Anhalt who told them that all was lost and that they must flee. Elisabeth and the children were immediately ferried across the river Moldau, taking with them the crown jewels but leaving in her bedroom 'the Queen's frivolous books…to scandalize the piety of the conquerors'.[412] Frederick followed and with his family took refuge in Brandenburg while Christian von Ahalt fled to Sweden. Their departure caused no regret among the Bohemians who only a year before had greeted them with such enthusiasm. 'Seldom can such innocent and well-intentioned rulers have made themselves more readily disliked'.[413]

The Battle of the White Mountain was the first in a war that over thirty years would devastate Germany and postpone for more than two hundred years its emergence as an European power. What began as a religious conflict between different Christian denominations with each party claiming to be agents for

411   *Ibid.* p. 121
412   *Ibid.* p. 127
413   *Ibid.* p. p. 103

the will of God ended as a largely secular struggle for ascendancy between nation states. Initially, Catholics could claim that it saved souls: in Bohemia and Moravia Protestantism was extirpated, not with the torture and burnings that had so signally failed in the Netherlands, but by an economic persecution which 'fastened up the Protestants like a vice from which the only means of a escape was the denial of their faith'.[414] German replaced Czech as the official language. The University of Prague was made over to the Jesuits. Artists and architects were summoned from other parts of Ferdinand's empire and in Prague there arose 'the stately palaces, the spacious courtyards, the cool loggias of Spanish Milan, the baroque churches of Jesuit Rome'.[415]

But outside Bohemia, within the Holy Roman Empire itself, there was nothing but death and destruction. Both sides employed able military commanders such as Tilly, Mansfeld, Pappenheim, Werth or Bernard of Saxe-Weimar who raised armies of mercenaries from all over Europe.

Of particular note was Albrecht von Wallenstein, born into a family of minor Protestant nobility in Bohemia, who converted to Catholicism in his youth. After the Battle of the White Mountain, he had bought up the estates confiscated from Protestant landowners and in due course 'he controlled a quarter of the land of Bohemia with over a hundred vassals'.[416] Personally frugal, he amassed a fortune, lending large sums to Ferdinand which put the Emperor in his debt. He was not to be compared as a military commander with men like Spinola, Tilly, Mansfeld, Pappenheim, Werth, Bernar or Turenne; his genius was in raising, organizing and above all paying for armies that he put at the service of the Emperor Ferdinand.

It was the failure of others to fund their armies that led inexorably to the atrocities of the Thirty Years War. Unable to pay them, the commanders lost control of their troops who were obliged to live off the land – seizing corn and cattle and slaughtering those peasants who tried to protect their property. With no particular commitment to either side in the conflict, defeated solders after a battle would happily join the winning side: 'the men drifted from one company to another wherever they saw that booty and food were best, without asking what party the captain belonged'. Famine drove the populace to eat cats, dogs, grass, acorns and finally human flesh – bodies of criminals cut down from the gibbets or the newly buried dug up from their graves.

---

414   *Ibid.* p. 149
415   *Ibid.* p. 173
416   *Ibid.* p. 172

The greatest carnage of a civilian population took place when the city of Magdeburg – once the principality of its Archbishop but since 1524 ruled by a Protestant Administrator. In March, 1631, the city was besieged by Tilly and the cavalry commander Count Pappenheim. Led by Pappenheim, Magdeburg was stormed on 20 May, its defences overwhelmed, and the city plundered. Tilly's troops went from house to house looking for booty to make up for their unpaid wages. There were reports of murder, rape and torture. A fire, possibly started to smoke out stubborn defenders, quickly spread, fanned by the wind. Ninety percent of the buildings were burned, and twenty of the city's twenty-five thousand inhabitants died – either slaughtered, suffocated or burned to death. Magdeburg would epitomise in Protestant demonology the callousness and cruelty of the Catholics, but 'one thing only is certain, that neither Tilly nor Pappenheim would have deliberately destroyed the city on whose wealth they had planned to feed and pay their army'.[417]

During the thirty years of the war, there were lulls in the fighting when one side appeared victorious and peace might have been restored, at which point there was a new intervention to restore the balance and the conflict continued. In 1630, when the Emperor Ferdinand and the Catholics were in the ascendant, the Protestant King Gustavus Adolphus of Sweden crossed the Baltic in support of the Protestant princes. Personally courageous, an inspiring commander, and a strategic genius, Gustavus Adolphus had been at war since he came to the throne – with Denmark, Russia and Poland and now with the Holy Roman Emperor. Secure in his rear after domestic reforms, and with an able chancellor, Oxenstierna, he led an army whose cavalry and artillery were not disparate mercenaries but Swedes, 'strong in the sense of national unity' and with 'a collective knowledge of its purpose'. [418] He was secure too in his ability to pay his troops with large subsidies being paid into the Swedish Treasurer by France.

In 1631 Gustavus Adolphus and the Elector John George of Saxony defeated the imperial army led by Tilly at the first Battle of Breitenfeld. It was a pivotal victory: 'from the day of Breitenfeld no man again feared the conquest of the Fatherland by the Habsburg dynasty or the Catholic Church…'[419] but 'the Saxons had paid for the Breitenfeld campaign by a loss

---

417   *Ibid.* p. 289
418   *Ibid.* p. 275
419   *Ibid.* p. 302

of close on a million lives from plague and hunger.'[420] On 14 November, 1632, Gustavus Adophus faced Wallenstein's army in Lützen in the south of Saxony – led by Wallenstein and Count Pappenheim. Again, it was a victory for the Swedes: Pappenheim was killed but so was Gustavus Adolphus – his body with multiple wounds found naked under a heap of dead.

The Swedes did not abandon the German Protestants after the death of their king. Gustavus Adolphus's High Chancellor, Alex Oxenstierna, in partnership with Cardinal Richelieu, continued to pursue the policy of thwarting the Habsburgs. Wallenstein, meanwhile, having lost confidence in the Emperor Ferdinand, and regarding himself as an autonomous power, began to negotiate with the Protestant powers. In Vienna, he was convicted *in absentia* of High Treason, and an order issued to bring him to Vienna dead or alive. In Cheb where Wallenstein was then quartered, two Irish and Scots colonels killed the Czech officers loyal to Wallenstein while an Englishman, Walter Devereux, dragged Wallenstein from his bed and skewered him with a halberd.

Now rid of the treacherous Wallenstein, Ferdinand gave the command of the imperial army to his young son Ferdinand, now crowned King of Hungary. At the same time, his cousin, son of the King of Spain and also called Ferdinand, was appointed Governor of the Spanish Netherlands and, taking command of a well-trained force of Spanish soldiers, he marched north through the Alps to join his cousin Ferdinand of Hungary.

The Protestant forces failed to prevent the conjunction of the two Catholic armies. At Nördlingen in Swabia battle was joined, and the two young Ferdinands triumphed. The Swedish commander Gustav Horn was captured; the Swedish army destroyed. 'From the religious point of view the Battle of Nördlingen was as shattering a victory for the Catholics as Breitenfeld had been a defeat: dynastically it raised the prestige of the Habsburgs to the heights': however, it turned out to be 'nothing but the last flare of a guttering candle'; and with both the Swedes and the German proxies now out of the game , the curtain was raised 'for the last act of the German tragedy in which Bourbon and Habsburg fought out their struggle openly at last to the inevitable end.'[421]

'I have heard it said,' wrote Miguel de Unamuno in *The Agony of Christianity*, 'that after the Reformation had cut Europe in two, Christendom ceased to

---

420   *Ibid*. p. 329
421   *Ibid*. p. 378

exist and the era of national states began – the era of the goddess France and the goddess Germany, the goddess England and the goddess Rome, and the poor sub-goddess Italy.[422] The struggle between the Habsburg dynasty and its opponents ceased to be the conflict of two religions and became the struggle between two nations. A new standard of right and wrong came into the political world. The solidarity that came with a shared faith was lost when the pope opposed the Catholic Habsburgs' crusade, and Catholic France, under the guidance of a cardinal, Richelieu, paid for the armies of Protestant Sweden. 'Insensibly and rapidly...the Cross gave way to the flag, and the battle cry 'Sancta Maria' of Maximilian's army during the Battle of the White Mountain gave way to 'Viva España' from the Cardinal Infante's troops at Nördlingen'[423].

No longer fighting the Habsburgs merely through proxies, the French invaded the empire, taking Alsace and the fortress of Breisach on the Rhine. The original protagonists died – Ferdinand II in 1637, to be succeeded by his son, Ferdinand III; Cardinal Richelieu in December, 1642, and King Louis XII six months later in May 1643. Five days after the death of the French king, a French army under the young Duke of Enghien – the son of the Prince of Condé – faced well-trained troops of Spanish troops commanded by Don Francisco de Melo before the small town of Rocroy on the border with Flanders. The French prevailed. 'It was the end of the Spanish army' and Spanish greatness[424].

Hearing of the defeat, the new emperor, Ferdinand III, authorised negotiations for a treaty with the Protestant powers. The sovereign of Sweden was now a woman, Queen Christina, who yearned for peace. A congress of all the parties was summoned to meet in the Westphalian towns of Münster and Osnabruck. The negotiations proceeded at a snail's pace: it took six months to decide how the delegates were to be seated, and who took precedence as they entered the room. Finally, between May and October, 1648, treaties were signed that brought the Thirty Years War to an end.

There were some territorial changes: Sweden came away with a small band of territory in Pomerania and France with cities on the Rhine. The Elector Palatine, the son of the ill-fated Frederick, retained his Electoral vote but an eighth vote was given to Bavaria. The Protestant United Provinces of the Netherlands were recognised as a sovereign nation. The Treaty accepted,

---

422   Miguel de Unamuno, *The Agony of Christianity*, p. 44

423   C.V. Wedgwood, *Op. Cit.*, p,383

424   *Ibid*. p. 458

for the first time since Charlemagne had coerced the pagan Saxons into the Church, that Catholicism could not be imposed by force.

The loss of life in Germany during the Thirty Years War was probably greater in in relation to the size of the population than in any conflict before or since. C.V. Wedgwood estimates that the population of the Empire 'probably numbered about twenty-one million in 1618 and rather less than thirteen-and-a-half million in 1648'. That is a decline of 7.5 million, or 35% of the population – a larger loss of life than in World War I and even World War II which in 1936, when Wedgwood published her history, was yet to come. It is normally taken as the last of the wars of religion, yet as Wedgwood concludes, 'the demarcation is artificial as such arbitrary divisions commonly are. Aggression, dynastic ambition and fanaticism are all alike present in the hazy background behind the actual reality of war, and the last wars of religion merged insensibly into the pseudo-national wars of the future'.[425]

Some minor issues remained unresolved and many questions unanswered. Had Pope Urban VIII, whose long reign ran parallel with the war, backed Ferdinand II's and Maximilian's crusade, and forbidden Cardinal Richelieu to support the Protestant powers, might the outcome have been victory for the Catholic religion? Certainly, Urban's successor, Innocent X, thought so. He condemned the Peace as 'null, void, invalid, iniquitous, unjust, damnable, reprobate, inane, empty of meaning and effect for all time'. His diatribe was ignored.

68.   Bernini and Galileo

It was during the long pontificate of Pope Urban XII that the basilica of Saint Peter's in Rome was finally completed. Although the Catholic Counter-Reformation was well under way, Urban, the son of a Florentine merchant, was in some ways a throwback to the Renaissance popes – enriching members of his family from the patrimony of the Church, leaving the papal treasury empty by the time of his death. He was also lavish in his patronage of baroque art and architecture; it was he who commissioned Bernini to design the *baldacchino* (canopy) with its curling black marble pillars over the high altar and tomb of the apostle in Saint Peter's basilica. His successors were

---

425   *Ibid.* p. 525

to continue his adornment of Rome with the fountain of the Four Rivers in the Piazza Navona, and the Bernini's large curved colonnade outside Saint Peter's.

It was under Urban that the style in art and architecture known as Baroque became the cultural expression of the Counter-Reformation – a defiant affirmation of a joyful creation to contrast with the bleak vision found in the pure, austere décor of Protestant places of worship. Throughout the Catholic principalities of southern and eastern Europe, and the Latin nations and their overseas empires, churches were adorned with marble and plaster statues of Jesus, Mary, Joseph, the apostles, saints and angels, attended by scantily clad *putti* – plump pink and gilt cherubs; and *trompe-l'oeil* painted on their walls and ceilings opened windows to the heavens. Gone were the Gothic pointed arches and spires: now churches followed classical designs with domes, porticos and pillars – windows placed so that shafts of celestial light should fall upon the gilded statues of the saints. Architects, painters and composers all embraced the baroque, with the cheerful music of a Mozart emanating from Catholic Salzburg contrasting with the more austere compositions of a Johann Sebastian Bach in Protestant Leipzig.

Urban was both a patron and friend of writers and scientists, among them the Pisan polymath Galileo Galilei. Galileo was the son of a lute-player and devout Catholic who in his youth had considered becoming a priest. His father had persuaded him to study medicine at the University of Pisa, but an irrepressible curiosity drew him to mathematics and the natural sciences; and a precious brilliance led him to make radical discoveries, and to develop instruments such a thermoscope, the forerunner of the thermometer. Although his claim to have invented the telescope was unfounded, and he got some things wrong, such as his theory on the tides, Galileo was an inspired scientist and inventor. His Latin was poor, but he was a fine stylist and humorous writer in his native Italian. His first book sold widely and made him famous. He was taken up by the Medicis and by Cardinal Barberini, the future pope Urban XII, who wrote an ode in Latin celebrating Galileo's discovery of sun spots.

There was a well-established interest in astronomy in the Vatican: Pope Gregory XIII had built an observatory in 1582, and the revised Gregorian Calendar was based upon astrological data. The discovery by the Polish Nicholas Copernicus in the early sixteenth century that the earth revolves around the sun had been met with interest. The Society of Jesus had its astronomers: there are craters in the moon named after Jesuit priests. In 1619 the Professor of Mathematics at the Jesuit College in Rome, Father Orazio Grassi, entered into a dispute with Galileo on the nature of comets. In a work described as 'a masterpiece of polemical literature', Galileo subjected Grassi's theories to 'withering scorn' which made enemies of the Jesuits. In one of his further works, Galileo's acerbic wit managed to offend Pope Urban by expressing his views through a character called Simplicio which could be taken to mean Simpleton. His brilliance led to conceit, and in 1632 he went too far. In a set of dialogues, disregarding a warning from the Inquisition, and with no scientific warrant, he asserted that Copernicus's theory that the earth revolved around the sun was not just an interesting theory but a fact.

It would turn out that it was indeed a fact, but a fact that contradicted the Church's belief based on Scripture that the whole universe revolved around the earth. Galileo was summoned before the Inquisition, ordered to retract his view of the Copernican hypothesis, banned from publishing any further works and sentenced to perpetual imprisonment – commuted to house arrest. To pope Urban, Galileo's crime was not so much insisting upon a heterodox theory but deliberately repudiating the authority of the Church: 'he has dared to meddle in matters beyond his competence… it is an injury to religion as grievous as ever there was and a perverseness as bad as could be encountered.'[426]

Thirty years earlier, a dissident mathematician and astrologer, the Italian Dominican Giordano Bruno, had been burned at the stake in the centre of Rome's *Campo de' Fiori* for insisting upon his pantheistic and therefore heretical views. Galileo was never in danger of such a fate. He remained a devout Catholic and was willing to conform. Moreover, he still had friends in high places. Under house arrest, Galileo was permitted to receive visitors, and he wrote a work much admired in the twentieth century by Albert Einstein, *The Two Sciences* – published in Protestant Holland to avoid the Catholic censors. When he fell ill, he was allowed to consult doctors in Florence. He died there at the age of 77 in 1642 – his body interred in a fine tomb in the Church of Santa Croce.

---

426   Eamon Duffy, *Saints and Sinners*, p. 235

69.   Cardinal Richelieu

The condemnation of Galileo by the Roman Inquisition was to gain for the Catholic Church a reputation for anti-scientific obscurantism that was not wholly deserved. As we have seen, Pope Urban's view was not that he was wrong but that he was imprudent. The pope may also have had ulterior motives – not just pique at being portrayed as a simpleton, but a wish to establish his commitment to orthodoxy among the cardinals dismayed by his failure to back the Catholic Spanish in the Thirty Years War, and acquiescence in the paying of subsidies to Protestant princes by Richelieu, a cardinal of the Catholic Church.[427]

Cardinal Richelieu was born Armand Jean du Plessis, the fourth son of a minor nobleman, François du Plessis, who was killed when fighting for the king against the Huguenots in the French wars of religion. As a recompense, the king assigned the see of Luçon with all its revenues to the family. Armand's older brother Alphonse was prepared for priesthood and the position of Bishop but chose instead to become a Carthusian monk. Armand, who was studying philosophy in Paris, and was intending to follow in a military career, was now required to replace Alphonse as preferred candidate for the bishopric. Aged only twenty-two, a dispensation from the pope had to be obtained from the pope to be consecrated a bishop at such an early age.

Given the reputation he would later acquire for realism and ruthlessness, it is important to note that, although using the funds of the diocese for the benefit of his family, Armand du Plessis was a diligent pastor, becoming the first bishop in France to implement the reforms prescribed by the Council of Trent. His closest friend was a devout Capuchin friar, François Leclerc du Tremblay. Although he would later leave the administration of his diocese to a coadjutor, he remained a conscientious priest: at a time when all his waking hours were taken up with the governance of France, he felt obliged to ask the pope to dispense him from the daily reading of his Office.

Though not yet thirty, Armand du Plessis was chosen by the clergy of the Poitou to represent them at the Estates General in 1614. There he spoke vehemently in favour of the rights of the Church, and was chosen by the First Estate, the Clergy, to present their petitions to the king. His abilities were noted and he was employed first by the regent, the young king's mother

---

427   A theory suggested by Father Guy Consolmagno, Research Astronomer and Planetary Scientist and the Vatican Observatory: Catholic Writers's Guild,17 September, 2009

Marie de Medici, and later by the king. As was then the custom, the popes were prepared to make cardinals at the request of Catholic monarchs: Louis nominated Armand who in 1622 received the red hat from Pope Gregory XV. In 1624 he became the king's first minister, and in 1629, King Louis XIII made him Duc de Richelieu – the name by which he became known to history.

Louis XIII had been king of France since the age of nine, following the assassination of his father, Henry IV. Taciturn, with a speech impediment, he was a conscientious Catholic, reproving a courtier who told him that an attractive lady-in-waiting was his for the taking on the grounds that as king he must be an exemplar of chastity: it is possible that he was not in fact attracted to women but rather to men. He faced challenges to his authority from his mother, reluctant to give up the powers she had enjoyed as regent; from the nobility who disregarded royal authority; and from the Huguenots who, with the strongholds given to them by the Edict of Nantes, were a state within a state.

Established as the king's all-powerful chief minister, Richelieu became known, because of the scarlet robes of a cardinal, as the 'éminence rouge' – the red eminence – while the friend of his youth whom he employed as his secretary, François Leclerc du Tremblay, or Father Joseph, was known because of the colour of his Capuchin habit as the 'éminence grise' – the grey eminence. Both were devout: Father Joseph had been an outstanding preacher before working for Richelieu. Richelieu, as we have seen, had in his youth implemented the reforms of the Council of Trent in the diocese of Luçon, and had written a catechism, *Instruction du chrétien*: however, his consecration at such an early age to what was essentially a fief of his family and his failure to reside in Luçon shows how far the Tridentine reforms had some way to go. Still more flagrant was his appointment by the king as the Abbot of Cluny so that he could enjoy the vast revenues of that venerable foundation – 'an abuse that was itself an abuse in Tridentine terms'.[428] Although always more interested in power than money, Richelieu accumulated a vast fortune which he spent on building a palace at Richelieu south of Blois in which he never resided, and enriching members of his family, ennobled at his request by the king.

King Louis XIII and Richelieu were agreed on two policies – at home to destroy any opposition to the power of the crown; and abroad to thwart

---

428   Michael A. Mullet, *Op. Cit.* p. 154

the Habsburgs whose principalities encircled France. To emasculate the nobility, Louis ordered the destruction of all fortified castles other than those on France's frontiers, and forbade the raising of private armies. Those who resisted or conspired against him were executed: so too, in a notorious case, those who disobeyed the king's ban on the fighting of duels. The measure was promoted by Richelieu whose brother had been killed in a duel.

The most formidable opposition to Louis XIII came from the Huguenots who, after the annexation of the Protestant principality of Béarn by France in 1617, and the imposition of Catholicism as the established religion, took up arms against the king. Their leader, the Duc de Rohan, hoped to emulate the revolt against the Spanish in the Netherlands and establish a Protestant province in south-western France. There were three Huguenot uprisings. The third led to a direct intervention by the English: a fleet of eighty ships commanded by Georges Villiers, the 1st Duke of Buckingham, landed 6,000 soldiers on the island protecting the port of La Rochelle, the Île de Ré. The intervention was a fiasco: the English army, failing to take Saint-Martin-de Ré and enfeebled by disease, went back to England. La Rochelle was now besieged by the royal forces directed by Richelieu himself clad in armour. After fourteen months of famine, disease and starvation during which its population was reduced from over twenty thousand to five thousand, the city of La Rochelle surrendered. Elsewhere in France, Huguenot places of refuge such as Privas and Alès, were taken – the inhabitants of Privas massacred and the city demolished. In 1629, the leader of the Huguenots, the Duc de Rohan, capitulated. Under the treaty which followed, the Huguenots kept the right to worship guaranteed by the Edict of Nantes, but they lost all their strongholds and places of safety: never again would they be able to oppose the king.

70. The Church in France

In retrospect it seems a historical paradox that the establishment of France as *primus inter* pares among the emerging nation states, should be the work of three Catholic priests – Cardinal Richelieu, Father Joseph and, during the regency of Anne of Austria, the Italian Cardinal Mazarin. They may have been loathed for their policies, but their clerical status did not seem anomalous at the time. Since the Concordat of Bologna when Pope Leo X surrendered to the king the right to appoint his nominees to the powerful and lucrative ecclesiastical posts, the administrative structures of Church and state had become inextricably intertwined. The French royal family were conscientious Catholics: during the reign of Louis XIII 'the French crown, along with pious noble families, and the royal family in the persons of Marie de Medicis, an Italian, and the queen, Anne of Austria, in fact a Spanish Habsburg, sponsored the restoration of conventual life... Under royal and noble patronage, Paris became a city of religious houses, forty new establishments of the older orders set up there...'. The Minims, an austere order founded by Francesco di Paula in the fifteenth century, 'established 150 houses in ten provinces of their order.'[429]

However, the revival of the Catholic Church in France was not primarily a matter of royal patronage, but arose from the zeal of individuals from different backgrounds. Jean-Baptise de la Salle, the son of vintners in Rheims, founded an order – the de la Salle Brothers or Salesians – dedicated to the education of the children of the poor that spread throughout the world. Another champion of the Counter-Reformation in France was Pierre de Bérulle also from Champagne, who wrote *A Brief Discourse on Interior Abnegation* at the age of twenty-two. Bérulle rose to become an influential prelate, bringing Teresa of Avila's discalced Carmelites to France, and founding a French Oratory modelled on that of Philip Neri in Rome. He was made a cardinal by Pope Urban VIII, and was briefly a Councillor of State, but he opposed Richelieu's policy of supporting Protestant powers against the Habsburgs and was obliged to resign.

In 1608, Pierre de Bérulle became the spiritual director of a young priest who came from a background very different from his own. Vincent de Paul was the son of peasant farmers in Gascony. His father sold livestock to pay for Vincent's education, first by the Franciscans at Dax, later at the University of Toulouse. Pierre de Bérulle found him a post as chaplain and tutor to the children of Philippe and Françoise de Godi, Duke and Duchess de Retz. It was while ministering to the peasants on their estates that Vincent came to face with the abysmal poverty and moral degradation of the peasants, and the idleness and ignorance of the rural clergy. His vocation was now clear, and the rest of his life was to be devoted to raising the material and moral standards of the peasantry, and the priests who ministered to them. He established a community of like-minded men in the disused priory of Saint Lazare in Paris who became known as the Lazarists. They spread out throughout

---

429   *Ibid.* p. 154

France, preaching, teaching and founding confraternities to provide food and clothing for the poor. Galley-slaves mouldering in Parisian prisons on their way to Marseille were tended by the Lazarists and, with a now extensive network of rich donors, Vincent de Paul raised funds to ransom more than a thousand Christians held as slaves in North Africa.

With a devout widow, Louise de Marillac, Vincent de Paul founded a community of women, the Daughters of Charity (also known as the Sisters of Charity), to establish soup kitchens, hospitals and schools to teach the children of illiterate peasants to read and write. By 1660, the year of the death of Louise de Marillac there were forty houses of the Sisters of Charity in France; a hundred years later, on the eve of the Revolution of 1789, there were almost five hundred, with communities of these religious sisters with their large starched head-dresses established throughout the world.

In the portrait of Vincent de Paul painted by Simon François de la Tour, we see the shrewd, even cunning, eyes of a Gascon peasant expressing both compassion and a strong will. Vincent became a prominent, even powerful, figure in France: Anne of Austria, the regent for the young king, Louis XIV, consulted him on the appointment of bishops. He differed with Cardinal Mazarin on foreign policy, but that did not impede the success of his apostolate. From his small room at Saint Lazare 'he sat day after day, busy at his interminable correspondence, writing to prelates and poor priests, the great in the land and the unimportant, those long letters in which he stands so clearly revealed. Firmness on occasion, but always gentleness, an all-embracing charity, and an overriding concern for the spread of God's kingdom...'[430] The charitable work begun by Vincent de Paul and Louise de Marillac continues to this day.

71.   Jansenism and Blaise Pascal

When King Louis XIII of France died in 1643, his heir, Louis XIV was only four years old. Contrary to the intentions of the late king, his widow, the Spanish Anne of Austria, was made regent, and retained in office the chief minister, Cardinal Mazarin. By raising taxes to pay for the war with Spain – five years were still to pass before the Peace of Westphalia – they provoked an armed uprising first by the *parlements* and then by leading French noblemen

---

430   Coulson, John, *Op. Cit.* p.442

who resented the rule of two foreigners, and wished to reclaim privileges abolished by Cardinal Richelieu. Known as the *Frondes* after the sling-shots used by the Parisians in the first round, the conflicts continued until 1653, ending with a victory for the forces of the crown. Its short term consequences were to confirm the power of Anne of Austria and Cardinal Mazarin: in the long term, the traumatic effect on the young king, who at one point had had to flee from his capital, led to the despotism of his reign – and the belief that not just the powers of government but the state itself subsisted through divine authority in the person of the sovereign: *l'état, c'est moi.*

This concept of the divine right of kings, though in its Gallican form it denied the claims of popes to an ultimate jurisdiction, was accepted by and large by the Church: the execution of the English king Charles I in London in the midst of the *Frondes* horrified Catholic Christendom. Moreover, the interests of the Catholic hierarchy, with their advocate Bishop Bossuet, considered one of the greatest orators of all time, were inextricably interwoven with those of the crown. Certainly, the Archbishop of Paris, Cardinal Retz, had sided with the *Frondeurs* but he was an exception, and was in due course reconciled with Louis XIV.

Yet the hierarchy was not the Church and there arose in this period a movement in France that was to become 'the most persistent problem affecting the Catholic Church for almost two centuries'.[431] Its adherents were called 'Jansenists' by their adversaries, the Jesuits, after the Dutch bishop of Ypres, Cornelius Jansen, whose life's work had been a study at the University of Leuven in the Spanish Netherlands of the writings of Augustine of Hippo which, after only the gospels and the epistles of Paul of Tarsus, formed the bedrock of Catholic teaching. The fruit of his researches was contained in a long book written in Latin, *Augustinus*, published only after his death. Its readership was initially limited to scholars, one of whom had been a friend and colleague at Leuven. This was a priest from Bayonne in France, Jean du Vergier de Hauranne, who, after being made the commendatory abbot of the Abbey of Saint-Cyran, became known as the Abbé de Saint-Cyran.

Before considering the theological issues which caused the problem, we must return to the reign of Henry IV. It will be recalled that that king's mistress, Gabrielle d'Estrées had a sister, Angélique, who was the Abbess of Maubuisson. Among the girls sent to be educated at Maubuisson was another Angélique,

---

431   William Doyle, *Jansenism. Catholic Resistance to Authority from the Reformation to the French Revolution.* p. x

Angélique Arnaud, the daughter of an eminent lawyer, Antoine Arnaud. The Arnauds had powers of patronage over another convent seventeen miles outside Paris, Port Royal-des-Champs, and to secure their interest and provide for one of their twenty children, they arranged for their daughter Angélique to join the community as its future abbess: she was then aged seven: documents were forged to conceal her youth from the Vatican. Four years later, in 1602, at the age of eleven, she became the abbess of Port Royal-des-Champs. Though never depraved like Angélique d'Estrées, the young abbess, who was joined by her younger sister Agnès, led the comfortable and undemanding life then common among nuns with no particular vocation.

The community had a male spiritual director, Sébastien Zamet, the Bishop of Langres, who arranged for sermons from itinerant preachers, and it was one of these, a Franciscan, that ignited a spiritual catharsis in the mind of the now seventeen-year-old abbess, Mère Angélique. She heard a call from God to bring her community back to the severe rule of the Cistercian order – a regime of prayer, mortification and strict enclosure: to their astonishment, even her parents were now refused entry and left standing at the convent gate.

Mère Angélique's first influences were those of the exiled bishop of Geneva, Francis of Sales, with whom she corresponded, and whom she saw two or three times in 1619; and the fathers off the French Oratory under Pierre de Bérulle. Sébastian Zamet, who retired as the community's spiritual director in 1634 asked the Abbé de Saint-Cyran to replace him – the same Saint-Cyran, by now a celebrated if controversial theologian, who had adopted wholeheartedly the teaching of Cornelius Jansen. Saint-Cyran was famous because, despite the scientific advances of the time, few French men or women doubted that after death each soul would spend eternity either in paradise – after a purifying smelting in purgatory – or unceasing torment in hell. What did it take to be saved? Repentance and absolution after confession to a priest, a successor to those disciples to whom Jesus had given the power to forgive sins.

But what kind of repentance was sufficient to wipe away our sins? To the Jesuits, eager to keep the weak and worldly in the flock, *attrition* was sufficient – viz. repentance inspired purely by the fear of damnation. To Saint-Cyran and the Jansenists this was a scandalous misuse of the sacrament: only *contrition* sufficed – regret not simply at the breaking of a rule but at offending God, a regret to be expressed in a turning away from the world and adopting a penitential way of life. The nobleman with a mistress, who kept his chaplain close at hand to shrive him should he suffer a stroke *in flagrante delicto*, would not be saved: in fact few would be saved, because salvation depended not upon faith or good deeds but Grace which God conferred on some but not others for unknowable reasons of his own. Indeed, the all-seeing and all-knowing deity, outside space and time, *already knew* who would be saved and who would be damned: we were therefore *predestined* to end up in heaven or hell.

This theological dispute between the Jansenists and the Jesuits was in many ways a replay of that between Augustine of Hippo and Pelagius in the fourth century: Augustine had triumphed; Pelagius had been condemned. No one now would promote the Pelagian heresy that we can earn salvation through our own merits alone, but the Jesuit approach to salvation, which allowed a man or a woman to play some part in their eternal destiny, choosing to co-operate with God's grace or not, was described as *semi*-Pelagian by the Jansenists and therefore condemned. The Jesuits counter-attacked with the charge that the Jansenists were crypto-Calvinists; however, while their 'doctrine of predestination was indeed very close to, if not identical, to Calvinist teaching…in such important matters as the interpretation of the Eucharist and of penance, the sacrament of the priesthood, the apostolic succession, the cult of the saints and the Holy Virgin, and the very concept of the Church including the hierarchy and the papacy they were emphatically, unequivocally Roman'.[432]

Cardinal Richelieu, who knew Saint-Cyran and read his works, saw the potential for sedition in a theology that taught that princes, bishops, and even the king himself – mired in worldly pursuits and pleasures – were not just destined for hell but were already damned. Saint-Cyran was arrested in May 1638 and imprisoned in the Château de Vincennes: it was then that Richelieu remarked that 'if Luther and Calvin had been locked up when they began to dogmatize, the state would have been saved a great deal of trouble'. The twentieth century English author of *Enthusiasm*, Ronald Knox, thought that 'Richelieu was right, only he struck too late'. [433] Saint-Cyran was released on Richelieu's death in 1642 but died a year later. This might have been the end of Jansenism – certainly Pope Clement XI thought it should be left to wither on the vine – but it proved to be only the end of the beginning.

432 Leszek Kolakowski, *God Owes Us Nothing. A Brief Remark on Pascal's Religion And on the Spirit of Jansenism*, p.90

433 Ronald Knox, *Enthusiasm*. p. 185

Already there had arisen a new champion to defend Jansen and *Augustinus* – Mère Angélique's brother Antoine, the youngest of the Arnauld's twenty children. He was destined for the bar but chose instead to study theology at the Sorbonne and in 1641 was ordained a priest. Visiting Saint-Cyran in the Château de Vincennes, he learned the tenets of Augustinianism, and underwent a conversion comparable to that of his sister Angélique and Saint-Cyran himself. The result was a book entitled *On Frequent Communion*, published in 1643, which became a best-seller. Its point of departure was an account of a courtier who after receiving the Eucharist went straight on to a ball. This demonstrates, argued Arnauld, the frivolity with which this awesome sacrament was treated in worldly circles – that 'deplorable abuse of imperfect confessions, of overhasty absolutions, of vain satisfactions and sacrilegious communions...'[434]

The Jesuits responded with their usual charge that Arnauld and his adherents were crypto-Calvinists, leading to a second work by Arnaud, *the Théologie morale des Jésuites,* accusing them of scandalous leniency towards penitents – an error known as *laxism*. Though laxism was later condemned in Rome, it was clear that the Jesuits leniency in the confessional appealed to their worldly clientele, while Jansenism, with its severe deity, appealed to those who took their faith seriously, and were disgusted by the moral hypocrisy rampant at court. The Order of Preachers, the Dominicans, rivals of the Jesuits, and the secular clergy who felt upstaged by the ingratiating Jesuits, though never Jansenist, were disinclined to side with the Society of Jesus. The convent of Port Royal-des-Champs flourished, with zealous postulants applying to join the community. A daughter house was established in Paris itself and schools – *les Petits écoles de Port Royal* – were founded by those who, eschewing the name Jansenist, called themselves the Friends of the Truth. Among the teachers was Arnauld's collaborator, the theologian Pierre Nicole, who taught Greek to the future playwright, Jean Racine – an orphan in the care of his grandmother who had taken up residence in the convent. Male Friends of the Truth known as *solitaires* came to live as hermits in the vicinity of Port Royal-des-champs, among them the mathematical genius, Blaise Pascal, whose sister was a nun in the convent.

In 1653 Pope Innocent X published a bull *Cum Occasione* condemning as heretical five propositions in Cornelius Jansen's *Augustinius*. Always reluctant

---

434   William Doyle, *Op. Cit.* p. 23

to be drawn into a controversy that risked exposing a seeming contradiction in Catholic teaching, Innocent had succumbed to pressure from the French king to intervene, and it was in fact 'the teaching of Augustine that the pope declared heretical'.[435] The response of Antoine Arnauld, followed by the sisters of Port Royal, was that the Five Propositions were indeed heretical but they were not contained in Jansen's *Augustinus*; and that, while a pope's ruling on doctrine had to be accepted, he could be wrong about facts.

The Jesuits counter-attacked. Arnauld was condemned by the Sorbonne without a proper hearing and deprived of his doctorate – an injustice which provoked Blaise Pascal to take up his pen and write a series of anonymous pamphlets called the *Provincial Letters*. In a prose that made them 'a classic of French literature',[436] Pascal satirized the laxity of the Jesuits, holding them up to ridicule. The Polish philosopher, Leszek Kolakowski, judged that in his polemic Pascal was 'not always reliable and often unjust and, though Pascal would establish in his posthumously published *Pensées* the strength and profundity of his Catholic faith, 'the *Provinciales* became…part of the libertine-liberal-anti-clerical-Voltarian canon. Its specifically Augustinian background and Jansenist inspiration could easily pass unnoticed'.[437]

Although the Friends of the Truth liked to represent Antoine Arnauld as a great theologian, Ronald Knox thought he 'should be remembered, rather, as a great controversialist. He argued with everyone… He spent some thirty out of the last fifty years of his life either in hiding or in exile, arguing all the time'.[438] While a fugitive in Brussels he came across Pasquier Quesnel with whom he had no need to argue because Quesnel, once an Oratorian, had been expelled for his Jansenist beliefs. Quesnel, who 'was to become more important to the second phase of Jansenism than Jansen himself'[439] published in 1692 a work entitled *Réflexions morales sur le Nouveau Testament*. Its Jansenist content was not immediately apparent; the work was recommended by Louis-Antoine de Noailles, Archbishop of Paris, and Quesnel, like Arnauld, became one of 'the petted theologians of a smart society that had gone mad over theology'.[440] However, when a more discerning reading of his *Réflexions morales* revealed

---

435   Kolakowski, *Op. Cit.* p. 14

436   *Ibid.* p. 60

437   *Ibid.* p. 63

438   Knox, *Op. Cit.* p. 197

439   Doyle, *Op. Cit.,* p. 39

440   *Ibid.* p. 176

its Jansenist leanings, it was referred to Rome; and in 1719 Pope Clement XI issued a bull *Unigenitus* that condemned 101 propositions gleaned from Quesnel's work. Quesnel himself was arrested and imprisoned by the Bishop of Mechelen in the Spanish Netherlands but subsequently escaped and took refuge in Protestant Amsterdam where he died six years after *Unigenitus*.

Unigenitus became the means by which Louis XIV could finally suppress the Jansenist movement in France. Its most stubborn adherents proved to be the nuns of Port-Royal. In 1661 they had accepted that the five propositions presented to them in a Formulary condemned in the encyclical *Cum Occassione* were heretical, but they insisted like Antoine Arnaud that they were not to be found in *Augustinius*. In 1665 they were ordered to sign the Formulary without this reservation and most of them refused. The community in Paris was disbanded and confined in their mother house, Port Royal-des Champs, with no priest to administer the sacraments.

In 1669, under a new pope, Clement IX, there was a truce called the Peace of the Church during which Port Royal, patronised and protected by a member of the royal family, the Duchess of Longueville, again became fashionable and the 'roads to it from the capital were jammed with coaches'. Borders and novices once more queued up to live in the holy precincts and join the famous community.'[441] The nineteenth-century man of letters, Charles Augustin Sainte-Beuve, who wrote a long and detailed history of Port Royal believed that the nuns were guilty of a kind of 'corporate self-satisfaction', always ready to 'assume their neighbour's damnation', and considering that Port Royal was the only real convent in Christendom. He calls them *une aristocratie de dévotion* which Ronald Knox suggests might be translated into English as 'spiritual snobs'. Another historian of Port Royal, Henri Bremond, talks of the imperiousness of Mère Angelique; of her prodigious freedom in passing judgements on her neighbours – 'an implicit assumption that while most of them were damned, she would be canonized as a saint.[442]

Mère Angelique died in 1661; her sister Agnès, who succeeded her as Abbess, in 1672. The Jansenist ethos of the community persisted and in 1708 Louis XIV persuaded pope Clement XI to dissolve the community of Port-Royal-des-Champs. The nuns were dispersed to other convents and a year later, in 1709, to prevent any attempt to make it a place of pilgrimage,

---

441   Doyle, *Op. Cit.* p. 38
442   Knox, *Op. Cit.* p. 190

the substantial buildings were demolished. This did not prevent 'reports of miraculous cures experienced by pious invalids in parishes served by Jansenist clergy'.[443] There had been signs before: it was the cure of Blaise Pascal's niece of a severe eye infection by the touch of Port Royal's most prized relic, a thorn from Christ's Crown of Thorns, that had finally brought the philosopher to take up his pen in the Jansenists' defence. However, these signs of divine favour were eclipsed by the visions of a nun in rural Burgundy, Margaret Mary Alacoque.

72.   The Sacred Heart

Margaret Alacoque was born in the Charolais district of Burgundy, in a village equidistant from the Abbeys of Cluny and Paray-le-Monial, in 1647. Her father, a royal notary, died when she was aged eight. Margaret was sickly as a child but also devout: upon recovering from a wasting illness, she pledged to the Virgin Mary that she would devote her life to Christ and added Mary to her name. At the age of seventeen, in May 1671, she was admitted as a novice to the convent of the Visitation in Paray-le-Monial – the order founded by Francis of Sales and Jane Frances de Chantal. Many of the sisters had little or no religious vocation, and were therefore sceptical, even scornful, when in 1673 Margaret Mary reported the first of four visions. These were of Jesus of Nazareth pointing to flames emanating from his heart, symbols of the burning love he felt not for the few but for all humanity. In further visions, she was told that she must spread this revelation of God's all-encompassing love throughout the world.

How was this to be done when her fellow religious regarded her visions as delusions? Providentially, the means was provided by her confessor and spiritual director, the rector of the Jesuit house in Paray-le-Monial Aged in his mid-thirties, and a member of the Society of Jesus for fifteen years, Claude Colombière was an experienced preacher, an author of spiritual treatises, and committed to a rigour derived from Ignatius of Loyola's Spiritual Exercises. In him Margaret Mary finally found someone whom she could trust, and who believed that her visions were real and that the message they conveyed should be promoted by the Society of Jesus. Thus began the cult of the Sacred Heart

---

443   Doyle, *Op. Cit.*, p. 55

which brought led to the Basilica of Sacré Coeur in Paris, and plaster statues of Jesus pointing to his flaming heart into almost every Catholic parish church.

Claude Colombière had the misfortune to be in London in 1678, serving as chaplain to the Duchess of York, Mary of Modena. During the anti-Catholic riots of that year, provoked by the allegations of a Popish plot by Titus Oates, he was arrested and thrown into the King's Bench Prison. Because of his position at court, he was later released, but his already poor health had deteriorated during his incarceration, and he lived only two more years after his return to France.

Claude Colombière was not alone in promoting the cult of the Sacred Heart. The year before Margaret Mary's first vision, in October 20th, 1672, a mass was said in honour of the Sacred Heart by the followers of John Eudes, 'one of the outstanding figures of the counter-reformation in France': and Eudes later composed both a mass and an office that was used by Margaret Mary's order, the Visitadine nuns. In early life, a member of the French Oratory, Eudes later left to found his own order of priests dedicated to the preaching of missions and the education of priests. John Eudes was an adversary of the Jansenists. Dismayed by the plight of prostitutes, he established an order of nuns in 1641 to care for them: God's love was not just for the few but for all.

73.   The Revocation of the Edict of Nantes

Jansenism was not the only heresy that appeared in the seventeenth and eighteenth centuries. There was also Quietism, a teaching promoted by a Spanish priest residing in Rome, Miguel de Molinos, and made fashionable in France by a rich widow, Madam de Guyon. Less widespread than Jansenism, it nevertheless had many adherents among devout Catholics such the exiled queen of Sweden living in Rome; and the second wife of king Louis XIV of France, Madame de Maintenon. Ronald Knox in *Enthusiasm* describes Quietism as 'a kind of ultra supranaturalism... The Quietist wants to do away with human effort as such so as to give God the whole right of spiritual initiative... God alone must do everything; we cannot even co-operate with him, only allow him to operate in us and forget that he even allows us to follow him.[444]

---

444   Knox, *Op. Cit.* p. 350

In France the Quietist teaching of Madame de Guyon led to a clash between the two leading bishops – Bossuet and Fenelon. Bossuet triumphed and in 1687 Quietism was condemned as a heresy by Pope Innocent XI in the bull *Coelestis Pastor*. Molinos, despite retracting his offensive teachings, was tried and condemned by the Holy Office in Rome and died in prison nine years later. Madame de Guyon also retracted her teachings, but was nevertheless shut away in the Bastille for seven years. Released in 1703, she spent the following fifteen years living with her son near Blois – writing letters, composing poems, and receiving visits from devotees, many from Protestant countries where her works were much admired.

There were also the Huguenots who, though they had been deprived of their 'safe places' such as La Rochelle by Richelieu in the previous reign, remained free to practice their religion as guaranteed by Henry IV's Edict of Nantes. This irked Henry's grandson, Louis XIV. The greatest of the Bourbon kings, known as *Louis le Grand* (Louis the Great) or *Le Roi Soleil* (the Sun King), he reigned for over seventy years and through continuous wars extended France's borders in the east to the river Rhine, making France the most powerful nation in Europe and, after Russia, the most populous.

We have seen how he was traumatised during his childhood by the Frondes – the uprisings first by the *parlementaires* in Paris, then by his close relatives among the nobility. When he came of age and took control of his kingdom, he decided that to avoid the risk of any recurrence he would move the seat of government outside Paris, converting a hunting lodge built by his father at Versailles into the largest and most magnificent palace in Europe. There the ancient landed nobility – the *noblesse de d'épée* – the nobility of the sword – were expected to attend on him from the *levée* in the morning until his withdrawal to his bed-chamber at night. Grandees with their own chateaux and vast estates were obliged to live in cramped quarters in Versailles: their absence created a presumption that they were up to no good. All patronage came from the king – a reason for those wanting some favour such as an exemption from taxes or a commission for a son to hang around the court, cultivating the king's favourites – ministers but also the mistress of the day. The ministers themselves were mostly able members of the middle-classes, rising to become members of the *noblesse de robe* – nobility of the gown.

Despite the mistresses and a number of illegitimate children, Louis was a devout Catholic – so terrified of damnation that he had his confessor, a Jesuit, assure him in writing that his soul would be saved. Though he deferred to the popes in Rome on matters of faith and morals, and used them when it suited his purposes as when he lobbied Pope Clement XI over *Unigenitus*, he governed the Church in France, choosing bishops and rewarding his favourites with benefices of now semi-defunct religious foundations. The Galician Church was not heretical; none of the exemplary bishops like Fénelon and Bossuet, or the devout champions of the poor like Vincent de Paul, disputed the Gallican view of Church and state united in the person of the king.

The fly in the ointment were the Huguenots – Protestants practicing their religion in parts of the kingdom – particularly the west, south-west and the mountainous region in the south-east, the Cevennes. This tolerance of a heretical religion, imposed by Henry IV to end the wars of religion, had never been popular with Louis' Catholic subjects, and to Louis it was an affront to his concept of absolutism. In 1681 he initiated a programme of petty persecution that encouraged Huguenots to convert to Catholicism or leave France. Dragoons – crude and violent soldiers – were billeted upon Huguenot households, leading to pillaging of their property and assaults on their wives and daughters.

On 22 October, 1685, Louis revoked his grandfather's Edict of Nantes with an Edict of Fontainebleau, and ordered the destruction of Protestant churches and the closure of Protestant schools. As a result, most of the Huguenots left France, finding refuge in Protestant countries – England, Sweden, the United Provinces of the Netherlands, Prussia – taking with them their considerable skills and so impoverishing the French economy. It is now thought that only a thousand, or fifteen hundred Huguenots out of almost a million remained in France.

In defence of Louis, it should be noted that few European nations at the time permitted freedom of religion: 1681, the year the persecution by the *dragonards* started, was also the year in which Oliver Plunkett, the 55-year-old Irish Archbishop of Armagh, was hanged, drawn and quartered at Tyburn. Louis's policy, 'devoid of humanity' and 'the greatest blot on his name', was popular: no single Catholic came forward to denounce it. [445] 'In those days... subjects wanted a Prince of their own religion' and vice versa.[446] The many condemnations of forced conversions by the popes over the centuries were ignored. If Bossuet forbade his priests from giving communion to new Huguenot converts, it was 'not out of humanity but for fear of profaning the

---

445   Emile Perreau-Saussine, *Catholicism and Democracy. An Essay in the History of Political Thought*, p. 23

446   Ernest Lavisse, *Histoire de France depuis les orgines jusqu'à la Revolution,* quoted in *Ibid.,* p. 25

sacrament'. [447] The Huguenots were not the victims of Catholic zeal, 'but were sacrificed on the altar of absolutism'. [448]

In the remote and mountainous district of the Cevennes where the Huguenots had been practising their religion in peace for three generations, resentment at intrusion of missionary priests and royal officials sent to enforce the Edict of Fontainebleau led to a revolt by the *Camisards* – peasants and rural craftsmen who commonly wore a smock – *camisa* in the local Occitan dialect. Incited, like the Anabaptists of Münster, by millennial prophets, and provoked by the cruel methods used to coerce conversions, the uprising began with the assassination in 1702 of the Abbé de Chayla, previously a missionary in Indo-China, then the Inspector of Missions in the Cevennes. The local nobility were not involved – but the *Camisards* showed themselves to be as capable of atrocity as any of the mercenaries in the Thirty Years War. In 1704, eighty priests were murdered and four thousand lay Catholics killed in cold blood – some the *Nouveaux Convertis* who had renounced their Calvinist faith. [449]

Comparable atrocities were committed by bands of Catholic irregulars formed for self-defence. And the means used by the state against the *Camisards* were abhorrent: a sentence of death for those who provided arms to the rebels, mere suspects condemned to the galleys, and finally the burning of villages to smoke out the rebels from their home – a list of outrages, wrote Ronald Knox, that 'sickens the heart'.[450] Some of the *Camisards'* atrocities such as the slaughter of women and children were committed at the behest of their prophets, acting rather like commissars in the Red Army in the twentieth century. Even their most able leader, Jean Cavalier, was attended by a prophet Daniel Gui.

The *Camisard* revolt ended in 1710 when Jean Cavalier was persuaded to surrender by an offer of a commission in the royal army. Sporadic fighting continued until 1715 and, while there was no revocation of the Edict of Fontainebleau which the die-hard Huguenots demanded, a small community survived with its own pastor. Cavalier, despite his royal commission and a personal interview with Louis XIV, thought it prudent to move abroad, receiving a commission in the British army and later an appointment as the Lieutenant Governor of the Island of Jersey.

---

447   *Ibid.*, p. 24
448   *Ibid.*, p. 25
449   Knox, *Op. Cit.* p. 363
450   *Ibid.*, p. 363

74. The Enlightenment

Despite Britain's dominance of the high seas, her conquest of French possessions in India, Canada and the West Indies, and the victories of her armies over those of Louis XIV on the Continent of Europe such as Blenheim (1704) and Malplaquet (1709), 'the eighteenth century belonged to France.'[451] With a few exceptions such as Britain and the United Provinces of the Netherlands, absolutism or despotism prevailed in every European polity from Russia, Prussia and Austria to the myriad principalities of the now largely defunct Holy Roman Empire. And what was a despot without a Versailles? Huge, and hugely expensive imitations of Louis's palace were built throughout Europe. The Bourbon kings of the kingdom of the Two Sicilies built a palace larger than Versailles at Caserta outside Naples with 1,200 rooms on five floors. The palace built at Ludwigsburg outside Stuttgart by the dukes of Württemberg had only 450 rooms but was nevertheless the largest baroque palace in Germany. The Dukes of Courland built two palaces – one in Mitau, the other at Rundale. In St. Petersburg, Catherine the Great completed a fitting residence for the Russian Tsars, the Winter Palace. In Berlin, plans for the renovation of the Charlottenburg palace were expanded to emulate Versailles. Frederick the Great, king of Prussia, also built a smaller palace in Potsdam based on the Chateau de Marly at Versailles so that he, like Louis XIV, should have an elegant refuge from affairs of state. Frederick named his single-storey baroque masterpiece *Sanssouci*, the French for 'without worries' or 'carefree'.

It is a mark of the ascendancy of the French language that it was used in this way by a German king. Frederick regarded German as 'a half-barbarian tongue in which not even a literary genius could do decent work. Accordingly, he made French the official language of the Prussian Academy of the Arts.'[452] French now became the language of diplomacy, and was used by the nobility throughout Europe. Women looked to Versailles to discover what was in fashion, and no noble household was without a French chef. However, it was the ascendancy of the language, and the consequent familiarity with the works of French authors, that gave rise to what came to be called the Enlightenment.

To devout Catholics, of course, the Enlightenment was rather a Darkening, an Obscuring. 'All those familiar with church history in eighteenth-century France', wrote David Knowles, 'find themselves taken aback by the apparent

---

451   James Hawes, *Op. Cit.* p. 79
452   *Ibid.*, p. 79

sudden change from the warmth and enthusiasm and deep spirituality of the seventeenth century to the chill and aridity and bitter feuds of the epoch that followed so soon. Jansenism, the intellectual climate of the philosophers and Deists, the anti-clerical Voltarian hostility, and the activity of European freemasonry, all combined to alter the quality of religious, and of monastic life shortly after the death of Louis XIV.[453]

Blaise Pascal, as we have seen (see page 201), traced the source of this infidelity to the work of Michel de Montaigne: the nineteenth century French critic, Charles Saint-Beuve, thought 'the *Pensées* are consciously, or almost consciously, an answer to Montaigne.'[454] Compromised by his association with Jansenism, and so recognised neither as a saint nor a Doctor of the Church, Pascal nonetheless wrote in his posthumously published *Pensées* (*Thoughts*) a lucid and cogent defence of the Catholic faith. He was baffled by the growing indifference that he saw around him: for 'it is indubitable that this life is but an instant of time, that the state of death is eternal, whatever its nature may be, and thus that all our actions and thoughts must follow such different paths according to the state of this eternity, that the only possible way of acting with sense and judgement is to decide our course in the light of this point, which ought to be our ultimate objective.'[455]

Pascal conceded that some sought the truth but did not find it: his exasperation was directed at those who put the whole question of their eternal destiny out of their minds, thinking only of 'dancing, playing the lute, singing, writing verse, tilting at the ring, etc.' Even innocent pleasures were poisoned by our fallen nature. 'A man enjoys life at home: he has only to see a woman who attracts him or have a few days fun, and you will find him wretched at having to return to his normal occupation. Nothing is commoner than that.' Leszek Kolakowski believes that the ill-health that dogged Pascal throughout his life may account for his 'unhappy religion': 'he was not on friendly terms with his own body which tormented him, as we know, most of his life…'[456] 'Pascal writes against human nature,' wrote Voltaire, 'more or less as he wrote against the Jesuits.'[457] Pascal's *Pensée* 607 might be applied to Voltaire: 'Great wit, bad character.'[458]

---

453   David Knowles, *Op. Cit.* p. 148

454   R.A. Knox, *Op. Cit.* p. 203

455   Blaise Pascal, *Pensées*, Translated and with an Introduction by A.J. Krailsheimer.p.428

456   Kolakowski, *Op. Cit.* p. 121

457   *Ibid..* p. 132

458   Pascal, *Op. Cit.* p. 214

If Blaise Pascal had not written his *Provincial Letters* or his *Pensées*, he would have gone down in history as a great scientist and mathematician. To assist his father, a tax-collector in Rouen, he invented a calculating machine now seen as the ancestor of the modern computer. His work on probability theory, as well as discoveries relating to hydraulics and vacuums, place him among the leading scientists of his time even if, preoccupied with eternity, he regarded them as *bagatelle*. It is perhaps an exaggeration to say, as does Leszek Kolakowski, that 'Pascal considered philosophy a futile business,'[459] He did not deny philosophy's achievements but and was unimpressed by Descartes.[460] 'I cannot forgive Descartes: in his whole philosophy he would like to do without God; but he not could help allowing him a flick of the fingers to set the world in motion: after that, he had no more use for God.[461]

France, and in particular Paris, was at the heart of the Enlightenment, but it was to spread throughout Europe and even to the Americas. The English philosopher and statesman, Francis Bacon was, with Réne Descartes, one of the progenitors of an intellectual movement that came to include the Germans Spinoza and Kant; the Scotsmen David Hume and Adam Smith; the Italian Cesare Beccaria; and the Americans Benjamin Franklin and Thomas Jefferson. European monarchs embraced Enlightenment ideas – Catherine in Russia, Frederick in Prussia and the Austrian emperor, Joseph II. The ideology of the Enlightenment was to be found in a thirty-five volume encyclopedia – the *Encyclopédie* – compiled over twenty years from 1751 by Denis Diderot and Jean-Baptiste le Rond d'Alembert, a mathematician, physicist and philosopher. One hundred and fifty scientists and philosophers contributed articles expressing radical and to some seditious ideas about the primacy of reason, religious toleration, constitutional government, and individual liberty.

Other influential works were Charles-Louis Montesquieu's *The Spirit of the Laws*, Voltaire's *Dictionnaire philosophique* and Jean-Jacques Rousseau's *The Social Contract*. Charles Augustin Sainte-Beuve, looking back from the nineteenth century, regarded Voltaire, Rousseau, the jurist Montesquieu and the scientist Buffon to be the 'four great men of the eighteenth century'[462] Voltaire, the pen-name of François-Marie Arouet, was born in Paris, the son

---

459   Kolakowski, *Op. Cit.* p. 82

460   Blaise Pascal, *Op. Cit.* p 817

461   *Ibid.* p.330

462   C.A.Sainte-Beuve, *Portraits of the Eighteenth Century*, Vol. 2., p. 245

of a minor treasury official, and educated – as were many of the Enlightenment *philosophes* – by the Jesuits in the Collège Louis le Grand. While training to be a lawyer, he wrote essays, verses and satires attacking the government – one of which led to nine months' imprisonment when he was twenty-three years old. He also wrote plays: the first, *Oedipe,* was staged at the Comédie Française soon after his release and was a success. Others followed, and brought both fame and fortune – the former gaining him 'a relative immunity from the more deadly forms of persecution'; the latter, combined with the astute use of the money he made, a material independence.

To find a publisher for a banned work of history, Voltaire travelled to the Netherlands, and after an ugly quarrel with the powerful family of de Rohan, to England: in both nations Voltaire saw at first hand societies showing far greater tolerance, and enjoying far greater liberty, than there was in France. He published his findings in his *Letters Concerning the English Nation*, published in Rouen in Normandy as *Lettres philosophique* without the permission of the censor. It was banned and publicly burned. Once again, Voltaire was forced to leave Paris. He found refuge in the château of the Marquis du Châtelet at Cirey-sur-Blaise on the border of Champagne and Lorraine: the Marquis's twenty-seven year-old wife, Émilie du Châtelet, was Voltaire's mistress. Voltaire was now thirty-nine and rich: he paid for the renovation of the château which may have made his presence more palatable to the husband. Émilie was a scientist and mathematician who translated the works of Isaac Newton into French. Their liaison was to last for sixteen years.

To illustrate his claim that religion was the source of bigotry, cruelty and intolerance, Voltaire turned to history. His *The Century of Louis XIV,* a classic in French literature, was followed by an ambitious history of civilization, *The Essay on the Customs and Genius of Nations.* His satirical novel *Candide* that ridicules religion, governments, wars, philosophers and their philosophies, was banned for its corrupting cynicism, but was read with enthusiasm not just by Voltaire's contemporaries, but in the centuries which followed.

In 1744, Voltaire left the château at Cirey-sur-Blaise: his affair with Émilie du Châtelet had evolved into friendship. He visited his admirer, Frederick II of Prussia, in *Sanssouci.* In 1758, he bought an estate at Ferney close to the French border with Switzerland, and lived there with his niece, Marie Louise Mignot: it was from there that he conducted a campaign to rehabilitate a French Protestant, Jean Calas, who had been cruelly executed in Toulouse after being found guilty of murdering his son to prevent his conversion to

Catholicism. The miscarriage of justice was a well-chosen weapon to belabor both Church and state.

Probably initially his mistress, Voltaire's niece Marie Louise Mignot remained Voltaire's companion into old age. Visiting Paris, shortly before his death, Voltaire was persuaded by Benjamin Franklin to become a Freemason, He died in Paris on 30 May, 1778, and because of his life-long enmity towards the Catholic Church was denied a Christian burial. His body was taken to the Abbey of Scellières by Marie Louise where her brother, Voltaire's nephew, was the abbot, and buried in hallowed ground.

Jean-Jacques Rousseau was the odd man out among the savants of the Enlightenment, yet possibly in the long-term the most influential. He was Swiss, born in Calvinist Geneva in 1712, and proud to be a citizen of that city. His mother died soon after his birth; he was raised by his father, a watch-maker, and his father's sister. Apprenticed first to a lawyer, then an engraver, he absconded at the age of fifteen to Catholic Savoy where he was taken under the wing of a formerly Protestant noblewoman separated from her husband, Françoise-Louise de Warens. He called her *maman* and at the age of twenty became her lover. Both were received into the Catholic Church. Madame de Warens was cultivated and had a large library used by Jean-Jacques to educate himself during long bouts of largely imaginary illness.

Moving to Paris in his early thirties, he found another motherly mistress, Thérèse Levasseur, a seamstress. She and her mother went to live with Rousseau as his servants: she bore him four, possibly five, children which were sent off to the foundling hospital run by the Church. He spent a year in Venice, employed as a secretary by the French ambassador but was treated as a domestic servant which he greatly resented. Back in Paris, he met Denis Diderot, and became a contributor to the *Encyclopédie* and in 1750 won a competition with an essay *Discourse on the Arts and Sciences* which brought him a measure of celebrity. Like other philosophers of the period, Rousseau rejected the concept of original sin: it was human institutions that had corrupted man's aboriginal innocence. He did not deny the existence of God, or the value of religion which instilled virtue, but wrote that one religion is as good as another which, as a heresy known as Indifferentism, antagonized the Church.

However, Rousseau was an excellent writer and master of the memorable phrase. 'Man is born free but everywhere is in chains,' begins *The Social Contract*. 'God makes all things good; man meddles with them and they become evil,' is the opening of *Emile, or On Education*. In *Emile,* the Indifferentist ideas put in the mouth of a Savoyard vicar led the book to be banned in both France and Geneva. To avoid arrest, Rousseau fled to Switzerland. He refused an invitation to stay with Voltaire, and put himself under the protection of Frederick II of Prussia who, for complex religious and dynastic reasons, was the sovereign of the small canton of Neuchâtel. In September 1765, denounced as the Antichrist by the Protestant pastor of Môtiers, he moved to England where the Scottish philosopher and religious skeptic David Hume found him a place to stay.

Rousseau was now a pan-European celebrity, lionized in London and with powerful champions such as Frederick in Prussia and, in France, the Prince de Conti. Although there was a warrant for his arrest, he was able to return to France. His last years were spent living in a cottage of the Marquis de Girardin on his estate in Ermenonville, revising and completing some of his works and studying botany. He died there on 1 July, 1778.

The Comte de Buffon was a great natural scientist, Charles-Louis de Secondat, Baron de la Brède and de Montesquieu, was a jurist whose *De l'Esprit des Lois* first proposed the separation of powers in government between the executive, the legislature and the judiciary – an idea adopted by those who drew up the constitution of the United States. Of the four great men of the eighteenth century designated by Sainte-Beuve, Rousseau implicitly and Voltaire explicitly worked to undermine the faith of their readers in the Catholic Church. Among the other *philosophes*, Baron d'Holbach, born in the Rhineland-Palatinate and heir to a large fortune, wrote direct attacks on the Catholic Church such as *Christianisme dévoilé* (Christianity Unveiled) which were published anonymously and abroad. D'Holbach contributed to the *Encyclopédie* but exerted his greatest influence through his lavish *salons* – twice-weekly receptions where the leading *philosophes* would gather to exchange ideas – among them Diderot, Condorcet, D'Alembert, even Rousseau; and also like-minded Britons passing through Paris – David Hume, Horace Walpole, Edward Gibbon, Laurence Sterne, John Wilkes, Adam Smith, David Garrick; and the American Benjamin Franklin.

The ideas of the Enlightenment were disseminated in a number of other *salons*, such as that of Madame Necker, the wife of the Swiss banker and statesman, Jacques Necker who, as Louis XV's Minister of Finance, tried but failed to save the French government from bankruptcy. Suzanne Necker, born Suzanne Curchod, was also Swiss – the daughter of a parson. She was beautiful, intelligent and well-educated – known in Lausanne as *'la belle Curchod'*. The young Edward Gibbon, fell in love with her: he had been sent to Lausanne by his father to 'cure him of the errors of popery'. After the death of her parents, Suzanne was taken to Paris by a Madame de Vermenou who was being courted by Necker. Necker promptly re-directed his affections towards Suzanne and made her his wife. Within only a few months of her arrival in France, she took charge of the banker's household and 'received all those who were most in vogue among Parisian men of letters', drawing them by her beauty and intelligence into her salon. 'There was a crowd of *beaux esprits*, all more or less licentious and irreligious' – many of them Catholic priests. 'I am very fond of some of our modern philosophers,' she wrote, 'but I am not fond of their philosophy'. She remained faithful to her husband and was mocked for her 'frigid demeanour of modesty' by the Abbé Galiani 'who could not forgive her for being virtuous.'[463] Chastity, the lily of the virtues, was ridiculed not just by Galiani. 'Much of the literature that was banned in the pre-Revolutionary period as "philosophical" was frankly pornographic'[464] and many of the ribald tales involved priests and nuns. The Marquis d'Argens' salacious story of a young woman's seduction by a depraved Jesuit was actually entitled *Thérèse philosophe*. The Vicomte de Valmont in Pierre Choderlos de Laclos' *Les Liasons Dangereuses* was an Enlightenment libertine. The Maquis de Sade, author of *Justine*, 'liked to consider himself a latter-day *philosophe*, and although few liberal thinkers were willing to admit him as a colleague, he was in fact representative of a major facet of Enlightenment thinking.'[465]

Of course marital fidelity was difficult when most matches were made not for love but in the financial, territorial or dynastic interests of the families involved. Louis XV had a sequence of mistresses before settling down with Jean Antoinette Poisson, the Marquise de Pompadour, as *maitresse en titre* and effectively the governor of the nation. The weak-minded Louis was only following the example of his great-grandfather, Louis XIV, and the liaison was encouraged by his ministers because the intelligent and agreeable Marquise was a more effective ruler than her lover. The Church itself set a poor example. Arthur Richard Dillon, whose father had commanded the Irish Brigade that fought for James II against William and Mary in Ireland and, after the Battle of the Boyne, had served in the French army, became first the Bishop of

---

463   *Ibid.*, p. 72

464   Susan Vandiver Nicassio, *Tosca's Rome. The Play and the Opera in Historical Perspective*, p. 208

465   *Ibid.* p. 208

Evreux, then Archbishop of Toulouse, and finally Archbishop of Narbonne. Despite the ruling of the Council of Trent that bishops must reside in their diocese, he lived a conjugal life with his widowed niece, Madame de Rothe, in the Chateau de Hautefontaine in the north of France where he kept a pack of hounds.

The Church, like the Nobility, was exempt from taxes and its representatives in the French *parlements*, though beneficiaries of royal patronage, thwarted any attempt by the bankrupt government to impose even the *vingtième* levy on its vast wealth, buying off the monarch with *dons gratuits* – gifts of money that set no precedent and acknowledged no obligation. The endowments of the devout over the centuries, though they sustained many charitable endeavours – Rousseau's five children were cared for by a Catholic orphanage – were mostly siphoned off by the nobility, leaving the *curés* in the many parishes living in poverty. Another example of this endemic corruption is that of Charles-Maurice de Talleyrand-Périgord who, excluded from a military career because of a club foot, and so directed to one in the Church instead, was made abbot *in commendam* of the Abbey of Saint-Denis in Rheims which 'was worth 18,000 lives a year, but its real value, like that of other French benefices of the day, was a good deal more':[466] he was just over twenty years old and had yet to be ordained a priest. Aged 34, he was appointed Bishop of Autun, worth 22,000 livres a year, and given the benefice of the abbey of Celles in Poitou, worth 12,000 livres annually – the fruits of the piety of previous generations now accruing to a man who may well not have 'believed in God at all, let alone the God of the Catholic doctrine to which he was meant to subscribe'.[467]

The future author, statesman and diplomat, François-René de Chateaubriand, describes in his *Mémoires d'outre-tombe* how, as the impecunious son of Breton nobleman he became a Knight of Malta which secured him an annual income of several thousand *livres*. For this 'it was necessary for me to receive the tonsure' which was given in the cathedral of Saint-Malo by the young bishop, M. Cortois de Pressigny, at the request of Chateaubriand's devout mother. 'Dressed in uniform, with my sword at my side, I went down on my knees at the prelate's feet; he cut two or three hairs from the crown of my head; this was called the tonsure, for which I received

---

466   Robin Harris. *Talleyrand. Betrayer and Saviour of France*. P.16
467   *Ibid.*, p. 22

a formal certificate.[468] The bishop performed the ceremony reluctantly, knowing that, despite his uniform, Chateaubriand had no intention of going to the Mediterranean to fight the Turks: 'to give the mark of the ecclesiastic to a soldier and a layman seemed to him to be a profanation not far removed from simony.' Thus at least one bishop had scruples about the misuse of the Church's resources. Of course, he himself was a member of the nobility – a *protegé* of the queen. At the time of the revolution in 1789, only one French bishop 'was from a bourgeois background; the rest were aristocrats, 67 percent of them from families whose nobility emerged in illustrious mists before the year 1400.'[469]

75.   Freemasonry

The origins of Freemasonry, like those of the French nobility, also claimed to emerge from the 'illustrious mists' of the far distant past: it was said that a fraternity was formed by those who built Noah's Ark, the Egyptian pyramids, Solomon's Temple. The Templar Knights also formed part of the pedigree. More credibly, at the time of the construction of the Gothic cathedrals, skilled but itinerant masons, unknown to local guilds, established their credentials by a system of secret signs and passwords.

The reason for the reappearance of such fraternities in the eighteenth century, not of stone-masons but of philosophically-minded Englishmen, is not clear. The first Grand Lodge, formed by the amalgamation of three smaller lodges, was established at the Goose and Gridiron public house in London on 24 June, 1717. The emblem of the Masons was a compass superimposed on a set-square denoting its commitment to science. Masons denied that theirs was a new religion, though the lodges in which they held their meetings became increasingly like churches, their robes and regalia like vestments, and their ceremonies like a liturgy. Just as a candidate for the Catholic priesthood passes through the orders of sub-deacon and deacon before being ordained, so the would-be Freemason went through degrees of initiation, learning the passwords, signs and secret handshakes, before becoming a Master Mason.

Freemasonry was a brotherhood, not a religion. Women were excluded, but Catholics, Protestants and even religious sceptics could become Freemasons

---

468   François-René de Chateaubriand, *Memoirs,* translated by Robert Baldick, p. 123
469   Michael Burleigh, *Earthly Powers,* p. 25

so long as they acknowledged a 'supreme being'. Beyond this amorphous deism, Freemasonry has been variously described as 'A particular system of morality veiled in allegory and illustrated by symbols'; or 'a science which is engaged in the search for divine truth' and ' to bring about a universal league of mankind.'[470] There is no mention of Christ, and it seems likely that the secrecy enjoined on all Masons was not just to give membership a frisson of conspiracy, but to avoid prosecution by governments of countries where religious dissidence was seen as sedition. It was an age of scepticism towards Christian claims that, say, Jesus walked on the water or fed five thousand with five loaves and two fishes; but was credulous when it came to the occult claims of charlatans such as Alessandro di Cagliostro or Giacomo Casanova, the self-styled Chevalier de Seingalt.

The far-fetched myths perpetrated by the Freemasons related only to their far-distant past. So far as the future was concerned, they proposed only that decency and common-sense should govern human affairs. Where religious bigotry and partisan passions had caused the chaos and cruelty of the past, science and reason would ensure a peaceful and prosperous future. Paradoxically, English and Scottish Jacobites, exiled to the Continent after the uprisings of 1715 and 1745, became prominent Freemasons: Charles Radclyffe, the Earl of Derwentwater, served as Grand Master of the French Freemasons in 1738. The Lodge in Florence was founded by Charles Sackville, Duke of Dorset.

Freemasonry became a craze: in Vienna the father and two of the daughters of the devout Empress Maria Theresa became Freemasons and her son, the Emperor Joseph II, if not a mason, was a fellow-traveller.[471] Wolfgang Amadeus Mozart became a Freemason: so too his father Leopold and Pierre Beaumarchais, Mozart's librettist for *The Marriage of Figaro*. However, when the implications of Masonic tenets became clear, Louis XV's chief minister, Cardinal Fleury, denounced the Freemasons as traitors and banned their assemblies; while in Rome, Pope Clement XII issued the bull *In eminenti* which, noting that Masonic Lodges were 'spreading far and wide and daily growing in strength', condemned Masonic teaching as 'depraved and perverted', and forbade Catholics from becoming Masons under pain of grave sin. The ban was repeated by Pope Benedict XIV in 1751 with the Apostolic constitution *Providas Romanorum*. Freemasonry was condemned

---

470   See *The Catholic Encyclopaedia*
471   See Harold Acton, *The Bourbons of Naples*, p. 151

for its secrecy and in particularly for its indifferentism – the belief that no one religion has a monopoly of the truth.

Lodges in different countries varied in their attitude towards existing religions. The British Freemasons were divided between Protestant Hanoverians and Catholic Jacobites, and they showed no animosity towards Christianity as such. In France, however, the requirement that a Mason must believe in a Supreme Being was suspended by the Grand Orient Lodge to admit the professed atheist, Helvetius. We have seen how Voltaire, as death approached, was persuaded by Benjamin Franklin to be initiated into Freemasonry rather than receive the last rites of the Catholic Church. Returning to America, Franklin was among a number of Masons who led the revolution against British rule in 1766. Paul Revere, John Hancock and John Marshall were Masons, and George Washington a leader of the Pennsylvania Lodge. It is thought that nine of the fifty-six who signed the Declaration of Independence drafted by Jefferson were Masons. 'We hold these truths to be self-evident, that all men are created equal, that they are endowed by their Creator with certain unalienable Rights, that among these are Life, Liberty and the pursuit of Happiness.' The men created equal with an inalienable right to liberty did not include Washington's or Jefferson's African slaves.

76.   The Suppression of the Jesuits

The implication of the American Revolution – that subjects might justify rebellion against their sovereign with the ideas of the Enlightenment – did not inhibit the despotic king of France from providing critical support for the revolutionaries. In eastern Europe, those friends of Voltaire, the Russian Tsarina Catherine and the Prussian king Frederick, saw no connection between the Enlightenment and constitutional monarchy or freedom of speech. Nor did those who came to rule the Austrian empire.

In 1740, the long line of Habsburg emperors came to an end with the death of Charles VI. With no sons, he had asked for and received assurances from other European monarchs that they would recognise his daughter, Maria Theresa, as his successor. The assurances were given but repudiated after his death. Frederick of Prussia invaded and seized Silesia in the seven year War of the Austrian succession. The twenty-three year old Maria Theresa, married to Francis, the Duke of Lorraine, held on to the rest of her domains and proved an able ruler. She secured the imperial crown for her husband and made him co-ruler: in practice he deferred to his wife.

Maria Theresa was a devout Catholic, who, though her husband was unfaithful, attempted to impose chastity on her subjects. She kept control over the Church through the appointment of bishops and restricted the powers of the pope. She had Jesuit confessors and, though benign when it came to her Greek Orthodox subjects, was intolerant of both Protestants and Jews. Her extensive reforms of the state apparatus were inspired by Enlightenment rationality but her view of the *philosophes* was constrained by her faith. Her foreign policy involved several wars and though she never recovered Silesia, held on to the rest of her domains. One of her daughters, Maria Carolina, was married to Ferdinand, King of Naples and Sicily: another, Maria Anna, or Marie Antoinette, to the French Dauphin. Her son Leopold, after an exchange of territories, became Grand Duke of Tuscany.

On the death of his father in 1765, Maria Theresa's eldest son Joseph succeeded him as Holy Roman Emperor and became co-ruler with his mother of the Austrian empire. Described as 'ambitious and despotic', he played second fiddle to Maria Theresa yet persuaded her against her will to go along with the expulsion of the Jesuits from their domains. She also agreed to the partition of Poland with Russia and Prussia, lamenting this destruction of an historic nation but, as Frederick of Prussia put it, 'she wept and she took'.

Although not as devout as his mother, Joseph was a convinced Catholic – more so, certainly, than his chancellor Kaunitz – but his concept of the Church excluded the pope from any role in the administration of national churches, limiting his powers to questions of faith and morals. This was also the view of the coadjutor bishop of Trier, Nikolaus von Hontheim, who in 1763 published a treatise *De Statu Ecclesiae et Legitima Potestate Romani Pontificis* under the pen name Febronius. This rejected the concept of papal sovereignty over the Church, claiming rather that such sovereignty lay with a Council of all the Catholic bishops. Febronius's relegation of papal authority went further than those of the Gallicians, harking back to the Conciliarism that followed the Council of Constance in the 15th century. Febronius claimed that a monarchical papacy was unknown in the early Church, and believed that its abolition would bring the Protestant churches back into the Catholic fold. His book was condemned by Pope Clement XIII in 1764, and the German bishops were ordered to suppress it; but Febronianism, as it came to be called, was in tune with the spirit of the times, and *De statu ecclesiae...* was widely read, went into a number of German editions, and was translated into French, Italian, Spanish and Portuguese.

Although never a follower of Bishop von Hontheim, the Emperor Joseph II shared his views on national churches. After the death of his mother in 1780, he was free to complete his drive for a modern, centralised state which brought him into conflict with the Church – not so much the bishops who were already tamed but with the papacy over the monasteries and convents. Throughout Europe, the monastic ideal had become defunct. The few successors of Benedict of Nursia and Bernard of Clairvaux who remained 'lived like princes on revenues originally designed to support hundreds'.[472] Contemplative orders in particular enraged the *philosophes* as serving no social purpose. Huge abbeys like Melk on the Danube or Klosterneuburg in Lower Austria witnessed to the past power of the Catholic Church but also to their wealth which Joseph believed could be used for more practical purposes than prayer. He therefore passed laws suppressing religious foundations – at first those of the contemplative orders – and placing the proceeds in one central fund to pay for schools, hospitals and the poorer parishes. In Austria 388 monasteries and convents were dissolved, the remaining monks sent to other communities, their works of art sold off to dealers in antiquities, their libraries scattered.

In 1781, Pope Pius VI travelled from Rome to Vienna to urge Joseph to desist. He was treated politely but his pleas ignored. The following year, 1782, Joseph passed an Edict of Toleration giving religious freedom to Lutherans, Calvinists and Jews. Five years later, his brother-in-law, King Louis XVI of France, followed suit with the Edict of Versailles. Apart from the period between the Edict of Nantes and its revocation, this was the first time since the reign of the emperor Theodosius in the fourth century that the two most powerful rulers in western Christendom had ceased to insist that their citizens belong to the Catholic Church.

Already, by the time of these edicts of toleration, those guardians of Catholic hegemony, the Jesuits – so powerful as the teachers, confessors and counsellors of kings – had been expelled by the Catholic despots from their domains. The main charge against them was that by their fourth vow they were subject to the pope, not the monarch or the bishops of the nation in which they lived; and the second that, back in the sixteenth century, with

---

472   Eamon Duffy, *Op. Cit.* p. 249

England's Protestant queen Elisabeth in mind, Jesuit theologians had argued that in certain circumstances regicide was no sin.

The initial moves against the Jesuits were made in Portugal by the first minister of the king, the Marquis of Pombal. He was a child of the Enlightenment and the reforms he enforced made him enemies among the nobility. The competence he showed after the catastrophic earthquake of 1755 reinforced his authority. We have seen how the agreement with Spain on the boundaries between their possessions in South America had led to the Guarani wars. Although by the time of the wars the Jesuits had been withdrawn from the reductions, they were accused by Pombal and his propagandists, among themVoltaire, of having profited from their control of the reductions and defied the authority of the crown.

In 1758 an attempt was made to assassinate the Portuguese king, Joseph I. The aristocratic family of Távor were held responsible, but so too the regicidal Jesuits. Pombal, on the king's authority, ordered their expulsion from Portugal and the Portuguese Empire. The Society's assets were seized and a thousand priests shipped to the port of Civitavecchia in the Papal States. In 1764, the Jesuits were expelled from France; in 1767 from Spain and its possessions in the Philippines and the Americas. Spanish warships delivering Jesuits from Mexico were fired on by batteries at Civitavecchia: Pope Clement XIII would not allow them to disembark, and it was five months before they found refuge on dry land. Six hundred Jesuits died during their passage to Europe.

In the Kingdom of the Two Sicilies, King Ferdinand's chief minister, Baron Bernardo Tanucci, a man in the mould of Pombal, sent the Jesuits from the kingdom of Naples under guard to the border of the Papal States: they were forced over the frontier and told that they faced death if they tried to return. In 1769 the Jesuits were expelled from Malta by the Grand Master of the Knights of Saint John. Next came the Duchy of Parma, ruled by a Bourbon, and finally the Society was disbanded in Austrian Poland, many of the priests welcomed in those parts of the partitioned Commonwealth ruled by the Orthodox Tsarina Catherine and the Protestant Frederick the Great.

What were the popes to do in the face of this onslaught against their Praetorian Guard, the Society of Jesus? Clement XIII, who was elected in 1758, reminded the Bourbon Duke of Parma that the fourteenth century Encyclical, *In Coena Domini*, that enjoined excommunication of anyone infringing on the powers of the Church, was still in force. This merely enraged the European monarchs: the French king sent troops to occupy the papal city of Avignon and the *Comtat Venaissin;* and Ferdinand of Naples occupied the papal enclave of Benevento. Clement stood firm. In 1765 he denounced Febronianism, and in 1765 he published a bull, *Apostolicum pascendi,* reminding the world of the Jesuits' exceptional achievements in the service of the Church. He had placed Helvetius's *De L'Esprit* and the *Encyclopédie* on the Index: there was to be no compromise with the Enlightenment. In 1769 he summoned the cardinals to a special consistory to consider how to deal with the crisis but on the day before the first session he suffered a stroke and died.

The Austrian emperor, Joseph II, came to Rome during the conclave held to elect a new pope – his presence impressing on the cardinals that the great Catholic powers would only accept a candidate prepared to dissolve the Society of Jesus. The Franciscan Cardinal Ganganelli who was chosen, taking the same name as his predecessor, had given no such assurance, 'but he let it be known that he thought the dissolution possible, and even a good idea.'[473] Once elected, he prevaricated, attempting to appease the monarchs with small gestures – the annual reading of *In Coena Domini* was dropped; the Marquis de Pombal's brother was made a cardinal; he imposed a ban on new recruits to the Society. None of this was enough to satisfy the monarchs who 'had scented blood and would be content with nothing less' than the dissolution of the order. In 1773 Pope Clement XIV gave in and dissolved the Society of Jesus: excluded from the Catholic nations of Europe and their empires, there now remained no field for their mission. Their General, Father Ricci, 'a blameless and holy man', was imprisoned in the Castel Sant' Angelo where he remained until he died. No explanation was given for this surrender to the implacable enemies of the Church: after many centuries of sometimes excessive claims to authority over Christendom, Clement had given 'the clearest demonstration imaginable of the powerlessness of the Pope in the new world order... It was the papacy's most shameful hour.'[474]

473   *Ibid.* p. 246
474   *Ibid.* p. 246

77.   The People of God

A history of the Catholic Church is dominated by the lives and accomplishment of a few notable men and women – popes, bishops, kings, queens, princes, theologians, inspired writers, inspiring preachers, the founders of religious orders. The *philosophes* and their admirers were neither kings nor clerics, but they largely came from a small circle within the privileged elite. Little is heard of the peasants and artisans who were mostly illiterate – capable of understanding a sermon in their own language but not Latin, the language of the Church. Langland, Chaucer, Cervantes, the author of *Don Quixote*, or Alain-René Lesage, the author of *Gil Blas*, give us glimpses of the common man but we learn little of his attitude towards religion.

A snapshot of popular belief in Italy in the late eighteenth century comes as a result of a synod of bishops held in the Tuscan town of Pistoia held in 1786. Tuscany was ruled by the Grand Duke Leopold, the brother of the Emperor Joseph II. He too was imbued with the ideas of the Enlightenment and, though Tuscany was only a small principality, believed it could be a model for liberal reforms. As a child he had been destined for the Church, and so had a thorough education in theology; but, due to deaths in the family, he came to inherit from his father the Grand Duchy of Tuscany which was exchanged for that of Lorraine. There he pursued a number of reforms, encouraging commerce, simplifying taxation, and re-writing the country's penal code, forbidding the use of torture and abolishing the death penalty.

Leopold then turned to the Church, and in 1786 wrote to the Tuscan bishops proposing a number of reforms. His ideas as to what these might be gave off a whiff of Febronianism and, though one of his ideas was to increase the authority of the bishops at the expense of the pope, this was not enough for the majority to accept what he proposed. However, Leopold had an ally in Scipione de'Ricci, the Bishop of Pistoia who, as a first step towards a national council, summoned a diocesan synod. More than two hundred priests assembled in the church of Sant' Benedetto in Pistoia and passed, virtually unanimously, a series of decrees where the whiff of Febronianism became an overpowering odour. The Catholic Church was a purely spiritual entity that had no right to trespass on secular affairs: its role was merely to protect the Apostolic faith, not the Roman pontiff. It had no authority to institute new dogmas; the mass should be said in the vernacular; women religious were not to take their final vows before the age of forty – and perhaps not at all since the synod also called for the dissolution of all monastic foundations except those of the Benedictines. It condemned indulgences, relics, the Stations of the Cross and the cult of the Sacred Heart. Legends and superstitious fables should be removed from holy books and statues of mythical saints from churches.

Ricci's revolutionary agenda pleased the Grand Duke, but not the other Tuscan bishops who the following year gathered in Florence to prepare for a national council. By a large majority, they rejected the proposals put forward at Pistoia; so too the pope when they came to his attention. However it was the citizens of Prato who finally put paid to Leopold and Ricci's attempts at reform. Angry crowds gathered outside the cathedral as statues were removed, and when the news spread that a precious relic, the Girdle of the Virgin Mary, was a fake and would be destroyed, riots broke out. The bishop's palace was stormed and looted, his episcopal throne broken up and burned, the statues stored in the cellar triumphantly returned to the cathedral, 'and crowds knelt all night in a blaze of candle-light before the condemned altar of the Girdle'.[475]

The Grand Duke Leopold sent troops to Prato to restore order, but the disturbances made clear that the reforms envisaged by an 'enlightened' prince and a like-minded bishop would be opposed by the bulk of the laity. Those Tuscan bishops who had been dithering now backed away from Ricci's proposals. Leopold was saved from a grave loss of face by the death of his brother, the emperor Joseph: Leopold was his heir and left Florence for Vienna. The reform movement collapsed. Scipio de' Ricci resigned as Bishop of Pistoia. In 1794, Pope Pius VI published a bull *Auctorem fidei* which condemned the Synod of Pistoia and eighty-five of its propositions. In 1805, just before his death, de' Ricci signed an act of submission to the papal ruling: by then it had become clear what dire consequences might come from precipitous reforms.

The riots in Prato give a glimpse of the nature and strength of popular devotion in one city in Italy in the late eighteenth century. But what of Rome itself, and the papal states? They too were ruled by a despot, a Catholic despot. Had this principality, ruled by the successor to Saint Peter, which had known such turbulence in the past, become the exemplar of Augustine's *City of God*, or come to resemble Thomas More's *Utopia*, or perhaps the Jesuit reductions in Paraguay? The Holy Spirit, believed by Catholics to guide the cardinals in their choice of the supreme pontiff, in the late seventeenth and eighteenth centuries

---

475   Duffy, *Op. Cit.* p. 250

made some excellent choices. Glancing through the *Oxford Dictionary of the Popes*, we learn that Innocent XI (1676-1679) was 'frugal in his personal life', 'entirely free from nepotism' and did what he could to 'sweep away moral and administrative abuses'. Innocent XII (1691-1700) was 'devout and charitable, simple in his personal life'; Clement XI (1700-1721) was 'devout and austere'; Benedict XIII (1724-1730) lived 'as a simple friar'; Benedict XIV (1740-1758) had 'an unusually sympathetic character'; Clement XIII (1758-1769), was 'mild and well-intentioned' and 'spent lavishly on poor relief'. Clement XIV (1769-1774) was 'outwardly reserved' but lacking self-confidence as we saw with his suppression of the Jesuits. There were exceptions to this run of good popes such as Alexander VIII (1689-1691) who enriched his relatives by appointing them to benefices in his gift and lived, to the delight of the Romans, in a lavish style.

The last pope of the eighteenth century, Pius VI (1775-1799), came from the same mould as Clement XIII. Giovanni Angelo Braschi was 'tall, handsome and vain, proud of his elegant legs and noble mane of white hair'.[476] He came from a noble but indigent family in Cesena in Emilia and after taking his degree in Law entered the papal civil service as secretary to Cardinal Antonio Ruffo, the papal legate in Ferrara, and then 'worked his way with charm and efficiency through the papal civil service'.[477] As pope, he stood firm against Febronianism but his main interests were in the ceremonial of the Church in which he appeared centre stage; and in his principality – adorning Rome with baroque fountains and Egyptian obelisks; building a sacristy for Saint Peter's basilica, and the Pio-Clementino museum; and, outside Rome, embarking on a worthy but unsuccessful attempt to drain the Pontine marshes.

Less worthy was the enrichment of his nephew Luigi Braschi, building him a grandiose palace, and making him a duke. This corruption was condemned by the *zelanti* – the rump of cardinals who had defended the Jesuits and were zealous in their pursuit of reform – but delighted the Romans who preferred the rule of worldly popes who spent the money that came pouring in from 'the very large and very varied tribute coming to the head of the Church from all the Christian world, three quarters of it from France'.[478] The Roman pontiffs were to their subjects not just the successors of Peter, the Galilean fisherman, but also of the Roman emperors, and in this latter capacity they were expected

---

476   *Ibid.*, p. 252

477   *Ibid.* p. 251

478   Maurice Andriex, *Daily Life in Papal Rome in the Eighteenth Century*, p. 69

to provide the Romans with *panem et circenses* – bread and circuses. Popes over the centuries had recognised and accepted this obligation, combined, of course, with Christian charity. As a result, the city of Rome, though unlike More's Utopia or the Jesuits' reductions came close to what we would now call a welfare state.

Rome was now a tenth of the size of what it had been at the height of the Roman empire – its population reduced from two million to around a hundred-and-thirty-six thousand, living opposite the Vatican in the bend of the Tiber where poultry scratched a living among the ruins of the city's imperial past. At the apex of Roman society were the thirty or so families, many claiming descent from antiquity, some like the Colonna or Orsini familiar from the conflicts of the Middle Ages. Raised with Jesuit tutors, and with little curiosity about what went on outside their city beyond what was considered fashionable in Versailles, the young Roman aristocrat 'acknowledged strict obedience to the will of the Church as the only basis of moral law; and loathed revolution, considering as the devil's work the novel notions of the Age of Reason.'[479]

The Roman nobility had a strong sense of *noblesse oblige*. Their magnificent palaces filled with outstanding works of art were open to all. So too the lavish celebrations when, say, foreign dignitaries visited the city, with 'wine flowing in fountains before the illuminated palaces' and concerts performed in the public squares. The disparity of wealth between the princes and cardinals on the one hand, and ordinary Romans on the other, was probably as great as any society in any time; but there were two provisos. First of all, poverty might be considered a misfortune in worldly terms, but it was esteemed as a privilege in spiritual terms, whether chosen as in the case of monk or friar or involuntary. Moreover, Rome was a good place to be poor because a family could live well on 'the inexhaustible charity of Rome with the many Church institutions vying with one another to care for the sick and the poor. While a third of Rome's population were clerics, and a third servants, shop-keepers or artisans, a final third of around 70,000 'adult Romans all perfectly healthy' did nothing at all. It was hard to distinguish between the active and the indolent because anyone employed by the church wore a soutane, and so 'was indistinguishable from their truly ecclesiastical fellow-clerics'.

Ostentation was frowned upon: 'rags or a soutane,' noted , Jean-Baptiste Dupaty, a French visitor, 'are the only wear'. 'Barrier of rank were non-

---

479   *Ibid.,* p.43

existent…. The cardinal's valet offered his snuff-box and his cardinal cheerfully took a pinch'. Medical treatment was only hampered by the Romans' deep mistrust of doctors: if someone died under the care of a doctor, the doctor was blamed; if the patient recovered, it was thanks to prayers to the Madonna. When it came to education, 'we may fairly say that that the opportunities for learning were better than anywhere else in Europe – much as this would have surprised the French *philosophes*.' There were fifty-two primary schools in Rome charging no fees, 'and every village in the papal states, too, had a school of its own.'[480]

The Romans were lazy, with the siesta lasting from noon until five in the afternoon; and they were cowardly. 'I don't want to bathe in the river,' says a character in one contemporary drama, 'I might get drowned. I don't want to get on a horse, I might fall off. And I don't want to go to war, I might get shot at.' [481] The pope had an army but it was a shambles. So too the legal system which, with its mix of secular and canonical jurisdictions, meant that few laws were enforced or lawsuits settled. 'A degree of anarchy was the most striking result of pontifical despotism'. No doubts entered their minds as a result of the Enlightenment: 'From the greatest prelate to the scum of the streets, the Romans regarded the new thinking as so much moonshine. "Monsù Voltaire", as they called him, was a lunatic.'[482]

The penitential system in Rome was ahead of its time: 'it was in Rome that the use of cells was first begun. Prisoners nowhere else enjoyed such comforts and were in fact so well-treated that prison could hardly be thought of as a punishment at all.' Why, it might be asked, was there a need for prisons in this benevolent welfare state where 'serious theft was rare, burglary rarer and rioting unheard of.' The streets were not lit at night, except for pools of dim light from a candle before an image of a saint or the Madonna in a niche at a street corner; but they were safe because of the Romans' 'scorn of thieving'.[483] But if there were few robberies, 'murders abounded' – 'flaring up among the lower classes as a result of romantic rivalries or insults exchanged while they danced and drank'. This 'knife crime' was ubiquitous and impossible to suppress because of the *omerta* kept by any witnesses.

---

480   *Ibid.,* p. 54
481   *Ibid.,* p. 133
482   *Ibid.,* p. 201
483   *Ibid.,* p. 93

The Romans' contempt for thieves did not extend to the bandits who infested the papal states. Here again it was not just *omerta* but a sympathy, even admiration, for the brigands who 'rich with loot, would … go back to their villages, buy land and houses and marry the prettiest girl in the district, who naturally took them in preference to honest stay-at-homes'. An ambush by bandits was so likely on, say, the route from Rome to Ancona, the port where travellers would take passage to Venice or Trieste and on to Vienna, that diplomats and dignitaries would exchange clothes with their valets, or at the very least 'dress down' to conceal their wealth. The attempts by successive popes to deal with banditry in their domains was constant and futile: very rarely, one might be caught and condemned to death. On the day of execution all cardinals were told to keep off the streets because if the criminal ran into one on the way to the scaffold he 'could demand a pardon which could not be refused'. [484]

And then there were sins which were not crimes. 'Libertinage and adultery,' we are told by the French historian Maurice Andrieux, 'had become accepted features of life'. They were condemned in sermons, but tacitly tolerated as a concession to the weakness of human nature. The visitor from France, Jean-Baptiste Dupaty, was told by a priest: 'It is for religion's sake that we are so lenient about love; people would forsake religion if we were more severe. We have tried it more than once, with most discouraging results'.[485] Here too, marriages were arranged in the interests of the families concerned, and so there was no expectation that wives would love their husbands. It was sometimes written into a marriage contract that a wife should be allowed a *cavaliere servente* and there was a general acceptance by husbands that they might not be the fathers of the children who bore their name. Husbands and lovers would meet at the *conversazione* in the great house, or at one of the several theatres where, wrote an English visitor to Rome, Samuel Sharp, 'instead of listening to the music they all laugh and talk as if they were at home'. Women were not permitted to appear on stage so *castrati* played the female roles.

The Church itself provided entertainment with the fiestas on saints' days which like Sundays were holidays and, with 120 listed in 1770, meant no work was done for around a third of the year. The greatest of these fiestas was on the 29th June, the feast of the Apostles Peter and Paul. The illumination of St.

484   *Ibid.*, p. 133
485   *Ibid.*, p. 109

Peter's that crowned the saint's festival was the time-honoured climax of all religious celebration. 365 technicians, hanging from ropes, lit 6,000 fire lamps to illuminate Michelangelo's dome. it was a spectacle that surpassed anything in any other city in the world.

A further occasion for stupendous celebrations came on over the eleven days leading up to Ash Wednesday, the opening of the penitential season of Lent. This was the Carnival when 'the Romans were seized by a passion for excitement, a furious appetite for amusement to be found nowhere else.[486] All the leading families competed to provide the most imaginative and exotic float which followed the city's officials, the Governor and Senator, in a parade down the Corso. Equally exotic were the costumes of the spectators, many providing impromptu theatrical displays. All except for the clergy, prostitutes and Jews might wear masks which ensured anonymity so that one could not be sure whether the slim body in a Harlequin costume, or the face behind the mask from the *commedia dell' arte*, were those of a woman or a man. Moral constraints were abandoned in a frenzy of fun. The German poet Goethe felt he 'had spent the day with lunatics' while Germaine de Staël, the daughter of the Parisian *salonnière* Madame Necker, was horrified by the familiarity shown by the different social classes during the Carnival – 'turning the nation upside down as though there were no social order any more'.[487]

Rome's Jews, forbidden to wear masks, played a humiliating role in the Carnival's opening ceremony on the Capitoline Hill. The Chief Rabbi would kneel before the Senator and Governor to symbolise his community's subjection, whereupon the Senator would dismiss him saying 'Go, for this year we tolerate you', kicking his posterior to speed him on his way. Such an indignity, so clearly at odds with Christian charity, was for the Romans all part of the fun and games. A judgement of the treatment of the Jews by the supreme pontiff is a case of seeing a glass half-full or half-empty. As Maurice Andrieux points out, 'of all rulers, the popes were most lenient towards' the Jews. 'During the most fanatical periods, when they were hounded in every land in Europe, St. Peter gave them shelter and protection'.[488] Certainly Jews were treated with contempt and forced to live apart, but 'they knew neither exile, extortion, mob violence or the stake'.

---

486   *Ibid.*, p. 140
487   *Ibid.*, p 143
488   *Ibid.*, p 86

Rome's Jews comprised around five percent of the city's population, and were confined since the start of the seventeenth century in a cramped ghetto. Numerous restrictions were placed on their activities but because the lethargy of the forces of law and order, they prospered despite these restrictions, particularly when it came to finance. Sumptuary laws forbade overt displays of their wealth, and there was a ban on them mixing with gentiles, but these regulations too were largely ignored. When a house collapsed during a wedding feast in the ghetto, the casualties included one of the city's precentors, a well-known canon, several *abbés* and quite a number of socially prominent Christians.'[489]

Here, then, thanks to the historian Maurice Andrieux, we catch a glimpse of the moral paradoxes at the heart of Latin Christendom in the eighteenth century. Rome under the popes was not an Utopia nor a community of saints but a city where the Catholic religion was 'a habit so deeply rooted that it entered the people's inmost soul'. [490] 'The paternal old men who were her rulers,' wrote Andrieux, 'had never been so liberal, so kind or so considerate: never in human history, can the tragic element have been so completely missing'. There had been horrors in the past and there were horrors to come, but some of the unique qualities of that theocratic despotism survived. 'These towns in the papal states,' wrote the French diarist Edmond de Goncourt in the nineteenth century,

> seem to be the last in which the poor are still to some extent at home. There is a compassion, a natural sympathy, almost a familiarity in the attitude of the middle classes towards the poor, the unfortunate, and the ragged that astonishes a man from a so-called philanthropic country. It is almost with a caress that a café-owner here gently propels a beggar into the street…the poor man reaching into his pocket to help the poorer.[491]

'Everything that is gentle and sensitive and movingly beautiful in modernity,' Goncourt adds a few page later, 'comes from Christ'.[492]

---

489   *Ibid.*, p 89

490   *Ibid.*, p.121

491   Edmond and Jules de Goncourt, *Pages from the Goncourt Journals*, p. 124

492   *Ibid.*, p.126

PART FOUR

78.　The French Revolution

By 1786, it had become clear that the French state was bankrupt. The costs of the Seven Years War, and the intervention in the American War of Independence, had drained the Royal Exchequer of its reserves. The system of taxation was archaic and inefficient. The richest of the king's subjects who belonged to the first two of the three 'estates', the clergy and the nobility, had long been exempt from taxation on the grounds that the first, the clergy, sustained the nation with their prayers, and the second, the nobility, with their blood, leaving the burden to be borne by those of the third estate who were neither clergy nor nobles – merchants, artisans and above all the peasantry.

How could the system be reformed? The Swiss banker, Necker, when a minister of the king, had tried different expedients such as a *vingtième* tax on all, and issuing bank-notes and bonds, but all failed. In 1786, King Louis XVI summoned an Assembly of Notables to consider the crisis. It advised the calling for the first time since 1614 of the elected representatives of the whole nation, the Estates General. Necker's proposal that the number of delegates from the Third Estate should be doubled because they represented the overwhelming majority of the French people was accepted by Louis XVI, but when the thirteen hundred delegates arrived at Versailles on 2nd May, 1789 he greeted only those representing the clergy and nobility.

This slight stiffened the resolve of the commoners, more acutely aware than their pampered superiors of the suffering of the French population – impoverished by high taxation, cold after a severe winter and hungry after a poor harvest the previous year. They rejected the government's proposal that the three Estates should meet separately, and on June 10th passed a motion put forward by a priest, the Abbé Sieyès, that they should declare themselves a National Assembly. On 19 June a majority of the First Estate, the clergy, voted to join them. The king ordered the doors to the hall where they met closed and locked. At the suggestion of one of their number, Joseph-Ignace Guillotine, the deputies reassembled in an indoor tennis-court and took an oath not to permit their dissolution until France had been given a new constitution.

On 22 June, 150 deputies from the First Estate, the clergy, and two from the Second, the nobility, joined the National Assembly meeting in Versailles' church of Saint Louis. Attempts by the king to keep the estates separate failed. He ordered Swiss and German mercenaries to move to Paris. A member of the Third Estate, the Comte de Mirabeau, demanded that these troops be withdrawn, and that the Assembly should form its own militia. On 11 July, the king dismissed Necker who had been sympathetic towards the Third Estate and the National Assembly, and appointed conservative members of the nobility in his stead. There were clashes between Parisians and the King's Guard outside the Tuileries Palace. On 13 July a mob seized muskets held in the Invalides, and the next day, 14 July, marched on the Bastille, the medieval fortress in the middle of Paris, in search of gunpowder. The Bastille contained not just supplies of gunpowder but also prisoners held at the whim of the king by a *lettre de cachet*. There were only seven at the time – four forgers, a lunatic imprisoned at the request of his family, a failed assassin of Louis XV, and a 'deviant' member of the nobility, again held at the request of his family. Another 'deviant', the Marquis de Sade, had been transferred to a different prison ten days before.

The governor of the Bastille, Bernard de Launay, realising that his paltry garrison could not hold out for long against a mob which had been joined by defectors from the *gardes françaises*, surrendered at 5.30 pm. He was dragged to the Hotel de Ville, stabbed and decapitated – his head, together with that of Jacques de Flesselles, a municipal official, placed on a pike. The king was told of the fall of the Bastille the next morning by the Duke de la Rochefoucauld. 'Is it a revolt?' he asked his minister., 'No, sire,' the duke replied, 'it is not a revolt. It is a revolution.'[493]

The news of the successful destruction of this symbol of royal despotism led to uprisings throughout France. In Paris the militia was renamed the National Guard, and the hero of the American War of Independence, the Marquis of Lafayette, was appointed to command it: he attached a tricolour cockade to his hat. The king reappointed Necker but it was too late. Radicals such as Camille Desmoulins and Jean-Paul Marat now had the ear of the deputies and of the mob. In August, the Assembly abolished all feudal privileges and rights, established freedom of speech and religious affiliation,

---

493   Christopher Hibbert, *The Days of the French Revolution*, p. 69-82

and on 27th adopted a Declaration of the Rights of Man, drawn up on the American model by Lafayette. 'The idea of including an explicit recognition of the predominance of the Catholic church into the opening of the Declaration was rejected'.[494]

Lafayette was a freemason and excluding Christianity was consistent with his Enlightenment ideas; however, 'viewed externally, the French Church on the eve of the Revolution was perhaps the most brilliant and most powerful in the world. Italy excepted, probably no other country possessed so many glorious churches filled with works of art of every kind… In every province there were numerous abbeys and monasteries, and religious confraternities flourished in the cities. Religious ceremonies were performed with great pomp and splendour, especially processions, the most impressive being that of Corpus Christi.'[495] Each of the many communes had its own church, and many were named after Roman martyrs. Catholic saints such as King Louis IX or Joan of Arc were embedded in France's history. France was 'the eldest daughter of the Church'.

Now the fissures in that imposing edifice became apparent: the Gallicans, Febronists and Jansenists, though at odds with one another, coalesced around the idea of a radical reform of the Church. Talleyrand, still a priest and bishop, declared that 'The Church's property belongs to the nation' and called for the wholesale expropriation of its assets – though not those of the Protestants.[496] The abolition of feudal rights enjoyed by many religious institutions, and the tithe which provided an income not just for parish *curés* but also for the 'host of parasites who called themselves *abbés* and had only donned the soutane for the sake of the revenues and benefices that went along with it'. [497] They were bought off with the promise of a pension paid by the government.

The passion for democracy and rationalisation among the members of the National Assembly led to the drawing up of a Civil Constitution for the Clergy. By this, the 130 episcopal dioceses were to be reduced to 83, corresponding with the new *départements,* instituted in 1790. The bishops were to be chosen by the electors of the *départements*, and they in turn would elect ten 'metropolitan bishops' to replace the existing archbishops. Each

---

494   Burleigh, *Op. it.* p. 52

495   Ludwig von Pastor, *The History of the Popes from the Close of the Middle Ages*, Volume XL, p. 87

496   Burleigh, *Op. Cit.*, p. 179

497   *Ibid.*, p. 106

parish priest was to be elected by those among his parishioners who went to mass – whether or not they were a Protestant, 'a Jew or a declared unbeliever: the spokesman for the Jansenists, made so bold as to say "we are the National Assembly and we possess the full power to change even religion".[498] The pope – the 'bishop of Rome' – played no role, and no longer would annates or Peter's Pence be sent to Rome.

There were 207 *curés* in the National Assembly and 44 bishops, together with a number of committed Catholics among the lay members, but so great was the social divide between the aristocratic prelates and the lower clergy that no Catholic party was formed and no leader came forward to defend the Church. There was 'vociferous dissent' over a proposal to abolish clerical celibacy, but only confusion when a law was passed insisting that the clergy must take an oath of loyalty to the new Civil Constitution. The intention was 'to tear the Church in France away from the great unity of Catholicism and reduce it to the status of a Government police institution'. For 'the Jansenists… the Gallicans and the Calvinists, the Civil Constitution was an act of revenge against the Holy See'. For a Voltairean like the Comte de Mirabeau it 'was only a stage on the way to the complete de-Catholicisation of France.' [499]

In fact the Assembly's blithe disregard for the deeply-held convictions of many millions of their compatriots turned out to be 'one of its greatest blunders – if not the greatest blunder and most disastrous…' It had failed to realise that besides the journalists and lawyers belonging to the political clubs and the vengeful Parisian mob, 'there was a farming population that held fast to the Church of its fathers with an unshakeable tenacity and a readiness to fight for it'.[500]

Clearly, writes the historian Michael Burleigh, 'the Assembly thought that the king and the nation would acquiesce in this new decree as they had done in previous resolutions.' Louis XVI, who had sworn at his coronation to defend the Church, and still notionally could veto new legislation, dithered, writing to Pope Pius VI for guidance. Pius, already outraged at the dissolution of France's religious orders without any reference to Rome, was advised by the French ambassador to the Holy See, Cardinal Bernis, to protest only in generalities.

On 22 July, upon the advice of his ministers, Louis let it be known that he would sanction the Civil Constitution. A majority of the bishops in the

---

498   *Ibid.* p. 136
499   *Ibid.* p. 140
500   Von Pastor, *Op. Cit.* p. 141

National Assembly temporised, saying that it might be accepted with certain amendments, but the radical majority in the National Assembly was in no mood to compromise. At an evening session on 26 November, 1790, it passed a resolution that all members of the clergy must take an oath of loyalty to the Civil Constitution within a week. Those who refused would lose their livings, and if they then persisted in their ministry, would be prosecuted as disturbers of the peace.

The first deputy to take the oath before the National Assembly was the parish priest of Emberménil, the Abbé Grégoire: fifty-one *curés* followed suit. On 2 January, 1791, the oath was taken by two bishops – Charles Maurice de Talleyrand, the Bishop of Autun, and a titular bishop from Alsace, Jean-Baptiste Gobel. However, Bishop Bonal of Clermont said that his conscience forbade him to take the oath and the remaining forty-two of the forty-four bishops agreed. It was, wrote the historian Ludwig von Pastor, 'a day of glory for the French clergy, the bishops in particular.'[501] 107 lesser clerics among the members of the Assembly had already taken the oath, but twenty now retracted: in the final tally, only a third submitted to the new law.

In Rome, Pius VI still prevaricated. French troops had been sent to support the inhabitants of the papal enclave of Avignon who had ousted the papal legate and demanded to be part of France: did Pius believe Avignon could be retrieved if a rupture could be avoided? Or was it, as Eamon Duffy suggests, that he did not want to see France follow the path taken by England?[502] However, as the months passed it became clear that the revolutionary government would accept no compromise and so, on 10 March, 1791, Pius denounced the Civil Constitution as schismatical and the ordinations by Constitutional bishops sacrilegious. He suspended all bishops and priests who had taken the oath, and denounced the 1789 Declaration of the Rights of Man. Diplomatic relations between France and the Holy See were broken off; Avignon and the Comtat Venaissin were lost; but now all doubts had been dispersed. The Constitutional Church was not part of the Catholic Church. Anyone who belonged to it, or took the oath, committed a grave sin. Priests who had taken the oath were given forty days to retract.

Political developments now exacerbated the divisions over religion. Louis XVI and Marie-Antoinette, who had been taken by a mob of revolutionary

---

501   *Ibid*, p. 171

502   Duffy, *Op. Cit.* p. 255

women from Versailles to the Tuileries palace in Paris, had, when attempting to attend mass and receive communion from a 'refractory' – that is, orthodox – priest in Saint-Cloud, been stopped by a crowd and confined in their coach for two hours. On the night of 20 June, a clandestine attempt to flee from France and seek the protection of Marie-Antoinette's brother, the Emperor Leopold II, in what were now the Austrian Netherlands, was thwarted when Louis was recognised by a postmaster from his portrait on an *assignat*, and forcibly returned to Paris from the town of Varennes.

Leopold, like other European monarchs such as Ferdinand, king of Naples – also his brother-in-law – and the self-indulgent successor to Frederick the Great, King Frederick William II of Prussia, followed with dismay the course of events in France. After the royal family's arrest at Varennes, Leopold publicly warned the revolutionary government against mistreating Louis, and on 27 August was joined by Prussia in the Declaration of Pillnitz in expressing solidarity with the French king. This merely enraged the French revolutionaries who now saw Louis XVI and Marie-Antoinette as traitors in league with foreign powers. Many members of the French nobility, among them non-juring bishops and archbishops, had succeeded where Louis had failed, leaving France either for the Austrian Netherlands or principalities on the east bank of the Rhine. These émigrés prepared a return with an Austrian and possibly Prussian army to suppress the revolution and restore the rule of the king.

In Paris, the non-juring clergy came to be seen as a potential fifth column of such an invading army. In the autumn of 1791 elections were held for a Legislative Assembly which was to draw up a new constitution. Among the 750 new members there were four hundred lawyers. Most were under thirty years of age. A contest for power now followed between the more moderate revolutionaries such as Lafayette and the extremists – the Jacobins backed by the poorest Parisians known as the *sans-culottes* because they could not afford the breeches worn by the nobility and middle-class; and these radicals were reinforced by the arrival of *fédérés*, zealous revolutionary delegates from Marseilles and Brittany – the former singing the stirring song written by Rouget de Lisle for the Army of the Rhine, the Marseillaise, which became France's national anthem.

On August 10, these *fédérés* and elements from the National Guard controlled by the now autonomous Paris Commune, attacked the Tuilleries palace, slaughtering the Swiss Guard who defended the king. Louis and his family ended up imprisoned in the Temple, the keep of what had been the Templars' fortress in Paris. On 22nd August the Paris Commune ruled that Louis should now be addressed as 'citizen Capet', rather than 'Your royal highness' or even 'Monsieur'. On the Rhine, Lafayette ordered his army to march on Paris to save the king. It refused. Lafayette fled to the Austrian Netherlands where he was imprisoned for the next five years.

The seizure of the initiative by fanatics was largely a response to the threat from the advancing armies of Austrians, Prussians and émigrés led by the Duke of Brunswick. On 2 September, 1792, the great bulwark against any invasion from the east, the fortress at Verdun, fell without a fight. Upon hearing the news, the Paris Commune ordered the massacre of all prisoners held in the make-shift prisons around Paris. In the Carmelite convent 115 non-juring priests awaiting transportation to Guiana were killed. Among them were the king's confessor, the superior of the Eudists, the bishops of Saintes and Beauvais, and the eighty-seven-year old Archbishop of Arles.

Next it was the turn of the Abbey of Saint-Germain-des-Près which had been turned into a goal. Here were held women from the royal household including the dauphin's governess and the queen's ladies-in-waiting: all were spared except the Princess de Lamballe whose body was stripped, her corpse eviscerated, and her head placed upon a pike. 127 members of the Swiss Guard who had survived the storming of the Tuileries Palace were slaughtered. Massacres followed in the Châtelet, the Conciergerie prisons and the Salpêtrière Hospital where 27 religious sisters were killed. Seventeen seminarians were killed at the Seminary of Saint Firmin on the rue Saint Victor; between 150-170 men at the Royal Hospital of Bicêtre.

The victims of the 'Septembriseurs' were not just priests and aristocrats but common criminals such as the forgers of *assignats*. Of the approximately 1400 massacred between 2-6 September, it is estimated that 238 were priests, though this figure excludes those in the Abbey of Saint-Germain-des-Près who, when told that their lives would be spared if they took the oath, refused and were killed.[503] The numbers are contested: so too is the question of who should be indicted in the tribunal of history for the atrocities. Charlotte Corday, a young woman from Normandy, blamed Marat and came to Paris where she stabbed him in his bath. Others point to Danton, the leader of the Paris Commune and Minister of Justice in the Legislative Assembly: he may not have organized the massacres, but he could have stopped them. The

---

503   Von Pastor, Op. Cit., p. 198

mob was not out of control. The Neckers' daughter, Germaine de Staël, whose coach was stopped by the mob when she tried to leave Paris, was saved by the procurator, Luis Pierre Manuel, and left the next day with a passport signed by the Secretary-General of the Commune, Jean-Lambert Tallien.

The alarm of the French revolutionaries eased when the revolutionary army under Generals Kellermann and Dumouriez defeated the advancing coalition of Prussians, Austrians and émigrés at Valmy in Champagne. The army, a mixture of professional soldiers from the pre-revolutionary army and zealous volunteers, now moved beyond France's eastern frontier, occupying Basel in Switzerland and Frankfurt am Main in Germany. In Paris the Convention, which had now replaced the Legislative Assembly, stated that its forces had the right to intervene 'where people desire to recover their freedom'. Basel, hitherto ruled by its Archbishop, was proclaimed a republic. In November, Dumouriez invaded the Austrian Netherlands and on the 14th occupied Brussels. Further south, Savoy and Nice were absorbed into France.

On 22 September, 1792, Louis XVI was deposed by the Convention and France declared a Republic. Letters written by Louis encouraging France's enemies to invade France had been found in the Tuileries palace. On 10 December, the Convention passed a motion put forward by Maximilien Robespierre to put their former king on trial before the Convention charged with conspiracy against public liberty. He was declared guilty by an unanimous vote, but condemned to death by a majority of one. He was beheaded by the guillotine on the Place de la Revolution on 21 January, 1793. He had mounted the scaffold with dignity: drum rolls were ordered to drown out the last words of the king whom the German historian Ludwig von Pastor judged to be 'the noblest of the Bourbons'.[504] Marie-Antoinette suffered the same fate nine months later.

While Louis XVI lay awaiting execution in the Temple during the winter of 1792, 'as many as a third of the French lower clergy and three quarters of the bishops went into exile, between twenty-five and thirty thousand priests. Seven thousand of them, escaping via the Channel Islands, were welcomed in Protestant England where ironically anti-Catholic laws were still in force. It was now the non-juring clergy remaining in France whose life 'resembled that of the recusant clergy in Elizabethan England, that is, a life in disguise,

---

504   *Ibid.* p.201

hiding and on the run.[505] Persecution intensified in the spring of 1793. Decrees passed by the Convention in March and April of 1793 ruled that any priest who had evaded deportation should be arrested, tried and executed within twenty-four hours of his conviction. Not just the ministers but symbols of orthodox Catholicism were eliminated. The names of communes were changed: for example, Bourg-la-Reine became Bourg-Egalité, Mont-Saint-Michel became Mont-Libre, and Saint-Gengoux-le-Royal in Burgundy was re-named Saint-Gengoux-le-National.[506] With an iconoclasm equalling that of the Calvinists in the sixteenth century, churches were sacked, religious paintings and statues destroyed, gold and silver chalices, monstrances and reliquaries seized and melted down, and the carved heads of saints and angels that embellished the facades of churches and cathedrals were hacked off. Ancient abbeys such as Cluny were plundered for building materials for the mansions of revolutionary profiteers. Saint Bernard's monastery of Clairvaux became (and remains) a prison. 'Christianity,' wrote von Pastor, 'had not been subjected to such merciless persecution since the time of Diocletian'[507].

The Constitutional Church failed to fill the spiritual void: it was loathed by the inhabitants of provinces such as Alsace. Excrement, dead cats and sometimes coffins were left outside the presbyteries of Constitutional priests, and guns fired in the middle of the night. As a result, throughout France, nearly half the Constitutional clergy abandoned their calling. Between 4,500 and 6,000 married; others left the priesthood and became school-teachers or joined the army being recruited to defend the Revolution. By 1794, 'only 150 of France's 40,000 pre-Revolutionary parishes were openly celebrating mass.'[508]

In the west of France – in Brittany and particularly the area bordering the Atlantic known as the Vendée – resistance to the new dispensation went further than depositing excrement and dead cats. Here the local nobility had not decamped to Versailles but had remained on their estates, were close to their tenants, and like them were devout members of the Catholic Church. The measures imposed from Paris were considered obnoxious and the *levée*

---

505 Burleigh, *Op. Cit.*, p. 95

506 The name of this small village was changed four times in the course of the nineteenth century: the attachment 'national' has remained since 1882. Saint Gengoux is the patron saint of cuckolds.

507 Von Pastor, *Op. Cit.*, p. 202

508 Burleigh, *Op. Cit.* p. 66

en masse of March, 1793, the conscription of 300,000 men – the first time that an European government had raised a conscript army – led to protests south of the Loire, the protests to riots and the riots to outright rebellion. A 'Royal and Catholic Army' was formed with emblems of the Sacred Heart sewn onto its uniforms and the motto '*Dieu, le Roi*' – God and the King. Guerrilla forces operated from the forests and soon a large swathe of territory around Nantes and Cholet were under their control. Republican forces sent from Paris to suppress the revolt were defeated by the rebels led by the twenty-one-year old Henri du Vergier, comte de la Rochejacquelein. Battles in May at Bressuire, Thouars, Fontenay-le-Comte were won by the royalists, and on 19 June they took the town of Saumur from republican forces led by the future Napoleonic Marshal, Louis-Alexandre Berthier.

A force of 40,000 counter-revolutionaries now advanced on Nantes, laid siege to the city but failed to take it. Beyond Nantes, the Royal and Catholic Army won a number of further encounters with republican forces, but within Nantes itself not just insurgent prisoners taken during the siege, but anyone deemed sympathetic to the royalist cause, was condemned to death by Jean-Baptiste Carrier, the *représentant en mission* or commissar of the National Convention. Around two thousand prisoners were shot in a quarry in Gigant near Nantes but, finding this means onerous and a waste of precious gunpowder, Carrier concentrated the prisoners in the Coffee Warehouse and on barges on the quay on the Loire. On 16 November a barge was taken out into the middle of the river and scuttled: 160 'refractory' Catholic priests were drowned. Only one, a strong swimmer, survived.

The next day a further 58 priests suffered the same fate when the barge upon which they were held, modified like the first with trap-doors in its floor, was towed to the mouth of the Loire and sunk: there were no survivors. Further drownings emptied the Coffee Warehouse of its prisoners – men, women, children and infants. A refinement in these *noyades* (drownings) were the 'republican marriages' where men and women were stripped naked, tied together and thrown into the river. 'The massacres perpetrated by Carrier at Nantes,' wrote von Pastor, 'are an ineffaceable stain on the history of the Revolution.'[509] Even the Revolutionaries appear to have acknowledged this because Carrier was guillotined in December, 1794.

Von Pastor estimates that there were 16,000 victims of the *noyades de Nantes*. An arresting number in itself, it was only a small proportion of the

---

509   Von Pastor, *Op. Cit.* p. 202

total number killed in the eventually successful suppression of the rising in the Vendée. 'A quarter of a million people perished during the revolt's brutal suppression,' writes Michael Burleigh. 'This was the first occasion in history when an anti-clerical and self-styled non-religious state embarked on a programme of mass murder that anticipated many twentieth century horrors'. It puts in proportion other totemic massacres such as that of the Jews in the Rhineland during the First Crusade, or of the Huguenots during the Saint Bartholomew's Day massacre in Paris. Both Burleigh, and the French historian Reynald Secher, consider that the implementation of the Committee of Public Safety's policy to exterminate the residents of the Vendée, approved by the National Convention on 1 October, 1793, was 'tantamount to genocide'.[510]

Parallel to the rising in the Vendée was that of the Chouans in Brittany who, with the help of troops sent from England, saw a succession of victories over revolutionary forces sent against them, and took advantage of local knowledge of the rugged landscape to wage guerrilla war. There were revolts in the south, too: the city of Lyon ousted the republicans and the inhabitants of Toulon invited the British navy into their port.

In all these conflicts, there were atrocities, but these were no longer confined to the western or southern provinces of France. The Revolution had entered that phase known as the Terror when the Jacobins led by Robespierre took control of the all-powerful Committee of Public Safety with his adjutant, the young radical, Louis Antoine de Saint-Just. They now drew up lists of aristocrats, clergy, suspected traitors and political adversaries to be tried, condemned and sent to the guillotine. Between June 11 and July 27, 1,376 were executed by the *rasoir national*, a figure exceeding that from the previous fourteen months. Sixteen nuns from the Carmelite convent in Compiègne; Louis XVI's sister, Madame Elisabeth; the veteran revolutionaries Jacques Hébert, Georges Danton and Camille Desmoulins; and the revolutionary *salonnière* Madame Roland were guillotined. 'Oh Liberty,' she declaimed as she mounted on the scaffold, 'what crimes are committed in your name'.

The de-Christianisation of France was completed under the Terror. The last remnant of a Christian ecclesial community, the Constitutional Church, had been an abject failure. On 6 November, the Convention declared freedom of religion. Jean-Baptiste Gobel resigned both as Constitutional Archbishop of Paris and as a priest, proclaiming his conversion to Reason. Four hundred

---

510   Burleigh, *Op. Cit.* p. 97 See also Reynald Secher, *Vendée, du génocide au mémoride.*

Parisian priests followed his example[511], together with Thomas Lindet, the Constitutional Bishop of Limoges. The Cult of Reason now became the national religion with its sanctuaries, ceremonies and saints. Already, in 1791, the newly built church in Paris dedicated to Saint Genevieve had been appropriated to serve as France's Panthéon. The first to be interred in this national mausoleum was the revolutionary Mirabeau though when posthumously he fell out of favour his remains were removed and replaced by those of Marat. On 4 April, 1794, at Robespierre's request, the Convention had the ashes of Jean-Jacques Rousseau re-interred in the Panthéon. In August, 1793, on the orders of the Convention, mobs broke into the abbey of St. Denis, the mausoleum of the French kings since the time of Dagobert, despoiled the tombs and scattered the bones. The cathedral of Notre Dame, now vacated by its archbishop, was declared a Temple of Reason, and a ceremony was held to venerate a scantily clad opera singer, Mademoiselle Maillard, as goddess of Liberty. In the provinces 'the conversion of churches into similar "temples of reason" was accompanied by anticlerical outrages and the desecration of sacred furnishings'.[512] A Protestant English woman then in France described the frenzied festivities celebrating the new cult during which the adherents of the new religion danced with 'a savage delight' around a bonfire of prayer-books, saints' images, confessionals, and other pieces of church furniture'. 'It was in this fashion,' wrote von Pastor, 'that the glorious cathedrals of Chartres, Rheims, Metz, and Strasbourg were desecrated. At Laon and Abbeville, the goddess of Reason was a harlot'.[513]

There was one revolutionary leader who disapproved of the worship of an abstraction and that was Robespierre. He was a Deist, believing like the Freemasons in a Supreme Being. Atheism was a source of disorder, and Robespierre came to fear that the excesses of the anti-religious fanatics were part of a conspiracy to discredit the revolution. In this he was not alone: his fellow Jacobins 'were respectable, middling people …overwhelmingly middle-aged… ', with a disproportionate number (around 6 percent) of former priests. 'Decorum was everything, adultery, drunkenness and gluttony disdained. Foul language was formally prohibited'.[514] Robespierre was high minded: he esteemed virtue and recognised that without a law-giver there

---

511   Burleigh, *p. Cit.* p.87

512   *Ibid,* p. 87

513   Von Pastor, *Op. Cit.* p. 208

514   Burleigh, *Op. Cit.* p. 89

could be no law. On 21 November, 1793, in a speech to his fellow Jacobins, he denounced atheism and quoted Voltaire's quip that 'if God did not exist, we would have to invent him'. At his request, the Convention passed a law acknowledging the immortality of the soul and the existence of a Supreme Being. An extravagant ceremony to venerate this deity was held on 8 June, 1794, on the parade ground adjacent to the École Militaire in Paris, the Champs de Mars.

Robespierre's antics during this Festival of the Supreme Being antagonised some members of the Convention, and contributed to his downfall and the end of the Terror in July, 1794. However, this did not end or reverse the de-Christianisation of France. Already, in September, 1791, the National Assembly had voted to 'admit those who took the civic oath and committed themselves to fulfil those duties imposed by the constitution' to full citizenship with the same rights as anyone else'. This included the Jews of whom there were in fact relatively few in France. Since their expulsion in the Middle Ages, some Sephardic Jews had crossed the Pyrenees to escape the Spanish Inquisition, and a larger community of Ashkenazi Jews came with Louis XIV's conquest of former imperial provinces on the Rhine.

The admission to full citizenship of the Jews did not mean the end of anti-Semitism. Quite to the contrary, instead of 'disappearing with the Enlightenment, anti-Semitism simply found a new guise, one which no longer blamed the Jews for the crucifixion of Christ but held them responsible for all the crimes and perversities committed in the name of monotheistic religion...' In his entry 'Juifs', written for the *Dictionaire Philosophique*, Voltaire wrote that 'we find in them only an ignorant and barbarous people, who have long united the most sordid avarice with the most detestable superstition and the most invincible hatred for every people by whom they are tolerated and enriched.'[515]

However, the logic of Liberty, Equality Fraternity meant extending full civic rights to Jews; and while 'the Jews and Judaism were not the central concerns of the French Revolution,'[516] the overwhelming reaction of Jews living in France was one of elation – a sentiment shared in other nations as Jews were liberated in the wake of the victorious revolutionary armies. Jews who for centuries had suffered from discrimination, supported the

515   Wistrich, *Op. Cit.* p. 45
516   David Nirenberg, *Op. Cit.* p. 375

dismantling of the structures and privileges of the *ancien regime*, and took advantage of their new freedom to move outside the ghettos.

If it was the logic of Liberty that ensured the liberation of the Jews, it was the Cult of Reason that led to reforms that were not all reversed by subsequent regimes. The *rasoir national,* the guillotine, remained in use in many European countries until the abolition of capital punishment.[517] The Metric System for measuring distance and weight, developed by the French Academy of Sciences during the revolution, was adopted by most nations with one or two Anglo-Saxon exceptions. Less enduring was the Republican Calendar which divided the year into twelve months named after the seasons, and each month into three ten-day weeks with the tenth day, *décadi*, replacing Sunday – the Jewish and Christian Sabbath – as the day of rest. An attempt to divide each day into ten hours, each with 100 minutes, and each minute with 100 seconds, was abandoned in April, 1795; however the Republican Calendar was used in France and the nations conquered by France for twelve years.

Establishing the tenth day as the day of rest, and so abolishing the Christian Sabbath, as well as all the feast days of the Catholic Church – Easter, Christmas, All Saints, Corpus Christi, the Assumption – were not unintended consequences of the passion for decimalisation, but part of a programme to eradicate anything associated with France's Christian past. After the successful coup against Robespierre and his execution, 'the principle of toleration gained ground, even in the National Convention'[518]; however, persecution resumed under the five-man Directory. Priests were once again arrested and sentenced to deportation to French Guiana and, because passage across the Atlantic was impeded by the British navy, held in hulks on the Loire or in the fortress on the Île de Ré. The president of the Directory, Louis Marie de la Révellière-Lépeaux, loathed the Christian religion and wished to replace it with a deist cult invented by a Welsh clergyman, David Williams – Theophilanthropy. Theophilanthropist ceremonies were held in a number of churches in Paris, including the cathedral of Notre Dame, singing hymns extracted from the work of Racine and Jean-Jacques Rousseau, and venerating 'saints' such as Socrates and George Washington.

---

517   The Munich students, Hans and Sophie Scholl, whose White Rose movement opposed the Nazis, were guillotined in the Stadelheim Prison in Berlin in 1943.

518   Von Pastor, *Op. Cit.* p. 281

79.   The Roman Republic

It was not unreasonable of Louis Marie de la Révellière-Lépeaux and his fellow Theophilanthropists to anticipate that a Theophilanthropist Mass might soon be said under Bernini's *baldacchino* on the high altar of Saint Peter's basilica in Rome, for Rome was now threatened by the armies of the French Republic.

While the ferocity of the Revolution of 1789 might not have been anticipated, some form of revolt within the kingdom of France hardly came as a surprise. What astonished Europe, however, were the victorious campaigns following Valmy of the French revolutionary armies beyond the borders of France. Certainly, France was, after Russia, the most populous country in Europe, and so the radical new idea of conscription could draw from a deep pool of young men; and while their aristocratic generals may have fled abroad to form an army of émigrés, the bulk of the former Royal Army remained in France. At Valmy, half the French infantry were zealous volunteers but the other half, and most of the cavalry and artillery, regarded as the best in Europe, were professionals who had served under the *ancien régime*. Moreover, the revolutionary armies benefited from promoting officers according to their ability, not their pedigree. In 1793, the royalists were ousted from Toulon, and the British fleet forced to flee, thanks to the courage and strategic intelligence of a professional soldier, a twenty-four year-old Corsican artillery officer, Napoleon Bonaparte.

Already, in 1795, the French had occupied the Austrian Netherlands, and at the Treaty of Basel made peace with Spain and Prussia. Austria remained in the alliance against the French republic with Russia, Piedmont and some other Italian principalities. The Italian Alps and the valley of the Po were the main theatres of war. In a series of battles under the brilliant young Corsican, Napoleon Bonaparte, the French triumphed over the coalition's forces. They occupied Lombardy, the Veneto, and then Venice: the thousand-year-old serene Republic, seeped in decadence, surrendered without a fight.

Two principalities to the south remained unconquered – the Papal States governed by *il papa bello*, Pius VI, in Rome; and the Kingdom of Naples and Sicily ruled by the Spanish Bourbon Ferdinand II, the husband of Marie-Antoinette's sister, Maria Carolina. Ferdinand's prime minister was an Englishman, John Acton, who, barred from employment by the government at home because he was a Catholic, had, like a number of his co-religionists, been obliged to find it abroad. Acton favoured an alliance with the English against the French, and Ferdinand hoped for one with his relatives in Vienna; however the French were in the ascendant not just in northern Italy, but also in the Mediterranean. In September, 1793, a French fleet under Admiral Latouche-Tréville sailed into the bay of Naples and, under threat of bombardment, Ferdinand had been obliged to make peace with the government that had so recently executed his sister-in-law, Marie-Antoinette.

Pius VI was now vulnerable in Rome. What if they should march on the Holy City? He had an army, his Swiss Guard and the garrison of the Castel Sant' Angelo but without a powerful ally these were wholly inadequate to defend the Vicar of Christ. 'We have neither troops nor ships,' he wrote to the Russian Czarina Catherine, begging her to send a Russian navy into the Mediterranean. Much as he would have liked the Austrians to triumph, Pius did not join the coalition for fear of provoking the French; but unlike Ferdinand, he still refused to recognise a republic that had slaughtered so many bishops and priests. Would his turn come next? Some cardinals advised him to leave Rome but he refused: 'My post is by the tomb of Saint Peter'.

Pius was not to know that Bonaparte had ignored orders by the Directory in Paris to march on Rome and depose the pope. He despised Pius, 'whom he regarded as a treacherous opportunist ready to stir against him every time the Austrians looked as though they might be winning' but he 'felt no animus against the Church and treated the clergy in the lands he occupied with respect, if only out of calculation.'[519] The reforms he imposed in northern Italy, comparable to those of Joseph II in the Austrian empire, 'were hated as much as the introduction of his administrative culture was admired'.[520]

There were native Italian revolutionaries but they were few. As we have seen, the Romans ridiculed the ideas of the Enlightenment, and were horrified by the slaughter of priests: they remained loyal to their pontiff. The failure of the Romans to topple their despotic ruler both puzzled and exasperated the French revolutionaries. A French banker, Morette, living in the city, together with Hugou de Basseville, conspired with the few Roman republicans to depose the pope. Morette gave dinners at the French Embassy at which he toasted the French Republic and called upon his guests to follow the example of Brutus who had assassinated Julius Caesar. On Sunday 13 January, 1793, Basseville, accompanied by his wife, their young son, and a

---

519   Adam Zamoyski. *Napoleon. The Man Behind the Myth*, p. 148

520   Andrew Roberts, *Napoleon the Great*, p. 118

young French naval officer who had joined him from Naples, went for a drive in an open carriage on the Corso. All wore *tricolor* cockades in their hats. As the carriage made its way down the Corso, the Romans were enraged at the sight of the *tricolor* cockades, and demanded that they be removed. The Frenchmen refused. A stone was thrown at the barouche and the coachman, alarmed, turned down the Vicolo dello Sdrucciolo and into the courtyard of Moretto's residence, the Palazzo Palombara. The angry crowd followed and assaulted the passengers as they left the carriage. All escaped into the palazzo except Bassveille who was stabbed in the stomach.

In France, Basseville's death transformed a tiresome *provocateur* who had been disowned by the government into a martyr. Demands for reparations, indemnities and the expulsion of French royalist émigrés were conveyed to Rome where they were rejected. The mood in Paris was vindictive: 'The conspiracy of the king's priests must be avenged by the destruction of Rome: the time had come for the city to disappear from the face of the world...' [521] Bonaparte was told to move on Rome and, still a republican and sharing the craze for antiquity, he toyed with the idea, announcing that 'our intention is to restore the Capitol, and to set up there in their honour the statues of the men who won renown, and to free the Roman people from their long slavery'. He invaded the Legations in the north of the Papal states, capturing the Cities of Ravenna, Ferrara and Bologna but as yet refrained from a march on Rome.

Pius VI, with no allies to come to his aid, sued for peace. Vain, self-indulgent, mildly corrupt, indecisive and now an old man, Pius VI staggered under the burdens now placed on his shoulders. Thousands of refugees from France were now in the city, among them 5,000 priests, yet the supplies of food were barely enough to provide for the Romans themselves. The revenues that had once poured into the papal coffers from France had now ceased; so too from once rich episcopal principalities such as Cologne where only 22 of its 118 churches were still in use. [522] In Rome itself conditions were dire. Pius staggered but he did not fall. Popes before him had faced barbarians at the gate: barbarians had on occasions burst through the gates and pillaged the Holy City, most recently the German *Landsknechte* of Charles V. To withdraw now like Pope Clement VIII into the Castel Sant' Angelo, leaving the Romans to their fate, was neither viable because of the advances in artillery, nor

---

521   *Ibid.,* p. 243

522   *Ibid.,* p. 253

something that Pius would consider as the father of his people.

For months Pius had temporised – hoping that the royalists might triumph in the Vendée or the armies of the Coalition in the valley of the Po. He did what he could to protect his flock and preserve the patrimony of Peter. In negotiating with the French, he made a distinction in his dealings with the French between his role as the ruler of an Italian principality and that as the head of the Catholic Church. Here there could be no concessions. He refused to withdraw the edicts he had issued condemning the actions of the French revolutionaries since 1789. He would never, the French were told, 'be party to such a defamation of the Church, even if his own life was at risk.'

As a result of this stand, the negotiations collapsed. The truce was now at an end. France and the pope were at war. The payment of indemnities ceased, and the works of art to be sent to Paris, some already loaded onto wagons, remained in Rome. A militia was formed to support the papal army which an experienced but decrepit Austrian commander, Lieutenant General Michelangelo Alessandro Colli-Marchi, led north, hoping to join forces with the Austrians in Lombardy. However Mantua, hitherto held by the Austrians but besieged by the French, now fell to the French. Bonaparte, triumphant after this victory, did not consider Colli-Marchi was an adversary worthy of his genius. He sent a subordinate who had risen from the ranks, Brigadier-General Claude Victor-Perrin, with nine thousand veterans to confront the seven thousand ill-trained soldiers of the papal army outside the town of Faenza. The papal army was obliterated.

Pius VI was once again left with no choice but to sue for peace. Bonaparte's terms were severe. The papal army was to be disbanded, its Austrian officers dismissed. Avignon and the Comtat Venaissin were to be ceded to France in perpetuity, and a large part of the Romagna incorporated into the new Cisalpine republic. The existing indemnity of 21 million scudi was increased to 36 million. All republican prisoners were to be released, and all members of the Roman nobility antagonistic towards the French were to be banished and their property confiscated. The port of Civitavecchia was used exclusively by the French navy, and at any future conclave the French government were to exercise a veto.

The papal delegation agreed to all Bonaparte's demands but the last: it could concede on temporal matters, but not on those concerning the governance of the universal Church. Bonaparte backed down. The Treaty of Tolentino was signed on 19 February, 1797, and in August of the same year

Napoleon Bonaparte's brother Joseph arrived in Rome as the new ambassador to the Holy See. On his staff was an ardent republican, General Maturin-Léonard Duphot. Duphot's task was to stimulate a revolutionary spirit in the inhabitants of the Holy City. With a French army hovering on the northern border of what remained of the papal states, Pius was powerless to prevent this breach of diplomatic etiquette. He told his subjects that the French must be treated courteously, and the aristocracy, understanding the reason for Pius's injunction, received members of Bonaparte's entourage in their *palazzi*. However, the people of the street were confused. Having been told by their priests that the French revolutionaries were agents of Satan, intent upon the destruction of the Church, they could not understand why they should now stand aside as their city's finest works of art, of which even those who did not own them were proud, were loaded on carts to be taken to Paris. Despite the papal edicts, strutting Frenchmen were insulted in the street, and the home-grown republicans who had come to Rome from other parts of Italy to partake in the glory of overthrowing the theocratic tyrant, were threatened and abused.

On 27 December, 1797, there was a large demonstration by these foreign agitators, shouting 'Long live liberty!' and 'Long live the Republic!'. Stones were thrown at the papal troops. A company of dragoons dispersed the crowd, but the republican agitators regrouped on the Pincio. Once again, the dragoons were attacked, this time with knives as well as stones. Two papal troopers were dragged off their horses and killed. Enraged, their companions drove the crowd back down the *lungara* towards the French embassy, the Palazzo Corsini. There General Duphot came out with a drawn sword to defend the republicans. 'Long live Liberty!' he shouted. 'Courage! I am your general'. He advanced on a corporal and four soldiers: the corporal ordered his platoon to raise their muskets and open fire. Duphot was shot in the head. His body was carried into the embassy, where he was found to be dead.

For Pius VI and his Secretary of State, Cardinal Doria Pamphili, this was a catastrophe: the cardinal went at once to the Palazzo Corsini to apologise to Joseph Bonaparte, but Bonaparte was not to be appeased. Duphot was to have married Joseph's brother's old flame, Desirée Clary, whose sister was Joseph's wife; but alongside his personal grief was the realisation that Duphot's death provided an impeccable *casus belli*. Spurning the repeated apologies emanating from the Quirinale Palace, Joseph Bonaparte left Rome with his family and diplomatic staff.

The death of Duphot was, as Joseph had anticipated, seized upon by the Directory in Paris as a pretext for a French occupation of Rome. Orders were sent to Bonaparte who delegated the task to his loyal and enduring aide, General Bertier. On 15 February, 1798, the anniversary of Braschi's election as pope, Bertier led his army into Rome and went straight to the Capitol where he declared Pope Pius deposed. After a thousand years, Rome was liberated from the rule of theocratic despots. The tyranny of priests was over. Standing in front of the statue of the Roman emperor Marcus Aurelius, draped with a tricolor flag, and wearing a circlet of laurel leaves on his head, Berthier declared that Rome was now a republic. 'Descendants of Cato, Brutus and Cicero…turn your eyes to the monuments of glory that surround you! Regain your ancient greatness and the virtues of your fathers!'[523]

Pope Pius VI, when told that he had been deposed and was now a prisoner in the Quirinale Palace, bowed his head and said that he accepted the inscrutable designs of divine providence. On 17 February, a French officer told him to prepare to leave the city. The pope answered that he wished to die by the tomb of Saint Peter. 'You can die anywhere,' the officer replied. He made clear that if Pius did not comply, force would be used to expel him. As a result, before dawn on 20 February, 1797, the ailing eighty-year-old pontiff climbed into a coach at the Cortile de San Damas with two priests and his doctor. It was still dark. Escorted by a small contingent of French soldiers, the coach passed through the streets unnoticed. Thus, with no ceremony and no farewells, the supreme pontiff of the Catholic Church left the Eternal City.

The reign of Pius VI had been the longest in the history of the papacy, with the last six months a slow martyrdom as, feeble and sick, he was taken in jolting coaches on dusty roads first to Florence, then Parma, Piacenza, Turin and finally in July to Valence on the left bank of the River Rhône where he was held in the citadel. His health had worsened. On the evening of 19 August, six weeks after his arrival in Valence, he received the last sacrament of the Church. Shortly after midnight, 'making a final effort…he gave the triple blessing to those present and with them, too, the whole ungrateful world from which he was now departing. His arm dropped listlessly on to the bed and the crucifix slipped from his grasp. After a few minutes of grievous agony, the face quivered slightly and the physician assured himself that death had taken place.'[524]

---

523   Harold Acton, *Op. Cit.*, p 300
524   Von Pastor, *Op. Cit.*, p. 388

The Roman republic established by General Berthier in Rome was given a constitution modelled on that of antiquity with a Senate, a Tribunal and five Consuls. The statue of the archangel Michael on the top of the Castel Sant' Angelo was renamed 'the Liberating Genius of France', painted red, white and blue, and a Liberty bonnet put on its head. The Roman Republic itself adopted a tricolor – black, white and red; crucifixes were replaced by Liberty trees; the statues of Catholic saints with busts of Cato and Brutus; and patriots rather than penitents processed through the streets of the once-holy city acclaiming the Nation rather than God.

A grandiose memorial service was held for the republican martyr, General Duphot, in Saint Peter's Square – men in togas extolling his heroic virtues while young women in diaphanous costumes danced around a *papier-mâché* altar. On the Piazza di Spagna there was a ritual burning of the archives of the Roman Inquisition: half-naked youths with wings attached to their should blades lit the bonfire and, at the summation of the ceremony, a naked woman symbolising Truth was seen rising from the Ashes of Superstition. The Romans watching from the Spanish Steps booed, jeered and pelted the performers with rotten vegetables.

Despite the elections to the republican institutions, Rome was in fact governed by General Berthier. He was shrewd enough to realise that a direct assault on Catholic practice would antagonise the Romans and make his rule more difficult. Thus, the republican celebrations were held in the open outside the city's great basilicas which were left in the hands of the clergy. However, the property of the Church was plundered – reliquaries, monstrances, even cruets and chalices used in the Mass. Gold and silver bars to the value of 15 million *scudi* were taken from the vaults of the Castel Sant' Angelo, and anything of value from the Vatican and Quirinale palaces. Pearls and precious stones were removed from their settings on papal vestments and regalia; and the plundered works of art were once again loaded on to carts for shipment to Paris. Those not considered of sufficient quality for Paris's new Musée du Louvre were sold off at auction, going at knock-down prices to the merchants and bankers who had ready cash. So too the property of papal loyalists – for example the palace of the Grand Master of the Knights of Malta on the Aventine Hill.

Under pressure from both the Directorate, and from Bonaparte who needed funds to pay his army, General Berthier, and later General Masséna who replaced him, pillaged the city as effectively as the Goths, Vandals or the

German *Landsknechte*. French troops were billeted in monasteries, convents and some private homes. Generals requisitioned palaces where they gave lavish receptions to celebrate their victory – these frequently degenerating into drunken orgies which provoked the resentment of their unpaid troops. A group of two hundred junior officers protested at the greed and depravity of their superiors, and at one point Massena, fearing a mutiny, fled the city.

With no munificent princes or cardinals to distribute their largesse, the economy of the city collapsed. The paper currency issued by the French became worthless. The people went hungry. The only group that welcomed and subsequently profited from the French occupation were Rome's Jews, liberated from the ghetto and now full citizens of the republic. A group that had ventured into Trastevere were attacked by a mob. French troops were summoned to restore order. The *fracas* became a riot. Some soldiers were killed. Twenty two protesters were arrested and later shot on the Piazza del Popolo. More demonstrations and isolated assassinations led to further reprisals. The cells of the Castel Sant' Angelo were filled with papal loyalists, or those thought to have concealed their treasures from the French. Two priests who had uprooted Liberty trees and replaced them with crucifixes were shot.

Some Romans, it was reported, were collaborating with the French. The Vicar General of Rome, Cardinal Somaglia, had let it be known that he no longer wished to be addressed as 'Your eminence' but 'Citizen Somaglia'. Young men from noble families were to be seen on the Corso wearing tricolor scarves, with their powdered wigs replaced by short 'Brutus' haircuts while some young married women, it was reported in a news sheet, 'and some not so young now exchanged the elaborate dresses of the *ancien régime* with light, clinging Grecian tunics – some dropping their Roman *cicisbei* in favour of handsome young French officers.

With French rule now established in northern and central Italy, Napoleon Bonaparte returned to Paris and presented plans to the Directory for the invasion, first of England and then of Egypt. On 19 May, 1798, a large French fleet left the port of Toulon and, taking Malta from the Knights of Saint John *en route*, captured Alexandria and on 21 July defeated the Mameluk rulers of Egypt in the Battle of the Pyramids. The French then took Cairo, and penetrated as far as Syria, but the ships that had conveyed them to the Orient were destroyed by a British fleet under Horatio Nelson at the Battle of the

Nile.

Encouraged by the absence of Bonaparte and victories of the Austrians and Russians in northern Italy, Ferdinand I, king of Naples and Sicily, led his army north, took Rome almost unopposed, and brought an end to the Roman republic: it had lasted less than a year. However, the French under General Championnet counter-attacked, re-took Rome, pursued the Ferdinand's army down the peninsula and took Naples. While Ferdinand and his family escaped on a British man-of-war to Palermo, the French set up a republic in the kingdom of Naples which, after the ancient Greek colony that had existed on the site, Parthenope, was called the Parthenopean Republic. It was supported by lawyers, doctors, former priests and some radical members of the nobility, but loathed by the city's impoverished masses, the *lazzaroni*.

Holding court in Palermo with Nelson and the Hamiltons, Ferdinand and Carolina left their fate in the hands of the Austrian and Russian armies fighting the French in northern Italy. But one of their entourage, Cardinal Fabrizio Ruffo – the same Ruffo whose expensive and, as it turned out, pointless reinforcement of Civitavecchia had led to his dismissal by Pius VI as Treasurer of the Papal States – was alarmed by reports from the mainland of republican attempts to destroy the faith of Ferdinand's subjects, with Crucifixes replaced by Liberty trees

On 7 February, 1799, Cardinal Ruffo crossed the straits of Messina with a small group of retainers, landing on the coast of Calabria where he was welcomed by retainers of his brother, the Duke of Calabria. They escorted him to Bagnara where he raised the standard of *il Armate della Santa Fide in Gesu Cristo* – the Army of the Holy Faith in Jesus Christ – the *Sanfidestas*. Hundreds, then thousands, joined his army. The army marched north and one by one the towns in its path capitulated. Supplied by Russian and Turkish ships, and combining with other bands of royalist guerrillas, the *Sanfidestas* reached Naples.

The French garrison had gone. After reverses in the north its long line of supply had become vulnerable. In an address to the Senate of the Parthenopean Republic, the French general Étienne Macdonald congratulated the Neapolitan republicans on reaching a point where they could stand on their own feet; then he led his troops out of the city. For a while, the gullible republicans believed what he had said, but their troops were no match for the *Sanfidestas* who broke into the city and defeated the republican defenders at a battle on the Magdalena Bridge.

The republicans withdrew into the city's fortresses, holding out in the hope of relief by a French fleet. To avoid further bloodshed, Ruffo offered them free passage out of the kingdom if they would surrender. The terms were accepted but, just as the republicans were embarking on ships to take them to Toulon, the British fleet under Nelson sailed into the harbour. On the instruction of King Ferdinand, Nelson overruled Ruffo, and the Russian and Turkish commanders who, with one of Nelson's own officers, had signed the armistice, and arrested and imprisoned the republicans. After a cursory court martial, the republican Admiral Caracciolo, was hanged from the yardarm of Nelson's flagship, *Foudroyant.*

Cardinal Ruffo protested but he was ignored. Eight thousand republicans were apprehended; 99 were executed, over 200 sentenced to life-imprisonment, 288 deported, and 67 exiled. The leading lights of the Neapolitan intelligentsia were among the victims, but that was of no consequence of King Ferdinand, and was a cause for celebration by Queen Carolina who, since the death of her sister, had kept by her bedside the embroidered words *je me vengera* – I will take revenge.

80.   Napoleon

King Ferdinand and Queen Maria Carolina returned from Palermo to Naples where, secure on a British warship, they both supervised the sanguinary punishment of their rebellious subjects. A reorganised army pursued the retreating French and occupied Rome, together with the Austrians coming from the north who restrained the Bourbons in their thirst for revenge. The Roman republic was abolished and the republicans banished from the city but, while some sailed to France, others remained in Civitavecchia, awaiting a swing of the pendulum that would bring them back to power. Ferdinand toyed with the idea of annexing Rome and the papal states to his kingdom, but such a solution was unacceptable to the Austrians, the British, the Russians and the Romans themselves. Though the standard of the Bourbon king flew from the Castel Sant' Angelo, it was understood that it would soon be replaced by that of the new pope.

Pius VI, before his death, had instructed the scattered cardinals to hold the conclave to elect his successor in Venice which, in exchange for Milan, had been given by Bonaparte to the Austrian Emperor, Francis II. Francis expected that in return not just for his protection but for footing the bill for the conclave, the Cardinals would choose a pope who would favour Austrian interests, and even agree to the annexation of parts of the Papal States to the Veneto and Venice, now under Austrian rule. He was to be disappointed. The cardinals, holding the conclave in the Benedictine monastery on the island of San Giorgio, deliberated for three months and then elected unanimously Barnaba Chiaramonte, the Bishop of Imola – a good natured monk who made his own bed and mended his own cassock, and was known – if at all – for a sermon he had preached back in 1797 in which he had said that democracy was quite compatible with the Christian religion. So appalled were the Austrians that 'the Citizen Cardinal of Imola', who took the name Pius VII, should be the new pontiff that they refused the use of Saint Mark's cathedral for his coronation, which took place instead in the chapel of the monastery of San Giorgio with a *papier-maché* triple crown. Angry, and remembering the crowds of devout Catholics who had lined the route of Pius VI when he went to Vienna in 1782, the Austrians prohibited his successor from travelling overland to Rome. Instead he was obliged to go by sea in the ancient tub *La Bellone*.

Yet no sooner had the new pope reached Rome, than there was a further swing of the pendulum. Napoleon Bonaparte, abandoning his army in Egypt and evading the British fleet had slipped back to France on the frigate *La Muiron*. There he engineered a coup against the Directory. On 25 December, 1799, under a new constitution, the Constitution of Year III, he was made First Consul and undisputed ruler of France. In was in this way that that 'singular accomplishment of moralizing lawyers, renegade priests and hack journalists'[525], the French Revolution, came to an end.

Bonaparte's first task was to form an army to replace the one he had abandoned in Egypt. This was done in a matter of months, and in May, 1800, a force of 51,400 men, 10,000 horses and 750 mules, often in single file, crossed the Alps by the Val d'Aosta. Bonaparte followed and on 14 June, 1800, he defeated the Austrians at Marengo.[526] The north of Italy was now in the hands of the French and the pope, Pius VII, although installed in the Quirinale palace in Rome, had the protection of no great power. But Bonaparte who in 1797 had sent General Berthier to depose the pope, pillage Rome and found a republic, had

---

525   Burleigh, *Op. Cit.* p. 39

526   Puccini's opera *Tosca* is set in Rome at the time of the Battle of Marengo.

changed his mind about the Catholic Church. First it had become clear that neither the cult of Reason nor that of the Supreme Being nor Theophilanthropy had successfully replaced Christianity as a basis of morality. Instead there was a void which had led to anarchy. 'Children have no idea of the Divinity,' the Prefect of the Aisne reported to the First Consul in 1800, 'no notion of what is just and unjust, hence their wild and barbarous behaviour and their resemblance to a people of savages'.[527] Chateaubriand, the short-lived Knight of Malta who had escaped the Terror first in America and then in England, made the same point: 'Think of all those children who, born during the revolution, have neither heard anything of God nor of the immortality of their souls, nor of the punishments or rewards that await them in the future'.[528]

Bonaparte had also come to realise that the defence of the Church and the Catholic religion was what motivated many of his adversaries, whether at home in Brittany and the Vendée, or abroad among the Catholic powers, and even in the Protestant nations in the Coalition. He therefore ruled that the persecution of Catholics should end and, in one of his first decrees as First Consul, ordered a state funeral for Pope Pius VI who since his death had lain in a sealed coffin in Valence.

In June, 1800, Bonaparte addressed a gathering of Catholic clergy in Milan.

> I am sure that the Catholic religion is the only religion that can make a stable community happy; and establish the foundations of good government. I undertake to defend it always…I intend that the Catholic religion shall be practised openly and in all its fullness…France has had her eyes opened through suffering, and has seen that the Catholic religion is the single anchor amid storm'.[529]

The end result of this change of heart in the new ruler of France was a Concordat (a treaty between the Catholic Church with a monarch or nation) negotiated over eight months by Pius VII's Secretary of State, Cardinal Ercole Consalvi, and the French. The negotiations were protracted because the issues were complex. There were two Catholic hierarchies in France – the remnant of that of the *ancien régime* whose priests and bishops were mostly in exile;

---

527 Ralph Gibson, *A History of French Catholicism*, p. 121

528 François-René de Chateaubriand, *The Genius of Christianity*, p.277

529 Owen Chadwick, *The Popes and the European Revolution*, p.484. Quoted in Eamon Duffy, *Op. Cit.* p.262

and the Constitutional bishops who, although despised by Bonaparte, could not be abandoned because to do so would seem to repudiate the Revolution. Moreover there were still veterans of the revolution who abhorred any compromise with superstition, holding firm to Voltaire's clarion call – *écrasez l'infâme.*

In Rome, Pius VII and Cardinal Consalvi faced the opposition of cardinals implacably opposed to any accommodation with a regime that had murdered hundreds of priests, deposed and then abducted a pope, and pillaged the property of the Church. Their intransigence was hardly mollified by Bonaparte's choice as Foreign Minister of Talleyrand, the former Bishop of Autun, who now had an English Protestant wife. Exasperated by the slow pace of the negotiations, Bonaparte threw tantrums and made threats but finally on 15 July, 1801, the Concordat was signed: it was 'to govern relations between France and the Holy See for a century, and to provide a pattern for the papacy's relations with the new international order of the nineteenth century.'[530]

Under the terms of the Concordat, Catholicism was acknowledged to be 'the religion of the vast majority of French citizens'. This fell short of re-establishing it as the religion of the state, but with a further reference to the benefits of Catholic worship to the nation, it would permit pilgrimages and processions, even if these were to be subject to regulation by the police. There was to be no interference by the state in the relations between the Church in France and the pope in Rome and, while the consecration of French bishops would still be validated by the reception of the *pallium* from the pope, they would be appointed by Bonaparte as First Consul, as they had been by French kings under the 1516 Concordat of Bologna.

To this end, Pope Pius asked for the resignation of all France's existing bishops, enabling Bonaparte to appoint ten new archbishops and fifty bishops – many fewer than had existed under the *ancien régime*. The new bishops would appoint parish priests, but these had to be approved by the government. There would be no restitution of the property purloined during the revolution, but the clergy would receive salaries from the state. The rich endowments of the many monastic communities had gone forever – their abbeys and cloisters like those in England now in ruins. A number of bishops appointed during the *ancien régime* refused to accept the Concordat but their sees were declared vacant by the pope. In the depths of rural France,

---

530   Duffy, *Op. Cit.* p. 264

a schismatic sect came into being, the *anti-concordataires*, who kept to the disciplines and liturgies of the pre-revolutionary Church.[531] Paradoxically, although both the Concordat of 1516, and the anti-papal Gallican Articles of 1682 were cited to justify French demands, the successful deposition of so many bishops by papal *fiat* was an unprecedented extension of the powers of the popes and, though 'few people grasped the full implications at the time, a new era in the history of the papacy, and the Church, had begun.'[532]

Almost at once, Bonaparte decided that he had given away too much and when the Concordat was published in France it was accompanied by seventy-seven 'Organic Articles' which re-imposed some of the earlier restrictions: for example, papal bulls were not to be published in France without the consent of the government. Pius VII and Cardinal Consalvi protested but there was no rupture. Among the French negotiatiors was Cardinal Joseph Fesch, Bonaparte's uncle through a half-sister, Laetitia Buonaparte, who as Archdeacon of Ajaccio at the time of the Revolution, had objected to the Civil Constitution of the Clergy. He had lain low during the Terror, living as a layman, and served as a commissary officer in Bonaparte's army in Italy; but returned to the priesthood after his nephew's rise to power. He was consecrated as Archbishop of Lyons in 1802 and was made a Cardinal the same year by Pius VII. Pius VII was even persuaded that in France the Feast of the Assumption of the Virgin Mary on 15 August should be replaced by that of Saint Napoleon, even though 'no one could come up with a convincing account of who "Saint Napoleon" was.'[533]

Bonaparte had a further use for the pope when, in May, 1804, he acquiesced in the staged request by the French Senate that he should become Emperor of the French. He would be the new Charlemagne and, like Charlemagne, Bonaparte decided that he should be crowned by the pope. To remind the pontiff that the velvet glove covered an iron fist, the request was made in person not by a cardinal but by a general. Pius hesitated: he had been appalled by the recent abduction from Baden and subsequent execution of the

---

531   No schismatic bishops were consecrated by the *anti-concordataires*. When their priests died out, they held 'spiritual' masses in clearings in the forests. Discreet, even secretive, *anti-concordataire* communities known as *les Blancs du Brionnais* remain extant in southern Burgundy. In the cemetery of the village of St. Julien-de-Civry their graves are marked by wooden crosses rather than stones.

532   *Ibid.* p. 265

533   *Ibid.*, p. 266

Bourbon prince of the blood, the Duc d'Enghien; but pragmatism prevailed: concessions for the Church might be won if he concurred; and in the autumn of 1804 Pius left Rome for France.

Bonaparte had said that a pope's moral authority was equivalent to 'a corps of 200,000 men', and did not wish to see it ranged against him. No crowds of devout Catholics were to line his route, and there was to be no ceremony when the two men met: indeed, their first encounter at Fontainebleau was almost insulting, with Bonaparte detaching himself from a hunting party to greet the pontiff and, still dressed *pour la chasse*, taking him first to the palace of Fontainebleau, and later by night to Paris.

With Christian humility, Pius overlooked these slights but, on the eve of the coronation, learning from Josephine that she and Bonaparte had been married by the mayor of Paris's 2nd *arrondissement,* not a priest, he declared that if they wished him to take part in the coronation the following day, they must first be married according to the rites of the Church. As a result, at four o'clock in the afternoon, in the Tuileries palace, an exasperated Bonaparte was married to Josephine by his uncle, Cardinal Fesch.

The next day, 2 December, the new nobility of the empire, sumptuously dressed, assembled in the bitter cold in the cathedral of Notre Dame. Bonaparte arrived an hour late and, though he permitted himself to be anointed by Pius VII with the royal chrism, took the crown into his own hands and crowned himself and then Josephine. The pope, apparently unperturbed by the usurpation of his role, embraced the new emperor and empress to the chant of *Vivat Imperator in aeternum.*

'I dethroned no one,' Napoleon was tell the Marquis de Montholon while in exile on the island of Saint Helena. 'I found the crown in the gutter. I picked it up and the people put it on my head.' This was no doubt correct, but by making himself an emperor whose rule was accepted throughout most of Europe, that other empire, the Holy Roman Empire, had become redundant. All the German principalities west of the river Rhine had been incorporated into France; the episcopal domains had been secularised, new kingdoms created and the free cities absorbed into the new states. The current Holy Roman Emperor, Francis, recognising that the imperial crown was an empty symbol, began to refer to himself not as the German emperor but 'the emperor of Austria.

The *coup-de-grâce* came in the summer of 1806 when sixteen German states – among them Bavaria, Würtenberg and Baden – repudiated the Holy Roman

Empire and joined Bonaparte's Confederation of the Rhine. On 1 August, the French representative to the Imperial Diet at Regensburg announced that his government no longer recognised the existence of the Empire. Five days later, Francis resigned as Emperor. No one was chosen to replace him. One thousand and six years after pope Leo had crowned Charlemagne in Saint Peter's basilica in Rome, the Holy Roman Empire, and with it the vision of an united Christendom, came to an end, and 'a new era in the world's history was marked by the fall of its most venerable institution.'[534]

There was, of course, a still more venerable institution and that was the Catholic Church. Having kept his side of the bargain by coming to Paris and giving some semblance of authenticity to Bonaparte's coronation, Pope Pius VII then presented a list to the Emperor Napoleon of what he expected as a *quid pro quo*. He wanted the restoration of the Legations to the Holy See; the re-establishment of monastic communities in France; the repeal of the law permitting divorce, and a return to the use of the Gregorian calendar. In the event, he succeeded only in the last: on 1 January, 1806, the Revolutionary calendar was abolished in France and all the principalities under its control. Pius VII returned to Rome a disappointed man; however, his flock in France were delighted with their new emperor and, particularly after his spectacular victory over the Austrians and Russians at Austerlitz, were caught up in the patriotic delirium. Only gradually did they realise that Napoleon meant to keep a tighter control over the Church in France than the Gallicans of the *ancien régime* had ever envisaged: by decree it was stipulated that Napoleon, like the Bourbon kings, was to be acknowledged as 'the Lord's anointed'. 'The prisons of Vincennes, Fenestrelles, and the Island of Sainte Marguerite received priests whom the emperor judged guilty of disobedience to his orders.'[535]

Outside France, Napoleon was all-conquering: the cause, however, was no longer 'liberty, equality and fraternity' but 'glory'. In Milan Napoleon declared himself King of Italy, and placed on his head the ancient steel crown of the Lombards, implying the same sovereignty over the whole sub-continent as that as Charlemagne. When French troops occupied Ancona, Pope Pius protested: the city was part of the papal states. He protested when the French once again chased Ferdinand II out of Naples, a vassal state of the Holy See,

534   James Bryce, *The Holy Roman Empire*, p.415

535   *Catholic Encyclopaedia*

making Napoleon's brother Joseph king in his place. And when Napoleon demanded that the pope close the ports of the papal states to all but French shipping, the pope refused: to do so would be tantamount to a declaration of war on the Coalition and the papacy must remain neutral.

That Pius VII – the gentle monk, Barnaba Chiaramonte – should stand up to the Corsican bully, Napoleon Bonaparte, was thanks partly to the papacy's many centuries of experience of facing-down secular powers, and partly because he had resolute advisers such as Cardinal Consalvi and, after Consalvi had resigned to mollify the French, Cardinal Pacca. When Napoleon demanded that Pius renounced his temporal power over the papal states, the pope refused. In January, 1808, French forces marched on Rome and once again occupied the Eternal City. Pius became a prisoner in the Quirinale Palace. On 10 June, he published a Bull excommunicating Napoleon Bonaparte. Less than a month later, on 6 July, French gendarmes entered the Quirinale and he was told to prepare to leave Rome. Locked into a coach with his Secretary of State, Cardinal Pacca, Pius set off on the route taken by his predecessor eleven years before. When the two prelates discovered that their combined resources amounted to twenty sous, they laughed. 'Their laughter annoyed their gaoler.'[536]

Pius VII was taken to Savona on the Italian Riviera where he was imprisoned in the episcopal palace. The life of a monk and the life of prisoner are not so different, and Pius was content to return to the simplicity of a monastic regime, but he was deprived of Cardinal Pacca and his other advisers and had to deal with Napoleon's demands alone. He refused to approve any new French bishops, so that by 1810 there were twenty-seven vacant sees. He also rejected Napoleon's request to annul his marriage to Josephine so that he could marry Marie Louise, the daughter of the Austrian emperor. A Church council was summoned in Paris and declared that irregularities made the Emperor's marriage to Josephine invalid. This satisfied the Austrians who despatched the young princess to Paris. The wedding took place in the cathedral of Notre Dame on 1 April, 1810. All the cardinals were told to attend. Thirteen absented themselves, to be told two days later by the Minister of Religious Affairs that they were no longer cardinals, that their pensions were forfeit, their property confiscated and that they were to be taken under police escort to live in small towns in the provinces. They became known as the 'black cardinals'. In the papal states, nineteen of the thirty-two bishops refused to

---

536   Duffy, *Op. Cit.* p. 269

swear allegiance to Napoleon and were imprisoned.

There followed two years of wrangling between Pope Pius VII, a prisoner in Savona, and Napoleon, master of Europe in the temporal domain but thwarted in the spiritual by the pontiff's intransigence on the question of the appointment of bishops. The council of French bishops which had agreed to the annulment of Napoleon's marriage to Josephine was reluctant to usurp the power of the pope to bestow the *pallium* since this would create a schism. Even Napoleon's uncle, Cardinal Fesch, stood firm. Nothing could prevent Napoleon from absorbing Rome and the papal states into the French empire, and giving the child born to Marie Louise the title of King of Rome: he could even plan to move the seat of the papacy to Paris; but he could not bend the self-effacing and insecure Benedictine monk to his will.

Napoleon lost patience: if the pope could not be cowed by his envoys, he would deal with him face-to-face. Once again, Pius VII was bundled into a coach and, dressed as a simple priest, set off for France. He was suffering from a bladder infection; the coach had to stop every ten minutes as it crossed the Alps. The privations of the twelve-day journey degraded his already poor health; he received the Last Sacrament of the Church; and arrived at the Palace of Fontainebleau 'more dead than alive'.[537]

Napoleon was not there. He had declared war on the Russian Tsar Alexander who had continued to trade with England, and now led his *Grande Armeé* to Moscow. A prisoner at Fontainebleau rather than Savona, Pius was able to convalesce but remained cut off from his advisers and any news from the outside. Pius did not realise, when Napoleon returned to France, that the campaign in Russia had been a catastrophe and that Napoleon would soon lose his throne. Pius had already read the French proposals for a new Concordat. On 18 January, 1813, the two men met at Fontainebleau and on 25 of the same month a draft was signed. Napoleon then published this as a *fait accompli* but, advised by the 'black' cardinals who had now been released, among them Cardinal Consalvi, Pius wrote a letter in his own hand saying that he had signed the Concordat 'out of human frailty, being only dust and ashes', and that his signature was now revoked. This revocation was not made public but it hardly mattered because Napoleon's empire was at an end.

On 24 January Pius set off for Rome, escorted by the squad of gendarmes who had kept him a prisoner for four years – his journey facilitated by the

---

537   *Ibid.* p. 271

Imperial prefects on the orders of Napoleon still fighting rear guard actions against the Austrians and Prussians. On 24 May Pius VII reached the gates of Rome. There to welcome him was the King of Spain, Carlos IV, and thirty young men from the Roman nobility who unharnessed the horses and dragged the pope's coach in triumph to the basilica of Saint Peter's. The captivity of Pius VII was now at an end.

Napoleon, now once again Bonaparte, was sent into exile by the victorious allies on the island of Elba off the Tuscan coast. Ten months later he evaded the lax supervision of his captors and returned to France. As Bonaparte and his companions set off from Cannes where they had landed on 1 March, 1814, those discontented with the restored Bourbon king, Louis XVIII, and nostalgic for the days of glory, joined him – among them Marshal Ney who had promised Louis to whom he had sworn fealty that he would return with the Corsican usurper in a cage. Louis XVIII fled. Bonaparte was once again the Emperor Napoleon and set about raising an army. France had not yet recovered from the losses during the retreats from Russia and Spain and, despite conscription, Napoleon could only raise a force a quarter of the size of those of the coalition ranged against him. On 17 June, at Waterloo in Belgium, he was defeated by an army commanded by the British Duke of Wellington, aided by a Prussian force under Marshal Blucher.

This time, Napoleon was exiled to the island of Saint Helena, a British possession in the south Atlantic. Here he would remain until his death in 1821. As he reminisced with his few companions, he expressed his regret for his dispute with Pope Pius VII – 'an old man full of tolerance and light'. He asked for a chaplain so that he could hear mass: 'I was born in the Catholic religion. I wish to fulfil the duties it imposes, and receive the succour it administers'. The request was conveyed to Pope Pius and from him to the British government. A French priest, the Abbé Vignali, was sent to Saint Helena to serve as Napoleon's chaplain. It was Vignali who, on 3 May, 1821, gave Napoleon Bonaparte the Last Sacrament of the Church. Two days later, on 5 May, just before six in the evening, he died.

81. The Restoration

After the final defeat of Napoleon in 1815, representatives of the victorious nations gathered in Vienna to settle the affairs of the continent of Europe. Britain sent the Anglo-Irish Lord Castlereagh, Austria Prince Metternich, Prussia Prince von Hardenberg: Russia's delegate was the Tsar himself, Alexander I. Lesser powers also sent distinguished diplomats to protect their interests – France, once again ruled by a Bourbon monarch, sent the ubiquitous Talleyrand; and Pope Pius VII his Secretary of State, Cardinal Consalvi, 'the greatest statesman whom Rome has produced in the modern age'[538]. Each government had its own objectives but all were agreed that revolution was 'the major problem of the age'. [539]

To pre-empt any repetition of the events of 1789 – and despite Prussia's demand for ' blood and revenge' – France was treated leniently, paying some reparations and losing one or two strongholds on its eastern frontier. Elsewhere territory was exchanged to reward the victors: principalities meant tax-payers and conscripts. Thus Russia was awarded those parts of Poland hitherto ruled by Austria and Prussia; Austria was compensated with Lombardy and the Veneto in northern Italy. Prussia gained territories in Germany, including the former prince bishoprics of Cologne and Trier, which gave it many Catholic subjects and a common border with France. The Austrian Netherlands was united with Holland: here again, Catholics found themselves subjects of a Protestant king. Cardinal Consalvi concentrated on regaining the former possessions of the papacy. He failed when it came to Avignon and the Comtat Venaissin; they remained part of France. However, all the Papal States were returned to the Pope together with the duchy of Benevento: Pius was admired for the way he had stood up to Napoleon.

Historians have praised the settlement in Vienna because, unlike the treaties following earlier and later wars, it did not contain the seeds of future conflicts between the great powers. It did, however, reveal a new order. Britain was now the pre-eminent sea power and was to rule the waves for the next century, securing and adding to its own great empire while aiding the disintegration of that of Spain in South America, and enforcing a ban on the transatlantic slave trade. Russia was now a great power. Russian troops

---

538   E.E. Hales, *The Catholic Church in the Modern World. A Survey from the French Revolution to the Present*, p/ 78

539   Adam Zamoyski, *Rites of Peace. The Fall of Napoleon and the Congress of Vienna*, p. 493

had fought against the French in Italy, had occupied Paris, and Russia's absolute ruler, Tsar Alexander I, was one of the arbiters of the future of Europe. He had a vision of a reinvigorated Christendom ruled by absolute monarchs answerable only to God. Thus the Quadruple Alliance promoted by Castlereagh was complemented by Alexander's Holy Alliance which both Castlereagh and Pius VII declined to join.

In Rome, Pope Pius VII, once again the absolute ruler of Rome and the Papal States, supported, and emulated where he could, the policies of Prince Metternich: 'it is not surprising that the Pope, though by no means by nature a blind conservative, felt driven towards the view that Rome should, for the sake of order, lend her support to the re-establishment of traditional monarchies.'[540] Terrified by the idea of a return of Jacobinism, these new despots were eager to re-establish Catholicism to sustain legitimism – an alliance between throne and altar. In fact Josephism as well as Jacobinism had reduced the wealth and influence of the Church prior to 1789. In 1750 there had been over 15,000 monasteries and 10,00 convents in Europe: by 1814, thanks to dissolutions under French occupation and 'opportunistic confiscations by Catholic rulers in Bavaria, Württemberg and elsewhere in southern Germany...[by] 1814 virtually no religious houses survived in France, Germany, Belgium, Switzerland, Spain or Italy'.[541]

From the decades of persecution and spoliation there had emerged one significant and enduring gain for the papacy – the 1801 Concordat with Napoleon. It had secured not just the standing of the Catholic Church in France and Napoleon's empire, but, as we have seen, the novel power of the bishop of Rome to deprive other Catholic bishops of their sees. With the pre-revolutionary episcopal principalities such as Cologne, Trier, Mainz and Salzburg abolished, the pope was now the only bishop with both temporal and spiritual powers; and Consalvi proceeded to negotiate concordats with other European powers, among them Orthodox Russia in 1818 and Protestant Prussia in 1821.

Pius VII was less preoccupied with these political arrangements than with the spiritual condition of the Church. The sheep were scattered. There were dioceses without bishops and parishes without priests. No attempt was made to recover the property confiscated under the republican and Napoleonic regimes,

---

540   Hales, *Op. Cit.* p. 75

541   Zamoyski, *Op. Cit.* p. 436

but steps were taken to counter the bacillus of Enlightenment ideas. Soon after his return to Rome, on 31 July, 1814, Pope Pius VII restored the Society of Jesus; and in Rome itself there was a purge of free-thinkers 'which included virtually the entire civil administration and educational establishment. In their enthusiasm for reversing everything that the French had done, the new authorities also turned off street lighting and forbade vaccination.'[542]

Yet Pius VII who, as Bishop of Imola had in 1793 declared that democracy was compatible with the Christian religion, though inflexible when it came to orthodox teaching, rose above the vengeful spirit of the times by giving asylum in Rome to members of the Bonaparte family. He reformed the administration of the Papal States, encouraged the arts, patronising among others the sculptor Canova whose work included the statue of a semi-naked Pauline Borghese, Napoleon's promiscuous twenty-five year-old sister, who after her brother's downfall settled in Rome.

Pius VII died in 1820 and a majority of *zelanti* – devout cardinals mistrustful of reform – chose Annibale della Genga to succeed him as Leo XII. Leo dismissed Consalvi, put a stop to the introduction of lay Catholics into the administration of the Papal States, and once again confined Rome's Jews to the ghetto. 'A simple, devout man',[543] he railed against Freemasonry and religious indifference, yet saw the advantage to the Church of keeping on good terms with Protestant powers, negotiating concordats with Hanover in 1824 and the Netherlands in 1828.

With popes now chosen from cardinals who had served in the papal administration, and whose experience of other nations was largely limited to the courts of kings; and with their aspirations – particularly those of the *zelanti* – the salvation of souls through a return to the virtuous and devout practices of earlier times – there was little recognition of how attitudes had changed. For better or worse, Pandora's Box had been opened – not just by the French Revolution of 1789 but the American Revolution of 1766. Both had established that men could successfully overthrow their rulers – that sovereignty lay not with hereditary rulers but with the people. The idea of the equal worth of every individual was Christian: the difference of opinion between the Catholic Church and post-enlightenment thinkers was whether those individuals could progress towards a measure of perfection, or

542   *Ibid.*p. 237
543   J.N.D.Kelly, *Op. Cit.* p.305

whether left to themselves they were irretrievably mired in original sin. 'The notion of a man's perfectibility was anti-Christian and for that reason more revolutionary; for it is a basic Christian proposition that man cannot hope to be perfect in a temporal world, least of all when he cuts himself off from the church, which is what most revolutionaries did'.[544]

Yet, though both the Church and its adversaries justified their actions with lofty ideals, 'it is important to realise that in the field of politics men in large numbers act in response to ideas only if those ideas acts reflect their desires' and paramount among the desires of the young liberal-minded members of the emerging middle classes was the career open to talents. Every soldier in Napoleon's army, as Karl Marx was to point out, carried a marshal's baton in his knapsack. 'The real cause of most of the revolutionary agitation after 1815 was the general sense of frustration which characterised most sections of intelligent society'.[545]

Another new and powerful phenomenon which the pastors of the universal Church failed to recognise was nationalism. The battle-cry of the ragged but all-conquering armies of French revolutionaries was originally 'liberty, equality and fraternity', and under Napoleon '*la gloire*', but it was also '*la patrie*' – the nation! – and this was infectious. The resentment felt by those occupied by the French gave rise to a similar passion, particularly in Prussia but also – ominously for the papacy – in Italy. Failing to understand the resentment provoked by a systemic injustice, 'the feudal aristocracy was reinstalled in privileged positions'[546] in Rome and the Papal States under Pope Leo XII. Throughout Italy, 'when the old order was restored, those Italians who had benefited from the role of Napoleon were edged aside by restored or returned adherents of the old regime, regardless of whether they lacked the former's merits or talents'.[547]

Nor did the popes sympathise with the sense of injustice felt by many Italians that Lombardy and the Veneto should be ruled by Austria: the Austrian Empire, after all, included Hungarians, Ruthenes and Serbs. It was also useful, in case of unrest, to have Austrian troops just over the northern border of the Papal States. It suited the papacy to see the secret societies that had sprung up during the French occupation – the 'charcoal burners' or *Carbonari* – as no better than bandits; and the zealous advocates of an Italian

544   L.C.B.Seaman, *Op. Cit.*, p.34

545   *Ibid.* p. 39

546   J.N.D.Kelly, *Op. Cit.* p.305

547   Michael Burleigh, *Op. Cit.* p.163

nation such as Giuseppe Mazzini, the founder of 'Young Italy', or Mazzini's disciple, Giuseppe Garibaldi, as no better than Danton or Robespierre. Yet there were among the Italian nationalists devout Catholics such as Silvio Pellico, an educated Milanese and *carbonaro*, who was arrested by the Austrians, convicted of sedition, and served ten years in solitary confinement and vile conditions in the Spielberg fortress of Brno in Bohemia – an ordeal described in his *Ten Years Imprisonment* written after his release.

The failure of the Church, after 1815, to adapt her policies to the new spirit of liberalism 'is probably the most important problem relating to Church history in the nineteenth century'.[548] The popes' obsessive conviction that the independence of the Church depended upon their absolute rule of a substantial swathe of the Italian peninsula led them to support the most reactionary rulers, and condemn revolts even when these were initiated by Catholics consigned by the Vienna settlement to the rule of non-Catholic regimes. The 1830 revolt in the former Spanish/Austrian Netherlands which resulted in its secession from Holland and the creation of a new nation, Belgium, was the work of Catholics who resented the rule of a Protestant king, yet the pope did not support it. And when the Catholic Poles rose against the Orthodox Tsar, Nicholas I, in October, 1830, 'Rome counselled the Polish clergy to preach to their flocks submission to the Russian overlord'.[549]

82. Lamennais and Maistre

There were Catholics during the period of restoration that followed the fall of Napoleon who believed that the Church should dissociate itself from the interests of absolute monarchs and move with the times. Hugues-Félicité Robert de Lamennais, a Breton priest – a 'sensitive, frail passionate prophetic *abbé*', considered by Michael Burleigh to be 'one of the most remarkable figures of the nineteenth century'[550] – combined with like-minded friends Robert de Montalembert and Henri-Dominque Lacordaire to found a journal *L'Avenir* (The Future) which called for the separation of church and state, freedom of conscience, freedom of the press, and support for the Polish uprising against the Tsar.

---

548   E.E.Y.Hales, *Op. Cit.* p. 73

549   E.E.Y. Hales, *Op. Cit.* p. 89

550   Michael Burleigh, *Op. Cit.* p. 138

All these ideas were abhorrent to Pope Gregory XVI who, though he had received Lamennais when he visited Rome, issued two Encyclicals, *Mirari Vos* and *Singulari Nos*, which condemned the ideas put forward by *L'Avenir* as 'absurd, ridiculous, execrable, perverse and worthy of eternal reprobation'. In deference to the pope's judgement, *L'Avenir* ceased publication while Lamennais, unable to assent to the teaching of *Mirari Vos*, renounced his priesthood and left the Church.

Many of Lamennais' ideas would become commonplace among Catholics in the following century, which is why he is now described as 'prophetic'. However, it was also prophetic for the popes to see that a state separated from the Church might become indifferent not just to Christian beliefs but to Christian values. The despotic kings such as Louis XIV may have constrained the liberties of their subjects, but they themselves were constrained by the precepts of the religion to which all subscribed. 'The sense of the sacred which the church communicated brought with it a sense of moral limits… Challenging the political or quasi-political role of the church opened the way to a potential totalitarian political monism'. [551] The popes were well aware that although, in the France of the restored Bourbons, the power and influence of the Church had been re-established, there were sceptics waiting in the wings – Voltaireans and Freemasons whose tenets had been condemned by the popes well before the French Revolution.

The realisation that 'the assertion of religious neutrality on the part of the state was inherently mendacious, a mere mask for anti-Catholicism'[552] was the view of Lamennais' contemporary, Joseph de Maistre. Born in Chambéry, and so a subject of the dukes of Savoy, he had in his youth belonged to a Masonic lodge and, because of property he owned in France, had been elected as a member of the States General summoned by Louis XVI in 1789. Fleeing to Chambery when things turned nasty, he moved on to Turin, then Lausanne where he frequented the salon of Germaine de Staël. It was here that he developed his ideas on legitimacy. From Lausanne he moved to Venice and then once again Turin where his sovereign, now King of Piedmont-Sardinia, appointed him ambassador to the court of Tsar Alexander I in St. Petersburg. He remained there for fifteen years: his correspondence and memoirs were a source for Leo Tolstoy's novel *War and Peace*.

---

551   Emile Perreau-Saussine, *Op. Cit.* p. 29

552   *Ibid.* p. 35

After the defeat of Napoleon, Maistre returned to Turin and in 1819 he published *Du Pape* (*On the Pope*), in which he argued that since God is the source of all authority, and the pope is his representative on earth, universal sovereignty resides in his office, giving him the power to depose monarchs who abuse their power. Such claims are reminiscent of those made by popes such as Gregory VII or Boniface VIII; but for the first time, in reference to papal teaching, Maistre talks of their 'infallibility' – an idea that was to increase in its appeal among ultramontane Catholics later in the century.

Part of Maistre's appeal was his skill as a writer – a measure of humour leavening the dogmatism of his ideas. His prose was admired by other writers who did not share his views such as Alphonse de Lamartine, and the English critic Matthew Arnold who saw him, together with Edmund Burke, as one of the founding theorists of conservatism. In the twentieth century the philosopher Isiah Berlin made the 'quirky charge' that Maistre's ideas led to Fascism, a charge 'dismissed by Robert Paxton, a leading American historian of Fascism, who had spent a lifetime studying the actuality of that phenomenon.'[553]

83.   Stendhal and Manzoni

The Bourbon kings who ruled France after Waterloo were the brothers of the 'martyr king', Louis XVI: his son, briefly Louis XVII, had died while still a child from ill-treatment and tuberculosis while held by the Jacobins in the keep of the Templar fortress in Paris, and was succeeded by his uncle, Louis XVIII. The victorious allies would not countenance a return to the absolutism of the *ancien régime* and insisted upon a Charter whereby France was given a constitution with an upper chamber made up of appointed members of the nobility; and a lower chamber with a franchise limited to men with substantial property. Though Louis himself was inclined towards conciliation, many of the returning émigrés wanted to punish the Bonapartists and any surviving Jacobins. A fundamental precept of these extreme royalists, known as the *ultras*, was the union of throne and altar. 'There were concerted attempts to swamp entire swathes of France with Christian missionaries. Missions descended on areas that had few priests of their own'.

---

553   Burleigh, *Op. Cit.*, p. 125.

Louis XVIII died in 1824 and was succeeded by his brother, Charles X, 'an over-earnest reformed rake'.[554] Now devout, he buttressed the powers of the Church, and had his *ultra* government make his subjects adorn their balconies on the feast of Corpus Christi, while blasphemy became a capital crime. The French novelist, Henri Beyle, who wrote under the pen-name Stendhal, portrayed life under Charles X in his novel *Le Rouge et le Noir* (*The Red and the Black*) – the red signifying a route to advancement via the army, the black by way of the Church. His hero is Julien Sorel, the son of a carpenter whose intelligence and sensitivity leads the parish priest, the Abbé Chelan, to take him under his wing and prepare him for the priesthood. He teaches Julien Latin and, with an exceptional memory, Julian learns to recite the Bible by heart. The Abbé Chélan is described by Stendhal as a Jansenist, by which he means not necessarily an advocate of predestination, but an austere and uncorrupt priest. 'If you dream of paying court to those in power, your everlasting ruin is assured….' Chélan tells Julian. 'Knowledge of the world might for a layman not be absolutely incompatible with salvation but in our calling it is necessary to choose'.[555]

Julien's vocation to the priesthood is shaky: he would much rather opt for the Red as a hussar but commissions are reserved for the sons of the nobility. He is devoted to the memory of Napoleon for whom the only things necessary for advancement were courage and talent. '"Ah", he cried. "Napoleon was truly the man sent by God for the youth of France". When the Abbé Chélan secures him the post of tutor to the children of the mayor of Verrières, M. de Rênal, he has to hide his portrait of Napoleon, and his copy of Napoleon's memoirs, under his mattress: if it was discovered that he was a Bonapartist, he would be dismissed.

Inspired by his hero, Julien embarks on a campaign to seduce the beautiful, artless Mme. de Rênal, a woman now in her thirties, younger than her husband but fifteen years older than her children's tutor. She has been educated 'by nuns who were passionate devotees of the Sacred Heart of Jesus… Madame de Rênal had enough native good sense to forget very quickly all that she had been taught at the convent because of its absurdity'.[556] She remains devout and, after succumbing to Julien's advances, feels acute remorse.

As an acolyte in a liturgical celebration, Julian meets the Bishop of Agde who, though only a year or two older than Julian, has been made a

---

554   *Ibid.* p. 134

555   Stendhal, *The Red and the Black,* translated by Roger Gard, p. 13

556   *Ibid.* p. 45

bishop thanks to the influence of his uncle, the all-powerful local magnate, the Marquis de la Mole. 'For a man of our cloth, there's no road to fortune except through the high nobility', Julien is told, and he determines to take it. The government of Charles X is in the hands of the *ultras*. It is these he must impress. He already knows the Bible by heart: now 'Julien thought he might gain some advantage from his study of Maistre's *Du Pape*'. He enrols in the seminary in Besançon whose austere, puritanical director, the Abbé Pirard, 'suspected of Jansenism', becomes fond of Julien and recognises his talents. Incongruously, brought together by a lawsuit, the Abbé Pirard and the Marquis de la Mole have become friends and, when the Marquis tells Pirard of his need for a secretary, Pirard recommends Julien: thus Julien gains entry to the household of one of the most powerful men in France.

The marquis takes to Julien; so too his nineteen-year-old daughter, Mathilde – groomed to marry a duke by her mother who 'won't conceal… that to have ancestors who went on a Crusade is the sole quality she admires'. Julien who by now has memorised Maistre's *Du Pape* as well has the Bible, survives among the *ultras* by concealing his liberal views. In due course, the imperious and haughty Mathilde de la Mole falls in love with Julien: unlike the devout Mme. de Rênal, she 'does not believe in religion at all' but 'values it as being extremely useful in the interests of her class'.[557]

Julien is a sceptic. He dislikes 'the god of the Christians… a despot and, like all despots, full of ideas of vengeance; his Bible speaks of nothing but abominable punishments'[558] . Stendhal portrays the regular clergy as hypocritical and corrupt with the exception of the two 'Jansenist' priests – the Abbé Cholan, and the Abbé Perard who as rector of the seminary 'had found the strength to struggle alone for six years against Marie Alacoque, the Sacred Heart of Jesus, the Jesuits and bishops'.[559]

In the salons of Paris Julien meets a political refugee, Count Altamira, 'a liberal who had been sentenced to death in his own country, and very pious. This strange contrast between religious devotion and the love of liberty astounded him'.[560] The character of Altamira may have been suggested by Silvio Pellico, imprisoned in the Spielberg fortress, whom Stendhal had met in Milan. Pellico, born in 1788, was Stendhal's near contemporary; so too

---

557   *Ibid.* p. 360

558   *Ibid.* p. 507

559   *Ibid.* p. 223

560   *Ibid.* p. 279

another Italian writer who was both a liberal and a Catholic, Alessandro Manzoni (1785-1873).

A Voltairean sceptic in his youth, Manzoni married a Swiss Calvinist who, two years after their marriage, converted to Catholicism. This precipitated a spiritual crisis in Manzoni himself from which he emerged a devout believer. He wrote a treatise on Catholic morality, sacred lyrics for the Church and a play, *Il Conte di Carmagnola*, before starting a long novel set in northern Italy in the seventeenth century, *I promessi sposi* (*The Betrothed*). On publication in 1827 it was immediately recognised as a work of genius, and became 'a national institution'[561] establishing Manzoni not just as an inspired novelist, but also as the arbiter in the '*questione della lingua* – that interminable controversy about the foundation on which standard Italian ought to rest'.[562] Each region had its own dialect; Cavour, the premier of Piedmont, spoke Italian badly: French was his mother tongue. Manzoni settled for the Italian as spoken in Florence, and re-worked his long novel in Tuscan Italian which then became the language of the united nation.

Besides the significance of *The Betrothed* in the evolution of Italian language and literature, there was its contribution to Catholic thought in the early nineteenth century. While most of the great French novelists were, like Stendhal, sceptics, Manzoni was a devout Catholic. He did not share the views of the popes: he remained a liberal. He condemned the Austrian occupation of Lombardy, wished to see a united Italy, and wrote an ode in praise of Napoleon when he heard of his death. The setting for *The Betrothed* was not contemporaneous, but Manzoni's values are projected into the seventeenth century. 'Imaginary evil is romantic and varied', wrote the French philosopher Simone Weil, 'while real evil is gloomy, monotonous, barren, boring. Imaginary good is boring; real good is always new, marvellous, intoxicating. "Imaginative literature", therefore, is either boring or immoral or a mixture of both.' *The Betrothed* is an exception to this rule. In Lucia, 'a poor peasant girl', and the heroine of the novel, Padre Cristoforo, a Capuchin friar, and Carlo Borromeo, the Cardinal Archbishop of Milan, 'Manzoni created three living examples of that pure and wholehearted Christianity which is his ideal'.[563] The novel played a role in the conversion to Catholicism of the Anglican John Henry Newman. 'It quite transposed me in parts,' he wrote to

561   Bruce Penman, introduction to *The Betrothed*, p. 12
562   *Ibid.* p. 11
563   *Penguin Companion of European Literature*

a correspondent. 'That Capuchin in the *Promessi Sposi* has stuck in my heart like a dart... I have never got over him'.[564]

84.   Overseas

1830 was a year of political revolutions in Holland, Poland and France. Pope Pius VIII, as we have seen, condemned the national uprisings, refusing asylum in the Papal States to *ultra* bishops and priests; but he was willing to accept the replacement of the French king, Charles X, with his Orleanist cousin, Louis-Philippe. Louis-Philippe promised to abide by the Concordat of 1801, and in return the pope acknowledged his claim to the title of 'Most Christian King'. Despite continuing to condemn democracy and revolutions, and promote the common interests of throne and altar, Rome reached agreements with the new republican regimes in South America.

There was the anomaly of the United States – a polity based upon principles which the popes of the period supposedly abhorred. It was a republic which enshrined democracy, freedom of speech and freedom of religion in its constitution; and, despite the austere Protestantism of the early colonists, and the prevalence of Freemasons among its founding fathers, had by and large left Catholics to practice their religion unimpeded: indeed, one of the thirteen founding states, Maryland, had been established by a Catholic convert, Lord Baltimore, as a refuge for his co-religionists, and was named after the Catholic wife of King Charles I, Henrietta Maria of France.

There were large Catholic communities in Quebec in Canada, and to the south in the French colony of Louisiana which was sold in 1803 to the United States. The residual anti-Catholic prejudice among the majoritarian Protestants in New England – aggravated later in the nineteenth century by the mass immigration of Irish, Italian and German Catholics, led to the burning of Catholic churches by the 'Know-nothings': but in their relations with the governments of the United States, the popes had as yet nothing to complain of. Here, clearly, was a case where 'Catholicism did not necessarily benefit from official recognition as the sole religion of a state. Indeed it could positively flourish in a society such as the United States that accorded it no special privileges'.[565]

---

564   Quoted in David Newsom, *The Convert Cardinals. Newman and Manning*, p. 135
565   Pereau-Saussine, *Op. Cit.* p. 117

1830, the year in which the King of France, Charles X, was replaced by Louis-Phillipe, also saw the capture of the city of Algiers on the north African coast by a French force under General de Bourmont. Algeria, like Morocco to the west and Tunisia to the east, was still notionally a province of the Ottoman Empire, but had become an autonomous principality ruled by a *dey*. Three years before, in 1827, a conference between the *dey* and the French consul over unpaid debts led to the former losing his temper and striking the consul with his fly-whisk. Like Jenkin's Ear, an insult that had provoked war between Britain and Spain in the 18th century, this diplomatic affront led the French government, still that of Charles X, to first blockade and then to invade Algeria. For centuries Algiers had been the base for piracy and slave raids on Christian countries on the Mediterranean and beyond – the Barbary corsairs even establishing a base on the island of Lundy off the north coast of Devon in England from which they seized ships sailing from Bristol, taking the crews to be sold as slaves[566]. Louis XI had led a crusade to North Africa; the Spanish had bombarded Algiers; the nascent navy of the United States had fought the pirates under President Jefferson. Now, with the occupation of the whole country, the piracy and slave trade was finally brought to an end.

The conquest of Algeria was popular in France and, during the eighteen year of Louis Philippe's reign, white, Christian colonists were brought over from France. There were revolts by the indigenous population both in Algiers and in the Algerian Sahara as the French pushed down into the African interior to their colonies in west Africa. It was not until 1904, after a final 'pacification', that Algeria was finally subdued, forming part of an empire that encompassed much of west Africa, Madagascar, Indo-China, some islands in the Caribbean, and French Guiana on the east coast of South America.

France was not alone in establishing an overseas empire: Britain had led the way; the Netherlands followed; Germany too, and Italy, but they were late in the game. Pertinent to this history is what these European conquests meant for the Catholic Church. The Spanish and Portuguese had made Catholics of the indigenous populations of their empires in the sixteenth and seventeenth centuries, and there is no evidence that in the nineteenth the subjection of less developed peoples by nations with a superior military technology was considered an injustice, and the exploitation of their resources wrong. There was rejoicing that General Bourmont had succeeded in north Africa

---

566   See Simon Webb, *The Forgotten Slave Trade, The White European Slaves of Islam.*

where Saint Louis had failed, and that Christians living on the coasts of the Mediterranean need no longer fear abduction by Barbary pirates.

Bourmont's conquests opened up hitherto inaccessible territory for evangelisation. A zeal for conversion merged with the secular concept of the *mission civilisatrice* – the view of most Europeans that it was good for the indigenous populations of their overseas possessions to be raised to the 'civilised' standards of their new rulers. It was portrayed as a lonely and heroic task. Sanders, in Edgar Wallace's novel *Sanders of the River,* is a District Commissioner in an African colony. Like a Jesuit missionary in Paraguay in the seventeenth century, he rules the native Africans in his district with the aid of six Houssas (native soldiers) and two Gatling guns mounted on an old paddle steamer. He is judge, jury and executioner but 'before the English came there were many wars, tribe against tribe, people against people. There were battles, murders, raidings, and wholesale crucifixions, but the British changed all that. There was peace in the land'.[567]

Pope Gregory VI (1831-1836), who had condemned Lamennais, and refused to allow railways in Rome, encouraged the missions, denounced slavery and promoted the appointment of priests from among indigenous populations. As the nineteenth century progressed, so too did the enthusiasm for missionary work among Catholics – particularly among the French. Missionary orders multiplied: Pope Pius IX approved seventy-four new religious congregations for women. 'Dedicated missionaries took the faith to the 'darkest' continents… Of six thousand Catholic overseas missionaries in 1875, some 4,500 were French'.[568]

Christianity put down roots in pagan west Africa – there are flourishing communities to this day[569]. However, the Muslims in Algeria, and neighbouring Tunisia and Morocco which became French protectorates, remained steadfast in their adherence to Islam. The Church naturally welcomed the chance to preach the Gospel in countries where Christian proselytism had hitherto been banned; and even the most anti-Catholic governments of the French Third Republic, while persecuting the Church in metropolitan France, encouraged the Catholic missions as useful adjuncts to its *mission*

567 Edgar Wallace, *Sanders of the River,* p.106

568 Burleigh, *Op. Cit.* p. 347

569 Cardinal Robert Sarah, the Guinean prefect to the Congregation for Divine Worship and Discipline of the Sacraments under Pope Francis in 2020, was the son of converts from animism, and was trained in a seminary run by French missionaries, the Holy Ghost Fathers.

civilisatrice. 'Anti-clericalism is not for export', declared Leon Gambetta – the same Gambetta who had declared: '*Le clericalisme, voila l'ennemi!*'. 'The Church and the Republic had common interests for, wherever foreigners went in the French empire, habits and surplices were as ubiquitous as képis and military uniforms'[570] – something which inevitably led the indigenous, suffering from the harsh treatment of their new masters, to see Christianity as the hypocritical ideology of their oppressors.

An example of this failure is found in the mystic, Charles de Foucauld, who after an unhappy childhood and dissipated youth, resigned his commission in the French cavalry, made his name as an explorer of unsubdued areas of north Africa, considered marriage, but was suddenly overwhelmed by desire to serve God. This 'was not "returning to the path of righteousness", as his family put it. Possessed by a passionate love, he threw himself unrestrainedly into the way of total asceticism'.[571] He joined the Trappists but considered them insufficiently severe and, after ordination as a priest, went to live as a hermit among the Tuareg, compiling a Franco-Tuareg dictionary, sharing his meagre supplies with anyone who asked, condemning colonial atrocities and slavery, and himself redeeming slaves, yet remaining close to the army and accompanying it on three campaigns of pacification.

Charles de Foucauld hoped to found a new religious order but, while he had many admirers, no one joined him. Even the Sudanese slave he had freed, who served at Foucauld's mass, was never baptised. With unrest during World War I, Foucauld built a fort around his hermitage to protect the people of Tamanrasset: the French army provided him with thirty rifles. Opening the gates to what he thought were couriers bringing mail, Foucauld was dragged out by Arab raiders and shot. Eighty years later, six French Cistercian monks from Notre Dame de L'Atlas were abducted from their monastery in Tibhirine in Algeria. They too were shot. The Catholic mission in Islamic North Africa may have produced few converts, but there were saints.

---

570   *Ibid.*

571   Jean-Jacques Antier, *Charles de Foucauld,* Translated by Julia Shirek-Smith, p. 105

85.   1848

The revolutions that took place in Europe in 1830 were either national uprisings as in Poland, or a case of an increasingly powerful middle-class, the *bourgeoisie*, taking power from the nobility as with the replacement of King Charles X of France with the 'citizen king', Louis-Philippe. The more widespread revolutions that took place eighteen years later, were of a different order and in some ways the portal to the modern era. It is now that we encounter not just ambitious young bourgeois seeking power and position, but also urban wage labourers, the product of the industrial revolution, demanding food and work – a class called the 'proletariat' by the editor of a German newspaper published in Cologne, the *Rheinisches Zeitung*, Karl Marx.

The first revolt, in January, 1848, was in Sicily against the rule of the Bourbon king in Naples. This was followed by revolts in February in Lombardy against the Austrians; and in the same month, the overthrow of Louis-Philippe in Paris. Uprisings followed in Germany, Denmark, Bohemia, Hungary, Sweden Switzerland, Poland and Ireland: in Vienna, Prince Metternich resigned. In some cases the demands of the revolutionaries were for independence; in others, after poor harvests, for food. All called for constitutional government with freedom of the press and, where there was some form of democracy, a widening of the franchise: under Louis Philippe, only one in a hundred Frenchmen had the vote.

It was in Paris, in 1848, that there appear the first instances of socialism with the establishment of National Workshops to provide work for the unemployed. But the bourgeoisie and the indigent working-class, who had combined to depose Louis-Philippe and establish France's second republic, fell out in the course of the late spring and early summer. Elections in April to a Constituent Assembly returned a majority of moderates who formed a Party of Order. The new government closed the National Workshops on the grounds of expense. The workers, now deprived of their only income, left their wretched dwellings and built barricades in the streets of Paris. The government enlisted a General newly returned from Algeria, Louis-Eugène Cavignac, to impose order. With 120,000 troops at his disposal, Cavignac suppressed the revolt.

In December, 1848, France held a presidential election. Cavignac was the candidate of the party of Order; Alexander Ledru-Rollin stood for the radicals; and François-Vincent Raspail for the working classes. There was a fourth candidate, a 'vague, well-meaning doctrinaire… who in some of the less flattering photographs of him, looks like a shady Italian waiter recently dismissed from service in a fourth rate hotel'[572]. This was Louis-Napoleon Bonaparte, the nephew of Napoleon. As so often, the urban politicians of both Left and Right, had failed to take into account the views of those living in *la France profonde* – the peasants. Napoleon won the election with more than five and a half million votes – four million more than Cavignac who came second. Ledru-Rolland came fourth and the workers' candidate, Raspail, came last. Three years after his triumph, Louis-Napoleon dissolved the National Assembly and proclaimed himself Emperor of the French.

86.   Pio Nono

In Rome, a year or two before these tumultuous events, the sequence of highly conservative popes that had followed Pius VII came to an end with the election as successor to Pope Gregory XVI of Gionvanni Maria Mastai-Ferretti as Pius IX. As archbishop of first Spoleto and then Imola, he had been regarded as a liberal, and at the first tally at the consistory he received only fifteen votes; but there was a standoff between the candidates favoured by the Austrians and the French, and the choice of Mastai-Ferretti seemed the only way to break it.

The conservative, even reactionary, members of Gregory XVI's curia may have been dismayed, but outside the Vatican there was rejoicing. The new pope granted amnesties to exiles and political prisoners; he ordered gas lamps to light the streets of Rome, and the building of a spur to bring the railways from Civitavecchia into Rome. 'Probably no Pope in modern times has enjoyed so wide a popularity as that enjoyed in those first months by Pius IX, or "Pio Nono" – the Italian name by which he was generally known… From the meeting halls of working men in New York to the common rooms of colleges at Oxford were echoed the cries of *Viva Pio Nono!* which rang from the *piazzas* of Italy'.[573] Many nationalists now called for a united Italy with the Pope at its head.

---

572   Seaman, *Op. Cit.* p.64

573   E.E.Y.Hales, *Op. Cit.* p. 101

In Vienna, Prince Metternich saw trouble ahead, fearing that Pio Nono was raising expectations that he could not meet. As revolutions broke out throughout Europe in 1848, Pio Nono extended liberties to his subjects which Lamennais would have applauded. He sanctioned freedom of the press, and in March, 1848, granted a bicameral constitution for the papal states with an elected chamber that could veto measures proposed by the pope. But now the contradictions were exposed. The first item on the agenda of the chamber was the forcible expulsion of the Austrians from northern Italy – a crusade to be led by the pope. In April, 1848, Pio Nono declared that it was unthinkable for the spiritual leader of the universal Church to wage war on a Catholic power. He repeated the counsel of all his predecessors since Pius VII: Italians should remain subject to the powers that be.

The nationalists and liberals felt betrayed, and all at once Pio Nono went from being the most loved to the most vilified of pontiffs. A toxic atmosphere existed in Rome throughout the summer. Count Rossi, the prime minister of Rome's new constitutional government, attempted to reach a compromise between the nationalists and the pope but was assassinated in November. Pio Nono, no longer safe, slipped out of Rome disguised as a simple priest. He found asylum in Gaeta in the Kingdom of the Two Sicilies.

Mazzini and Garibaldi were summoned to Rome, and on 9 February, 1849, the triumphant nationalists proclaimed a Roman Republic with Mazzini as its first Triumvir. Neither Mazzini nor Garibaldi were Romans or Catholics. It was no longer a case of a democratically elected government sharing power with the pope, but the establishment of a secular republic. The great powers were alarmed and, when Pius called for their help from Gaeta, they responded. The new French emperor, Napoleon III, once a *carbonaro* himself, sent a French force under General Oudinot which, after some resistance from Garibaldi and his volunteers, entered Rome and restored Pio Nono to his throne. 'For the next twenty years, Pio Nono's position as ruler of the Papal States depended entirely on the presence of French and Austrian troops to suppress rebellion.'[574]

---

574   Duffy, *Op. Cit.* p. 288

87.   The Immaculate Conception

Pio Nono's political control of Rome and the papal states may have been precarious, but his spiritual authority over the universal Church was unquestioned. Ultramontanism had triumphed. The pope was now held 'in almost mystical reverence' – 'one aspect of a devotional revolution within Catholicism, away from the sober decorum of eighteenth-century religion towards a more emotional and colourful religion of the heart, a new emphasis on ceremonial, on the saints, on the virgin Mary'.[575] On 8 December, 1858, after a consultation with Catholic bishops, Pio Nono proclaimed the dogma of the Immaculate Conception of Mary, the mother of Jesus of Nazareth. Augustine of Hippo had taught that all human beings were born tainted with Original Sin – that this tendency to wrongdoing was transferred by the parents by the carnal act of conception; but whether or not Mary was exempt had been a matter of theological debate for centuries with the majority of theologians, and certainly the *sensus fidei*, asserting that she was indeed sinless and 'full of Grace' from the moment of her conception.

Besides responding to a popular belief, the proclamation of the dogma was also an assertion of the Church's belief in itself as the source of truth. There was nothing in the Gospels, apart from the Angelic salutation that Mary was 'full of Grace', to establish the state of her soul at conception either way. To Protestants who believed in *sola scriptura* the declaration of the dogma was an example of papist presumption. However, it was not something isolated or unusual. The cult of the Virgin Mary – the 'Mother of God' – had been constant in both the Catholic and Orthodox churches, and it was now enhanced by claims of her appearance to devout young women – to Catherine Labouré in 1830; to two children tending their parents' flock of sheep in la Salette in Savoy in 1846; and in 1858 the white figure of a woman surrounded by dazzling light to Bernadette Soubirous, the fourteen-year-old daughter of a miller at a grotto near Lourdes in the Pyrenees. 'Who are you', Bernadette asked the apparition who replied: 'I am the Immaculate Conception'.

---

575   Duffy, *Op. Cit.* p. 291

88.   The Mortara Affair

A further affront to Protestant opinion came when, in 1850, Pio Nono restored a Catholic hierarchy in Britain, appointing bishops to new diocese with a metropolitan archdiocese in Westminster. The small number of recusant Catholics who had survived the Reformation and the penal measures which followed had hitherto been governed by a Vicar Apostolic. Freed by the Catholic Relief Act of 1829, the number of Catholics had increased through conversion, and above all immigration from Ireland, so that by mid-century they amounted to around ten percent of the population. Compared to the number of Catholics in the nations on the Continent, they were few, but they were influential: one of Pio Nono's two chamberlains, and his confidant, George Talbot, was an Englishman – 'a man of violent prejudice and limited understanding';[576] and two eminent Anglican clergymen, Henry Manning and Henry Newman, had become Catholics. The restoration of a Catholic hierarchy was a slap in the face for those high Anglican churchmen who held that the Church of England, despite its separation from Rome, remained part of the Church founded by Christ. The affront was exacerbated by the triumphalist tone of the first pastoral letter of the first Archbishop of Westminster, Nicholas Wiseman, in which he declared that 'Catholic England has been restored to its orbit in the ecclesiastical firmament from which its light had long vanished'. Wiseman had been born in Spain to Irish parents.

Britain may have had few Catholics but, since 1815, it was the leading world power. It was also a Christian country which had never adopted the ideas of the French Enlightenment. Britons liked to feel their governments pursued righteous policies abroad – stamping out the slave trade, assisting the liberation of the South American republics and supporting the Christian Greeks in their struggle for independence from the Ottoman empire. In the Ottoman empire itself, while the French acted as protector of the Catholics, and the Russians of the Orthodox Christians, the British championed the Jews – sending a fleet to Alexandria in 1840 at the instigation of Sir Moses Montefiore to induce the Ottoman Vizier in Cairo, Muhammed Ali, to release Jews charged with the ritual murder of a Capuchin friar in Damascus.[577]

---

576   Robert Gray, *Cardinal Manning*, p.150

577   See Jonathan Frankel, *The Damascus Affir. "Ritual Murder", Politics, and the Jews in 1840.*

There was therefore particular outrage when in 1857 a Jewish child of six, Edgardo Mortara, was taken by the police from his home in Bologna, still part of the Papal States. The Mortaras were Jewish, and it had come to the attention of the Bolognese Inquisitor, Father Pier Feletti, that when as an infant their son had been ill and in danger of death, the Mortaras' devout Catholic housemaid, Anna Morisi, had secretly baptised him. This meant he was a Catholic, and under the law Christian children were not to be raised in non-Christian households. Edgardo was removed from his parents and raised by the Church. Attempts by his parents, and by representatives of the Jewish communities in Bologna and Rome, to obtain the child's return to his family came to nothing. The Church authorities held on to Edgardo and put it about that he was happy to be a Catholic, playing hide-and-seek with the amiable Pio Nono in the Quirinale palace.

The forcible removal of a Jewish child from his home and the care of his parents became a *cause célèbre* throughout the world. To Cavour, the anti-clerical prime-minister of Piedmont, the affair was a useful stick with which to belabour the papacy. In France, the affair made Napoleon III less inclined to support Pio Nono, and strong protests were delivered by the French ambassador to the Holy See, the Duc de Gramont. In Britain, Sir Moses Montefiore who had so successfully intervened in the Damascus Affair, travelled to Rome where he was politely received by Pio Nono's Secretary of State, Cardinal Antonelli, but was told that the case was closed. There was intense interest in the case in the United States. 'In the month of December 1858 alone, *The New York Times* published more than twenty articles on the case; the *Baltimore American* published thirty-one articles on Mortara from October 1858 through January of the following year'.[578]

Edgardo Mortara was never returned by the Church to his parents and as he grew into adolescence and adulthood made no attempt to do so on his own accord. Quite to the contrary, he embraced the faith into which he had been so furtively baptised by Anna Morisi, and by his own volition entered a seminary to be trained as a priest. When Rome fell to the Piedmontese in 1870, his father Momola came to retrieve his son but Edgardo had fled to Austria with other seminarians.

Pio Nono never forgot his spiritual son, writing fond letters, asking for news and setting up a trust fund to pay for his fees. A successful preacher in five European languages, among them Basque, Father Pio Mortara later tried

---

578   David I.Kertzer, *The Kidnapping of Edgardo Montaro*, p. 129

but failed to persuade his mother and siblings of the truth of the Catholic Faith. He spent his last years in the monastery of Bouhay in Belgium, a community with a particular devotion to Our Lady of Lourdes. He died there in March, 1940, at the age of eighty-eight.[579]

89.   The Syllabus of Errors

If smart society in the seventeenth century had been 'mad about theology', the same constituency in the nineteenth was mad about philosophy. Advances in science and technology – vaccination, the railways, steam-ships – appeared to confirm that once men and women freed themselves from superstition they could progress towards a better world. There were, of course, intelligent lay Catholics but it was the non-Christian philosophers whose work seemed to express the spirit of the times.

What were Catholics to make of these new ideas? At a provincial synod in Spoleto in 1849, a petition was drawn up to be presented to the pope, Pio Nono, asking him to list the chief errors of the time. The task was first undertaken by Olympe-Philippe Gerbert, the Bishop of Perpignan, and later Cardinal Prospero Caterini, and then a series of commissions, culminating in the publication in 1864 of *A Syllabus containing the most important errors of our time, which have been condemned by our Holy Father Pius IX in Allocutions, at Consistories, in Encyclicals and other Apostolic Letters.* Its publication coincided with that of the Encyclical *Quanta Cura*: however, it was not itself an encyclical but rather a compendium of the various pronouncements made by the pope during the eighteen years of his pontificate. It denounced as errors Pantheism, Naturalism, Rationalism, Indifferentism, excessive tolerance in religious matters, Socialism, Communism, Secret Societies, Bible Societies, liberal Clerical Associations, erroneous views on the rights of the Church and the pope; and on Christian ethics. Each item referred to a papal pronouncement, and could only be properly understood in the context in which that pronouncement had first been made; but the eightieth item seemed to permit no nuance. It condemned outright the view that 'The pope may and must reconcile himself with, and adapt himself to, Progress, Liberalism, and Modern Civilisation'.

---

579   *Ibid.* p. 301

What came to be called simply *The Syllabus of Errors*, though not an infallible pronouncement, was promulgated as orthodox Catholic teaching. It was welcomed by the new Archbishop of Westminster, Henry Manning: he would later describe the *Syllabus* as 'among the greatest acts of the pontificate'[580], but was a body-blow to liberal Catholics such as Bishop Dupaloup of Orleans and Charles de Montalembert in France, and in Germany, the theologian Ignaz von Döllinger. Dupanloup wrote a pamphlet which largely explained away the provocative document by placing it in context – 'a *tour de force* which went a long way towards defusing non-Catholic hostility to the Syllabus, and give breathing-space for liberal Catholicism. Six hundred and thirty bishops wrote to thank him for it, and Montalembert called it 'a first class vanishing trick'.[581]

The publication of *The Syllabus of Errors* continues to be regarded by many Catholics as an embarrassing episode in the history of the Church, yet this sometimes fails to take into account the threat to Christian belief in the philosophical theories then in vogue. God had made foolish the wisdom of the world, the Apostle Paul had told the Corinthians[582] but the German philosopher, Friedrich Nietzsche had declared that God was dead and a number of philosophers of the period proceeded on that assumption. Among those who remained Christian, there were instances of corrosive dissent from orthodox teaching, Biblical scholars in Germany confidently established that Moses was not the author of the Pentateuch, and that Jesus of Nazareth was not who he had claimed to be – the Jewish Messiah, the Son of God. In England, the biologist Charles Darwin, in his *Origin of the Species*, appeared to establish beyond doubt that there had been no 'creation' as described in the Book of Genesis, but that men and women had evolved from other creatures, and those creatures from a primordial slime.

Some of the philosophers would have a long-lasting effect on human affairs: others, popular at the time, are now forgotten. Herbert Spencer, an English biologist, sociologist and philosopher expanded Darwin's theory of evolution into the fields of sociology and ethics, and coined the phrase 'the survival of the fittest'. He published his first book, *Social Statics*, in 1851 and through his publishers was introduced into a circle of liberal intellectuals which included John Stuart Mill and Mary Ann Evans who wrote under the

---

580   Robert Gray, *Op. Cit.* p. 175

581   Duffy, *Saints & Sinners*, p. 296.

582   1 Corinthians,1:20

pen-name George Eliot. Further publications, in particular *Man Versus the State*, made him by the 1870s 'the most famous philosopher of the age'. His books were translated into many different languages, and he 'was probably the first, and possibly the only, philosopher to sell over a million copies of his works in his lifetime'.[583]

Spencer's social Darwinism contributed to the development of scientific racism. Though later in life a critic of British imperialism, and particularly the Boer War, he had argued in *Social Statics* that imperialism served civilization by clearing the inferior races from the earth: 'The forces that are working out the great scheme of perfect happiness, taking no account of incidental suffering, exterminate such sections of mankind as stand in their way'. Such theories would gain traction later in the nineteenth century, particularly in Germany, but they were not ascribed to Spencer because in his later years he went out of fashion.

Spencer's relevance to the history of the Catholic Church is as the author of one of the many post-Christian theories about the human condition swirling around Europe at the time. 'The basis for Spencer's appeal to many of his generation was that he appeared to offer a ready-made system of belief which could substitute for conventional religious faith at a time when orthodox creeds were crumbling under the advances of modern science'.[584] Clearly to the Church such philosophies were pernicious, and their dissemination should not be allowed on the grounds of 'free speech'. Most Catholics at the time were still illiterate and therefore vulnerable to claims made by the apostles of progress. This explains the misgivings expressed in the *Syllabus of Errors* about freedom of speech and freedom of the press. 'The Church will never admit it as a benefit,' said Pio Nono in October, 1863, 'that error and heresy should be preached to Catholic peoples'.[585]

The pope's hold on Rome and the Papal states had since the Congress of Vienna depended upon the support of the Great Powers. Napoleon III had sent soldiers to suppress the Roman republic of Mazzini and Garibaldi in 1848, but in the subsequent decade it was Piedmont that had come to promote the cause of Italian unification under its cunning prime-minister, Camillo Cavour. Any possible rekindling of Pio Nono' s early sympathy for the Italian

583   Wikipedia, *Herbert Spencer*
584   Wikipedia, *Herbert Spencer*
585   E.E.Y.Hales, *Op. Cit.* p. 131

nationalists was killed off by Cavour's anti-clericalism: in the 1850s he ordered the dissolution of all contemplative monastic foundations in the kingdom. This did not inhibit Napoleon III, although he had married a devout Spanish wife, from agreeing with Cavour at a secret treaty at Plombières-les-Bains to help him oust the Austrians from Lombardy in return for ceding Savoy and the province of Nizza (Nice) to France. After two sanguinary battles at Magenta and then Solferino the Austrians were defeated. Crowds cheered the French and Piedmontese soldiers as they marched into Milan.

Unplanned and unwanted by Cavour was the invasion of Sicily in May by the romantic adventurer, Giuseppe Garibaldi, with a thousand redshirt volunteers, who routed the forces of the Bourbon king; and, four months later, took Naples and proclaimed Victor Emmanuel as King of Italy. To prevent Garibaldi marching north towards Rome, which he feared would antagonise Napoleon III, Cavour moved into the papal provinces of Umbria and Marche, linking up with Garibaldi's forces and leaving only a rump territory around Rome under papal control.

In May, 1865, Florence became the capital of Italy but this was considered a temporary solution by the Italian patriots. 'Roma o morte!' – Rome or death – declared Garibaldi. The following year, the new Italian state joined Prussia in a war against Austria; and after the Austrian defeat by the Prussians at the battle of Sadowa (Königgrätz) Venice and the Veneto was ceded to Victor Emmanuel. There were no cheering crowds when the Piedmontese marched into Venice: 'the Venetians, governed since 1797, by rulers they had not chosen, showed little enthusiasm for the latest lot'.[586]

It was the same when, in 1867, Garibaldi made an assault on Rome. 'One notable feature of the campaign...was the lack of popular support in the towns and countryside of the Roman state. Garibaldi was neither acclaimed by crowds nor assisted by peasants nor mobbed by aspiring volunteers'.[587] He might have defeated the papal army at Mentano north-east of Rome had it not been for the arrival of a thousand French soldiers sent by Napoleon III to aid Pio Nono. A French garrison remained in Rome for the next three years.

---

586   David Gilmour, *The Pursuit of Italy*.

587   *Ibid*. p. 209

90. The First Vatican Council

On the 29 June, 1867, the Feast of Saints Peter and Paul, Pope Pius IX summoned the eight hundred bishops of the Church in communion with Rome to assemble for a General Council in the Vatican on the Feast of the Immaculate Conception, December 8, 1869. It would be the first Church Council since that of Trent in the sixteenth century and, because of the uncertain political situation, a hazardous enterprise; but, against the advice of his Secretary of State, Cardinal Antonelli, Pius insisted. He was now seventy-five years old.

At the top of the agenda for the Council was to be a precise definition of the beliefs of the Church – to sift the true from the false in the face of claims made by Biblical scholars, liberal theologians and would-be Catholic reformers. 'The purpose of the Council of the Vatican was to define the nature of the Church herself. But, before it could do that, it was necessary for it to reassert the fundamental dogmatic basis of Christianity itself, since this was now, for the first time, being called into question.'[588] Initially, the issue which came to dominate the Council, papal infallibility, was not on the agenda; but it soon came to the fore and parties were formed, for and against. No one doubted that the Church, guided by the Holy Spirit, could define what was true or false: God 'had spoken through the prophets' and continued to do so through the bishops and, *primus inter pares*, the Bishop of Rome. The question was whether the pope on his own was infallible. Most of the bishops thought he was; few thought he was not; but a fair number felt that, though the pope might be infallible, now was not the time to make it an article of faith.

The leaders of the 'inopportunists' were Bishop Dupanloup of Orleans and Ignaz von Döllinger who had had misgivings about the *Syllabus of Errors*. Acknowledged as pre-eminent in his fields of theology and ecclesiastical history, Döllinger's liberal views on the Church had made him suspect in Rome. A conference which he organised in Mechelen in Belgium in 1863 was closed down on the orders of Pio Nono.

Döllinger had many followers both in Germany and abroad – prominent among them Sir John Acton, the grandson of the John Acton who as prime-minister to the Bourbon monarchs of Naples and Sicily had successfully guided them through the difficult years of revolutions and wars. A baronet and

---

588   *Ibid.*, p. 133

owner of the family's sixty-thousand acre estate at Adenham in Shropshire, John Emerich Edward Dalberg-Acton had been excluded from Cambridge University because he was a Catholic, and so had studied under Döllinger in Munich instead. He was not a stranger in the city: his mother was the daughter and heir of the first Duke of Dalberg, inheriting a large castle at Hermsheim; and Acton was to marry the Bavarian Maria von Arco-Valley.

After completing his studies in Munich, Acton returned to England where he entered the House of Commons as a Liberal, edited the Catholic journal *The Rambler* and embarked upon research that was to make him the leading historian of his generation. His admiration for his professor, Ignaz Döllinger, had developed into a close friendship: they travelled together and Acton introduced Döllinger to liberal Christians in England. On the question of papal infallibility, the two were of one mind: 'Acton's opposition to the Infallibility of the Pope was mainly historical and moral rather than grounded in dogma, as was Dr. Döllinger's.'[589] Acton was a friend of the then British Prime Minister, William Evart Gladstone – a devout Anglican who had considered conversion to Catholicism but regarded the idea of papal infallibility as the height of papist presumption, and a threat to a Catholic subject's loyalty to his king.

Ironically, if Acton, who took up residence in Rome during the Council, was to become 'the "Chief Whip" for the minority'[590] (the 'inopportunists'), it was another Englishman, Henry Manning, Archbishop of Westminster, who led the majority calling for the dogma of papal infallibility to be declared. Manning, the son of a London merchant and MP, had been an Anglican clergyman, rising in the Anglican hierarchy to become Archdeacon of Chichester. Shaken by the decision of the Privy Council to appoint a vicar who did not believe in the objective efficacy of the sacraments, Manning became a Catholic. He had been married but his wife had died before they had children – 'conveniently', the malicious would say, but her portrait was found attached to his watch-strap when he died. After studying in Rome, he was ordained a priest at the Jesuit Church at Farm Street in London. He then founded the community of the Oblates of Saint Charles – Saint Charles Borromeo – in Bayswater to care for the Irish workers building Paddington Station. Manning was notable throughout his life for his pastoral concern for the poor.

---

589   Roland Hill, *Lord Acton,* p. 197

590   *Ibid.* p. 203

Unlike his contemporary and in some sense adversary, John Henry Newman, Manning as a Catholic was conservative to the tips of his toes – deeply mistrustful of innovative and liberal theologians. He welcomed the *Syllabus of Errors:* like Maistre, he saw the papacy as the guarantor of truth in the face of the usurpation of religious matters by the state. 'Manning saw papal infallibility as the way to escape the danger of 'Caesarism', to release the Church from the grip of a state which had lost all legitimacy in religious affairs'.[591] His zeal contrasted with Newman's lukewarm acceptance of the idea of papal infallibility: Newman told the journalist W.G. Ward that he thought it 'likely to be true' which, as Manning's biographer Robert Gray remarks, 'hardly leaves an impression of blazing faith'.[592]

Newman was the gentler and more learned of the two: his teaching on the evolution of doctrine qualified him as a Doctor of the Church. He was, like Manning, made a cardinal and, unlike Manning, a saint. Manning 'certainly struggled to bring his imperious nature into conformity with the gospel of humility'[593]: the French historian of the Council, Emile Oliver, wrote of Manning that 'the love of domination emanates from every pore, and when his thin lips allow a smile to hover, one feels it is from pure condescension'.[594] However, when it came to the dogma of papal infallibility, it would appear that the Holy Spirit favoured Manning over Newman. The decree submitted to the Council for a vote was hedged in with qualifications but it was a victory for the Infallibilists all the same.

> We, with the approval of the sacred Council, teach and define that it is a divinely revealed dogma: that the Roman Pontiff, when he speaks *ex cathedra*, that is, when acting in the office of shepherd and teacher of all Christians, he defines, by virtue of his supreme apostolic authority, doctrine concerning faith and morals held by the universal Church, possesses through the divine assistance promised to him in Saint Peter, the infallibility with which the Divine Redeemer wished his Church to be endowed in defining doctrine concerning faith or morals, and that such definitions of the Roman Pontiff are therefore irreformable because of their nature, but not from the agreement of the Church.[595]

---

591   Emile Pereau-Sausine, *Op. Cit.* p. 64

592   Robert Gray, *Op. Cit.* p. 229

593   *Ibid.* p. 206

594   *Ibid.* p. 231

595   *The Church Teaches. Documents of the Church in English Translation.* St. Mary's College, Kansas

The decree was to be put to the Council on 18 July, 1870. The day before, fifty-seven bishops had left Rome to avoid voting against a measure which they knew would pass. The next day, 533 bishops voted in favour, two against. The tally took place under a black sky, with flashes of lightning outshining the dim light of the candles, and thunder drowning out the sound of the choir. Some saw this as a sign of God's displeasure: Manning compared it to the 'peals of thunder and the lightning flashes'[596] that had accompanied Moses' reading of the Ten Commandments to the Jewish people on Mount Sinai.

Like the *Syllabus of Errors*, the decree of the First Vatican Council on Papal Infallibility was considered an affront to non-Catholic Christians, and to the increasingly nationalistic secularists who believed it cast doubt on the loyalty of Catholics to the nations to which they belonged. It remained unacceptable to Döllinger: 'As a Christian, as a theologian, as an historian, and as a citizen,' he wrote, 'I cannot accept this doctrine.' In April, 1871, he was excommunicated by the Archbishop of Munich, but the widespread support he enjoyed is evident in his election as *Rector Magnificus* by his colleagues in the university, and honorary doctorates conferred by the universities of Oxford, Edinburgh, Marburg and Vienna. For a time he considered joining a schismatic group dating from the Jansenist controversy of the eighteenth century known as the Old Catholic Church, but finally declared 'I do not wish to join a schismatic society...' He died in Munich at the age of ninety-one, still refusing to submit to the Council's dogma on Infallibility and so denied the last Sacrament of the Church

In 1870 the Prussian Minister President Otto von Bismarck successfully tricked Napoleon III into declaring war. The French were defeated on all fronts – the emperor was captured after the rout of the army he led at Sedan. Napoleon III abdicated; republicans came to power and there was an armistice which was rejected by the citizens of Paris. They formed a revolutionary Commune and continued the war against both the Prussians and the French government installed in Versailles. The Prussian treatment of the French populace was harsh, but the worst atrocities were self-inflicted by the French. The Communards shot hostages, among them the Archbishop of Paris; the government forces, suppressing the Commune, imprisoned, deported and shot the Parisian insurgents up against the wall of the cemetery of Père Lachaise. Up to 20,000 Communards were killed.

---

596   *Exodus*, 20:18

To fight the Prussians, Napoleon III had had need of all the troops he could muster, and so had withdrawn the French garrison from Rome. The Council was adjourned *sine die*, and the archbishops, bishops and religious superiors returned to their native countries. As soon as the French troops had departed, Piedmontese troops laid siege to the Holy City, defended now by the small papal army and Catholic volunteers, the Papal Zouaves. The walls were breached at the Porta Pia. Pio Nono ordered his defenders to surrender and withdrew into the Vatican palace. Victor Emmanuel marched into Rome and moved into the Quirinale. Rome was proclaimed the capital of an united Italy.

91.   The Kulturkampf

The Roman pontiffs would remain 'prisoners in the Vatican' for the next fifty-nine years. To Pio Nono and his successors, the usurpation of the throne upon which they had sat for more than a thousand years by the coarse, tawdry monarch of an insignificant Alpine kingdom was both a blasphemy and an outrage. It was not merely the humiliation of Christ's vicar on earth, but also the more concrete threat to the spiritual well-being of the pope's erstwhile subjects because Victor Emmanuel and his Liberal governments, elected on a narrow franchise, was deeply anti-clerical and pursued policies that were inimical to the Church.

'The terms "anti-clerical"' and "Liberal" require a word of explanation' wrote Anthony Rhodes in his *The Vatican in the Age of the Dictators*.

> The Englishman or American imagines an anti-clerical as a reasonable enough person, who merely wishes to prevent the clergy from interfering in his private life, to avoid them as he might a doctor or a lawyer. In Latin countries, however, the anti-clerical is more fanatical than reasonable, a dedicated iconoclast and often an atheist. By the world 'Liberal', too, the Anglo Saxons understand something favourable, a kind of Mr. Gladstone, upright if somewhat sanctimonious. But the 'Liberal' to the Vatican is quite different, being virtually synonymous with 'Socialist' or 'atheist' and 'Communist'.[597]

---

597   Anthony Rhodes, *The Vatican in the Age of the Dictators*, 1922-1945, ps. 24-25

It was assumed by the popes that in due course the great powers would restore the papal states to their legitimate sovereigns, but in 1870 neither of the two Catholic powers, France or Austria, was in a position to come to the pope's aid. Nor did religion play much of a role in the chancelleries or cabinet rooms of Europe. 'Great Britain has no permanent friends or permanent enemies,' said the British statesman Lord Palmerston, 'but only permanent interests'. When the peace between the Great Powers established by the Congress of Vienna finally came to an end with the Crimean War of 1853, it saw two Christian nations, France and Britain, attack a third, Russia, to aid the Islamic Ottoman Empire. The era of the crusades had well and truly come to an end.

However, with the Ottoman empire disintegrating in both north Africa and the Balkans, Islam had ceased to be a threat to the Catholic Church: instead it was menaced by governments in the heart of what had once been Latin Christendom. With the defeat of Denmark in a short sharp war in 1865; of Austria in 1866, and France in 1870, Prussia had become the dominant power on the continent of Europe. Napoleon III was now a sad exile in England; an emperor's crown lay once more in the gutter, and was picked up by Otto von Bismarck and placed on the head of his sovereign, Wilhelm I of Prussia. On 18 January, 1871, in the *galerie des glaces* (the hall of mirrors) in the palace of Versailles Wilhelm was proclaimed the German *Kaiser* – ruler of an empire that stretched thirteen hundred kilometres from Mulhouse in the newly conquered Alsace in the west to Memel on the Baltic Sea in the east. Its population approached fifty million, its industrial production was close to that of Britain and, following Britain and France, Germany had established colonies on the continent of Africa.

Otto von Bismarck, the architect of the unification of Germany and the crowning of a Kaiser, came from a family of Junkers – the descendants of the Teutonic knights who had been the first Catholic religious order to revoke their vows at the time of the Reformation, take wives and establish themselves as a landowning military caste on the eastern marches of Prussia. It was in a sense anomalous that a man from the fringes of the new empire should be first its Minister President and then imperial Chancellor. Certainly Bismarck was a Protestant, and Prussia had been a Protestant nation: the Prussian Reichstag in 1867 had 569 Protestant deputies as against 51 Catholics;[598] but the new German empire had substantial communities of Catholics amounting to thirty percent of the population.

---

598   Burleigh, *Op. Cit.* p. 323

Certainly, in the south and west, the rulers of Catholic states such as Baden, Württemberg and Bavaria had joined Prussia in its war against France, and acclaimed the new Kaiser in Versailles' hall of mirrors. But what of their subjects? The great prince-bishops of Münster, Cologne, Trier, together with the lesser nobility of the former Holy Roman Empire, had looked to the Habsburg emperors in Vienna as their sovereign. Ancient habits of allegiance die hard. Could they now be trusted to be loyal to the Hohenzollerns in Berlin? Clearly, the French were not resigned to the loss of Alsace and Lorraine: sooner or later, there would be another war with possibly Catholic Austria allied with Catholic France and the Catholics within Germany a fifth column commanded by their infallible pope.

Thus in 1872, Bismarck embarked on a campaign to enfeeble and control the Catholic Church in Germany: the Reichstag deputy Rudolf Virchow termed it a *Kulturkampf* – a struggle for the identity of the nation. Its principal aim was to replace the Church's influence by insisting upon secular marriage, and extending the state's control over education. The backing for Bismarck's policy in the Reichstag came from the nationalistic Liberal party: 'Germanic pride, racial and intellectual, was the soil in which the Kulturkampf took root...'[599] 'Liberal rhetorical violence was directed not just towards the Catholic Church but Catholics in general.' 'Convents and monasteries were castigated as cold citadels of cruelty or hot debaucheries, in wilful ignorance that they played a leading role in the nation's charitable, educational and hospital provision.'[600] There was a revival of all the old calumnies of the *philosophes*: 'Kettler, the Bishop of Mainz, was convinced that the Kulturkampf was the brainchild of a "masonic-Jewish conspiracy", and certainly secular liberal Jews were enthusiastic supporters of the Kulturkampf'. [601] But then so were some Catholics, particularly in Bavaria, because of the influence of Döllinger. 'The anti-clerical government there actually prohibited priests from publishing the decisions of the Vatican Council and gave its full support to the Old Catholic movement', handing over churches to the schismatic group.

The climax of the Kulturkampf came in early 1872 with the appointment of Adalbert Frank as Minister of Education, and the passing of 'the May laws' which subjected all schools to the state, even when it came to religious instruction; and required teachers to 'satisfy state inspectors as to their

599   E.E.Y.Hales, *Op. Cit.* p.217
600   Burleigh, *Op. Cit.* p 326
601   *Ibid.* p. 333

scientific, philosophical and historical knowledge and outlook'. The Jesuits were forbidden to say mass and so were effectively exiled. Seminaries were to be subject to approval by the state, and the state was to take over bishops' disciplinary powers over both clergy and students. Further laws in 1874 passed measures against 'recalcitrant priests': in the following year, one hundred and three priests were imprisoned or expelled. In May, Catholic religious orders were dissolved and monks and nuns were forced into exile. A steam ship, the *Deutschland*, carrying a party of religious sisters to the United States, sank in a storm in the Thames estuary. The nuns were drowned.[602]

During the Kulturkampf, over a million German Catholics were deprived of the sacraments because so many priests were either exiled or imprisoned. Bishops had been deprived of their sees, and the archbishops of Cologne and Posen had been banished. The diocese of Posen was inhabited largely by Poles, and here the Kulturkampf included an attempt to either integrate or get rid of the Kaiser's Polish subjects. Forty thousand Polish 'subjects of foreign powers' – effectively from other parts of Poland – were expelled without compensation; and later, in 1886, Bismarck allocated substantial funds to replace Polish with German farmers.[603]

While Germany's Catholics undoubtedly suffered from the Kulturkampf so too did non-Catholic Germans. Of the 914 religious foundations, 623 were devoted to the care of the sick. 'Many industrial cities, including Düsseldorf and Essen, would have no hospital arrangements whatsoever without the dedication of nursing orders. The army insisted upon exempting the nursing orders from expulsion: "Without the Sisters of Mercy," said one general, "I cannot wage war".[604] This contributed to political consequences that Bismarck cannot have foreseen. In south and west Germany, the dynasties may have been 'easily won over to the new "Protestant Empire" but it was very different in the case of the deeply conservative elements in the nation. The Catholic priesthood, the great nobles, and vast numbers of peasants and labourers in southern and western German united to form an imposing front, and the Centre Party arose as the party of German Catholics'.[605] It was led by Ludwig Windhorst, whose 'balance and control, combined with tenacity… must raise him to the highest rank among political leaders in the nineteenth

602 This tragedy was the subject of the poem by the English Jesuit Gerard Manley Hopkins, 'The Wreck of the Deutschland'

603 George Slocombe, *A History of Poland*, p. 288

604 Burleigh, *Op. Cit.* p. 325

605 Arthur Rosenberg. *Imperial Germany. 1871-1918.* p. 9

century'.[606] Though denounced by Bismarck as a *Reichsfeind* – an enemy of the state – Windhorst never closed the door to compromise and, drawing support for the Centre Party from non-Catholics, dramatically increased its representation until it became the largest single party in the Reichstag.

Gradually the storm abated, and one by one most of the anti-Catholic laws were either repealed or were no longer enforced. Windhorst's policy of infinite patience was made easier when Pio Nono died in 1878 and was succeeded by a more emollient pontiff, Leo XIII. At the same time, it had become clear to Bismarck that a war with Austria and France was unlikely, and that the internal threat came less from Germany's Catholics than the revolutionary Socialists who, despite Bismarck's attempts to appease the growing industrial workforce with advanced measures of social welfare, increased their representation at every election.

And finally there was Bismarck's realisation that the *external* threat to Germany now came not from France in the west but Russia in the east. In 1877-1878, a coalition of Slav states led by Russia defeated Ottoman forces in the Balkans. Bulgaria became an independent nation state. Serbia sought to expand its frontiers. The wave of Pan-Slav nationalism was a threat to the Austrian empire whose German dynasty ruled over a number of different ethnic groups, among them a large number of Slavs. If the Poles, Slovenes, Serbs, Croats and Czechs were to form their own nations, then the rump of German speaking Austrians might join the German *Reich*, adding eight million more Catholics to its population. For a Protestant Prussia to remain dominant in Germany, the Austrian empire had to be preserved: 'So Bismarck made a U-turn that astonished the world: he called off the *Kulturkampf*, broke with the Liberals .. and in October, 1879, signed an anti-Russian defensive alliance with his oldest enemy, arch-Catholic Austria'.[607]

92.   Rerum Novarum

The pope who succeeded Pio Nono, Vincenzo Luigi Pecci, came from the minor nobility of the Romagna and took the name Leo XIII. His career in the Church had until then been as a papal diplomat at which he had been a failure, and a legate governing the Papal States at which he had been a

---

606   E.E.Y.Hales, *Op.Cit.* p. 222

607   James Hawes, *Op. Cit.* p. 116

success. As Bishop of Perugia he had reformed and reinvigorated religious life in his diocese – particularly solicitous when it came to the plight of the poor. He weathered the annexation of Perugia by the Piedmontese in 1860 and, while sharing the convictions of Pio Nono, expressed them in a more conciliatory tone. He was made Cardinal Camerlengo in 1877 – a move possibly engineered by Cardinal Antonelli, the Secretary of State, because the Camerlengo who organised conclaves, and ran the Vatican during and interregnum (*sede vacante*) never became pope. Pecci proved an exception: in the conclave that followed the death of Pio Nono in 1878, he was elected on the third ballot.

No doubt sensing that, at the age of sixty-eight, his reign might not last long, Leo immediately took measures to modify the Church's confrontation with the modern world. In two encyclicals in 1885 and 1888, Leo XIII subtly distanced himself from the intransigent position of his predecessor towards liberty and science. 'In the long term, Leo XIII's explicit acceptance of various political forms was a highly significant contribution to the Church's reconciliation with democracy…'.[608] When it came to Germany, as we have seen, his conciliatory approach helped end the *Kulturkampf*, and he encouraged the Centre Party to support Bismarck's policy of providing social welfare for the working class. When it came to France, his call for French Catholics to support the Third Republic – the *Ralliement* – was less successful: the great majority of French Catholics wanted a king. Yet it was lay French Catholics whose ideas and example were to contribute to Leo XIII's ground-breaking encyclical, *Rerum Novarum*.

Catholic teaching on social matters over the centuries had mostly been formulated around the feudal structures of the Middle Ages – the nobility, the burghers and the peasants – and, as with the teachings of Jesus, had been concerned less with objective outcomes than with the salvation of souls: the motive for the provision of welfare through monasteries and hospitals (*hotels Dieu*) undertaken by the Church following the fall of the Roman empire was not altruism alone but the love of God.

With the industrial revolution, there had arisen the new classes of rich and poor, the entrepreneurs and workers – the rich small in number, the poor many, and now uprooted from the land, living in dire conditions in grim industrial cities – at the mercy of fluctuations in the economy, and often

---

608   Burleigh, *Op. Cit.* p. 350

exploited by hard-hearted employers. Francis of Sales, in the sixteenth century had said that the poor, because beloved by Jesus, were a privileged class and should accept their condition; but now it was apparent that alms-giving was insufficient to alleviate the privations of the new industrial proletariat – cut off from the rural communities from which they had migrated, and so from the Church.

In 1864, Bishop Ketteler of Mainz had published a treatise, *Christianity and the Labour Question* – 'a pioneer volume that gave the German Catholics a programme'[609]; but there were other programmes on offer from those who were not Catholic or even Christian – indeed who saw the Christian churches, particularly the Catholic Church with its support of despots, as one of the mainstays of social injustice. There were many radical programmes on offer – that of the Frenchmen Henri de Saint Simon, Louis-Auguste Blanqui and Pierre-Joseph Proudhon ('all property is theft'); the Russians Nikolay Chernyshevsky and Mikhail Bakunin; and the Germans Karl Marx and Friedrich Engels whose ideas were adopted by the German Social Democratic Party founded in 1863. Only in England was there a religious element, mostly Low Church and Methodist, in the movement for social improvement: on the Continent the Church was not only considered in cahoots with the capitalists, but diverted the poor from fighting to improve their condition in this life by assuring them of recompense in paradise in the next. 'Religion,' wrote Marx, 'is the opium of the people'.

There were Catholic social reformers such as, in France, Albert de Mun, René de la Tour du Pin and Léon Harmel: Albert de Mun 'was tireless in his capacity, from 1887, as a member of the Chamber of Deputies, in advocating industrial and social reform from within the political system';[610] while Léon Harmel put his ideas into practice in the textile factory he owned in eastern France. Harmel also organised a number of pilgrimages by factory workers to Rome where, dressed in their overalls, they were welcomed by Leo XIII. Leo strongly supported Harmel in his schemes to improve and sanctify the lives of industrial workers; and did nothing to impede Cardinal Manning when he 'very visibly mediated in the 1889 London dock strike'.[611] It would be noted, however, that Harmel, like Bishop Ketteler of Mainz, blamed 'usurious capitalism' on Freemasons and Jews.

---

609   Hales, *Op. Cit.* p. 197
610   Burleigh, *Op. Cit.* p. 401
611   *Ibid.* p. 409

Léon Harmel, together with Bishop Ketteler and Cardinal Manning, undoubtedly influenced the encyclical issued by Pope Leo XIII in 1891 – *Rerum novarum* (*New Things*). For the first time in the Church's history, a pope went beyond the question of charity and its role in salvation to consider social questions less obviously concerned with religion – the relationship between capital and labour, and the duties of the state towards its citizens – in particular the need to alleviate 'the misery and wretchedness pressing so unjustly on the majority of the working class'.[612] Leo insisted on the right to private property, and condemned the socialist and communist proposals that all property should belong to the state; but along with the rights to private property went the duties of employers to respect the dignity of workers, to match their employment with each one's strength, gender and age; to pay a wage that could sustain a man and his family, and even provide a surplus so that a worker could make savings and improve his condition over time.

An employee must be given time off to attend to his religious duties and have the right to form a trade union. Child labour was condemned, and Leo recommended that where possible women should work in the home.[613] He introduced the 'principle of subsidiarity' whereby the presumption should be that the state would never intervene in matters that could be settled by smaller units of society such a local commune or the family – a concept that was anathema to future totalitarian regimes.

'*Rerum Novarum*', wrote the historian E.E.Y.Hales, 'was not only the most important of Leo XIII's encyclicals, but has provided the basis for Catholic teaching on social justice ever since…' It dealt with religion, politics and the right ordering of society 'with a serenity and authority, but also a warmth and sympathy, which blend to make it one of the great documents of history'. However, alongside his novel and radical understanding of 'new things', Leo remained 'a man of deep and conservative piety', devoting eleven encyclicals to the Blessed Virgin Mary and instituting the feast of the Holy Family. He had taken part in compiling Pio Nono's *Syllabus of Errors*, never deviated from his predecessor's beliefs, and towards the end of his long reign became uneasy about liberal trends, setting up a Biblical Commission, publishing new norms of censorship, and revising the Index of forbidden publications.

---

612   *Rerum Novarum,* 3

613   E.E.Y. Hales, *Op. Cit.* p. 198 (where in text?)

Leo also disappointed those Catholics and Anglicans who believed that the Church of England was merely schismatic, and so its orders valid, by condemning these orders, in an 1895 apostolic letter, *Ad Anglos*, and subsequently an encyclical *Apostolicae Curae*, which declared Anglican orders 'absolutely null and utterly void'. 'The tone and implications of these two documents could not have been more insulting and condemnatory of Anglicanism and, by inference, a huge spectrum of Protestantism throughout the world'.[614] Leo is also criticised by twentieth century historians for retaining all 'the trappings of monarchy' – insisting that that 'Catholics received in audience kneel before him throughout the interview' and 'never in twenty-five years exchanging a single word with his coachman'.[615] However, in his long reign 'he transformed the international prestige of the papacy, and won it a recognition it had lacked for centuries'.[616]

93.   Modernism

From its inception, the Catholic Church had been vulnerable to perversions and distortions of the teaching of Jesus of Nazareth and his Apostles. The evangelist John and the apostle Paul had both warned against 'false prophets' and in every era attempts were made to change doctrine. The popes, who as successors of Peter had been given the power to bind and loose, saw it as their principal duty to protect and preserve the Apostolic faith. Martin Luther's heresy was his insistence that divine revelation was to be found only in the Bible (*sola scriptura*), and it is a paradox that Modernism, the heresy that arose in the late nineteenth century, came from the researches of biblical scholars.

Did the heresy of Modernism actually exist? Some came to regard it as 'potentially [the] most potent of all heresies',[617] others as the figment of the imagination of a paranoiac pope. The pope in question was Pius X who succeeded Leo in 1903. His background was in marked contrast to that of his predecessor for, while Leo had come from the nobility, Giuseppe Sarto's father was a village postman and his mother a seamstress. After his ordination in

---

614   Paul Johnson, *A History of Christianity*, p. 475

615   Duffy, *Op. Cit.* p. 318

616   J.N.D.Kelly, *Op. Cit.* p. 312

617   E.E.Y.Hales, *Op. Cit.* p. 178

1858, he had served for seventeen years in parishes, first as a curate, then as a parish priest. He was made the spiritual director of the seminary at Treviso, then bishop of Mantua, and finally the Cardinal Patriarch of Venice. He was the first pope in the nineteenth century to have been a parish priest.

Sarto took the name of Pius out of respect for the long-suffering Pius VII and to establish a continuity with Pio Nono whose intransigent orthodoxy he shared. Early measures sprang from his pastoral experience: reform of education in seminaries and schools; a reinvigoration of the Church's spirituality through the catechism, the breviary and missal; and the promotion of frequent Communion not just for adults but children from the age of seven. His 'plump, handsome face and warm, open-hearted manner, won an immense popular following... He was in many ways the first Pope for the people...'[618] but he mistrusted intellectuals, particularly liberal theologians, upholding the precepts of Pio Nono's *Syllabus of Errors*.

An intimation of the impending Modernist crisis came not from Europe but the United States of America during the reign of Leo XIII. In 1892, an Exhibition was staged in Chicago to celebrate the four hundredth anniversary of the discovery of America by Christopher Columbus. One of the exhibits was a 'Parliament of Religions' where representatives of the world's faiths celebrated their shared beliefs and common values. Among them was Cardinal Gibbons, the Catholic Archbishop of Chicago, who joined with Buddhists, Hindus and Moslems in reciting the 'Our Father' and gave an apostolic blessing at the end of the proceedings, thereby marking, wrote the historian E.E.Y. Hales, 'the highest watermark ever attained in the history of Catholic co-operation with non-Catholic religions,'[619] and came perilously close to what the Church called the heresy of *Indifferentism* – viz. the belief that no one religion has a monopoly of truth.

Cardinal Gibbons' participation in the 'Parliament of Religions' did not in itself concern Pope Leo XIII: it was recognised that, while Catholics could never abandon their belief that theirs was the one true faith, they had to keep their heads down in a predominantly Protestant country. Certainly, with immigration from Catholic countries, Catholics were now a substantial and increasingly powerful minority in the United States; but the problems the American bishops faced, and called upon the Vatican to solve, were not theological niceties but the antagonism between immigrants from Germany

---

618   Duffy, *Op. Cit.* p. 121
619   E.E.Y. Hales, *Op. Cit.*. p. 171

and Ireland: German Catholics were lapsing because they were given Irish parish priests.

It was only when news of Cardinal Gibbons' gesture reached France that its implications were brought to the attention of the pope who in 1899 wrote a letter, *Testem Benevolentiae*, citing the errors 'called by some Americanism' found in the preface written by a French priest, the Abbé Klein, to a biography of Father Isaac Hecker, a German immigrant to the United States who had converted to Catholicism, become a priest and founded a religious order, the Missionary Priests of Saint Paul the Apostle', or Paulists. The errors were essentially proposals to make the Catholic faith more palatable to Americans by adapting her discipline and even her teaching to modern norms – promoting natural virtues such as honesty and temperance over supernatural merits of prayer, contemplation and the sacramental life.

The reaction of the American bishops was one of dismay. They denied any intention to teach a watered-down faith, and that there was such a heresy as 'Americanism'. They suggested that it was an invention of those who hated the Abbé Klein in particular, or the Church in America in general, whose accommodation with republicanism was anathema to the French royalists. They were right that 'Americanism' was never a heresy with erroneous dogmas: it never denied any article of faith. However, there was some fire behind the smoke: it led to the dismissal of the rectors of the American College in Rome and the Catholic University of America – measures taken at the instigation of Monsignor Francesco Satolli, the first Papal Legate in Washington, initially sympathetic to the liberals but later disillusioned by their secularist tendencies, stating on his return to Rome that there was 'nothing supernatural' in the American Church.

Modernism itself was a European phenomenon, found in the teaching of a professor at the *Institut Catholique* in Paris, Alfred Loisy, and an Irish Jesuit, George Tyrrell. Loisy had been a pupil of Louis Duchesne, an academic who had applied the rigorous standards of German scholars to biblical texts, while Duchesne himself had studied under the Italian archaeologist, Cavaliere Rossi, whose excavations of the catacombs had cast new light upon the history of the early Church. Loisy's researches led him to question the Church's teaching, and cease to believe 'in the unique nature and eternal truth of the revelation contained in the New Testament'.[620] Tyrell, a convert from Protestantism who had become a Jesuit, taught that Catholic dogmas

---

620   *Ibid.* p. 180

were the product of the times in which they were promulgated, and not the expression of eternal truths. He was a friend of the Austrian Baron von Hügel, resident in England and, despite holding no academic post, one of the most influential lay Catholics of his day. Through von Hügel Tyrell was introduced to the ideas of Loisy and, like Loisy, denied the permanent validity of any of the Church's dogmatic definitions. In 1906, he was expelled from the Society of Jesus and suspended as a priest.

It is unclear to what extent Modernist ideas spread beyond circles of advanced Catholic intellectuals and individual priests and theologians: some said that fifteen thousand priests in France favoured Loisy's teaching; others said at most fifteen hundred. To Pius X, widespread or not, the virus was malignant and had to be suppressed. In July, 1907, he issued a decree, *Lamentabili,* which condemned sixty-five Modernist propositions; and three months later an encyclical *Pascendi,* followed in 1910 with an edict (*moto proprio*) imposing an oath abjuring Modernism on all Catholic clergy. The tone of *Pascendi* was one of outrage: the Modernists, motivated by a mixture of curiosity and pride, had showed a 'sacrilegious audacity' in promoting their ideas. They were 'the most pernicious of all the adversaries of the Church…because they are within her and because they lay the axe to the root not the branches'.

If Modernism was indeed an existential threat to the Catholic faith, as Pius X and his advisers clearly believed, it was only to be expected that he should seek to eradicate it with all the means at his disposal. First there was the oath which 'was devised to impose a straitjacket of orthodoxy on suspects, and subscription to this oath became a routine and repeated part of every cleric's career, from the lowest priest to the most exalted cardinal.'[621] A secret agency was set up by a Monsignor Umberto Benigni with the pope's approval to investigate suspect theologians, priests, and seminarians – using *agents provocateurs* to entrap them, and encouraging seminarians to denounce their teachers and teachers their students. Although the German bishops managed to secure an exemption from taking the oath for the Catholic theologians in their universities, the anti-Modernist measures paralysed freedom of thought and of expression among Catholic scholars, and alienated them from the institutional Church.

A number of twentieth century Catholic historians, writing after Vatican II, and imbued with the liberal spirit that prevailed in its wake, are critical of the

---

621 Duffy, *Op. Cit.* p. 329

heavy-handed suppression of Modernism by Pope Pius X. Professor Eamon Duffy in his history of the Popes, *Saints and Sinners*, uses the term 'witch-hunt' and describes 'all these movements' being 'ruthlessly crushed'. Paul Johnson, in his *A History of Christianity*, talks of 'a systematic persecution'. 'Deeply hostile to intellectualism of every kind, Pius X and the advisers he gathered round him saw in every attempt at the liberalisation of Catholic theology and social thought, nothing but heresy and betrayal.'[622] Johnson ascribes the pope's paranoia to his experience as bishop of Mantua, when Pius had come into conflict with socialists and freemasons, and had his appointment as Patriarch of Venice blocked by Italy's anti-clerical government for three years. Pius, he suggests, 'saw the universe in black and white terms. The Tridentine papacy and the Church it represented was white; the rest was black, and in the rest he mingled democracy, republicanism, science, modern biblical exegesis, communism, atheism, free thought...He believed Protestantism to be a mere staging-post on an inevitable progression towards atheism.'[623]

Edward Hales, on the other hand, writing shortly *before* Vatican II, concurs with Pius's view that Modernism was 'the synthesis of all heresies': 'On their own showing, Loisy and Tyrrell and, to a greater or lesser extent, their many intellectual friends in every Western country, were undermining every dogma of the faith, destroying the whole structure and trying to replace it by an indefinable and unknowable flux'.[624]

94.   The Dreyfus Affair

What came to be called 'the Dreyfus Affair' started when the cleaning lady at the German embassy in Paris, Madam Bastien, was recruited by French military intelligence, the Statistical Section, to smuggle the contents of the military attaché's waste-paper basket out of the embassy and hand them over in the nearby church of Sainte Clotilde to her 'control', Major Henry. In September, 1894, there was found among the discarded papers a memorandum or *bordereau* torn into six pieces which, when put together, revealed a hand-written list of what the author termed 'interesting information'. All were top

---

622   *Ibid.*, p. 326
623   Paul Johnson, *Op. Cit.* p. 470
624   E.E.Y.Hales, *Op. Cit.* p. 185

secret military documents, accessible only to members of the General Staff. It was unsigned.

Who was the traitor? After an amateurish investigation, suspicion settled upon Alfred Dreyfus, an artillery officer, briefly an intern on the General Staff, who had had access to some of the documents and whose handwriting was remarkably similar to that of the author of the *bordereau*. Dreyfus had other characteristics that to the investigating officers, consciously or unconsciously, made him a plausible traitor. He was a Jew from Alsace-Lorraine: his first language was German. An uncle was still living in the now German city of Mulhouse to manage the family business.

Dreyfus was arrested, tried by court martial, found guilty and sentenced to public degradation and life imprisonment in the penal colony in French Guyana. The public spectacle of his degradation at the École Militaire in Paris, when the symbols of his rank were torn from his uniform, was accompanied by cries from the crowd of spectators of 'Coward! Judas! Dirty Jew!' Theodor Herzl, a Hungarian Jewish journalist covering the event for the Austrian *Neue Freie Presse,* would later claim that the venom spewed out by the crowd convinced him that Jews would never be safe in Europe, and must therefore have a state of their own: thus the Dreyfus Affair became 'an important event not just in Jewish history but in French, indeed European history'.[625]

The strong current of anti-Semitism in France was incongruous. In 1789, France had been the first European nation to remove all discriminatory laws affecting Jews. Future regimes had not restored them, and French Jews had flourished, particularly in the field of trade and finance. 'Economic changes,' wrote Abram Sacher, 'were more crucial in winning political equality for Jews than all the glittering generality about the rights of man and the sanctity of the human personality'.[626] 'Well-equipped by their experience and connections, many Jews entered into commercial and financial enterprises and distinguished themselves.[627] Among the bankers and entrepreneurs who made huge fortunes 'there was a disproportionate number of "outsiders" – notably 'men of Protestant or Jewish origin',[628] with close relatives living in other countries such the Rothschilds (Germany and Britain) or the Ephrussis (Austria and Russia).

625   Paul Johnson, *A History of the Jews,* p. 387

626   Abram Sacher, quoted in Flannery, *The Anguish of the Jews,* p. 167

627   Flannery,*Op. Cit..,* p. 167

628   *Encyclopaedia Brittanica,* Vol 7, p. 666

This rise of a cosmopolitan Jewish plutocracy both baffled and enraged conservative Catholics. Had not Pope Gregory the Great taught that the Jews must be preserved to demonstrate the degradation that followed their failure to recognise their Messiah? Were they not contemptible – the chief rabbi of Rome kicked down the steps of the Capitol during the Roman Carnival? The traditional social hierarchy that went with an economy based on land held by the ancient French nobility was now reversed with the nobility keeping their heads above water by selling their estates and marrying their sons and daughters to rich Jews.

Anti-Semitism was not just found among disgruntled Catholics, but also among secular academics and intellectuals. 'Instead of disappearing with the Enlightenment, anti-Semitism simply found a new guise, one which no longer blamed the Jews for the crucifixion of Christ, but held them responsible for all the crimes and perversities committed in the name of monotheistic religion… In the arch-sceptic Voltaire the resulting image of the Jew is one of utter scorn and contempt.'[629] In 1853, the French diplomat Comte Joseph de Gobineau published his *Essai sur l'inégalité des races humains* which talked of Aryan virtue and Semitic 'degeneration'. Ernst Renan, in his *Vie de Jésus,* the most successful book published in France during the whole nineteenth century, wrote that the 'exclusivism and self-imposed isolation of the Jews, exacerbated by the teachings of the Talmud and by an ingrained complex of superiority, is the ultimate cause of the detestation with which they were widely regarded'. His view of contemporary Jews 'was a little more nuanced but still riddled with ant-Semitic clichés emphasising their egoism, clannishness, worship of Mammon and their leading role in modern revolutionary movements'.[630]

Another best-seller in late nineteenth-century France was *La France Juive* by Edouard Drumont. It was a call to arms. France was a conquered nation ruled by an alien minority, the Jews. Just as the Saxons in England had been enslaved by sixty thousand Normans under William the Conqueror, so the French had been enslaved by half-a-million Jews[631] living in France who had worked deviously to establish themselves as a ruling caste. Contempt for the gentile and hatred of Christianity were unalterable features of their genetic make-up. Working through Freemasonry at the time of the Revolution of 1789,

---

629   Robert S. Wistrich, *Op. Cit.* p. 45

630   Robert S. Wistricht, *Op. Cit.* p. 46-47

631   'At the time of the Dreyfus case Jews in France numbered no more than 86,000 out of a total population of nearly forty millions.' Paul Johnson, *A History of the Jews,* p. 380

they had now established their ascendancy through banking and commerce, establishing monopolies with the collusion of French Protestants, crushing any competition from French Catholics. He cited as evidence the collapse of the Union Générale bank, set up as a haven for the savings of Catholics, which had collapsed in 1884, brought down, according to Drumont, by the machinations of the Rothschilds. Drumont believed that he was defending the interests of Catholics but he received no support from the Catholic hierarchy. 'I am not the intimate of any cardinal bishop or Jesuit…On the contrary, the members of the upper clergy are hostile to our ideas'. However, he had many followers among the lower clergy and religious orders: an attack on Jewish influence appeared in the Jesuit journal, *Civilità Cattolica* in 1890; and crude anti-Semitic polemic appeared in *La Croix*, the paper published by the Assumptionist Order.

In 1891, with the money he had made from *La France Juive*, Drumont founded a newspaper, *La Libre Parole* (*Free Speech*) to promote his anti-Semitic views and expose the deputies in the National Assembly who had been bribed to bail out the bankrupt Panama Canal company with public funds. One of the bankers behind the company was Jacques de Reinach – a German who had taken French citizenship, had made a fortune from investments in French and American railways, and had become a prominent member of France's Jewish elite.[632] The Panama Canal Scandal was grist to the mill for *La Libre Parole*, showing that Jews, particularly those of German origin like Reinach, were not just corrupt but potentially disloyal.

Thus, at the time of Dreyfus's conviction, almost no one doubted his guilt; and Dreyfus did not help his own case by his demeanour in court – stiff, detached, confident that common sense would exonerate him, disdainful of those who were unable to see that the charges against him were absurd. Because the army was held in such high esteem, it seemed inconceivable to the overwhelming majority of French men and women that it could have arrested the wrong man. So afraid were the prison authorities in French Guiana that Dreyfus might escape with the help of the Germans, or the British or mercenaries hired by the Jewish 'syndicate', that he was incarcerated in a hut built on the site of a former leper colony on an island just off the coast known as Devil's Island. There, in the tropical heat, sometimes manacled to his bed, Dreyfus languished – to most Frenchmen, a well-deserved punishment for his crime.

---

632   Paul Johnson, *Op. Cit.* p. 388

Two people knew that he was innocent – Alfred Dreyfus's wife Lucie and his brother Mathieu. At the time of her husband's arrest, Lucie was twenty-five years old. Mathieu, Alfred's older brother, thirty-seven years old, was his antithesis – handsome, charming, suave, debonair: it was said that if Alfred had been more like Mathieu, he would never have been convicted. He and Lucie immediately began a campaign to prove Alfred's innocence. They had considerable resources at their disposal: the Dreyfuses were rich; Lucie's family, the Hademards richer. To keep the case alive in the press they recruited as a publicist a dynamic young journalist, Bernard Lazare – at first sight an odd choice in that Alfred was loath to ascribe his conviction to anti-Semitic prejudice and Lazare was the author of *L'Antisémitisme, son histoire et ses causes* (*Anti-Semitism: Its History and Causes*) which the anti-Semitic Drumont considered 'a remarkable book, nourished with facts and dominated from end to end by a fine effort at impartiality...'[633]

Lazare's history appealed to Drumont because, while it lacked the abusive tone, fanciful historicism, scurrilous anecdotes and pseudo-scientific theorizing of *La France Juive*, it accepted a number of Drumont's contentions. Lazare accepted that, having helped to demolish the old order – the *ancien régime* – the Jews sought to dominate the new: 'As conquerors, not as guests, did they come into modern societies....' So long as landed capital remained the political power, the Jew was deprived of any right; the Jew was liberated on the day when political power passed to industrial capital, and that proved fatal. Having for so long constituted an alien and persecuted nation within other nations, the Jews were now able to dominate their former oppressors through their ascendancy in banking and trade. Jews helped Jews: Jewish solidarity is all the stronger in that it goes so far back. Jews were anti-Catholic. The Jews, might not be 'solely responsible for the destruction of religious doctrine and the decay of faith', but 'they may at least be counted among those who helped to bring about such a state of desuetude and the changes which followed'.

It was not Lazare's analysis of anti-Semitism, and the linking it to the conviction of Dreyfus, that broke open the case but another item filched from the contents of the German military attaché's waste-paper-basket – a note proving that the leak of secrets was continuing, written in handwriting that was not similar to that of the *bordereau* but *identical*, and on which the author had conveniently written his name and address. The scrap of paper

---

633   *La Libre Parole,* 10 January, 1895, quoted in Bredin, *Op. Cit.,* p. 134

was shown to the newly appointed chief of the Statistical Section, Colonel Georges Picquart, who then told his superiors that there was evidence that the conviction of Captain Dreyfus was a miscarriage of justice. He was told to bury it. The French Army could not admit that it had blundered.

The full story of the Dreyfus Affair is not pertinent to the history of the Catholic Church and is told elsewhere.[634] In due course, Dreyfus was recalled from Devil's Island for a second Court Martial held at Rennes in Brittany. Again, he was found guilty: the officers on the panel of judges could not bring themselves to believe that the one-time Minister of War and Chief of the General Staff, General Mercier, was lying when he swore on oath that he had incontrovertible proof of Dreyfus' guilt which he could not make public for reasons of national security. Since it was clear to the government that Dreyfus was innocent, he was pardoned, but only fully exonerated in 1906, and never to this day have the verdicts of the courts martial been reversed by a military tribunal.

This obtuseness enraged the Dreyfusard intellectuals (the term was first used at this time), and confirmed their view that the army was the last redoubt of Catholic conservatives. The particular *bête noire* of the Dreyfusards was the Jesuit Père Stanislas du Lac – a suave and intelligent priest from a family of the lesser French nobility – who was the spiritual director of General de Boisdeffre, the army Chief of Staff. It was said that through his connections he could ensure that the graduates of Jesuit schools won places at the elite military academies: in fact, of the 180 officers in the General Staff in 1898, only a dozen had been educated at Jesuit schools.[635] Joseph Reinach claimed that Father du Lac was 'astir in every intrigue',[636] directing the anti-Dreyfusard campaign as part of a wider plan to foster a coup d'état and replace the anti-clerical Republic with a pro-Catholic authoritarian regime. The theory has been considered plausible by a number of twentieth-century historians.[637]

---

634   See the author's *The Dreyfus Affair*.

635   John McManners, *Church and State in France: 1870-1914.*, p. 126

636   Jean-Louis Bredin, *The Affair. The Case of Alfred Dreyfus.*, p. 304 fn

637   Hannah Arendt in *The Origins of Totalitarianism*, wrote that 'the Jesuits were not prepared to tolerate the existence of officers immune to the influence of the Confessional' and had a 'coup d'état policy' that they 'and certain anti-Semites were trying to introduce with the help of the army.' The historian Robert Tombs regards the charge that 'the Jesuits through their influence over Catholic army officers were running the anti-Dreyfus plot in order to destroy the Republic' a 'more plausible accusation' than some of the wilder charges against the order; Ruth Harris writes of Père du Lac that 'there is no hard evidence that he was responsible for directing the military cover-up, as the Dreyfusards claim' but does not enumerate the soft evidence.

However, the historian Ralph Gibson calls the idea of a Jesuit conspiracy 'demonstrably a total delusion'[638].

Indeed, as the Affair progressed, it was discovered that, if there was a bias in the appointment of officers in the army, it was *against* Catholics rather than in their favour. The 1905 *affaire des fiches* revealed that Captain Mollin, a member of a notably political and anti-Catholic Masonic Lodge, the Grand Orient had, with the help of the secretary of the Grand Orient, set up a network of informers to report on officers in the army. Their names were entered on cards or *fiches*, and these labelled 'Corinth' or 'Carthage'. An officer reported to be 'perfect in all respects; excellent opinions' would be marked as a Corinthian and put forward for promotion; another who, 'though a good officer, well reported on, takes no part in politics' would nonetheless be designated a Carthaginian because he 'goes to Mass with his family' and sent his six children to Catholic schools. A bachelor officer who went to Mass was by definition of a reactionary disposition. Carthaginians were posted to backwaters and denied promotion.

But what of the institutional Church? There were sporadic attempts by bishops to distance themselves from the anti-Semitism of the Assumptionists which so tarnished the shrine at Lourdes; and they refused to support Drumont when he stood as a candidate for the municipality of Paris. Monsignor Coullié, the Archbishop of Lyon had shunned a Congress of Christian Democracy held in Lyon because of its anti-Semitic tone.[639]

With hindsight these measures were grievously inadequate. Broadly speaking, the French bishops took the line that the guilt or innocence of Alfred Dreyfus was a judicial matter in which, by the terms of the Concordat, they were not permitted to intervene. Among the French laity, the liberal Comte de Mun who had backed pope Leo XIII's appeal to French Catholics to abandon their intransigent royalism and support the republic – the *Ralliement* – had also boycotted the Congress in Lyon for the same reason as the Archbishop, but he later accepted the anti-Dreyfusard contention that there was a 'Jewish syndicate that was working for German wages' to undermine and demoralise the French army. The Catholic poet Charles Peguy was a militant Dreyfusard who formed a small army of students to defend Dreyfusard professors from attack by anti-Semitic gangs. However,

638   Ralph Gibson, *A Social History of French Catholicism. 1789-1914*, p. 110

639   Stephen Wilson, *Ideology and Experience: Antisemitism in France at the Time of the Dreyfus Affair.*, p. 360

by and large the division in France was tribal – Jews, Protestants and atheists were Drefusards and Catholics anti-Dreyfusards – among them 'Catholics without faith' like Charles Maurras who regarded Catholicism as integral to French identity and saw the Dreyfusard campaign to discredit the army as part of a long-term 'de-Christianisation' of society by 'Talmudic Judaism'.[640]

95. The Disestablishment of the Catholic Church in France

The Catholic Church in France was to pay dearly for its neutrality over the Dreyfus Affair on the one hand, and the anti-Semitism of so many Catholics on the other. In January, 1900, twelve members of the Assumptionist order were tried and convicted of subversion: 'The court case,' wrote Ruth Harris, 'enabled the government to trot out the most elaborate fantasies of clerical subversion and financial corruption'.[641] New laws were passed that prohibited all associations that were not specifically authorised by the state: henceforward rights enjoyed by socialists and freemasons did not apply to monks and nuns. These anti-clerical statutes, designed to silence 'propagandists for the Counter-Revolution' were 'the defining and only significant issue' during the general election of 1902.[642] Economic and fiscal questions such as tariffs and income tax, roused no passions: the cement of the Left wing coalition, said the Comte de Mun, was 'religious war'.[643] The popular vote was close; in the first round of the elections, the Right trailed the Left by only 200,000 votes: but the second round returned a majority of between 80 and 90 in the Chamber of Deputies for the *Bloc des Gauches*.[644]

How was it that a majority in a supposedly Catholic country should vote for the anti-clerical parties of the Left? Catholicism remained the faith of the majority of the French. There was a *curé* in every village, and most of the French still used Catholic ceremonies for the rites of passage through life – birth, marriage and death. Relations between Church and state were still governed by Napoleon's concordat; the salaries of the clergy were paid

---

640   Flannery, *Op. Cit.*, p. 188-189

641   Ruth Harris, 'The Assumptionists and the Dreyfus Affair', *Past and Present*, Volume 194, Issue 1, pp. 175-211

642   Robert Tombs, *France: 1814-1914.*, p. 465

643   McManners, *Op. Cit.*, p. 125

644   Tombs, *Op. Cit.*, p. 465

by the state. There were many areas of shared endeavour. The Catholic missions were encouraged by the anti-clerical governments as part of their *mission civilisatrice*; and in France the care of the old, the poor, the sick, the orphaned, the insane, the imprisoned, was largely undertaken by Catholic agencies funded by charitable donations. 'In the 1870s, the wards of almost all of France's 1,500 hospitals were run by about 11,000 members of active religious congregations.'[645] This was welcomed by the radical governments which were reluctant to raise taxes. 'A Frenchman's heart is on the Left,' wrote André Siegfried, 'but his purse is on the Right.'

The principal conflict between Church and state was over education. The radicals were determined to cleanse French youth of superstition by teaching the precepts of the Enlightenment in the fine *lycées* provided by the government.[646] They were enraged by the success of the Catholic schools – run for the poor by the Assumptionist order, and for the upper classes by the Jesuits. The two systems were teaching different curricula and, above all, different values: they were creating '*deux jeunesses*' (two youths) – a phrase coined by the historian Ernest Lavisse in the 1880s – that grew into two hostile camps within one nation. It was particularly galling for the radicals that atheist *préfets* and higher civil servants sent their sons to Jesuit schools where they 'would learn good manners and form useful friendships.'[647]

The French peasant may have shown little interest in the ideological conflict between Catholic conservatives and atheist radicals, but at a time of increasing social discontent, Catholicism was seen as a pillar supporting the established social order and therefore the enemy of both the urban and rural poor. 'The clergy of France has finally convinced the voters,' said the Abbé Frémont, 'that between the Church on the one hand and progress, the Republic and the future on the other, there is no possible relationship but the most deadly hatred.'[648]

Another cause of anti-clerical sentiment in the exclusively male electorate was the Catholic Church's strict views on sexual morality at a time of growing eroticization and permissiveness in French society. This was the *belle époque*. Every year thousands of young women moved to Paris to work as prostitutes. As is clear from the novels of Emile Zola, or Anatole France, or the Journals of

---

645   Katrin Schultheiss, *Bodies and Souls*, p. 3

646   *Ibid.*, p. 51

647   Robert Anderson, *The Conflict in Education: Catholic Secondary Schools (1850-1870).*, p. 71

648   quoted in McManners, *Op. Cit.*, p. 44

Edmond de Goncourt, there was no stigma attached to keeping a mistress or sleeping with a girl picked up off the streets. The danger was venereal disease: Edouard de Goncourt's brother Jules died at the age of forty from syphilis.

Though it was a commonplace of anti-clerical propaganda since the time of the Enlightenment to claim that priests and particularly monks were depraved hypocrites when it came to sex, the historian Ralph Gibson believes that 'the vast majority of the clergy in the nineteenth century were pious and chaste and did their best to get on with their religious duties.'[649] However, among these duties was an attempt to enforce chastity through the confessional. The view of the saintly and popular priest, Jean Vianney – known as the Curé d'Ars – that dancing was sinful was confirmed in the later nineteenth century when traditional dances in which there was little physical contact between the sexes were replaced by the waltz and the polka which placed a man and woman in one another's arms – effectively a prolonged perambulatory embrace. The moral dangers of such 'occasions of sin' obsessed the nineteenth century clergy. Girls were made to sign pledges not to dance which alienated the young, 'particularly young men in the countryside who deeply resented the *curé's* rôle in cutting off the supply of girls for the village *bal*.' [650]

French husbands greatly resented the prying of the *curé* in the confessional into the intimate details of their conjugal life. Measures taken by married couples to avoid conception were sins confessed by women but blamed on men.[651] French husbands refused to submit to such an interrogation, abandoned the sacrament of confession, were therefore barred from Easter communion and so effectively excluded from the Church. The Bishop of Le Mans, Jean-Baptiste Bouvier, in a letter to Pope Pius IX, asserted 'without hesitation that the prying by confessors into sexual habits and their prohibition of birth control was producing protests and driving people away from the Church.'[652]

It was, then, not so much the Church's attitude to the Dreyfus Affair that made the Church unpopular, but the widespread perception that it was the ally of the rich, the enemy of progress, and a prurient kill-joy when it came to

---

649   Gibson, *Op. Cit.*, p. 103

650   *Ibid.*, p. 93

651   Cf. Marcel Jouhandeau in *Marcel and Élise*: 'Thus Élise does not confess her sins but mine...'

652   Theodore Zeldin, *Conflicts in French Society,* p. 49

sex. A majority of French men voted for the anti-clerical agenda of the *Bloc des gauches* in the general election of 1902. The strategy of the prime minister, Pierre Waldeck-Rousseau, was vindicated; but, in his moment of triumph, he resigned on the grounds of ill-health. He was replaced as Prime Minister by Émile Combes.

Combes, born in the Tarn, had studied in a Catholic seminary for the priesthood but had been rejected because he was judged 'too proud'.[653] Spurned by the Church, Combes lost his faith, joined the Freemasons, studied medicine, and practised as a doctor in the country town of Pons in the Charente-Inférieure. Here he espoused 'all the ideas, prejudices, hates, and principles of the small town anticlerical'[654] He was typical of those in the French provinces who worked to ensure that the village priest was 'banished from the school, excluded from the committee directing official charities, regarded with malicious distrust or jealous hatred by the mayor and the school-master, kept at arms-length as a compromising neighbour by all the minor officials employed by the commune or the state, spied on by the innkeeper, exposed to the anonymous denunciations of the local newspaper' and was left to spending 'his mornings reciting prayers to empty pews and his afternoons planting cabbages and pruning roses'.[655]

What had been done on a small scale in a provincial town, Combes now enacted for the whole nation. He formed a cabinet which included ten fellow Freemasons, and in his first days in office signed decrees closing down more than one hundred Catholic schools.[656] His provincial roots, and disdain for the moderating blandishments of the metropolis such as a seat in the Academy endeared this 'obstinate and self-satisfied little man'[657] to his admiring disciples who called him 'the little Father'. One of his few excursions into society was to attend the *soirées* of Marquise Arconati-Visconti where other regulars were Joseph Reinach and the now pardoned Alfred Dreyfus.[658]

On 1 July, 1901, a new Law of Associations was passed which obliged every religious order to obtain 'a legislative authorizing' act which would determine its function. All but five of the religious orders who applied for authorization

---

653   McManners, *Op. Cit.*, p. 133

654   D.E Brogan, *Op. Cit.*, p. 362

655   *Revue des Deux Mondes*, quoted in McManners, *Op. Cit.*, p. 133

656   Michael Burns, *Dreyfus. A Family Affair. 1789-1945.*, p. 296

657   Brogan, *Op. Cit.*, p. 362

658   Harris, *Op. Cit.*, p. 359

were refused. [659] The unauthorised orders were either dissolved or forced to move abroad. There were in France at that time 159,628 members of religious orders living in 19,424 establishments of one kind or another. Women were particularly affected by the new laws. As the historian Katrin Schultheiss observed, 'membership in an active religious congregation afforded single women of all classes the opportunity to perform a vast array of social services, including nursing and teaching'.[660] As many as 100,000 girls and single women were employed in enterprises in the silk and clothing industries run by religious orders: these were now closed down. In Catholic Brittany, there was popular resistance to the closures: 1,500 colonial troops were sent to deal with three convents in the province, and 3,000 laid siege to a monastery near Tarascon.[661]

Expelling the nursing orders from French hospitals was particularly unpopular. 'The *congrégations hospitalières*...rapidly developed their own paramedical establishments (pharmacies, sanatoria, home nursing, etc.) and then moved into a bewildering variety of social services: old people's homes, orphanages, homes for the blind and deaf-mutes, lunatic asylums, homes for ex-prostitutes, prison services, soup kitchens, job placements for domestic servants and so on, almost *ad infinitum*... They were prepared to take on the repulsive, the incurable, and the financially unrewarding in a way that doctors were often not.'[662]

Now anti-clerical zeal over-rode Republican parsimony. 'It is the strict duty of every republican,' said the Parisian doctor and politician, Désiré Bourneville, 'to remove from the priests and nuns every means of action accorded them in civil society of which they are the implacable adversaries'. Bourneville led a protracted campaign to replace nuns with lay nurses in French hospitals and succeeded thanks to the anti-clerical majority on Paris's Municipal Council. There were, at the turn of the century, approximately 20,000 Catholic nuns providing nursing care in French hospitals. Sacking them was not popular. In both Paris and Lyons, 'anti-clerical doctors, hospital administrators and politicians – many of whom unequivocally supported the laicization of the nation's schools – rallied in the defence of the congregational nurses'.[663] On 15

---

659 those exempt were mostly missionary orders considered useful for the *mission civiliatrice* in the French Empire.

660 Schultheiss, *Op. Cit.*, p. 10. See also the scathing satire of such an institution in Octave Mirbeau's *Diary of a Chambermaid*.

661 Tombs, *Op. Cit.*, p. 469

662 Gibson, *Op. Cit.*, p. 126

663 Schultheiss, *Op. Cit.*, p. 11

January, 1908, several thousand Parisians, among them doctors, councillors and politicians – assembled outside the historic Hôtel-Dieu hospital to take leave of the Augustinian Sisters who had served there as nurses since 1217.[664]

The prime target of the anti-clerical legislation were the Catholic schools. By a Law of 7 July, 1904, members of religious orders were prohibited from the 'teaching of every grade and every kind in France'. The members of the few authorized congregations came under this ban. Every religious, man or woman, who wanted to continue to teach children had to renounce their religious calling, and it was left to the courts to decide whether such a renunciation was sincere. Henri de Gaulle, the father of Charles de Gaulle, lost his job as the lay headmaster of the Jesuit school in Paris and sent his son Charles to be educated by the Jesuits in Belgium.[665]

Here, for French Catholics, was the persecution which they had feared: it might not be as cruel and sanguinary as that of the Jacobins, but it was, all the same, a determined effort by a government of atheists and Freemasons to prevent the education of French children in a faith that had flourished in France since the baptism of Clovis 1400 years before, and to root out significant aspects of Catholic practice from the life of the French nation. Many devout customs were now criminalised. Monastic life was unlawful and religious processions, dating from the Middle Ages, were banned by anti-clerical local authorities.[666]

What could the Catholic Church do in the face of this persecution? In 1901, Pope Leo XIII was ninety-one years old. With a government in Paris led by a Freemason and dominated by Freemasons, all that he had foreseen in his Encyclical *Humanus Genus* had come to pass. He had held out an olive branch to the French Republicans but they had rejected it: his policy of *ralliement* had failed. Leo died, in 1903. His successor, Pius X, whose model Pius VII had stood up to Napoleon, was unlikely to back down before the little doctor from the Tarn. Clearly the French government was in breach of the Concordat but it blamed the rupture on the pope. A motion passed in the Chamber of Deputies on 10 February, 1905, declared that "the attitude of the Vatican" had rendered the separation of Church and State inevitable; and on 11 December 1905, the separation Law was passed and published in the *Journal Officiel*.

---

664   *Ibid.*, p. 20

665   See Don Cooke, *Charles de Gaulle*, p. 27

666   Brogan, *Op. Cit.*, p. 378

For the Catholic poet Charles Péguy, the fact that the struggle of the Dreyfusards should lead to this 'Combes demagogy' was a catastrophic perversion of the movement's ideals. 'The Dreyfusards who became Combists were already inflated with pride, and did evil.'[667] Certainly, the Church itself was partly to blame for their defeat by the French secularists. 'It was not the arguments that it lacks but charity. All the reasons, all the systems, all the pseudoscientific arguments weigh for nothing in the scales against an ounce of charity.'[668]

However, the Catholic Church had survived worse bouts of persecution, and in some ways that by the Combes government had a salutatory outcome. The historian Denis Brogan describes the effect as 'bracing.'[669] The disciples of Comte and Michelet, who had assumed that the Catholic faith itself would wither and die, were to be disappointed. In the world of letters there was a Catholic renaissance with authors such as Péguy, Ferdinand Brunetière, Joris-Karl Huysmans, Paul Bourget, Paul Claudel, Georges Bernanos and François Mauriac; and philosophers and theologians such as Lucien Laberthonnière, Maurice Blondel, Louis Duchesne, Henri Brémond, Jacques Maritain and Ernest Psichari.

Some, certainly, remained anti-Semitic: 'I am an anti-Semite,' wrote Huysmans, 'because I am convinced that it is the Jews who have turned France into a sad country, agitated by the lowest passions, the sad country without God that we now see.'[670] But others, such as Péguy, Claudel, Bernanos and Mauriac, abhorred anti-Semitism; and the anti-Semitism of the Assumptionists that had contaminated, by association, the shrine at Lourdes and the message of Bernadette Soubirous, was wholly absent in the cult of another Catholic girl, Thérèse Martin, a Carmelite nun, who died of consumption at Lisieux at the age of twenty-four in 1897. Her *Story of a Soul,* published posthumously, revealed a spirituality far removed from the polemics of *Action Française* or diplomatic disputes over the disestablishment of the Church. She was, as Ruth Harris writes, 'no anti-Semite, despite having grown up in an ultra-Catholic and right-wing family.'[671] Canonized by Pope Pius XI in 1925, Thérèse became 'the most widely loved Catholic intercessor of modern times'.

---

667   Charles Péguy, *Notre Jeuneusse.*, p. 96

668   *Ibid.*, p. 134

669   Brogan, *Op. Cit.*, p. 378

670   quoted in Wilson, *Op. Cit.*, p. 555

671   Harris, *The Man on Devil's Island*, p. 229

96.   The Great War

In the last decades of the nineteenth century and the first of the twentieth, the Great Powers were poised for war. With diplomacy a prelude to combat, alliances were formed by the different nations. The *entente cordiale* between Britain and France survived the Fashoda incident, and France, with Germany as always its likely enemy, allied itself with Russia – despite the republican distaste for Tsarist autocracy. Germany continued Bismarck's policy of sustaining the Austro-Hungarian empire, fearing that its Slav subjects might emulate those fellow Slavs who had broken away from the Ottoman empire and formed their own nations. The Russian Tsar was the patron and protector of his fellow Slavs, also Orthodox Christians, while the Ottoman Empire, being the enemy of the Russians, was allied with Germany.

An incident deep in the Balkans led to the world-wide conflict that was to be called the Great War. Serbia, since the mid-nineteenth century an independent state with its capital in Belgrade, claimed as part of its historic kingdom the neighbouring province of Bosnia. For centuries part of the Ottoman Empire, Bosnia had been occupied by troops of the Austro-Hungarian empire in 1878 and then annexed by Vienna. In June, 1914, the heir to the imperial throne, the Archduke Franz Ferdinand, went on a tour of the province and while riding in an open carriage in the streets of its capital, Sarajevo, was assassinated by a Serb nationalist, Gavrilo Princip.

The government in Vienna held the Serb government responsible and issued an ultimatum with humiliating terms which the Serbs rejected. On 28 July, the Austria-Hungarian army shelled Belgrade. Russia ordered the mobilisation of its armed forces. The Germans followed suit, at the same time demanding that the Russian mobilisation cease. When the Russians proceeded, Germany, on 1 August, 1914, declared war on Russia. France now mobilised in compliance with its treaties with Russia. The British Cabinet, led by the prime-minister, Herbert Henry Asquith, hesitated; a number of ministers were reluctant to be drawn into a Continental imbroglio in which no British interests were involved; but the German invasion of Belgium on 3 August, following the plan drawn up by Field Marshal Alfred von Schlieffen in 1906, not only broke the terms of the 1839 Treaty of London which guaranteed Belgium's neutrality, but raised the prospect of the Germans gaining control of the Channel ports and so threatening Britain's command of the seas. Britain too declared war on Germany and dispatched an expeditionary force to fight in France.

What part was played by the Catholic Church in this fast moving resort to war? Little or none. 'Rome was mostly a helpless spectator while Catholics, in a struggle she had striven to avert, destroyed each other. Even good Catholics, even the best of them, were often victims of the age, taught for too long by their governments and by the spirit of the times that the interests of the State or of race were paramount, that religion was 'a private affair'.[672] Paradoxically, if there was to be any example of international fraternity preventing the belligerent governments from declaring war, it was not Catholics refusing the fight Catholics, or Protestants refusing to fight Protestants, but Socialists refusing to fight Socialists. There was a large Social-Democratic bloc in the German Reichstag but, on 4 August, 1914, 'the Reichstag unanimously voted the necessary credits for the war': 'the masses of Socialist workmen…were not prepared to tolerate an invasion of Germany by troops of the Russian Tsar'[673].

Pope Pius X died around a month after the opening of hostilities, and Giacomo della Chiesa was chosen to succeed him as Pope Benedict XV. The choice 'was as explicitly a reaction against the proceeding regime as it was possible to get. Della Chiesa was a wisp of a man with one shoulder higher than the other …and none of the papal robes kept in readiness for the election was small enough to fit him'.[674] Benedict abhorred the war, and condemned the slaughter in general terms but, hoping to be called upon to mediate, he remained neutral with the result that both sides accused him of favouring the other. He did intervene 'to stop German deportations of Belgian civilians, and protested against the Turkish massacres of the Armenians; what he would not do was to condemn this side or that'.[675]

There were two issues of particular interest to the papacy. The first was to keep Italy out of the war, and to this end Benedict sent a young papal diplomat, Eugenio Pacelli, to Vienna to persuade the Emperor Franz Joseph to withdraw from the Trentino. His mission failed. In April, 1915, Italy joined the Triple Entente (France, Britain and Russia) and declared war on the Austro-Hungarian Empire. The second was 'the Roman question' – viz. the continuing aspiration of the popes to repossess Rome. This 'paralysed Benedict's efforts for peace'. By a secret agreement made when Italy entered

---

672   Hales, *Op. Cit.* p. 250

673   Rosenberg, *Op. Cit.* p. 72

674   Duffy, *Op. Cit.* p. 333

675   Burleigh, *Op. Cit.* p.458

the war, the Italian government persuaded its new allies not to negotiate with the pope: as a result when, in August, 1917, Benedict proposed a peace settlement, it was ignored: 'Had the pope's proposals for peace been accepted, several million lives would have been saved, and it is hard to see what country would have been the loser; the United states would have been spared entry into the war, and the Bolshevik revolution in Russia would probably have been averted'.[676] The irrelevance of the Vatican's diplomatic standing was made clear when Italy made sure that the Holy See played no role in the negotiations that followed the end of the war.

It was not just papal diplomacy that was shown to be irrelevant: so, it would seem, was the Christian religion. 'Everywhere clergy and theologians played a considerable part in justifying participation in the war, whether in terms of its justness and virtue, or by claiming that God was with their nation's defensive struggle'.[677] German Catholics were persuaded that the war was in defence of Austria-Hungary, Europe's pre-eminent Catholic power, disregarding the anti-Catholic element in their country's conduct of the war – the burning of the library at the Catholic university of Louvain in Belgium, or the three hundred shells that were fired at the cathedral at Rheims. This sacrilege, combined with reports of German atrocities, made it easier for their enemies to see them as agents of the devil.

In France, the divisions and enmities that had been exposed by the Dreyfus Affair were laid aside. The religious orders were permitted to return to France and the hitherto anticlerical government of Raymond Poincaré declared a *Union sacrée* – Sacred Union – while 'the French clergy abandoned the scowling apartness that had been their stance during the Third Republic. Since they were subject to conscription, their role was not confined to that of military chaplains: 32,699 French clerics, 23,418 seculars and 9,281 regulars, served in the Republic's armed forces; a further 12,554 worked in military hospitals.'[678] Many of the officers promoted for their political correctness during the *Affaire des Fiches* were sacked and more competent Catholics put in their place. Fourteen of the nineteen senior officers whose courage and competence won them promotion in late 1914 had previously been victims of Masonic detraction.

---

676   Hales, *Op. Cit.* p. 251

677   Burleigh, *Op. Cit.* p.439

678   *Ibid.* pp 454-455

Rejected as a mediator, Pope Benedict's energies were directed to the relief of the suffering caused by the war. His *Opera dei Prigionieri* enabled six hundred thousand prisoners of war to make contact with their families, and twenty-six thousand invalids among them were sent at the Vatican's expense to convalesce in Swiss sanatoria. During the war the Vatican expended eighty-two million lire on humanitarian relief, bringing it to the verge of bankruptcy.

And there was prayer. In the spring of 1916, three Portuguese children acting as shepherds for their family's flock of sheep near the village of Fatima, north of Lisbon, had a series of a visions of 'a lady more brilliant than the sun' who told them that prayer would bring an end to the war. She asked the faithful to 'pray the Rosary every day to bring peace to the world...' This apparition of the Virgin Mary brought thousands of pilgrims to Fatima, many of whom witnessed what came to be called 'the miracle of the sun' – a pyrotechnical display in which the sun seemed to hurtle towards the earth and then return to its normal position. In the ten years following the apparitions, two million pilgrims came to Fatima to pray at the Sanctuary of Our Lady, one of the largest Marian shrines in the world. In 1930, the Church declared the claims of the three children 'worthy of belief'.

If authentic, the visions were sobering because on 13 July, 1917, the Virgin Mary imparted three 'secrets' to the young shepherds – the first being a vision of Hell with, as the eldest, Lucia, later described it, 'shrieks and groans of pain, and despair, which horrified us and made us tremble with fear'. The second was an assurance that the war would come to an end but would be followed by another war unless Russia was consecrated to the Immaculate Heart of Mary. 'Russia will be converted, and there will be peace; if not, she will spread her errors throughout the world, causing wars and persecutions of the Church'. [679] The third secret was to remain secret. It was written down by Lucia and delivered to the Bishop of Leira in a sealed envelope, and in 1957 sent to Rome.

Around 13,000,000 civilians died from famine, disease and massacres during the First World War – a figure only exceeded as a proportion of the population by the Thirty Years War. For those in uniform, wrote the Australian historian, Geoffrey Blainey, it was 'the most terrible war the world had known... Of the 8,500,000 soldiers and sailors who died, Germany lost the most, followed by Russia, France, Austro-Hungary and then Britain and its Empire. These five powers, along with Italy which entered the war in 1915, lost nine out of every

---

679   Santos, *Fatima in Lucia's Own Words*, p. 123 (Wikepedia)

10 soldiers killed in the war. In addition more than 20,000,000 soldiers were wounded…. From crowded apartments in Moscow to sheep farms in New Zealand there were millions of mantelpieces on which stood framed black-and-white photographs of earnest or smiling young men, killed in the war which everyone now called the Great War, not realising that a greater war was barely 20 years ahead'.[680]

680   Geoffrey Blainey, *A Short History of the World*, pp. 543-544

PART FIVE

97.   The Armenian massacre and the Russian Revolution

During World War I, Turkey was allied with Germany and so at war with Russia. A defeat by the Russians at the Battle of Sarikamish in January, 1915, was blamed on the perfidy of the Armenians in the Turkish army who, like the Russians, were Christian. To counter further disaffection, the Ottoman government withdrew and later shot all Armenian soldiers in their armed forces, expelled prominent Armenians living in Constantinople, and set about the deportation of the entire Armenian population – men, women, children – from its homeland in the north to the Syrian Desert. Walking on foot in columns escorted by paramilitary units, they were given no food or water, and were periodically robbed, raped and killed. Of around a million who set out, only 200,000 survived.

Was this genocide? The word had yet to be invented, and subsequently Turkish historians insisted that the measure was a cruel necessity imposed by the exigencies of war. Was it religious persecution? Islam, as we have seen, taught toleration of the Peoples of the Book, and the perpetrators of the Armenian massacre were not zealous Muslims but members of the Young Turk movement who deposed the Sultan and secularised the state. However, for generations Armenians had suffered for their faith within the Ottoman Empire: as recently as 1909 between fifteen and thirty thousand Armenians had been massacred in Adana. The death-march of 1915-1916 was the culmination of this persecution; and many Christian Assyrians and Greeks suffered the same fate.

If the destruction of Christianity was not the principal motive for the extermination of the Armenians, it was unquestionably an objective of the two ideologies that flourished in the wake of the First World War, both of which saw the Christian churches as rivals, and obstacles to the well-being of mankind. We have come across the seeds of these ideologies in earlier centuries but never since the days of the Jacobin persecution following the French Revolution of 1789 had there been a systematic attempt to eradicate the Catholic religion. Of the two ideologies one, Communism, was able to embark upon such a programme; the other, National Socialism, was obliged to bide its time, but its intentions for the future were not in doubt.

The first to suffer from the atheistic assault were not Catholic priests and religious but those of the Russian Orthodox Church. Under the Tsars, Church and state were entwined. Since the fall of Constantinople to the Ottoman Turks, the Patriarch of Moscow had, in power and authority, replaced that of Constantinople, and the Tsar was seen as the successor to the Byzantine emperors. In the late nineteenth century, Slavophile Russians such as the novelist Fyodor Dostoevsky held a 'fanatical belief in the moral elevation of the Russian spirit, and the Messianic destiny marked out for it in the future... '[681] Russia was not merely Russia but Holy Russia.

Intimately connected with the monarchy, the Russian Orthodox Church became vulnerable after the fall of the Tsar in 1917. Hunger among the urban workers had led to strikes and demonstrations; and reverses in the war against Germany and Austria-Hungary had led to mutinies in the Russian armed forces. In St. Petersburg deserters from the front and mutinous sailors mingled with striking workers, demanding food and an end to the war. Tsar Nicholas II abdicated. The Duma elected a provisional government, and others followed but none was willing to end the war: indeed, under Aleksandr Kerensky, plans were laid to pursue it. To prevent this, or at least to add to the chaos, the German General Ludendorff arranged for a group of Russian Socialist revolutionaries – known as the Bolsheviks (majority) as opposed to the Mensheviks (minority) – under their leader Vladimir Lenin to travel through Germany in a sealed train from Switzerland where they had been in exile. Travelling via Sweden and Finland, they arrived at Petrograd's Finland Station on 16 April, 1917.

Lenin was the revolutionary *nom de guerre* of Vladimir Ilyich Ulyanov, the son of school teachers in the town of Simbirsk. Already immersed in revolutionary politics as a student, iron entered his soul when his older brother Aleksandr was executed for conspiring to assassinate the Tsar. Highly educated, and trained as a lawyer, Lenin accepted as holy scrip the

---

681   Quoted in Joseph Frank, *Dostoevsky. The Miraculous Years. 1865-1871*

works of Marx and Engels, and elaborated upon their theories of proletarian revolution with treatises of his own such *What is to be Done?* This was written in Munich: as a wanted man in Russia, Lenin spent many years in western Europe – in Munich, London and Zurich.

Once back in Russia, Lenin successfully out-manoeuvred the other larger revolutionary parties, renamed his Bolshevik faction the Communist Party in May, 1917, and in October of the same year successfully stormed the Winter Palace in Petrograd and seized power. The Duma was abolished and power vested in workers' councils known as Soviets. The Bolsheviks' trump card was their commitment to pull out of the war, and they were as good as their word. Leon Trotsky, a seasoned Bolshevik, and his friend Adolf Joffe negotiated a treaty with the Germans at Brest-Litovsk. Peace came at a price. Under its terms Russia was deprived of thirty-four percent of its population, fifty-four percent of its industrial undertakings, and eighty-nine percent of its coal. For the Bolsheviks it was a price worth paying because it enabled them to consolidate their power in Russia's heartland and, under Trotsky's ruthless but inspired leadership, form a Red Army to deal with other adversaries – White Russian forces in the east and south of the country (aided by the French and British), and the army of the newly formed nation of Poland. The Whites made no headway but the Polish army swept into the Ukraine, was repulsed and forced back to within sight of Warsaw. Most of the foreign diplomats fled the city: the Vatican's Apostolic Visitor, Cardinal Archille Ratti, remained. So too did the French mission which included a young cavalry officer, Charles de Gaulle. Led by Marshal Pilsudski, the Poles broke the siege and once again drove the Red Army back to the borders of Russia. Devout Polish Catholics called this the 'miracle of the Vistula'.

Given the many and acute problems that faced Lenin and the Bolsheviks, it might have been thought that an assault on Christianity in Russia might have been postponed. 'On the eve of the Bolshevik *coup d'état*, the Orthodox Church claimed a hundred million adherents, two hundred thousand priests and monks, seventy-five thousand churches and chapels, and over eleven hundred monasteries.' Industrial workers may have lost their faith, but the rural population remained believers 'so to strike at the Orthodox Church was not simply a matter of taking on its clerical hierarchy but assaulting the traditional beliefs of much of the population.' Prudence turned out to be no match for ideological zeal. 'Within a few years the institutional structures were swept away, the churches were demolished, vandalised or put to other uses. Many of the clergy were imprisoned or shot; appropriately enough, the first camp of the gulag archipelago was opened in a monastery in Arctic regions.'[682]

In May, 1922, there was an early 'show trial' at which fifty-four parish priests and laymen were sentenced to death. The Petrograd metropolitan Veniamin who protested was secretly shot during the night of 12 August. Relentless propaganda was employed in 'this battle for the people's soul... The aim of Bolshevik propaganda was to replace the worship of God with veneration of the state, to substitute revolutionary icons for religious ones. Communism was the new religion, Lenin and Trotsky its new arch-priests.'[683] In Moscow, the cathedral of Christ the Saviour was dynamited under Stalin, Lenin's successor, with plans to replace it with a Palace of Soviets. 'The new Bolshevik religion arose amid the ruins of the old, but it was never free of its imprint...'[684] A League of Militant Godless was founded in 1925. 'Religious rituals were Bolshevized. Instead of baptisms, children were "Octobered"'

In 1921, famine had been the pretext for the government to appropriate the liturgical vessels in cathedrals and parish churches. Those not required for the Eucharist were willingly surrendered but when even the latter were seized there was popular resistance. When 'armed bands gutted local churches, carrying away the icons and crosses, the chalices and mitres, even the iconostases in bits....angry crowds took up arms to defend their local church... Troops with machine-guns fought against old men and women armed with pitch forks and rusty rifles: 7,100 clergy were killed including 3,500 nuns, but only a handful of Soviet troops. One such clash...prompted Lenin to issue a secret order for the extermination of the clergy...' 'Lenin instigated this totally gratuitous reign of terror' because 'apart from the Academy of Sciences, the Church was the only remaining institution outside the control of the party.' [685]

A further famine between 1932 and 1933 – this time man-made – led to the Holomodor – the effective genocide of the rural population of Ukraine. The Communist 'command economy' could not feed its urban population. Ukraine was the bread basket of Europe, but the peasant farmers, known as the *kulaks*, with no market for their produce, were growing only enough crops

---

682   Michael Burleigh, *Sacred Causes,* p. 40

683   Orland Figes, *A People's Tragedy, The Russian Revolution 1891-1924*

684   Burleigh, *Op. Cit..* p.40

685   Figes, *Op. Cit.* p. 748

to meet their own needs. The Soviet solution was the collective farm but there was overwhelming resistance by the Ukrainian *kulaks* to the amalgamation of individual holdings into state-run enterprises. Christian belief animated this resistance: 'The rural societies of the Soviet Ukraine were still for the most part religious' and 'some believed that Satan had come down to earth in human form as a party activist...'[686] For Poles living in western Ukraine, 'an attachment to Polish culture or Catholicism became evidence of participation in international espionage... People were sentenced to ten years in a prison camp for owning a rosary'.[687] 125,000 Catholic Poles and Lithuanians were deported to Siberia.[688]

It is now estimated that between seven and ten million Ukrainians died in the Holodomor. It was not primarily a religious persecution, but the assault on the Orthodox church accompanied the liquidation of *kulaks*. In Kiev the golden-domed monastery of St. Michael was destroyed. The cathedral of Sancta Sophia was scheduled for demolition, with a park to be built over its ruins, but a body of non-Christian scientists and academics protested and it was retained as a museum.

'Blessed are those who hunger and thirst after righteousness, for they shall be filled' (Matthew, 5:6). The scale of the atrocities committed by the Bolsheviks overwhelm any attempt to see good in what as young idealists they had hoped to achieve. Tsarist Russia, behind the baroque façade, had been a brutal autocracy, imposed by the knout, with no guaranteed liberties and gross inequality. Serfdom had been abolished in 1861, but the bestial bare-foot squalor in which most of the peasants lived was a painful contrast to the leisured existence of the gentry so beautifully portrayed in the great Russian novels of the nineteenth century. These novels also depict the preoccupation of a younger generation with social questions and some, like Turgenev's *Fathers and Sons*, or Dostoevsky's *The Devils*, also give a foretaste of what might happen when, as the Russian philosopher Semyon Frank put it, 'the great love of mankind of the future gives birth to a great hatred for people; the passion for organizing an earthly paradise becomes a passion for destruction'.[689] Even if it is acknowledged that some revolutionaries showed courage and even heroism as they sought to satisfy their hunger and slake

686   Timothy Snyder, *Bloodlands. Europe Between Hitler and Stalin.* p. 29
687   Snyder, *Op. Cit.* p. 36
688   Anthony Rhodes, *Op.. Cit*, p. 18
689   Quoted in Burleigh, *Op. Cit.* p. 39

their thirst for justice, one is struck by how much rage and now little love of mankind there was in the Marxist ideology that inspired them. 'The philosophers have only interpreted the world, in various ways,' wrote Marx. 'The point, however, is to change it'. Attempting to change it turned out to be cruel, messy and ultimately unsuccessful.

What strikes the historian, looking back at the Russian Revolution, is the relative rarity among its leaders of ordinary Russians. Lenin was certainly Russian, born and raised in Simbirsk on the Volga, but by 1917 he had spent much of his adult life abroad. Josef Stalin, who succeeded Lenin, was a Georgian, born Iosif Dzhugashvili; so too Lavrentiy Beria, head of the NKVD and Sergo Ordzhonikidze, the Soviet commissar in the Caucasus. Feliks Dzerzhinsky, the founder of the Bolsheviks' secret police, the Cheka (later the OGPU, NKVD, KGB) was a minor Polish nobleman. A large number of the Bolshevik leaders were secularised Jews – Leon Trotsky, born Bronstein, who fashioned the Red Army into a formidable force; Yakov Sverdlov, who ordered the killing of the Tsar and his family; Lazar Kaganovich, Stalin's brother-in-law, who supervised the demolition of the cathedral of Christ the Saviour; Grigory Zinoviev, born Apfelbaum, member of the Politburo and President of Comintern; Moisei Uritsky, commander of the Petrograd Cheka; Nikolai Yezhov, organizer of Stalin's 'Great Purge' of 1937-38; Genrikh Yagoda, who employed slave-labour to build the canal connecting the river Volga with the White Sea; Naftali Frenkel and Matvei Berman, administrators of the network of prison camps (the gulag); the diplomats Adolph Yoffe, Grigory Sokolnikov, born Brilliant; Maxim Litvinovk, born Wallakh; the Hungarian revolutionary, Bela Kun, born Kohn; and the journalists Karl Radek, born Sobelsohn, and Ilya Ehrenburg – all were Jewish. Lenin, Stalin and Sergei Kirov had Jewish wives.

Some regard the concept of 'Jewish Bolshevism' as an 'anti-Semitic canard'[690] and, because it became a trope of Nazi propaganda, historians have been reluctant give it credence; but there is evidence that the link was made at the time.[691] The British philosopher Bertrand Russell, who spent five weeks in Russia in 1920 with a Labour Party delegation, described the Bolshevik leaders as "an aristocracy of Americanised Jews".[692] 'We dined at the house of a dentist,' wrote Brigadier H.N.H. Williamson, describing his experiences

---

690   See Wikipedia, *Jewish Bolshevism*
691   See H.N.H. Williamson, *Farewell to the Don*
692   Ronald Clark, *The Life of Bertrand Russel*, p. 380. Quoted in Burleigh, *Op. Cit.*, p. 38

during the British intervention to support the White armies in 1919. 'Unlike some of the other houses we had seen, it showed no signs of damage or occupation. "I am a Jew," the dentist explained, "so the Bolsheviks have not worried me".[693]

Russian Jews had good reason to abhor the Tsarist regime. Jews were banned from 'Holy' Russia from the late Middle Ages as they were from England, France and Spain. The Tsars only acquired Jewish subjects when their empire expanded into Ukraine and Poland[694]: it will be remembered that Jews from Germany had been invited to settle in Poland in the fourteenth century by King Casimir. That they became subjects of the Tsar did not mean that they were permitted to live in Russia: they were confined to the border-lands in what became known as The Pale of Settlement in Lithuania, Poland and Ukraine. The prohibition was eased under Catherine the Great; some gained permits to live in Russia and, in a brief period of liberalisation in the nineteenth century, Jewish students were allowed to enrol in Russian universities. However, the belief that Jews were prominent among the Nihilist assassins of Tsar Alexander II led to an anti-Semitic backlash, with men, women and children slaughtered in Cossack pogroms throughout the southern provinces of the Russian empire.

Secularised Jews were therefore drawn to an ideology that transcended the national state: as Bernard Lazare had pointed out at the time of the Dreyfus Affair, 'the Jews are essentially cosmopolitan in character; they are the cosmopolitan element in mankind... and with the aid of their instinct of solidarity, they have remained internationalists.'[695] The loyalty of the Marxist revolutionary was not to a tribe or nation but to the proletariat, a class.

98.   Red Risings in Germany

Rosa Luxemburg who with Karl Liebknecht founded the German Communist Party, was a Polish Jew who had taken German nationality. She and Liebknecht reluctantly joined the Spartacus League (*Spartakusbund*) in January, 1919, in an attempt to emulate the Bolsheviks and seize power in Berlin. The uprising was suppressed by militias made up of former army officers known as the

---

693   H.N.H.Williamson, *Farewell to the Don*, p.100

694   Comparable to Louis XIV of Alsace

695   Bernard Lazare, *Op. Cit.*, p. 108

Freikorps. Both Liebknecht and Luxemburg were taken prisoner: Liebknecht was then shot in the back while Rosa Luxemburg, after being beaten with rifle butts, was also shot and her body thrown into the Landwehr canal.

The failure of the Spartacist rising was a setback for the Communists throughout Europe because Karl Marx, their authority on all things, had predicted that, with the largest and most politically-conscious proletariat, it was in Germany that the revolution would triumph. That it had succeeded in Russia with its largely agricultural economy and predominately peasant population was anomalous; so too the rising, at around the same time as that in Berlin, in Munich, capital of the largely rural, overwhelmingly Catholic and semi-autonomous kingdom of Bavaria.

Ruled by the Wittelsbachs for six centuries, Bavaria had adhered somewhat reluctantly to the Reich after Prussia's victory over the French in 1870. Anti-Prussian sentiment remained strong, but in Munich in particular there was a tolerant, cosmopolitan culture. Writers and artists congregated in Schwabing, a Bohemian district in the north of Munich. The novelists Heinrich and Thomas Mann lived in Munich at the time; so did the poet Rainer Maria Rilke and the painter Wassily Kandinsky. A period of Lenin's exile had been spent in Munich: it was there that he had written *What is to be Done?*

Bavarians had not been exempt from the ravages of the World War and the political chaos that followed the collapse of the western front. In the autumn of 1918, mutinous sailors from Kiel arrived in Munich and, as in Petrograd, mixed with deserters from the army and striking workers. King Ludwig III wisely left the city with his family. On 7 November, 1918, a demonstration for peace organized by the Social Democratic party led to a successful assault on government buildings by a faction on the extreme Left, the Independent Socialists. The leader of the Independent Socialists, Kurt Eisner, was declared minister-president of a People's State of Bavaria. 'Red flags were run up on the twin towers of the Frauenkirche (Church of Our Lady) chief landmark of Munich and premier church of Catholic Bavaria.'[696]

Kurt Eisner, a journalist and political activist who had come from Berlin to Munich in 1905, was a most improbable candidate to govern the Bavarian nation. He suffered from 'the double handicap of a Prussian background and Jewish origins' wrote Richard Grünberger. 'With his beard and broad-rimmed floppy hat he cut an outlandish figure: Old Testament prophet cast adrift in Schwabing... He was with his Prussian accent and Jewish

---

696   Richard Grunberger, *Red Rising in Bavaria*, p.35

appearance, an almost tailor-made hate object'. So too other leaders of the Independent Socialists such as the poet Ernst Toller, and Gustave Landauer, whose'patriarchal beard and searching rabbi's eyes gave him an Old Testament prophet's aspect...They were in fact – to use a phrase that soon acquired odious connotations, "Jewish literati".[697]

Elections were held in April, 1919, and Eisner's Independent Socialists came almost bottom of the list with 2.5% of the vote. On 21 February, 1919, as he walked to the *Landtag* to present his resignation, Eisner was shot by a right-wing fanatic, Count Anton von Arco-Valley.[698] Arco-Valley was shot in turn but survived. Subsequent investigations turned up a diary in which he had written of Eisner 'he is a Bolshevik. He is a Jew, not a German'. A hundred thousand mourners turned out for Eisner's funeral. In his eulogy the writer Gustav Landauer eulogized this champion of the poor and down-trodden: 'Kurt Eisner, the Jew, was a prophet who mercilessly fought small minded wretched men because he loved mankind.... He was one like Jesus, like Hus...who were killed by stupidity and greed'.[699]

In death, the martyred Eisner was more popular than he had been in life: violent demonstrations followed his assassination. A Bavarian government was formed by Johannes Hoffman, the leader of the Social Democratic faction in the *Landtag*. In early April, the success of a Communist uprising in Budapest incited the poet Ernest Toller, the playwright Eric Mühsam and Gustav Landauer to oust the Hoffman government in Munich and proclaim a Soviet Republic with Toller as its head of state. Whether the Independent Socialists should take part in parliamentary politics had been a matter of debate: Eisner before his death had inclined more and more to the idea of workers' councils – the equivalent of the Russian Soviets – seizing power. The *Landtag* was now consigned to the dustbin of history but, only six days after Toller had established his government, it was ousted by the Communists led by Eugen Leviné. Endorsed by Lenin, and keen to emulate the Bolsheviks, Leviné issued edicts expropriating the money, food and flats of the bourgeoisie. Members of the Bavarian nobility and upper classes were taken hostage to deter a White reaction: the Catholic Archbishop of Munich, Cardinal Faulhaber, was considered as a candidate for abduction but was rejected for fear of antagonising his flock. A Red Army was recruited from

---

697   Grunberger, *Op. Cit.* p. 60

698   a member of the same family as the wife of the historian Lord Acton.

699   *Ibid.*, p.83

factory workers and a Catholic church was made into a revolutionary temple dedicated to the Goddess of Reason.[700]

A little more than a week after coming into existence, on 18 April, the Soviet regime in Munich came under attack from forces of the Social Democrat government of Johannes Hoffman established in the city of Bamberg. Hoffman had called upon Lieutenant General Burghard von Oven who commanded a *Freicorps* force of twenty thousand men, to join him in the suppression of Leviné's Soviet state. Aware that these 'White Guards of Capitalism' would pose a more serious threat, Leviné ordered further hostages to be taken. A unit of the Red Army broke into the offices of the right-wing Thule Society in the Four Seasons Hotel and arrested the society's secretary, Countess Hella von Westarp, and six others, among them Prince Gustav of Thurn and Taxis, Lieutenant von Sydlitz and a Professor Burger. On 30 April, as the *Freicorps* advanced on Munich, the hostages were shot.

On 1 May, using armoured cars, artillery and flame-throwers Von Oven's *Freicorps*s, together with volunteers from the countryside wearing *lederhosen*, moved into the city. An exchange of fire took place around the residence of the Papal Nuncio: 'At one point Red guards entered the building itself which, under international law, constituted foreign territory; when the nuncio, Cardinal Eugenio Pacelli, protested at the trespass a Red soldier threatened him with a revolver'.[701] It was an experience that the papal diplomat was not to forget.

By 6 May the short-lived Bavarian Soviet Republic had come to an end. More than six hundred people were killed in the conflict, half of them civilians. This was small beer when compared to the reprisals taken by the *Freikorps*. Gustav Landauer was shot out of hand: Leviné was charged with treason, found guilty and executed by a firing squad in the Stadelheim Prison. The lives of the anarchist *literati* were spared after the intervention by fellow authors: the poet Eric Mühsam was sentenced to fifteen years in prison but Toller to only five.

What was described by Cardinal Pacelli as the 'bestial hostage murder' of eminent Bavarians by soldiers of the Red Army was made a pretext for disproportionate retribution: it is thought that between 1,000 and 1,200 Communists and Anarchists shared the fate of Landauer and Leviné. This revenge was popular: the *Müncheners* were relieved that the weeks of

---

700   *Ibid.,* p. 121

701   *Ibid.,* p. 141

Communist rule – the *Schreckensherrschaft*, the rule of horror – had come to an end, and thereafter their city became a haven for right-wing extremists.

Among them was a thirty-year-old corporal from Linz in Austria, Adolf Hitler – twice the recipient of the Iron Cross and wounded in the last days before the armistice. Recently released from hospital and still in uniform, he had been in Munich throughout the tumultuous days of the Red republic. Already an anti-Semite, he believed that the war would have been won had it not been for a 'stab in the back' by Socialists, Communists and Jews – a theory seemingly confirmed by the fact that the leaders of the Bavarian Soviet Republic – Eisner, Lindauer, Leviné, Mühsam, Toller – were all Jews.

99.   The Revenge of Jan Hus

One of the objectives of Pope Benedict XV's diplomatic initiatives during the Great War was the preservation of the Austro-Hungarian Empire, the only great power that remained Catholic. There was reason to be believe that, even in the event of an Allied victory, it might survive: 'the dissolution of the Dual Monarchy was not envisaged when the war began: it was not even precisely specified in (President Wilson's) Fourteen Points'.[702] Prominent among the Fourteen Points, however, was the principle of self-determination which the French and British accepted at Versailles though they had no intention of applying it to the inhabitants of their imperial possessions: only when it came to Europe did these imperial powers find no reason to object.

The settlement made at the Treaty of Versailles has been criticised for many reasons, not least for sowing the seeds of the Second World War by its apparently vengeful treatment of the Germans. The vengefulness came principally from the French leader, Clemenceau. The final bill for reparations, issued in May 1921, was $34 billion – less than Germany had imposed upon the Russians at Brest-Litovsk but ten times the tribute she imposed on France in 1871.

In retrospect, it can be seen as mistaken for the allies to negotiate with the shaky socialist government in Berlin and so let those who had led Germany into the war off the hook. 'Versailles should have been signed by plenipotentiaries representing Ludendorff rather than the shadowy creatures representing Ebert who stood for nothing real in Germany at all'. The German

---

702   L.C.B.Seaman, *Op. Cit.* p.200

High Command that had created the catastrophe 'survived undefeated in their hour of defeat'[703] – free to propagate the theory that Germany's defeat was caused by a 'stab in the back'.

The liberation movements of the Slav, Serb and other minorities within the Austro-Hungarian empire, which had been lobbying for statehood among the allies during the war, now successfully used President Wilson's principle of self-determination to establish new nations – a greater Serbia, now named Jugoslavia (the land of the south Slavs) and Czechoslovakia, formed by the provinces of Bohemia, Moravia and Slovakia. Austria and Hungary were reduced to rump states – Austria with a mere six million inhabitants and few natural resources. Lloyd George may have known little about Eastern Europe, and President Wilson even less, but 'the cause of peace and justice was served in eastern Europe by the treaties, and better served than they had been for centuries.'[704]

Among the great powers, the apparent beneficiary of this new arrangement in Eastern Europe was France. The Treaty of Versailles was described by some doubters as 'Clemenceau's peace' 'for no map of Europe save that drawn by Napoleon I had ever been more clearly marked 'made in France'. By 1927 France had made alliances with all the new Slav states; but it would soon become clear that the new settlement would only survive if France remained strong enough to maintain it.

The Czechs in particular modelled their new nation on France, but it was the France of Emile Combes, not Saint Louis. The president and prime-minister of the new nation, Tomas Masaryk and Edvard Benes, who were free-thinkers, introduced into their new state the same anti-clerical laws which had been in force in France between 1904 and 1925. The two men, 'wrote Anthony Rhodes, 'had good cause for disliking the Vatican. During the three hundred years since the Battle of the White Mountain which had obliterated their state, the Habsburgs had ingeniously used the Catholic Church to keep the Czechs in bondage.'[705] Prague, the capital of Bohemia, had fine baroque buildings but they were the work of Austrian and Italian architects. Now, finally, the Czechs were free of the Habsburgs and the Church. 'We have got rid of Vienna,' said Masaryk, 'Now we will get rid of Rome!' In 1925, once the laws separating the state from the Catholic Church had been passed, Masaryk

---

703   *Ibid.* p. 196

704   *Ibid.* p. 201

705   Anthony Rhodes, *The Vatican in the Age of the Dictators. 1922-1945,*

re-established a National Hussite Church, and a statue of the Bohemian theologian who had been burned as a heretic at the Council of Constance was erected in Prague's Old Town square.

This bizarre endeavour was more successful than might have been expected: some Catholic priests, 'intoxicated like everyone else with the new independence', said mass in the vernacular and took wives. A new law stated that where more than half the population of a village was Hussite, the church should be given over to the Hussites. By the end of 1925, there were 150 of such parishes, and around 200,000 members of the Hussite church.

In 1927, however, there was a schism in the Hussite Church and reaction against this Hussification by the devout Catholics among the rural population, particularly in Slovakia. They established a political party, the Christian Socials, and when in 1926 the anti-clerical coalition that had governed Czechoslovakia since its inception collapsed, Benes had to choose between an alliance with the Sudeten Germans, a third of the population, or the Christian Socials. Since the former felt no loyalty to the Czech state, openly stating that they wished to be part of Germany, he had no alternative but to turn to the Christian Socials. For this there had to be rapprochement with the Vatican. Benes went to Rome. It was agreed that Church property should be restored and the right to appoint bishops be reserved to the pope. Diplomatic relations which had been ruptured were now restored. 'The controversy over Jan Hus,' the papal Secretary of State, Cardinal Gaspari, told the British ambassador to the Vatican, Sir Odo Russell, 'has been relegated to oblivion where it always belonged.'[706]

100. The Mexican Revolution

Even while the Church in Czechoslovakia suffered from the measures taken by Masaryk and Benes, a far more drastic persecution of Catholics was underway on the other side of the world. The eruption took place in Mexico, a nation formed after the collapse of the Spanish empire in the early nineteenth century. The Church, established by the missionaries who had accompanied the *conquistadors*, had by the nineteenth century acquired a wealth and influence of which, wrote Lord Acton, ' there has been no example in Europe for the last five hundred years...' The evangelical fervour of the missionaries

---

706   *Ibid.* p. 93

had long since degenerated into a parasitic and self-serving grip over the peasant population. Priests demanded large fees for their services such as marriage. 'The peon had no idea of civil marriage...so he took a wife and begot children without the sanction of the Church', hoping in due course 'to save enough money to pay the priests and thus obtain legitimisation of his wife and children'.[707]

It is estimated that as late as 1870, a quarter of Mexican landholdings was owned by the Church. Its wealth and power were resented by the educated classes, among them Freemasons and Positivist sceptics who, emulating the Combes government in France, inserted anti-clerical clauses in the constitutions of 1854 and 1917. The Jesuits were expelled; so too priests from Spain. Churches, monasteries and convents were declared the property of the state, together with Catholic schools, orphanages and hospitals. Processions were banned.

At first, these statutes were largely ignored but in 1926 a new President was elected, Plutarcho Calles – a zealous anti-clerical who 'saw red at the very mention of a priest'. Ninety-two churches, seventy-two convents and 129 Catholic colleges were closed, and 185 Spanish priests deported. The Vatican retaliated by ordering the Mexican clergy to go on strike: the churches, now the property of the state, were silent and empty. There were no baptisms or marriages, confessions or confirmations. A new National League for the Defence of Religious Liberty organised a mass boycott of the economy which effectively denied tax revenues to the government and paralysed commerce.

These acts of defiance developed into open revolt. A rebel army was formed, the Cristeros, rallying to the cry of *Viva Cristo Rey* and *Viva la Virgen, Reina de Mexico.* Convoys were ambushed and trains derailed: the government lost control of whole provinces in the west of the country. Between January and May, 1928, two generals, 324 officers and 2892 soldiers were killed by the Cristeros who in turn lost 48 of their leaders and 6148 of their men. There were atrocities on both sides. At Toluca a young priest was nailed to a cross, soaked in petrol and burned alive. In Mexico City, seven priests were taken to a cemetery and shot. A distinguished Jesuit, Father Pro, was shot without trial. Before the war, there were 4,500 priests dispersed throughout Mexico; by 1934 a mere 334 were licensed by the government to serve a nation of fifteen million. 'The rest had been eliminated by emigration, expulsion and assassination. By 1935, seventeen states had no priests at all'.[708]

---

707   Anthony Rhodes, *Op. Cit.*, p.95

708   *See Brian* Von Hove, *Blood*-Drenched Altars (Wikipedia)

Atrocities were also committed by the Cristeros. In the town of Paras de la Fuente, the Socialist mayor was killed by 'fifty Cristeros shouting "Long Live Christ the King"'... On 20 April, 1927...three hundred Cristeros derailed the Mexico City – Guadalajara express and murdered fifty travellers, among them women and children, before setting fire to the coaches. A particular hatred of the Cristeros were lay school-mistresses who in obedience to the clause in the constitution that 'the education imparted by the State shall be a socialist one', and that they should imbue in their pupils 'an exact and rational concept of the Universe and of social life', taught not just socialism but sex education. The assaults of these progressive young women continued after the Cristero rebellion had come to an end: it is thought that around 400 rural teachers were killed between 1935 and 1939, some after their ears had been cut off.[709]

Lord Acton had compared the power and wealth of the Catholic Church in Mexico to that it had enjoyed in the Middle Ages. A better analogy is perhaps the condition of the Church in France prior to the French Revolution of 1789. It was then rich and corrupt, and after 1789 suffered a persecution that led to a civil war. The difference was the reluctance of other nations to criticise what went on. In the last decades of the eighteenth century, a number of nations condemned the measures taken by the French revolutionaries; in the 1920s and 1930s, the pope – now Pius XI – called for condemnation of what was taking place in Mexico. Some other South American states responded, but 'the reaction of the European powers was different. They did nothing.'[710] Afraid that the Socialist Calles might move on from expropriating the property of the Church to confiscating that of foreign investors, they decided that it would be wise not to intervene in Mexico's internal affairs. Even Spain, humiliated by the expulsion of its priests, restricted itself to a mild note to the Mexican government asking that the religious susceptibilities of its citizens in Mexico should be taken into consideration.

In 1927, the persecution abated not because of the intervention of European powers, but thanks to the commercial clout of the United States. Encouraged by the success of the measures taken against the Church, Calles drew up plans to nationalise land owned by foreigners without compensation – land, and what lay beneath it. 'To nothing do Americans react more sharply than to anything connected with oil.'[711] The US President Hoover appointed

709 Antony Rhodes, *Op. Cit.*, p.99
710 *Ibid.* p. 100
711 *Ibid.*, p. 102

a banker, Mr. Dwight Morrow, as ambassador to Mexico who threatened Calles with sanctions if he did not back down. Backing down meant not just protecting American interests but ending the religious persecution. The Archbishop of Mexico City was to be allowed to return from exile. Priests were to be appointed by their bishops, not the state; and religious education allowed in premises belonging to the Church. The persecution eased. In Mexico, Mammon had saved the Catholic Church.

101.   The Spanish Civil War

From the reign of *los reyes catolicos* Ferdinand and Isabella in the sixteenth century, Spain had been the most steadfast champion of the Catholic Church. The expulsion of Jews and Moors, the use of the Holy Inquisition to weed out Protestants and insincere *conversos*, the founding of the elite religious order, the Society of Jesus, by the Basque Ignatius Loyola, and the deployment of Spanish troops against Protestant princes in Germany, Bohemia and the Netherlands, was responsible for the success of the Counter-Reformation in much of Europe, and the establishment of Catholicism as the sole religion in Spain's many dominions overseas.

The Spanish empire collapsed in the course of the nineteenth century, as Spain's South American provinces, aided by the British, established their independence – a process ending with the direct intervention of the second Anglo-Saxon power, the United States of America, in the Spanish-American war of 1898, and the loss to that Protestant power of Cuba, Puerto Rico, Guam and the Philippines. One remaining possession was Spanish Morocco but even that was hard to hold, with a fierce war against an uprising in the Riff from 1921-1926. Spain had to sustain a large army of occupation which developed its own *esprit de corps*, and whose triumphs and setbacks had repercussions in the mother country on the other side of the straights of Gibraltar.

Spain had remained neutral during World War I, but suffered economically as a result of the Great Depression of 1929. Municipal elections in April, 1931, returned a majority of republicans and King Alfonso XIII fled the country. A republic was declared and a government which included five freemasons was formed by the socialist Manuel Azaña. 'True to its socialist principles, the new government immediately introduced legislation on the separation of Church and State...on the well-tried French model. The Jesuits were, as usual, expelled first and their property confiscated. Azaña…made the momentous statement in Parliament, 'And with these measures Spain ceases to be Catholic'.[712]

As with Benes in Czechoslovakia, Azaña was following the example of the anti-clerical Emile Combes in France, and had popular support for his anti-clerical laws. 'Two thirds of the Spaniards in the 1930s were…not practising Catholics – that is, though they might use churches for baptisms, weddings, and funerals, they never confessed or went to mass'. 'Within a matter of days after the promulgation of the anticlerical laws, they had become the excuse for unbridled plundering and destruction …of churches, monasteries and convents all over Spain'.[713]

Nevertheless, the Church in Spain remained a substantial presence with around '20,000 monks, 60,000 nuns and 35,000 priests. There were nearly 5,000 religious communities of which about 1.000 were monasteries, the rest convents.'[714] Nor were Spain's bishops prepared to concede that their nation was lost to the Catholic religion. The formidable Cardinal Segura, Cardinal Archbishop of Toledo and primate of Spain, rallied the faithful with a call to 'fight like intrepid warriors' those 'attempting to destroy religion'.

Unrest among the working classes was not unique to Spain: what was exceptional was the spread among the discontented workers of the ideas not of Karl Marx but the Russian anarchist Mikkail Alexandrovich Bakunin. 'Throughout the south of Spain…during the eighties, nineties and the first ten years of the twentieth century, anarchism continued to spread as if it were a new religion.'[715] 'By 1873 there were 50,000 Bakuninists in Spain, at first known as "internationals", and later by the more accurate name of anarchists.'

The differences between Bakunin and Marx, which led the latter to see the former expelled from the Second International, was about how revolution should be achieved and what should follow. With a measure of prescience, Bakunin predicted that the 'dictatorship of the proletariat' as proposed by Marx would merely replace one authoritarian regime with another. He condemned all government. Workers and peasants must be free to form small voluntary self-governing communities which would combine and cooperate only if they so chose. 'When we speak of justice…we mean that justice which is based solely on the conscience of mankind… This justice

---

712   *Ibid.*, p. 116

713   Anthony Rhodes, *Op. Cit.* p. 116

714   Hugh Thomas, *The Spanish Civil War*, p. 47

715   Hugh Thomas, *Op. Cit.* p. 60

-406-

which is universal has, thanks to the abuse of force and religious influences, never yet prevailed…'[716]

Like Jean-Jacques Rousseau, Bakunin rejected the idea of original sin, and condemned the Church which, with its claim to unique knowledge and authority, controlled its gullible flock with on the one hand the possibility of damnation, and on the other a recompense for its present wretched condition in this world with paradise in a world to come. The Church sustained the tyrannical power of the state just as the state in turn protected the Church. Both must be obliterated, and actions were more eloquent than words. Traces of the nihilism of the Russian terrorist Sergey Nechayev, with whom Bakunin had once worked, are found in his passion for destruction.

The considerable physical presence of the Catholic Church in Spain – the churches, monasteries, convents and shrines – made it vulnerable to the anarchists' rampages and, despite the decline in the numbers of the devout, Catholicism remained embedded in the customs and traditions of the people. Processions, which the government now sought to licence, as well as fiestas formed the cycle of daily life. The party that had supported the Catholic and conservative Infante Carlos during the civil wars in the nineteenth century remained considerable. 'There was nothing fraudulent about the Carlists' religious, semi-mystical hostility to the modern world (especially liberalism and the French revolution) and their fervent loyalty towards *Dios, Patria* and *Rey*. Yet, while the anarchists thought that a pistol and encyclopaedia would give them a new world, the Carlists put similar faith in a machine-gun and a missal'.[717]

Many army officers, and the families from which they came, considered Catholicism to be part of their national identity, and so to be anti-Catholic was to be 'anti-Spain'. The officer corps was substantial – 17,000 for around 150,000 men – and it had its own ethos: 'Many Spanish officers saw in their own traditions a certain idea of a timeless, supremely Castilian Spain, without politics, creating order and banishing all things non-Spanish (by which they understood separatism, socialism, freemasonry, communism and anarchism)'.[718] Thus, when there was a 'red' rising in Asturias in 1934, with thirty thousand miners taking up arms, it was the army that was called

---

716   Michael Bakunin, *Oeuvres*, I, p54-55. Quoted in Herbert Read, *Anarchy and Order,* p. 43
717   Hugh Thomas, *Op. Cit.* p,. 95
718   *Ibid.*, p. 91

in by the republican government in Madrid to suppress it – not conscripts whose loyalties could not be assured, but the Foreign Legion from Morocco, directed by the then joint chief of staff, General Francisco Franco.

New elections to the Cortes were held in February, 1936. In Moscow Comintern – the Third Communist International in Moscow founded by Lenin to spread Communism throughout the world – instructed the Spanish Communist Party to combine with other Left Wing parties to form an electoral coalition, the Popular Front. Voting in the February elections saw a collapse of the centre, and an increase in the share of the vote for the two extremist parties, the Popular Front on the Left and the National Front on the right, with the Popular Front ahead by a single percentage point. The Catholic bishops had decared that to vote for the Popular Front was a sin, but this failed to affect the outcome: 'the Left had won an unexpected victory; and the... CEDA (the Catholic party) an unexpected defeat. The centre had won a mere 5.4% of the vote. When it came to the allocation of seats in the Cortes, 'the Left had a majority of seats, reflecting a definite if slender majority of votes cast'.[719]

When it became clear that the Popular Front was victorious, its supporters took to the streets to celebrate, demanding an immediate amnesty for all those imprisoned as result of the rising in Asturias two years before. In Oviedo, the crowd itself opened the prisons, while in Madrid the Prime Minister Azaña signed a decree freeing all political prisoners, including anarchists, socialists, communists, the leader of the Catalan separatists and common criminals mingling with the euphoric political militants. Now was the time for revenge and revolution. 'From the moment of the election onwards, a trail of murder and arson spread across the face of the country.'[720] On 21 May the Socialists in Madrid agreed to a seizure of power by the working class 'by whatever means possible', leading to a 'dictatorship of the proletariat'. Beyond the collectivisation of property, there was to be ' free love, without more regulation than the will of the man and the woman... At the same time, through a good sexual education beginning at school, eugenic selection would be inculcated, in order to produce healthy and beautiful children'.[721]

---

719   *Ibid..* p.148
720   *Ibid.,* p. 153
721   *Ibid.,* p. 173

Thus the mid-summer of 1936, wrote the historian Hugh Thomas, 'saw the culmination of a hundred and fifty years of passionate quarrels in Spain... Now the old masters of economic power, led by the army and generally supported by the church, that embodiment of Spain's past glory, believed that they were about to be overwhelmed.' On Monday 13 July a monarchist member of the Cortes, Calvo Sotelo, was arrested by members of the Civil Guard, and then shot in the back of the police truck by the bodyguard of the socialist leader, Indalecio Prieto. This triggered the rising already planned by officers in the army's high command led by Generals José Sanjurgo and Emilio Mola. Francisco Franco, the third member of the *junta,* had only latterly been persuaded to join the conspiracy. Now commander-in-chief in Morocco, he had been despatched by the Minister of Defence to Las Palmas on the Canary Islands, but on 14 July flew back to Morocco in an aeroplane chartered from Croydon airport in Britain.

On 18 July, Franco issued a manifesto denouncing the 'foreign influences' on the republican government, and promising a 'new order'. Much admired by his fellow officers, he quickly secured Morocco for the nationalists. The coup was also successful in a number of military districts in mainland Spain, but by no means in all: many officers and military units remained loyal to the republic. A swathe of towns in the north of the country from Galicia to the Pyrenees fell to the nationalists led by General Mola, but not the Basque region or cities like Oviedo and Santander. In the south, Cadiz and Seville were taken by the nationalists, which enabled units of the elite forces stationed in Morocco, including the Muslim *regulares*, to cross to the mainland. Madrid, Barcelona and Valencia remained in the hands of the republic, and in Toledo the rebels held only the *alcazar.*

General Franco, in his manifesto, had said nothing about the destruction of churches: 'the rebellion as yet had not formally become a crusade'[722]; but when the extent of the military uprising became apparent, and the execution of those who opposed it became known, it was on the Church that the enraged socialists and anarchists took their revenge. 'Throughout republican Spain, but particularly in Andalusia, Aragon, Madrid and Catalonia, churches and convents were indiscriminately burned and despoiled' even though 'practically nowhere had the church taken part in the rising'. In Valencia, eleven churches and the archbishop's palace were destroyed. 'Almost all the

---

722   *Ibid.*, p. 207

fifty-eight churches in Barcelona save the cathedral were burned. Some were ruined, others, such as the lovely Santa Maria del Mar, merely damaged. Much petrol was wasted in an attempt to burn Gaudi's unfinished *Sagrada Familia* which was, alas, made of cement'.[723] In Madrid, during the night of 19-20 July, fifty churches were set on fire.

These attacks were accompanied by an onslaught on members of the clergy and the bourgeoisie. 'Admit that God does not exist and that you priests are hypocrites who deceive the people': such questions were put in countless towns and villages of republican Spain. 'At no time in the history of Europe, or even perhaps the world, had so passionate a hatred of religion and all its works been shown.' The word 'God' was abolished and anyone pronouncing "*Adios*" in the street was liable to be stopped, and told say '*Salud*' because there is no God.'[724] A credible tally of Catholic religious killed, mainly in the early days of the Spanish Civil War, is 6,832, among them 12 bishops, 283 nuns, 4,184 priests and 2,365 monks.[725] Comparable atrocities were committed by the Nationalists; schoolmasters were shot and *casas del pueblo* burned down. However, the killing of so many religious inevitably led Spanish Catholics to support the Nationalists, and the Nationalists to enlist the support the Church: 'Franco began to speak of God and the church in the same reverent tone which had until then been reserved for regiments and barracks'.[726]

As the war progressed, the pro-Nationalist rhetoric of Spanish Catholics grew more vehement: 'No pardon for criminal destroyers of churches and murderers of holy priests and ministers,' a priest told his congregation in Burgos: 'Let their seed be stamped out – the evil seed – the seed of the Devil. For verily the sons of Beelzebub are also the enemies of God!'[727] When the republicans at last entered Cordova, which had been defended by some 300 Carlists against the Republicans 2,000, they found this slogan scrawled on the wall: "When you kill a "red", you will spend a year less in purgatory".'[728]

An exception to this pattern of mutual hatred between Catholics and Republicans was found among the Basques who remained devout Catholics but, in pursuit of independence, allied themselves with the Republicans

723   *Ibid.* p. 286

724   Anthony Rhodes, *Op. Cit.* p. 125

725   Hugh Thomas, *Op.Cit.*, p. 259

726   *Ibid.*, p. 274

727   Quoted in *Ibid.*, p. 496

728   *Ibid.*, p. 794

against the Nationalists. They were supported by their priests whose calling did not protect them when the Nationalists finally triumphed: 'priests were shot precipitously without trial, and without coffins, funeral services or official registration.'

The Spanish Civil War lasted from 1936 to 1939 and, while the outcome was often in the balance, ended with the victory of the Nationalists under the undisputed leadership of their *caudillo*, Francisco Franco. Franco's ability to hold together a coalition of royalists, Carlists and fascists – the *falange* – suggests a political acumen as well as soldierly skills. Although initially half the Spanish army remained loyal to the republic, Franco had had at his disposal the elite units from Morocco with their experience of conflict and *esprit de corps*. There were also the *regulares*: it was an irony that when the Cardinal Archbishop of Toledo, Isidro Goma, returned to his cathedral, he was escorted by Muslim troops.

The Nationalist forces were also reinforced by an increasing number of 'volunteers' sent from Italy by Mussolini and from Germany by Hitler – with machine-guns, tanks and aeroplanes. In France, which also had a Popular Front government under Leon Blum, the impulse to help their republican comrades was stymied by the fear of the British government that any intervention would precipitate a war. Non-intervention therefore became the policy of the French and British, but they were unable to prevent volunteers travelling to Spain to form an International Brigade fighting for the Republic. So too the Soviets who, though paying lip service to the policy of non-intervention, shipped arms and aircraft from ports on the Black Sea to Barcelona and Valencia, together with a large contingent of military personnel.

In western Europe, an admiring cult arose around those who fought in Spain for the International Brigade. Authors such as André Malraux, Ernest Hemingway and George Orwell sent back despatches, and wrote novels, that portrayed the conflict as one between good and evil – the good being the republican cause. Despite the atrocities perpetrated on their co-religionists, Catholic authors in France such as Georges Bernanos, François Mauriac and Jacques Maritain supported the Republicans. Some of those in the International Brigade were Communists, but others – and their supporters in their home countries – saw the uprising as an assault on parliamentary democracy, and it was sometimes tricky for Republican propagandists to match 'one picture, for foreigners, [which] depicted constitutional democracy struggling against international fascism' and another 'for consumption at home, [which] showed the Spanish people at one pace only from a new world.'[729]

The aid sent by Stalin, together with the success of the Bolshevik Revolution, enhanced the prestige and in due course the power of the Spanish Communist Party. 'Usually a red flag, decorated with a hammer and sickle, would be hung outside the town hall, indicating the magnetic attraction of Russia to all the proletarian parties not only the communists.'[730] Many of these admirers of the Bolsheviks were Bakuninites and, even among the Spanish Communists, there were divisions: the *Partido Obrero de Unificación Marxista* – the POUM – had a Trotskyist leadership and was anathematized by Stalin. It was the 'propaganda and tactical skill of its leaders that were the chief reasons for Communist successes': many joined the Party between July and December 1936 'without reading much Marx or knowing much about Russia, in the hope of finding protection against anarchism and lawlessness.'[731] As the war progressed, the Communists formed their own secret police, and established their own prisons where their enemies were confined in cells in which they were unable to stand up, tortured and shot – enemies less likely to be Nationalist spies or fifth columnists than members of POUM.

102.   Pope Pius XI

If Spanish Catholics had come to support Franco, and to accept his evolution over the course of the Civil War from a military *caudillo* to a fascist dictator, the same was not true of the pope in Rome. The Spanish church in the twentieth century had embarrassed the Vatican and 'on three occasions during the civil war, Franco had attempted to obtain recognition of his regime, and on three occasions it was refused'. It was only on 28 August, 1937, 'that the Vatican formally recognized the "Burgos authorities" …as the official government of Spain.'[732]

The reigning pope at the time was Achille Ratti, Pius XI, who had been chosen after a long dead-lock in the consistory following the sudden death

---

729   *Ibid.*, p. 525
730   *Ibid.*, p. 290
731   *Ibid.*, p. 628
732   *Ibid.* p. 676

of Benedict XV in 1922. Ratti's *curriculum vitae* had not suggested that he was *papabile*. He was born in Desio in the province of Milan where his father managed a silk factory. Desio was close to the Alps, and Ratti became an enthusiastic mountaineer. He was academically precocious and, after short spell teaching in a seminary following his ordination, he became a librarian – first in the Ambrosiana Library in Milan, then in the Vatican Library in Rome. He was an expert in mediaeval palaeography and taught theology, but the first forty-five years of his career were spent almost entirely in libraries and teaching theology.

Then, in 1918, for no apparent reason other than that he spoke fluent German and French, Ratti was plucked out of his scholarly retreat by Benedict XV and sent to Warsaw as papal nuncio to the new Polish state. As the Red Army approached Warsaw in August,1920, Ratti was one of the few diplomats to remain in the city. The experience impressed upon him Europe's vulnerability to Bolshevik communism. Warsaw, as we have seen, was saved by the 'Miracle on the Vistula' but it might have been otherwise.

On his return to Italy in 1921, Ratti was made a cardinal and appointed to the archiepiscopal see of Milan. Only a year later came the death of Benedict XV and the election of Ratti, on the fourteenth ballot, as pope Pius XI. He ascended the throne of Saint Peter 'faced with one of the most turbulent periods in this history of the Church since the Reformation'[733]. There was political instability throughout Europe with an antipathy towards Catholicism found in most parties on the Left. Italy still had a king, but there was little support for parliamentary democracy with Communist agitators on the Left, and on the Right flamboyant demagogues such as Gabriele d'Annunzio.

Pius XI had misgivings about parliamentary democracy with governments often in coalition with minor parties of anti-clerical liberals who sabotaged attempts to reach an accommodation with the Church. Moreover, the pope himself was an autocrat – in his role as supreme pontiff but also by temperament: 'after he became pope, there was only one word on every tongue, *oboedire*, obey'. [734] His Secretary of State, Cardinal Gaspari, also 'loathed parliamentary parties', even Catholic parliamentary parties, and concurred with Pius's view that the interests of the Church were better protected by concordats – treaties – with established governments rather than by supporting Catholic parties such as the Centre party in Germany, CEDA in Spain, or the Popolare in Italy.

---

733   Anthony Rhodes, *Op.Cit*

734   *Ibid.*, p. 19

The model was Pius VI's concordat with Napoleon I which, though now abrogated, had protected the Church in France for most of the nineteenth century. From Pius XI's first year as pope a series of Concordats were concluded, to secure freedom of action for the Church in Europe: Latvia in 1922, Bavaria in March 1924, Poland in 1925, Romania in May 1927, Lithuania in September 1927, Prussia and Italy in 1929, Baden in October 1932, Germany in 1933 and Yugoslavia in 1935. 'Behind all of them was a concern not merely to secure Catholic education, unhampered papal appointment of bishops and free communications with Rome, but to halt as far as was possible the secularising of European life which the popes had been resisting under the title 'liberalism' for more than a century'.[735]

The Concordats with Italy and Germany were the most significant. In Italy, there had been a gradual easing of the papacy's implacable hostility towards the state. Catholics had been permitted to take part in Italian politics, forming the *Popolare* party led by a Sicilian priest, Don Sturzo; and the bricked-up entrance to the balcony on Saint Peter's basilica had been opened to enable Pius XI on his accession to give his blessing *Urbi et Orbi*, the first pope to do so since 1870. He also authorised negotiations for a resolution of 'the Roman question' with the fascist government that had come to power after a *coup* in 1921. Fascism, named after the symbol from Roman antiquity of a pike bound by rods signifying strength through unity, was – and remains – a label attached almost any non-Communist authoritarian form of government – for example that of Franco in Spain – but its roots were in fact in socialism. Benito Mussolini, the leader of the Italian fascists and, after 1921 the despotic ruler of Italy, was originally a socialist and 'from his father…had learned to be a thoroughgoing anti-clerical'. He had described Jesus 'as an ignorant Jew whose family thought him mad, and who was a pigmy when compared to the Buddha. Religion, he said, was a disease of the psyche, an epidemic to be cured by psychiatrists, and Christianity in particular was vitiated by the preaching of the senseless virtues of resignation and of cowardice'.[736]

By 1921, Mussolini's anti-clerical views had been modified when he realised that he would need the support of Catholics to take power. 'Mussolini saw it as vital to gratify and disarm the Vatican, firstly because Italians were overwhelmingly Catholic, secondly because with the Pope's help he could

---

735   Eamon Duffy, *Saints and Sinners*, p. 338-339

736   Denis Mack Smith, *Mussolini*, p. 8

eliminate – or at least divide – the Catholic *Popolari*, the second largest party in parliament... He tried to create the impression that he was a profoundly religious man' [737] and 'began to advocate that the government should subsidise churches and religious schools'.[738]

Few Italian Catholics were taken in by his conversion but many 'were frightened of socialist talk of revolution and were ready to look on Mussolini as a lesser evil.' So too the Vatican, and after three years of difficult negotiations, a treaty was signed with Mussolini's fascist government that finally solved the Roman question. It established a sovereign papal state of just over a hundred acres around Saint Peter's basilica on the Vatican hill. The pope also had jurisdiction over Rome's major basilicas and his summer residence, Castel Gandolfo. This Vatican city state had its own radio station and post office, ensuring its freedom of communication with the wider world. And under the treaty some of the anti-clerical legislation in Italy was repealed. Marriages were once again subject to Canon Law, crucifixes returned to the walls of state schools, and religious instruction to the curriculum. Finally it was agreed that 1,750,000,000 lire would be paid in compensation for the sequestration of the papal states.

Both parties to the Lateran Treaty of 1929 were criticised for giving away too much but for the pope remedying the festering sore of the Roman question, and reinstating the official standing of the Church throughout Italy, were substantial gains. Part of the cost was the final withdrawal of the support by the Vatican for Mussolini's political rivals, the *Popolare*: already in 1924 Pius had forbidden priests from joining political parties and Don Sturzo was told to leave the country. 'Pius wished to withdraw the church as far as possible from politics, so that Catholics may be united on a religious and moral basis'.[739] He had demonstrated his disapproval of political Catholicism by placing the French monarchist newspaper, *Action Française*, on the Index and later excommunicating its influential editor, Charles Maurras, who had championed the Church but did not believe in God. The apple of the pope's eye was the lay organisation, Catholic Action – a blend of the Knights of Saint Columbus in the US, the Women's Institute in Britain and Baden Powell's Boy Scouts: Mussolini had agreed to its freedom of action in the Lateran Treaty.

The chief gains for Mussolini were the treaty itself – an agreement between Italy's parvenu fascist regime and the world's most ancient institution – and

---

737   *Ibid.*, p. 50

738   *Ibid.* p. 44

739   Anthony Rhodes, *Op. Cit.*, p. 15

the withdrawal of the Vatican's support for the *Popolare*. It had already been 'a great help to fascism when the leading Catholic in active politics, the priest Don Sturzo, was ordered by the pope to leave Italy. Without this courageous and irreconcilable enemy of the regime, the *Popolare* languished...'[740] It languished not just because Pius XI withdrew his support, but because the policies of the fascist government were often in tune with the teaching of the Church.

Pius and his Secretary of State Cardinal Gaspari were well aware of the thuggery and violence in Italian fascism, but considered them a price that had to be paid for political stability. If the choice was between Communism and Fascism, Pius preferred the latter. At one time, Pius said that dealing with Mussolini was like dealing with the devil, yet 'an ally on the whole he remained because on the whole Mussolini's enemies were the enemies of the Church. Such, for instance, were the Freemasons, who had been for a century and more the most implacable enemies of the Church in Italy, and who now found the activities of their lodges, their banks, and their press curtailed by the fascist regime.'[741] Neither Pius nor Gaspari thought the French and British parliamentary democracies were models that Catholics should follow. Despite the fact that during the 1920s the Vatican received half its income from the Church in the United States, the pope, like his predecessor, had grave misgivings about capitalism and unfettered liberty for the individual, condemning them in the 1931 encyclical *Quadragesimo Anno*.

The 1920s had seen the start of the Jazz Age with a wave of wild hedonism and sexual permissiveness spreading from the US. In 1930, the year before *Quadragesimo Anno*, Pius had issued an encyclical, *Casti Connubii (Chaste Wedlock)*, reminding the faithful in the most emphatic tones of the Church's teaching on marriage, the family and sexual morality. It had been prompted by the Church of England's declaration at the 7th Convocation of Canterbury held in 1930 that it was not sinful for men and women to use artificial means to prevent conception – the Anglican miscreants referred to obliquely in the encyclical as 'some who, openly departing from the Christian teaching which has been handed down uninterruptedly from the beginning, have in recent times thought fit solemnly to preach another doctrine concerning this practice.'[742]

---

740   Denis Mack Smith, *Op. Cit.* p. 65

741   E.E.Y. Hates, *Op. Cit.*, p.270

742   *Cast Connubii*, p. 28

That the Church of England should act unilaterally in this way confirmed Pius's misgivings about the ecumenical movement: 'the union of Christians,' he wrote, 'can only be promoted by the return to the one true Church of Christ of those who are separated from it, for in the past they have unhappily left it'.[743] He saw no reason to revise Leo XIII's ruling that Anglican orders were invalid, and it was therefore only to be expected that the Church of England should unilaterally decide that use of artificial means of birth control was not, as Pius insisted, 'an offence against the law of God and of nature', nor 'those who commit it guilty of a grave sin'. Pius also condemned abortion 'which attacks the life of the offspring while it is yet hidden in the womb of its mother'. He quoted Augustine of Hippo's castigation of 'those depraved married persons who, having attempted unsuccessfully to forestall the conception of offspring, criminally and ruthlessly put it to death. "'Their licentious cruelty or cruel licentiousness, sometimes goes to such lengths as to procure sterilizing poisons, and if these are unavailing, in some way to stifle within the womb and eject the foetus that that has been conceived. They want their offspring to die in the womb, to perish before it is born."'[744]

It is clear from the tone of *Casti Connubii* that Pius meant not just to remind the faithful of the Church's teaching on matters of marriage and sexual morality, but to stem the rising tide of an indulgent, individualistic ethos. He did not name Sigmund Freud or Havelock Ellis, but warned how 'without any sense of shame' Christian sexual mores 'are treated with derision and contempt. The spoken and written word, theatrical performances of every kind, novels, love-stories, humorous talks, cinematography films, broadcast talks – all the latest inventions of modern science are used to this end. On the other hand, divorce, adultery, and the most shameful vices are glorified or, at an rate, depicted in such colours as to make them appear free from all blame'.[745] He condemned 'trial marriages' and warned that 'the same false teachers...attack also the loyal and honourable obedience of the wife to her husband, which some of them even describe as an ignominious servitude of one partner to the other'.[746] They would free a wife 'from the domestic care of children and family, enabling her, to the neglect of these, to follow her own bent and engage in business and even in public affairs'.[747]

---

743   *Mortalium Animos*
744   *Casti Connubi:* p.32
745   *Ibid.* p. 24
746   *Ibid.* p. 36
747   *Ibid.* p. 37

In *Casti Connubii* Pius wrote that 'the family is more sacred than the State', a view that Mussolini would come to question; but at the time of the publication there was much in the encyclical that matched Mussolini's own views. 'During his anti-Christian youth he had been a convinced believer in artificial contraception as a positive duty for each family, but in 1924 he introduced penal sanctions against anyone who advocated it, and in 1926 mounted a nationwide campaign to increase the birth rate'.[748] He put his own house in order by marrying his wife Rachele in a church, and having his children baptised. He became not just respectable but puritanical. Sexually promiscuous himself, and aware that 'many fascists were extremely dissolute men', Mussolini nevertheless declared that he would make Rome the most moral town in the world. 'He tried to regulate dancing on the grounds that modern dances were "immoral and improper, evil germs that will breed immorality in the minds of my people".' Women were encouraged to give up '"negro dances" imported from America' and 'prudish rules were prescribed for the shape of bathing costumes and the lengths of skirts.'[749]

Mussolini had broken with the socialists not so much on the question of free love, but because of his fervent nationalism, corporatist concept of the state, and the use of violence against his political enemies – even murder as in the case of the socialist leader Giacomo Matteotti. Pius XI abhorred the fascist use of violence; he realised that Mussolini was responsible for the murder of Matteotti but he considered him 'preferable to all conceivable alternatives'. 'When Mussolini invaded Abyssinia in 1935, the pope did not condemn him 'and delivered speeches couched in such bewildering and lofty generalities that it was impossible to say what he thought'.[750] This extension of Italian *imperium* into Africa was denounced by the League of Nations, and sanctions were imposed on Italy, but Pius, who had from the start of his reign boosted the Church's foreign missions, and had been the first pope to consecrate indigenous bishops in India, China and Japan, 'had always regarded Abyssinia with its slave-owning habits as particularly suited for proselytization'; considered that any influence exercised there by Catholic powers such as Italy could only further the process'; and so went no further than to call for 'Peace based on Truth, Justice and Charity'.[751]

---

748   Denis Mack Smith, *Op. Cit.*, p. 159

749   *Ibid.* p. 160

750   Eamon Duffy, *Op. Cit.* p. 343

751   Anthony Rhodes, *Op. Cit.* p. 69

103.   Mit Brennender Sorge

In 1930 the long-serving Vatican Secretary of State, Cardinal Pietro Gaspari, retired because of his failing health. He was replaced by Cardinal Eugenio Pacelli who as Papal Nuncio in Munich during the Communist rising in 1918 had been threatened with a pistol by a Red guard. In 1925 the Nunciature had moved to Berlin where, as the doyen of the diplomatic corps, Pacelli had been closely involved in the travails of Germany's Weimar Republic. He negotiated concordats with three German *Länder* – Bavaria, Baden and Prussia – and was recalled to Rome only in December, 1929, after residing in Germany for twelve years.

Eugenio Pacelli was a consummate Vatican diplomat, born in Rome into the Vatican's 'black nobility': his grandfather had been Secretary of the Interior under Pio Nono; his cousin Ernesto Pacelli was a financial counsellor to Leo XIII; his father, Filippo Pacelli, the dean of the Roman Rota; and it was his brother Francesco, a legal advisor to Pius XI, who had negotiated the Lateran Treaty. Eugenio Pacelli had been entrusted with a number of delicate diplomatic missions by the pontiffs he served, negotiating the concordat with Serbia just before the outbreak of World War I, negotiating with the Soviet foreign minister Georgy Chicherin over food relief for the starving in Russia, and taking charge of the unsuccessful papal initiative to end that war in 1917. He 'was devoted to Germany and its culture' but 'had no illusions about Nazism...which he recognised as anti-Christian...'[752] He described Germany as 'a noble and powerful nation whom bad shepherds would lead astray into an ideology of race' and the Nazis as 'false prophets with the pride of Lucifer'. The author David G. Dalin has calculated that 'of the forty-four speeches Pacelli gave in Germany as papal nuncio between 1917 and 1929, forty denounced some aspect of the emerging Nazi ideology'.[753]

In Germany, as in Italy, the Communists were seen as the principal threat to the Church, but that did not lead Catholics in Germany to support Hitler as the Catholics in Italy had Mussolini where, 'in the elections of March 1929 most of the clergy encouraged their congregations to vote Fascist'.[754] In Germany, by contrast, in the final free elections of the Weimar republic, 'the confessional

---

752   Eamon Duffy, *Op. Cit.* p. 341

753   David G. Dalin, Joseph Bottum, *The Pius War: Responses to the Critics of Pius XII*, p. 17 [Lexingtonton Books, 2010

754   Duffy, *Op. Cit.* p. 340

factor…seems to have had a significantly greater influence on electoral results in the towns and communities of the German Reich than the various indicators of class.'[755] Thus in 1928, if you were trying to forecast who would vote for Hitler, 'asking whether they are rich or poor, town or country, educated or not, man or woman and so on will scarcely help at all. The only question really worth asking is whether they are Catholic or Protestant.'[756] In July, 1932, in the largely Catholic south and west of Germany, only 17% voted for Hitler.

However, the antipathy of the Catholic voters for the Nazis was accompanied by wishful thinking in both their lay and clerical leaders. The Catholic Centre Party, led by Franz von Papen, not only voted to install Adolf Hitler as Chancellor but also for 'the Law for the Alleviation of the People's and the Reich's Misery, otherwise known as the Enabling Law' which gave the government dictatorial powers. Fourteen of the seventy-four Centre Party members of the Reichstag who wanted to vote against the enabling act were dissuaded by Papen who assured them that as vice-Chancellor he would vet any of the government's decrees: and some feared that 'their safety might be in jeopardy' from the SA and SS mobs outside the chamber.[757]

The Catholic bishops did not protest. A statement by the Bishops' Conference held at Fulda declared that Catholics '"need no particular admonition to be loyal to the legally constituted authorities, to fulfil their civic duties conscientiously, and to reject absolutely any illegal or revolutionary activity".'[758] Nor did the theologians. Karl Adam, Professor of Theology at Tübingen University whose book The Spirit of Catholicism (1924) had established him as 'perhaps the most notable theologian of his generation', published an essay in 1933 arguing that Catholicism and National Socialism were compatible, and that anti-Jewish legislation was justified to enable Germans to reinforce their sense of racial identity.

Political opposition by Catholics in the Reichstag was also constrained by Pius XI's lack of support for parliamentary shenanigans. His conviction that the interests of the Church were best served by concordats with established authoritarian governments had seemed confirmed by the success of the Concordat with Mussolini, and Pius XI and Cardinal Pacelli wasted no time in negotiating something similar with Hitler. Pius anticipated that the

---

755   Jurgen W. Falter, *Die Wahlen des Jahres 1932/33 und der Augsteig totalitärer Parteien.* Quoted in James Hawes, *Op. Cit.* p.164

756   James Hales, *Op. Cit.* p.164

757   *Ibid.*, p. 154

758   Michael Burleigh, *The Third Reich*, pp. 153-154

German dictator 'would prove to be, in religious matters, a second Mussolini, requiring a fair element of Church support in order to govern effectively.'

Concordats, as we have seen, had been negotiated by Cardinal Pacelli with three of the German *Länder*, but no concordat had been made with the German *Reich* since the Reformation – both because of Bismarck's *Kulturkampf* and, under the Weimar republic, because of the antipathy towards the Church among Liberals, Socialists and Communists. Now there was a German government that could deliver on its assurances and, it later emerged, wielded a stick as well as a carrot – an unofficial threat was made by Hitler that 'if he could not obtain a concordat, he intended to close the confessional schools and abolish confessional youth movements. This touched Pius XI on the quick for, if the Pope had shown that he was relatively indifferent to the fate of Catholic parties, he was deeply concerned, in this irreligious twentieth century, with religious instruction for the young, and with maintaining Catholic youth organisations.'[759]

Hitler's interest in a concordat were similar to Mussolini's. It would enhance the respectability, even the legitimacy, of his regime; and would remove the Centre Party as a possible source of opposition. He appointed Papen to conduct the negotiations with the Vatican. On 20, July, 1933, after only eight days of negotiations, the concordat was signed: negotiations for the concordat with Italy had taken three years. For the Church, the liberties it had asked for were now enshrined in German law. For the Third Reich, 'within six months of its birth, it had been given full approval by the highest spiritual power on earth.'[760]

The concordat was welcomed by the Cardinal Archbishop of Munich, Michael von Faulhaber, who said that Catholics were now free to join the Nazi party. However, it was criticised in both France and Poland, Germany's likely adversaries should there be a war. In Rome itself, Cardinal Cerretti, a member of the Curia and earlier Papal Nuncio in Paris, predicted that this, like all concordats with anti-Catholic regimes, would do nothing to prevent them from ignoring the clauses protecting the Church: 'the Church did not possess the physical power to enforce them'.

Ceretti was soon proved right both in Germany and Italy where there was relentless pressure to ensure that the formation of the young should pass from

759   Anthony Rhodes, *Op. Cit.*, pp. 174-175

760   *Ibid.* p. 177

the Church to the State. Catholic Action suffered relentless attrition in favour of the youth movements of the fascist regimes. In Germany, parents who sent their children to Catholic schools faced discrimination when it came to employment by government agencies such as the post-office. Despite the exhortation of some bishops for the faithful to stand firm, the many threats and inducements had their effect, with a precipitous decline in the number of pupils attending Catholic schools – in Munich from 65% in 1933 to 35% in 1935 and 3% in 1937. Religious sisters who had taught at Catholic schools were declared redundant, and told to find work elsewhere. In Munich priests were imprisoned and pastoral letters confiscated. Protests were ignored: letters from the Papal Nuncio and Cardinal Pacelli received no reply.

In September, 1935, the German *Reichstag* met in Nuremberg in northern Bavaria during the annual rally of the National Socialist Party. There it passed laws 'for the protection of German Blood and German Honour' which excluded from German citizenship those not of the German race. True to the Nazis' prurient obsessions, the laws banned marriages and extramarital sexual relationships between Jews and Germans, and the employment of German women under the age of 45 in Jewish households. Later the laws were amended to include Roma (gypsies). Earlier, Hitler had called for a boycott of Jewish businesses, and a 'Law for the Restoration of the Professional Civil Service' excluded non-Aryans from the legal profession and civil service. Thus Jewish lawyers and civil servants became unable to earn their living. Ironically, German Jews made up a small proportion of the population, and they were better integrated than those in many other nations. Nevertheless, the Nazis intended to get rid of them through expropriation and intimidation. 'More than one hundred thousand Jews left Germany in late 1938 or 1939... German Jews would have departed even faster than they did had the British allowed them to go to Palestine, and the Americans seen fit to increase – or even fill – immigration quotas.'[761] Emigration to Palestine was encouraged by the Nazis, and there was a plan to establish a settlement of deported Jews in Madagascar.

Harassment of the Jews had started as soon as the Nazis had come to power, with anti-Semitic laws combined with Nazi thuggery in the streets – the most grotesque being the pogrom on the night of 9-10 November, 1938, when throughout Germany and Austria 267 synagogues were destroyed, 7,000

761   Snyder, *Op. Cit.* p. 111-112

Jewish enterprises destroyed or damaged, and 30,000 Jewish men arrested and sent to concentration camps. It had been triggered by the assassination in Paris of a German diplomat, Ernst vom Rath, by a 17-year-old Polish Jew living in the city, Herschel Grynszpan. Because of the shards of glass littering the streets from broken shop windows, it became known as the *Kristallnacht* – the 'Night of the Broken Glass'.

Pius XI and the German bishops were dismayed by *Kristallnacht*, and the Nazi's anti-Semitic legislation. There were frequent protests and condemnations from the Vatican, and from some Catholic bishops in Germany. In the years before the outbreak of war, could they have done more? A distinguished philosopher, Edith Stein, raised as an observant Jew, subsequently an atheist, was converted to Catholicism in 1922 and entered a Carmelite convent as Sister Benedicta of the Cross. She lost her job teaching at Münster's Institute for Scientific Pedagogy as the result of laws passed by the Nazis. She then wrote to Pius XI complaining of the silence of the Church.

> As a child of the Jewish people who, by the grace of God, for the past eleven years has also been a child of the Catholic Church, I dare to speak to the Father of Christianity about that which oppresses millions of Germans. For weeks we have seen deeds perpetrated in Germany which mock any sense of justice and humanity, not to mention love of neighbour. For years the leaders of National Socialism have been preaching hatred of the Jews... But the responsibility must fall, after all, on those who brought them to this point and it also falls on those who keep silent in the face of such happenings.... For weeks, not only Jews but also thousands of faithful Catholics in Germany, and I believe, all over the world have been waiting and hoping for the Church of Christ to raise its voice to put a stop of this abuse of Christ's name. Is not this idolisation of race and governmental power which is being pounded into the public consciousness by the radio open heresy? Isn't the effort to destroy Jewish blood an abuse of the holiest humanity of our Saviour, of the most blessed Virgin and the Apostles?... We all, who are faithful children of the Church and who see the conditions in Germany with open eyes, fear the worst for the prestige of the Church, if the silence continues any longer.

Edith Stein received no reply to her letter, and it is not known whether or not it was read by Pius XI or Cardinal Pacelli. It would seem that in the early years of Nazi rule, both the pope and the German bishops, preoccupied with the plight of German Catholics, did not feel that it was up to them to defend Germany's Jews who, after all, had their own powerful protectors in in London and New York. There was also a fear that many of their flock, if they had to choose between the Church and the Nazis, might choose the Nazis – comparing 'the state of political humiliation and economic distress that overwhelmed them when Hitler seized power with the new situation, relatively prosperous economically and dominating politically'.[762]

Moreover, anti-Semitism was pervasive in Germany, and indeed throughout Europe for many and often contradictory reasons. Jewish refugees from Russian pogroms were resented because they were poor; Jewish bankers and businessmen because they were rich. Jews kept themselves to themselves and dealt with gentiles only to take their money. Jewish department stores put small shop-keepers out of business. Jews were clever, quick-witted, and in 'an age of formal equality…had emerged as dangerous competitors in the liberal professions, especially journalism, medicine and law…'[763] They were 'rootless cosmopolitans' who felt no love of any country, exploiting their international connections to establish monopolies in life's necessities, or fomenting revolution following the theories of Jews like Karl Marx. And had not their ancestors killed Christ? The Church might reject the idea of deicide and collective guilt, but every Good Friday, over many centuries, Catholics had prayed for the *perfidis Judaeis*, and in the Gospel of Saint Matthew heard the cry of those demanding Christ's crucifixion: 'His blood be on us and on our children'.[764]

It took four years of Nazi rule for both Pope Pius XI and his Secretary of State, Cardinal Pacelli, to realise that, while Catholics were not subject to racial hatred, they were considered, after the elimination of Communists and Socialists, second only to the Jews as enemies of the new order. National Socialism had now become as great a threat to the Catholic Church as Soviet Communism. 'During these years, relations of the Vatican with Germany grew more tense and embittered, the prospects of conciliation more remote, the repression of freedom of conscience and religion more active and relentless'.[765] Among those murdered by the SS in the 1934 'Night of the Long

---

762   Pierre Blett, S.J., *Pius XII and the Second World War*, p.53

763   Robert S. Wistrich, *Op. Cit.*, p. 58

764   Matthew, 27:26

765   *Ibid.* p.195

Knives' was Eric Klausener, the head of Catholic Action in Berlin. 'By the end of 1936, physical violence was being used openly and blatantly against the Catholic Church'. 'Nazi assaults on the clergy and Christianity were crude – up to and including smearing excrement on altars and church doors or desecrating roadside shrines… Churches were plastered with anti-clerical posters…. Pious images were vandalised to the annoyance of farmers who regarded them as guarantors of good harvests. St Anthony lost his head, St. Bernadette ended up in the pond, Christ was heaved onto a dung heap.'[766] Priests were spat upon by fanatical Nazi women. When the *Dompropst* of Berlin's Catholic cathedral, Bernhardt Lichtenberg, spoke in a sermon of 'the Jews and other unfortunates in the concentration camps' he was arrested and sent to join the unfortunates in Dachau.

Aware of these developments, the Vatican could do nothing but protest. In January, 1936, Pius XI summoned the German ambassador to the Vatican, Diego von Bergen, for a dressing down. He told him that he no longer believed that Germany was saving the world from Bolshevism and that it was now Christianity itself which was threatened. He complained that while Bismarck, during the *Kulturkampf*, had allowed the Vatican's criticism of his policies to appear in the German newspapers, Hitler did not: no word of the pope's misgivings about what was going on in Germany appeared in the German press. 'If you want a *Kulturkampf* again,' the ambassador was told, 'you can have one.' [767]

In January, 1937, five German bishops, among them three cardinals, came on an *ad limina* visit to Pope Pius XI in the Vatican. The bishop of Berlin, Johan Konrad, Graf von Preysing, and the bishop of Münster, Clemens August, Graf von Galen, both came from the German nobility; Michael von Faulhaber, the archbishop of Munich, was the son of a baker, but had been made a knight (*Ritter*) by Prince Ludwig of Bavaria during World War I. It was thus a group of strong, confident prelates who went to the bedside of the old and ailing pope to report on the state of the Church in Germany. They found that Pius's patience had run out. He told Cardinal Faulhaber to write a draft of an encyclical denouncing the Nazi government – not in Latin, as was customary, but in his own language, German. Faulhaber completed the draft, written in his own hand, by the morning of 21 January. He delivered

---

766   Michael Burleigh, *Op. Cit.*. p. 261
767   Anthony Rhodes, *Op. Cit.* p. 199

it to Cardinal Pacelli who made one or two amendments, changing the title from *Mit grosser Sorge* (*With Great Concern*) to the stronger *Mit brennender Sorge* (*With Burning Concern*).

Mit Brennender Sorge 'began mildly enough with an account of the broad aims of the Church, but went on to become one of the greatest condemnations of a national regime ever pronounced by the Vatican. Its vigorous language is in sharp contrast to the involved style in which encyclicals were normally written.'[768] Somewhat defensively, Pius begins by explaining why he signed a concordat with the Nazi government soon after it came to power, saying it was to secure in law freedom of action for the Church in Germany. But the Germans had not kept to the terms of the treaty – particularly when it came to education. The Nazis had shown bad faith, clearly never intending to keep to their agreement with the Vatican, but rather replacing Catholicism with their own pagan ideology. 'Whoever exalts race, or the people, or the State,' wrote Pius, 'or a particular form of State, or the depositories of power, or any other fundamental value of the human community...and divinizes them to an idolatrous level, distorts and perverts an order of the world planned and created by God...'[769]

Although Pius did not name Hitler, he was clearly meant when Pius denounced those who dared, 'in sacrilegious disregard of the essential differences between the God-man and the children of man, to place a mortal, were he the greatest of all times, by the side of, or over, or against Christ...'[770] 'It is only faith in God, preserved pure and stainless, that man's morality is based. All efforts to remove from ... the moral order the granite foundation of faith and to substitute for it the shifting sands of human regulations, will sooner or later lead these individuals or societies to moral degradation.'[771]

Mit Brennender Sorge was smuggled into Germany and on Palm Sunday, 1937, read from the pulpits all the Catholic churches in Germany – in the great cathedrals, read by the bishops themselves. Its message spread further but only by word of mouth because the very next day the Gestapo raided printers, presbyteries and parish offices and confiscated every copy of the encyclical it could find; and a number of vindictive measures were taken such as cutting off grants to students of theology, banning banners at religious processions,

---

768   *Ibid.*, p. 204

769   *Mit Brennender Sorge,* 8

770   *Ibid.,* 17

771   *Ibid.* 29

changing the names of towns and villages with Catholic connotations such as Heiligenstadt, Mariendorf or Gottesberg, and printing scurrilous stories about priests and nuns in the Nazi press.[772]

However, the impact of the encyclical outside Germany was considerable, turning opinion against Germany in Catholic countries such as Chile, but also in the United States. Pius had made clear that he now regarded Nazism as as great a threat to the Church and Christian civilisation as Communism. 'Let us call things by their true name,' he said in an address to the College of Cardinals in November, 1938. 'I tell you, in Germany today a full religious persecution is in progress. A persecution which does not shrink from using every weapon, lies, threats, false information, and in the last resort physical force'. To his dismay, Mussolini, under pressure from Hitler, now passed anti-Semitic laws, prohibiting marriage between Jews and Aryans. He sent hand-written letters to both to King Umberto and Mussolini saying that such laws were anathema to the Church 'which makes no distinction between the races of the great human family', and lodged a formal protest when the laws were passed.

104. The Teutonic Religion

In September, 1937, four months after the publication of *Mit Brennender Sorge*, the German National Socialist Party held a spectacular rally in Nuremberg which was attended by the ambassadors of Britain and France. During the ceremonies, a National Prize was awarded to Alfred Rosenberg, the Party's Commissar for the Supervision of Intellectual and Ideological Education, and author of *The Myth of the Twentieth Century* which, if Hitler's *Mein Kampf* was the gospel, now 'became the official catechism of the new Teutonic religion.'[773]

What were the teachings of this new religion? At its heart was the faith in reason and science with its prophets such as the Frenchman, Auguste Comte and the Englishman, Charles Darwin. Darwin, with his theory of evolution, had many followers: we have seen how Herbert Spencer, 'the most famous philosopher of the age', coined the phrase 'the survival of the fittest', and

772 Anthony Rhodes, *Op. Cit.*, p. 206
773 *Ibid.*, p. 214

thought it legitimate that those working for improvement of mankind should 'exterminate such sections of mankind as stand in their way.'

Following on from Spencer was Francis Galton – a child prodigy who could read at the age of two, and was competent in Latin, Greek and long division at the age of five. Later a student of medicine and mathematics, he developed an expertise in, among other things, sociology, psychology, anthropology, meteorology and genetics: it was Galton who gave us the word 'eugenics'. Like Spencer, the inspiration for his life's work was *The Origin of the Species* by his half-cousin, Charles Darwin. Financially independent, and a master of statistics, he conducted experiments and organized surveys in an attempt to find an answer to the perennial question of whether men and women are formed by nature or nurture. He decided on the former, and at the second Huxley lecture at the Royal Anthropological Institute proposed that financial incentives be offered to able and intelligent men and women to marry and have children. It followed that the less able and intelligent should be discouraged from breeding – whether as individuals or as a group. 'There exists a sentiment,' he wrote, 'for the most part quite unreasonable, against the gradual extinction of an inferior race.'[774]

Eugenics was one among many of Galton's areas of expertise. The value of his work was acknowledged by awards from a number of institutions, and he was elected Fellow of the Royal Society, an honorary fellow of Trinity College, Cambridge; a 'Galton Chair of Eugenics' was established at London's University College, and he was knighted by King George V in 1909. He seemed to regard his theories on eugenics as his greatest accomplishment. Towards the end of his life, he wrote a novel, *Kantsaywhere*, which described a utopian eugenic society that bred superior human beings. It was turned down by the publisher, Methuen, and after his death Galton's niece burned pages from the manuscript that described the superior men and women making love.

The failure of *Kantsaywhere* to find a publisher was perhaps because it was considered a bad novel, not because Galton's ideas on eugenics had gone out of fashion. Quite to the contrary, societies were formed in Britain and the United States to promote eugenics and faculties of Eugenics were established in many academic institutions. Eugenics became fashionable. Winston Churchill who had attended one of Galton's lectures, became the honorary vice-president of the British Eugenics Society, and in 1921 the Catholic

774   Israel W. Charney et. al. *Encyclopaedia of Genocide*: quoted in Wikipedia entry on 'Francis Galton'

Archbishop of New York, Patrick Joseph Hayes, endorsed an International Eugenics Conference held in that city. The most widely adopted proposal of the eugenicists was the sterilisation of those with hereditary diseases. Marie Stopes was a prominent advocate of women's rights, particularly the right to control their fertility through birth control; so too the American feminist Margaret Sanger.

However, eugenics also had its critics – biologists such as J.B.S. Haldane and R.A. Fisher, and the English author and journalist G.K. Chesterton. Catholic support for eugenics declined when in *Castii Connubii* Pius XI condemned enforced sterilisation. 'Public magistrates have no direct power over the bodies of their subjects; therefore, where no crime has taken place and where there is no cause present for grave punishment, they can never directly harm, or tamper with the integrity of the body, either for the reasons of eugenics or for any other reason.'[775]

Pius XI's strictures had little effect in predominantly Protestant Great Britain or the United States. In the latter, the Immigration Act of 1924 assumed the racial superiority of members of the Nordic races – the 'old stock' of the founding fathers: inferior races such as the Chinese and Japanese were largely banned from entering the US. Already in the US there were laws against miscegenation – inter-racial marriages – but in the course of the 1930s American eugenicists went further to rid society of its genetically defective members, with inmates in a mental institution in Illinois being given milk infected with tuberculosis.[776] In 1931 in the same state the Homeopathic Medicine Association applied for the right to terminate the lives of 'imbeciles' and other defectives. At the same time, 'best baby' competitions were organized throughout the southern states with prizes going to the parents of flawless children. African American and immigrant parents were barred from the competitions.

Laws enforcing the sterilisation of women with hereditary diseases were passed in thirty of the United States, with the Supreme Court in 1927 upholding the constitutionality of the Virginia Sterilization Act of 1924 which allowed the compulsory sterilization of patients in state mental institutions: Virginia did not repeal its sterilization law until 1974. Between 1907 and 1963, 64,000 women were forcibly sterilized under eugenic legislation in the

---

775   *Casti Connubii*, p.34

776   Edwin Black, *Eugenics and the Nazis – the California Connection*. San Francisco Chronicle, 9 November 2003 (Wikipedia)

United States.[777] A disproportionate number were African-Americans – in the state of North Carolina 5,000 out of 7,600 women.

Although eugenics was to be found in France and South America, the influence of the Catholic Church constrained its influence on social policy. In Britain, the source of the sound stock that the Americans wished to foster and preserve, there was no comparable programme to eradicate defective genes but eugenics had its advocates among some of the most eminent and influential intellectuals – not just those on the Right such as Winston Churchill, but particularly on the Left, among liberals and socialists such as Bertrand Russell, John Maynard Keynes, Harold Laski and Sidney and Beatrice Webb. It was promoted by the *Manchester Guardian* and the *New Statesman*: the latter condemned those who argued against 'the legitimate claims of eugenics' for clinging to 'the individualistic views of parenthood and family economics'.[778] For socialists like the Webbs, eugenics should be part of the planning that would improve the condition of mankind. The liberal William Beveridge, the designer of Britain's future welfare state, wrote that defective men and women who were unemployable and so dependent upon the state should be lose their civil rights, 'including not only the franchise but civil freedom and fatherhood'. The playwright, Bernard Shaw, advocated 'the selective breeding of man'; the novelist, H.G. Wells, held that such breeding should be directed towards the elimination of 'detrimental' types; and Bertrand Russell that it should be enforced by issuing men and women with colour-coded 'procreation tickets' so that the gene pool of the elite would not be diluted by inferior human beings.[779]

The Englishman who disseminated Galton's ideas abroad was Houston Stewart Chamberlain, born in Hampshire in 1855, the son of a Rear-Admiral in the British navy. After the premature death of his father, he spent some of his early years in France, returning to Cheltenham College in England to be prepared for a career in the navy or the Indian Civil Service. He disliked Cheltenham, and he disliked England. He was converted by the music of Wagner – 'one of the great geniuses of all time' – to an esteem for Germany, the 'land of love' whose culture was infused with a special spirituality that brought out the best in humanity.

777　Paul Lombardo, 'Eugenic Sterilization Laws', *Eugenics Archive* (Wikipedia)

778　Victoria Brignell, 'The eugenics movement Britain wants to forget', *New Statesman*, 9 December, 2010

779　*Ibid.*

Chamberlain settled in Dresden where he studied the works of Kant and Nietzsche, and immersed himself in the music of Richard Wagner. He visited Wagner's widow Cosima in Bayreuth and, enraptured, espoused her *Völkisch* ideas and in due course married her daughter. Already an anti-Semite, he ingratiated himself with the Wagnerite circle by confirming their prejudices with fanciful and esoteric theories on race. While living in Dresden, he had learned Sanskrit to study Hindu myths and legends in their original form. From these studies he claimed to have discovered the existence of an Indo-European master-race, the Aryans, who conquered the Indian sub-continent, and were the ancestors of western Europeans. One of their symbols was the swastika.

In 1893, on Cosima Wagner's recommendation, Chamberlain read Arthur de Gobineau's *Essai sur l'inégalité des races humaines* (*Essay on the Inequality of Human Races*) which also declared the existence of an Aryan master race. Chamberlain was then living in Vienna, capital of the polyglot Austro-Hungarian empire, with ten percent of its population Jewish; and, inspired by Gobineau, and after further studies, he wrote a book entitled *Die Grundlagen des neunzehnten Jahrhunderts* (*The Foundations of the Nineteenth Century*). It was written in German and published in 1899.

Chamberlain's hypothesis was that the ancient Indo-European 'Aryan' race, while it now encompassed all European nationalities, and even the Berbers of North Africa, was principally to be found in the Teutonic peoples. Just as it was the Aryan blood of the ancient Greeks and Romans that led to their achievements, and later those of the great European writers and artists of the Renaissance, so too the prodigious advances in philosophy, science, technology and the arts that took place in the nineteenth century were made by members of the Aryan race.

Who was the adversary of the Aryan? The Jew, who 'wished to put his foot on the neck of all nations of the world and be Lord and possessor of the whole earth': and, among the agencies employed by the Jews to subjugate the human race was the Catholic Church. Jesus of Nazareth himself had not been Jewish; he was a Galilean and hence an Aryan; but his followers had created a 'Judaized' Christianity, extant in Rome but overthrown in Germany by the Aryan Martin Luther. The two 'pure' races – the Jews and the Germans – were engaged in a war for world domination which could only end with the victory of one over the other.[780]

---

780   Saul Friedländer, *Nazi Germany and the Jews*, p. 89 (Wikipedia)

The Foundations of the Twentieth Century became a best-seller, and made Huston Stewart Chamberlain famous throughout the world. A circle of rich and aristocratic Germans formed around him; he was befriended by the Kaiser; and copies of his book were distributed in secondary schools, and to recruits in the army. In 1908, he married Eva von Bülow, officially Cosima Wagner's daughter by her first husband but in fact the child of Chamberlain's idol, Richard Wagner, already Cosima's lover at the time of Eva's conception.

During World War I, Chamberlain volunteered for the German army but was rejected as too old. In 1923, in a wheelchair because of a progressive paralysis, he met Adolph Hitler at Bayreuth – the mutual admiration of the two men cemented by their shared passion for the music of Wagner. Chamberlain joined the Nazi Party and wrote for the party's newspaper, the Völkischer Beobachter, declaring that Hitler was the greatest of all his heroes. When Chamberlain died in 1927, Hitler and other Nazi leaders attended his funeral in Bayreuth.

Alfred Rosenberg was Houston Stewart Chamberlain's disciple and ideological heir. Like Chamberlain, he was not German but of mixed Estonian, Baltic German and French blood. He was born in 1893 in Reval, Estonia, then part of the Russian empire, and studied architecture in Riga and Moscow. After World War I, Rosenberg emigrated to Germany where he became one of the earliest members of the Nazi party. When Hitler was imprisoned following the failed Beer Hall Putsch in 1923, he appointed Rosenberg as interim leader – a scholarly dilettante more interested in theory than practice, and so unlikely to threaten the position of the Führer. After Hitler's release, Rosenberg edited the Nazi newspaper, the Völkischer Beobachter.

In 1930 Rosenberg published The Myth of the Twentieth Century as a sequel to Chamberlain's The Foundations of the Nineteenth Century. The book, following Chamberlain's theories, postulated a hierarchy of races with the Aryans at its apex and the degenerate Jews at its base. Successive periods of Aryan supremacy, such as the Roman Empire, had decayed because of the interbreeding of Aryans with members of lesser, degenerate races; and the influence of a Jewish religion, Christianity. The Aryan race survived in the Teutonic races of northern Europe, above all the Germans. It was both the duty and destiny of the Aryan Übermensch to retain the purity of his race by eschewing miscegenation and excising, as a surgeon would a tumour, the influence of the lesser, degenerate races – in particular the Jews.

Like Chamberlain's magnum opus, Rosenberg's The Foundations of the

Twentieth Century was a best-seller. For the Germans, late-comers like the Italians in forming a nation state – thwarted by the British and French from forming an empire overseas; and more recently humiliated by the terms of the Treaty of Versailles – it was heartening to learn that despite such setbacks they were the master race. German culture, admired throughout the world, and so clearly superior to that of other tribes and nations, confirmed the theories of the racist polymaths. The critics of those theories, and there were many, showed how the meticulous scientific observations found in Charles Darwin's *The Origin of the Species* had degenerated in the work of his intellectual successors into fanciful hypotheses and improbable speculations – producing in the case of Rosenberg a mishmash of Schopenhauer's neo-Buddhism, Nietszche's philosophy of the superman and his hero Wagner's theories about the Holy Grail. 'Nietzsche, Wagner and Houston Stewart Chamberlain,' wrote the Christian philosopher Theodore Haecker, 'are in fact mainly responsible for the present condition of the German mind.'[781]

Yet even Hitler mocked some of Rosenberg's ideas. 'Rosenberg's fantasies about an Aryan church are ridiculous. Trying to set up the party as a new religion! A Gauleiter is no substitute for a bishop; a local group leader can never serve as a parish priest.'[782] He said he had 'merely glanced cursorily at the book' – *The Myth of the Twentieth Century* – and insisted 'that it was not to be regarded as an expression of the official doctrine of the party.' [783] Goebbels called Rosenberg's *magnum opus* 'a philosophical belch'. Nevertheless, a million copies had been sold by 1944; and, while its attacks on Christianity alienated not just Catholics but Evangelical Christians, it influenced the formation of an emerging generation of Germans and when they came to serve in the SS or the *Wehrmacht* justified their inhuman treatment of other races.

781   Theodor Haecker, *Journal in the Night*, p.12

782   Albert Speer, *Spandau. The Secret Diaries*, p.15

783   Hugh Trevor-Roper, *Adolf Hitler's Secret Conversations 1941-1944*, p. 400 (Wikipedia)

105. The Anschluss

Adolf Hitler had made it clear in *Mein Kampf* that he would gather all Germans into a single state. The frontiers established by the Treaty of Versailles had left many outside the *Reich* – the Sudeten Germans within Czechoslovakia; Germans in East Prussia and the city of Danzig cut off from Germany by a corridor of Polish territory giving Poland access to the sea. And there was the German speaking rump of the ancient Austro-Hungarian empire – a barely viable republic with a disproportionately populous capital, Vienna.

The Treaty had also imposed the demilitarisation of the Rhineland but when Hitler sent German troops to reoccupy the Rhineland in 1938, neither Britain nor France was prepared to take military action. Both these two western democracies had yet to recover from the horror of the trenches: few could face the idea of another war. France was preoccupied with conflicts between Left and Right, and the resources devoted to defence were spent on building a series of linked fortresses and concrete bunkers stretching from Belgium to Switzerland, the Maginot Line, which left no resources for assertive military action.

It was later thought that if such action had been taken, Hitler would have backed down. But, encouraged by his success in the Rhineland, he now moved to bring Austria into the fold. Even before the Nazis came to power, there had been Austrians on both the Left and Right who thought that their country should unite with Germany. By the 1930s, the slogan *Heim ins Reich* had been appropriated by the Nazis to demand an *Anschluss*. The cause was discredited when, in 1934, Austrian Nazis attempted a coup, assassinating the Catholic Chancellor Engelbert Dolfuss. However, by 1938, Dolfuss's successor, Kurt Schuschnigg, had promised a referendum. Under pressure from Hitler, the idea of a referendum was abandoned. Schuschnigg resigned and was replaced as Chancellor by the Nazi Arthur Seyss-Inquart. On 12 March German troops marched into Austria unopposed. The *Anschluss* had been accomplished without a drop of blood being shed.

Austria was a Catholic country, and the addition of so many Catholics to the population of the Third Reich shows Hitler's confidence that Austrian Catholics would be as enthusiastic as non-Catholics about the *Anschluss*, particularly those living in Vienna. He had lived in Vienna from 1908 – 1913, and had seen the spectacular success of Karl Lueger, 'the first democratic politician to triumph anywhere in Europe on an explicitly anti-Jewish platform': Hitler judged him 'the greatest German *Bürgermeister* of all times'. The Jews at the time amounted to 8 percent of the city's population – 'heavily over- represented in the liberal professions… half the students in the medical faculty in 1910 were Jewish. The Jews dominated the liberal educated class, even more than in Germany at the time. They seemed to be the creators, the critics, the impresarios and managers of German high culture, which enraged Austrian anti-Semites such as Lueger who denounced the 'Judaisation' of the press, art, literature and the theatre, as well as the leadership of the governing Social Democrats 'most of whose intellectual leadership was Jewish'.[784]

In 1938, Hitler's intuition was proved right. Crowds lined the streets to welcome the units of the *Wehrmacht* as they marched into Vienna, and 200,000 cheering Austrians gathered in Vienna's Heidenplatz to hear Hitler himself declare 'As leader and chancellor of the German nation and Reich I announce to Germany now the entry of my homeland into the German Reich'. Soon after Hitler's arrival in Vienna, the Cardinal Archbishop of Vienna, Theodore Innitzer, called on him in the Imperial Hotel and, according to Baron von Shirach, embraced him.[785] The Austrian bishops issued a declaration endorsing the *Anschluss*, with a letter from the Cardinal to the Nazi Gauleiter Josef Bürckel ending 'Heil Hitler!'

On hearing of these blandishments, both Pope Pius XI and Cardinal Pacelli were dismayed. The Vatican had flirted with the idea of a Catholic German state embracing the Rhineland, Baden, Wurttemberg, Bavaria and Austria; but on Hitler's accession to power had condemned outright the idea of Austria being absorbed by the Third Reich. Cardinal Innitzer was summoned to Rome, and given a dressing-down by both Pacelli and the Pope. He was told to recant, or at least to modify his position, which he did in an article in *L'Osservatore Romano*, declaring that 'the Austrian bishops' profession of loyalty to the Führer must not be interpreted as anything incompatible with the laws of God, and with the liberties and rights of the Church'.[786]

In Vienna it quickly became apparent that the bishops' welcome of the *Anschluss* had done nothing to alter the planned course of Nazi rule. While 70,000 Communists, Social Democrats, critics of National Socialism, gypsies and Jews were arrested and taken to concentration camps, Catholic

---

784   Robert S. Wistricht, *Op. Cit.*, p.63

785   Anthony Rhodes, *Op. Cit.* p. 150

786   *Ibid.*, p. 151

associations were closed down, premises such as the College of the Capuchin Friars in Vienna expropriated, and the monastery of St. Lambrecht turned into a hostel for the Hitler Youth. Catholic women's and girls' associations were closed and the Catholic press suppressed.

There was some resistance. Cardinal Innitzer became increasingly critical of the regime he had earlier endorsed. Although he ordered all Austrian churches to ring their bells and fly swastika flags on Hitler's birthday in April, 1938, he declared on a day of prayer in his cathedral on 7 October, 1938, that for Catholics 'there is only one Führer, Jesus Christ'. The cry went up among the mostly young congregation: 'Christ is our Führer!'. Some days later, a group from the Hitler Youth smashed the windows of Cardinal Innitzer's residence in the Stephansplatz, climbed a ladder into the first floor, and there destroyed painting, sculptures, chalices and items of episcopal regalia. Furniture and the cardinal's robes were thrown into the street and set on fire. Innitzer took refuge on the third floor, defended by the young priests in his household. One had five stitches after being attacked by a broken bottle; another broke a leg when thrown out of the window.

The police were called but arrived only after the culprits had left. Complaints at the outrage, made both by the Archbishop and the Vatican, resulted in 'crocodile tears' from the authorities, and an empty assurance that the guilty would be punished. In reality, Cardinal Innitzer's vacillations had lost him the respect of both his enemies and his friends. Even as he ordered the raising of the swastika banners on Catholic churches to celebrate Hitler's birthday, the Gauleiter Josef Bürckel said his gift to his Führer would be 'a *closterlos* Austria' – an Austria without any of the convents or monasteries that had been there for more than a thousand years.[787]

Hitler's next move was to incorporate the three million Sudeten Germans living in mountainous border regions of Czechoslovakia. The frontiers of the new republic, based on the ancient provinces of Bohemia and Moravia, had been guaranteed by France and Britain at the Treaty of Versailles; and formidable fortifications had been built on their border with Germany by the Czechs. However, both the guarantor nations lacked the will and the means to resist the impetuous demands, not just of the Germans of the Sudetenland but also of the opportunistic Poles to snippets of the sub-Carpathians, and the Hungarians to parts of Slovakia. In September, 1938, the British and French

787   *Ibid.*, p. 153

prime ministers, Neville Chamberlain and Èdouard Daladier, flew to Munich to confer with Hitler: they were later joined by Mussolini. An agreement was reached permitting German troops to occupy the Sudetenland, and territories were ceded to both Poland and Hungary. The Czech government had no choice but to accept the terms of the accord. Chamberlain flew back to England and declared that there would be 'peace for our time'.

Pius XI was now old and unwell. He had thought Chamberlain 'feeble and smug, and no match for the tyrannies he confronted' but approved of his attempts to avert war.[788] In early February, 1939, he sat up all night preparing a speech to be addressed to the Italian bishops during ceremonies celebrating the tenth anniversary of the concordat with Italy – a speech 'in which he intended to include a detailed criticism of Fascist faithlessness'. '"Try at all costs to keep me alive until Saturday," he told his doctor, but no treatment could now save him, and on 10 February he died.

106.   World War II

On 2 March, 1939, on the first day of the conclave, the cardinals gathered in Rome chose Pius's Secretary of State, Cardinal Eugenio Pacelli as Pius XI's successor. 'He was the inevitable choice. Immensely able, an exquisitely skilled political tactician; he had been groomed for the succession by Pius XI.'[789] His years as Nuncio in Germany had given him a first-hand knowledge of both Bolshevism and National Socialism. He spoke fluent German and admired German music and culture, but 'he loathed and despised Nazi racial theory'[790] No one at the time of his elevation thought of him as 'Hitler's Pope'.[791]

However, as his assistant Secretary of State Cardinal Domenico Tardini later wrote, the new pope was 'by nature gentle and almost shy: he was not born with the temperament of a fighter. That is what distinguished him from his great predecessor'.[792] In August, 1939, as war seemed certain, he made an impassioned speech declaring that 'nothing is lost by peace; everything

---

788   Eamon Duffy, *Op. Cit.* p. 345

789   *Ibid.* p. 346

790   *Ibid.*, p. 347

791   The title of John Cornwell's 1999 book on Pius XII

792   Quoted in Anthony Rhodes, *Op. Cit.* p. 223

may be lost by war'; but once war began he stuck rigorously to the policy of Benedict XV during World War I, never straying beyond denunciations of inhumanity and atrocities to name names, and always making sure to 'avoid sprinkling holy water on the arms of either side.'[793]

This policy was hard to sustain because the first victims of Nazi aggression were Catholic Poles. Up to the last minute, Pius had advised the Poles to accept the German demands, particularly in regard to Danzig, but his advice had not been taken. There is no scope here to evaluate the record of the successors to Marshal Pilsudski who governed Poland at the time: we have seen how they took advantage of Hitler's confrontation over Czechoslovakia to take a portion of the spoils; and they too had considered deporting Polish Jews to Madagascar. However, they had rejected approaches by Hitler to join him in a war against the Soviet Union, feeling confident in the guarantees given by France and Great Britain. Stalin too had hoped to form a defensive alliance with Poland but had been rebuffed. The result was an astonishing *volte-face* by the arch-enemies, Hitler and Stalin. On 23 August, 1939, their foreign secretaries Ribbentrop and Molotov signed a non-aggression pact in Moscow.

The pact contained a secret clause partitioning Poland in the event of a war. Hitler lost no time in putting the clause into effect. On 1 September, on a contrived pretext of Polish aggression, units of the Wehrmacht crossed the frontier into Poland from the north, west and south. True to their treaty with Poland, Britain and France demanded that the Germans withdraw and, when the demand was refused, declared war on Germany. However, neither country was in a position to assist the Polish army which was defeated in less than a month by the dive-bombers of the *Luftwaffe*, and the tanks and mobile artillery of the *Wehrmacht*. 'Germany had all but won the war by the time the Soviets entered [their zone] on 17 September... Poland never surrendered, but hostilities came to an end on 6 October, 1939'.[794]

The subsequent treatment of the conquered Poles in the two areas of occupation was similar but the motivation was different. 'The link between loyalty and ethnicity was taken for granted in the Europe of 1938' and Stalin regarded all Poles as potential traitors. An anti-Soviet 'Polish Military Organisation' had been invented to justify the mass murder of Poles within the Soviet Union. By the time of *Kristallnacht* which had appalled public

---

793   Eamon Duffy, *Op. Cit.* p. 347
794   Timothy Snyder, *Op. Cit.* p. 123

opinion throughout the world, 'some 247,157 Soviet citizens had been shot in national operations' by the NKVD. After the Ukrainian Kulaks, the 'Poles suffered more than any other group within the Soviet Union during the great Terror'. This was not apparent in the west. 'In these years of the Popular Front, the Soviet killings and deportations were unnoticed in Europe. Insofar as the Great Terror was noticed at all, it was seen only as a matter of show trials and party and army purges'.[795]

More was to come. When the Red Army entered the eastern half of Poland in September, 1939, it claimed to be restoring order after the disintegration of the Polish state. It 'disarmed Polish units and engaged them wherever necessary' but, with sixty already thousand already dead, there was no will left among the Polish soldiers to continue the conflict. In due course, those soldiers were allowed to return home, but not their officers who were taken to three prison camps run by the NKVD in the eastern part of Soviet Ukraine. More than two thirds of these officers came from the army reserve: they were not professional soldiers but doctors, lawyers, scientists, authors, academics, politicians and priests. 'They saw their camps as churches and prayed in them'[796], and assumed that they too would soon be allowed to return home.

However, though their army had been defeated, an underground resistance had already started, and the Soviet Chief of Police, Lavrenty Beria, warned Stalin that the imprisoned Polish officers 'were just waiting to be released in order to enter actively into the battle against Soviet power'. He made clear 'in writing that he wanted the prisoners of war dead...and the mechanisms of the Great Terror began again'.[797] The imprisoned officers, imagining that they were on the first leg of their journey home, were taken by buses and trains to the edge of a forest called Katyn. There they were shot with a bullet in the back of the neck, their bodies buried in a mass grave in the forest.

If Stalin's programme of exterminating Poland's officer corps, most of whom as we have seen were in fact reservists with civilian professions, was formulated on the assumption that they were potential bourgeois counter-revolutionaries, and so opposed to Communist rule, Hitler's comparable programme was based not on class but on race. The Polish nation, in his masterplan, was to be destroyed. The peasantry would be kept alive to work as

---

795   *Ibid.*, p. 107
796   *Ibid.* p. 138
797   *Ibid..* p. 135

the serfs of the German farmers who would colonise their land, but the Polish cities were to be destroyed and the educated *intelligentsia* exterminated. When the Germans took Cracow, the ancient capital of the Polish kingdom, they arrested the entire faculty of the Jagiellonian University – an older institution than any in Germany: international outrage later led to their release.

Hitler appointed Himmler the 'Reich Commissar for the Strengthening of Germandom', and his adjutant Arthur Greiser set about the task of Germanification 'by emptying three psychiatric hospitals and having the patients shot. Patients from a fourth were gassed by carbon monoxide. This was the first German mass murder by this method'.[798] *Einsatzgruppen* (task forces) were formed 'to fulfil their mission as "ideological soldiers" by eliminating the educated classes of a defeated enemy...By killing the most accomplished Poles, the *Einsatzgruppen* were to make Poland ...incapable of resisting German rule'. Hitler told them 'to kill without pity or mercy all men, women, and children of Polish descent or language'. They were also to liquidate the spiritual leaders of the Polish people: around 3,000 members of the clergy were killed and least 1,811 members of the Polish clergy died in concentration camps.

To accommodate those apprehended, the Germans built more concentration camps, including one on the site of a Polish army barracks at Oświęcim, outside Cracow, 'better known by its German name, Auschwitz... The first transport to Auschwitz was made up of Polish political prisoners from Cracow...' In November, at first hundreds and then thousands rounded up in Warsaw were sent to Auschwitz: the camp became both 'a giant labour camp very much on the Soviet model' and 'an execution site for Poles'.[799]

In Rome, Pope Pius XII and his Secretary of State, Cardinal Luigi Maglione, were told of the Nazi assault on the Catholic Church in Poland by the Primate of Poland, Cardinal August Hlond. 'Hitlerism aims at the systematic and total destruction of the Catholic Church in those parts of Poland it has annexed... Many priests are imprisoned, suffering humiliations, blows, maltreatment. A certain number were deported to Germany...' Hlond reported that bishops had been sent to concentration camps and Catholic charities had been closed down, their funds seized and their leaders either shot or deported. In the few churches that remained open, sermons were to be in German: Polish hymns

---

798   *Ibid.* p. 130

799   *Ibid.* p. 151

were forbidden. The cathedral in Poznan was closed and the seminary made into an academy for police cadets.

Pope Pius XII thus came under great pressure, not just from Cardinal Hlond but also the Polish government in exile in London, and the governments of France and Britain now at war with Germany, to issue an outright denunciation of the German's actions in Poland. Against issuing such a targeted denunciation was the principle established by Benedict XV that the Vatican should always avoid direct intervention in international conflicts, and the fear that such an intervention would only make things worse. 'We would like to utter words of fire against such actions,' Pius told his Assistant Secretary of State, Giovanni Battista Montini, 'and the only thing restraining us from speaking is the fear of making the plight of the victims worse.'[800]

In fact the Pope did condemn the invasion of Poland, but 'in the approved periphrastic manner of the Vatican' in the encyclical *Summi Pontificatus* on the 27 October 1939. 'The blood of countless human beings, including many civilians, cries out in agony, a race as beloved by us as the Polish, whose steadfast Faith in the service of Christian civilisation is written in ineffaceable letters in the book of History.' In Germany, the head of Reich Security, Reinhard Heydrich, prohibited the publication of the encyclical. He could not prevent the Vatican's short-wave transmitter run by the Jesuits from reporting how priests were being imprisoned without trial in Poland and Church property seized; how the church of Mary Magdalen in Cracow, one of the most beautiful in Poland, had been turned into a concert hall and a police school had been installed in the bishop's seminary. It also reported that Polish 'youths and maidens' were being forcibly sterilised to stamp out the race.[801] In England, the *Manchester Guardian* declared that 'tortured Poland has found an advocate in Rome', but 'the language seemed inadequate to the statesmen of the west', and also to the Poles.

Between September, 1939, when France and Britain declared war on Germany, and the spring of 1940, little had happened on the western front; the period became known in the west as the 'phoney war'. In April, 1940, this phoney war ended when the Germans invaded Denmark and Norway, and in May Belgium, the Netherlands, Luxembourg and France, by-passing the Maginot Line through the forests of the Ardennes, routing the French army

---

800   Anthony Rhodes, *Op. Cit.* p. 237

801   *Ibid.* p. 239

with their versatile use of tanks and driving the British Expeditionary Force back to the coast at Dunkirk. On 14 June they marched into Paris. The French government of Paul Reynaud that had fled to Bordeaux collapsed. Marshal Pétain, the veteran general of the Great War, was elected by a majority of the French National Assembly to take charge, and sue for an armistice and save France from the fate of Poland. This he achieved on 22 June. There were some minor humiliations: the armistice was signed in the same railway carriage in the Forest of Compiègne that had seen the capitulation of Germany in 1918; but, to the relief of most of the French, the terms of their surrender were relatively mild. The *Wehrmacht* would occupy only half of the country: the rest would be a free zone with its capital in the spa town of Vichy, and a government appointed by its new president, Marshal Pétain. In contrast to their behaviour in Poland, the German army behaved correctly towards its Aryan neighbour.

On May 22, 1940, while the Germans advanced into the Netherlands, Belgium, Luxemburg, Denmark and Norway, Mussolini and Hitler formed a military alliance known as the Pact of Steel or, when joined by Japan, the Axis powers. Both Pius XI and Pius XII had exhorted Mussolini to keep out of the war, but on 10 June he declared war on Britain and France, and moved into the French Alpes-Maritimes. 'The Pope and the Vatican ... adopting 'their curiously ambivalent behaviour during the Abyssinian war... remained silent.[802] Not so the Italian bishops who advertised their patriotism in their pastoral letters. 'Thirty Italian bishops sent a telegram to the *Duce* congratulating him on his action and predicting the 'inevitable victory of Italian arms...'

    'With Italy's entry into the war,' wrote the historian Anthony Rhodes, 'the high position and prestige enjoyed by the Papacy throughout the world declined. The voice of the Vatican which, under Pius XI, had fearlessly pronounced the moral verdict of Christian civilisation against Nazism was discreetly lowered, though not stilled, and its words and sentiments discreetly adjusted to the exigencies of an anxious neutrality'.[803] To Pius XII, and to many Catholics throughout Europe, Communism remained the principal threat to the Church, and 'when, in June 1924, the Soviet Union was attacked by Germany, to many good Catholics the war took on something of the nature of a crusade'. Hitler, for all his contempt for Catholics, was no doubt aware of

---

802   *Ibid.*, p. 247

803   *Ibid.*, p. 249

this when he named his invasion 'Operation Barbarossa' after the crusading Holy Roman Emperor, Frederick of Hohenstaufen.

Stalin, too, saw the advantage of enlisting the support of Christians in his existential battle with the Germans. He declared himself 'the champion of Freedom of Conscience and Religion', and set up a Department of Church affairs in Moscow 'to organise friendly relations between the government and the confessions'. Around fifty Polish Catholic chaplains were released from the concentration camps, and were attached to a Polish contingent being formed under the Polish general Wladyslaw Anders to fight the Germans. In March, 1942, Anders' corps was evacuated through Iran and Palestine to form the Polish 2nd Army under British command. Anders himself, from a Baltic German family, was not a Catholic but his men were, and it was one of the many ironies of the war that in due course their finest military exploit, dislodging the Wehrmacht from the mountains of central Italy, should have led to the total destruction of Benedict of Nursia's monastery of Monte Casino.

With the outbreak of war, Pius XII lost what little influence he might have had over Catholics in Germany and Austria, and he could do little to assist the Catholics in Poland. As the war progressed, many Catholics were appalled by what they witnessed under German occupation. In France, Cardinal Gerlier, the Archbishop of Lyons, and so Primate of France, had initially welcomed the election of Pétain but he condemned the anti-Semitic measures taken by the prime-minister appointed by Pétain, Pierre Laval. His protest against the deportation of Jews from France 'was read from all the pulpits of his diocese and, in spite of Laval's censorship, broadcast throughout France'.[804] The Archbishop of Toulouse, Jules-Gérard Saliège, preached against the ill-treatment of Jews. 'The Jews are real men and women... They are part of the human species. They are our brothers like so many others. A Christian should not forget this.'

Some did but many did not. The fissure dating from the Dreyfus Affair had not healed. Revenge was in the air among the anti-Dreyfusards who had, in their view, been persecuted by the radical, masonic governments of the Third Republic. In March, 1941, the Vichy government set up a *Commissariat Générale* to administer Jewish affairs – viz. appropriate the money and possessions of French Jews: its third director was Charles du Paty de Clam, the son of the officer chosen to interrogate Alfred Dreyfus, Ferdinand du

---

804   *Ibid.*, p. 316

Paty de Clam.[805] However, more potent among French Catholics than anti-Dreyfusism was anti-Bolshevism. The Spanish Civil War had barely ended; the Communists, routed in Spain, were active in France, and as obedient to Stalin as the French fascists were to Hitler. Should not French Catholics support the German struggle to end the Bolshevik menace? A number from the nations defeated by the Germans enlisted to join the crusade. 'Although exact figures are lacking, probably as many as 125,000 west Europeans served in the Waffen SS… The largest group, some 50,000 men, was Dutch; Belgium provided 40,000 SS men, almost equally divided between Flemings and Walloons; 20,000 came from France.'[806] In France, the Legion of French Volunteers Against Bolshevism became the Charlemagne brigade of the Waffen SS: around 300 members were among those defending Hitler in the bunker beneath the German Chancellery in April and May of 1945, rising from their trenches to confront the Russian tanks shouting 'Long Live Christ the King!'

Poland was not the only European nation with a predominantly Catholic population: there was also Croatia, Slovakia, Lithuania and Hungary. What role was played by these communities of the faithful during the course of the war? Croatia had been part of Yugoslavia ('the nation of South Slavs'), a kingdom established by the Treaty of Versailles incorporating Serbia, Croatia and Montenegro and with a king. Resenting what he took to be the dominance of Serbia within Yugoslavia, a Croatian nationalist, Ante Pavelić, founded a fascist party in 1929 – the Ustasha or 'Upright'; and, when the Italians and Germans dismantled Yugoslavia ten years later, he was made the ruler of an independent Croatian state. Modelling himself on Hiter, and particularly Mussolini, Pavelić took the title of the *Poglavnik* – the Serbo-Coatian equivalent of *Duce*.

Unlike Hitler or Mussolini, Pavelić was a practising Catholic and, when he and other Ustasha leaders returned from exile in Italy to take power in Croatia, they were welcomed with a grand dinner by the Cardinal Archbishop of Zagreb, Aloysius Stepinac. The archbishop later published a pastoral letter asking the faithful to obey the *Poglavnik* not just as their ruler but 'representative of the Holy Catholic Church'.[807] It was an endorsement Stepinac would come to regret. Under Pavelić the pent-up hatred of the

---

805   Piers Paul Read, *The Dreyfus Affair*, p. 352

806   George H. Stein, *the Waffen SS. Hitler's Elite Guard at War 1939-1945*, p. 139

807   Anthony Rhodes, *Op. Cit.* p. 325

Catholic Croats for the Orthodox Serbs was unleashed leading to the most fearful pogroms of Orthodox Christians known in history'. Squads of the Ustasha, sometimes accompanied by and encouraged by Franciscan priests, destroyed 290 Orthodox churches, killed 128 Orthodox priests and burned hundreds of thousands of devout Orthodox men, women and children. It is estimated that over the four years of the war, 700,000 were slaughtered – 10% of the population.[808]

The role of the Franciscans goes back to the time when, over centuries, Croatia was occupied by the Ottoman Turks and, while the Church's hierarchy fled into Austria, the Franciscan missionaries remained and suffered with the people. Now the hierarchy had returned, but the Franciscans remained close to the Croatian people and, having shared their suffering, they were now complicit in their revenge. Cardinal Stepinac, on the other hand, was appalled by the atrocities, and the racist policies of the government. 'We Catholics protest against such measures, and we will combat them.' The Ustasha were now emulating the Nazis and so, like the Nazis, they should be regarded as enemies of the Church. Moreover, the government's treatment of Orthodox Serbs, Jews and gypsies was driving them into the arms of the Communist partisans.

Faced with Stepinac's opposition, Pavelić petitioned the Vatican to have him replaced. He made three requests: all were turned down. But why did the Vatican not do more than sustain an archbishop critical of the regime? Unlike Poland, where hard facts were hard to ascertain, there was no barrier to stop information crossing from Croatia into neighbouring Italy. However, supporters of the *Poglavnik* were deeply embedded in the Vatican administration, and there was a strong incentive to accept that reports of atrocities were untrue. In March, 1942, the Under-Secretary of State, Monsignor Giovanni Battista Montini, confronted a Croatian representative, a Doctor Rusinovich: 'But what is happening in Croatia? Can it be possible that crimes of such a nature are being committed? Was it true that the *Poglavnik* was 'the instigator of a policy of extermination?' Doctor Rusinovic immediately denied the charges, and Montini seemed satisfied.[809]

And always there was the spectre of Communism which was the ideology of one of the two guerrilla forces fighting the Germans and the Ustasha. However abominable the actions of the Ustasha they were Catholics whereas

---

808   *Ibid.*, p. 327
809   *Ibid.*, p. 334

the partisans led by Josip Broz Tito were atheist Communists. A report by a member of the 37th British Military Mission to Yugoslavia, Captain Evelyn Waugh, described now Tito's forces pursued 'a deliberate policy of extermination of the Church in Yugoslavia': however this was not a factor of much interest to the government in London. In the autumn of 1943, a British plenipotentiary, Brigadier Fitzroy Maclean, was sent to the former Yugoslavia to decide which group of partisans 'was killing the most Germans and suggest by which means we could help them to kill more'.[810] Maclean chose those led by Tito.

In Hungary, the Benedictine primate, Cardinal Jusztinian Serédi, Archbishop of Esztergom, was more forthright than Cardinal Stepinac in his denunciation of the racist policies of the Nazis. 'We Hungarians have sometimes been called a *Herrenvolk*,' he declared in a sermon in Saint Stephen's Cathedral on New Year's Day, 1943.

> That is untrue, and nor do we want to be such a people... There is no such thing on earth as a *Herrenvolk* – only those who serve God and those who serve the Devil. No nation is inferior to another...Murder is murder, and he who, for political reasons, orders mass executions will not receive the rites and consolations of the Church. Nor will the Church grant the sacraments to those who, on ideological grounds, abduct human beings for forced labour.[811]

The Germans protested about the Cardinal's sermon to the Hungarian Head of State, Admiral Horthy, but were told that under the Hungarian Constitution the archbishop was free to say what he liked. Horthy, like Cardinal Séredi, believed that the Jews deported from Hungary were being sent to labour camps in the east. However, in April, 1944, two Slovak Jews managed to escape from Auschwitz, reached Bratislava and there told the Papal Legate, Monsignor Burzio, that the deported Jews were destined not for hard labour but for extermination. Monsignor Burzio passed this information on to the Vatican Secretary of State and the Pope.

The existence of gas ovens and crematoria at Auschwitz was now beyond doubt. Protests at the deportation of Hungarian Jews reached Admiral Horthy from all over the world. Pius XII wrote to Admiral Horthy, in his usual periphrastic prose, asking him 'to shorten and mitigate the sufferings

---

810   Fitzroy Maclean, *Eastern Approaches*, p. 287

811   Quoted in Anthony Rhodes, *Op. Cit.* p. 303

that have for so long been peacefully endured on account of their national or racial origin by a great number of unfortunate people belonging to this noble and chivalrous nation'. Horthy took the Pope's plea to heart, and promised to do what he could to stop the deportations, and perhaps make a separate peace with the Allies, but the Germans became aware of his intentions and Horthy was deposed, and replaced by Ferenc Szálasi, leader of the fascist Red Arrows. Adolf Eichmann and his team arrived in Budapest and the 'deportations now began in earnest.[812]

Slovakia was among the most Catholic nations in Europe. For centuries part of the Austro-Hungarian empire, it only came into existence as an independent state in 1939 at Hitler's insistence after he annexed the Sudetenland and occupied Bohemia and Moravia. Its first president, Josef Gaspar Tiso, was a Catholic priest. Under German tutelage, Slovakia became a National Socialist state with Tiso as its President and its own storm troopers, the Hlinka Guard. SS officers were sent from Germany to advise on 'Jewish questions': a 'Jewish Code' was passed into law which excluded Jews from almost every aspect of Slovakian life, and obliged them to wear the Star of David in public. The Slovak government in concert with the German authorities began the deportation of Jews to Auschwitz – 58,000 between March and October of 1942. There were protests from some bishops such as Pavel Jantausch and, when it became known what fate awaited the deported Jews, protests from the Vatican. At first Tiso was defiant: 'There is no foreign intervention which would stop us on the road to the liberation of Slovakia from Jewry'. However, opposition from the Catholic bishops increased: on 8 May, 1943, the Slovakian bishops issued a pastoral letter condemning totalitarianism and anti-Semitism. Tiso then had second thoughts and ordered the end to the deportations.

In August, 1944, there was a rising against Tiso's government which was suppressed by the Germans. In the wake of the German troops came the Einsatzgruppe H. which deported 13,500 of the remaining Slovakian Jews to Auschwitz, and murdered others in camps in Slovakia itself. Two thirds of the Jews living in Slovakia were killed under the government of Tiso. 'Everyone understands that the Holy See cannot stop Hitler,' said the Curial cardinal, Domenico Tardini, 'but who can understand that it does not know how to rein in a priest?'[813]

---

812   Anthony Rhodes, *Op. Cit.* p. 104

813   James Mace Ward, *Priest, Politican, Collaborator: Jozef Tiso and the Making of Fascist Slovakia*, p. 232 (Wikipedia)

Lithuania was one of the three small states situated between Russia and the Baltic Sea. Their original inhabitants were among the last tribes in Europe to remain pagan, converted in the late Middle Ages not by gentle missionaries like Boniface, the English apostle of the Germans, but by brutal German crusaders who, having subdued and converted the native population, remained as their feudal overlords with large estates. Ruled at times by Sweden, or Poland, they were part of the Russian empire from the late eighteenth to the twentieth century, with Baltic barons proving to be efficient and loyal servants of the Tsars.

At the Reformation, Estonia and Latvia had become mainly Lutheran while Lithuania, for centuries joined with Poland, had remained Catholic. Under the agreement reached between Molotov and Ribbentrop in 1939, the Baltic States were assigned to the Soviets. In June 1940 the Soviet Union annexed all three of the independent Baltic states and proceeded to deport to the Siberian prison camps 6,000 from Estonia, 17,000 from Latvia and 17,500 from Lithuania – nationalists, bourgeois, potential counter-revolutionaries and, in the case of Lithuania, Catholic priests.

Prominent in the NKVD cadres responsible for the deportations were Jews which led some Lithuanians to associate Jews with atheistic Bolshevism. Thus, when the Germans drove the Soviets out of Lithuania following Operation Barbarossa, many saw them as liberators. Accompanying the Wehrmacht were Lithuanian nationalists who had fled to escape from the Soviets, and 'who were ready to believe, or to act as if they believed, that the Jews were responsible for Soviet repressions'. As a result, from the start of the programme to exterminate Lithuania's two hundred thousand Jews, 'German killers had all the help they needed... By 4 July, 1941, Lithuanian units were killing Jews under German supervision and orders. In the forest of Ponary outside the city of Vilnius, known as the Jerusalem of the North, around 73,000 Jews, and about eight thousand Poles and Lithuanians were shot and buried in mass graves. Latvians and Estonians also joined in the massacre of Jews. 'By the end of 1941, tens of thousands of Ukrainians, Belarusians, Russians and Tartars had been recruited into local police forces. Ethnic Germans in the Soviet Union were the most desired.'[814]

---

814   *Ibid.*, p. 198

107. Pius XII and the Jews

The systematic killing of all European Jews became German policy in the third year of the war. Hitler's original plan, as we have seen, was to deport them to Madagascar, or send them to Birobidzhan, the autonomous Jewish oblast in the Soviet Far East on the border with China founded by Stalin – a proposal which Stalin declined. Palestine was the favoured destination of Edler von Mildenstein, head of the Jewish Section of the Nazi SD, and mentor of Adolf Eichmann who in 1937, on Mildenstein's instructions, made contact with Zionist agencies and visited Palestine, a trip that was aborted after only one day. After the Anschluss, put in charge of the deportation of Jews from Vienna, Eichmann established a Central Emigration Office through which Jews could exchange their property and possessions for a passport and exit visa. 'Within a few months, the office had emigrated 150,000 Jews.'[815]

The outbreak of war meant it was no longer possible to send Jews overseas to Palestine – the British ruled the waves, and had anyway been under pressure from the Arab Palestinians to curb Jewish immigration; and, with the conquest of Poland, and later the Baltic states, the number of Jews under German governance had vastly increased. Banned from living in Russia under the Tsars, Jews had come to live near the border – the Pale of Settlement: there were the same number of Jews in Lithuania as there were in the whole of Germany, and around three million in Poland. One idea was to settle all European Jews in eastern Europe: 'in mid-September, 1941, Hitler took the strangely ambiguous decision to deport German Jews to Minsk.'[816] In the meantime, they were concentrated in ghettos in Warsaw and Cracow, administered by the Jews themselves.

Hitler had assumed that it would take around three months to defeat the Red Army. This turned out not to be the case. After stupendous losses, and a retreat of over a thousand miles to the outskirts of Moscow and the gates of Leningrad, the Russians held firm. Checked not just by their resolute enemy, but also by the winter weather for which they were unprepared, the Wehrmacht ceased its advance and in due course began a slow retreat. 'As the war turned Stalin's way, Hitler recast its purpose.' His original plan had been to defeat the Soviet Union and then deal with the Jews. Now, as the destruction

---

815   David Cesarini, *Adolph Eichman: The Mind of a War Criminal* . BBC History (Wikipedia)

816   Timothy Snyder, *Op. Cit.* p. 206

of the Soviet Union was indefinitely delayed, the utter extermination of the Jews became the primary objective.

In January, 1942, Reinhard Heydrich, the director of the Reich's Main Security Office, was told by Hermann Göring to draw up a plan for the 'total solution of the Jewish question'. On the 20th Heydrich convened a conference in a large house on the Wannsee, a lake in the wooded suburbs in the west of Berlin. Attending the conference were representatives from the Gestapo, the SS; civil servants from the Reich Chancellery, Interior Ministry and Foreign Ministry; and Adolph Eichmann, now director of the Reich Central Office for Jewish Emigration. Eichmann opened the proceedings with a report of what had already been achieved since the Nazis had come to power in 1933. Over half a million German, Austrian and Czech Jews had emigrated. That was, of course, a small proportion of the eleven million Jews estimated to reside in Europe, half of which were now under German control.

Since emigration was now impossible, another solution – *ein Endlösing*, a final solution – had been agreed and was to be put into effect: all European Jews were to be killed. Since the extermination of Jews was already underway in the conquered territories, none of this came as a surprise to the assembled officials: 'on any given day in the second half of 1941, the Germans shot more Jews than had been killed by pogroms in the entire history of the Russian empire.'[817] Much of the discussion during the ninety minute meeting was about who was to be classified as a Jew. None of those present made any objection to what was proposed, and the only questions raised were over administrative protocols. Heydrich made clear that the SS would be in charge.

Four months after the Wannsee conference, Reinhard Heydrich, acting governor for the German protectorates of Bohemia and Moravia, was assassinated by members of the Czech resistance. In honour of this Nazi martyr, the programme of extermination of Jews which he had initiated was called Operation Reinhard. Among the many concentration camps, there were six 'death camps' equipped with gas chambers and crematoria – at Chemno, Belzec, Sobibor, Treblinka, Majdanek and Auschwitz-Birkenau: Timothy Snyder estimates that 'about 5.4 million Jews died under German occupation'. 'The core of the killing campaign east of the Molotov-Ribbentrop line was Operation Reinhard, the gassing of 1.3 million Polish Jews at Belzec, Sobibór and Treblinka in 1942.... Auschwitz served as the main extermination site for Jewish populations *beyond* Poland... Within the Reich Security Main

817   *Ibid.*, p. 227

-450-

Office, Adolf Eichmann and the men of his section organised deportations from France, Belgium and the Netherlands…. Almost all of the six hundred thousand or so Jews killed by the Germans in 1944 died at Auschwitz.'[818]

Around 100,000 of those who were killed at Auschwitz were not Jews – among them 74,000 non-Jewish Poles and 15,000 Soviet prisoners of war. Nor were the Jews alone in being selected for extinction. 'At least a hundred thousand Roma and Sinti, and more likely two or three times that number were killed by the Germans.' And there were those considered 'unworthy of life'. In Germany itself, the methods for killing large batches of mentally or physically disabled human beings had been developed in Euthanasia Centres in Bamberg, Brandenburg, Graveneck, Hadamar and Sonnenstein; and in Austria Am Spiegelgrund, Gugging and Harheim. 'Scholars have established a fundamental connection between the motivation, the practical experience and the psychological preparation, and the technology used in the Nazi euthanasia centres…and the extermination camps used in the Holocaust.[819]

Almost the only example of an effective protest against the Nazis' homicidal programmes was made by the Archbishop of Münster, Count Clemens August von Galen. Münster was the capital of Westphalia, one of the most Catholic provinces in Germany, and the archbishop was described by the SS General Jürgen Stroop, sent to rebuke him for his criticism of Rosenberg's ideas, as 'a great gentleman, a true aristocrat, a Renaissance prince of the Church'. Von Gallen, as we have seen, had been in Rome for the German's *ad limina* visit to Pope Pius XI in January, 1937, and contributed to the encyclical *Mit Brennender Sorge*. Now, in the spring of 1941, after learning of the Nazis' systematic killing of the disabled and insane, he preached a series of powerful sermons which were printed and distributed throughout Germany.

'Thou shalt not kill'. God engraved this commandment on the souls of men long before any penal code…They are the unchangeable and fundamental truths of our social life… As for the first commandment, 'Thou shalt not have strange gods before me,' instead of the One, True, Eternal God, men have created, at the dictates of their whim, their own gods to adore: Nature, the State, the Nation or the Race.

In later sermons von Galen attacked the harassment of priests, the closure of churches, the concentration camps, and the tactics of the Gestapo which

---

818   *Ibid.*, p. 275

819   See Christopher R. Browning, *The Origins of the Final Solution: The Evolution of Nazi Jewish Policy. September 1939-March 1942.* University of Nebraska Press. (Wikipedia0

terrorised 'even the most loyal and law-abiding citizens'. Among the Nazis, there were calls for his arrest, or assassination, but Goebbels realised that it would lead to disaffection among the devout Catholics of Westphalia which during the war the country could ill-afford. On 24 August, 1941, Hitler ordered the suspension of the euthanasia programme designated T4, but widespread euthanasia continued. By the end of the war, it is estimated that between 275,000 and 300,000 men, women and children considered 'unworthy of life' had had their lives brought to an end.

It does not detract from the courage of Archbishop von Galen, the 'Lion of Münster', that as bishop of the diocese which had seen off the Anabaptists in the sixteenth century – a fanatical sect with which he compared the Nazis – he was to some extent protected by the devotion to the Catholic Church of his Westphalian flock. His sermons were read outside Germany and proved useful for Allied propaganda but they contained no reference to the persecution of the Jews.

So too Stalin, after November 1941, never singled out the Jews as victims of Hitler, and none of the Allied powers seem 'to have seriously contemplated direct military action to rescue the Jews'.[820] They rather hoped that Pope Pius XII would condemn by name those Catholics who were aiding and abetting the German genocide. In Belgium, Léon Degrelle, the Catholic leader of the fascist Rexist Party and active collaborator with the Germans, was excommunicated by the Bishop of Namur, but the Croatian *Poglavnik*, Ante Pavelić and Marshal Pétain, whose governments co-operated in rounding up French Jews for deportation to Auschwitz, and whose definition of who was Jewish in the case of Vichy France cast a wider net than did that of the Germans, remained in communion with the Church.

The reasons for Pius XII's reluctance to condemn the Nazis by name were various. First of all, as we have seen, there was the policy established by Pope Benedict XV during World War I that in conflicts between different nations the Vatican should condemn atrocities and aid the victims of war but not take sides. Second, there was the conviction, hard to shake off, that however criminal the Nazis, and however hostile towards the Catholic Church, they had not as yet banned worship in Germany while the Soviets had done what they could to eradicate the Christian religion: it was possible to sustain this view well into the war, and as a result there was some dismay in the Vatican

---

820   Timothy Snyder, *Op. Cit.*, p. 239

when, in September, 1942, the American businessman, Myron Taylor, the personal envoy of the US president, arrived with a letter from Roosevelt stating that the Allies' policy was now the Germans' unconditional surrender. Nazism was to be eradicated root and branch, and to that end 'America and Britain had a close alliance and excellent relations with Soviet Russia'. 'It was their intention when the war was won, that Russia should play its part in ordering the new world'[821].

A third reason for Pius XII's failure to condemn the Germans by name for the mass killings in their death camps was that it took time for the evidence to reach the Vatican, and longer still for it to be believed. No information came from Catholics in Germany itself where 'the existence of wartime extermination camps was a closely guarded secret…'[822] After the war, in the author Gitta Sereny's extended interviews with Albert Speer, the Third Reich's Minister for Arms and Munitions, it proved difficult to establish that he knew about the extermination of the Jews.[823]

There was also – a fourth factor – a widespread mistrust of Allied, particularly British, propaganda. Hitler in *Mein Kampf* had expressed admiration for the way that, during World War I, British exaggeration of German atrocities in Belgium – depicting German soldiers as brutes and monsters – had been more effective in stiffening the resolve of British troops than the Germans' dismissal of the British 'Tommies' as timid weaklings. Was it not possible that the Allies were exaggerating the scale of the Germans' atrocities? On 30 August, 1943, the American Secretary of State wrote: 'There exists no sufficient proof to justify a statement regarding execution in gas chambers.' When Myron Taylor had his audience with the pope, 'Pius XII, for his part, did not hide from the American diplomat that he thought certain things were being exaggerated by Allied propaganda'.[824]

The fifth, and most conclusive reason for Pope Pius XII not to condemn Hitler and the Germans by name for perpetrating genocide in eastern Europe was the belief that it would do nothing to help the Jews yet intensify the persecution of Catholics. In July of 1942, the leaders of the Catholic Church and the Reformed Church of Holland had sent a joint telegram to the

---

821   Anthony Rhodes, *Op. Cit.,* p. 267

822   Timothy Snder, *Op. Cit.,* p. 462

823   See Gitta Sereny, *Albert Speer His Battle with Truth.*

824   Pierre Blet, S.J., *Pius XII and the Second World War. According to the Archives of the Vatican,* p. 160

Reichskommissar of the Netherlands, Arthur Seyss-Inquart, threatening to protest from the pulpits of their churches at the deportation of Jews that was then underway. Seyss-Inquart replied that, if they were to follow such a course of action, Jews who had converted to Christianity and had until then been spared, would be apprehended and sent east. 'The Reformed Church agreed to this and let the matter drop. But the Catholic Archbishop of Utrecht refused and issued a Pastoral Letter sharply condemning the Nazi persecution of the Jews'. [825] Whereupon 244 Catholic Jews were arrested and deported, among them the philosopher and Carmelite nun, Edith Stein (Sister Benedicta of the Cross) who before the war had written to Pius XII urging him to protest against the Nazis' ill-treatment of German Jews. She was gassed and her body incinerated at Auschwitz.

Pius XII was aware that many could not understand why he did not excommunicate Hitler who, with other Nazi leaders, had been baptised a Catholic. 'I have often considered excommunication, to castigate in the eyes of the entire world the fearful crime of genocide', he later told his doctor, 'but after much praying and many tears, I realise that my condemnation would not only fail to help the Jews, it might even worsen their situation...' In his Christmas message broadcast over Vatican radio on Christmas Eve, 1942, Pius went as far as he thought wise in alerting the world to fate of 'those hundreds of thousands who, without any fault on their part, sometimes only because of their nationality or race, have been consigned to death or to a slow decline'. He did not name the Jews, but the import of what he said was clear. His words were commended by some – an editorial in the *New York Times* called Pius 'a lonely voice crying out of the silence of a continent'[826]; but it disappointed others for failing to say who was perpetrating these atrocities. In enraged the Germans, who called Pius 'a mouthpiece for the Jews', but the lack of specificity enabled them to claim in diplomatic circles that the pope's words were meant for the Soviets.[827]

His words had an effect in Italy itself, where there was a camp at Ferramonti di Tasia in which several thousand Jews were interned. It was Mussolini's state policy to deport them, 'but the concrete decisions taken by his subordinates were always those of refusing and even sabotaging every step taken on behalf

---

825   Anthony Rhodes, *Op.Cit.*, p. 345

826   *New York Times*, 25 December, 1942

827   Michael Phayer, *The Catholic Church and the Holocaust, 1930-1965*, p. 63 (Wikipedia)

of deportation'.[828] The situation changed in 1944 when, after Mussolini had been deposed and then re-instated, the Wehrmacht moved into Italy, occupied Rome and initiated a round-up of Rome's Jews who for centuries had lived in the city under the popes' protection. Pius instructed Catholic institutes to hide them: 'the barriers of the canonical cloister were lifted, thus allowing men to enter convents of women religious, and also permitting women to enter the cloisters of male religious…' Around a hundred Jews and anti-fascist fugitives were given refuge in the Vatican City: others were hidden in 'the extraterritorial buildings adjacent to the various basilicas'. After a visit from the pope's nephew, the pro-Nazi rector of the German National Church in Rome, Monsignor Alois Hundal, told the German authorities that the pope was minded to denounce the Germans' actions which would make life difficult for the Wehrmacht. As a result, 'Himmler himself gave the order to suspend the arrests "out of consideration for the special character of Rome"'[829].

Meanwhile, 'while the pope was silent in public, his Secretariat of State was exerting pressure on the nuncios and apostolic delegates in Slovakia, Croatia, Romania and Hungary, telling them to intervene'. Monsignor Angelo Roncalli, Apostolic Delegate in Turkey, saved many Jews by issuing visas and baptismal certificates, and by direct intervention with the authorities: he later insisted 'that on each occasion he had acted only on the precise orders of Pius XII'.[830] These efforts by the Holy See were recognised and appreciated by Jewish organizations. The Jewish writer, Pinchas Lapide, who was the Israeli Consul in Milan for some years, would later say that 'the Catholic Church saved more Jewish lives during the war than all the other churches, religious institutions and rescue organisations put together. Its record…stands in startling contrast to the achievements of the international Red Cross and the Western Democracies.' Lapide estimated that about 850,000 were thus saved.'[831] 'It is therefore, I think, established beyond all doubt,' concludes the historian Anthony Rhodes, ' that the humane work of the Pope, in helping suffering European Jewry during the Second Word War, not only by large donations but by hiding them from their persecutors, was in fact in the finest charitable traditions of the Catholic Church'.[832]

---

828   Pierre Blet, S.J., *Op. Cit.*, p. 157
829   Anthony Rhodes, *Op.Cit.*, p. 216
830   *Ibid.*, p. 340
831   Pierre Blet, S.J., *Op. Cit.* p. 286
832   Anthony Rhodes, *Op. Cit.*, p. 341

PART SIX

108.   The Iron Curtain

The Second World War ended on 8 May 1945 in Europe, and on 2 September 1945 in Asia. By any measure, it had been the most vicious war in human history. Major cities had been totally demolished, infrastructure destroyed and between 70 and 85 million people killed – 50-56 million as a result of the conflict, 19-28 million as a result of starvation and disease. Around 28 million Russians died, 20 million Chinese, 8 million Germans. Britain, France and the United States suffered around 350,000 – 450,000 fatalities; Italy, among the Axis powers, much the same. 11.44% of the Soviet population perished; 16.7% of the Polish population; 17.5% of that of the Ukraine. The comparable figures for Great Britain were 0.94%, for France 0.93%; for the United States, 0.32%.

For Pope Pius XII, what he and his predecessors had feared had now come to pass: 60 million Catholics were now living under Communist regimes in the east European nations that the Soviets had liberated from the Germans. Germany itself was divided into zones – American, British, French and Russian; and the capital, Berlin, was itself divided into four sectors: it was a mark of the genius of Charles de Gaulle that France, which had collaborated with the Germans during most of the war, was declared one of the four victors. Given the high price in blood the Soviets had paid, and the facts on the ground, Stalin's demands when it came to eastern Europe accepted at Yalta in 1945 could hardly be refused. During the war, he had eased the persecution of Christians in Russia to enlist their support; such tolerance was not now extended to the Catholics in eastern Europe: 'for many people in central and eastern Europe, the arrival of the Red army inaugurated a period of terror…'[833] The persecution was naturally most rigorous in those parts of Poland which were now incorporated within the Soviet Union. In Western Ukraine, the seven million members of the Uniate Church – Orthodox Christians who were in communion with Rome – were suppressed. The Uniate Archbishop of

---

833   Michael Burleigh, *Sacred Causes*, p. 320

Lwów, now Lviv, Josef Slipyj, after refusing the offer of the see of Kiev in return for the renunciation of his Roman obedience, was sent to a camp in the Urals where he remained for the next seventeen years.

In Lithuania, once again a Soviet republic, 'the Latin priests...were expelled in hundreds on fabricated charges. Many were taken to Siberia...'[834] In Albania, the Catholic hierarchy were arrested or shot together with about a hundred priests and nuns. In Poland Nazi concentration camps, among them Auschwitz and Majdanek, were used by the NKVD to imprison members of the former Home Army who had spent four years fighting the Germans. These prisoners were then shipped eastwards in long freight trains: around 25,000 were held in camps south of Moscow.[835]

The persecution of Catholics was not confined to those nations occupied by the Red Army and so controlled by Stalin. In Yugoslavia, the Communist partisans under Marshal Tito who had benefitted from British aid liberated their own country and took revenge on members of the Ustasha and other political opponents. In Croatia priests were executed, imprisoned, or driven into hiding, and religious education ceased. Archbishop Stepinac was arrested, put on trial and sentenced to seventeen years imprisonment for collaborating with the Germans.

The move by the new Communist regimes against the Catholic Church came not just from the atheist imperative embedded in Marxism, but an awareness that 'the churches represented a constituency outside the totalitarian state, and in many cases were the main surviving repository of a sense of national independence...'[836] This was particularly true in Hungary where the primate, Jósef Mindszenty, Archbishop of Esztergom, 'a blunt-speaking Hungarian patriot' whose politics 'were those of a Catholic Habsburg-minded monarchist', had been an outspoken critic of both Nazism and Communism. In July, 1919, he had been arrested by both the Karolyi government and then that of the Communist, Béla Kun. In 1939 he had denounced the fascist Arrow Cross Party, and again in 1940, judging it to be as evil as the Communists.

Though not a nobleman in the mould of Bishop Graf von Galen of Münster or Prince Sapieha, Archbishop of Krakow, Mindszenty, the son of a magistrate, having seen off Bela Kun, was not about to be intimidated by

---

834   E.E.Y Hales, *Op. Cit.,* p. 282

835   Burleigh, *Op. Cit.* p. 321

836   *Ibid.*. p. 326

another Bolshevik, Mátyás Rákosi; but this adversary, with the backing of Stalin and the Red Army, was more formidable, declaring that 'the tolerant policy which has donned kid gloves for dealing with traitors, spies and smugglers clad in clerical garb was over'. In December, 1948, Mindszenty was arrested and, after torture by sleep-deprivation, put on trial. On 8 February he was found guilty of black marketeering, espionage and treason. He was sentenced to life imprisonment. During the Hungarian uprising in 1956 he was released and took refuge in the American embassy before Russian tanks restored the Communist government in Budapest. He was to remain there for the next fifteen years.

In Poland, because of the strong Catholic faith of the population, its atrocious suffering at the hands of the Germans, and the courageous resistance of the Home Army, the Communist government had to move with a certain caution. Archbishop Hlond, who had been under house arrest by the Gestapo in France, returned to Poland as Archbishop of Warsaw. He was able to appoint bishops to vacant sees but he soon came into conflict with the Communist government over the censorship of his pastoral letters, and the secularisation of Catholic schools. 'Since the days of Saint Peter,' he wrote in May, 1947, 'the Church has not been subjected to a persecution as it is today'. He died in 1948 and was replaced by the Bishop of Lublin, Stefan Wyszyński. In 1953, during a government onslaught on the Church in Poland, Wyszynski was imprisoned and held in house arrest until the 'thaw' under Wadislaw Gomulka in 1956.

In Cracow, even the Nazi head of the General Government, Hans Frank, had not had the temerity to move against Archbishop Prince Sapieha. He had remained inviolate and, when seminarians were being pursued by the Germans, had concealed them in his palace – among them Karol Wojtyla, whom he ordained as a priest on 1 November, 1946. Sapieha died in July, 1951. Wyszyński lived to see Sapieha's *protégé*, Karol Wojtyla, become pope.

109. Post-war

In western Europe the Communists, who had been the most militant members of the French Resistance and the Italian partisans, now felt that the time was approaching when they would emulate their comrades in East Berlin, Warsaw, Bucharest, Budapest, Belgrade and Prague: they were only thwarted in Athens by the intervention of first British and then American armed forces. Their leaders returned from exile in Russia – Jacques Duclos to France, Palmiro Togliatti to Italy. Communism became fashionable: artists like Pablo Picasso, philosophers like John-Paul Sartre, authors like Louis Aragon joined the Party. Even those who were not Communists, nor even fellow travellers, realised what the western democracies owed to the Red army and 'Uncle Joe': it was considered tactless to raise the question of the gulags and religious persecution.

The Poles, for whom Britain and France had gone to war with Germany, and who had suffered as much as any, were abandoned to the Soviets and treated shabbily in the west for fear of offending Stalin. They had provided 10% of the pilots for the Battle of Britain, and had suffered atrocious losses in the Battle of Monte Cassino, but they were excluded from the victory parade in Whitehall, and their war memorial was erected not in London but in the suburb of Northolt.

To set against the crimes of Catholic fascists such as Pavlevic in Croatia and Monsignor Tiso in Slovakia in the post-war reckoning should be remembered the Catholics who had bravely spoken out against the Nazis and mostly paid with their lives. The Jesuit Rupert Mayer who as early as 1936 had preached against the Nazis was sent to the Sachsenhausen concentration camp. Bernhard Lichtenberg, the Provost of Saint Hedwig's Cathedral in Berlin, ended a sermon in 1941 with an appeal to the congregation 'to pray for the Jews, and the wretched prisoners in the concentration camps, above all for my fellow clergy'[837]: he was imprisoned and died while being transferred to Dachau. An Austrian priest, Franz Reinisch, was executed in 1942 for refusing to swear the oath of allegiance to Hitler. In February, 1943, two students, Hans Scholl aged 25, and his sister Sophie, 22, members of the White Rose movement opposing Hitler, were arrested while handing out anti-Nazi leaflets at Munich University, sentenced to death by the President of the People's Court, Roland Freisler. They asked to be received into the Catholic Church but were advised against it by the Lutheran pastor on the grounds that it would upset their parents. They were guillotined in the Stadelheim prison. Claus Schenk, Graf von Stauffenberg, who tried but failed to kill Hitler with a bomb he planted in the Wehrmacht's headquarters in East Prussia and was shot in the courtyard of the War Office in the Bendlerstrasse in Berlin was a devout Catholic. Edith Stein, Sister Benedicta

---

837   Annedore Leber, *Conscience in Revolt. Sixty-four Stories of Resistance in Germany 1933-1945,* p. 201

of the Cross, was, as we have seen, sent to Auschwitz not just as a Jew but also a Catholic. A Polish Franciscan friar, Father Maximilian Kolbe, a prisoner in Auschwitz, voluntarily took the place of Franciszek Gajowniczek, one of ten inmates selected to starve to death in an underground bunker as retribution after the escape of a prisoner. Father Kolbe led the other nine in prayer and was the last to die – finished off with an injection of carbolic acid.

Thus the Catholic Church had its martyrs – there were 2,579 priests, mostly Poles, held in the 'Priest Barracks' in the Dachau Concentration Camp – but the numbers were trivial when it came to the six million Jews exterminated – for belonging not to a religion, which was a matter of choice, but a tribe or people, which was not. The German genocide of the Jews – the Shoa or Holocaust – was an event unique in human history which some saw as calling for a re-definition of good and evil. In the immediate aftermath of the war, the return of liberated prisoners-of-war and forced labourers; the flood of German refugees evicted from the Sudetenland, East Prussia and Silesia – 'the largest population transfer in modern history'[838]; and the threat of a Communist takeover in western Europe, meant that it was not in the forefront of peoples' minds: the French philosopher, Simone Weil, did not mention it in the paper she wrote for the Free French, *The Need for Roots*. Some Nazis were prosecuted for 'crimes against humanity' by the Allies at a tribunal at Nuremberg, but a number of the worst offenders escaped to South America, or hid out in the Alps, some with the help of the pro-Nazi Austrian bishop in the Vatican, Alois Hundal.

In Germany the Allies embarked upon a programme of de-Nazification but it was not vigorously pursued. Germany and Austria could not be run indefinitely by the Allied armies and there were not enough untainted civil servants to form a national administration. Elderly politicians, some of whom had belonged to the Catholic political parties abandoned by Pope Pius XI – the Centre Party in Germany, the Populare in Italy – emerged to head the post-war governments of western Europe. Konrad Adenauer, the former mayor of Cologne, became the Christian Democrat Chancellor of west Germany: he and his fellow-Catholic, Charles de Gaulle, attended a service of reconciliation in Rheims cathedral.

Alcide de Gasperi, in Italy, founded the Christian Democrat party with the help of both the Vatican and the CIA, and won a resounding victory over the Communists in the general election of 1948. Together with two other

---

838   Burleigh, *Op. Cit.,* p. 324

devout Catholics, Konrad Adenauer and Robert Schuman, he was among those European statesmen who established the European Coal and Steel Community: integrating their nations' economies was to make another war impossible for the west European nations. It was seen as a first step towards a united Europe – in the minds of many the rebirth of the Holy Roman Empire. The treaty between Belgium, France, Italy, Luxembourg, the Netherlands and West Germany to form the European Economic Community was signed in 1957 in Rome.

Exiles belonging to Germany's Social Democratic Party returned to form an opposition to Adenauer's Christian Democratic Party (Christian Social Union in Bavaria), and the West Germans directed their energies to rebuilding their infrastructure and their economy and adopting the values and outlook of the western democracies: with a well-constructed constitution, there was to be no repeat of the chaos of the Weimar days. The Teutonic religion disappeared like a puff of smoke. Eugenics went out of fashion but was discreetly practiced in the treatment of children with Down's Sydrome or Spina Bifida, and the pre-implantation screening of foetuses in the process of *in vitro* fertilisation.

We have seen how philosophers in the nineteenth and early twentieth centuries, liberated from the constraints of Christian teaching, used Darwin's concept of evolution, described by Herbert Spencer as 'the survival of the fittest', and Nietzsche's ideal of the *Ubermensch*, to develop racist ideologies; but what responsibility could be ascribed to Christians who created a culture of discrimination with their degrading treatment of the Jews? How could the Church have permitted the development of an ethic whereby a Croatian youth, after confessing a sexual peccadillo, could go on to slaughter Jews and fellow Christian Orthodox Serbs – perhaps encouraged to do so by his Franciscan confessor? True, the popes had insisted that Jews were not to be killed or forcibly converted; but they had confined them in ghettos and obliged them to sew the Star of David onto their clothes. Jews had been subject to an enduring and ubiquitous disdain, massacred by Crusaders, expelled from Catholic countries, defamed by Blood Libels and excluded from the Society of Jesus – a statute hastily abolished in 1946.

Materially, Europe recovered from the devastation of the war. It was a moral irony that West Germany – the miscreant, defeated nation responsible for the Holocaust – would be at an advantage when it came to economic revival thanks to the *tabula rasa* following the destruction of its cities. With Marshall

Plan Aid from the United States, it built new factories and plants. Unlike the French and the British, it was free of the ball and chain of an empire.

The historian Timothy Snyder suggests that it was in pursuit of an empire that Hitler invaded the Soviet Union.

> The answer to the question of 1941 has less to do with the intellectual heritage of the Enlightenment and more to do with the possibilities of imperialism, less to do with Paris and more to do with London. Hitler and Stalin both confronted the two chief inheritances of the British nineteenth century: imperialism as an organising principle of world politics, and the unbroken power of the British empire at sea. Hitler, unable to rival the British on the oceans, saw eastern Europe as ripe for a new land empire.'[839]

The British and French empires survived the war. In 1945, rather than learning the lesson that perhaps powerful nations should not force their rule on weaker ones, the two western democracies re-possessed the colonies that had been occupied by the Japanese. Winston Churchill, the great war leader, was an imperialist: the fear that he would use British conscripts to hold on to India was one of the reasons for his overwhelming defeat in the British General Election of 1945. India, the corner-stone of the British Empire, was given its independence but Britain became mired in other nationalist risings in Malaya, Kenya, Rhodesia and Cyprus.

In Indo-China, at the end of the war, the Emperor of the Anamite kingdom, Bao Dai, appealed to General de Gaulle to leave his country to govern itself. 'You have suffered too much during four deadly years not to understand that the Vietnamese people who have a history of twenty centuries and an often glorious past, no longer wish, can no longer support, any foreign domination'. The letter received no reply. De Gaulle sent General Leclerc to re-impose French rule in Hanoi, and appointed as High Commissioner Thierry d'Argenlieu, a naval officer who had once been a Carmelite monk.

What of the Church outside Europe? In China it flourished after the defeat of the Japanese with 20 archdioceses, 85 dioceses, over 3,000 missionaries and 2,557 priests but in 1949, after the defeat of the Nationalists by the Communists led by Mao Tse Tung, Catholic worship was permitted only in churches approved by the Chinese Patriotic Catholic Association – a body

---

839   Timothy Snyder, *Op. Cit.* p. 157

which was controlled by the Communist Party and which did not accept the authority of the pope. Catholics loyal to the pope were driven underground. The Church remained influential in the Philippines, and in Kerala in southern India. So too in South America which had been spared the ordeal of World War II.

In the United States and British dominions the post-war period was the era of formidable churchmen such as Cardinal Francis Spellman, the Archbishop of New York – reputed to be the model for Stephen Fermoyle in Henry Morton Robinson's successful novel *The Cardinal* (1950). In Australia there was Daniel Mannix, Archbishop of Melbourne from 1917 – 1963. Catholics comprised a quarter of Australia's population and was made up mainly of Irish immigrants until the end of World War II when they were joined by Catholics fleeing from devastated Europe: B.A. Santamaria, the Catholic who successfully thwarted the takeover of the Australian Labour movement by Communists, was the son of an immigrant from the Aeolian Islands in the Tyrrhenian Sea.

110. The New Theology

In Europe, during the 1950s, among those who were not Communists or fellow-travellers, Catholicism was in fashion. In Britain, although the high hopes that had followed the re-establishment of the hierarchy, and the conversion of the Anglican clergymen, Henry Manning and John Henry Newman, had not been realised, there were prominent and popular Catholic apologists such as G.K. Chesterton and Hilaire Belloc. The Captain Waugh who, as member of the British Military Mission to Yugoslavia had warned his government that Tito's Communist partisans persecuted the Church, was in civilian life a successful author; so too a fellow convert, Graham Greene, who had made his name with a novel about a fugitive priest in Mexico during the revolution, *The Power and the Glory*; and wrote others with Catholic themes such as *The End of the Affair*. Both were realists yet described the miraculous intervention of God in human affairs: this was acceptable to their readers. 'Religion mattered and mattered deeply in British society as a whole in the 1950s'.[840]

In the United States, Walker Percy (*The Moviegoer*) and Flannery O'Connor (*A Good Man is Hard to Find*) were both committed Catholics: 'My

---

840   Callum G. Brown, *The Death of Christian Britain*, p. 7

audience' said O'Connor in 1955, 'are those who think God is dead'. In Spain there was the philosopher Miguel de Unamuno (*The Agony of Christianity*); in France, Paul Claudel (*L'Annonce faite à Marie*), Georges Bernanos (*Journal d'un Curé de Campagne*); the novelist and diarist Julien Green; and François Mauriac (*Thérèse Desqueyroux, Le Noeud de vipères*). Mauriac had joined the Resistance and was 'as close as anyone could be to General de Gaulle.'[841]

In France, there was also a new dynamism among theologians such as the Dominican, Yves Congar, and the Jesuits Henri de Lubac and Henri Bouillard. The Catholic philosopher, Jacques Maritain, appointed by General de Gaulle to be French Ambassador to the Holy See, declared in 1948 that, when it came to the renewal of the Church, 'France is light-years ahead of other countries… If the Holy See puts on the brakes, this not because France is in error, but because France is way ahead'.

A case of the Holy See putting on the breaks arose with the Worker Priest movement which had been started by Father Jacques Lowe in the Marseilles docks in 1941. Throughout Europe, the alienation of the working-classes from the Catholic Church had preoccupied popes, bishops and priests. Jacques Lowe came up with the idea of sending priests in civilian clothes to work in factories alongside the workers and, by sharing their privations and aspirations, bring them back into the fold. In 1945, Pius XII cautiously approved this novel mission but by 1950 it became clear that many of the priests had become politicised: fifteen were working with the Communist trade unions and ten had married. The priests were ordered to return to their parishes. In 1955, just as the early popes had co-opted pagan seasonal bacchanalias for the feasts of Christmas and Easter, Pius XII declared 1 May, the day on which Socialist and Communists celebrated their aspirations and triumphs, the Feast of Saint Joseph the Worker.

Such gestures achieved little, leaving it open to Catholic philosophers and theologians to ask whether there was perhaps something about the way the Church presented itself that alienated potential converts. This was the premise of the *nouvelle théologie* which flourished during these post-war years in the universities and Catholic institutes in both in France and Germany. At its heart was a revolt against the straightjacket imposed by Thomism – the theology of Thomas Aquinas – which had been declared the foundation of Catholic orthodoxy by the popes in previous centuries, and so was the

---

841   Quoted in Peter Hebblethwaite, *Paul VI, The First Modern Pope*, p. 216

basis for instruction in seminaries and Catholic schools. Why, it was asked, should the Catholic faith be frozen in the teaching of a Mediaeval theologian obsessed with Aristotle? Should not theologians be allowed to go back beyond Aquinas and study the early Fathers of the Church – a *ressourcement,* a return to the sources? And should they not be allowed to absorb modern Biblical exegesis – viz. research by scholars into the texts of the Hebrew Bible and the Christian New Testament? Theologians were now no longer labelled 'liberal' and 'conservative' but *ouvert* or *fermé* – 'open' or 'shut'.

Was this Modernism under a new guise? Certainly some in the Vatican thought so, among them the Dominican theologian Reginald Garrigou-Lagrange who in 1946 suggested that the so-called *ressourcement* was merely a cover for theological novelties and speculation. For example, the French Jesuit palaeontologist Pierre Teilhard de Chardin wrote that the account in Genesis of the creation of Adam and Eve was a fable; the Swiss theologian, Hans Küng, disputed papal infallibility; and the German theologian Karl Rahner declared that he wished 'to dispel the notion that catholic theology was a monolith in which everything of importance was settled'.[842] It was Rahner who came up with the idea of 'the anonymous Christian' whereby anyone true to his or her conscience would be saved. This would seem to suggest, wrote the Swiss theologian Hans Urs von Balthasar, 'that there is ultimately no difference between Christians who are such by name and Christians who are not… Hence it cannot matter whether one professes the Christian name or not'.[843]

Pope Pius XII, who early in his reign had encouraged 'audacity' in theological thinking, later grew alarmed at the direction the new theology was taking, 'Pius at heart was deeply conservative, increasingly fearful of the genie he had let out of the lamp'.[844] In August 1950 he published an encyclical, *Humani Generis,* 'concerning some false opinions threatening to undermine the foundations of Catholic doctrine'. He reminded the faithful that it was not theologians who were the source of truth but the teaching authority of the Church. The use of reason had its limits 'for the truths that concern the relations between God and man wholly transcend the visible order of things, and, if they are translated into human action and influence, they call for self-

842   Philip Trower, *The Catholic Church and the Counter-Faith,* p. 241
843   Quoted in *Ibid.,* p.258
844   Eamon Duffy, *Op. Cit.* p. 351

surrender and abnegation'. Although he did not name names, Pius clearly had in mind the proponents of the *nouvelle théologie* whose teaching he believed introduced relativism into Catholic teaching and so undermined the Church's *magisterium*.

The principle that truth was not arrived at only through scientific research, Biblical exegesis or the use of reason, was demonstrated three months after the publication of *Humani Generis* by Pius XII when he declared *ex cathedra*, as a dogma to be accepted by all Catholics, that Mary, the Mother of God, did not die and decay but was bodily 'assumed' into Heaven. This belief had been held from at least the fifth century by Catholic and Orthodox Christians alike but had no basis in Scripture. The declaration of the Assumption was only the second exercise of papal infallibility established by the First Vatican Council – that dogma itself being the first: the dogma of the Immaculate Conception had been pronounced by Pio Nono before the Council in 1858. It was a provocation to Protestant Christians with their belief in *sola scriptura*, and distaste for Catholic 'Mariolatry'; and it embarrassed many Catholic theologians for the same reasons. However, it delighted the mass of the faithful and the annual commemoration of the Assumption of August 15th became one of the most important and popular Feast Days in the calendar of the Church.

Ill-health and exhaustion dogged the next eight years of Pope Pius XII's pontificate. He avoided demanding liturgies, concentrating his remaining energies on addressing lay Catholics, explaining the relevance of Catholic teaching to their professional associations, insisting that *they* were the Church, calling upon them to eschew hedonism and lead lives of heroic virtue. To rejuvenate the episcopate, he appointed bishops in their thirties – Julius Döpfner as Archbishop of Munich at the age thirty-five, and Karol Wojtyla an auxiliary bishop of Cracow at the age of thirty-eight. Giovanni Battista Montini, the under-secretary of state who had been Pius's close advisor and confidant throughout the war years, became suspect for his friendliness towards the new theologians, and was exiled from the Vatican to become archbishop of Milan without the traditional cardinal's hat.

111. Vatican II

Pope Pius XII died on 5 October, 1958, in his summer residence of Castel Gandolfo and, just as he had been the obvious candidate to succeed Pope Pius XI, so Giovanni Battista Montini might well have followed Pope Pius XII but, though he was said to have received one or two votes in the conclave, he was thought to be disqualified by his lack of the scarlet, wide-brimmed, tasselled cardinal's hat. To keep the seat warm for him the cardinals sought a stop-gap – one of their number who was old and in poor health – and on the twelfth ballot they elected Angelo Giuseppe Roncalli, the Patriarch of Venice, who took the name the name John.

Pope John XXIII is described by Professor Eamon Duffy as 'the most beloved pope in history'.[845] He was perhaps also among the most misrepresented. One of his first acts was to recall the liberal Archbishop Montini from Milan and make him a cardinal; and then, three months after his coronation, he summoned an Ecumenical Council of the Catholic Church to assemble in the Vatican. This Second Vatican Council was to be pastoral, not dogmatic. It would complete the agenda of the First, prematurely disbanded in 1870 after the defeat of France in the Franco-Prussian war, but, at Pope John's 'personal insistence', it was not to be 'a Council directed against the modern world.'[846]

Because of what followed from Vatican II, Pope John XXIII was to be portrayed as a liberal – *ouvert* in the terminology of the new theologians; but, as Montini would later tell the French theologian Jean Guitton, 'Pope John was much more conservative than me, much more traditional.'[847] Because he was the son of peasants in northern Italy who lived above their cattle, there was talk of his 'peasant shrewdness'[848]; but he had a doctorate in Theology and was the author of a substantial study of Saint Charles Borromeo, the apostle of the Council of Trent. Nor had he spent much time caring for souls in rural parishes as the epithet 'peasant' might suggest. Conscripted during World War I, he had served as an orderly and chaplain but was then appointed director of the Congregation for the Propagation of the Faith, and later joined the Vatican's diplomatic service, sent by Pius XI as apostolic delegate to Bulgaria, and then Turkey.

---

845   *Ibid.* p. 361
846   *Ibid.*, p. 358
847   Peter Hebblethwaite, *Op. Cit.*, p. 340
848   Eamon Duffy, *Op. Cit.* p. 364

Isolated from his fellow-Catholics in Sofia and then Ankara during World War II, he established friendly relations with leaders of the Orthodox Churches and Turkish politicians; and he did all he could to help fugitive Jews by issuing Vatican passports and visas. The terrible plight of the Jews during the war, and the enormity of the Holocaust, raised questions that all Christians, but particularly a pope, must answer. How was it that German Catholics – both clergy and laity – had done so little to protest against the Nazis' treatment of German Jews? How was that so many from Catholic countries such as Croatia and Slovakia had been not just complicit but active in the mass extermination of blameless civilians? Had the Church been right to concentrate its concern to its own rights and interests, and neglect those of non-Catholics? Should not a pope – the vicar of Christ – be the father not just of Catholics but all humanity?

During the war, as we have seen, Roncalli used his diplomatic status to save many Jews – the blood-relatives of the Lord – for which he was subsequently recognised as 'Righteous among the Gentiles'. In 1944, he was transferred as Papal Nuncio to Paris where delicate negotiations over Pétainist bishops demanded more than 'peasant shrewdness'. In 1953, Pius XII appointed him Patriarch of Venice and, during the next five years, finally in a pastoral role, Roncalli demonstrated the 'transparent goodness' of a good shepherd devoted to his flock. But always there was the sense that the Church had failed humanity, which in turn led to 'a kind of inferiority complex towards the world...a political way of looking at the world [that] strangely begged sympathy from the world'[849] – sympathy, and perhaps forgiveness.

The Second Vatican Council, in the course of four sessions held over three years, issued sixteen constitutions and decrees. Many were uncontroversial such as the decrees on the Eastern Churches, the Office of Bishops, on Education and the Training of Priests. Prior to its opening, the preparatory Commission in the Vatican, directed by the Prefect of the Holy Office, Cardinal Ottaviani, had drawn up drafts, known as *schema*, to present to the Council in the expectation that they would be adopted with only minor adjustments. In the event, 'one by one, often with considerable bitterness, the curial draft documents were swept aside, and replaced with radically different texts'.[850]

---

849   Athanasius Schneider, *Christus Vincit. Christ's Triumph Over the Darkness of the Age*, p.132

850   Peter Hebblethwaite, *Op. Cit.*, p. 361

The authors of these texts were often not if fact the bishops but their *periti* or theological advisers, some of whom were the very *nouvelle théologiens* who had been censured during the pontificate of Pius XII. Karl Rahner accompanied Cardinal König, the Archbishop of Vienna; Yves-Marie Congar advised the Belgian bishops; Edward Schillebeeckx the Dutch bishops; Charles Moeller Cardinal Paul-Emile Léger of Montreal. Among the other *periti* was the American Jesuit, John Courtney Murray; the German Redemptorist Bernard Häring; the Canadian Gregory Baum; the Swiss theologian, Hans Küng, and Küng's colleague in the theological faculty of Tübingen University, Josef Ratzinger.

Küng and Ratzinger 'were never a team'[851]. The difference in their temperaments was described by Küng himself in recalling that while Ratzinger went around Tübingen on a bicycle, Küng drove an Alfa Romeo. Later, they would take radically different views on the interpretation of Vatican II but, at the time of the Council, Ratzinger was considered quite as radical as Küng. The sons of a Bavarian village policeman, both Josef Ratzinger and his older brother Georg had been ordained by Cardinal Faulhaber, the Archbishop of Munich – the same Faulhaber who had written the first draft of Pius XI's *Mit Brennender Sorge*. Like his brother Georg, Josef was an unalloyed product of Bavaria's Catholic culture, spending much of his youth studying and teaching at the seminary at Freising outside Munich.

Recognised as a theological *wunderkind*, Josef Ratzinger was recommended in 1961 to Cardinal Frings, the Archbishop of Cologne who – partially blind and no great theologian – asked him to ghost-write an address that Frings had promised to give in Genoa on the significance of the up-coming Council. In the lecture 'the highly respected, world-famous old cardinal's historian's view was combined with theological insight, philosophical penetration and the brilliant use of a language that was as plain as it was emotional.' The audience, which included the conservative Cardinal Siri of Genoa, was delighted. So too was Pope John XXIII when he read the text. '*Che bella coincidenza del pensiero,*' he told Frings. 'What a beautiful harmony of thought! You have said everything that I've thought and wanted to say, but was unable to say myself'. Frings confessed to the Pope John that he had not actually written the lecture; that the author was a young theologian, Josef Ratzinger. 'Herr Cardinal,' said Pope John, 'I did not write my last encyclical myself either. You just need the right adviser'.[852]

---

851   Peter Sewald, *Benedict XVI. A Life.*, p. 356

852   *Ibid.*, p. 361

Peter Seewald, Josef Ratzinger's biographer, wrote that the Genoa speech, which was published under Cardinal Fring's name, but acknowledged to be the work of his theological adviser, 'was the most significant and long-lasting that Ratzinger ever wrote'.[853] It meant that when it came to the Council, this thirty-five-year-old academic, by then Professor of Theology at the University of Bonn, exercised a decisive influence over not just Cardinal Frings but other German bishops, leading to their rejection of the *schema* on the Constitution of the Sacred Liturgy introduced by Cardinal Ottaviani. 'If I am allowed to speak openly,' said Frings, '*Schema non placet*. In the schema put before us today I think the voice that can be heard is not that of a mother or guide, nor that of the good shepherd who calls his sheep by name, so that they hear his voice. Rather, it is the language of a schoolmaster or professor, which does not nourish or stimulate'.

This intervention by Frings, 'which he had memorized the night before, came word for word from Ratzinger's pen'.[854] It successfully thwarted the careful plans of Cardinal Ottaviani and the Holy Office. Although Council Fathers came from all over the world, the initiative was now taken by bishops from northern Europe – Belgium, the Netherlands, and Germany. 'The Council has shown that a doubtful form of leadership is emerging,' wrote Cardinal Siri of Milan, 'represented by the German-speaking group and their associates and neighbours'. Siri took particular exception to 'those who want to suit as much as possible the Protestants and Orthodox and so on...' with the result that 'the Divine tradition becomes nullified'.[855]

Ecumenism – the unifying of all Christians in one Church – was high on the agenda of the Council, and a cause dear to Cardinal Montini who, when elected as expected to replace John XXIII, chose the name Paul. His coronation followed tradition with the new pontiff seated on his throne carried shoulder-high by members of the Roman nobility, cooled by ostrich-feather fans, his body laden with sumptuous vestments, his head bowed down by the weight of the triple crown. His biographer, Peter Hebblethwaite, judged that the pomp 'was at odds with the spirit of the Council'[856] and no doubt Paul VI thought the same: the crown was later sold with the proceeds given to the poor.

---

853   *Ibid.* p. 360
854   *Ibid.* p. 402
855   *Ibid.*p. 408
856   Peter Hebblethwaite, *Op. Cit.* p.

Sympathetic to the *nouvelle théologie*, Paul declared upon his election that his entire pontificate would be devoted to the Council. Considered indecisive like Shakespeare's Hamlet, he had to mediate between the more radical reformers and the conservative cardinals such as Cardinals Siri and Ottaviani. Certainly, his instinct was for reform, but he had spent twenty years working in the curia under Pius XII and, when it came to ecumenism and collegiality, he might be willing to sign documents as 'the Bishop of Rome' rather than 'Supreme Pontiff', but was loath, in the last analysis, to renounce the claims of the Catholic Church as the *spes unica*, or surrender the unique powers of the successor to the Apostle Peter to bind and loose.

The changes which the liberal cardinals and their *periti* wished to see enacted by the Council were:

1. The unity of Christians which, when it came to the Church of England, meant rescinding the ruling of Pope Leo XIII that Anglican orders were 'utterly null and void'.

2. Religious liberty, which meant reversing the teaching that 'error has no rights'

3. Collegiality, transferring the governance of the Church from the Bishop of Rome and his curia to a College of the bishops of the universal Church.

4. A reform of the liturgy, including purging the Mass of the embellishments that had been added over the centuries, returning it to the spare and simple form used, it was thought, by the early Church

5. Mass to be said in vernacular languages rather than Latin, the *lingua franca* of the Church since the days of the Roman Empire.

6. Communion in both kinds – viz. under the form of both bread and wine: like Mass said in the vernacular, this had been one of the demands of Jan Hus.

7. A greater participation of the laity in the life of the Church, encouraging the congregations to participate in the new, pared-down vernacular mass.

8. A 'dialogue' with the World.

Some of these ambitions were realised, some partially realised, some realised after the Council in ways that might have dismayed the Council Fathers, some left pending, and some withered on the vine. Adrian Hastings, in *Modern Catholicism* (1991), lists 'key texts' that led 'to specific and major changes in the life of the Church...'

The first was the definition of the Church as 'the People of God'. Paul of Tarsus had talked of the Church as 'the body of Christ' but, the *periti* claimed, this new definition had 'biblical roots', was frequently used in early liturgical prayers, and was appealing because 'it did not evoke clergy or hierarchy but rather the basic equality of all the baptized'.[857] It had been a favourite theme of Martin Luther and so appealed to Protestants. Together with 'the People of God', the Council also talked of 'the priesthood of the faithful', with ordained priests relegated to the sub-category of the 'ministerial priesthood'.

The second of Hastings' texts placed the 'Eucharist as the centre of the Church and its unity'. This also pleased the ecumenicists because it could be seen as limiting the role of the popes: 'where post-conciliar theology will say that the Eucharist gives the Church its unity, pre-conciliar theology would undoubtedly have been most likely to declare that it was the papacy that did so'.

So too the 'third decisive orientation' – the insistence upon the primacy of Scripture 'in theory and in practice'. 'The Teaching Office – viz. papal encyclicals – 'is not above the world of God but serves it'. Here too there are echoes of Luther's *sola scriptura*.

Also appealing to the ecumenicists was the fourth decisive orientation – an endorsement of theological diversity meaning that 'theologically separated Christians are no longer to be seen as simply "outside" the Church but, on the contrary, recognized as being united visibly with the Church in a state of "imperfect" communion'.

The fifth text was the declaration of religious freedom in the decree *Dignitatis Humanae*, described by the American theologian, J. Courtney Murray, as 'the most controversial document of the whole Council'. Hastings' view was that 'It explicitly reversed the accepted teaching which related freedom only to truth and not to persons, claiming that error had no rights... and demonstrates that "development" may have to proceed at times more by reversal than by an extension of what has hitherto been taught'.[858] Another theologian, Thomas Pink, denied that it reversed the teaching of

---

857   Adrian Hastings, Ed., *Modern Catholicism*, p. 58

858   *Ibid.*, p. 62

the nineteenth century popes that error has no rights: this applied only to Catholic countries, while *Dignitatis Humane* treated with modern secular societies where the Catholic Church was just one among other religions.[859] Nevertheless, *Dignitatis Humanae* was opposed by a significant minority of bishops, and led one – Monsignor Marcel Lefebvre, the Archbishop of Dakar – although he signed the decree, to denounce the entire Council as the work of the Devil, and form the schismatic Society of Pius X.

Hastings' sixth text is found in the decree *Nostra Aetate* which deplored 'the hatred, persecutions, and displays of anti-Semitism directed against the Jews at any time and from any source'. The decree condemned outright the idea that 'our older brothers in the faith' should be considered collectively responsible for the crucifixion of Jesus of Nazareth. Popes had condemned anti-Semitism a number of times over many centuries, but 'this was…a stronger, more public, more obviously unqualified condemnation'.[860]

The seventh text condemned indiscriminate warfare: 'the destruction of entire cities…along with their population is a crime against God and man himself'. This again was controversial because during World War II the Allies had done just that: the British had 'fire-bombed' Hamburg and Dresden, and the Americans dropped atomic bombs on the Japanese cities of Hiroshima and Nagasaki. Moreover it was the view of the powers that made up the North Atlantic Treaty Organisation that peace was best ensured by the certainty of 'mutually assured destruction'.

'The final text', wrote Hastings, 'concerns the responsibility of the married couples in deciding to have or not to have a child.' It did not rule on the question of 'artificial' birth control which Pope Paul removed from agenda of the Council, reserving it for his own competence and judgement. However, the Fathers did 'develop a theory of marriage in which procreation was no longer seen as its sole purpose, but conjugal love was recognised as of equal importance'.

There were two words in the Council's decrees whose redefinition was to have significant repercussions in the life of the Church.

1. **Modern.** Throughout the decrees, but prominent principally in the Constitution *Gaudium et Spes* (*The Joys and the Hopes of the Church in the Modern World*) 'modern' or 'modernity' lost its hitherto

---

859   See Thomas Pink, *The Interpretation of* Dignitatis Humanae.

860   Adrian Hastings, *Op. Cit.* p.62

pejorative meaning. Based on the work of *nouvelle théologiens* – principally Chenu, Congar and Rahner – the emphatic condemnation of modernity found in Pio Nono's *Syllabus of Errors* was reversed, bringing about a shift in emphasis that 'may well be described as revolutionary'.[861]

2. **The World.** So too what was meant by 'the World'. In the Gospels but also the Old Testament, the World was understood in the sense of the principality of the Devil. 'If the world hates you,' Jesus told his disciples, 'remember that it hated me before you.' [862] 'You must not love this passing world,' wrote the Apostle John, 'The love of the Father cannot be in any man who loves the world, because nothing the world has to offer…could ever come from the Father…'[863] 'As for me, wrote Paul of Tarsus in his letter to the Galatians, 'the only thing I can boast about is the cross of our Lord Jesus Christ, though whom the world is crucified to me, and I to the world'.[864]

This distinction between the children of the Light and the children of the World is found throughout the teachings and rituals of the Church. Catechumens are warned to beware of 'the World, the Flesh and the Devil'. Francis of Sales, in the English translation of his *Introduction to the Devout Life*, talks of 'worldlings', meaning those who pursue power, pleasure and prosperity – preoccupied only with the things of this world, oblivious to those of the next. One does not have to subscribe to the anathemas of the *Syllabus of Errors* to talk of 'worldly values' in contrast to those of the spirit. The French have the word *mondain*; the Italians *mondanità*: the Spanish *mundane;* the Germans *weltlich.* They may mean something relatively innocent – fashion, society – but all exclude the spirit. Throughout the history of the Church, saints would renounce 'the world'.

Now the faithful were reminded of the passage, also from Saint John's Gospel, in which Jesus tells Nicodemus that 'God sent his Son into the world not to condemn the world but so that through him the world might be saved'.[865] Although Jesus goes on to say, in the next verse, that salvation

861   Enda McDonagh, *Modern Catholicism*, p. 96

862   John, 15:18-21

863   First Letter of St. John, 2:15-16

864   Galatians, 6:14

865   John, 3:18

depends upon belief 'in the name of God's only Son', the authors of *Gaudium et Spes*, wrote that salvation is not only for believers 'but also for all men of good will in whose hearts grace is active invisibly. For since Christ died for all, and since all men are in fact called to one and the same destiny, which is divine, we must hold that the Holy Spirit offers to all the possibility of being made partners, in a way known only to God, in the paschal mystery'.[866]

'One of the gravest errors of our time', the constitution states, 'is the dichotomy between the faith which many profess and the practice of their daily lives'. Slipping into bathos, it talks of those who break the speed limit or cheat on their taxes; but we are back with the shriven member of an *Einsatzgruppe* or the Croatian Ustasha, and the gravitational pull of the Holocaust which, like a black hole in outer space, draws the Church's teaching away from its primal belief that only the waters of baptism wash away Original Sin, and that faith in Christ is a prerequisite to salvation, to an almost Rousseauesque belief in the aboriginal innocence of mankind. Rousseau's 'Man is born free but is everywhere is in chains', and indeed Karl Marx's 'The philosophers have only interpreted the world, in various ways. The point, however, is to change it' would not have been out of place in *Gaudium et Spes*.

Not just the Holocaust but the challenge of Communism hovered over Vatican II. Puzzling from the perspective from the 21st century is the respect shown by Paul VI towards the Communist regimes in Russia and Eastern Europe. 'Breaking the implacable and principled anti-Communism of Pius XII, Paul VI encouraged dialogue with the Communist regimes, granting many of their leaders private audiences ... encounters that would have had Pius XII whirring in his grave'.[867] The aim of such initiatives was no doubt to improve the condition of Catholics behind the Iron Curtain and to promote peace but there were some theologians who took the view that Communism was more likely than capitalism to ensure social justice. *Gaudium et Spes*, 'so radiant with paschal optimism about the Church's impact on the world', [868] seemed to echo, albeit in gentler terms, the *Communist Manifesto*. 'By uniting their forces, let the laity so remedy the institutions and conditions of the world when the latter are an inducement to sin, that these may be conformed to the norms of justice, favouring rather than hindering the practice of virtue'.[869]

---

866   *Gaudium et Spes*, 22

867   Michael Burleigh, *Sacred Causes*, p. 418

868   *Hebblethwaite, Op. Cit.*, p. 449

869   *Lumen Gentium*, 36

In 1967 Paul VI published an encyclical on social justice, *Populorum progressio*, 'which advanced beyond the generalities of *Gaudium et Spes* and denounced unrestrained economic liberalism as 'a woeful system'. This condemnation of western capitalism, which is found in Leo XIII's *Rerum Novarum*, was combined with moves to compromise with the Communist regimes in Eastern Europe. Opposition to this *Ostpolitik* came largely from bishops behind the Iron Curtain, notably Cardinal Mindszenty immured in the American Embassy in Budapest, who refused Pope Paul VI's request that he resign from the primatial see of Esztergom in exchange for free passage to the West; and Cardinal Wyszynski, the Archbishop of Warsaw, whose advice that 'Communism was on the wane'[870] was ignored. If in Poland, he said, there was the 'Church of silence' which couldn't speak, in Rome he found a 'Church of the deaf' which wouldn't listen. Wyszyński was a sceptic when it came to the Council. He did not think that the Church was in need of reform.[871]

112. The New Mass

The Second Vatican Council was closed by Pope Paul VI on 8 December, 1965, the feast of the Immaculate Conception. Professor Duffy considered it to have been 'the most revolutionary Christian event since the Reformation'.[872] The Anglican priest and historian, Edward Norman, who attended the Council as one of the observers from other Christian denominations, concluded that 'though the pluralism of the modern world seeped into the proceedings, yet the resulting formulations of the faith were, in the event surprisingly unitary and conservative .... The cultural and intellectual changes that were to take place in the years immediately following the closing sessions, in the later 1960s and in the 1970s, were much more fundamental'.[873]

Many of these changes affected only the clergy, and it was the introduction of the *Novus Ordo* (New Order) mass that brought home to the Catholic laity, uninterested in theology, ignorant of the meaning of words such as 'hermeneutics' or 'exegesis' or 'eschatology', indifferent as to whether their Church should be called 'the Body of Christ' or the 'People of God', suddenly

---

870   Hebblethwaite, *Op. Cit.* p. 298

871   *Ibid.*, p.477

872   Eamon Duffy, *Op. Cit.*, p. 361

873   Edward Norman, *Modern Catholicism*, p. 457

discovered that the mass they attended every Sunday was no longer said in Latin but in their native language. The poetic opening *Introibo ad altare Dei, Ad Deum qui laetificat juventutem meam* – 'I will go up to the altar of God, to God who gives joy to my youth' – was gone; so too the 'Last Gospel' – *In principio erat Verbum, et Verbum erat apud Deum, et Deus erat Verbum* – 'In the beginning was the Word, and the Word was with God, and the Word was God'.

The altar, previously attached to the wall of the church facing east towards the rising sun, was now detached from its moorings and faced west like the communion table of the Protestant denominations. The officiating priest, hitherto with his back to the congregation, and whispering the words of the sacred mystery, now faced the People of God like a lecturer or, some said, a talk show host, his every action plain for all to see. The congregation was actively engaged in the liturgy as the Council had intended, giving vigorous responses to what had previous been said *sotto voce* by the altar server. There was now no place for the tax collector who, 'standing some distance away, not daring even to raise his eyes to heaven…beat his breast and said, "God be merciful to me, a sinner"'.[874]

Many who had loved the Latin Tridentine mass were dismayed. 'A year in which the process of transforming the liturgy has followed a planned course,' wrote the novelist Evelyn Waugh in his diary on Easter Sunday, 1965. 'More than the aesthetic changes which rob the Church of poetry, mystery and dignity, there are suggested changes in faith and morals which alarm me… I shall not live to see things righted'.[875] It was the last entry in his diary. He died on Easter Day a year later.

The *Novus Ordo,* which replaced the 'Tridentine Mass' promulgated by Pope V at the time of the Council of Trent, was largely the work of Archbishop Annibale Bugnini, described in the memoirs of a consultant at Vatican II, Louis Bouyer, as 'a man as bereft of culture as he was of basic honesty'.[876] As early as 1948, Bugnini had served as secretary of a Commission for Liturgical reform set up by Pope Pius XII. He was responsible for various changes to the Code of Rubrics in the 1950s, and was the Vatican's 'expert' on liturgical matters. He was therefore the was 'chief architect' of the decree *Sacrosanctum*

---

874   Luke, 18:13

875   *The Diaries of Evelyn Waugh,* p. 793

876   Louis Bouyer, *The Memoirs of Louis Bouyer* (Wikipedia)

Concilium which had called for a new mass but the change was not imposed on the Council Fathers: 'the final voting…revealed an impressive unanimity… There were only a derisory four votes against.'

The *Novus Ordo*, which became known as the Paul VI mass, was enthusiastically backed by the pontiff and imposed throughout the Catholic Church. Those who hankered for the old Latin, Tridentine mass were dismissed as reactionaries at odds with 'the Spirit of Vatican II'. Yet in due course a future pontiff, Benedict XVI, would permit its return as an 'extraordinary rite', and many theologians would recognise that much had been lost as a result of the reform. 'Its keynotes', wrote the Dominican theologian Aidan Nichols, 'were a utilitarian or pragmatist philosophical infrastructure of which happiness or usefulness is the key to truth; anthropocentricism; a predominance of ethical values over strictly religious ones; and a downplaying of the notion of special revelation in favour whenever possible of religion within the limits of reason…'[877] 'Above all', wrote the philosopher Catherine Pickstock, 'the liturgical reformers of Vatican II failed to realise that one cannot simply "return" to an earlier form, because the earlier liturgies only existed as part of a culture which was itself ritual in character'.[878] 'The drastic change of the millennia-old rite of Mass enacted by Pope Paul VI,' wrote Bishop Athanasius Schneider, 'unquestionably weakened the essentially sacrificial Christocentric … character of the mass, shifting it more towards the meaning of a fraternal banquet and a community-centred prayer meeting, which … is more similar to Protestant prayer services.[879]

113.   Reunion

This comparison of the new mass to a Protestant prayer service was welcomed by the enthusiasts for the reunion of the different Christian denominations. Ecumenism was a cause dear to both Pope John XXIII and Pope Paul VI: Christ himself had prayed that 'they may be one'.[880] We have seen that Pope John XXIII, when in Sofia and Ankara during the war, had befriended his

---

877   Quoted in Catherine Pickstock, *After Writing. On the Liturgical Consummation of Philosophy*, p. 175

878   *Ibid.* p. 176

879   Athanasius Schneider, *Op.Cit*, p. 155

880   John, 17:21

Orthodox *confrères*, and for him the main ecumenical imperative was to end the schism between the Eastern and Western churches. To the *nouvelle théologiens*, however, most of them from northern Europe and living cheek by jowl with Lutherans and Calvinists, reunion with the Protestant churches was equally important. The result was the Council's Decree *Unitatis redintegratio*

A special case among the Protestant churches was the Church of England whose High Church, Anglo-Catholic wing, in both its liturgy and beliefs, was close to Catholic practice and teaching. There were high hopes that the few differences such as the role of the pope could be overcome. In 1960, Geoffrey Fisher, the Archbishop of Canterbury, met Pope John XXIII in Rome. The pope gave him his episcopal ring. Later, in 1967, Pope Paul VI referred to the Anglican communion as a 'sister church'. An Anglican-Catholic International Commission (ARCIC) was set up to deal with the remaining impediments to union. In 1976 the Benedictine Abbot of Ampleforth, Basil Hume, was made Archbishop of Westminster – a man who could most plausibly combine the see of Westminster with that of Canterbury. Despite a letter sent to Pope Paul by the then Archbishop of Canterbury, Frederic Coggan, in 1975 informing him that the Anglican communion was minded to ordain women as priests, the optimism over reunion remained unabated until 1994 when thirty-two women were ordained as priests of the Church of England.

While it was possible for a Catholic priest to be married – Uniate priests had wives, and Anglican priests who converted and took Holy Orders were permitted to keep their wives – ordaining women was considered impossible by the Catholic Church. A Catholic priest acted *in persona* Christ and Christ had been a man. Jesus had chosen only men as apostles; therefore the Church 'did not feel authorised' to ordain women. This was a gentle, almost apologetic way of saying that the male gender was intrinsic to the priesthood – a view that would later be described as infallible. Because the Anglicans had gone ahead with the ordination of women, despite both Catholic and Orthodox teaching, it had shown itself to be a Protestant sect rather than part of the universal Church.

The ordination of women dashed the hopes of the ecumenicists when it came to the Church of England, and moves towards unity with the English Methodists, the German Evangelicals and the Orthodox churches fared no better. Had the path to unity been a cul-de-sac? There had unquestionably been benefits. The old antagonism between Catholic and Protestant had largely gone; so too the petty point-scoring which had been found in the polemic of even distinguished converts such as Monsignor Ronald Knox, the son of an Anglican bishop. Sincere friendships had been established between Anglican and Catholic prelates; it was said that Catholic bishops saw more of their Anglican equivalents than they did of their own priests.

One consequence for English Catholics had been the playing-down as impediments to reunion of certain articles of their faith such as the true presence of Christ in the Eucharist. Communion in both kinds, and saying mass in the vernacular, appealed to Protestants but made Catholic practice less distinctive: we have seen how during the Council this was a matter of concern to Cardinal Siri. With hindsight it would become clear not that the move to unify the Christian churches was mistaken, but that it was unlikely that it could ever succeed. It was pursued as a theological imperative by popes, and many bishops and priests; but there is little evidence that members of the laity of the different Christian denominations wanted anything to change. Popes, Patriarchs and Protestant bishops might pray together, but the Orthodox rank-and-file neither forgot nor forgave the sack of Constantinople during the Fourth Crusade[881], and among the Anglicans there remained many who still shared Cranmer's belief that the mass was 'a blasphemous fable'.

114. The Signs of the Times

With hindsight, it seems puzzling that between 1960 and 1990 Christian disunity should have been of major concern to the Catholic Church. Certainly, schisms and separation were visible cracks in the edifice of Christendom but, had the theologians and churchmen surveyed the foundations, they would have discovered the first signs of a far more corrosive rot. It was mentioned, almost in passing, by the Council Fathers in *Gaudium et Spes*: after recognising that the Church had adversaries in atheists of one kind or another – Marxists, Existentialists, Humanists – and those who have 'a faulty notion of God that made no reference to the God of the Gospels', it went on: 'There are also those who never enquire about God; religion never seems to trouble or interest them at all; nor do they see why they should bother about it.'[882]

---

881   Fyodor Dostoyevsky's Grand Inquisitor in his novel *The Brothers Karamazov*, and
        Tolstoy's Helene Bezukov in *War and Peace* illustrate common Russian attitudes
        towards Catholics

882   *Gaudium et Spes*, 19.

The 1950s had seen a rise in conversions to Catholicism and religious observance – baptisms, confirmations, church weddings and funerals. However by 1960, the year in which the Archbishop of Canterbury called on the Pope in Rome, there had begun a precipitous decline in Christian practice that sent 'organized Christianity on a downward spiral to the margins of social significance'. [883] In 1960, 190,000 English men and women were confirmed in the Church of England; thirty years later, in 1990, there were 57,618; and eight years after that, 40,881. [884] A comparable rate of 'disaffiliation' was found among Catholics in Britain and the United States. In France, a survey conducted in 1994 found that only 64% of the population considered themselves Catholics – a decline of 17% over the past four years. The proportion of 'convinced Catholics' had fallen from 30% to 24% over the same period, 89% considered religious belief irrelevant to ethical behaviour, 83% considered that conscience was the sole criterion for moral judgements, and only 1% looked to the teaching of the Church.[885] The dwindling congregations in parish churches throughout Europe coincided with the growth of Catholic movements such as *Communione e Liberazione* in Italy and *Opus Dei* in Spain; and new religious orders such as the *Frères de Saint Jean* in France, and the Legionaries of Christ in Mexico.

It was not that the young at the time were indifferent to good and evil. Quite to the contrary, they raged against injustice, or what they perceived to be injustice. However, their moral imperatives had often little to do with Christianity; indeed they were very often at variance with Christian teaching, particularly when it came to sexual mores. Despite the gruesome record of Lenin and Stalin, Marxism remained in fashion: Communists such as Fidel Castro, Ernesto Che Guevara and Ho Chi Minh were the heroes of the day.

1968 was a pivotal year in the sudden metamorphosis of the culture of the developed world. Protests at the American military intervention in Vietnam brought many thousands onto the streets. There were student riots in New York, Paris, Tokyo, Belgrade. In August large demonstrations disrupted the Democratic Convention in Chicago. In France, a million marched through the streets of Paris and revolutionary students occupied the Sorbonne. The president of France, Charles de Gaulle, flew secretly to Strasbourg to see if the Army of the Rhine could be relied upon to restore order. Even in the usually

883   Callum G. Brown, *Op. Cit.*, p. 1

884   *Ibid,* p. 191

885   Michael Gilchrist, *AD 2000*, July 1994

placid university town of Tübingen in south Germany, student unrest in April and May led the then Professor of Theology, Josef Ratzinger, to wonder whether the theological speculation rife after Vatican II had undermined respect for the authority of Church teaching, and so authority as such.

115.   Humanae Vitae

In July, 1968, as Russian tanks were sent into Prague to suppress the liberal Communist regime of Alexander Dubček, Pope Paul VI finally passed judgement on the question of artificial birth control. His encyclical, *Humanae Vitae*, condemned it as 'intrinsically evil'. Liberal opinion in the developed nations of the west was outraged. The report of the Birth Control Commission appointed by Paul VI to advise him on the question was divided, but the majority view was that the teaching should be changed. It had been leaked to the American *National Catholic Reporter* and was published on 16 April, 1967. 'In London, the Catholic periodical, the *Tablet*, followed suit on 22 April 1967'[886]. The leaks convinced many conscientious married Catholics, hitherto obedient to the Church's teaching, that Pope Paul VI would surely follow the advice of his Commission and ask their doctors to prescribe the pill: no one as yet envisaged prescribing it to the unmarried.

Pope Paul VI acknowledged, in *Humanae Vitae*, that 'evolution in human society had resulted in changes which have provoked new questions'; he referred to the Commission, but did not say that the married couples among its members had said that limiting sexual intercourse within marriage to the 'safe period'- viz. the days in a woman's menstrual cycle when conception was unlikely, which had been permitted by Pius XII in certain circumstances – caused tension within a marriage, nor that a majority of the Commission had recommended a change to the Church's teaching, only that 'within the commission itself, there was not complete agreement concerning the moral norms to be proposed'.

Pope Paul was aggrieved by the leak because already a paper from the Congregation for the Doctrine of the Faith – the new name he had given to the Holy Office at the close of the Council – had raised three objections to a change of the teaching. The first, that reversing the teaching of *Casti Connubii* would undermine the authority of the *magisterium*; second, that

---

886   Hebblethwaite, *Op. Cit.*, p. 487

any relaxation of the teaching would encourage hedonism and a 'permissive society'; and third, that it would encourage governments to impose policies on their citizens to limit population growth.

At the heart of Pope Paul's reasoning in *Humanae Vitae* was the concept of Natural Law as developed by Thomas Aquinas from the philosophy of Aristotle – considered the basis for Catholic theology by many popes but rejected by some of the *nouvelle théologiens*. Just as English law held that some crimes were absolute offences, and did not require *mens rea* (malign intent) to be crimes, Natural Law held that some actions were 'intrinsically evil', irrespective of their motive. Deliberately thwarting conception fell into this category. There was 'an inseparable connection, established by God, which man on his own initiative might not break, between the unitive significance and the procreative significance, which are both inherent in the marriage act'.[887] Given Pope Pius XI's condemnation of 'sterilizing poisons' in *Casti Connubii*, it was always unlikely that the invention of the contraceptive pill containing the hormones oestrogen and progesterone which simulated pregnancy and so stopped ovulation would lead to a change in the Church's teaching.

While *Casti Connubii* had attracted little criticism from Catholics at the time of its publication in 1930, *Humanae Vitae* led to widespread and indignant dissent. To non-Catholics, the main objection was that it would frustrate attempts to limit the rapid increase in the world's population. To many Catholics, the encyclical contradicted the spirit of Vatican II. There had been no consultation with the bishops – no collegiality: the judgement had been made by the pope alone. There had been no concession to the sovereignty of conscience ascribed to Newman; and the argument of the Encyclical had been based on Thomist theology which many considered to have been superseded by the new theology. The Belgian Cardinal Suenens, once Pope Paul's right-hand man, criticised the failure of the pope to consult the bishops and talked of a new 'Galileo affair'. The encyclical was criticised by Karl Rahner, Hans Küng and, in the United States, the theologian Charles Curran. In Canada, the Bishops' Conference stated that Catholics who felt unable to keep to the Church's teaching on contraception should not consider this a reason to withdraw from the sacraments or leave the Church.

Pope Paul had anticipated criticism and even dissent, and in contrast to the confident, almost triumphant tone taken by Pius XI in *Casti Connubii*, that of

---

887   *Casti Connubii*, 12

Humanae Vitae was almost apologetic. He acknowledged that that limiting the size of a family might be desirable 'when living conditions are harsh...'; and that 'only with the gravest difficulty' could the teaching be observed, 'sometimes only by heroic effort'. He asked Catholics to 'acquire complete mastery over themselves and their emotions', and practice 'periodic continence', but, as Augustine of Hippo had said, moderation can be more difficult than outright abstinence.[888] The Church was aware of human weakness, wrote Pope Paul; 'she has compassion on the multitudes; she welcomes sinners.' Was it open then, for Catholic couples to pray, like Augustine, 'make me chaste, O Lord, but not yet'?

Humanae Vitae had its supporters. Within the Church, there was Karol Wojtyla, Archbishop of Krakow, whose book *Love and Responsibility* was said to have influenced Pope Paul's thinking. The Benedictine historian, David Knowles, quoted another of Augustine of Hippo's well-known sayings: 'Peter has spoken. The case is closed'. Elizabeth Anscombe, Professor of Philosophy at Cambridge University and a convert to Catholicism, picked up on Pope Paul's prediction that the removal of the disincentive of an unwanted pregnancy 'can lead to the way being wide open to marital infidelity and to a general lowering of moral standards'; that 'men – and especially the young, who are so exposed to temptation – need incentives to keep the moral law, and it is an evil thing to make it easy for them to break that law'.

Anscombe concurred.

Make no mistake: it is the whole Catholic Christian idea of chastity that is under fire in the modern world. It is also under fire from those Catholics who reject *Humanae Vitae*. I used to think you could argue sufficiently to convince a Catholic that no sort of sexual acts could be excluded if once you admitted contraceptive intercourse. But the enemies of *Humanae Vitae* now seem to embrace that conclusion...at least as far as concerns sexual activity between two people; I suppose adult people. For though I know Catholics who solemnly defend and commend homosexual activity, I don't know any who make propaganda for bestiality, group-sex or paedophilia. No doubt, however, all that will come as the world at large becomes accepting of these things.[889]

---

888   Augustine's denunciation of contraception quoted in *Casti Connubii* may well have been inspired by remorse for his own past: he lived with a woman 'out of wedlock' for a number of years yet had only one child, a son Adeodatus.

889   G.E.M. Anscombe. *Faith in a Hard Ground. Essays on Religion, Philosophy and Ethics*, p. 197

Of the many factors that contributed to the outrage expressed by both Catholic and secular commentators on *Humanae Vitae*, three were of particular importance. The first was the influence of the new theologians, many from the lands of the Reformation, among the educated Catholic middle-class. Their books were best sellers, and often their unorthodox views were backed by bishops. The Dutch Church was at the time close to schism. The Swiss theologian Hans Küng later described the encyclical as 'the prime example by the *magisterium* which sparks off world-wide opposition and at times even subjects the pope to ridicule':[890] it will be remembered that at the time of the Council Cardinal Ottaviani had said that Küng was 'far closer to the Protestants than to the Catholics"[891].

The orthodox Swiss theologian Hans Urs von Balthasar saw the opposition to *Humanae Vitae* by some of his colleagues as a symptom of their 'anti-Roman prejudice'.[892] At times it seemed as if Calvin's concept of 'the elect' influenced their thinking, particularly if one compares their self-righteous dissent with the easy-going attitude towards sexual sin of Catholics in Italy in the eighteenth century (see Chapter 77). The confidence – perhaps over-confidence – of the Romans ruled by the pope in God's tolerance of human weakness, together with the sunny climate, made life a joy.

It was under the dark skies of the north that Catholics now became 'justified sinners'. A crucifix might still be found on the wall behind the *letto conjugale* in Catholic countries, but less and less did Catholic married couples in northern Europe and the United States feel that priests or even God had the right to pass judgement on what went on beneath the blankets. Was it not up to them to decide? Had not John Henry Newman said that conscience was paramount? Vainly did scholars insist that Newman had meant only 'to refute Gladstone's charge that the First Vatican Council's definition of papal infallibility deprived Catholics of their political freedom and made them subjects to a foreign power'. 'The idea that a Catholic may conscientiously dissent from the magisterium's moral teaching would have amazed Newman. The possibility never occurred to him.'[893]

The second factor that scuppered *Humanae Vitae* was the advent of cinema, and more particularly television. Prior to the 1950s, Catholics had some

---

890   Hans Küng, *Disputed Truth. Memoirs II*, p. 145
891   *Ibid.*, p. 75
892   Hebblethwaite, *Op. Cit.* p. 497
893   Ian Ker, *Newman on Vatican II*, p. 122

control on what material came into their homes from the outside world. We have seen the effect of romantic and frequently pornographic novels on the morals during the Enlightenment, and how, conscious of literature's power to corrupt the innocent, the Roman Inquisition had issued its *Index librorum prohibitorum* – a list of works no Catholic should read. Overwhelmed by the amount of questionable material, it was abolished under Pope Paul VI in 1966.

By then it was not so much books as television that posed a danger to faith and morals. To go to 'the flicks' in the 1930s and 1940s, like going to the theatre, meant leaving one's home. In Britain there was a Board of Censors to evaluate and even ban what could be shown on the screen; and until 1968 the office of the Lord Chamberlain performed the same function for what was shown on stage. In the United States Catholic pressure had led to the Hayes code which laid down that no motion picture 'should ever lower the moral standards of those who see it' and that 'the sympathy of the audience shall never be thrown to the side of crime, wrongdoing, evil or sin'. The code was modified in 1954 and replaced by the ratings system of the Motion Picture Association of American in 1968.

It was television that finally opened the window in even the most devout Christian household to the outside world, removing the power of parents to control the formation of their children. Certainly, they need not buy a television, or could attempt to control what programmes were watched by their children, but because last night's soap was the subject of chatter in the school playgrounds, those without televisions could not join in. Inexorably, as the century progressed, the boundaries based on Christian morals were pushed back. Romance meant passion; passion, sex – often on the first date. While the Hays code had forbidden the showing of even married couples in the same bed, soaps such as *Friends* portrayed sex outside marriage as the norm. Adolescent children now felt that they were more in tune with the *zeitgeist* than their parents.

116. Feminism

The third and perhaps most significant development that explains the different reactions to *Casti Connubii* and *Humanae Vitae* was the change that had come over the position of women. Until the twentieth century, objective social conditions had buttressed the Church's teaching on the relations between the sexes derived largely from the teaching of Paul of Tarsus that 'man was not created for woman's sake, but woman for the sake of man'. A wife should obey her husband, 'for while every man has Christ as his head, a woman's head is man'.[894] Paul also taught that a husband must cherish his wife, and Christ's emphatic insistence on the indissoluble nature of marriage gave unique power to married women: if a man wished to go to Heaven, he could have sex only with his wife.

Throughout history, until the twentieth century, a man toiled to provide for his wife and children, and risked his life in battle to protect them, while a woman, in the words of Pius XI in *Casti Connubii*, 'reigned as queen of the home'. Her subjection to her father or husband was not considered a humiliation: the veneration of Jesus's mother Mary enhanced the standing of all her sex. Christendom produced powerful queens such as Eleanor of Aquitaine or Isabella of Spain; saintly queens such as Margaret of Scotland or Margaret of Hungary; and formidable religious such as Teresa of Avila or Mary Ward.

However, outside the Church, and outside the home, a woman's opportunities were limited and, by the second half of the eighteenth century, there were a number of educated women with servants to do the household chores who chafed at the restrictions to which they were subject. They could paint (Elisabeth Vigée Le Brun, Angelica Kaufmann); they could write (Jane Austen, Mary Wollstonecraft, Emily Bronte) but they could not minister, preach or enter any of the professions.

Of course, most women did not have domestic servants and, seeing the hard and often humiliating labour undertaken by their husbands, were content to cook, clean and care for their families: were content, even, to let their husbands take decisions on matters pertaining to the outside world. Prior to World War I, despite the agitation of the Suffragettes, a majority of women did not want the vote. During that war, with their husbands off at the front, women took their places in the offices and factories. The traditional division of labour no longer applied. Women were given the vote and given access to jobs in commerce and administration. Even in the factories, or in agriculture, it had been shown that a man's superior strength was no longer indispensable; and as the century progressed, a woman's nimble fingers made her actually better suited to work at the typewriter, keyboard and assembly lines making electronic equipment.

---

894   1Corinthians, 11:3. See Margaret E. Thrall, *The Cambridge Bible Commentary*, p. 77

How did these changes affect the Church? In 1930, as we have seen, Pope Pius's XI's presumption was still that a woman's place was in the home. Thirty-five years later, the tone had changed. 'At present,' stated Vatican II's *Gaudium et Spes*, 'women are involved in nearly all spheres of life; they ought to be permitted to play their part fully according to their own particular nature. It is up to everyone to see to it that woman's specific and necessary participation in cultural life be acknowledged and fostered'.[895] Pope Paul VI acknowledged this in *Humanae Vitae*, talking of a 'new understanding of the dignity of woman, and her place in society'. But what was that place? The key to understanding the decline of Christianity in Britain, wrote Callum G. Brown in *The Death of Christian Britain,* was 'the simultaneous de-pietisation of femininity and the de-feminisation of piety from the 1960s'.[896] 'The fifties construction of the "respectable" woman of homely virtues, the last widespread vestige of nineteenth-century female piety, was for the bulk of young people abruptly dissolved.'

Statistics for Catholic practice, though they show a slightly slower rate of disaffiliation, broadly follow that of Anglicans. Young women, hitherto 'the guardians of chastity' because devout, or simply through the fear of getting pregnant, were now at the forefront of the sexual revolution. In France, Simone de Beauvoir, the mistress of the existentialist philosopher, Jean-Paul Sartre, called for the liberation of women from their status as adjuncts to men in *The Second Sex*. Further feminist tracts followed such as *The Feminine Mystique* (1960) by the American Betty Friedan which argued that women were stifled by their roles as wives and mothers; and *The Female Eunuch* by the convent-educated Australian, Germaine Greer, who wrote that children would better off if raised in families without their fathers.

'Chastity' wrote Julien Green, 'is too heavy a burden for present-day humanity, because faith has weakened'.[897] By the 1970s, the Catholic Church's teaching on this 'lily of the virtues' was a dead duck. Yahweh's great rival, Baal, the god of fertility, was in the ascendant: his prophets were Havelock Ellis (*The Psychology of Sex*), Alex Comfort (*The Joy of Sex*) and above all Sigmund Freud who had persuaded a generation that sexual repression led to neurosis.

---

895   *Gaudium et Spes*, 60
896   Callum G. Brown, *Op. Cit.* p. 192
897   Julian Green, *Diary 1928-1957*, p. 240

The unleashing of the libido also revealed that sex was not simply a matter of conjugal congress. There was a kind of innocence – the innocence of a celibate – in the way Pope Paul VI could envisage but not address the many roles played by sex beyond pleasure and procreation. Sexual intercourse had become, as perhaps it had always been, a rite of passage for the young, an exercise of power or masochistic subjection, the satisfaction of curiosity, a recreation, a means to resolve pathologies, a *nostalgie de la boue*. Elizabeth Anscombe's predictions were to be amply fulfilled.

117.   Exodus

Humanae Vitae was the last encyclical to be issued by Paul VI. He was a pope who had brought about more changes than any other, fulfilling the commitment he had made to devote his pontificate to the Council and what it enjoined. The mass was now in the vernacular; the laity received Holy Communion in both kinds. He had abolished the tonsure for religious, and the age-old discipline that in memory of Christ's Passion Catholics should abstain from meat on a Friday. He had committed the Church, in his encyclical *Populorum progression*, to radical social reform. He had flown to New York to address the United Nations, confirming Pope John XXIII's belief that a pope was pastor not just of Catholics but of all mankind.

However, it had become apparent that he would go down in history as 'the pope who banned birth control'. 'Paul's position,' wrote his later biographer Peter Hebblethwaite, 'was that he expected to be criticised and misunderstood by the secular media'[898] but not by so many within the Church. We have seen how Catholic disaffiliation, at any rate in Britain and the United States, had started in the early 1960s, and so it cannot be 'blamed' on *Humanae Vitae* or Vatican II, but the Council – with evangelisation through an opening to the World as its proclaimed intent – did nothing to stop the precipitous decline. Between 1960 and 2016, Sunday mass attendance in Britain declined by 60%. The decline was less precipitous in the United State: in the diocese of Columbus, Ohio, mass attendance on Sundays declined over the same period declined by around 30%.[899] Many of those who continued to go to mass

---

898   Hebblethwaite, *Op. Cit.* p. 519

899   Stephen Bullivant, *Mass Exodus. Catholic Disaffiliation in Britain and America since Vatican II*, p. 197

introduced liturgical novelties with dancing, chanting and the ubiquitous guitar. 'Liberated Catholics were doing much as they pleased, happy to thumb their nose at the Vatican.'[900]

Most painful for Pope Paul VI was the large number of priests who, following Vatican II, abandoned their calling and left the priesthood. 'In 1963 some 167 priests had opted for the secular life; by 1965 that had reached 1,189, and an all-time high of 3,700 four years later.'[901] The Society of Jesus, which numbered 37,000 at the opening of the Council, lost a third of its members over the next decade. The *Statistical Yearbook of the Church* published by the Vatican's Secretariat of State, records that between 1964 and 1986, 48,351 diocesan and religious priests left the priesthood 'with or without a dispensation.'[902]

It was the same with women religious, many of whom 'jumped over the wall', while some of those who remained exchanged their distinctive but often cumbersome habits for lay clothes. No sanctions were threatened to stop them. Peter Hebblewaite, a Jesuit who left the priesthood, remarked on the kindness shown by Paul VI to former priests, a tone replicated throughout the Church which, following the Council's injunction to increase the participation of the laity, found former priests and nuns employment in the Church's educational establishments and the now burgeoning lay administration.

An unanswered question is whether this large-scale laicisation of priests would have taken place if they had been allowed to marry. 'Loneliness' was frequently given as a reason for their renunciation of Holy Orders: 'many of the older generation of priests were brought up to regard celibacy as a condition of their priesthood rather than a separate charism.'[903] It is possible that there was a back-log of unhappy, 'burnt-out' priests who been deterred from seeking laicisation by the punitive process it entailed prior to Vatican II. But it was also the case that to reduce a man belonging the Order of Melchizedek and acting *in persona Christi* to an adjunct of 'the priesthood of the people'; and the insistence of the ecumenicists that he had the same standing as a Protestant pastor, cannot have done much to sustain a Catholic priest's morale.

---

900   Hebblethwaite, *Op. Cit.* p. 547

901   Michael Burleigh, *Sacred Causes*, p. 387

902   Michael Gaine, 'The State of the Priesthood' in *Modern Catholicism*, p. 246

903   *Ibid.*, p. 249

In a speech to the College of Cardinals on 15 December, 1969, Pope Paul VI described the departure of priests as his 'Crown of Thorns', but in fact 'from the first days of his pontificate, the papacy was a Calvary for him'.[904] He had incurred the enmity of the persecuted Hungarian Cardinal Mindszenty, he had failed to end the schism created by Archbishop Lefebvre, and the '*aggiornamento*' of Vatican II had created a Church divided between those who thought the Council had gone too far and those who thought it had not gone far enough. He was disliked by his fellow-countrymen: Italian journalists who accompanied him on his many foreign journeys avoided looking at him, believing that he had 'the Evil Eye'.[905]

The evangelisation that was to have followed the Council never took place. 'The ten years of Paul VI's pontificate', wrote the Italian author, Vittorio Gorresio, 'have been an uninterrupted attempt to open up a dialogue with the modern world. But in this attempt he has failed'.[906] The world which Paul VI had hoped to bring to Christ through a new love and understanding had turned nasty: on 16 March, Aldo Moro, one of the founders of the Christian Democratic Party, a two-term prime minister of Italy, a devout Catholic and friend of Paul VI, was kidnapped by the Communist Red Brigade. The government of Giulio Andreotti refused to negotiate with terrorists, and Moro was killed. It became clear from Moro's correspondence from captivity with his wife that he felt that not just Andreotti but Pope Paul might have done more to save him. Pope Paul officiated at Moro's funeral mass at the basilica of Saint John Lateran: Moro's family did not attend.

The murder of Moro blighted the last months of Pope Paul's pontificate, and it was a source of sorrow that his prayers for his friend had not been answered. However, it was merely the last of many trials and disappointments that he had had to endure. In the preceding years he had suffered from bouts of depression – dark nights of the soul. 'He said the rosary every day: he identified with the first 'sorrowful mystery', the Agony in the Garden'. He was to be found weeping at the shrine of *San' Pietro ad Vincula* – Saint Peter in Chains – on his walks in the Vatican gardens. These 'tears and lamentations... were not over his sins but over the state of the Church'. On the tenth anniversary of his pontificate, in a sermon preached in Saint Peter's,

904   George Weigel, *Witness to Hope. The Biography of Pope John Paul II*, p.241

905   Alexander Chancellor to the author

906   Quoted in Peter Hebblethaite, *Op. Cit.* p. 602

he spoke of the restlessness, disquiet, dissatisfaction, polarisation that existed in the Church: of how 'any jumped-up prophet who wrote in the papers or any movement that appealed to him was believed, while the authentic voice of the *magisterium* was ignored'. Through some crack, he said, 'the smoke of Satan' had entered the temple of God.[907]

---

907   *Ibid.*, p. 595

PART SEVEN

118. Karol Wojtyla

Pope Paul VI died on 6 August, 1978, in Castel Gandolfo. In the conclave to choose a successor held before the end of the month, the cardinals looked for a candidate who would 'lift the gloom that had descended during Paul's last years'[908] – someone holy but cheerful like John XXIII; and they found one from the same source in Albino Luciani, the Patriarch of Venice. The son of a migrant worker, he broke precedent by refusing a coronation, choosing instead to mark his installation with his reception of the pallium as bishop of Rome; and, to mark the continuity with his predecessors that he envisaged, he took the names of both – John and Paul. 'The first pope of demonstrably working-class origins, a man of practical common sense', he 'captivated people with his friendly smile'. He was called 'God's candidate' which in a sense was a tautology because all conclaves are believed to be guided by the Holy Spirit and in this case the workings of the Spirit were puzzling because, three weeks after his inauguration, on 28 September, the nun who brought him a cup of coffee at 5.15 every morning found Pope John Paul I dead in his bed. Theories that he had been murdered to thwart certain measures he had in mind were shown to be groundless: it was, in any case, 'impossible to guess what kind of policies he would have pursued had he lived'.[909]

A second conclave was held in October, 1978. A stand-off between Cardinals Siri and Benelli, and the announcement by a possible compromise candidate, Cardinal Colombo, that, if elected, he would decline, led the cardinals to look beyond Italy and on the eighth ballot held on 16 October the requisite majority chose the Polish Archbishop of Krakow, Karol Wojtyla, who, as an obeisance to his predecessor, took the name John Paul.

Pope John Paul II, the 264th successor to Peter, was the first non-Italian pontiff since Adrian VI (the Emperor Charles V's Dutch tutor) 455 years before and, at 58, was the youngest pope since Pio Nono who had been chosen

---

908   Eamon Duffy, *Op. Cit.* p. 370
909   J.N.D. Kelly, *Op. Cit.,* p. 326

aged 54. He spoke fifteen languages, would travel over a million kilometres to 129 countries, and play a critical role in the collapse of Communism in Eastern Europe. He would be shot at point-blank range by a Turkish assassin yet survive to address a crowd of five million people in Manila – the largest gathering ever recorded – and reign for 27 years. He was 'indisputably the most visible pope in history' and considered by many 'the most consequential pope since the Reformation and Counter-Reformation in the sixteenth century'.[910] Yet while he was loved by the many he came to be loathed by those who felt that he had betrayed 'the spirit of Vatican II'.

Karol Wojtyla was born in 1920 in Wadowice, the youngest of the three children of a retired army officer and school teacher. His sister Olga died before he was born and his mother Emilia when he was eight years old. He was raised by his devout father and older brother who became a doctor but then died of scarlet fever. In 1938, the Wojtylas – father and son – moved to Krakow where Karol enrolled in the Jagiellonian University. After the German invasion of Poland, and the occupation of Krakow, the university was closed and its entire faculty dispatched to a concentration camp. The younger Karol Wojtyla worked first in a limestone quarry, then for the Solvay chemical works. He joined an underground theatre group, acting and writing to keep alive a Polish culture that the Nazis were determined to destroy.

Wojtyla was devout, taking part in a 'living rosary' prayer group that cultivated the spirituality of the Carmelite, John of the Cross. The death of his father in 1941, a road accident that almost killed him, a narrow escape in August, 1944 when the Gestapo made mass arrests to pre-empt an uprising in Krakow, persuaded him that God did not want him to be an actor – hitherto his ambition – but a priest. He entered the underground seminary that the Archbishop of Krakow, Cardinal Prince Adam Stefan Sapieha, had established in his archiepiscopal palace. A man in the mould of Count Clemens August von Gallen, Archbishop of Münster, whom the Germans dared not touch, Sapieha – in the absence of the primate, Archbishop Hlond who had gone into exile, – 'was the de facto inter-rex of Poland for more than five years – the focal point of legitimate authority in a nation being run by gangsters'.[911]

After the Germans were driven out of Poland by the Red Army in 1945, a Communist government was formed in Warsaw. The western Allies, who

---

910   George Weigel, *Op. Cit.* p. 4

911   *Ibid.* p. 73

had gone to war in support of Poland, felt unable to resist Stalin either in his choice of a government or the re-drawing of national boundaries with huge swathes of pre-war Poland going to the Russians and Ukrainians in exchange for German territory east of the Oder. Despite the atheist ideology of the new regime, it proceeded carefully in its dealings with the Catholic Church – so embedded was it in the nation's identity.

Karol Wojtyla, having completed his studies at the seminary, was ordained priest by Cardinal Sapieha on 1 November, 1946. Recognising his potential, the cardinal sent the twenty-six year-old priest to continue his studies at the Angelicum in Rome under the French Thomist theologian, Reginald Garrigou-Lagrange – the Dominican, it will be remembered, who was sceptical of the *nouvelle théologie* and contributed to Pius XII's encyclical, *Humani generis*. During his vacations, Wojtyla left Rome to visit Padre Pio, the Franciscan mystic with the stigmata – the wounds received by Jesus when he was nailed to the cross; and to travel in France and Belgium, learning about the Worker Priest movement. Upon completing his studies at the Angelicum, he returned to Poland, where he served first in a small rural parish and then the Church of Saint Florian in Krakow. He was awarded a Doctorate in Sacred Theology by his nearby *alma mater*, the Jagiellonian University, but continued his philosophical studies, specialising in the work of the German phenomenologist philosopher, Max Scheler.

As parish priest of Saint Florian's, he was responsible for the pastoral care of the students, and took them on hiking, climbing and kayaking trips in the mountains. They called him 'uncle' to hide the fact that he was a priest. The combination of piety, learning, a warm personality and calm courage in dealing with the Communist authorities led to Wojtyla's swift rise in the Polish hierarchy. In July, 1958, he was appointed auxiliary bishop of Krakow – at 38 the youngest bishop in Poland. In 1964, after the death of Archbishop Eugeniusz Baziak of Lviv, since Cardinal Sapieha's death administrator of the archdiocese of Krakow, he became the city's Archbishop, and in June, 1967, Pope Paul VI made him a cardinal.

Already, as an auxiliary bishop, Wojtyla had taken part in the proceedings of the Second Vatican Council, insisting on the idea of religious freedom found in *Dignitatis Humanae* – something vital when it came to the Church's confrontation with the Communist government in Poland. We have seen how Wojtyla's book *Love and Responsibility* influenced Pope Paul VI's encyclical, *Humanae Vitae*. In March, 1976, Wojtyla preached the Lenten retreat to Pope

Paul and the Curia: thus he was not unknown to the cardinal electors when it came to the conclave held in 1978.

In 1982, four years into the pontificate of John Paul II, the English author and historian, Paul Johnson, published a book entitled *Pope John Paul II and the Catholic Restoration*. Johnson, dismayed by much of what had followed Vatican II, welcomed what to him seemed a restoration by both the pope and Cardinal Joseph Ratzinger who, in 1977, after a short tenure as Archbishop of Munich, had been summoned to Rome to serve as Prefect of the Congregation of the Faith.

The irony here is that neither John Paul II nor Ratzinger saw themselves as 'restoring' the pre-Conciliar Church. There were those such as Archbishop Lefebvre who thought Vatican II had been a disaster, and Cardinal Wyszynski, the primate of Poland, who regretted its 'lack of enthusiasm for popular piety, processions and pilgrimages that were so important to Polish Catholic life'.[912] John Paul II did not agree with either; nor did Josef Ratzinger. Both had played significant roles in drawing up some of the Council's decrees, and both would insist that Vatican II was to be the inspiration of the pontificate. The progressives, however, 'would become increasingly conscious of the gap between John Paul's words and his actions'.[913] They would accuse him of hypocrisy; while some conservative Catholics, antipathetic to the legacy of Council, thought that he and Josef Ratzinger were trying to square a circle. Few, one suspects, took the trouble to read the Council's decrees which, as we have seen, the Anglican observer Edward Norman had found 'surprisingly unitary and conservative'.[914]

Pope John Paul II was no more inclined to compromise with dissident theologians than he had been with Communist *apparachiks,* and in the first year of his pontificate he doubled-down on the key question of contraception in a series of fifteen minute homilies on marriage and sexual love, later published as *The Theology of the Body*. They were 'highly compact philosophical and theological meditations' which 'did not make easy listening and do not make easy reading'.[915] He knew well from hearing confessions in Poland the trials and tribulations of marriage, but held the sacrament in high esteem, comparing spousal love with that of the Three Persons of the Trinity.

912   Hebblethwaite, *Op. Cit.* p. 450

913   John Cornwell, *The Pope in Winter*, p.95

914   Adrian Hastings (ed.), *Op. Cit.*, p. 457

915   George Weigel, *Op. Cit.* p. 336

Sex without love was abhorrent. 'The woman at whom a man gazes lustfully is an object, not a person, and sex is reduced to an utilitarian means to satisfy a "need". Even within marriage, there can be 'adultery of the heart'.[916]

One of the visions of Teresa of Avila, referred to by Francis of Sales in his *Introduction to the Devout Life,* had been of married couples suffering torments in Hell for 'having violated the sanctity of marriage which happened, she said, not for the enormity of the sin, for murders and blasphemies are more enormous; but because they that commit it make no conscience of it, and therefore continue long in it...'[917] Thus, Pope John Paul II's talk of adultery within marriage was nothing new but it made the headlines.

George Weigel, the American biographer of Pope John Paul II, suggests that *The Theology of the Body* 'may well be seen as...a critical moment in modern thought',[918] but he conceded that it did not make easy reading and, by and large, fell on deaf ears. Sexual intercourse between a man and a woman leading to the conception of a child might be, alternately, the most bestial and the most sacred of human actions – satisfying a mere carnal appetite or expressing spousal love and possibly engendering an immortal being. In what John Paul II called the current 'aphrodisiac civilisation of the west', the momentous partnership with God in procreation during sexual intercourse was rarely in the forefront or even the background of a couple's mind.

The importance of chastity was not the only message that John Paul wished to convey to the world. 1979 also saw the first of his many pastoral visits – in this case to Mexico, still ruled by an anti-clerical regime. A million Mexicans turned out along the route from the airport to Mexico City; it took the motorcade an hour to cover less than five miles; the Church had flourished thanks to the blood of the martyrs in the persecution of the 1920s. From Mexico John Paul flew to New York where he addressed the United Nations, 'exuding physical vigour, vitality and a sense of command.'[919] Here, following the example of Popes John XXIII and Paul VI, he spoke not as the leader of a religion, but as the pastor of all humanity.

That same year saw the award of the Nobel Prize for Peace to Mother Teresa of Calcutta for her work among the destitute in that city; and the ruling by the Congregation for the Doctrine of the Faith under the Croatian

---

916   *Ibid.,* p. 338

917   Francis of Sales, *Op. Cit.,* p. 157

918   George Weigel, *Op. Cit.,* p. 343

919   *Ibid.,* p. 774

Cardinal Franjo Šeper that, because of his unorthodox views, Ratzinger's erstwhile colleague at Tübingen University, Hans Küng, 'could not now be considered a Catholic theologian' and therefore 'his mandate to teach as a Professor of Catholic theology was withdrawn'.[920] This censure of the darling of the progressives – handsome, articulate, a best-selling author – outraged the *bien pensant* liberals in the developed world. It was considered a heavy-handed attempt to silence a scholar who had dared to question the doctrine of papal infallibility.

In fact, Küng's 'errors' went further, holding that not just that the Pope but the Church itself could make 'concrete errors in definitions of faith'. Clearly, he was entitled to his opinion, but it contradicted a fundamental tenet of the *magisterium*. Thus the censure was not to silence him – he was not excommunicated, nor 'defrocked' and continued teaching at Tübingen as Professor of Ecumenical Theology – but merely to spare students being told that his theories were within the parameters of the Catholic Faith.

Six further censures were to be issued by the Congregation for the Doctrine of the Faith during John Paul II's long pontificate – most of them when it was led by Cardinal Josef Ratzinger who replaced Cardinal Šeper as Prefect in 1981. A number were related to Liberation Theology which will be the subject of a separate chapter. It meant that for more than a decade and a half the shy, scholarly Bavarian 'was subject to caricature as the fierce *Panzercardinal* (tank cardinal), heir to the Inquisitors, or as a gloomy German out of tune with modernity'.[921] Again, it is something of an irony that the theologian who had done so much to prize open Pandora's Box during Vatican II should now be charged with retrieving the errant beliefs that had escaped. He was as good a theologian as any of the dissenters, if not better, and though differing in style from John Paul II – Ratzinger's lucidity contrasting with the impenetrability of some of the pope's discourse; the cardinal self-effacing and retiring while the pope confident and assertive – a *Panzerpabst*. Both came from the same deeply Catholic culture of Central Europe, and both were the sons of uniformed figures of authority – the one an army officer, the other a police chief. When they had first met at the conclave after the death of Pope Paul VI, 'the fifty-one year old Bavarian and the fifty-eight year old Pole...discovered that they had very similar analyses of the Church's situation'.[922]

---

920   *Ibid.* p. 357
921   *Ibid.,* p. 444
922   *Ibid.,* p. 244

The two churchmen – the pope and the prefect – became an effective team – the one drawing upon his training as an actor to enrapture huge crowds (John Gielgud praised his 'perfect sense of timing'); the other on his scholarship and exceptional clarity of mind. Of course John Paul II also wrote many encyclicals, but he lacked Ratzinger's lucidity. Some of the impenetrability of his phenomenological models, Martin Heidegger and Max Scheler, was found in his writing. A Polish colleague taking part in a symposium at Lublin university to discuss a philosophical paper submitted by the then Archbishop of Krakow, declared that he had 'read it twice and still did not understand it'. Even critics well disposed towards him regarded him as an 'aspiring philosopher…well-meaning, clever, undoubtedly original, bold – but essentially an autodidact and academically out of his depth' – hardly surprising, perhaps, for 'a part-time academic running one of the largest dioceses in Eastern Europe in a time of major political and economic crisis'.[923]

Among Pope John Paul's more notable encyclicals was *Evangelium Vitae* which addressed 'the moral foundations of a free and virtuous society'. During Vatican II, he had championed the idea of Human Rights to counter any attempt by the Communist government in Poland to suppress the rights of Catholics. What he had not envisaged was that in the western democracies human rights would come to mean Rabelais' *Fait çe que voudras* – the right of the individual to do what he or she liked with the only proviso that such actions should not harm other human beings. The foetus or embryo was not considered a human being and, despite Pope John Paul's 'unsparing' denunciation of 'tyrant states that poison the culture of rights' by denying 'the inalienable right to live from conception until death',[924] the criteria which permitted a woman to terminate a pregnancy grew ever more lax as the century proceeded, and formerly Catholic nations such as Belgium passed laws permitting euthanasia – the 'right' to die.

If, from a religious perspective, the conservative understanding of Vatican II by Pope John Paul II lies at the heart of his pontificate, secular historians would point to his role in 'one of the most extraordinary paroxysms in modern history, the implosion of the Soviet system'.[925] It is hard now to remember, or even imagine, the rivalry of the states embodying two political systems

---

923   John Cornwell, *Op. Cit.*, p. 51
924   George Weigel, *Op. Cit.*, p.757
925   John Cornwell, *Op, Cit.*, p.103

on either side of the Iron Curtain, each championed by a 'superpower', the United States and the Soviet Union, armed with nuclear weapons capable of annihilation. Both the possibility of 'mutually ensured destruction', and Soviet hegemony in Easter Europe, had in fact both ensured a stability that prevented the kind of revanchism that might have arisen after the post-war re-drawing of borders and movement of populations; and, given the high price paid by the Soviets to defeat what they termed the 'fascists', it was only to be expected that after their victory they would want to install puppet regimes in 'buffer' states adjoining their borders. There were some convinced Communists among these puppet regimes but they were few: as always under any system most of those who made up the administration were opportunists ready to become Marxists for the sake of a government job.

Of the East European nations which now had Communist governments, Poland was the odd man out. Unlike, say, in Romania, Bulgaria, Lithuania or Slovakia, no Poles had collaborated with or fought alongside the Germans: they had resisted the Germans *à l'outrance*. Moreover, because of its long history of oppression by the Protestant Prussians and Orthodox Russians, the Catholic faith was embedded in the nation's identity – not a narrow, provincial Catholicism but one that looked to western Europe – to France and in particular to Rome. As a result, no Polish government, however antithetical to the Catholic Church, dared stop priests and bishops passing through the Iron Curtain, or prevent Karol Wojtyla from travelling to Rome to study, and later become pope. Nor could the government in Warsaw prevent the Polish pontiff from making pilgrimages to his native country – greeted by huge crowds in Warsaw, Krakow and Czestochowa where he prayed before the icon if the Virgin Mary. By the end of his reign, 'thirteen million Poles, more than one-third of the national population, had seen the pope in person.'[926]

No one in 1979, the year of John Paul II's accession, anticipated the collapse of the Soviet system within a decade, but the Polish pope 'had measured Communism's weaknesses as well as its strengths. And he knew that cultural resistance could be an effective antidote to the seemingly impregnable position of a criminal state.[927] 'The *Ostpolitik* of Pope Paul VI and his Secretary of State Cardinal Casaroli changed dramatically with Karol Wojtyla's election as pope. Recalling the Soviet suppression of revolts in East Germany in 1953, Hungary in 1956 and Czechoslovakia in 1968, the Church

---

926   George Weigel, *Op. Cit.*, p. 320

927   *Ibid.*, p. 295

in Poland, while insisting upon its rights, never trespassed into the political arena or called for a change of regime. However, communism was not just malign but inefficient: the lackluster socialist economy led to shortages, and the shortages to discontent.

In 1980, two years after the election of John Paul II, a strike broke out in the Gdansk shipyard. Emboldened by the support of the Polish pope in Rome, the strikers formed a Trade Union, Solidarity. All attempts to suppress it failed, and in due course 'Poland's communist government agreed to recognize the legality of the first independent, self-governing trade union in the communist world.' The leader of Solidarity, Lech Walesa, 'signed the agreement with a huge souvenir pen 'topped by the picture of a smiling Pope'.[928]

A year later, on 13 May, the Feast of Our Lady of Fatima, the smiling pope, while greeting the large crowds of pilgrims gathered in Saint Peter's Square from an open-topped Fiat, was shot at point-blank range by a Turkish assassin, Mehmed Ali Ağca. Pope John Paul II was hit by four bullets – one on the hand, another on the shoulder, and two entering his abdomen. He was taken to the Gemelli hospital where it was found that the bullets had avoided by millimeters any vital organs – the heart, the spleen, the liver, the kidneys – and were lodged in his lower intestine. After surgery, some months of convalescence, and a relapse caused by contaminated blood used in transfusions, John Paul II returned to his duties in the Vatican. There was no doubt in his mind but that he had survived the assassination thanks to Our Lady of Fatima. 'He spoke of how one hand had guided the trigger, while another, "a motherly hand", had guided the bullet so as to avoid the vital organs'.[929] He would later take the retrieved bullet to the shrine at Fatima where it was placed in the crown of the statue of the Virgin who had appeared to the three peasant children in 1916.

Ali Ağca, apprehended by the pope's body guards, was later tried and sentenced to life imprisonment. At one time a member of a group of Turkish nationalists, the Grey Wolves, Ağca had shot the editor of a left-wing Turkish newspaper in 1979; was denounced, arrested and sentenced to life imprisonment; but escaped from a military prison and fled to Bulgaria. Ağca appears to have had links with the Turkish mafia who smuggled him across the border, but also the Bulgarian intelligence Service, and it was thought that

---

928   *Ibid.*, p. 323

929   John Cornwell, *Op. Cit.*, p. 89

he had been recruited by the Bulgarians on the instructions of the KGB in Moscow to kill the 'troublesome' pope. None of this was proved.

Later, Pope John Paul II would visit Ağca in prison, and later still Ağca would become a Catholic. When the 'third secret' imparted by the Virgin at Fatima was revealed as a vision of a figure in a white soutane stepping over dead bodies and under assault, it was seen by many as a foretelling of what had taken place in Saint Peter's Square on 13 May, 1981. For John Paul II, the attempt on his life 'and his survival, was to leave a deep and lasting religious, even "mystical" impression, the consequences of which would take some years to become fully apparent'.[930]

119.   Liberation Theology

A little more than a year before the attempt to assassinate Pope John Paul II, on 24 March, 1980, the Archbishop of El Salvador, Oscar Romero, was shot dead while saying mass in the chapel of the Divine Providence Hospital in El Salvador. John Paul II was shot as the enemy of Marxist communism, Oscar Romero as its friend. To the list of issues that divided the guardians of orthodoxy in Rome and the progressive theologians in the wider Church – collegiality, celibacy, married priests – there had now been added the Theology of Liberation.

During Vatican II, 'No important Latin American theologian's voice was heard in the Council: the future liberation theologians were still students or only young priests and activists, not really aware of being at all different from the rest'[931] but there were among the Council fathers from the developed world those who believed that the Church should play a more active role in promoting social justice. The result were contradictions even within the same decree. *Gaudium et spes* stated that 'Christ did not bequeath to the Church a mission in the political economic, or social order.... The purpose he assigned was a religious one';[932] But also that 'God destined the earth and all it contains for all men and all peoples so that all created things should be shared by all mankind...'[933] Francis of Sales, as we have seen, believed that poverty was a

---

930   *Ibid.*, p. 86

931   Dussel, Enrique, 'Latin America' in Hastings, *Op. Cit.*, p 320

932   *Gaudium et spes,* 42. Kelly, *Op. Cit.*, p.942

933   *Ibid.,* 67, p. 975

God-given privilege because the poor were particularly loved by God; the Council held that Catholics 'should do all in their power to relieve their need' ' even to the point of fostering public and private organizations devoted to the bettering of the conditions of life'. The decree *Lumen Gentium* called for 'a greater commitment to working with all men towards the establishment of a world that is more human' and 'this emphasis would provide the charter for the development of theologies of social and political engagements, like Liberation Theology. It was one of the Council's most profound acts of theological reorientation,' wrote Eamon Duffy, 'and one which transcended the somewhat glib optimism of *Gaudium et Spes* itself'.[934]

The key work in this theological reorientation was *A Theology of Liberation* by the Peruvian Gustavo Gutierrez. The work was 'a serious attempt to transform the theologian into a socio-political activist. It freely acknowledged its debt to Marx...'[935] Other Liberation theologians were also from South America – Leonardo Boff from Brazil, Juan Louis Segundo from Uruguay. Their views were espoused by the Brazilian Archbishop of Olinda e Recife, Hélder Camara, the founder and first Secretary-General of the Latin American Episcopal Council, CELAM. South America was the world's most Catholic continent, yet one with a great gap between the rich and the poor, and prone to the rule of military *juntas*. For too long Catholic prelates, often on the pretext that it was in the best interests of the Church, had thrown in their lot with the privileged elites. At the CELAM conference held in Medellin in Colombia in 1968 the assembled bishops announced that from now onwards they would exercise 'a preferential option for the poor'. 'Medellin was the great turning-point in the modern history of Latin America... Its main achievement was to re-express the Christian concept of salvation in terms of liberation, *liberación* not only from individual sins and peccadilloes but from the sinful built-in structures of society'.[936]

The phrase 'a preferential option for the poor' was first used in a letter to the South American Jesuits in 1968. by 'Pedro Arrupe, a charismatic Basque who had led the Jesuits since 1965'[937]. It would be adopted not just by CELAM but by the World Congress of Catholic Bishops in 1971 as 'a constitutive dimension of the preaching of the Gospel, or, in other words, of the Church's mission for

---

934   Eamon Duffy, *Op. Cit.* p. 361

935   Peter Rawlinson, *The Jesuit Factor*, p. 21

936   Peter Hebblethwaite, *Op. Cit.*, p. 522

937   George Weigel, *Op. Cit.*, p. 426

the redemption of the human race and its liberation from every oppressive situation'. The Jesuits – with their 36,000 members at the time of Vatican II, the largest order of the Church – had been stung by the rebuke implicit in some of Vatican II's decrees. The heroism of its missionaries despatched to the four corners of the world, and the success of the Society at turning the tide at the time of the Reformation, had been replaced after its restitution by Pope Pius VII in 1814 by the exercise of influence through the education of the children of the elites who would as adults constitute the governing classes: in other words, a preferential option for the rich and influential (see Chapter 94). Not just in Europe but throughout the world, ambitious parents would send their children to be educated by the Jesuits. In the United States alone, the Jesuits at the time of Vatican II 'operated some twenty-eight universities and forty-six high schools'[938] but what had they done for the poor?

Vatican II had thrown the Jesuits into disarray. Seven thousand priests, as we have seen, left the Society, while those that remained pursued their own idea of what was meant by renewal with exotic liturgies, unorthodox teaching and secularised life-styles: eminent Jesuits such as Karl Rahner dropped their dog collars for a shirt and tie. Pope Paul VI had become alarmed. As early as 1965 'he had expressed amazement and sorrow at the conduct of the Society of Jesus and had warned the Jesuits against a decline in the spirit of obedience and against the adoption of worldly ways'.[939] 'He laid great stress on the fourth vow of obedience to the pope', and asked the Society 'to undertake a new task of obstructing atheism. This was variously interpreted.' A year later, he had complained that many Jesuits had abandoned 'so many of their hallowed customs concerning their spiritual and ascetic life and discipline'. In September, 1973 he wrote to the Society's Father General, Arrupe, 'a massive doom-laden warning that Pedro Arrupe's stewardship was on the wrong lines';[940] and during the Jesuits' Thirty-Second General Congregation held in Rome the following year, 'Pope Paul intervened three times during their meeting, warning them against "false humanism"'.[941]

After the death of Pope Paul VI, both John Paul I, in his brief tenure, and after him Pope John Paul II, inherited Paul VI's misgivings about the Jesuits, and under the latter things came to a head. In September, 1979, Pope John

---

938   Peter Rawlinson, *Op Cit..*, p. 127

939   *Ibid.*, p.32

940   Peter Hebblethwaite, *Op. Cit.*,0 628

941   *Ibid.* p. 423

Paul II told a Conference of Jesuits in Rome, "'I want to tell you that you were a matter of concern to my predecessors and you are to the pope who is talking to you'.[942] Pedro Arrupe was minded to resign as Father General, but according to the Society's constitution, such a resignation could only be accepted by a General Congregation which would then elect his successor. John Paul II, aware of the rebellious spirit at large in the Society, and the radical views of Arrupe's four Assistants, forbade summoning of a Thirty-Third General Congregation. Instead, when Arrupe suffered a stroke and was considered incapable of continuing in his post as Father General, Pope John Paul imposed the seventy-nine year old Jesuit Father Paolo Dezza as his 'personal delegate' to lead the Society until further notice.

'The intervention was shock therapy, intended to break a pattern of confrontation between the Society and the Church's highest authorities'.[943] It did not lead to open revolt, and indeed it was welcomed by some Jesuits, but if 'serious change in the direction of Jesuit life and ministry was the purpose of John Paul II's 1981 intervention, it is not easy to see how the intervention can be rated a success'.[944] A Thirty-Third General Congregation was held in 1983 and elected as General a Dutch Jesuit, Peter Hans Kolvenbach, Professor of Oriental Linguistics at the University of Saint Joseph in Beirut. Peter Rawlinson, a former Attorney General in the British government, who interviewed Kolvenbach for a radio programme about the Jesuits, found him 'a subtle and sophisticated man' with 'the bearing above all of a priest';[945] however, the best Kolvenbach could hope for was to mediate between the guardians of Catholic orthodoxy in Rome and those members of the Society who, like 'the majority of the Catholic clergy, espoused positions that were congruent with those of the semi-Marxist intelligentsia'.[946]

We have seen how texts taken from the decrees of Vatican II, and books written by South American theologians, led to Liberation Theology; but there was also a significant historical event that preceded Vatican II – the Cuban Revolution. In January, 1959, a guerrilla army led by the Jesuit-educated lawyer, Fidel Castro, his brother Raoul, and the Argentinian medical student, Ernesto Che Guevara, ousted the regime of the corrupt Cuban dictator

---

942   Quoted in George Weigel, *Op. Cit.* p. 426

943   *Ibid.*, p. 430

944   *Ibid.*, p.470

945   Peter Rawlinson, *Op. Cit.* p. 43

946   Michael Burleigh, *Sacred Causes*, p. 367

Fulgencio Batista and 'inaugurated the first socialist government on the continent'.

The world was delighted. Every student now put up posters of Fidel and Che Guevara on their walls of their rooms; many grew beards, wore berets and smoked cigars. Guevara was later killed trying to do the same for Bolivia as Castro had done for Cuba, but Castro himself held on to power despite attempts by the United States to oust him. An embargo was placed on Cuba: It was not just that Batista had been a close ally of the US, but that that Castro was a Marxist who looked to the Soviet Union. Would the bacillus spread from Cuba to other countries in the Americas? Initially willing to recognize the new government, the then President of the United States, Dwight D. Eisenhower, broke off diplomatic relations when Castro nationalized American property in Cuba. Castro also moved against the Catholic Church, nationalizing Catholic schools, censoring Catholic publications and expelling Catholic priests: around 130 were arrested in 1961 and dispatched to Spain on a freighter. Catholics were excluded from universities, were not allowed to teach, and were discriminated against on the job market.[947] 'In Cuba…the Castro regime had a rope around the Church's neck'.[948]

This persecution did not inhibit the proponents of Liberation Theology from seeing Castro's revolution as a model to follow. In Argentina, the Montoneros guerrillas, 'started out as a self-described Christian, nationalist and socialist group; but as time passed the socialist element eclipsed the Christian'. After the coup against the Peronist government in 1976, the military junta pursued a 'dirty war' against not just the Montoneros but anyone deemed sympathetic to their cause. Around 30,000 were killed in this repression. Sixteen priests and two French nuns were detained and subsequently 'disappeared'. The left-wing bishop Enrique Angelelli of La Rioja was murdered by a death squad: the Argentinian bishops accepted the government's report that he had died in a road accident. Many of the bishops had ties with the military and approved of the coup. 'Vatican II appeared to have passed the majority of Argentinian bishops by'.[949]

In Nicaragua, Augusto César Sandino, the leader of the resistance to the United States' occupation of the country in 1936, gave his name to the socialist

---

947   See Peter Rawlinson, *Op. Cit.*, p. 206

948   George Weigel, *Op. Cit.* 451

949   Dussel, Enrique, *Op. Cit.*, p 298

Sandinista National Liberal Front which in 1979 overthrew the dictatorship of Anastasio Somoza Debayle. Here the Catholic hierarchy had supported the insurrection, but looked askance when, despite the ruling that the clergy should not take part in politics, four priests joined the revolutionary government. One of them, Ernesto Cardenal, was made Minister for Culture and was publicly rebuked by Pope John Paul II when he visited Nicaragua in March, 1983.

The pope was alarmed not just by these priests' breach of the rules but, together with the Prefect of the CDF, Cardinal Ratzinger, at the Liberationist ideology of the Sandinistas. As recorded in the Gospels, Christ had told the Roman procurator Pontius Pilate that his kingdom 'was not of this world'. Paul VI had 'doubted very much whether one should present Jesus as an "earthly saviour"' because it 'might give rise to unrealizable hopes'.[950] In March, 1983, Cardinal Ratzinger published a critique of the theology of Gustavo Gutiérrez, accusing him of erroneous interpretations of Biblical texts to support 'temporal messianism', and giving precedence to orthopraxis (correct action) over orthodox belief. He pointed out that Liberation Theology had not sprung from the ranks of the deprived poor it purported to champion, but was rather 'the creation of Western intellectuals' who had developed their ideas in European universities and so was a form of 'cultural imperialism'.

Cardinal Ratzinger recognised the good in the pursuit of justice, but condemned the idea that the charitable imperative incumbent on all Catholics should be seen in Marxist terms as 'class struggle'; and the idea that taking up one's Cross meant taking up a Kalashnikov. The Brazilian theologian, Leonard Boff, was suspended; the Sri Lankan Father Tissa Balasuriya was excommunicated; the Indian theologian Sebastian Kappen was censured for his book *Jesus and Freedom*. Liberal Catholics in the developed world saw this as censorship and were outraged.

It exacerbated their indignation that the governments of the United States – particularly under President Ronald Reagan – had their own geopolitical reasons for countering the Liberationist movements in South and Central America, and provided military assistance to right-wing regimes, sometimes – as in their support for the Nicaraguan Contras who fought to bring down the Sandinista regime – covert and contrary to laws passed by the US Congress. There was no hiding the brutality of the Contras during the conflict which cost 30,000 lives, and the supporters of the Liberationists in the United States

---

950   Hebblethwaite, *Op. Cit.*, p. 252

and western Europe made little distinction between Reagan, Ratzinger and Pope John Paul II. It was certainly true that 'the pope and the president held certain common convictions' but these mainly concerned the 'captive nations' of Eastern Europe – what Reagan called the Soviets' 'evil empire'.

120.   El Salvador

Bordering Nicaragua in Central America, but with a coastline on the Pacific Ocean, was the state of El Salvador. A small, densely populated country, it was almost a caricature of a banana republic. Of its five million inhabitants, most were *mestizos* (of mixed Spanish and Indian descent). The land could hardly sustain them, and what land there was, in the second half of the nineteenth century, had been enclosed to form plantations not of bananas but of coffee. Huge fortunes had been made by a few energetic and unscrupulous entrepreneurs. By the 1960s, more than half of the rural peasantry had no land: sixty percent of the land was owned by two percent of the population. Nor was this disparity merely a matter of statistics. In the capital, San Salvador, huge mansions surrounded by fortified walls stood side by side with makeshift shacks with no drains, no water, no electricity and often no food.

El Salvador was ruled at the time in the interests of the landowning oligarchy, the famous 'fourteen families' who, though they may have had the mentality of the Spanish *Conquistadores*, were often more recent arrivals with names like Schwartz, Schmidt, Dalton and Hill. There was both an army and a national guard to protect the 'security' of the nation from both external enemies and 'enemies' within. The army's officers were drawn from the middle and lower-middle classes. Governments that came to power after often fraudulent elections were routinely ousted by military coups.

It was in this classic case of an unjust society that the progressive priests and their catechists went to work in the late 1960s, organizing workers and peasants into unions, staging protests and working for a fairer distribution of the country's wealth. They were not encouraged by the Church hierarchy which was either comfortable with the *status quo* or feared that their flocks were being led astray by a material concept of salvation. There was considerable resentment by the indigenous clergy of foreign missionaries, particularly the Jesuits – ideological *conquistadores* armed with doctorates from European universities, hoping to emulate their spiritual forefathers' Reductions in

Paraguay by gathering groups of *campesinos* into 'base communities', to study the Bible and through a process called 'conscientization' be made to realise that they were poor and oppressed and should do something about it.

This friction between the conservative Catholic hierarchy and the Jesuit zealots of Liberation Theology came to a head when the then Archbishop of San Salvador, Monsignor Chavez y Gonzalez, expelled a French missionary, a Father Bernardo Boulang, for engaging in political activities. In 1972, the bishops of El Salvador had ousted the Jesuits from the Seminary of San José de la Montagna on the grounds that they had been recruiting students into Marxist organizations. The Jesuits were obliged to withdraw to the university they had founded, the University of Central America, or UCA. There the progressives shared one house, the less progressive another, and the traditionalists were sent off to El Carmen in Sant Tecla.

Leading the progressives was Father Ignacio Ellacuria – like the Jesuit Superior General, Pedro Arrupe and, indeed, Ignatius Loyola, a Basque. Highly intelligent, Ellacuria had first come to El Salvador as a nineteen-year-old novice; he had later gone back to Europe to study theology at Innsbruck in Austria and, after his ordination as a priest in 1961, in Madrid. After returning to El Salvador to teach at UCA in 1967, he came to dominate the Liberationists. 'He was clearly both extraordinarily gifted and a natural leader' yet some found his 'controlled, ironic intellect arrogant and off-putting. '[951] 'Ellacuria's ideas were so radical, so seemingly coherent, the strength of his dialectic so impregnable, and at times shot through with a streak of aggression, that his opponents found themselves unable to reply and were left with the impression that they had been objects of an assault'. [952]

On 23 February, 1977, the Bishop of Santiago de Maria, Oscar Romero, was made Archbishop of San Salvador. His reputation as a moderate conservative had led to the recommendation to Rome by the papal nuncio, and his appointment was met with satisfaction in conservative circles. The Jesuits at UCA were displeased; Romero had played a role in their eviction from the seminary of San José de la Montagna; but as soon as his appointment was announced, forty progressive priests, led by Ignacio Ellacuria and Jon Sobrino, met to discuss tactics. It was agreed that five progressive diocesan

---

951   Teresa Whitfield, *Paying the Price. Ignacio Ellacuria and the Murdered Jesuits of El Salvador*, p. 28
952   *Ibid.*, p. 46

priests should ask to 'dialogue'[953] with Romero and warn him that he would find his diocese ungovernable without their help and that of the Jesuits.

The conservative Catholics in El Salvador would claim that the Jesuits, in their discernment of the new archbishop, had decided that he was weak but also ambitious, and had persuaded him that with the help of the Liberationists he would become a great figure in the Church. More likely, in bringing about a radical re-orientation in Romero's thinking, was the effect on him of the assassination, less than a month after his appointment as archbishop, of a personal friend, the Jesuit Father Rutilio Grande, who had been working among the poor in base communities and, in Romero's view, was 'a priest to the very marrow of his bones'. Ellacuria's fellow-Jesuit, Jon Sobrino, reported that Romero, after celebrating a requiem mass for Grande, had seemed nervous, weighed down by the enormity of what he was facing, and had asked for the help of the Jesuits. 'An archbishop was truly asking... for help from those he had held as suspicious, as Marxists, only weeks before... asking, almost begging us, for help in carrying the heavy load that was falling upon him, far heavier than any load his shoulders or anyone else's could bear'.[954]

Whether or not Romero asked for, or merely acquiesced in, the Jesuits' offer for help, they 'came to play key roles within the running of the archdiocese. The Jesuit provincial, Jerez, attended the Tuesday morning meeting of Romero's closest advisers, sometimes bringing another Jesuit with him. Rafael Moreno became press secretary and a permanent member of the team providing information and ideas before Romero would sit down to write the homily for each Sunday mass'.[955] Romero's second pastoral letter 'was drafted by Jon Sobrino who tried to put himself in Romero's mind after discussing the directions the letter should take.' The Sunday sermons would be broadcast throughout El Salvador on the Catholic Radio station – 'the voice of the voiceless' for the Liberationists; Marxist propaganda in the view of the government. Romero, originally welcomed as a moderate, now became the subject of 'slander and abuse of the right-wing press but also – and much more painful to him – the "systematic and incomprehensible opposition" of the Papal Nuncio and the majority of the Salvadorian bishops'.[956]

---

953   'In the end,' wrote Sir Peter Rawlinson, after his world-wide study of the Jeuits, 'I remained in a state of invincible ignorance about the modern doctrine of "dialogue"'. *The Jesuit Factor*, p. 208

954   *Ibid.*, p. 104

955   *Ibid.*, p. 107

956   *Ibid.* p. 105

On 15 October, 1979, a military coup and the protests which followed marked the beginning of a twelve year civil war. On one side was the army and the national guard, financed by the landowners and the United States; on the other, a coalition of left-wing and revolutionary groups in the Farabundo Marti National Liberation Front, or FMLN – named after a Marxist activist from the 1930s – supported by Nicaragua, Cuba and a large network of sympathizers in Europe and the United States. Ignacio Ellacuria and his companions at UCA never took up arms but they were widely perceived to justify and encourage those who did. In a major offensive in 1981, the FMLN captured and held large sections of territory. The army, largely out of the control of any civilian government, formed covert units – 'death squads' – to eliminate FMLN sympathizers – among them missionary priests and nuns from the United States.

The FMLN also had their death squads. An elderly academic, Francisco Peccorini, who had taught philosophy in California for twenty years, retired to his native San Salvador where he became an articulate critic of Ellacuria and the FMLN: he was shot while driving on a busy street in San Salvador, and died in hospital.[957] Other conservative pundits fled the country for fear of assassination, and even other Catholic missionaries lived in fear. A Franciscan friar, Father Spezzotto, who had preached against violent solutions to social problems had been shot – it was assumed, by the FMLN. The Franciscans and Salesians, long established in El Salvador, were indignant at the claim made by what they called 'Romero's church' that Catholic charitable work had only started with the gathering of bishops in Medellin in 1968 and their 'preferential option for the poor'.[958] The Salesians had been in El Salvador long before 1968 providing technical training in their institutions. They considered that providing work was the best way to help impoverished Salvadorians – something made more difficult by the sabotage of the infrastructure by the FMLN and the consequent sharp decline in the gross national product.

On 24 March, 1980, six months after the start of the civil war, Oscar Romero in his Sunday sermon once against criticized the government for its repression, saying that 'no soldier is obliged to obey an order to kill if it runs contrary to his conscience'. Broadcast throughout the country by the Catholic radio, this was taken by the army as an incitement to mutiny. That evening, after

---

957   *Los Angeles Times*, 16 March, 1989

958   See 'Catechists and Commissars' in *Hell and Other Destinations* by Piers Paul Read

saying mass at the Divine Providence Hospital, Romero again preached a sermon condemning the government for its violation of human rights. As he stepped away from the lectern, a man entered the chapel and fired at him with a revolver. The bullet hit his heart. He died at once. The assassin escaped in the car he had parked outside the chapel.

There was world-wide dismay at the killing of Romero: a quarter of a million mourners attended his funeral on 30 March, 1980. To the Liberationists, he was a martyr for the faith. Cardinal Ernesto Corripio y Ahumada, officiating at his funeral, spoke of him as a 'beloved, peace-making man of God'. Pope John Paul II, visiting El Salvador in 1983, prayed at the tomb of Oscar Romero, referring to him as 'a zealous and venerated pastor who tried to stop violence'. However, both John Paul II and his successor, Benedict XVI, were conscious of Romero's association with Liberation Theology: his canonization would have to wait for the pontificate of his fellow-South American, Pope Francis I, in the 21ˢᵗ century.

Romero's assassin was never caught, but it was thought, and later confirmed, that he had acted on the orders of a Major Robert D'Aubuisson, a right-wing officer and politician. D'Aubuisson was arrested but then released. In 1981 he founded a political party, the Nationalist Republican Alliance or ARENA. He served as President of El Salvador's Constituent Assembly from 1982-1983 and was a candidate for the Presidency. The civil war continued. So strong were the passions, and so dominant the influence of the Liberationist fellow-travellers in the western media, that the existence of a 'traditional Church' which abhorred the use of violence by the FMLN was ignored. Within El Salvador, some young *campesinos* drawn into the base communities balked when told that taking up one's Cross meant joining the FMLN. There was a defection of Catholics to the Pentecostalist church where, each Sunday, they would forget that they were poor, put on their Sunday best, and gather to pray to God and sing hymns. Bishop Athanasius Schneider later wrote that 'Liberation Theology, Modernism and liberalism in the liturgy and in the practice of the faith emptied Catholic life of its riches for so many people... Simple everyday Latin American Catholics were betrayed and robbed of the faith-filled devotion of the Catholic faith, such as festivals in honour of saints, processions in honour of Our Lady, and so on.'[959]

---

959   Athanasius Schneider, *Op. Cit.* p. 209

As during the Spanish Civil War, there was a virtually unanimous consensus among Western journalists and academics about the rights and wrongs of the conflict in El Salvador. The Salvadorian army with its murderous 'sweeps' through areas with populations susceptible to recruitment to the FMLN; its massacres of civilians, and murder by death squads of FMLN sympathizers, among them priests and nuns – all this aided and abetted by the government of the United States – was considered worse than the FMLN's selective assassinations of political and military and civil officials, landowners and businessmen. The United Nations would later estimate that the FMLN was responsible for about five percent of the total number of atrocities against ninety-five by the army. However, as in Spain in the 1930s, it was not appreciated by those who supported the Liberationists in Europe and the United States that the objective of the FMLN was not to establish a western democracy but a Marxist dictatorship modelled on that existing in Cuba. Indeed, it was legitimate for the devout, while abhorring injustice, to accept that, as Josef Ratzinger succinctly put it, 'Jesus was not Spartacus'.

On 16 November, 1989, fifteen hundred guerrilla fighters of the FMLN descended from the volcano which overlooks some of the smarter suburbs of San Salvador in an all-out assault on El Salvador's capital city. 'Sleepers' in the barrios dug up buried weapons and joined the attack. Parts of the city were occupied. Mortars were fired at the presidential palace. It is unclear as to whether the FMLN *commandantes* hoped their attack would precipitate a general uprising that would topple the government, or whether – like the Tet offensive of the Viet Cong twenty-one years before – it was a show of force prior to negotiations for a political settlement.

No general uprising was forthcoming and after three days of fighting the FMLN withdrew. Up to three thousand people had been killed, either in battle or caught in the cross-fire. Five days after the start of the offensive, in the early morning of 16 November, 1989, a group of uniformed soldiers from the Salvadorian army's Atlacati Battalion broke into the residence of the Jesuit priests at UCA and shot Ignacio Ellacuria, Segundo Montes, Ignacio Martin-Baró, Joaquin López, Juan Ramón Moreno, and Amando López y López – together with their housekeeper, Elba Ramos, and her daughter, Celina Marisela Ramos. The priests were dragged from the beds, shot with machine-guns and their bodies mutilated. The women were shot in the bed they shared.

Just as the assassination of Archbishop Romero came soon after the start of the Salvadorian civil war, so the murder of the UCA Jesuits and their housekeepers took place towards the end. Almost at the same time as the failed offensive, and the atrocity at UCA, came the breach of the Berlin Wall. With the subsequent collapse of the Soviet Union, the Cold War came to an end. The Cubans lost their patron and the Americans their fear of Red revolutions. The civil war in El Salvador spluttered on for another two years, ending with the Chapultepec Peace Accords signed on 16 January, 1992. Under its terms the army was regulated, a civilian police force established, and the FMLN laid down its arms to become a political party.

The Society of Jesus today place the six Jesuits from UCA on the list of their many members who died for the Catholic Faith. 'They went to Latin America and were martyred,' wrote the former Jesuit, Peter Hebblethwaite. 'From 1970 there were more martyrs in Latin America's right-wing regimes than under Communism in Eastern Europe.'[960] It is now accepted that from 1970 until the end of the civil war, two bishops, sixteen priests, three nuns, one seminarian and at least twenty-seven lay Catholics were killed by assassins and death squads from the Salvadorian army. The overall death toll of the conflict was between 70,000 and 80,000.[961]

With democracy finally re-established in El Salvador, the presidency was contested in free elections held in March, 2003, with Schafik Handal, the candidate of the Farabundo Marti National Liberation Front, and Antonio Saca, the candidate for ARENA, the right-wing party founded by the instigator of Oscar Romero's assassination, Roberto D'Aubuisson. Saca won with 58% of the vote as against 36% for the FMLN's Schafik Handal.

121.   The Ratzinger Report

After the fall of the Soviet Union, and prior to the rise of China as a major power, academics continued to discuss Marxist theories but Communism lost its credibility as an alternative system to capitalism and liberal democracy. In the Americas, Cuba under Fidel Castro remained Communist but it was shackled by sanctions imposed by the United States and, although it could point to considerable achievements in the spread of literacy, and medical care

---

960   Peter Hebblethwaite, *Op. Cit.* p. 632

961   George Childs Kohn, *Dictionary of Wars¸* 1999 (Wikipedia)

for its population, the Marxist straight-jacket together with the sanctions ensured that it remained poor. Pope John Paul II visited Cuba in 1998 and Castro's persecution of the Church abated but it did not cease.

The Church in eastern Europe was now free and flourished in Catholic countries such as Poland and Lithuania; and in Russia there was a revival of the Orthodox Church. In western Europe and the United States, however, Catholic practice continued to decline. The sacrament of Confession, now called Reconciliation, fell into desuetude after liberal priests offered their congregations 'general absolution'. A ruling by the Holy See that general absolution was intended for soldiers on the eve of battle when it was logistically impossible to hear individual confessions, and that a penitent should confess his sins face to face to a priest, was ignored. The moral metamorphosis of the wider society 'directly affected the churches' domain with 'the decline of church marriage, the rise of divorce and remarriage, the rise of cohabitation in place of marriage...decreasing stigmatisation of illegitimacy, homosexuality and sexual licence, the growing recourse to birth control and abortion, the irresistible pressures for government liberalisation of restrictions on drinking, Sunday closing and recreation'.[962]

Moreover, the Catholic Church remained as divided as at any time since the Reformation between dissenting theologians in the universities and the liberal laity on the one hand; and the guardians of orthodoxy in the Vatican – notably Cardinal Josef Ratzinger and John Paul II, on the other, with the bishops cowering between the antagonists – intimidated by the erudition of the theologians yet afraid to openly dissent from the views of the pope. The lay structures of the local churches – catechists, the secretariats of bishops' conferences – were invariably staffed by progressive Catholics, some of them former priests and nuns for whom 'the business of a Council is never finished'.[963] At the root of the differences was the question of orthodoxy itself. 'The Council', wrote F.J. Laisley, who taught at the Jesuit Heythrop College in London, 'was a plunge into the waters of pluralism or it was nothing'.[964]

Few lay Catholics read the often opaque theological treatises of the progressive theologians but they increasingly adopted the libertarian ethos of the secular society that surrounded them 'which found its origin not in Christian

---

962   Callum G. Brown, *Op. Cit.,* p. 191

963   F.J.Laishley in Adrian Hastins, *Op. Cit.* p. 215

964   *Ibid..* p. 225

traditions...but the ideas of John Stuart Mill'.[965] 'The *de facto* guideline for the living of human life ' had become "whatever makes you happy" – "so long as you're not hurting anyone else" – in which the criteria for happiness ...are self-determined, self-reported and therefore immune to criticism, and in which "hurting anyone else" is assumed to be self-evident, unproblematic or both'.[966]

In 1985, an attempt to stem this tide of disaffection was made by the publication of a book-length interview of Cardinal Josef Ratzinger by an Italian journalist, Vittorio Mesori: it was entitled *Rapporto Sulla Fede*, or in English translation *The Ratzinger Report*. In it, the Prefect for the Congregation for the Doctrine of the Faith acknowledged that there was 'a crisis of faith and of the Church' [967] – a division between those who saw the decrees of Vatican II as consistent with 'a *depositum fidei* which was viewed... as undisputed and already assured' and the proponents of 'a pernicious anti-spirit (*Conzils-Ungeist*)' who hold that 'everything that is "new" (or presumed such: how many old heresies have surfaced again in recent years that have been presented as something new!) is always and in every sense better than what has been or what is. It is the anti-spirit according to which the history of the Church would first begin with Vatican II, viewed as a kind of point zero.'[968]

Ratzinger acknowledged that some of the Council fathers 'no doubt harboured an optimism which from our present-day perspective we would judge as not critical or realistic enough', leading to 'an unrestrained and unfiltered opening to the world, that is to say, to the dominant modern mentality, which at the same time brings up for discussion the very foundations of the *depositum fidei* which for many was no longer clear.' 'Every theologian now seems to want to be "creative"' which has led 'a series of often conflicting schools and currents to the grave harm of the disconcerted people of God';[969] and to a failure to realise that behind the *human* exterior of the Church lies a '*more than human* reality, over which reformers, sociologists, organisers have no authority whatsoever'.[970] 'The Church is not *our* Church, which we could dispose of as we please. She is rather *his* Church' – the Church of Christ.

---

965   John Cornwell, *Op. Cit.*, p. 123

966   Brad.S.Gregory, *Op.Cit.* p. 182

967   Joseph Cardinal Ratzinger with Vittorio Messori, *The Ratzinger Report. An Exclusive Interview on the State of the Church*, p.44

968   *Ibid.*, p. 34

969   *Ibid*, p. 71

970   *Ibid.* p. 46

Ratzinger's critique extended to a number of different errors made by the exponents of the Spirit of Vatican II. The reading of the Bible, reserved for the clergy in the Middle Ages, then available for any Catholic who could read, was once again reserved for exegetes; 'The science of specialists has erected a fence around the garden of Scripture to which the non-expert now no longer has entry'.[971] National bishops' conferences 'have no theological basis, they do not belong to the structure of the Church as the will be Christ…;' [972] and lead some bishops to delegate their 'inalienable powers as shepherd and teacher to the structures of the local conferences'. Papers for such conferences are prepared by lay members of the conferences administration, and so 'in many episcopal conferences, the group spirit and perhaps even the wish for a quiet, peaceful life or conformism lead the majority to accept the positions of active minorities bent on pursuing their own goals'[973]. He reminded Messori that 'the really powerful documents against National Socialism were those that came from individual, courageous bishops'.[974]

Like the pontiff he served, John Paul II, and many popes both before and since, Josef Ratzinger saw free-market capitalism as antithetical to Christian values.

In a world like the West, where money and wealth are the measure of all things, and where the model of the free market imposes its implacable laws on every aspect of life, authentic Catholic ethics now appears to many like an alien body from times long past, as a kind of meteorite which is in opposition, not only to the concrete habits of life, but also to the way of thinking underlying them. Economic *liberalism* creates its exact counterpart, *permissivism*, on the moral plane….it becomes difficult, if not altogether impossible, to present Catholic morality as reasonable. It is too distant from what is considered to be obvious, as normal by the majority of persons, conditioned by the dominant culture with which now a few 'Catholic' moralists have aligned themselves as influential supporters. [975]

---

971   *Ibid.*, p. 76

972   *Ibid.*, p. 59

973   *Ibid.*, p. 62

974   *Ibid.*, p. 61

975   *Ibid.*, p. 83

The consequences of rejecting *Humanae Vitae* were now all too apparent. 'In the culture of the developed world it is above all the indissoluble bond between *sexuality* and *motherhood* that has been ruptured'. [976] 'It logically follows from this that every form of sexuality is equivalent and therefore of equal worth... Pleasure, the *libido* of the individual, becomes the only possible point of reference for sex.... Hence, it naturally follows that all forms of sexual gratification are transformed into the 'rights' of the individual. Thus, to cite an especially current example, homosexuality becomes an inalienable right... Its full recognition appears to be an aspect of human liberation'.

So too today's woman, Ratzinger continued, 'is being convinced that the aim is to 'liberate' her, 'emancipate' her, by encouraging her to masculinize herself, thus bringing her into conformity with the culture of production, and subjecting her to the control of the masculine society of technicians, of salesmen, of politicians who seek profit and power...' [977] This 'now dominant mentality attacks the very foundation of the morality of the Church which, as I have already said, if she remains true to herself, risks appearing like an anachronistic construct, a bothersome, alien body. Thus we stand before the difficult alternative: either the Church finds an understanding, a compromise with the values propounded by society which she wants to continue to serve, or she decides to remain faithful to her own values...as the result of which she finds herself at the margin of society'. The theology that opts for the first of these two positions – 'the so-called morality of ends...or *consequentialism*; holds that nothing in itself is good or bad, the goodness of the act depends entirely upon its end, upon its foreseeable and calculated consequences'.[978] Allied to consequentialism – the end justifies the means – and behind 'the moral convictions of many liberation theologies lies a 'proportionalist' morality... The 'absolute good' (and this means the building of a just socialist society) becomes the moral norm that justifies everything else, including – if necessary – violence, homicide, mendacity... What looks like 'liberation' turns into its opposite and shows its diabolic visage in deeds'.

In contrast to Pope John Paul II's sometimes opaque encyclicals, Josef Ratzinger's replies to Vittorio Messori's questions were lucid and concise. Although he steadfastly refused to ascribe the present ills of the Church to

---

976   *Ibid.*, p. 84
977   *Ibid.*, p. 99
978   *Ibid.*, p.90

Vatican II – and so they were not the fault of the reforming theologians of whom he had been one – his list of the troubles that had followed was long: 'the stubborn denial of sin'; an ecumenism 'marked by a ...perverse need [of the Church] to declare itself guilty of all the catastrophes of past history'; 'the lacklustre face of post-Conciliar liturgy...its hankering after banality and its lack of artistic standards'; a fascination with Asiatic religions; bishops' conferences ('truth cannot be found through ballots. A statement is either true or false)'; the burgeoning of episcopal bureaucracies – 400 working for the diocese of Munich 'producing documents, organizing meetings, planning new structures...' as against 30 in the Congregation for the Doctrine of the Faith in Rome. 'The Church, I shall never tire of repeating, needs saints more than functionaries'[979]

'Today more than ever,' Ratzinger concluded, 'the Christian must be aware that he belongs to a minority and that he is in opposition to everything that appears good, obvious, logical to the "spirit of the World", as the New Testament calls it. Among the most urgent tasks facing Christians is that of regaining the capacity...to oppose many developments of the surrounding culture.'[980]

122. The Ordination of Women

One such development, condemned by Cardinal Ratzinger, was the changing position of women in 'a culture that is the fruit of masculine attitudes of mind, masculine ideologies, which deceive women, uproot her in the depths of her being, while claiming that in reality they want to liberate her.'[981] Despite the fact that, as we have seen, there is little evidence of women resenting their traditional role until the late eighteenth century – in Britain a majority prior to World War I did not want the vote – there was, by the time of the *Ratzinger Report*, a widespread acceptance of the feminist hypothesis that women had suffered, and continued to suffer, from unjust discrimination. 'Patriarchy' was condemned, and with it the Church which, like Judaism from which it sprang, was unquestionably a patriarchal religion.

---

979   *Ibid.*, p. 67
980   *Ibid.* p. 115
981   *Ibid.*, p. 94

In 1990, a German theologian and one-time friend of Josef Ratzinger, Uta Ranke-Heinemann, published a book, *Eunuchs for Heaven*, attacking the the celibacy of priests. 'It is high time that the Pope and all other celibatarians realise, after eighteen hundred years of error, that they can justifiably drop their pet argument in favour of the unmarried state'. [982] Three years later a long and learned study by Susan Haskins sought to establish that Mary Magdalen, 'chief female disciple, first apostle and beloved friend of Christ' had been transformed by the patriarchal and misogynistic early Church Fathers 'into a penitent whore'. [983]

What was the Church's response? As recently as 1946, in an address to Catholic Women's Associations, Pope Pius XII had defended the old order of things: women should be free to work but Pius wondered whether 'a regime in which capitalism was dominant' offered 'a prospect of real welfare for woman'[984]; and while 'both sexes have the right and the duty to work together for the good of society…it is clear that a man is by temperament most suited to deal with external affairs and public business.'[985]

Such views were anathema forty years later, and in 1984 Pope John Paul II published an *aggiornamento* in a long apostolic letter on the Dignity of Women – *Mulieris Dignitatem.* John Paul II had lost his mother as a child, and had been raised largely by his father, and so had little experience of a woman as Pius XI's 'queen of the home'. As Archbishop of Krakow, in the 1970s, he had spent many hours with the highly intelligent, vivacious, sophisticated and cosmopolitan phenomenologist philosopher Dr. Anna-Teresa Tymieniecka, who had helped him with his major philosophical work, *The Acting Person:* Wojtyla had stayed on occasions with her and her husband Hendrik S. Houthakker in their house in the United States.

John Paul II therefore welcomed, in *Mulieris Dignitatem,* Vatican II's declaration that women were acquiring 'an influence, an effect and a power never hitherto achieved'. [986] The first chapter of the Book of Genesis, he wrote, gives us 'the structural basis of biblical and Christian anthropology', telling us that both man and woman were made in the image and likeness of God, but he passed over older passages that describes how the woman, Eve, was created from Adam's rib as his 'helpmate' and Paul of Tarsus's understanding

---

982   Ute-Ranke-Heinemann, *Eunuchs for Heaven. The Catholic Church & Sexuality.*, p. 37

983   Susan Haskins, *Mary Magdalen*, p. 15

984   *Questa Grande Vostra Adunta*, p. 8

985   *Ibid.* p. 12

986   *Mulieris Dignitatem*, p.3

that this meant 'woman was made for man, not man for woman' [987]. 'He even corrects St. Paul ' wrote Luigi Accattoli, 'when he states that the reasons in favour of the "subjection" of women to man in marriage be understood in the sense of a mutual subjection of both...'[988]

Mulieris Dignitatem reiterated the Church's esteem for marriage and motherhood, and also 'a woman's consecration in virginity'; and pointed to the indomitable women who appear in both the Old Testament and the Gospels, from Eve to the Virgin Mary whose assent to the declaration of the angel Gabriel in Nazareth was the *sine qua non* of humanity's redemption. But for all the insistence on the equal status of men and women, and the expression of regret for any 'misogyny' in the Church's past, the apostolic letter failed to resolve the two *casus belli* of the feminists – the Church's teaching that, when it came to contraception and particularly abortion, women were not sovereign over their own bodies: and that, while men and women were equal, women could not be priests.

The ordination of women, together with a reversal of the teaching of *Humane Vitae*, was among the 'reforms' demanded by the dissident theologians. The Church of England had approved the ordination of women in 1992, and the first women were ordained in 1994. That same year, Pope John Paul II issued an apostolic letter, *Ordinatio sacerdotalis (Priestly Ordination)*, which confirmed the teaching of *Inter insigniores* (1976) issued by the Congregation of the Doctrine of the Faith under Pope Paul VI. God became incarnate as a man, Jesus of Nazareth chose only men as his apostles, and so priests, acting *in persona Christi,* must be men. 'The Church has no authority whatsoever to confer priestly ordination on women and that this judgement is to be definitively held by all the Church's faithful'.

There followed a difference of opinion as to whether, since the pope had not been speaking *ex cathedra*, the ruling should be considered infallible: the Catholic Theological Society of America and most of the dissident theologians thought not and so the ruling could be reversed sometime in the future; Cardinal Ratzinger, Prefect of the Congregation for the Doctrine of the Faith, in answer to a request for clarification (a *dubio*), confirmed that *Ordinatio sacerdotalis* now belonged to 'the ordinary and universal *Magisterium*, and accordingly was to be held definitively as belonging to the deposit of faith'. This judgement was endorsed by the pope.

---

987   See Margaret E. Thrall, *The Cambridge Bible Commentary, I and II Corinthians*
988   Luigi Accattoli, *When the Pope asks Forgiveness*, p. 105

123. Sexual Offences

There were instances where Catholic practices changed with the times. One such was corporal punishment which was liberally administered in Catholic schools, particularly in those run by the Jesuits and the Christian Brothers; boys were beaten with canes, belts or ferulae not just by their teachers but by older pupils. In Britain both state and 'public' schools – viz. ancient institutions such as Eton, Westminster and Winchester – followed the principle of 'spare the rod, spoil the child'. Then, all of a sudden, the practice was considered cruel and archaic: in Poland beating school children had been abolished in 1783. In Britain it was abolished by law in 1987.

Less sudden, but more problematic for the Church, was the change in public attitudes towards homosexuality. Same-sex attraction was found throughout history, particularly in ancient Greece and Rome. However, in both the Jewish and Christian religions homosexual activities – anal intercourse and mutual masturbation – had always been considered a grievous sin. Genesis 18-19 describes how the citizens of Sodom asked Abraham's son Lot to hand over three angels who were his guests 'that we may know them'. Lot refused and with his household and the guests fled the city. God destroyed Sodom and a second 'city of the plain', Gomorrah, with fire and brimstone.

Paul of Tarsus, in his First Letter to the Romans, describes as symptoms of the 'impiety and depravity' of those who reject God women 'who have turned from natural intercourse to unnatural practices, and how their menfolk have given up natural intercourse to unnatural practices to be consumed with passion for each other, men doing shameless things with men and getting an appropriate reward for their perversion'.[989] In the eleventh century, Anselm, the archbishop of Canterbury from Aosta in Italy, condemned the English king William Rufus for his homosexual practices.[990] After torture by the Inquisition, James de Molay, the Grand Master of the Templars, confessed to all the charges, including spitting on the Cross, but vehemently denied sodomy. The English Parliament in 1533, under King Henry VIII, passed a 'Buggery Act' which defined anal intercourse as an unnatural act against the will of God and Man. It was a capital offence in England until 1828, and remained a crime punished by fines or imprisonment. In 1953, 2,500 men were charged in England with 'gross indecency' – usually homosexual pick-ups in parks or public lavatories.

---

989   *Romans*, 1:26-27

990   See R.W.Southern, *Saint Anselm. A Portrait in a Landscape*, p. 149 *et. seq.*

Despite this harsh treatment, there was what Noel Annan in *Our Age* called a 'cult of Homosexuality' in elevated social and cultural circles with roots in the nineteenth century. 'It flourished in Proust's Paris, Freud's Vienna and in the Berlin of Sacher-Masoch. In Wilhelm II's court the Kaiser's friend Prinz von und zu Eulenburg was forced out of public life after a libel case.'[991] And of course there was Oscar Wilde: despite the fact that his relations with under-age rent-boys would be considered a crime today and that he became a Catholic on his death bed, his imprisonment made homosexuals regard him as a martyr for their cause.

In Britain, facultative homosexuality was found in boarding schools, the armed services and the boy scouts, and it became so fashionable in cultural circles – 'a freemasonry that reached into the upper echelons of the elite.'[992] There was a certain *cachet* associated with being 'queer' or a 'pansy', and by the 1960s, in Britain, 'the best-known English born poet, the outstanding composer, the most famous choreographer, and the most prestigious painter – Auden, Britten, Ashton and Bacon – were all known to be homosexuals. So too England's leading actor, John Gielgud, who in October 1953 was arrested for soliciting in a public lavatory in Chelsea. He was fined £10. The case was reported in the newspapers but when he opened in *A Day by the Sea* in Liverpool shortly afterwards he was applauded by the audience.[993] Opinion, at least among theatre-goers, was changing.

Under pressure from a Homosexual Law Reform Society, the British government appointed a commission headed by a former headmaster, Sir John Wolfenden, to look into the law affecting homosexuals. Its recommendation that homosexual acts by consenting adults in private should no longer be a crime formed the basis of Sexual Offences Act of 1967. There was opposition but it passed through the House of Commons thanks to the support of the then Labour Home Secretary, Roy Jenkins.

There was nothing new in secular legislation deviating from Christian norms; divorce is an example; and there were many Christians who welcomed the change in the law. Homosexuals had been susceptible to blackmail and there had been suicides among those who were exposed. However, the growing tolerance of what the Church still referred to as the sin of Sodom – a sin which, according to the Penny Catechism, along with defrauding

---

991   Noel Annan, *Our Age*, p. 99

992   *Ibid.* p. 118

993   See Piers Paul Read, *Alec Guinness. The Authorised Biography*, p. 250

labourers of their wages, 'cried out to heaven for vengeance', caused alarm in the Church. Vatican II had said nothing about homosexuality. 'The trigger to open discussion of the matter among Catholics was *Humanae Vitae* (1968) which led to a general questioning of the sexual ethic developed in the Church since the early Middle ages, and still prevalent, just at a time when sexual orientation began to be talked about more widely by society as a whole'. [994]

Elizabeth Anscombe had predicted that the time would come, as a result of the rejection of *Humanae Vitae,* when there would be Catholics who would 'solemnly defend and commend homosexual activity'. And so it turned out. By the mid-1970s works by theologians such as the Jesuit J.J. McNeill's *The Church and the Homosexual,* argued for a compassionate approach towards active homosexuals; and groups such as Dignity in the United States and Quest in Britain called for the reconciliation of the practice of their faith with 'the full expression of their homosexual natures in loving Christian relationships'.[995]

In 1976, Cardinal Šeper, then the Prefect of the Congregation for the Doctrine of the Faith, took the bull by the horns, publishing a *Declaration on Certain Questions Concerning Sexual Ethics.* 'In the present period, the corruption of morals has increased, and one of the most serious indications of this corruption is the unbridled exaltation of sex'. In regard to relations between men and women, he reiterated the teaching of *Casti Connubii* and *Humane Vitae;* but he also noted that 'at the present time there are those who, basing themselves on observations in the psychological order, have begun to judge indulgently and even to excuse completely, homosexual relations between certain people. This they do in opposition to the constant teaching of the Magisterium and to the moral sense of the Christian people'.[996]

The Declaration acknowledged that same-sex attraction might well be involuntary, and insisted that 'homosexuals be treated with understanding', but reminded its readers that in Sacred Scripture 'homosexual relations are condemned as a serious depravity and even presented as the sad consequence of rejecting God. This judgement of Scripture does not of course permit us to conclude that all those who suffer from this anomaly are personally responsible for it, but it does attest to the fact that homosexual acts are intrinsically disordered and can in no case be approved of.'[997] So too masturbation which

---

994   Timothy Potts, 'Homosexuality', in Adrian Hastings, *Op. Cit.* p. 276
995   *Ibid.,* p. 277
996   Congregation for the Doctrine of the Church, *Sexual Ethics,* p. 10
997   *Ibid.,* p. 11

constitutes an 'intrinsically and seriously disordered act'. In effect, only intercourse between married couples, and open to the transmission of life, is free from sin.

There were no open protests by 'self-abusers' but there was widespread indignation that what came to be called 'gay' sex was condemned as depraved. Not content with the *tolerance* recommended by the Wolfenden Report, homosexual activists came to demand *approval*, and then *celebration* of their lifestyle with Gay Pride rallies in many major cities. A battle with New York police when, in 1969, they raided Stonewall Inn in Greenwich Village, gave its name to a British charity set up to promote the rights of lesbian, gay, bisexual and transgender (LGBT) people. In Britain its lobbying successfully brought about the repeal of Section 28 of the Local Government Act of 1988 which stated that local authorities 'shall not intentionally promote homosexuality or publish material with the intention of promoting homosexuality'. 'Homophobia' was now bundled with racism as a prejudice that should be condemned. Society's moral stance on sexual relations between members of the same sex was inverted: what had been considered wrong was now considered right, and declaring it sinful was now itself a sin. 'It is legitimate and necessary to ask oneself,' said Pope John Paul II, 'if this is not perhaps part of a new ideology of evil, more subtle and hidden, perhaps, intent upon exploiting human rights themselves against man and against the family.'[998]

In the course of the 1970s there appeared, initially in the gay community in the United States, a debilitating and mostly fatal virus, the Acquired Immunodeficiency Syndrome, or AIDS. Some Christians saw it as God's punishment for the sin of Sodom: the Church never made such a claim, and it became untenable as the virus spread to heterosexuals – men, women and children – including through blood transfusions, hypodermic needles and from mother to child during pregnancy. AIDS spread from homosexual circles in Europe and the United States to Asia and Africa: by 2018 it would have led to 35 million deaths.[999]

In time, antiretroviral therapy would mitigate the effects of the virus and reduce fatalities, but initially the best protection against infection was 'safe sex' – viz. the use of a condom during intercourse to prevent the intermingling of bodily fluids. Such a measure, which blocked complete

---

998   CNN, 'John Paul II. A Strong Moral Vision', 2005 (Wikipedia)

999   *Centers for Disease Control and Prevention*, 2018 (Wikipedia)

sexual union, was forbidden to Catholics – a prohibition of little relevance when it came to homosexuals but a critical issue when it came to the spread among heterosexuals, particularly in Africa. Catholic aid agencies with a strong presence on the continent were unable to distribute condoms because of the Church's teaching. Pope John Paul II came under great pressure to modify the ruling because of the pandemic but he refused. He argued that doling out condoms would encourage promiscuity and, because they were not always effective, might actually increase the rate of infection. His solution was to promote chastity – no sex outside marriage and conjugal fidelity; and in Uganda, promoted by the Catholic hierarchy, this met with some success.

However, John Paul's intransigence enraged secular commentators in the developed world. 'His insistence that condoms should not be used in any circumstances' wrote John Cornwell in *The Pope in Winter*, 'condemned untold numbers of Catholics at risk for HIV infection to almost certain death'.[1000] . 'The Pope kills millions through his reckless spreading of AIDS,' wrote the columnist Polly Toynbee in the *Guardian* newspaper.[1001] Also in the *Guardian* was a violent attack on Pope John Paul II by its most respected columnist, Hugo Young – a Catholic who had been a pupil at Ampleforth of the Archbishop of Westminster, Cardinal George Basil Hume. Young did not mention AIDS or Africa, but told his readers that 'the disasters John Paul II has inflicted on the Catholic church over 20 years would be hard to exaggerate. His record is such an offence against elementary tenets of liberal democracy that even a Catholic who has not entirely lost his ability to accept the church's teaching finds certain particulars intolerable'.[1002] The piece was a review of *The Catholic Church. A Short History* by Hans Küng.

124. The Catechism of the Catholic Church

Hugo Young, although a Catholic, was more interested in politics than religion, and his reference to 'the tenets of liberal democracy' in his attack on Pope John Paul II shows little understanding of the nature of the Church. His instincts, like those of many *bien pensant* lay Catholics in Europe and the United States, were to accept the views of the zealots of the 'Spirit of Vatican

---

1000   John Cornwell, *Op. Cit,* p.xii

1001   *The Guardian*, 6 September, 2002

1002   *Ibid.*, 17 April, 2001

II' such as Küng, and indeed many of their bishops who, although they might not openly oppose Pope John Paul II or Cardinal Ratzinger, did not support them either; and revealed their covert sympathies when it came to teaching the tenets of the faith to children.

The result was catechetical confusion. The French historian, Alain Besançon, complained that the encouragement of theological diversity meant that the differences between French Catholic writers was far wider than those between the *Catechism* of the Council of Trent and Calvin's *Institutes of the Christian Religion*. 'Dictionaries containing diametrically opposed views on serious issues are published continually, and the Church takes no position'. Besançon ascribed this chaos to 'the crisis of faith' and 'the woeful state of catechetics'. He cited the 'grotesque catechism' approved by the French bishops, *Pierres Vivants* (Living Stones). 'It was a catechism poor on doctrine, very poor intellectually and even poorer in style... I am sure that even at the time of Charlemagne, few bishops would have accepted this miserable catechism...'[1003]

It was the same in other countries. In the archdiocese of Westminster in London, children in Catholic schools followed a 'modular programme of Religious Education' called *Weaving the Web* which presented Christianity as just one among other religions, and Jesus of Nazareth on a par with Lord Krishna of the Hindus and Guru Nanak of the Sikhs. The idea of salvation was given a Liberationist tinge. Before Jesus was even mentioned, pupils would learn 'that there are great contrasts between poor people who live in Peru and the rich people who live there'. 'The Eucharist was the sacrament of Liberation', 'the celebration of Christian Freedom'. Oscar Romero, Desmond Tutu and Martin Luther King are the prophetic figures of the modern world, rather than any of the Catholic martyrs in Mexico, Spain, Poland, China or the USSR, let alone the Polish priest, Fr. Jerzy Popieluszko, who was murdered by members of the Polish Secret Police in 1984. Jesus is presented as a kind of Che Guevara of the ancient world. Sanctity, it would seem, comes not from prayer, self-denial or sacramental grace but from political activism in the community. The sacrament of Confession is 'a way of saying sorry to everybody, including God'. One of the themes suggested for discussion are: 'are priests necessary?' Another, 'what do you think of the idea of women

---

1003   *AD 2000*, July 1994

being priests?'[1004] *Weaving the Web* was approved by the bishops of England and Wales for use in Catholic schools.

Varying and often contradictory views of the Catholic Faith were found not just in schools but Catholic institutes and parish churches, leading to widespread confusion over what it was that Catholics were supposed to believe, and failing to stem the flow of baptized Catholics who abandoned their religion. In France, in the eight years between 1986 and 1994, the number of those describing themselves as Catholics fell from 81% to 64%: only 9% regularly went to mass. The percentage of those who accepted Catholic teaching on sexual mores fell to single figures.

Was there still a *depositum fidei* – a deposit of faith? If so, why did not Pope John Paul not denounce and discipline bishops who failed to preserve it and pass it on? In fact, although Hans Küng and other dissident theologians liked to present John Paul II as a tyrant, the pope's method was to let the truth speak for itself. Few measures were taken to discipline dissidents. Küng himself, who repudiated so much of the Church's *magisterium*, was never excommunicated or deprived of his Holy Orders but merely lost his mandate to teach as a *Catholic* theologian. 'As for repression in the direct, personal sense,' wrote George Weigel in 1999, 'very few Catholic theologians have been disciplined during this pontificate (public action was taken against six in twenty years), and those who have been were treated far more mildly than in the past. The same can be said of wayward bishops. Thirty-five years after Vatican II, John Paul II's intellectual critics, and in some instances his avowed enemies, remain firmly in control of most theological faculties in the Western world.'[1005]

Even if Pope John Paul II had been minded to purge the Church of dissidents, it would have been an impossible task with theologians enjoying tenure, bishops only subject to sanction for the most egregious offences, and priests defended by their bishops and often their equally liberal-minded congregations. Although in some respects, as Alain Besançon pointed out, the alternative *magisterium* of the dissidents was quite as unorthodox as the teaching of some of the Reformers in the sixteenth century; and although they might have joined Christian denominations such as the Church of England that had enacted most of the desired reforms, the dissidents

---

1004 Richard Lohan, Sister Mary McClure, *Weaving the Web*, 'Community, Story, People', leven 3, p. 19

1005 George Weigel, *Op. Cit.*, p. 852

remained firmly in the Catholic Church. In Germany the state collected a *Kirchensteur* – a supplementary income tax paid by registered members of religious denominations which, in the case of the Catholic Church, raised billions of Deutschmarks and later Euros: hence, the 400 employees of the archdiocese of Munich.[1006]

To counter the doctrinal confusion that had existed at the time of the Reformation, the Council of Trent had resolved to 'publish a formulary and method for teaching the rudiments of the faith', a task given to Charles Borromeo, the reforming Archbishop of Milan (see Chapter 60). By means of short answers to simple questions, it laid out the beliefs and practices of the Catholic Church. 'Who made me? God made you. Why did God make me? God made you to know him, love him and serve him in this world, and to be happy with him forever in the next.' It was used for catechesis throughout the Catholic world, published in England in a small pamphlet with a red cover, and was known as the Penny Catechism. Its exposition was somewhat 'cut and dried'. There were three kinds of sin: original sin from which only the Virgin Mary was exempt (the Immaculate Conception); venial sin, 'an offence that does not kill the soul', and mortal sin which does kill the soul 'by depriving it of sanctifying grace, which is the supernatural grace of the soul'. Most sins against 'purity' were deemed to be mortal, including 'irregular motions of the flesh' (masturbation): so too a breach of the Fourth Commandment to keep holy the Sabbath day by deliberately choosing not to go to mass on a Sunday. 'Where will they go who die in mortal sin? They who die in mortal sin will go to hell for all eternity'.[1007]

After Vatican II, attempts were made to modify the Tridentine catechism. A Dutch Catechism of 1966, drawn up by progressive theologians, was subsequently censured by the Church. *The St. Peter Catechism of Catholic Doctrine* of 1975 sought to incorporate some of the teaching of the Council; but by and large the Penny Catechism fell into desuetude. Cardinal Ratzinger in *The Ratzinger Report* said it was a 'grave error', not just ' to suppress the catechism' but 'to declare quite universally that the category "catechism" was obsolete'.[1008]

1006   In 1985, the year of the publication of the Ratzinger Report, the church tax in Germany raised DM 5,713,000 for the Catholic Church. By 2018 the sum was €6,643 billion euros.

1007   *A Catechism of the Catholic Church* (1978), 125, p. 21

1008   Joseph Cardinal Ratzinger with Vittorio Messori, *Op. Cit.*, p. 73

Errors can be rectified. Early in the same year as the publication of *The Ratzinger Report*, 1985, John Paul II convened an Extraordinary General Assembly of the Synod of Bishops to mark the 20th anniversary of the close of Vatican II. There the decision was made to draw up a new Catechism of the Catholic Church. A commission of twelve bishops and cardinals was appointed to oversee the work of seven diocesan bishops with the requisite theological and catechetical expertise. To many confused Catholics, it came as a relief to know that they would learn what they were supposed to believe: to the zealots of the spirit of Vatican II, it was a move to stifle dissent. John Wilkins, the editor of the English periodical *The Tablet*, called it 'a put-up job'.[1009]

The Catechism of the Catholic Church was published seven years later in 1992 – first in French, the common language of the exegetes; then in English and other languages in 1994; and the final definitive edition in Latin, the language of the Church, in 1997. It did not follow the question and answer method of the Penny Catechism, but was an exposition in four parts – the first being the *Credo*, the profession of faith; the second the sacraments and sacred liturgy; the third the Decalogue (the Ten Commandments) and the life of Christ; the fourth the Our Father or Lord's Prayer. Progressive Catholics were dismayed and traditional Catholics reassured to find in it a reaffirmation of the Church's pre-Conciliar beliefs – in angels and devils, in Heaven and Hell. The Catechism talks of mortal sin and venial sins. It states that 'the Sunday Eucharist is the foundation and confirmation of all Christian practice. For this reason the faithful are obliged to participate in the Eucharist on days of obligation... Those who deliberately fail in this obligation commit a grave sin'.

The Catechism was intended to put an end to the arguments that had gone on since the end of Vatican II about what Catholics now believed. However, in the view of the Cambridge academic John Casey there was a sense of detachment in the manner in which some traditional teachings were presented.

> The new catechism leaves you with the curious impression that modern Catholics may give 'real' assent to different things from those that moved their forebears. The angels and devils, miracles, our First Parents – they are all there in this splendidly orthodox document. There is no trimming of the supernatural element in Christianity...

1009   Letter to the author, 13 July 1990

Yet the supernatural seems to have less imaginative reality in this catechism than it does in Trent... Take the catechism's teaching about the next life. It is the same in all essentials as what you find in the Catechism of the Council of Trent – which was written to combat the "errors" of Protestants. Everyone who believes in the resurrection of the body must be quite curious about what it would be like. Trent confidently satisfied this curiosity: 'The bodies of the risen Saints will be beyond the reach of suffering... Neither the piercing severity of cold, nor the glowing intensity of heat, nor the impetuosity of waters can hurt them...they shall shine like the sun.' There is nothing so pithy or vivid in the new version. Nor has Hell quite retained its terrors. It is there all right, but we are not invited to dwell on its tortures as we are in Trent.[1010]

Rather, wrote Casey, 'you feel that the elaborate discussions of sexual and family morality and social justice are closest to the hearts of the authors...these are the equivalents of the bitter disputes in the 16th century about grace, free will and predestination.' Missing mass on a Sunday, sexual relations outside marriage, the use of artificial means of contraception were all still serious sins; and the Catechism repeated the Church's traditional teaching that those who died in a state of serious sin would be damned; but there was no sense of urgency – no impression, from the tone in which it was written, that its authors were worried that the Catholic girl on the pill who only went to mass at Christmas and Easter, and came up to take Communion fresh from the bed of her boyfriend, was is in grave danger of eternal torment in Hell.

The Catechism of the Catholic Church was written for Catholics and did not seek to match its teaching with that of other Christian denominations; yet for Pope John Paul II the unity of Christians remained of paramount importance and in 1995 he issued an encyclical Ut Unum Sint (That They Should be One). During the seventeen years of his pontificate he had done more than any pontiff before him to demonstrate his respect for other Christian denominations and even other religions – praying in mosques, synagogues and Protestant churches. In Ut Unum Sint the pope insisted that that the Church's ecumenical commitment was irreversible, and called upon Catholics 'to recover a sense of urgency for their task'. He lamented in particular the continuing division between the 'sister' Catholic and Orthodox churches

1010   The Sunday Telegraph, 29 May 1994

where differences were largely historical rather than doctrinal. 'Why should Catholicism and Orthodoxy not return to the status quo ante 1054? '[1011]

Clearly, unity with the Protestant churches was more problematic because while, from a Catholic perspective, the Church had made substantial concessions, the Protestants had, as it were, 'moved the goal posts' with the ordination of women. John Paul II noted that some progress had been made, but noted that differences remained not just on the ordination of women but on the relationship between Scripture and Tradition, the Virgin Mary, the teaching authority of the Church, and the nature of the Eucharist.

Moreover, the urgency of John Paul II did not seem to be shared. Dr. Konrad Raiser, the Secretary-General of the World Council of Churches, gave a lecture in Rome in which he said it was time to 'close the books over our past struggles and to concentrate all our energies on addressing together the life and survival issues of today and tomorrow...' such as 'the apartheid between rich and poor' and 'the progressive degradation of the whole ecosphere'. Ecumenism was being superseded by environmentalism. 'The ecumenical movement described by *Ut Unum Sint* was now the only global ecumenical movement still committed to the movement's original goal'.[1012]

Pope John Paul's biographer, George Weigel, suggests that John Paul II came to recognise that there may have been some romanticism in the immediate post-conciliar years about the possibilities of full ecclesial reconciliation within the West and between East and West, and that *Ut Unum Sit* expressed 'a vision ahead of its time'.[1013] Was 'romanticism' a charitable euphemism for wishful thinking? The animosity between the leaders of the different Christian denominations was now a thing of the past, but it had become clear that in its wider ambitions the ecumenical movement had failed.

Josef Ratzinger as a young *peritus* at Vatican II had shared that romantic optimism about the possibilities of reunion. At the time, older churchmen had been more sceptical. We have seen how Pope John XXIII had summoned separated Christians to 'return to unity' in the Catholic Church. Professor Eamon Duffy had called this 'a mistake', but while John XXIII and particularly Pope Paul VI were prepared to make concessions on inessentials – mass in the vernacular, communion in both kinds, the officiating priest facing his

---

1011   George Weigel, *Op. Cit.*, p. 761
1012   *Ibid.*, p. 764
1013   *Ibid.*, p. 766

congregation – it was never likely that the Church would trim its belief that Christ was truly present in the Eucharist. Nor could a pope abandon or even share his authority over the universal Church. It was not just that, as Peter Hebblethwaite put it, ' no pope could be expected to saw off the branch on which he was sitting'[1014] but that it was clear from scripture that Jesus had conveyed that authority on Peter: *Tu es Petrus et Super hanc petram aedificabo ecclesiam meam* was chiselled onto the façade of St. Peter's basilica.

In the year 2000, the Congregation of the Faith issued a declaration on 'the Unicity and Salvific Universality of Jesus Christ and the Church', known by its opening words in Latin, *Dominus Jesus*. It was signed by the Prefect, Cardinal Ratzinger and approved by Pope John Paul II who, in a short preface, wrote that 'this document expresses once again the same ecumenical passion that is the basis of my encyclical *Ut Unum Sint*' through a 'clarification and openness' that would clear up 'so many erroneous interpretations'. The clarifications were more apparent than the passion. *Dominus Jesus* was an unambiguous reassertion that Catholicism was the *spes unica* – the One True Faith. The world's different religions were *not* equally true. Only Jesus of Nazareth was 'the Word of God made man for the salvation of all' with 'a significance and a value for the human race and its history, which are unique and singular, proper to him alone, exclusive, universal and absolute'. [1015]

Certainly, there may be aspects of truth in other religions, and 'the historical figures and positive elements of these religions may fall within the divine plan of salvation', but their forms of mediation 'acquire meaning and value *only* from Christ's own mediation and they cannot be understood as parallel or complementary to his'.[1016] There was a historical continuity – rooted in the Apostolic succession. The Church founded by Christ, and constituted as an organized society in the present world, subsists in the Catholic Church, governed by the Successor Peter and the Bishops in communion with him'.

Dominus Jesus disappointed many of those belonging to those non-Christian religions which Pope John Paul II had so assiduously courted throughout his pontificate, and dismayed ecumenical Protestants – particularly members of the Church of England which Pope Paul VI in 1967 had called 'a sister church' and were anticipating intercommunion. The declaration acknowledged that other Christian 'ecclesial communities' are 'by

---

1014 Hebblethwaite, *Op.Cit.* p. 382

1015 *Dominus Jesus*, p.28

1016 *Ibid.*, p. 27

Baptism, incorporated in Christ and thus are in a certain communion, albeit imperfect, with the Church'; but where they do not have a 'valid Episcopate and the genuine and integral substance of the Eucharistic mystery, they are not Churches in the proper sense...'[1017]

Behind *Dominus Jesus* was Josef Ratzinger's fear that many Catholics had already succumbed to the 'relativistic mentality, which is becoming ever more common'. His tone is commanding: 'The Catholic faithful *are required to profess* that there is an historical continuity – rooted in the apostolic succession – between the Church founded by Christ and the Catholic Church.' Repeatedly, he reminds his Catholic readers that this teaching must be '*firmly believed*'. Catholics must rule out in a radical way that mentality of indifferentism 'characterized by a religious relativism which leads to the belief that one religion is as good as another'.

If it was hoped that *Dominus Jesus* would lock away the error of indifferentism that had escaped from Pandora's Box under the guise of ecumenism at the time of Vatican II – a box which Ratzinger had himself helped prize open – it failed. In Africa, perhaps, where Christians faced Islam and Animism, it was possible to assert that only Jesus was the way, the truth and the life; but in Europe and the US, thirty years of progressive catechesis had led Catholics to accept the view of Hans Küng 'that the different denominations were branches of a single Christian Church'.[1018] Memories of Catholic school-children telling Protestant school-children that they would go to Hell were an embarrassment. Pluralism, diversity and tolerance had replaced faith, hope and charity as society's pre-eminent virtues – a tolerance which excluded the intolerant such as those who held that one race was superior to another, or that one religion held a monopoly of truth.

125. Abuse

One of the most convincing accounts of the sexual abuse of an adolescent boy by a Catholic priest is not a psychologist's case study but a novel, *Sébastien Roch*, written in the late nineteenth century by the French author, Octave Mirbeau. Sébastien, the son of a socially ambitious ironmonger, is sent to a Jesuit boarding school in Vannes, Brittany, where his fellow pupils would be

---

1017 *Ibid*, p. 31
1018 Piers Paul Read, 'The Inquisition and Dr. Küng, *Hell and Other Destinations*, p. 99

the sons of the aristocracy. There he is groomed by a Father du Kern, taken to a darkened room, plied with liqueur and cigarettes, and raped. He reports the crime to the Rector who believes him, but 'although in normal circumstances he was a good man, he had only one thought at that moment: to prevent the terrible secret from getting out, even if that meant a flagrant injustice or sacrifice of an innocent, unhappy boy'.[1019] Sébastien is charged with impure exchanges with a fellow pupil and expelled. The novel does not end there. In further chapters Mirbeau describes the effect the abuse had on Sébastien – his revulsion at physical contact with the girl he loves and who loves him.

Octave Mirbeau was raised a Catholic but left the Church and, at the time of the Affair, became an active Dreyfusard. It was said that Father du Kern was based on Père Stanislas du Lac, the spiritual director of General de Boisdeffre, (see Chapter 94) and so *Sébastien Roch* was dismissed as black propaganda for the Dreyfusard cause. It is unlikely to have been read by Catholic bishops, either in France or elsewhere in the world. However, the sin described in the novel was not unknown to the Church: it had been denounced by Peter Damian in his 11th century *Liber Gomorrhianus*; and Pope Pius V in the sixteenth century condemned cardinals who kept catamites; Martin Luther claimed that 'openly and shamelessly the Pope and cardinals in Rome practice sodomy', but that too could be dismissed as black propaganda.

Thus, while pedophilia among the Catholic clergy was not unknown, it was thought to be uncommon. More concerning was the grooming by priests of women in the confessional, and it was to prevent this that Charles Borromeo had introduced the 'box' with a grill between the penitent and confessor. It was considered a sin so grievous that it had to be reported to the Holy Office, later the Congregation for the Doctrine of the Faith, in Rome. The CDF was not given jurisdiction over other kinds of sexual abuse until 2001; they were dealt with by diocesan bishops. Fatally, most of the diocesan bishops decided, when a case was brought to their attention, that, like the Jesuit Rector in Mirbeau's novel, their first duty was to save the Church from scandal.

In some parts of the world – the former episcopal principalities in Austria and Germany, and the Irish diaspora in Australia and the United States – the Catholic Church was more than one among other denominations; it was in places at the core of the community. A case in point was the city of Boston on the east coast of the United States. Established by the earliest European

---

1019   Octave Mirbeau, *Sébastien Roch*, translated by Nicoletta Simborowski, p. 186

settlers, mostly Puritan Protestants from England, it became a centre of Irish immigration in the nineteenth century as a result of the Irish famine. The Irish became a majority and ruled the city. The mayor and a majority of the legislature were Catholics, and, with their secular hierarchy long-since destroyed by the British, their archbishop was king.

We have seen how the model for the hero of Henry Morton Robinson's novel *The Cardinal* was said to have been New York's Cardinal Spellman, but it could equally have been any one the archbishops of Boston where Robinson was born such as John Joseph Williams, William Henry O'Connell or Richard James Cushing. Under these imperious prelates, there was a steady flow of vocations to the priesthood and the religious orders: 'by the early 1960s there were close to 6,000 nuns in the Boston archdiocese, most of them working in Catholic schools'.[1020] Not just in Boston but throughout the United States the Catholic Church was held in high esteem. The suffering of Catholics under Communism in Eastern Europe gave substance to the polemics of the Cold War. 'Hollywood was in love with Catholicism' with priests in films portrayed in a positive, even heroic light – *Bells of St. Mary's, I Confess, On the Waterfront*, and many others. But Boston was not immune to the change in social attitudes that came about in the late 1950s and early 1960s. The grandsons of Irish immigrants moved out of the city into the suburbs and, though they retained their tribal affiliation, came to adopt some of the secular values of their neighbours. An example of this change from a spiritual to social identity was John F. Kennedy who was 'conspicuously Catholic but not at all religious'; and who, to allay the fears of non-Catholics, when he was a candidate for the presidency, assured a gathering of Baptist leaders in Houston that his personal beliefs would never influence his political decisions. 'So it was that in post-war America the most prominent member of the Catholic community struck an effective truce with the enemies of the Church'.[1021]

The main bone of contention in the United States was, and remains, abortion with the Church teaching that to destroy a human embryo or foetus is homicide; while liberals – among them many liberal Catholics – insisted that a woman was sovereign over her own body, and so had the right to decide whether to terminate a pregnancy or bring it to full term. The question arose as to whether Catholic legislators who voted in favour of abortion should be (or already were automatically) excommunicated for complicity in a mortal

---

1020   Philip F. Lawler, *The Faithful Departed. The Collapse of Boston's Catholic Culture*, p. 45
1021   *Ibid.*, p. 47

sin, or whether they could be exonerated if they took the line that, while personally opposed to abortion, they believed that a woman had 'the right to choose'? One of the exponents of this second option was in fact a Catholic priest, Fr. Robert Drinan, who, despite the Vatican's ruling that priests should not enter political life, was elected to the US House of Representatives. A committee led by the Cardinal Archbishop of Washington, Theodore McCarrick, was set up to consider the question: 'the cardinal decided against denying the Eucharist to dissident politicians'.[1022]

The Church's strict sexual morality was at first compromised and then ridiculed when it emerged in the early 1990s that adolescent boys had been sexually abused by Catholic priests. Cases cropped up in different dioceses, but the scandal centered upon Boston where its leading newspaper, the *Boston Globe*, 'easily the most powerful media voice in New England',[1023] made the exposure of clerical sexual corruption a crusade. Many of its journalists and readers were tribal Catholics, but 'Massachusetts had already completed its transformation from a bastion of social conservatism to the most liberal state in the nation, and with the Catholic community in Boston in the vanguard'.[1024] A special unit called 'Spotlight', set up within the newspaper, found an abundance of material for their exposés, running several hundred news items and seventeen front page stories. The John Jay College of Criminal Justice, in a report later commissioned by the US Catholic bishops, found that in the United States 11,000 credible allegations had been made against 4,392 priests during the period 1950-2002 which constituted '4% of the total number of priests during the time'.[1025] Over $1billion was paid out by the archdiocese of Boston to settle claims for compensation. By 2008 five American dioceses had sought bankruptcy protection because of such liabilities: the diocese of Los Angeles faced damages 'five times as great as the payoff to the victims in Boston'.[1026]

The John Jay College study noted that 81% of the victims of clerical abuse were male – around half between the ages of 11 and 14, and 27% between the ages of 15 and 17. The abusers showed little interest in adolescent girls who made up the largest category among the 200,000 children that the Crimes

---

1022   *Ibid..* p. 133
1023   *Ibid.,* p. 111
1024   *Ibid.,* p.5
1025   Dr. Pravin Thevasthasan, *The Catholic Church and the Sex Abuse Crisis,* p.26
1026   Philip F. Lawler, *Op. Cit.,* p. 245

Against Children Center estimated were abused in the United States in 2004 – often by members of their family: and students were a hundred times more likely to be abused in schools and colleges than they were by Catholic priests.[1027]

However, priests were *in persona Christi,* and their transgressions could not be justified or explained away as part of a general trend. The bishops' solution to the emerging scandal was *omerta* – intimidating those who complained, and moving offending priests from parish to parish. This was the policy of Cardinal Bernard Law who, though doctrinally orthodox, was more concerned with his errant priests than their victims. Like other bishops, he was persuaded by psychoanalysts that with treatment they could be cured: when one of the more notorious paedophile priests, John Geoghan, finally resigned 'Cardinal Law wrote a letter than contained this breathtaking sentence: "Yours has been an effective ministry, sadly marred by illness"'. [1028] The evidence now 'all pointed to the same inescapable conclusion: many priests had abused children and the archdiocese had protected the abusers'.[1029]

In January, 2002, Cardinal Law made the first in a series of apologies to the victims of sexual abuse; however, 'he did not apologize to the witnesses who were ignored and patronized and misled and even calumniated'.[1030] It would seem that the most serious sin remained damaging the reputation of the Church. Cardinal Law was not alone: 'two thirds of American bishops had been guilty of covering up sexual abuse'[1031] Was this only to protect the reputation of the Church, and save dioceses from litigation? Or was there a feeling that though wrong the seduction of teenage boys was a *peccadillo*? In the 1970s, a priest of the archdiocese, Father Paul Shanley, had argued that homosexual activities could be healthy and desirable, and 'even spoke favourably of affairs involving mature men with young boys...'[1032]

By and large, however, homosexual priests denied that there was any link between the abuse of adolescent boys and adult homosexual activities. The bishops, too: 'in their dealings with the sex-abuse crisis, the American bishops and their close advisers have evinced the same sort of reluctance to

1027   Dr. Pravin Thevasthasan, *Op. Cit.* p. 14

1028   Philip F. Lawler, *Op. Cit.,* p. 151

1029   *Ibid.,* p. 156

1030   *Ibid.,* p. 161

1031   *Ibid.,* p. 169

1032   *Ibid.,* p. 154

admit the influence of homosexuality'.[1033] They 'were determined to avoid any discussion of priestly homosexuality, and still more determined to avoid grappling with the accusation that networks of homosexuals wielded great power within the clergy'.

The Archdiocese of Boston has been chosen as a case study in the sex-abuse crisis both because of the relentless investigation by the *Boston Globe*, and because the editor of the diocesan newspaper, *The Pilot*, Philip F. Lawler, described it in convincing detail in his book *The Faithful Departed*. However it soon emerged that often for decades Catholic priests had been abusing adolescent boys not just in the United States but throughout the world; that bishops had kept their crimes secret and often dealt with the priests in question by appointing them to a new parish where, after cursory psychological 'treatment' and assurances of a cure, the abuse recurred.

Not just priests and monks but bishops were charged with abuse, among them Hans Hermann Groër, the Archbishop of Vienna. In France, an eighteen month inquiry commissioned by the French bishops discovered that between 1950 and 2020, 300,000 children had been abused by priests, deacons and monks. 'A minimum of 3,000 priests and church officials had performed criminal acts', and that 'until the early 2020s the Catholic Church showed a profound and even cruel indifference towards its victims'.[1034]

Indifference, but also incredulity. When Pope John Paul II was told that the Archbishop of Washington, Theodore McCarrick, had abused seminarians, he refused to believe it. So too the rumours that the founder of the Mexican Legion of Christ, Marcial Maciel Degollado, had not only abused seminarians but was addicted to drugs, had had affairs with four women, one a minor, and fathered children, two of whom he had abused.[1035] John Paul II had had ample experience of what was surely black anti-Catholic propaganda when a bishop in Communist Poland!

In seeking an explanation for how not just the smoke of Satan but Satan himself had entered the Church, some sought to blame Vatican II even though many of the abusers had been ordained prior to the Council. Certainly, as we have seen, the status of the priest had been diminished and this may have led to 'a loss of faith and lack of prayer life'. There may have been a lack of

1033   *Ibid.*, p. 230

1034   Jean-Marc Sauvé, quoted in *The Times*, 6 October, 2021

1035   Emilio Godoy, 'Pope Rewrites Epitaph for Legion of Christ Founder', IPS News (Wikipedia)

adequate discernment by seminary directors, particularly in Ireland and the Irish diaspora where a vocation to the priesthood led to a career in a prestigious profession and brought joy to a young man's mother. We have seen how the Irish Catholic culture of Boston had lost its spiritual core prior to the sex-abuse revelations; but in Ireland itself, and in Australia, where the Catholic Church had been held in high regard, the disclosures delivered a shock that in one generation changed respect to contempt. Every priest was seen as a molester and every accusation believed. The Cardinal Archbishop of Sidney, George Pell, was charged with abuse, convicted, and his appeals rejected until finally the Supreme Court of Australia ruled unanimously that he was innocent.

Sexual abuse by Catholic priests was by no means confined to Ireland or the Irish diaspora. In Central and South America, India, the Philippines, there were cases of abuse of both young men and girls. No European country was spared. In Britain cases of abuse were uncovered in the great Benedictine monasteries which, like Mirbeau's Jesuit college at Vannes, had for generations educated the sons of the Catholic elite. Monks were imprisoned, three from Ampleforth where Cardinal Basil Hume, the Archbishop of Westminster, had been abbot between 1963 and 1976.

Some years passed before the Church wholly faced up to the abuse of those in the care of Catholic priests. The crimes were condemned: Pope John Paul II denounced the abuse as 'a profound contradiction of the teaching and witness of Jesus Christ', and Cardinal Ratzinger talked of 'filth'. Formal apologies were made to the victims who as a result of the abuse had suffered from, among other things, 'Post-Traumatic Stress Disorder, Personality Disorder, Eating Disorders, substance misuse, depression and suicide attempts'[1036].

The abused were not the only victims: there were also the many thousands of innocent priests. Estimates of the percentage of predatory priests in the United States range from 1.8% in the diocese of Chicago[1037] to 4% overall.[1038] Working on the credible assumption that the percentages were similar elsewhere in the world, it would seem that, with over 400,000 Catholic priests in the universal Church, up to 1,600 were guilty of abuse but 384,000 were not. Perhaps some of these were guilty of suppressing suspicions of their fellow-

---

1036   Dr. Pravin Thevasthan, *Op. Cit.*, p.12

1037   Philip Jenks of Pennsylvania State University, *Paedophiles and Priests*

1038   John Jay College of Criminal Justice: see Dr. Pravin Thevasthan, *Op. Cit.*, p.26

priests, and of looking the other way; but the paedophiles were cunning, and were adept at rationalising what they were doing and deciding that it as not sinful and therefore need not be confessed. The overwhelming majority of Catholic priests, many of whom had chosen not to leave the priesthood during the turbulence that followed Vatican II, remained in post – teaching, preaching, caring for the sick and the poor; serving in the missions, often in acute discomfort and in danger of death, re-enacting throughout the world Christ's sacrifice on Calvary in the mass, and conferring the Eucharist and other sacraments on the now one billion faithful.

In parts of the Third World priests were killed by the fanatics of other religions; in the Second – Communist countries such as China or Vietnam – they were persecuted; and in the First they were vilified by the now overwhelmingly atheist intelligentsia as purveyors of superstition and, because celibate, sexual freaks. Baal, the god of fertility, was in the ascendant: a satisfactory sex life was regarded as the *sine qua non* of human happiness and celibacy the only remaining perversion.

126. Pope Benedict XVI

As the world passed into the third millennium after the birth of Jesus of Nazareth, the health of Pope John Paul II went into decline. Over eighty years old, he had had not only a bullet removed from his body but a benign tumour the size of an orange. Now he was diagnosed with Parkinson's Disease: his once robust and upright body became stooped and partially paralysed. He remained in office, his pronouncements now made in a voice that was slurred and hard to comprehend. What might have been pitiable was heroic: the man who had so often insisted upon the value of suffering became its living proof.

Pope John Paul II died on 2 April, 2005, at the age of 84. He had served as the successor of Peter for 26 years and 162 days. Four kings, five queens, seventy heads of state, fourteen leaders of other religions and an estimated crowd of two million mourners, some shouting 'santo subito', attended his funeral. The requiem mass was conducted by the Dean of the College of Cardinals, Cardinal Josef Ratzinger, who also delivered the homily in which he condemned the moral relativism that seemed now to prevail in the world. The ceremony ended with the singing of *In paradisum*; 'May angels lead you into Paradise, and upon your arrival may the martyrs receive you and lead you to the holy city of Jerusalem'. His body was then interred in the crypt of Saint Peter's basilica, close to the tomb of Peter, the first pope.

Who would succeed him? In the past, the cardinals had sometimes chosen candidates with contrasting views to their predecessors, sometimes preferring continuity. Liberal Catholics hoped for the first but Hans Küng realised that it was unlikely: 'The Roman system goes on and on. The Pope chooses those who will elect his successor solely according to his taste… They are "creatures of the pope" who will choose the next pope – of course from their own ranks'.[1039] Sure enough, on 19 April, 2005, after four ballots, the cardinals in conclave chose Cardinal Josef Ratzinger who took the name Benedict in honour of the founder of western monasticism, Benedict of Nursia, and Benedict XV, pope during World War I.

Josef Ratzinger had lived in Rome since 1981 when John Paul II had appointed him Prefect for the Congregation of the Faith; and was familiar with the workings of the Vatican, having served as Dean of the College of Cardinals since 2002. When it came to the Church, he and John Paul II had seen eye-to-eye, but when it came to temperament Benedict XVI was a contrast to his predecessor. One could imagine Pope John Paul II riding out at the head of an army like Pope Julius II; Benedict was shy and retiring – his only known possessions before his elevation a bicycle, a piano and a cat. He had let it be known that he would rather retire to a village in his native Bavaria than serve as pope but accepted the choice of the cardinals as the will of God.

In terms of theatre the new pope was no match for Pope John Paul II; he was a scholar, an intellectual, and his weapon of choice in the struggle against secularism was his pen. In numerous addresses and lectures he insisted upon the bond between faith and reason: 'From the beginning, Christianity has understood itself as the religion of the *Logos*, as the religion according to reason'. It had been part of God's plan for the redemption of mankind that he had taken human form at a time when Greek philosophy was in the ascendant. 'In the so necessary dialogue between secularists and Catholics, we Christians must be very careful to remain faithful to this fundamental line: to live a faith that comes from the *Logos*, from creative reason, and that, because of this, is also open to all that is truly rational'.

Pope Benedict XVI wrote three encyclicals, *Deus caritas est* ('God is love'), *Spe Salvi* ('Saved by Hope'), and *Caritas in veritate* ('Love in Truth') – the first equating the sexual love of spouses with the love of God. Further lectures

1039   Hans Küng, *Disputed Truth,*

and addresses expressed Benedict's views on the nature of the Church and the challenges it faced in the modern world. Few now accepted that there was a God who had revealed objective norms of right and wrong. 'Today a particularly insidious obstacle…is the massive presence in our society and culture of that relativism which, recognising nothing as definitive, leaves as the ultimate criterion only the self with its desires. And under the semblance of freedom it becomes a prison for each one, for it separates people from one another, locking each person into his or her own ego'.[1040]

In September, 2006, Pope Benedict gave a lecture on 'Faith, Reason and the University' at the University of Regensburg where he had once been a professor. To make the point that religious proselytism through the use of violence was unreasonable, he quoted the Byzantine Emperor Manuel II Palaeologos on Islam: 'Show me just what Muhammad brought that was new and there you will finds things only evil and inhuman, such as his command to spread by the sword the faith he preached'. This outraged Muslims and led to violent demonstrations throughout the Islamic world. Cardinal Bertone, the Secretary of State, subsequently announced that 'The Holy Father is very sorry that some passages of his speech may have sounded offensive to the sensibility of Muslim believers'. This was not an apology. *Il n'y a que la vérité qui blesse* – only the truth hurts.

'When a Mozart Mass was sung on feast days in our Traunstein parish church,' Ratzinger would tell his biographer, Peter Sewald, 'then for me as a little country boy, it was as if the heavens opened…'[1041] Consistently loyal to the decrees of Vatican II, Pope Benedict had nevertheless been dismayed by some of the changes to the liturgy that had followed. 'One shudders at the lacklustre face of the post-conciliar liturgy as it has become, or one is simply bored with its hankering after banality and its lack of artistic standards… More and more clearly we can discern the frightening impoverishment which takes place when people show beauty the door and devote themselves exclusively to 'utility'.[1042] He was appalled by the 'so-called "renewal programmes" in parishes and diocese which take the form of marketing fresh insights to small groups, often under the banner of buzz-words and posters reminiscent of the kind which promoted five-year plans in Communist countries…'[1043]

1040   Josef Ratzinger, Address to the Ecclesial Diocesan Convention in Rome, 6 June, 2005
1041   Peter Sewald, *Op. Cit.*, p. 182
1042   Cardinal Joseph Ratzinger and Vittorio Messori, *Op. Cit.* pp. 121,128
1043   Tracy Rowland, *Op.Cit,* p. ?

There was no question of returning to the *status quo ante* – the 'Latin' or 'Tridentine' mass established at the time of the Council of Trent in the sixteenth century and replaced by the *novus ordo* in 1969. Priests had been permitted to continue to celebrate the Tridentine mass but only under certain conditions. These were now relaxed by Pope Benedict in his edict (*motu proprio*) *Summorum Pontificum*. Groups of the faithful who wished for a Tridentine mass said in Latin need no longer obtain the permission of their bishop. The 'mass of Paul VI' would remain the norm, but a parish priest could schedule regular Tridentine masses in his church. Just as he wished to bring beauty back into the liturgy, so he esteemed tradition, wearing once again some of the sumptuous vestments that had been put away by his more austere predecessors, and wearing the traditional footwear of a pontiff – red outdoor shoes and scarlet slippers.

Pope Benedict made a number of pastoral visits abroad, following the practice established by Popes Paul VI and John Paul II. In 2010 on a pastoral visit to the United Kingdom he recalled how the British had fought against Nazism, going on to compare the denial of God of that regime with the scepticism of the present day. 'As we reflect on the sobering lessons of the atheist extremism of the twentieth century, let us never forget how the exclusion of God, religion and virtue from public life leads ultimately to a truncated vision of man and of society and thus to a reductive vision of the person and his destiny'. In Birmingham he announced the beatification of John Henry Newman, and in London he addressed the members of both Houses of Parliament in Westminster Hall where in the sixteenth century Thomas More had been tried and found guilty of treason. The Prime Minister, David Cameron, and his deputy, Nick Clegg, listened politely as Pope Benedict once again condemned moral relativism: 'If the moral principles underpinning the democratic process are themselves determined by nothing more solid than social consensus, then the fragility of the process becomes all too evident – herein lies the real challenge for democracy'. Three years later, David Cameron's Conservative government passed laws permitting same-sex marriage.

Sex had become the bugbear of the Catholic Church. Not only was the teaching of *Humanae Vitae* ignored by otherwise conscientious Catholics, but the Church's authority to rule on matters of sexual morality had been gravely undermined by the revelations of the abuse of minors by priests. In 2002, Josef Ratzinger, then Prefect for the Congregation of the Faith, had persuaded Pope John Paul II to extend his congregation's jurisdiction, which until then had been restricted to seductions in the confessional, to all cases of clerical abuse. The pontiff had agreed but for reasons that remain unclear had, together with curial cardinals, been reluctant to encourage investigations of eminent churchmen such as Cardinal Hans Herman Groër in Austria, Marcial Maciel in Mexico, or Cardinal Theodore McCarrick in the United States. Groër, though denying all the charges made against him, had resigned as Archbishop of Vienna and died in 2003. Marcial Maciel, no longer protected by the incredulity of Pope John Paul II, was subject to further investigations by Pope Benedict, and on 1 May, 2010, the Vatican declared that Maciel's 'very serious and objectively immoral acts' had been confirmed by 'incontrovertible testimonies' and were 'true crimes that manifest a life without scruples or authentic religious sentiment'. He was ordered to withdraw to lead a life of prayer and penance.

Equally decisive was Pope Benedict's handling of the case of Cardinal Theodore McCarrick, the Archbishop of Washington. Allegations of sexual misconduct had been made dating back to the previous century: Pope John Paul II had refused to believe them. Pope Benedict was less easily deceived, and on his accession insisted that McCarrick resign as Archbishop of Washington, cease to travel, lecture or say mass in public and, like Maciel, withdraw to lead a life of prayer and penance. Cardinal McCarrick complied but he was a powerful figure in the American Church, and came back into favour in the pontificate that followed, advising the Vatican on the choice of US bishops. It was not until June, 2018, that a review board of the Archdiocese of New York ruled that an allegation McCarrick had sexually abused a 16-year-old altar boy while serving in that diocese was 'credible and substantiated'. Only then was McCarrick removed from public ministry by the Vatican.

The accusations and revelations continued. In March, 2013, the Archbishop of St. Andrews and Edinburgh, Keith O'Brien, hitherto vigorous in his condemnation of homosexual activities, was accused of abusing four priests. At first he denied the allegations but later admitted that 'there have been times that my sexual conduct has fallen below the standards expected of me as a priest, archbishop and cardinal', and resigned.[1044]

After the death of the Canadian Jean Vanier, who with the Dominican priest, Thomas Philippe, had established L'Arche, a charity that provided homes for the mentally and physically disabled, it emerged that he had abused women

----

1044 See the *Guardian*, 3 March, 2013

who had come to him for spiritual counsel. L'Arche had spread to thirty-eight different countries and Vanier had come to be regarded as a living saint. Now L'Arche itself revealed that he had 'engaged in manipulative and emotionally abusive' sexual relations with six women in France. So too the co-founder, Fr. Thomas Philippe, and his brother, the French Dominican theologian, Marie-Dominique Philippe, who had founded a new religious order, the *Frères de Saint Jean*, which had attracted many youthful vocations and like L'Arche had established communities throughout the world. The sins of these supposed saints, unlike those of Maciel and McCarrick, had remained hidden during their life-time.

Pope Benedict XVI was uncompromising when it came to the 'filth' of sexual abuse, but he knew his limitations. He was a scholar, not an administrator, with his only experience of governance his few years as Archbishop of Munich. With this in mind, and to leave time for writing a trilogy on Jesus of Nazareth, he left the governance of the Vatican to Cardinal Tarcisio Bertone who had been Secretary at the Congregation for the Doctrine of the Faith when Ratzinger was Prefect. In 2002 Pope Benedict made Bertone Secretary of State. He was a man the pope could trust but he had never served in the department he now headed, and proved unable to master the tangle of intrigues in the Vatican, or prevent stories appearing in the press about abuse of power, financial corruption and homosexual orgies, some of which seemed fanciful while others rang true.

Pope Benedict XVI was criticised for reserving a day in each week to work on his trilogy, *Jesus of Nazareth*, and for his appointment of the inexperienced Cardinal Bertone. 'Practical government is not my strong point,'[1045] he would tell his biographer, Peter Seewald. Nor was governance of his household. After the death of his sister Maria who had cared for him over the decades, he had to deal with the 'hysterical fits, bitter reproaches and floods of tears' of Ingrid Stampa, a musicologist, professor of the *viola gamba*, who believed that God wished her to replace Maria Ratzinger.[1046]

In May, 2012, Vatican police raided the flat of Paolo Gabriele, Pope Benedict's butler for the past five years, and found letters and documents which revealed that he had been feeding information to an Italian journalist, Gianluigi Nuzzi. Gabriele, charged with aggravated theft, admitted that he

---

1045   Peter Seewald, *Benedict XVI. A Life*. Volume II, p.403

1046   Peter Seewald, *Op. Cit.* p.350

had stolen the documents, including those marked by Pope Benedict 'to be destroyed', and passed them on to Nuzzi to combat 'the evil and corruption' rampant in the Vatican. He was found guilty and sentenced to eighteen months imprisonment. A computer specialist in the Secretariat of State who had helped Gabriele was also indicted and condemned: and Ettore Tedeschi was dismissed as president of the Vatican Bank for 'failure to provide any formal explanation for the dissemination of documents last known to be in the president's possession'.

Josef Ratzinger, Pope Benedict XVI, now almost 86 years old, had become weary and frail. 'Those close to him had never seen him so exhausted, so flat and listless, almost depressive. His face looked haggard, and his whole appearance was weak and feeble. He complained of constant tiredness'.[1047] He felt no longer able to join in the great jamborees that were now part of the papal ministry. Waving to a crowd from the balcony of Saint Peter's was one thing, but addressing millions in foreign countries was another. He had been advised by his doctor not to take long-haul flights, yet there was to be a World Youth Day in Rio di Janeiro which he would be expected to attend. Benedict decided to abdicate: following the precedents set by Celestine V in 1294 (see Chapter 42) and by Gregory XII in 1414 (see Chapter 46), he would step down from the papal throne. He announced his resignation in Latin to the cardinals assembled for the canonisation of the 800 martyrs of Otranto (see Chapter 48) on 11 February, 2013; and said his last mass in Saint Peter's basilica on Ash Wednesday, then was flown in a helicopter from Vatican City to the papal summer residence outside the city, Castel Gandolfo. Later he moved to the *Mater Ecclesiae* monastery in the Vatican Gardens, formerly a convent, where, continuing to wear a white soutane, the 'pope emeritus' returned to a life of prayer, study and writing. He died there on 31 December, 2022.

1047 *Ibid.* p. 493

127. The End of Time

As a history reaches the present day, it becomes journalism. Archives remain unopened and memoirs are yet to be written: the story of the Catholic Church becomes subject to what editors think will interest their readers. Jorge Mario Bergoglio, who succeeded Benedict XVI as Pope Francis I in 2013, was of interest – the first pope from South America, the first Jesuit pope, the first pope to take the name Francis – humble, unassuming, an archbishop who had used public transport and ministered to the poor. When he appeared on the balcony of Saint Peter's basilica after his election, he greeted the crowd with an informal '*buona sera*' – 'good evening'; and later himself telephoned his newsagent in Buenos Aires to cancel the delivery of a daily paper. Pope Francis became front-page news. 'Even in the twenty-first century,' wrote the *New York Times* columnist, Ross Douthat, 'many millions of people – including the secular press – could still be inspired by an antique religious organization and its aged, celibate leader'.[1048]

The church Francis was to govern had grown over two millennia from the small group around the Cross on Calvary, and the slightly larger gathering in the Upper Room in Jerusalem at the time of Pentecost to number around one and a quarter billion men, women and children – one sixth of the world's population – served by 200 cardinals, around 5,000 bishops and 400,000 priests. Over 700,000 women in religious communities devoted themselves either through prayer or ministry to the service of God and of others.

In the economically developed world, faith in the truths taught by the Catholic Church has unquestionably declined, but it had never been confined to one part of the world. It may have become almost extinct in areas where it began such as north Africa, Anatolia and Palestine itself, but it now flourished in parts of Africa and Asia. Hilaire Belloc's claim that 'The Faith is Europe and Europe was the Faith,' was no longer true: only Catholics in Poland and Hungary continued to resist the secular values promoted by the European Union.

However, as Pope Benedict XVI had recognised, popes, emperors, kings and theologians may dominate a history of the Church, but its 'main base is always those people who are humble believers, those who need love and give love; simple people, who are open to the truth because they have remained children, as the Lord says. They have kept their eyes on what is essential

---

1048   Ross Douthat, *To Change the church. Pope Francis and the Future of Catholicism*, p.80

throughout the change of history and kept the spirit of humility and love of the Church'. [1049]

'I bless you, Father, Lord of heaven and of earth,' Jesus had said, 'for hiding these things from the learned and the clever and revealing them to mere children'.[1050] There remained many millions throughout the world who believed, like the first Christians, that Jesus of Nazareth was the Son of God, the Second Person of the Trinity; that he had died to atone for our sins that he had risen from the dead, and that he would remain with them, 'yes, to the end of time'. At every mass, they professed these beliefs established at the Council of Nicaea in the fourth century, and prayed to God their Father in the words used by Jesus of Nazareth himself. They believed that the mass was a re-enactment of Christ's sacrifice on the Cross – a reality at the heart of their faith coming not from a theologian's treatise or the edict of a pope but 'from the Lord'. [1051] They believed that the finite and the infinite, the temporal and the eternal, the natural and the supernatural, the material and the numinous, the immanent and the transcendent, all came together when at the moment of consecration in the mass the bread and wine became the body and blood of Christ – 'a sort of "nuclear fission,"' wrote Pope Benedict XVI, 'which penetrates to the heart of all being, a change to set off a process which transforms reality, a process leading ultimately to the transfiguration of the entire world, to the point where God will be all in all'. [1052]

1049   Peter Seewald, *Op. Cit.*, p. 359-50

1050   Matthew, 11:25

1051   1 Corinthians, 11:23

1052   Pope Benedict XVI, *Sacramentum Caritatis*, 22 February, 2007 - 1 Cor 15:28.

Bibliography

Ackroyd, Peter. *The Life of Thomas More.* London, 1998

Acton, Harold. *The Bourbons of Naples.* London, 1956

Adam, Karl. *The Spirit of Catholicism,* London, 1929

Anderson, Robert. *The Conflict in Education: Catholic Secondary Schools 1850-1870.*

Annan, Noel. *Our Age.* London, 1990

Anscombe, G.E.M. *Faith in a Hard Ground. Essays on Religion, Philosophy and Ethics.* Exeter, 2008

Antier, Jean-Jacques. *Charles de Foucauld.* Translted by Julia Shirek-Smith. San Francisco, 1997

Armstrong, Karen. *Muhammad. A Biography of the Prophet.* London, 1991

Augustine of Hippo, *Confessions.* Translated by R.Pine-Coffin. London, 1961

Barber, Malcolm. The New Knighthood. *A History of the Order of the Temple.* Cambridge, 1996

Barber, Malcolm. *The Trial of the Templars.* Cambridge, 1978

Beckett, Lucy. *In the Light of Christ. Writings in the Western Tradition.* San Francisco, 2006

Benedict XVI, Pope. *Sacramentum Caritatis.* Vatican City, 2007

Bernstein, Alan E. *The Formation of Hell.* Ithaca, New York. 1996

Black, Edwin. *Eugenics and the Nazis – the California Connection.* San Francisco Chronicle, 2003

Blainey, Geoffrey. *A Short History of the World.* Ringwood, Victoria. 2000

Blet, SJ, Pierre. *Pius XII and the Second World War. According to the Archives of the Vatican.* Leominster, 1997,

Blockmans, Wim. *The Emperor Charles V.* London, 2002

Bouyer, Louis. *The Memoirs of Louis Bouyer.* New York, 2015

Bredin, Jean-Louis. *The Affair. The Case of Alfred Dreyfus.* London, 1986

Brooke, Christopher. *The Medieval Idea of Marriage.* Oxford, 1991

Brown, Callum G. *The Death of Christian Britain.* London, 2001

Brown, E.A.R. *Medieval Studies.*

Browning, Christopher R. *The Origins of the Final Solution: the Evolution of Nazi Jewish Policy: September 1939 – March 1943.* Lincoln, Nebraska, 2007.

Bryce, James. *The Holy Roman Empire.* New York, 1961

Bull, Marcus. *The Oxford History of the Crusades.* Oxford, 2002

Bullivant, Stephen. *Mass Exodus. Catholic Disaffiliation in Britain and America Since Vatican II.* Oxford, 2019

Burleigh, Michael. *Earthly Powers.* London, 2005

Burleigh, Michael. *Sacred Causes.* London, 2007

Burns, Jimmy. *Francis, Pope of Good Promise.* London, 2015

Burns, Michael. *A Family Affair, 1789-1945.* New York, 1991

Calixtus II, *Sicut Judaeis*, Rome, 1120

Caraman S.J., Philip. *St. Ignatius Loyola.* London, 1990

Caraman, Philip. *The Lost Paradise.* London, 1975

Cesnari, David. *Adolph Eichmann: The Mind of a War Criminal.* London, BBC History

Chadwick, Henry. *Augustine.* Oxford, 1991

Chadwick, Owen. *The Popes and the European Revolution.* Oxford, 1981

Chamberlin, E.R. *The Bad Popes.* London, 1970

Chateaubriand, François René. *Memoirs.* Translated by Robert Baldick. London, 1964

Chateaubriand, François René. *The Beauties of Christianity.* London, 1815

Chesterton, G.K. *Saint Thomas Aquinas*, London, 1933

Clark, Ronald. *The Life of Bertrand Russel.* London, 1975

Clarkson, SJ, John F. (ed.) *The Church Teaches.* Rockford, Illinois, 1973

Cohen, J.M. Introduction to Montaigne's *Essays.*

Cohn-Sherbok. *The Crucified Jew. Twenty Centuries of Christian anti-Semitism.* London, 1992

Cook, Don. *Charles de Gaulle.* London, 1984.

Cornwell, John. *The Pope in Winter.* London, 2004

Coulson, John. *The Saints. A Concise Biographical Dictionary.* London, 1957

Dobson, R.B. *The Jews of Medieval York and the Massacre of 1190.* York, 1974

Douthat, Ross. *To Change the Church.* New York, 2018

Doyle, William. *Jansenism.* London, 2000

Drummond, Sarah. *Divine Conception. The Art of the Annunciation.* London, 2018

Drumont, Édouard. *La France Juive.* Paris, 1886

Duffy, Eamon. *Fires of Faith.* London, 2009

Duffy, Eamon. *Saints and Sinners.* London, 1997

Duffy, Eamon. *The Catholic Church on the Eve of the Millenium.* Worth, 1999

Duffy, Eamon. *The Stripping of the Altars.* London, 1992

Dussel, Enrique. `Latin America' in *Modern Catholicism.* Oxford, 1991

Elton, G.R. *Europe from Renaissance to Reformation.* New York, 1967

Erland-Brandenberg, *The Cathedral. The Social and Archoitectural Dynamics of Construction.* Cambridge, 1994

Eusebius. *The History of the Church from Christ to Constantine.* Translated by G.A. Williamson. Harmondsworth, 1965

Faber, Geoffrey. *Oxford Apostles.* London, 1933

Figes, Orlando. *A People's Tragedy*. London, 1996

Flannery, Edward. *The Anguish of the Jews*. New York, 1985

Flannery, OP, Austin, (Ed.). *Vatican Council II*. Dublin, 1977.

Fletcher, Richard. *The Conversion of Europe*. London, 1997

Francis I, *Amoris Laetitia*. Vatican City, 2006

Frank, Joseph. *Dostoevsky. The Miraculous Years. 1885-1872*. Princeton, 1995

Frankel, Jonathan. *The Damascus Affair*. Cambridge, 1997

Freeman, Charles. *The Closing of the Western Mind. The Rise of Faith and the Fall of Reason*. London, 2002

Friedländer, Saul. *Nazi German and the Jews*. New York, 1997

Gaine, Michael. *The State of the Priesthood in Modern Catholicism*.

Gibson, Ralph. *A Social History of French Catholicism. 1789-1914*. London, 1989

Gilmour, David. *The Pursuit of Italy*. London, 2011

Goncourt, Edmond and Jules. *Pages from the Goncourt Journalsl*. New York, 1962

Goyau, Georges. *St. Louis XI*.

Gray, Robert. *Cardinal Manning*. London, 1985

Green, Julian. *Diary 1928-1957*. London, 1961

Gregory, Brad S. *The Unintended Reformation*. Cambridge, Mass. 2012

Grunberger, Richard. *Red Rising in Bavaria*. London, 1973

Grunebaum, Gustav E. von. *A Study in Cultural Orientation*. Chicago, 1947

Haecker, Theodor. *Journal in the Night*. New York, 1970

Hales, E.E. *The Catholic Church in the Modern World*. New York, 1960

Hapsburg, Otto von. *Charles V*. London, 1970

Harris, Robin. *Talleyrand*. London, 2007.

Harris, Ruth. *The Man on Devil's Island*. London, 2010

Haskins, Susan. *Mary Magdalen*. London, 1993

Hastings, Adrian (ed.) *Modern Catholicism*. Oxford, 1991

Hawes, James. *A Short History of Germany*. Devon, 2017

Hebblethwaite, Peter. *Paul VI. The First Modern Pope*. London, 1993

Heseman, Michael. *Die Jesus-Tafel*, Friburg, 1999

Hibbert, Christopher. *The Days of the French Revolution*. London, 1980

Hill, Roland. *Lord Acton*. London, 2000

Hodges, Michael. *The Knights Hospitaller in Great Britain in 1540*. London, 2018

Holland, Tom. *In the Shadow of the Sword*. London, 2012

Holland, Tom. *The Making of the Western Mind*. London, 2019

Ivereigh, Austen. *The Great Reformer*. London, 2014

John Paul II, *Mulieris Dignitatem*. Vatican City, 1988

Johnson, Paul. *A History of Christianity*. London, 1976

Johnson, Paul. *A History of the Jews*. London, 1987

Joinville, *The Life of St. Louis* from *Chronicles of the Crusades*. Translated by M.R.B. Shaw. New York, 1963

Jones, Alexander (Ed.), *The Jerusalem Bible*. London, Darton, Longman & Todd. 1966

Josipovici, Gabriel. *The Book of God. A Response to the Bible*. Yale University Press, New Haven and London, 1988

Josipovici, Gabriel. *The World and the Book*. St. Alban's, 1973

Kamen, Henry. *The Spanish Inquisition. An Historical Revision*. London, 1997

Keen, Maurice. *Chivalry*. London, 1984

Keen, Maurice. *Penguin History of Medieval Europe*. London, 1991

Kelly, J.N.D. *The Oxford History of the Popes*. Oxford, 1986

Kempis, Thomas á. *The Imitation of Christ*. Translated by Leo Shirley-Price. Harmondsworth, 1954

Ker, Ian. *Newman on Vatican II*. Oxford, 2014

Kertzer, David I. *The Kidnapping of Edgardo Montaro*. London, 1997

Knapp, Robert. *The Dawn of Christianity. People and Gods in an Age of Miracles and Magic*. London, 2017

Knowles, David. *Christian Monasticism*. Oxford, 1969

Knox, Ronald. *The Belief of Catholics*. San Francisco, 2000

Knox, Ronald. *Enthusiasm*. Oxford, 1950

Kohn, George Childs. *Dictionary of Wars*. London, 1999

Kokakowski, Leszek. *God Owes us Nothing*. Chicago, 1995

Küng, Hans. *Disputed Truth. Memoirs Vol. II*. London, 2008

Laishley, F.J., `Unfinished Business' in *Modern Catholicism,* London, Oxford, 1991

Lane Fox, Robin. *Augustine. Conversions and Confessions*. London, 2015

Lane Fox, Robin. *Pagans and Christians,* London, 1986

Lavisse, Ernest. *Histoire de France depuis les origins jusqu'a la Revolution*. Paris, 1900-1912

Lawler, Philip F. *The Faithful Departed*. New York, 2008

Leber, Annedore. *Conscience in Revolt*. London, 1957

Leon XIII, *Rerum Novarum*. Vatican City, 1891

Libreria Editrice Vaticano. *Catechism of the Catholic Church*. London, 1994

Lohan, Richard and McClure, Sister Mary. *Weaving the Web*. London, 1988

Luidprand, *Antopodosis*. See A. Wright (trad.), *The Works of Liudprand of Cremona*, London-New York, 1930.

MacCulloch, Diarmid. *Reformation. Europe's House Divided, 1490-1700*. London, 2003

Maclean, Fitzroy. *Eastern Approaches*. London, 1949

Manzoni, Alessandro. *The Betrothed*. Translated by Bruce Penman. London, 1972

Martin, Ralph. *Will Many be Saved?* Grand Rapids, 2012

Maryks, Robert Aleksander. *The Jesuit Order as a Synagogue of Jews.* Cambridge, 2018

Masson, Georgina. *Frederick II of Hohenstaufen. A Life.* London, 1957

McDermott, Timothy. *Summa Theologiae. A Concise Translation.* London, 1989

McDonagh, Enda. *Modern Catholicism.* Oxford, 1991

McManners, John. *Church and State in France. 1870-1914.* London, 1972

Meissner S.J., W.W. *St. Ignatius Loyola. The Psychology of a Saint.* London, 1992

Menache, Sophia *Clement V.* 1998

Mirbeau, Octave. *Sébastien Roch.* Translated by Nicoletta Simborowski. Sawtry, 2000

Montaigne, Michel de. *Essays.* Harmondsworth, 1958

Moorehouse, Geoffrey. *The Pilgrimage of Grace.* London, 2002

Mullet, Michael A. *The Catholic Reformation.* London, 1999

Murphy-O'Connor, Jerome. *The Holy Land.* Oxford, 1986

Newsome, David. *The Convert Cardinals. Newman and Manning.* London, 1993

Nicassio, Susan Vandiver. *Tosca's Rome.* Chicago, 1990.

Nirenberg, David. *Anti-Judaism. The History of a Way of Thinking.* London, 2013

Norman, Edward. `An Outsider's Evaluation' in *Modern Catholicism.* Oxford, 1991

Norman, Edward. *Secularisation. Sacred Values in a Godless World.* London, 2002

O'Neil, George. *Golden Years on the Paraguay.* London, 1934

Orchard, Dom Bernard OSB, *The Evolution of the Gospels. One Scholar's View.* London, CTS, 1990

Parker, Geoffrey. *Emperor. A New Life of Charles V.* New Haven, 2019

Pascal, Michel de. *Pensées*. Translated by A.J.Krailsheimer. Harmondsworth, 1966

Pastor, Ludwig von. *The History of the Popes from the Close of the Middle Ages*. Vol. XI. London, 1953

Péguy, Charles. *Notre Jeunesse*. Paris, 1910

Perreau-Saussine, Emile. *Catholicism and Democracy*. Princeton, 2012

Phayer, Michael. *The Catholic Church and the Holocaust, 1930-1965*. Bloomington, Indiana. 2000

Pickstock, Catherine. *After Writing. On the Liturgical Consummation of Philosophy*. Oxford, 1998

Pink, Thomas. *The Interpretation of* Dignitatis Humanae. Steubenville, Ohio. 2013

Pius XI. *Casti Connubii*. Vatican City, 1930.

Pius XI. *Mit Brennender Sorge*. Vatican City, 1937.

Prawer, Joshua. *The Latin Kingdom of Jerusalem*. London, 1972

Prior, Edward S. *History of Gothic Art in England*. 2015

Ratzinger, Cardinal Joseph. *The Ratzinger Report. An Exclusive Interview on the State of the Church*. Leominster, 1985

Ratzinger, Joseph Cardinal. *Address to the Ecclesial Convention*. Vatican City, 2005

Ratzinger, Joseph Cardinal. *Dominus Jesus*. Vatican City, 2000

Rawlinson, Peter. *The Jesuit Factor*. London, 1990

Read, Herbert. *Anarchy and Order*. London, 1954.

Read, Piers Paul. *Alec Guinness*. London, 2003

Read, Piers Paul. *Hell and Other Destinations*. London, 2006

Read, Piers Paul. *The Dreyfus Affair*. London, 2012

Read, Piers Paul. *The Templars*. London, 1999

Renan, Ernest. *The Life of Jesus*. London, 1864

Rhodes, Anthony. *The Vatican in the Age of the Dictators. 1922*. New York, 1973

Riley-Smith, Jonathan. *The First Crusade and the Idea of Crusading.* Philadelphia, 1986

Roberts, Andrew. *Napoleon the Great.* London, 2014

Rosenberg, Arthur. *Imperial Germany.* Boston, 1964

Roth, Cecil. *A Short History of the Jewish People.* London, 1936

Rowland, Tracey. *The Theology of Josef Ratzinger.* Oxford, 2008

Roy, Olivier. *Is Europe Christian?* London, 2019

Runciman, Steven. *A History of the Crusades.* Vols. 1-3 London, 1991

Sainte-Beuve, C.A. *Portraits of the 18th Century.* New York, 1905

Sales, Francis de. *Introduction to the Devout Life.* New York, 1989

Sanderlin, George (ed.) *Witness. Writing of Bartolome de las Casas.* Maryknoll, 1993

Sauer, Joseph (Ed.) *Catholic Encyclopaedia.*

Schäfer, Peter. *Jesus in the Talmud.* Princeton, 2007

Schneider, Athanasius. *Christus Vincit.* New York, 2019

Schultheis, Katrin. *Bodies and Souls.* Cambridge, Mass. 2001

Secher, Reynauld. *Vendé, de genocide au mémoricide.* Paris, 2019Lon

Seewald, Peter. *Benedict XVI. A Life.* Volume 1. London, 2020

Seewald, Peter. *Benedict XVI. A Life.* Volume 2. London, 2021

Seper, Franjo Cardinal. *Sexual Ethics.* Vatican City, 1975

Sereny, Gitta. *Albert Speer. His Battle with Truth.* London, 1995

Siena, Catherine of *Selected Writings.* London, 1980

Slocombe, George. *A History of Poland.* London, 1939

Slocombe, George. *A History of Poland.* London, 1941

Smail, R.C. *Crusading Warfare. 1097-1193.* Cambridge, 1956

Snyder, Timothy. *Bloodlands. Europe Between Hitler and Stalin.* London, 2010

Socci, Antonio. *Rorate Caeli.*

Southern, R.W. *Saint Anselm*. Cambridge, 1990

Speer, Albert. *Spandau. The Secret Diaries*. London, 1976

Stark, Rodney. *Bearing False Witness. Debunking Centuries of anti-Catholic History*. London, 2017

Stein, George H. *The Waffen SS. Hitler's Elite Guard at War. 1939-1945*. Ithaca, New York. 1966

Steinsaltz, *The Essential Talmud*. New York, 1976

Stendhal. *The Red and the Black*. Translated by Roger Gard. London, 2002

Sumption, Jonathan. *The Albigensian Crusade*. London, 1978

Tacitus, *Annals*. London, 2003

Thevasthasan, Dr. Pravin. *The Catholic Church and the Sex Abuse Crisis*. London, 2011

Thomas, Hugh. *The Slave Trade. The History of the Atlantic Slave Trade*. London, 1997

Thomas, Hugh. *The Spanish Civil War*. London, 2012

Thrall, Margaret E. *The Cambridge Bible Commentary*. Cambridge, 1965

Tombs, Robert. *France: 1814-1914*. London, 1996

Treasure, Geoffrey. *The Huguenots*. London, 2013

Trevor-Roper, Hugh. *Adolf Hitler's Secret Conversations. 1941-1944*. New York, 1972

Trower, Philip. *The Catholic Church and the Counter-Faith*. Oxford, 2006

Vryonis, Speros. *Byzantium and Europe*. New York, 1967

Wallace, Edgar. *Sanders of the River*. London, 1911

Wallace-Hadrill, J.M. *The Barbarian West*. Oxford, 1986

Wallace-Hadrill, *The Frankish Church*. Oxford, 1983

Ward, James Mace. *Priest, Politician, Collaborator: Jozef Tiso and the Making of Fascist Slovakia*. Ithaca, NY. 2013

Watt, H. Montgomery. *Muhammad. Prophet and Statesman*. Oxford, 1961

Waugh, Evelyn. *The Diaries of Evelyn Waugh*. London, 1976

Webb, Simon. *The Forgotten Slave Trade. The White European Slaves of Islam.* Barnsley, 2021

Wedgwood, C.V. *The Thirty Years War.* London, 1938

Weigel, George. *Witness to Hope. The Biography of Pipe John Paul II.* New York, 1999

Whitfield, Teresa. *Paying the Price. Ignacio Ellacuria and the Murdered Jesuits of El Salvador.* Philadelphia, 1995

Williamson, G.A. *The History of the Church by Eusebius.* London, 2020

Williamson, H.N.H. *Farewell to the Don.* New York, 1971

Wilson, Stephen. *Ideology and Experience: Anti-Semitism in France at the Time of the Dreyfus Affair.* London, 1982

Wistrich, Robert. *Anti-Semitism. The Longest Hatred.* London, 1991

Wright, Tom. *Paul. A Biography.* London, 2018

Yuval, Israel Jacob. *Two Nations in Your Womb.* Berkley, California. 2006

Zamoyski, Adam. *Napoleon. The Man Behind the Myth.* London, 2018

Zamoyski, Adam. *Rites of Peace.* London, 2008

Zeldin, Theodore. *Conflicts in French Society.* London, 1970